Building Data-Driven Edge Systems for Business Success

Minakshi
King Khalid University, Saudi Arabia

Tarun Kumar
University of Petroleum and Energy Studies (UPES), Dehradun, India

Kapil Joshi
Uttaranchal University, India

Akash Saxena
Compucom Institute of Technology and Management, India

Dilip Kumar Jang Bahadur Saini
Dayananda Sagar University, India

IGI Global
Scientific Publishing
Publishing Tomorrow's Research Today

Vice President of Editorial	Melissa Wagner
Director of Acquisitions	Mikaela Felty
Director of Book Development	Jocelynn Hessler
Production Manager	Mike Brehm
Cover Design	Jose Rosado

Published in the United States of America by
IGI Global Scientific Publishing
701 East Chocolate Avenue
Hershey, PA, 17033, USA
Tel: 717-533-8845
Fax: 717-533-7115
Website: https://www.igi-global.com E-mail: cust@igi-global.com

Library of Congress Cataloging-in-Publication Data

Names: Minakshi (Computer engineer), 1980- editor
http://id.loc.gov/rwo/agents/n2025010651
Title: Building data-driven edge systems for business success / [edited by]
Minakshi, Tarun Kumar, Kapil Joshi, Akash Saxena, Dilip Kumar Saini.
Description: Hershey, PA : IGI Global Scientific Publishing, [2026] | Includes bibliographical references and index. | Summary: "This book explores the fundamental principles and practical implementations of data-driven edge systems, bridging the gap between theoretical concepts and real-world business applications. By bringing computation closer to data sources, organizations can achieve faster insights, reduced latency, and improved operational efficiency"-- Provided by publisher.
Identifiers: LCCN 2025000144 (print) | LCCN 2025000145 (ebook) | ISBN 9798337311470 hardcover | ISBN 9798337311487 paperback | ISBN 9798337311494 ebook
Subjects: LCSH: Edge computing--Industrial applications | Technological innovations--Management
http://id.loc.gov/authorities/subjects/sh2008112644
Classification: LCC QA76.583 .B85 2025 (print) | LCC QA76.583 (ebook) | DDC 004/.36--dc23/eng/20250314
LC record available at https://lccn.loc.gov/2025000144
LC ebook record available at https://lccn.loc.gov/2025000145

British Cataloguing in Publication Data
A Cataloguing in Publication record for this book is available from the British Library.

Table of Contents

Detailed Table of Contents

The Making use of cutting-edge technology like cloud computing and machine learning is essential for producing insightful data and facilitating wise decision-making. In order to meet the increasing requirement for continuous data processing, low-latency interpersonal interaction, and resilient systems in the IoT ecosystem, the paper first provides an overview of the development of IoT and its recent surge in global adoption. It then highlights the growing significance of integrating internet, fog, and frontier computing. The survey carefully breaks down each computing paradigm, emphasizing the special traits, benefits, and difficulties of edge computing, cloud computing, fog computing, and the Internet of Things.

The rapid deployment of data-driven edge (DDE) systems raises significant security concerns. As cloud providers expand edge technologies, accompanying security risks grow exponentially. Unlike traditional deployments, modern systems face sophisticated attacks compromising data, workloads, and computing results. Current security solutions inadequately address cloud-edge integration. Researchers have defined comprehensive security requirements, including data ownership protection and cross-domain access control. A new architecture integrating edge-cloud systems with cloud-native security services has been proposed to mitigate risks. Cloud security vulnerabilities are particularly alarming, with data breaches accounting for approximately 30% of security incidents and substantial financial losses. Potential risks include unauthorized data extraction, backdoor introduction, and hijacking of customer information. Undetected compromised cloud services can propagate malware and exploit system vulnerabilities, posing significant threats to public security and data integrity.

Real time data processing of data in intelligent analytics, decision making and AI model training and updating is an area where edge computing can be put to effective use. This chapter focuses on their deployment with machine intelligence, sensors, and networking in IIoT and smart health care particularly concentrating on edge computing. It explores deploying AI models at the edge level and how to overcome some areas of constraint computational resources such as memory devices. Approaches for incorporating the sensor and the fusion of data to improve efficiency in edge devices are presented. Central concepts such as decentralised, distributed, and distributed intelligence accentuate the collaborative model building; federal learning acknowledges the model training co-operation but with the data protection interior. This chapter also explores large-scale edge-cloud systems, security, and resources in hybrid models. Last, the chapter explores use cases in industry across verticals and technology trends such as AI, 5G and quantum computing that define the future of edge intelligence.

Urban healthcare infrastructure is increasingly relying on edge computing to handle massive amounts of medical data in real time, minimizing latency and enabling

application of bi-stacked Artificial Neural Networks (ANNs) on edge devices for handling healthcare data from different sensors, including wearable sensors and medical IoT sensors. The bi-stacked ANN model has two tiers of neural networks where the lower-level aggregates low-level features from raw sensors and the higher level consolidates such features for application in disease prediction and patient monitoring. With this distributed form of data processing, there is considerable alleviation against dependency on cloud infrastructures and this hence boosts the efficiency and speed of healthcare systems. In addition, healthcare edge computing benefits in diminishing bandwidth consumption, enhancing patient privacy, and providing timely medical treatments.

The framework of distributed edge computing is the core of the replacement of centralized cloud computing infrastructure regarding the digital transformation. This chapter reviews the shift of strategies to be cloud-first to edge-first and the strategic, technological and financial reasons behind it. This chapter forms the basis on how enterprises can leverage edge computing to have competitive advantage in a more data-driven economy by carefully reviewing the latest trends in the market, technology capabilities and business needs. It provides a checklist of the steps companies could take to implement scalable and smart edge solutions by pointing out to practical use cases, architecture paradigms and referring to the future perspectives.

Edge computing in healthcare offers significant benefits by improving medical outcomes, enhancing operational efficiency, and supporting real-time clinical decisions. This chapter explores how edge systems build resilient healthcare networks, enabling rapid patient support through data-driven protocols while meeting security and compliance requirements such as HIPAA and GDPR. The proliferation of wearable

including cryptographic methods, federated learning, access control mechanisms, and anonymization schemes. Cryptographic techniques such as homomorphic encryption and secure multi-party computation enable secure processing of data, and federated learning minimizes data exposure in AI-driven applications. Access control frameworks such as role-based and zero-trust models prevent unauthorized access, and anonymization techniques minimize re-identification threats. Edge-to-cloud privacy frameworks and secure communication protocols also ensure data security.

Edge computing eliminates the need to send data to the cloud for processing/execution, hence reducing latency and time complexity. Furthermore, advances in information technology and communication have enabled the solution to be saved, computed, and decided locally by developing an on-premise IOT solution. Edge computing with Artificial Intelligence provides continuous processing by preventing unexpected device failures and recognizing the need for predictive maintenance. The fast growth of IoT devices has raised the height of data creation, resulting in a massive flow of data. These sensitive data generated by IoT devices is mostly kept in the cloud paradigm, but the latency encountered in the transmission between cloud data centres and end-users has rendered the arrangement pointless. This has remained the motivation for many businesses or organisations to move away from the cloud paradigm and toward edge computing, which allows data to be processed or performed locally at the user's end, allowing for quicker computation and real-time decision making.

latency and enabling immediate decision-making in urgent healthcare scenarios, and identifying specific challenges faced by urban healthcare systems, including data overload, resource allocation inefficiencies, and accessibility issues in densely populated areas. The chapter uses a combination of qualitative and quantitative research methods as its methodology framework. A study of urban healthcare facilities through different case examples evaluates positive results as well as best practices in implementation. The book chapter investigates the fundamental framework of edge computing within healthcare systems which specifically targets main goals to improve patient outcomes together with operational refinement and immediate data evaluation capabilities.

Preface

The rapid digitization of the modern world, fuelled by the proliferation of smart devices, cloud-native architectures, artificial intelligence, and the Internet of Things (IoT), has ushered in an era of data-driven decision-making. In this context, edge computing has emerged as a pivotal technological shift that transforms how data is processed, analysed, and acted upon. No longer confined to centralized data centres or cloud platforms, computation now occurs closer to the source of data generation be it a smart sensor, a wearable device, or an industrial controller. This paradigm shift from cloud-first to edge-first methodologies is at the heart of this edited volume, *Building Data-Driven Edge Systems for Business Success*. This book also aims to provide a comprehensive and multidisciplinary overview of intelligent edge computing systems that are purpose-built for business optimization, healthcare innovation, smart city deployment, and industrial transformation. Total 15 chapters included the perspectives from academia as well as industry persons so it presents insights into the practical, theoretical, and strategic complete dimensions of edge intelligence computing.

Global industry trends whereas Industry 4.0 to industry 5.0, digital health transformation, autonomous systems and smart urban infrastructure increasingly rely on distributed intelligence at the edge.

The rapid growth of data, driven by billions of connected devices (like smartphones, sensors, and IoT devices), has created a big challenge for traditional centralized cloud systems so these systems can't handle the sheer volume of data and the need for instant processing in critical situations. On the other side edge computing also solves this problem by processing data locally, closer to where it's generated, rather than sending it to a central cloud server. This approach is all about to reduces latency (processing happens in milliseconds) and enables faster decision-making and action. In short, edge computing enables faster, more efficient, and more reliable processing of critical data, making it a vital technology for various industries.

This resource is all about the major objective is to demystify the architectural models that enable intelligent edge ecosystems, including hybrid cloud-edge systems and distributed processing frameworks. On the other hand, to explore the integration of AI and machine learning at the edge, with an emphasis on resource-constrained environments, model optimization, and federated learning.

The book comprises 15 curated chapters, grouped thematically to reflect the different dimensions of edge computing applications. While each chapter is self-contained, together they represent a cohesive narrative that begins with foundational studies and progresses to more advanced and specialized explorations.

The chapter 1 defines and discusses how Industrial Internet of Things (IIoT) technologies are used to manage and optimize resources (such as energy, materials and machines) in an industrial environment and chapter 2 explores how cloud security methods can be applied to edge computing environments and the importance of securing data, devices, and communications at the edge and how cloud technologies help enforce security policies. Chapter 3 shows a detailed survey of recent advancements in edge computing and intelligent data processing. It also highlights how these technologies work together to support real-time and scalable solutions in sensitive environments like hospitals etc. The chapter 4 titled "AI-Powered Urban Healthcare: An Efficient Edge Computing Model" defines and explains how Artificial Intelligence (AI) combined with Edge Computing can revolutionize urban healthcare systems by making them faster, smarter, and more efficient.

This chapter 5 serves as a practical guide for businesses to design and implement data-driven systems at the edge of the network. It explains how leveraging Edge Intelligence can improve operational efficiency, reduce latency, enhance customer experience, and support real-time decision-making for business growth. In chapter 6 focuses on the use of Artificial Neural Networks (ANN)—specifically a bi-stacked architecture—to enable real-time health monitoring and predictive diagnostics through edge computing technologies. This chapter no.7 explores the transition from traditional cloud-first computing strategies to edge-first methodologies, highlighting how real-time processing, low latency and data privacy needs are driving the adoption of edge computing across industries. This chapter 8 focuses on how edge computing technologies are transforming healthcare by improving clinical decisions and hospital operations through real-time data processing and analysis closer to where the data is generated (e.g., hospitals and patient monitoring devices). Benefits of Edge Computing in Healthcare with low latency (quick response), data privacy and security – data can stay within the hospital network and reduced cloud dependency – faster and more reliable. Finally, this chapter shows how edge computing is helping hospitals make faster, smarter, and more informed decisions, improving patient care and overall hospital efficiency.

Chapter 9 discusses the technical implementation of healthcare edge systems, particularly how medical devices (e.g., monitors, ventilators, wearable sensors) are connected through edge computing frameworks, and how DevOps practices are used for deployment and maintenance. It also presents a technical guide on how to set up and manage an edge-powered healthcare infrastructure using DevOps principles, enabling hospitals to handle large-scale medical devices, ensure smooth maintenance, and deliver scalable solutions. The chapter 10 and 11 focuses on how AI and ML technologies are being used to transform business operations, improve decision-making, and drive growth in the current digital era and focuses on how Industrial Internet of Things (IIoT) technologies and smart manufacturing systems are transforming traditional industries by improving efficiency, resource usage, and overall performance.

This chapter 12 focuses on designing and implementing privacy-preserving frameworks for edge computing environments rather than sending everything to the cloud. The chapter emphasizes the trade-off between strong security measures and high system performance, aiming to strike the right balance. The chapter 13 provides a comprehensive look at the evolution of edge computing, its emerging trends, and the key challenges and opportunities it presents across various sectors. On the other hand, how edge computing is transforming industries by bringing data processing closer to the data source, enabling low-latency, real-time analytics, and greater privacy—while also highlighting the technical, operational and regulatory challenges that must be addressed for wide-scale adoption. In chapter 14 is all about that how to effectively design, deploy, scale, and maintain medical device integration (MDI) systems in modern healthcare environments. It serves as a practical roadmap for developers, hospital IT administrators, healthcare providers, and technology solution architects. This chapter also provides a step-by-step framework to build and manage systems that integrate medical devices (like ventilators, monitors, infusion pumps, etc.) with hospital IT infrastructure such as Electronic Health Records (EHRs), edge/cloud platforms, and clinical decision systems and chapter 15 explores how urban computing technologies, when combined with edge computing, can transform healthcare services in urban environments—especially by providing faster, smarter, and more context-aware medical care. This book stands out as a practitioner-researcher collaborative effort, featuring diverse authorship from India, the Middle East, Central Asia, and the United States. It balances state-of-the-art research with field-tested insights, ensuring its relevance to both academic and applied communities.

Edge computing is redefining the digital world by decentralizing intelligence, empowering end-user devices, and enabling real-time action at the point of data origin. The transition from cloud-centric to edge-enabled systems is not merely an architectural change, it is a reorientation of how we think about computing, security, and decision-making in a data-intensive future.

We express our deepest appreciation to all contributors (authors) of this volume who have invested their full expertise, time, and effort into the realization of this book. Each chapter is a product of careful research, collaborative scholarship and experimentation.

We also thank the peer reviewers and editorial team, whose feedback has elevated the academic quality of this book. Their rigorous inputs ensured that the content meets the standards expected by a global publishing platform such as IGI Global.

Minakshi
King Khalid University, Saudi Arabia

Tarun Kumar
University of Petroleum and Energy Studies (UPES), Dehradun, India

Kapil Joshi
Uttaranchal University, India

Akash Saxena
Compucom Institute of Technology and Management, India

Dilip Kumar Jang Bahadur Saini
Dayananda Sagar University, India

Chapter 1

A Case Study on Resource Management Industrial IoT Application

Harishchander Anandaram
https://orcid.org/0000-0003-2993-5304
Amrita Vishwa Vidyapeetham, India

K. S. Shreenidhi
https://orcid.org/0000-0002-6844-0454
Rajalakshmi Nagar Thandalam, India

Kapil Joshi
https://orcid.org/0000-0003-1097-8347
Uttaranchal University, India

Kawerinder Singh Sidhu
https://orcid.org/0000-0002-8910-6279
Uttaranchal Institute of Management, India

R. Kiruthigha
https://orcid.org/0000-0002-4355-2548
SRM Institute of Science and Technology, India

Vineeta Singh
https://orcid.org/0000-0003-1084-279X
School of Engineering and Technology, Chhatrapati Shahu Ji Maharaj University, India

Amrendra Tripathi
University of Petroleum and Energy Studies, India

ABSTRACT

The Making use of cutting-edge technology like cloud computing and machine learning is essential for producing insightful data and facilitating wise decision-making. In order to meet the increasing requirement for continuous data processing, low-latency interpersonal interaction, and resilient systems in the IoT ecosystem, the paper first provides an overview of the development of IoT and its recent surge in global adoption. It then highlights the growing significance of integrating internet, fog, and frontier computing. The survey carefully breaks down each computing paradigm, emphasizing the special traits, benefits, and difficulties of edge computing,

DOI: 10.4018/979-8-3373-1147-0.ch001

cloud computing, fog computing, and the Internet of Things.

1. INTRODUCTION

An important development in the field of machine intelligence (MI) is the Web of Things (IoT), which represents a step towards a paradigm shift in modern civilisation. Since "things" refers to physical objects in this context, they form a network made up of processing devices and sensors that enable data exchange between them. There are two types of nodes in this network: virtual and physical nodes (Wen et al., 2023). Virtual nodes are software programs or networks used in wireless networks, whereas physical nodes are actuators, detectors, transit nodes, as well as other wearable or imbedded equipment. Because of its versatility, the Internet of Things has attracted a lot of attention lately. IoT systems now need to adjust to a wide range of requirements brought forth by these applications.

The IoT architecture is built upon the first layer also referred to as the sensor layer. It includes RFID tags, readers, embedded systems, sensor networks, and other kinds of sensors placed throughout the field. Each of these kinds of sensors performs the tasks of data collection, identification, and information storage. Transferring the data gathered by the sensed objects to the top layer is the responsibility of the following layer, which is known as the doorways and network layer. Computing services (Amazon Web Services, Microsoft Azure, and Google Cloud, respectively). With a large number of distant servers, cloud computing can intelligently offer users real-time processing, storage, and internet access based on their needs in terms of resource types and quantities (Wen et al., 2024). Sensors, protocols, devices online services, and layers are just a few of the elements that make up the Internet of Things architecture. This architecture's three levels are essential for evaluating data, producing insights, identifying industrial risks, and quickly resolving issues with linked devices. Three different architectures—cloud, fog, and edge computing—are integrated to perform these requirements. IoT device analytics and evaluation are made easier by cloud computing architecture, which provides crucial application-specific operations across a variety of functional areas.

This layer needs to function well and guarantee a strong network while allowing for independent communication between various organisations. The entry point layer and the application itself layer communicate with one other through the management service layer. By gathering vast volumes of raw data and obtaining pertinent information and what has been saved while maintaining the security and integrity of the information, it manages networks and data. Lastly, the IoT top layer is made up of the application layer. Notwithstanding different developmental paths, the convergence of the Internet of Things IoT results in a theoretical structure known as the Cloud of Things (Kristiani et al., 2020). It offers a user interface that enables a variety of users to access various apps that can be utilised in diverse sectors, such as transportation, healthcare, and agriculture.

Based on the fundamental elements, in the Fig. 1 IoT cloud model presents a wider range of simultaneous connectivity choices, which impacts the latency of receiving data from IoT devices from the cloud. Device-to-cloud interfaces act as data transmission endpoints, allowing cloud services and Internet of Things devices to share information (Liu et al., 2022). For this reason, in some situations, combining internet of things and cloud services could maximise resource use. While cloud providers make it easier to move data across the internet, fog computing enables IoT devices to process, make decisions, and then send relevant data to the cloud. Despite subtle differences, the functional congruence underlying edge computing and fog computing architectures—both of which act as enhancers of cloud-based data transmission—is apparent in a number of cases (Lawal et al., 2024). When the discission is all about network layer then it has 6 major components where all are connected to the middle layer. The major components like as tracking, managing, applications, significantly, energy and functional are well explained in figure 1.

Figure 1. The basic architecture of IoT

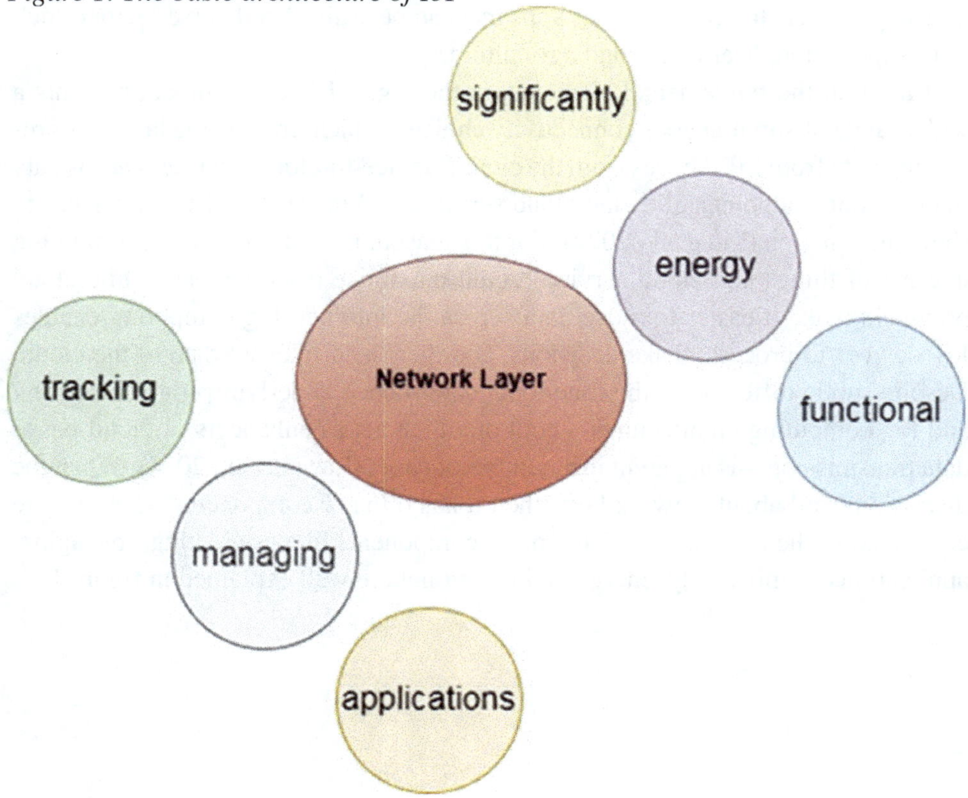

The Internet of Things is a multidimensional technology with applications in an abundance of industries, including transportation, intelligent houses, intelligent towns, healthcare, and agriculture. It is used in agriculture to monitor and improve crop management, animal tracking, and environmental conditions. IoT provides solutions in the healthcare industry, including remote patient monitoring, drug administration, and tracking of linked medical equipment. This technology makes it possible for smart homes to have automated device control, managing energy, and home security. IoT helps smart cities monitor environmental conditions and waste disposal, deploy smart transit networks, and manage urban resources more effectively. IoT in transportation offers advantages including traffic control, road safety, and real-time vehicle tracking. Its versatility has benefits that range from increased operational effectiveness to better quality of life. It is essential for process optimization, well-informed decision-making, and the development of more intelligent and ecologically sound settings because it makes it possible for sophisticated networking, real-time data collecting, and in-depth analysis (Zhang et al., 2022).

Even after the three computing structures were integrated, some areas of computer networks still face a number of difficulties. These difficulties include, among other things, problems with 5G network infrastructure, inaccurate data storage in industrial IoT, resource allocation difficulties, and mistakes in optimization procedures, increased energy consumption, and complexity in business and service models. IoT technology is essential in many areas, such as e-commerce, industrial structures, data security, the creation of novel companies, and other industries, in the current era of rapid communication networks (Lai & Chang, 2023). Even while many IoT applications have advanced significantly in the past several years, it is important to remember that technology in general is still in its infancy. The aforementioned difficulties might remain because of this preliminary phase of growth. If the discussion about application of the resource management industrial IoT application then it may include the smart manufacturing for optimizing resource usage in industrial manufacturing systems to improve productivity and efficiency. Industrial automation with utilization resource management techniques to support industrial automation and control systems and predictive maintenance with leveraging resource management to support predictive maintenance and reduce downtime in industrial based equipment. Simple discussions of IoT provides the extended part as IIoT and all resources may be connected to resource management in IIoT with energy scale so some resources may be interconnected with Quality services and scalable resource that will be measured automatically. Here are few factors treated as key Aspects of Resource Management in IIoT with energy efficiency: optimizing resource usage to minimize energy consumption and reduce costs, particularly in real-time IoT applications with stringent Quality of Service (QoS) requirements. Scalability: Developing flexible and scalable IoT infrastructure to support diverse use cases and applications, such as autonomous driving, eHealth, and smart grids. Dynamic Resource Allocation: Utilizing techniques like Deep Reinforcement Learning (DRL) and Mobile Edge Computing (MEC) to dynamically manage resources and adapt to changing industrial environments. Device-to-Device (D2D) Communication: Leveraging D2D communication and MEC to enhance resource utilization and QoS in IIoT applications.

Some benefits of effective resource management in IIoT that improved Responsiveness: Enhancing industrial communication processes and responsiveness by managing resources effectively. Reduced Delays: Preventing task delays and ensuring timely decision-making in industrial applications. Increased Efficiency: Optimizing resource utilization to reduce costs and improve overall efficiency.

2. LITERATURE REVIEW IOT-AGRICULTURAL

The Internet of Things (IoT) is a network of linked things that exchange information and communicate with one another. Smart agriculture, which aims to increase agricultural output while improving resource utilisation, is one of its most important uses. An essay by the author suggested a crop tracking apparatus that uses soil sensors to measure temperature, humidity, and soil moisture. This method helps to maximise water use by automating irrigation where soil moisture levels are low (Cui et al., 2024). A Raspberry Pi is linked to the sensors, enabling wireless communication. The findings of the experiments and observations show that this project offers a complete answer to problems pertaining to agricultural irrigation. Improved agricultural yields and less waste of water resources could result from field application.

IoT in agriculture refers to the actual use of Internet of Things (IoT) technologies to upgrade general farming practices, increase efficiency and improve crop yields. This generally involves deploying sensors, devices and data analytics to control, monitor and manage different aspects of agricultural operations. Here are few applications of IoT in Agriculture including the general terms: Key Applications of IoT in Agriculture: Precision Farming: Using sensors and drones to monitor soil moisture, temperature, and crop health, enabling targeted irrigation and fertilization. Livestock Monitoring: Tracking animal health, behaviour, and location using wearable sensors and RFID tags. Crop Monitoring: Monitoring crop growth, detecting pests and diseases, and predicting yields using sensors and satellite imaging. Automated Farming: Using IoT-enabled automation to control irrigation, pruning, and harvesting systems. In resource allocation, supply chain management has key role to identify the importance of resource management providing information about agriculture farming. It is already satisfied where tracking system may be possible and can be justified through the term of crop management system.

Supply Chain Management: Tracking produce from farm to table using IoT-enabled sensors and blockchain technology. here are the benefits of IoT in Agriculture for Increasing efficiency with automating tasks and optimizing resource usage. It improves Crop Yields for enhancing crop health and yields through precision farming. Reduced Waste for minimizing water and fertilizer usage. It enhances decision-making for providing real-time data for informed decision-making. Improved Food Safety for tracking produce and detecting potential contaminants.

Basic examples of IoT in Agriculture era: Smart Irrigation Systems: Using soil moisture sensors to optimize irrigation. Drone-Based Crop Monitoring: Using drones equipped with cameras and sensors to monitor crop health. Livestock Tracking: Using GPS and sensor-enabled collars to track animal location and health.

Challenges and Future Directions in agriculture era: Connectivity and Infrastructure: Ensuring reliable connectivity in rural areas. Data Management: Handling large amounts of data generated by IoT devices. Security: Protecting IoT devices and data from cyber threats. Integration: Integrating IoT solutions with existing agricultural practices.

Overall, IoT has the potential to transform agriculture by increasing efficiency, reducing waste, and improving crop yields.

2.1. Three-Layer Architecture

The effectiveness of the architecture of the Internet of Things layer is crucial for the fastest possible convergence of data and communications systems while maintaining security and authenticity. The three-layer paradigm figure. 2 which consists of the perceptions, network, and application levels, is one of the well-known and fundamental IoT architectures (Wang et al., 2019). Despite being realistic and doable in its implementation, this system is unable to offer a complete answer because of the complexity of the Internet of Things. All details are mentioned in figure 2.

Figure 2. Three-layer architecture and service-oriented architecture of IoT

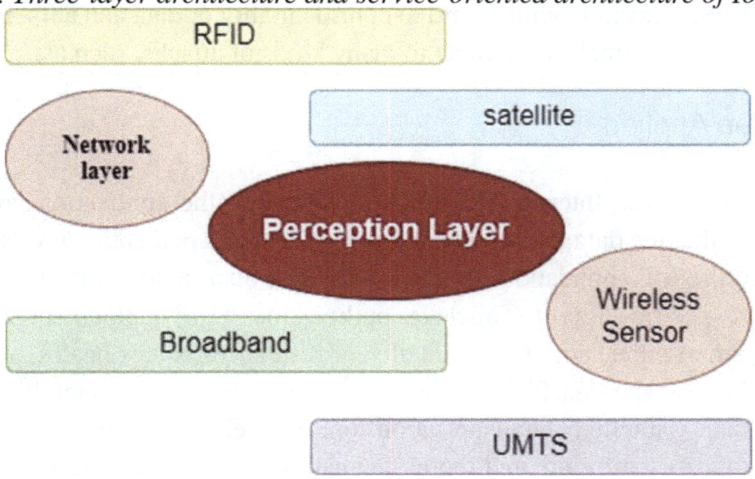

A. Layer of Perception

Located at the bottom and also known as the control layer, the perception layer is mostly focused on object detection and gathering information from users, desired services, and the surroundings (Biswas & Wang, 2023). It includes detection tools like bar codes, RFID, distance sensors, and other physical items. The choice of monitoring tools depends on the particular service needs. This layer, which has sensory capabilities, picks up signals from the surroundings, including intelligent objects (Xing et al., 2023). In order to carry out the required management procedures through executive devices, the perception layer receives control signals from the connectivity layer and performs preliminary data processing and packing after data gathering. Included within this layer are data sensors like Wireless Sensor Network (WSN), Reactive Sensor Network (RSN)

B. Network Layer

In the IoT design, the network layer—also called the transmission layer—acts as a bridge that joins the application and experience layers. This layer acts as a conduit, transferring information from tangible items and distributing it via sensors, much like the brain's neurons and neural network (Aboualola et al., 2023). This layer uses both wired and wireless transmission techniques, including Wi-Fi, 3G, UMTS, The infrared Broadband, satellite, Bluetooth as well, and Networks protocols. Furthermore, the network layer takes on the duty of connecting different networks, smart entities, and network devices (Liu et al., 2024). As a result, the network layer has serious security flaws, especially with regard to confidentiality of data and authentication, which leaves it extremely vulnerable to many kinds of attacks, such as:

C. Degree Applied

At the top of the Internet of Things architecture, the application layer is in charge of evaluating data from the connected devices and perception levels in order to produce the IoT application. Its responsibilities also include offering the user application-specific support. This layer outlines many IoT deployment scenarios, including smart cities, smart cars, intelligent residences, smart health, and smart eyewear (Amin & Hossain, 2020). In order to implement a variety of intelligent technologies, such as intelligent transportation control, intelligent properties, intelligent logistics, safety monitoring, and motor navigation, it acts as an interface between the Internet of Things and different users, whether they be systems or humans, with specific requirements (Zhang et al., 2022).

3. COMPUTATIONAL EDGES

Globally, the expansion of internet access of Things (IoT) is propelling the manufacturing and use of a wide range of sensors and hardware devices. These sensors and hardware components have the ability to sense their physical surroundings and transform that information into data. Members of the public can access data stored on the cloud and retrieve the information they require based on their specific needs once these massive volumes of data have been moved there for processing or storage. But as IoT continues to advance and be used more widely, new problems with cloud computing are starting to surface. For instance, issues with low performance, high latency, bandwidth constraints, data protection, centralised vulnerabilities, and extra expenses arise when data produced by worldwide endpoints is processed and stored in a centralised cloud (Cai et al., 2024). High speed and low latency are in fact necessary for the processing of data, analysis, and result return in many IoT application scenarios, particularly in the digital age of Vehicles.

4. PROGRAMMING IN FOGGY

In contrast to typical cloud computing, fog computing design distributes networking, processing, storage, and computing functions among several end devices (Hu & Hao, 2012). By placing compute, storage, and network connections close to end devices, it acts as a conduit to bring the cloud and actual devices closer together. Essentially, fog computing works in tandem with cloud computing by carrying out certain processing activities close to the network's edge, close to end users. The topology used by this paradigm is made up of geographically scattered nodes that perform networking and storage duties in addition to computational responsibilities. Fog nodes are network-integrated devices that can be placed anywhere there is an Ethernet cable. A device needs to be able to compute, store, and connect in order to be considered a fog node. The differences between cloud with edge computing architectures, with or without computing architecture, are depicted in Figure 3. Therefore, using all three architectures is necessary for the successful deployment of an IoT solution, which is a fully integrated collection of technologies meant to solve an issue or provide value to the organisation. — cloud, fog, and edge (Zhuang et al., 2023). Ethernet, store, edge, cloud and fog are directly connected with network which has range to identify the grid length and gives the proper information to the user in figure 3.

Figure 3. Fog computing design

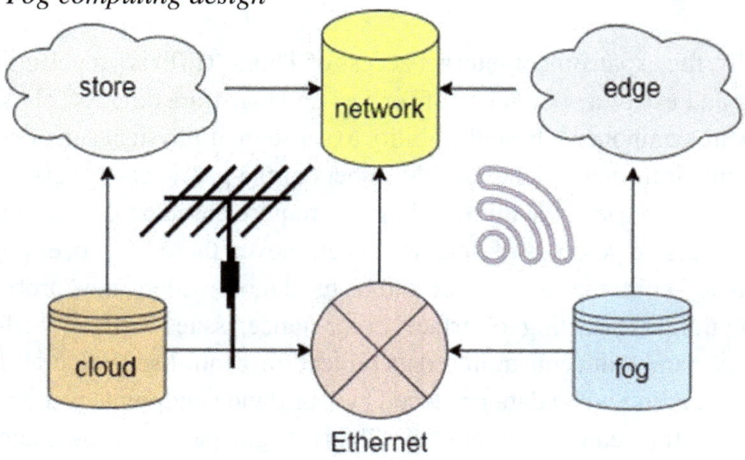

As a transit system, fog computing reduces the amount of data sent to the main data centre by going through and reacting to data locally, improving bandwidth and privacy. By operating close to end customers, this method also reduces latency and opens up scalability possibilities (Kuchuk & Malokhvii, 2024). However, there are drawbacks to being close to the network's edge, such as vulnerability to intrusion attempts, problems with authentication, and widely distributed rejection of service. Although fog computing has uses in a wide range of industries, including data processing, web optimisation, road safety, healthcare systems, micro-data centre control of resources, and processing pictures for surveillance, it experiences execution time delays as a result of ineffective task scheduling alongside resource allocation for user tasks (Zhou et al., 2021). An inventive bio-inspired composite algorithm has been put out for managing assets in the fog-IoT framework in order to tackle this problem (Gong et al., 2023).

This method uses components of modified cat swarm optimisation (MCSO) to manage available fog resources and modified particle swarm optimisation (MPSO) to distribute load across fog nodes (Ali et al., 2022). The results of the suggested technique indicate promise in lowering energy usage, completion time, average response period, and cost in contrast to traditional fog computing scheduling strategies. However, the learning mechanisms in the proposed model must be reframed and reinforced in order to be applied in a fog-IoT environment. Concerns about potential privacy issues and a loss of sovereignty over data are raised by fog computing concepts, which store user data on cloud servers (Al-Saedi et al., 2022). Conventional methods of protecting confidentiality and privacy are frequently inadequate to stop assaults on cloud servers. A three-tier storage infrastructure has been proposed as a solution to these issues, with the goal of protecting data privacy while optimising cloud storage use. This framework stores data on a user's local device, cloud server, and fog server. Data is encoded on the user's device using the Hash-Solomon code algorithm, which preserves fragmented data and divides it into discrete chunks for the best possible storage use (El-Sayed et al., 2017).

4.1 The Need for Computing on the Edge

Three viewpoints shall be used to describe the significance of EC: the “big volume era” ushered in by the Internet of Things; increased demands for high network responsiveness and reliability; and privacy and security considerations (Nain et al., 2022).

Computing on the edge, also known as edge computing, is becoming increasingly important due to several factors with reduced latency including edge computing processes data closer to its source, reducing latency and enabling real-time decision-making. Improved Performance through processing data at the edge, devices can respond faster and more efficiently. Enhanced security including edge computing reduces the amount of data transmitted to the cloud or central servers, minimizing the risk of data breaches. Increased reliability for edge computing can continue to function even with limited or no internet connectivity. Bandwidth optimization for edge computing reduces the amount of data transmitted over the network, optimizing bandwidth usage. Benefits are

1. Faster Decision-Making: Edge computing enables faster decision-making by processing data in real-time.
2. Improved Efficiency: Edge computing optimizes bandwidth usage and reduces latency, improving overall efficiency.
3. Enhanced Security: Edge computing reduces the risk of data breaches by processing data closer to its source

   so overall, computing on the edge is becoming increasingly important as more devices become connected and require fast, efficient, and secure processing.

4.2 The Global Internet of Things-Driven Data Warehouse Era

Even while supply chain management was the original purpose of the Internet of Things concept, it now encompasses a far larger scope. Smart buildings, smart grids, sensible traffic, and smart factories are just a few of the new application areas that have emerged as a result of his introduction of IoT into conventional sectors (Chen et al., 2024). According to the Internet of Things concept, objects that are linked to the Internet create a vast network that enables connections at any time and from any location. The number of sensors, smart phones, health apps, and online social media sites is growing quickly as the Encyclopaedia of Things continues to develop, and the outcome of this global data is anticipated to improve prediction, according to the Worldwide Data Corporation. The big data field has benefited from this enormous volume of data (Rupanetti & Kaabouch, 2024).

Moving data to the cloud to be handled is the simplest and most straightforward method of working with it in the big data era. Global yearly cloud Internet protocol traffic was predicted to exceed, according to Cisco (Chen et al., 2018). On the other hand, the cloud's processing capacity grows linearly. Compared to the current data growth rates, this is far slower. Given the speed at which data is growing, computing in the cloud is no longer entirely dependable. Rapid response times are necessary in certain IoT application scenarios. For instance, self-driving automobiles equipped with sensor devices like cameras are used in intelligent driving scenarios. When driving autonomously, these small sensors can consistently gather environmental data (Putra et al., 2024). According to a web-based computing model, all of this information is sent to the cloud for computation, and the control chip of the car receives the results. This approach is incredibly time-consuming and can even hinder the intelligent car from making timely decisions due to its complicated operating environment, which could have dire repercussions (Liu et al., 2022).

4.3 Increased Standards for Response Time and Network Stability

In the realm of virtual reality (VR) and augmented reality (AR), mobile AR/VR applications need to transmit high-resolution video continuously, which puts a lot of strain on reaction time, network reliability, and data processing power (Mohammadi et al., 2024). The power of cloud computing can no longer keeps up with the needs of today's growing data. However, there would be significant network congestion if all data is uploaded to the cloud. Cloud computing is unable to satisfy the latency and timeliness constraints of these scenarios because of the enormous weight that the data stored by numerous IoT devices places on the network's limited bandwidth. Furthermore, there may be a lot of inaccuracies and noise in this data. Only one-third of data that is gathered by the majority of sensors is correct, according to certain research. Many clouds server horsepower and network bandwidth are wasted when this useless material is stored on the cloud (Gong et al., 2020).

5. PROTECTION OF PRIVACY AND SECURITY

Outsourcing is possible with cloud computing. Users need to store their own data in the data centre in order to use cloud computing. Numerous privacy and data security problems result from this. Data loss via distant communication between equipment and the cloud may jeopardise the accuracy and integrity of the data. High levels of centralisation in handling and storing data are additionally a major issue. Other devices will suffer if the main device malfunctions as a result of a malicious attack or a benign issue. Theft or usage by other unapproved individuals, businesses, or organisations is considered privacy issues. Because of the cloud's service-oriented architecture, data owners no longer have control over the data they upload.

6. AI IS NECESSARY FOR NETWORK EDGE DATA TO REACH THEIR COMPLETE POTENTIAL

Large volumes of various types of information (audio, pictures, video, etc.) about the physical world are continuously gathered on the machine's side due to the quickly growing quantity and diversity of mobile and Internet of Things devices. AI that can swiftly evaluate these enormous volumes of data and extract insights for sound decision-making is functionally required in this situation. One of the most widely used AI technologies, deep learning, automatically finds anomalies and patterns in data gathered by edge devices, including demographics, traffic flow, humidity, pressure, and temperature; and air quality. Operational efficiency is improved by using insights from the gathered data to inform real-time predictive decision-making (traffic control, driver warnings, public transportation planning, etc.) in reaction to quickly changing environments (Cao et al., 2020).

7. AI CAN GROW THROUGH EDGE COMPUTING MORE RICH METADATA AND INDUSTRY SITUATIONS

It is generally acknowledged that four factors—algorithms, machinery, data, and application scenarios—are responsible for the current explosion in deep learning. Although the impact of technology and algorithms on deep learning growth is obvious, data and application cases have received less attention. Adding more neuron layers to the DNN is the most popular method for enhancing the capacity of deep learning algorithms. Thus, more parameters must be learnt by the DNN, increasing the amount of training data needed. This illustrates how crucial data is to the development of AI. When you understand the value of data, you may wonder, "Where does it come from?" Mega data centres were the usual location for the generation and storage of data in the past (Shi et al., 2016). However, that trend is currently reversing due to the IoT rapid development. A tremendous quantity of IoT information will soon be released at the edge, per Cisco research. The processing of this data by artificial intelligence programs in cloud server's results in high bandwidth resource consumption and a substantial strain on cloud server farms. By shifting processing power between cloud data centres down to the edge, or edge side, edge computing has been offered as a solution to these problems in order attain low-latency data processing. H. AI processing with high performance is made possible in figure 4.

8. TAKING ARTIFICIAL INTELLIGENCE TO NEW LEVELS

8.1. Structures

Various architectures for fast inferring models have been developed to satisfy latency concerns. Three significant architectures that are shown in Figure were the focus of the study. 4.

(1) Calculation on-device, in which DNNs are run on the final devices.
(2) In periphery server-based constructions, endpoints send data to edge processors for processing.
(3) Collaborative computing, which encompasses the potential for cloud work.

Router and server connectivity have been controlled with consideration for user accessibility, and detailed information is provided in Figure 4. The complete description is available and explained in figure 4.

Figure 4. On-Device computer

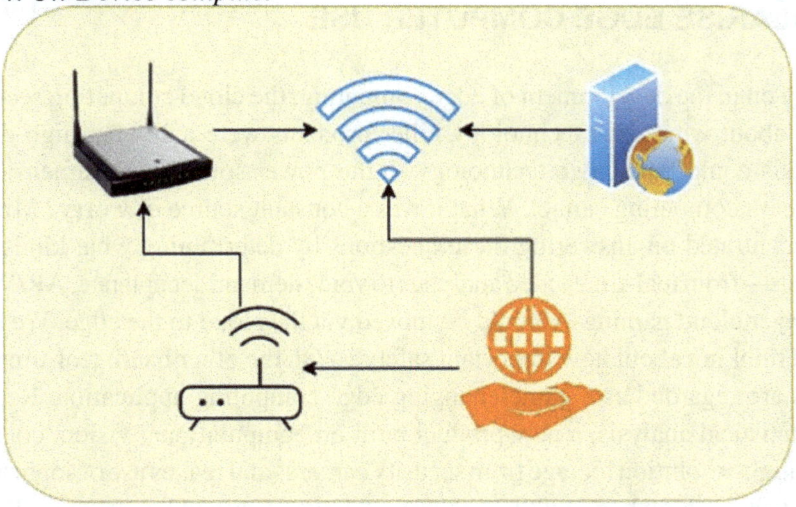

8.2. Model Computer and Hardware

A number of studies have examined the potential for introducing artificial intelligence to low-resource devices, and efforts have been made to reduce the inference time of the model on the device. In order to deploy an AI model on devices with embedded functionality, machine learning developers must address the appropriate hardware selection that aligns with model design and compression (Khan et al., 2019).

8.2.1. Model Design

ML experts work on developing models with a decreased number of inputs in the DNN model, thereby lowering memory and execution time, while striving to keep high accuracy. There are various efficient models created expressly to run a NN on hardware with minimal processing capacity and leadership, such as mobile networks or Squeeze Network, originally established for tasks pertaining to computer vision. Mobile Nets are built on a simplified architecture that creates lightweight deep neural networks (NNs) using depth-wise separable convolutions. Squeeze Net uses unique convolution coefficients to down sample the data (Liu et al., 2019).

9. AI TECHNOLOGIES COULD HELP POPULARISE EDGE COMPUTER USE

Early on in the development of edge computing, the cloud computing sector was curious about what edge technology killer products were and what high-demand workloads could push edge technology to the power source next dimension that mainstream computing cannot. What it was a constant source of worry? Microsoft has concentrated on answering these questions by determining what kinds of applications—from real-time video analytics to voice demand acceptance, AR/VR, and multiplayer cloud gaming—should be moved via the cloud to the edge. We haven't stopped thinking about how important safety is. On the other hand, real-time video insights are regarded as a game-changing edge computing application. Real-time video statistical analysis, a new product built on computational vision, constantly gathers high-resolution footage from security cameras and makes use of sophisticated data protection, high bandwidth, high processing power, and low latency. The only practical way to satisfy these demanding requirements is through edge computing. In light of the aforementioned advancements in edge computing, we may forecast that new AI uses across domains like the Internet of Things, intelligent robots, urban planning, and home automation will be crucial to the growth of edge computing. The main reason for this is that a lot of AI applications for smart phones and the Internet of Things are a family of useful applications that are sensitive to latency, privacy, and energy consumption. As a result, they naturally work well with computing near the edge. This must be completed (Joshi & Patil, 2024).

10. FRAMEWORKS FOR INTERNET, EDGE, AND FOG TECHNOLOGY

Devices with different addressing systems can easily communicate and share data thanks to the Internet of Things' architecture for universal computing. No matter the place, time, or entities involved, this special capacity enables the connectivity of objects and people using these devices in a variety of settings. IoT facilitates connection and engagement across any system, the internet, path, service, or communication method. Essentially, cloud computing architecture supports both device-to-device and app-to-app communications by facilitating collaboration among devices and apps in the Internet of Things. Furthermore, the edge computing and fog computing topologies function as cloud network extensions. The versatility and effectiveness of IoT computation and communication are improved by these architectures, which are distinguished by decentralised networks made up of a group of computers (Krishna et al., 2024).

11. INTERNET COMPUTING

Internet computing refers to the use of internet-connected devices and infrastructure to process, store, and manage data, applications, and services. This encompasses various technologies, including Cloud computing: Remote storage, processing, and management of data and applications. Distributed Computing: Processing tasks across multiple devices or nodes. Edge Computing: Processing data closer to its source, reducing latency.

Discussing characteristics, applications, and benefits would warrant a detailed discussion in itself. Therefore, the relevant data is being mentioned here.

Key Characteristics:
Scalability: Internet computing resources can be scaled up or down as needed.
Accessibility: Resources are accessible from anywhere with an internet connection.
On-demand services: Resources and services are provided on-demand. If the study deals with few applications, then it includes
Cloud Storage: Storing and accessing data online.
Online Applications: Web-based software and services. IoT (Internet of Things): Connecting and processing data from devices.
Benefits of internet computing:
Increased Flexibility: Access to resources from anywhere.
Cost-Effectiveness: Reduced infrastructure costs.
Improved Collaboration: Enhanced sharing and collaboration.
Challenges:
Security: Protecting data and applications from cyber threats.
Dependence on Internet: Requires stable internet connectivity.
Data Management: Managing and processing large amounts of data. so here internet computing enables efficient, scalable, and accessible computing resources, transforming the way we work, communicate, and access information.

Through the internet, cloud computing provides a range of computer services, which include as servers, networks, software, the form of databases, and data analytics. It is an application-based software system that offers quick deployment and adaptable tools and resources. These services are run by other organisations, and data is kept on distant servers that are reachable from anywhere in the globe through the internet. Different model of service and deployment techniques that are adapted to the unique requirements of clients are how cloud computing functions. Private, community, open to the public, and combination approaches are among the cloud's deployment options, serving private users, people in general, single organisations, and many organisations, respectively (Joshi & Patil, 2022). Because of its adaptability, cloud computing infrastructure benefits a wide range of users. Among the main characteristics of cloud computing are cost-effective solutions that combine mobility, scalability, multitenancy operates, a large resource pool, and service availability, making them appropriate for both public and corporate use. Notwithstanding its benefits, several experts have pointed out some disadvantages with cloud computing. Among the worries are the potential for commercial and regional rules to prevent essential components from being supplied when needed. Furthermore, there may be security, integrity, and authenticity problems associated with the shared resource notion. However, cloud computing has proven to be beneficial in a variety of domains, including data storage, research, e-learning, and e-governance.

A. Internet Intelligence: All DNN prediction of models and learning takes place in show figure 5 the public internet.
B. Level 1 - Cloud-Edge Cooperation Conference and Online Training: Infer the model using DNN collaboratively across the edge of the cloud while training it in the cloud. Some data gets exported to the cloud as a result of edge-cloud integration.
C. Level 2 - Network instruction and in-edge conferences: The DNN model is trained in the cloud, yet it makes inferences in an in-edge way. In this context, "in-edge" refers to model inference carried out inside the network edge. Data may be fully or partially offloaded to edge nodes or neighbouring devices (via D2D connection) to accomplish this.
D. Level 3 - Cloud preparation and on-device inference: The model used by the DNN is properly inferred remotely on the device, yet it is trained on the cloud. In this context, "on-device" refers to data that is not transferred.
E. Level 4 - Programming and computation of DNN models in cloud edge and cloud networking is known as cloud edge collaborated training and inference (Liu et al., 2019).
F. Level 5 – The judgement and the education of DNN models are in-edge approaches.
G. Level 6 – Everything on the device: The neural network (DNN) model is trained and inferred on the physical device (Musaddiq et al., 2018).
    1. All the data and (Hussain et al., 2020) functionality related to DNN prediction models and learning are comprehensively illustrated in Figure 5, which reminds us of a human-centric approach that inherently enhances user efficiency (Javadpour et al., 2020) and it also shows all segments one by one in figure 5.

Figure 5. All DNN prediction of models and learning

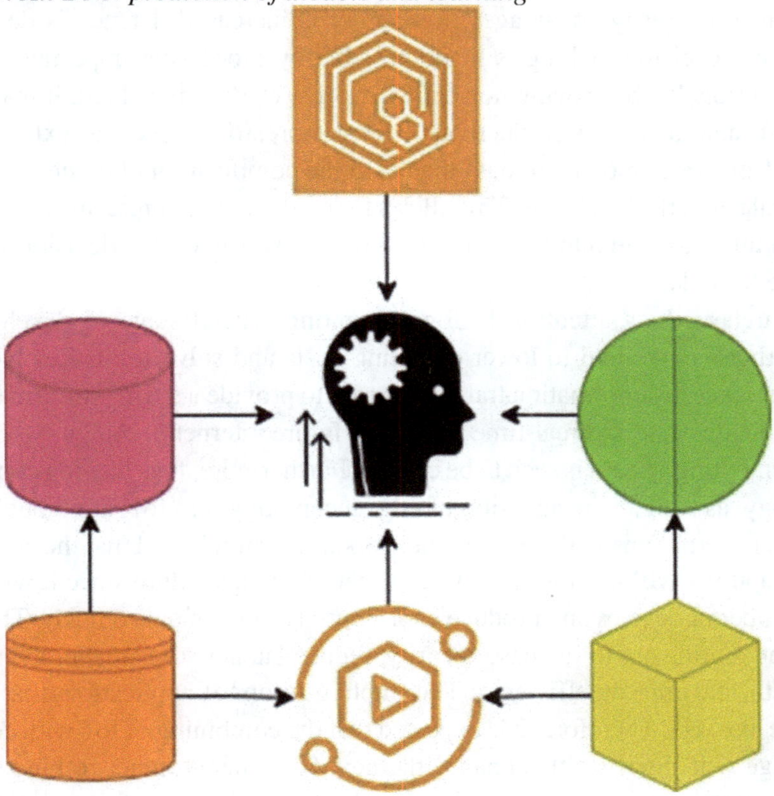

All DNN (Deep Neural Network) is the model for learning and prediction with all segments and further prediction of models and learning refers to the actual process of using deep learning techniques to upgrade and train models that can make accurate predictions or decisions based on general complex data. Key Aspects with Model Training: DNNs learn from large datasets, adjusting weights and biases to minimize errors. Prediction: Trained models make predictions on new, unseen data. Learning: DNNs learn patterns, relationships, and representations from data. This DNN model exists the actual data of prediction and learning at initial stage.

12. CONCLUSION

Internet infrastructure, computer science at the edge, and neural networks have come together to create edge-to-cloud intelligence, which has completely changed the potential of Internet of Things technologies. IoT devices can now gather, process, and analyse data in real time at the edge thanks to this integration, which also makes use of cloud facilities for scalability as well as statistical analysis. Edge-to-cloud intelligence has many advantages. Reliability is increased, latency is decreased, and quicker decision-making is made possible by processing important data locally. Additionally, by moving non-time-sensitive work to the cloud, it maximises resource usage and boosts productivity. Furthermore, IoT devices can extract useful insights from vast amounts of data thanks to the combination of cloud computing and neural network algorithms. This allows for predictive and prescriptive analytics, which in turn promote intelligent automation and well-informed decision-making. It will be feasible.

Researchers draw attention to fog computing crucial stage of development, highlighting its potential to lower operating costs and solve IoT issues including latency, storage, as information traffic. In order to provide a smart platform that can manage the disperse and real-time aspects of future internet of things systems, the dense computing system is seen to be crucial. Furthermore, fogs like fog computing technology, as well as the adoption of edge technology into IoT, are thought to be solutions for problems with seamless networks. It is anticipated that the concept of edge computing will be crucial to the Internet of Things' future since it will link a large number of devices and produce enormous amounts of data quickly. The goals of this integration are to increase security, reduce latency, use smaller amounts of bandwidth, and improve efficiency. The emphasis is on IoT applications that require real-time answers. Therefore, it is expected that the combining of IoT with compute at the edge will significantly enhance the next 6th generation networking system. 6G technology is regarded as a crucial enabler for realising the full capabilities of IoT and has the potential to revolutionise a number of industries. Applications like holographic transfers, via telemedicine for distant health care, cities with smart autonomous public transportation, improved distance learning opportunities, brain-computer screens, and other cutting-edge technologies are anticipated to emerge from the combining of IoT in the larger setting of 6G.

REFERENCES

Aboualola, M., Abualsaud, K., Khattab, T., Zorba, N., & Hassanein, H. S. (2023). Edge technologies for disaster management: A survey of social media and artificial intelligence integration. *IEEE Access : Practical Innovations, Open Solutions*, *11*, 73782–73802. DOI: 10.1109/ACCESS.2023.3293035

Al-Saedi, A. A., Boeva, V., Casalicchio, E., & Exner, P. (2022). Context-Aware Edge-Based AI Models for Wireless Sensor Networks—An Overview. *Sensors (Basel)*, *22*(15), 5544. DOI: 10.3390/s22155544 PMID: 35898044

Ali, O., Ishak, M. K., Bhatti, M. K. L., Khan, I., & Kim, K. I. (2022). A comprehensive review of internet of things: Technology stack, middlewares, and fog/edge computing interface. *Sensors (Basel)*, *22*(3), 995. DOI: 10.3390/s22030995 PMID: 35161740

Amin, S. U., & Hossain, M. S. (2020). Edge intelligence and Internet of Things in healthcare: A survey. *IEEE Access : Practical Innovations, Open Solutions*, *9*, 45–59. DOI: 10.1109/ACCESS.2020.3045115

Biswas, A., & Wang, H. C. (2023). Autonomous vehicles enabled by the integration of IoT, edge intelligence, 5G, and blockchain. *Sensors (Basel)*, *23*(4), 1963. DOI: 10.3390/s23041963 PMID: 36850560

Cai, Z., Cao, X., Zhang, Z., Chen, Q., Li, H., Li, X., . . . Zhu, G. (2024, March). Integrated Sensing and Learning for Better Generalized Edge AI. In *2024 IEEE 4th International Symposium on Joint Communications & Sensing (JC&S)* (pp. 1-6). IEEE. DOI: 10.1109/JCS61227.2024.10646278

Cao, K., Liu, Y., Meng, G., & Sun, Q. (2020). An overview on edge computing research. *IEEE Access : Practical Innovations, Open Solutions*, *8*, 85714–85728. DOI: 10.1109/ACCESS.2020.2991734

Chen, C. H., Lin, M. Y., & Liu, C. C. (2018). Edge computing gateway of the industrial internet of things using multiple collaborative microcontrollers. *IEEE Network*, *32*(1), 24–32. DOI: 10.1109/MNET.2018.1700146

Chen, X., Letaief, K. B., & Huang, K. (2024). On the View-and-Channel Aggregation Gain in Integrated Sensing and Edge AI. *IEEE Journal on Selected Areas in Communications*, *42*(9), 2292–2305. DOI: 10.1109/JSAC.2024.3413988

Cui, Y., Cao, X., Zhu, G., Nie, J., & Xu, J. (2024). Edge Perception: Intelligent Wireless Sensing at Network Edge. *arXiv preprint arXiv:2410.21017*.

El-Sayed, H., Sankar, S., Prasad, M., Puthal, D., Gupta, A., Mohanty, M., & Lin, C. T. (2017). Edge of things: The big picture on the integration of edge, IoT and the cloud in a distributed computing environment. *IEEE Access, 6*, 1706-1717.

Gong, C., Lin, F., Gong, X., & Lu, Y. (2020). Intelligent cooperative edge computing in internet of things. *IEEE Internet of Things Journal*, *7*(10), 9372–9382. DOI: 10.1109/JIOT.2020.2986015

Gong, T., Zhu, L., Yu, F. R., & Tang, T. (2023). Edge intelligence in intelligent transportation systems: A survey. *IEEE Transactions on Intelligent Transportation Systems*, *24*(9), 8919–8944. DOI: 10.1109/TITS.2023.3275741

Hu, F., & Hao, Q. (2012). *Intelligent sensor networks: the integration of sensor networks, signal processing and machine learning*. Taylor & Francis. DOI: 10.1201/b14300

Hussain, F., Hassan, S. A., Hussain, R., & Hossain, E. (2020). Machine learning for resource management in cellular and IoT networks: Potentials, current solutions, and open challenges. *IEEE Communications Surveys and Tutorials*, *22*(2), 1251–1275. DOI: 10.1109/COMST.2020.2964534

Javadpour, A., Wang, G., & Rezaei, S. (2020). Resource management in a peer to peer cloud network for IoT. *Wireless Personal Communications*, *115*(3), 2471–2488. DOI: 10.1007/s11277-020-07691-7

Joshi, V., & Patil, K. (2022). Delay-energy aware task offloading and vm migration policy for mobile edge computing. *Wireless Personal Communications*, *123*(4), 3309–3326. DOI: 10.1007/s11277-021-09290-6

Joshi, V., & Patil, K. (2024, April). Efficient Handoff Detection for Computation Offloading using Machine Learning and Bio-Inspired Optimization Techniques in Mobile Edge Computing. In *2024 IEEE 13th International Conference on Communication Systems and Network Technologies (CSNT)* (pp. 100-104). IEEE. DOI: 10.1109/CSNT60213.2024.10546105

Khan, W. Z., Ahmed, E., Hakak, S., Yaqoob, I., & Ahmed, A. (2019). Edge computing: A survey. *Future Generation Computer Systems*, *97*, 219–235. DOI: 10.1016/j.future.2019.02.050

Krishna, G., Singh, V., Pandey, D., Krishna, K. H., Joshi, K., & Gupta, T. (2024, May). Power trading framework of cloud-edge computing in the artificial intelligence market. In *2024 4th International Conference on Advance Computing and Innovative Technologies in Engineering (ICACITE)*, pp. 1910-1918. IEEE. DOI: 10.1109/ICACITE60783.2024.10617344

Kristiani, E., Yang, C. T., Huang, C. Y., Ko, P. C., & Fathoni, H. (2020). On construction of sensors, edge, and cloud (ISEC) framework for smart system integration and applications. *IEEE Internet of Things Journal*, *8*(1), 309–319. DOI: 10.1109/JIOT.2020.3004244

Kuchuk, H., & Malokhvii, E. (2024). Integration of IOT with Cloud, Fog, and Edge Computing: A Review. *Advanced Information Systems*, *8*(2), 65–78. DOI: 10.20998/2522-9052.2024.2.08

Lai, M. H., & Chang, K. S. (2023). AI Sensor Applications in Edge Computing. *IEEE Nanotechnology Magazine*, *17*(6), 23–28. DOI: 10.1109/MNANO.2023.3316869

Lawal, O., Veluthedath Shajihan, S. A., Mechitov, K., & Spencer Jr, B. F. (2024). Edge Integration of Artificial Intelligence into Wireless Smart Sensor Platforms for Railroad Bridge Impact Detection. *Sensors (Basel)*, *24*(17), 5633. DOI: 10.3390/s24175633 PMID: 39275541

Liu, F., Tang, G., Li, Y., Cai, Z., Zhang, X., & Zhou, T. (2019). A survey on edge computing systems and tools. *Proceedings of the IEEE*, *107*(8), 1537–1562. DOI: 10.1109/JPROC.2019.2920341

Liu, P., Zhu, G., Jiang, W., Luo, W., Xu, J., & Cui, S. (2022). Vertical federated edge learning with distributed integrated sensing and communication. *IEEE Communications Letters*, *26*(9), 2091–2095. DOI: 10.1109/LCOMM.2022.3181612

Liu, P., Zhu, G., Wang, S., Jiang, W., Luo, W., Poor, H. V., & Cui, S. (2022). Toward ambient intelligence: Federated edge learning with task-oriented sensing, computation, and communication integration. *IEEE Journal of Selected Topics in Signal Processing*, *17*(1), 158–172. DOI: 10.1109/JSTSP.2022.3226836

Liu, S., Liu, L., Tang, J., Yu, B., Wang, Y., & Shi, W. (2019). Edge computing for autonomous driving: Opportunities and challenges. *Proceedings of the IEEE*, *107*(8), 1697–1716. DOI: 10.1109/JPROC.2019.2915983

Liu, S., Wen, D., Li, D., Chen, Q., Zhu, G., & Shi, Y. (2024). Energy-Efficient Optimal Mode Selection for Edge AI Inference via Integrated Sensing-Communication-Computation. *IEEE Transactions on Mobile Computing*, *23*(12), 14248–14262. DOI: 10.1109/TMC.2024.3440581

Mohammadi, M., Assaf, G., Assaad, R. H., & Chang, A. J. (2024). An Intelligent Cloud-Based IoT-Enabled Multimodal Edge Sensing Device for Automated, Real-Time, Comprehensive, and Standardized Water Quality Monitoring and Assessment Process Using Multisensor Data Fusion Technologies. *Journal of Computing in Civil Engineering*, *38*(6), 04024029. DOI: 10.1061/JCCEE5.CPENG-5989

Musaddiq, A., Zikria, Y. B., Hahm, O., Yu, H., Bashir, A. K., & Kim, S. W. (2018). A survey on resource management in IoT operating systems. *IEEE Access : Practical Innovations, Open Solutions*, *6*, 8459–8482. DOI: 10.1109/ACCESS.2018.2808324

Nain, G., Pattanaik, K. K., & Sharma, G. K. (2022). Towards edge computing in intelligent manufacturing: Past, present and future. *Journal of Manufacturing Systems*, *62*, 588–611. DOI: 10.1016/j.jmsy.2022.01.010

Putra, K. T., Arrayyan, A. Z., Hayati, N., Damarjati, C., Bakar, A., & Chen, H. C. (2024). A Review on the Application of Internet of Medical Things in Wearable Personal Health Monitoring: A Cloud-Edge Artificial Intelligence Approach. *IEEE Access : Practical Innovations, Open Solutions*, *12*, 21437–21452. DOI: 10.1109/ACCESS.2024.3358827

Rupanetti, D., & Kaabouch, N. (2024). Combining Edge Computing-Assisted Internet of Things Security with Artificial Intelligence: Applications, Challenges, and Opportunities. *Applied Sciences (Basel, Switzerland)*, *14*(16), 7104. DOI: 10.3390/app14167104

Shi, W., Cao, J., Zhang, Q., Li, Y., & Xu, L. (2016). Edge computing: Vision and challenges. *IEEE Internet of Things Journal*, *3*(5), 637–646. DOI: 10.1109/JIOT.2016.2579198

Wang, D., Zhang, D., Zhang, Y., Rashid, M. T., Shang, L., & Wei, N. (2019, December). Social edge intelligence: Integrating human and artificial intelligence at the edge. In *2019 IEEE First International Conference on Cognitive Machine Intelligence (CogMI)* (pp. 194-201). IEEE. DOI: 10.1109/CogMI48466.2019.00036

Wen, D., Li, X., Zhou, Y., Shi, Y., Wu, S., & Jiang, C. (2024). Integrated sensing-communication-computation for edge artificial intelligence. *IEEE Internet of Things Magazine*, *7*(4), 14–20. DOI: 10.1109/IOTM.001.2300146

Wen, D., Liu, P., Zhu, G., Shi, Y., Xu, J., Eldar, Y. C., & Cui, S. (2023). Task-oriented sensing, computation, and communication integration for multi-device edge AI. *IEEE Transactions on Wireless Communications*.

Xing, H., Zhu, G., Liu, D., Wen, H., Huang, K., & Wu, K. (2023). Task-oriented integrated sensing, computation and communication for wireless edge AI. *IEEE Network*, *37*(4), 135–144. DOI: 10.1109/MNET.011.2300046

Zhang, T., Wang, S., Li, G., Liu, F., Zhu, G., & Wang, R. (2022, May). Accelerating edge intelligence via integrated sensing and communication. In *ICC 2022-IEEE International Conference on Communications* (pp. 1586-1592). IEEE. DOI: 10.1109/ICC45855.2022.9839016

Zhang, Y., Jiang, C., Yue, B., Wan, J., & Guizani, M. (2022). Information fusion for edge intelligence: A survey. *Information Fusion*, *81*, 171–186. DOI: 10.1016/j.inffus.2021.11.018

Zhou, X., Ke, R., Yang, H., & Liu, C. (2021). When intelligent transportation systems sensing meets edge computing: Vision and challenges. *Applied Sciences (Basel, Switzerland)*, *11*(20), 9680. DOI: 10.3390/app11209680

Zhuang, Z., Wen, D., Shi, Y., Zhu, G., Wu, S., & Niyato, D. (2023). Integrated Sensing-Communication-Computation for Over-the-Air Edge AI Inference. *IEEE Transactions on Wireless Communications*.

Chapter 2
Securing the Edge: Integrating Cloud Security in Data-Driven Edge Systems

Tarun Kumar
https://orcid.org/0000-0002-8507-8522
University of Petroleum and Energy Studies (UPES), Dehradun, India

Minakshi
https://orcid.org/0000-0001-7586-6309
King Khalid University, Saudi Arabia

ABSTRACT

The rapid deployment of data-driven edge (DDE) systems raises significant security concerns. As cloud providers expand edge technologies, accompanying security risks grow exponentially. Unlike traditional deployments, modern systems face sophisticated attacks compromising data, workloads, and computing results. Current security solutions inadequately address cloud-edge integration. Researchers have defined comprehensive security requirements, including data ownership protection and cross-domain access control. A new architecture integrating edge-cloud systems with cloud-native security services has been proposed to mitigate risks. Cloud security vulnerabilities are particularly alarming, with data breaches accounting for approximately 30% of security incidents and substantial financial losses. Potential risks include unauthorized data extraction, backdoor introduction, and hijacking of customer information. Undetected compromised cloud services can propagate malware and exploit system vulnerabilities, posing significant threats to public security and data integrity.

DOI: 10.4018/979-8-3373-1147-0.ch002

1. INTRODUCTION

In recent years, end-devices have generated unprecedented volumes of diverse data, driving the rapid development of data-driven edge applications that bring intelligence closer to users. Edge computing accelerates traditional cloud-centric architecture by shifting intelligence toward edge and fog infrastructures, significantly improving multi-source and multi-format data management for production and daily operations (El-Sayed et al., 2017). Advances in hardware and software have expanded edge infrastructures, enabling diverse use cases ranging from critical systems to residential applications. Developers now deploy numerous edge services with similar specifications to deliver computing resources and data solutions. Cloud-native computing techniques simplify the packaging and deployment of these services, ensuring that they meet evolving application demands (Colombo, 2021).

However, the growing complexity and diversity of edge data raises serious security concerns. New threats and vulnerabilities necessitate innovative methods, techniques, and frameworks tailored to edge cloud environments. Additionally, the varied infrastructure of cloud service providers, along with cloud-native and open-source approaches, complicates edge security deployment and management. Unlike traditional edge systems, AI-powered systems handle data-driven tasks like preprocessing, model training, and inference. However, challenges persist in defining detection criteria and determining optimal data sharing among edge nodes.

To address these issues, a multi-layer detection architecture and a distributed detection method using local model sharing are proposed. The authors also identify key security challenges for DDE applications. Using a common edge-based video analytics case study, a security framework with system and threat models, supported by protective mechanisms, emerges. Future research directions to overcome these challenges are also explored.

This chapter presents a novel security framework that bridges edge and cloud protection mechanisms. The architecture combines four key innovations:

- Dynamic access controls that adapt to device capabilities and data sensitivity
- Lightweight encryption protocols optimized for edge processing
- Distributed anomaly detection using collaborative learning between nodes
- Cloud-based threat intelligence for zero-day attack prevention.

2. UNDERSTANDING EDGE COMPUTING

This study focuses exclusively on data-driven edge systems, explores the current security landscape, highlights recent advances, and pinpoints key challenges and opportunities. Edge computing bridges conventional cloud computing and end-device-centric Internet of Things (IoT) systems, combining edge devices with fog-tier and cloud-tier computing resources. Experts recognize this paradigm as transformative because it moves computations, data processing, and artificial intelligence (AI) inference closer to data sources.

The edge computing market has gained commercial viability across manufacturing, energy, natural resources, and smart cities (Arthurs et al., 2021), Alrowaily & Lu (2018). Modern society generates massive data-driven cycles that span the edge-to-cloud spectrum, increasing the variety, sources, and volume of edge data. To meet these demands, cloud services must ensure accessibility, affordability, cross-regional federation, interoperability across platforms and data formats, and traceability—regardless of data processing methods or origins. Figure 1 illustrates the convergence of edge and cloud security.

Figure 1. Convergence of edge and cloud security

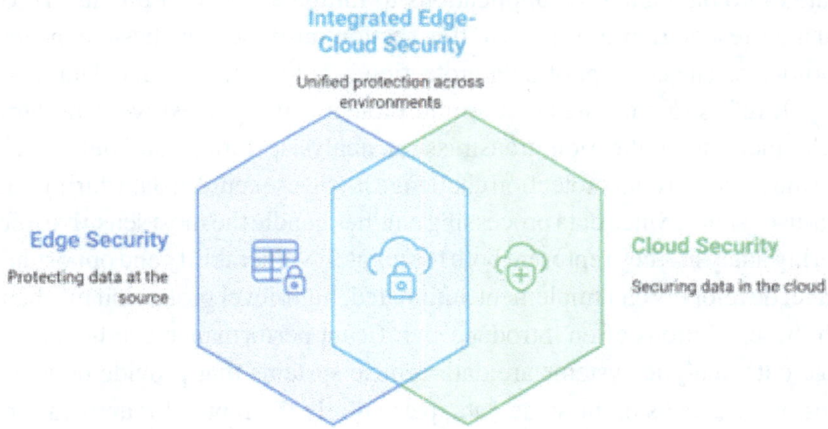

A rapidly evolving edge ecosystem now integrates ubiquitous heterogeneous edge devices and highly distributed fog computing systems, enabling edge-native data acquisition, storage, transmission, processing, modeling, analysis, monitoring, and visualization. Experts consider this ecosystem a cornerstone of information technology and services, poised to revitalize edge data-centric industries while simultaneously introducing urgent security and privacy challenges (Alwarafy et al., 2020; Roman et al., 2018).

This study focuses on data-driven edge systems that form a unique lightweight data-centric computing ecosystem. These systems have triggered unprecedented business disruption and exposed a vast, underexplored cyber threat landscape. Data-driven edge systems encompass three key facets: edge-centric, data-centric, and intelligence-centric, all of which are undergoing significant transformation. This chapter specifically examines the evolving challenges in edge data security and privacy.

2.1. Definition and Key Concepts

Edge data processing leverages dedicated edge and cloud resources to deliver intelligent edge services with high efficiency, low latency, and minimal bandwidth requirements. This approach effectively addresses the growing need for real-time data processing and analysis across IoT applications in smart cities, remote healthcare, and video surveillance. Data-driven edge services typically process sensitive, privacy-critical data at the edge, creating significant protection challenges during data usage. Conventional security solutions such as hardware-based systems and trusted execution environments prove inadequate as they depend on inherent trust assumptions. Recent innovations demonstrate how security measures can be directly integrated into data handling applications to mitigate potential threats. To offer a systematic presentation of this area, this section introduces its basic concepts and terminologies. The concept of data protection is at the core of edge data or system security. It refers to measures that aim to protect privacy-sensitive data during its lifecycle, including collection, transmission, analysis, storage, and deletion.

The most critical data protection challenge involves securing data during analysis (the "in-use" state). Since data processing engines handle the most sensitive information during analysis, they represent both the greatest vulnerability and opportunity. At this stage, developers can implement automated, high-level protection mechanisms, though these solutions often introduce significant performance overhead.

Edge data analytic systems are data-centric systems that provide data analysis services, with a focus on how the data, particularly the inputs for applications, are provided, processed, and presented to users. Thus, they have great potential to take advantage of effective data protection measures. This sub-domain covers thin processing framework-based implementations of data-centric applications that focus on data analysis rather than on external presentation, with emphasis on data processing or processed data when observing data-analytic systems.

2.2. Benefits of Edge Computing

Edge computing is becoming increasingly popular, and new concepts and systems are spreading rapidly. A corresponding interdisciplinary research field has emerged to address manifold research questions, including various fog computing aspects such as data processing, security, privacy, mobility, algorithms, and system architecture. The key insights and topics investigated in fog computing were presented, suggesting promising future research directions. The authors hope to motivate more interdisciplinary research in this area. Over the last decade, cloud providers have opened data centers located far from end users. Although cloud computing offers powerful capabilities, current infrastructures struggle to support performance-critical applications. Cloud interactions often cause high latency, making local computation essential for resource-intensive applications such as augmented reality, mobile gaming, vehicle remote control, and predictive maintenance.

Edge computing addresses these performance issues by integrating edge and cloud resources. This paradigm enables reactive systems, reduces communication overhead, and processes massive data streams locally. With advancements in connectivity, storage, and processing capabilities, edge data centers can now filter, reduce, and analyze data before transmitting it to the cloud (Gedeon et al., 2019). Edge computing distributes application processing tasks across multiple cloud and edge nodes. By extending traditional cloud infrastructures, this approach brings computing resources closer to end users. Smartphones, tablets, dashboards, and smartwatches connect to local area networks, which route data to edge microdata centers, resolving performance issues. Figure 2 illustrates the proposed edge computing ecosystem.

Unlike distant cloud data centers, edge microdata centers allow even small and mid-sized organizations to securely protect users' sensitive data through rental models. Edge resources support location-based tasks, such as those in wearable health devices, which deliver personalized services. Edge applications operate peer-to-peer, enabling organizations to share tasks and resources while creating new revenue streams

Figure 2. Edge computing ecosystem

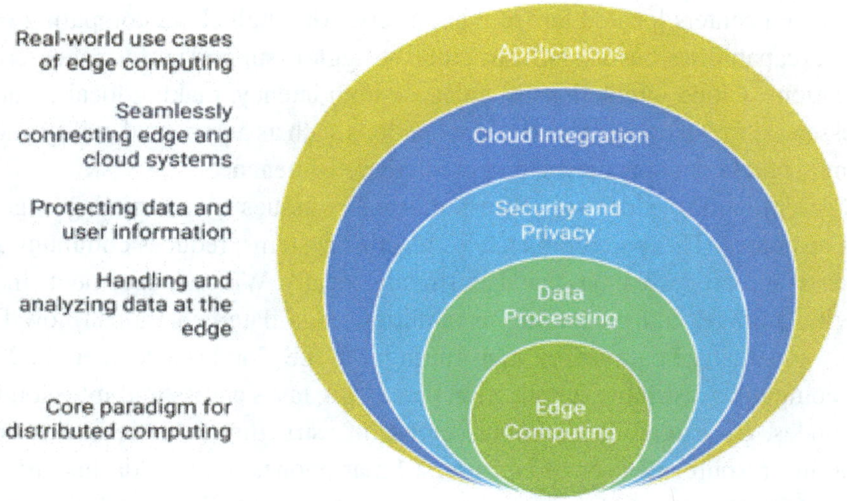

However, this decentralized approach raises concerns about governance and privacy, as borderless raw data may contain sensitive information. Multi-party computation techniques at the edge allow participants to store shared data without exposing it to peers. Additionally, edge devices can remove personally identifiable information before transmitting large data streams to the cloud.

2.3. Challenges in Edge Computing

Although edge computing offers significant opportunities, it also presents serious challenges. First, the system connects numerous edge nodes to the cloud, which interface with multiple IoT devices. These devices range from stationary nodes (e.g., on lamp posts) to mobile units (e.g., vehicles and public transportation) (Alwakeel, 2021) and incorporate various sensors for audio, video, and data streaming. Their diverse models and limited resources create operational complexities.

This heterogeneous environment demands multiple routing protocols, but the dynamic nature of edge computing renders existing protocols inadequate. The variety of communication methods—such as Wi-Fi, wired, Bluetooth, and cellular—introduces corresponding security vulnerabilities, with each protocol susceptible to distinct attack vectors.

The system must protect edge node communications from eavesdropping while ensuring data confidentiality and integrity. Although edge nodes can establish end-to-end secure communication by concealing details like encryption keys and transmission protocols from IoT devices, implementing these security measures remains challenging. Figure 3 illustrates these security challenges in edge computing.

Figure 3. Security challenges in edge computing

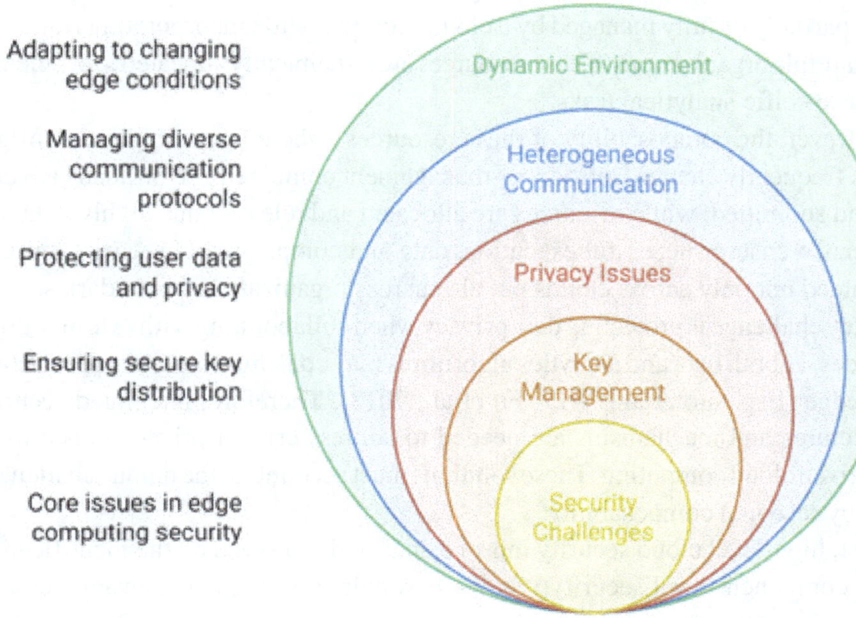

Another critical challenge is key management. A specialized key management and distribution mechanism may need to be designed, as edge nodes are often considered semi-trusted parties. Thus, understanding how cryptographic keys are generated, distributed, and managed in this environment is essential. Privacy concerns arise due to several factors. First, edge nodes operate in close proximity to end users, increasing the risk of exposing sensitive data. A sophisticated attacker could compromise these nodes, leading to the misuse of user-related data. Additionally, edge nodes have limited computational and network resources compared to cloud servers, making efficient data management crucial. For instance, when sharing data with a partner, a fine-grained access control mechanism should determine which data is shared and which remains concealed.

3. ROLE OF CLOUD SECURITY

The outsourcing of computational workloads and data to the cloud has led to the emergence of large-scale, cloud-based parallel ecosystems that leverage data-driven systems. Such ecosystems—comprising interconnected services and capabilities—can be partially or fully managed by a cloud provider while incorporating resources from multiple organizations. These resources are dynamically allocated to efficiently execute specific analytical tasks.

However, the composability of these resources (where ownership and configurations frequently change) introduces management complexity. Workloads are created and submitted, while resources are allocated and released in a highly dynamic manner. To ensure successful execution, data and computational security must be guaranteed not only across clouds but also across organizational boundaries.

A key challenge is protecting data privacy when collaborating with external cloud resources, as both data and analytics algorithms may constitute sensitive proprietary knowledge (Esposito et al., 2017; Fu et al., 2018). Therefore, integrated security architectures and mechanisms are needed to address critical privacy concerns in data-driven cloud computing. These solutions must account for the unique challenges posed by resource composability.

First, high-level cloud security must be analyzed, followed by the identification of key component-level security issues—particularly in the data privacy domain. While some of these components have been studied, existing work often examines them in isolation or focuses solely on in-cloud resource and data security rather than cross-organizational privacy.

By adopting an integrated approach, synergies between security knowledge, mechanisms, and toolsets can be leveraged through composable cloud security policies. This strategy also helps mitigate risks arising from security overlaps or fragmentation in cloud ecosystems. Figure 4 illustrates the various cloud security challenges.

Figure 4. Navigating cloud security challenges

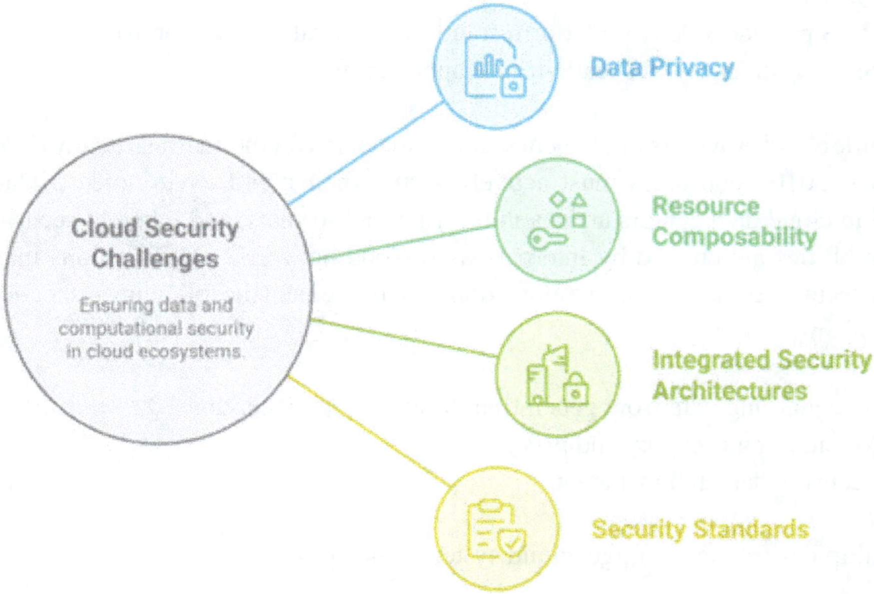

With many cloud computing services available nowadays, users often store personal and sensitive information in the cloud. Such valuable data attracts malicious users to attack the cloud and violate its confidentiality. Therefore, there are security concerns regarding how to protect users' data confidentiality before it is or after being processed in the cloud. Cloud users also want to know whether a cloud service meets its security requirements or not. To mitigate these risks, security modules in the form of software agents or overlays, such as security middleware, that advocate security from the client and server's perspective will be able to flexibly and efficiently support cloud services. There is also a need for associated standards.

3.1. Definition of Cloud Security

Cloud computing is revolutionizing global business and government operations by abstracting computer resources (CPU, disk space, storage) into Internet-accessible services that are available anytime, anywhere, on any device (Chinnam & Sambana, 2024). This model delivers on-demand, self-service computing resources with rapid provisioning capabilities, enabling subscribers to consume IT resources flexibly while vendors manage the infrastructure. Similar to utility services (phone, water, electricity), users pay only for what they use. Service providers offer three main models (Kumar et al., 2025), (Kuchuk & Malokhvii, 2024).

- IaaS vendors supply raw resources (CPU, memory, storage) through virtualization
- PaaS providers deliver platform solutions with data center control
- SaaS companies offer ready-to-use applications

While cloud providers implement security standards for their infrastructure (Kofi Fletcher, 2010), end-users must actively secure their cloud environments. Data stored in cloud data centers arrives in unstructured formats, and inherent security vulnerabilities are created by Internet-based cloud networks. Organizations must ensure secure, confidential communications and implement the following protection mechanisms:

- Safeguarding data from generation through cloud reception
- Maintaining accuracy and privacy
- Securing data and metadata

Multiple threat actors target cloud systems, including:

- Conspiring users
- Malicious CSP personnel
- Government entities

Cloud systems face the following unique security challenges:

- Programmers with system access pose insider threats
- Escaped secrets become permanently compromised
- Cloud migration often leaves sensitive data behind
- Proper data disposal remains critical

These persistent vulnerabilities make cloud security a vital research priority.

3.2. Importance of Cloud Security in Edge Systems

Edge systems include hardware (servers, routers, switches) and applications that integrate data-driven edge applications across data pipelines. These systems collect, store, and analyze massive IoT datasets in real-time at or near network edges. Modern data-driven edge applications typically combine multiple edge systems, gaining significant academic and industrial attention for their ability to derive insights from expanding IoT data streams.

These systems achieve enhanced analytical capabilities through cloud collaboration; however, this integration introduces security complexities in the cloud-edge-device architecture. Data-driven applications must ensure secure data generation and analysis through two complementary approaches:

1. Cloud Security employs encrypted communication to globally protect data and model privacy.
2. Edge Security implements device-level protections including the following:
    - Malware defense systems
    - Physical access control
    - Request validation mechanisms

The edge network requires robust local security solutions, because unprotected edge systems risk leaking sensitive data and ML models through cloud integration channels.

Cloud-integrated edge systems primarily face three security challenges:

- Dynamic communication protocols adapting to cloud and edge constraints
- Proprietary models from cloud providers
- Unique requirements for peer-to-peer collaboration

Current research emphasizes the following cloud-side protections:

- Maintaining data and model integrity after migration
- Preventing ML model reverse-engineering
- Detecting inference-time attacks

While public cloud services offer cost-effective storage and processing (eliminating maintenance overhead), the industry continues to debate the responsibility for cloud security costs, although providers ultimately bear system-level accountability for integrity failures.

4. THREAT LANDSCAPE FOR EDGE SYSTEMS

While industries widely deploy sensor-based and mobile edge systems in smart cities and healthcare applications, these implementations reveal significant security vulnerabilities. Traditional cloud security methods fail to protect edge systems because edge architectures, operating environments, and security requirements differ fundamentally from cloud environments. When organizations transfer cloud security solutions to large-scale, heterogeneous edge systems, these approaches frequently prove inadequate and may introduce new vulnerabilities.

Researchers now prioritize developing security frameworks specifically designed for edge-cloud collaborative architecture. Edge systems present unique risks because their proximity to end-users significantly increases attack surfaces. Successful attacks can compromise not only edge infrastructure but also connected cloud services. Consequently, the research community has intensified its focus on securing distributed intelligent edge systems. Figure 5 illustrates these emerging edge computing security threats.

Figure 5. Security threats in edge computing

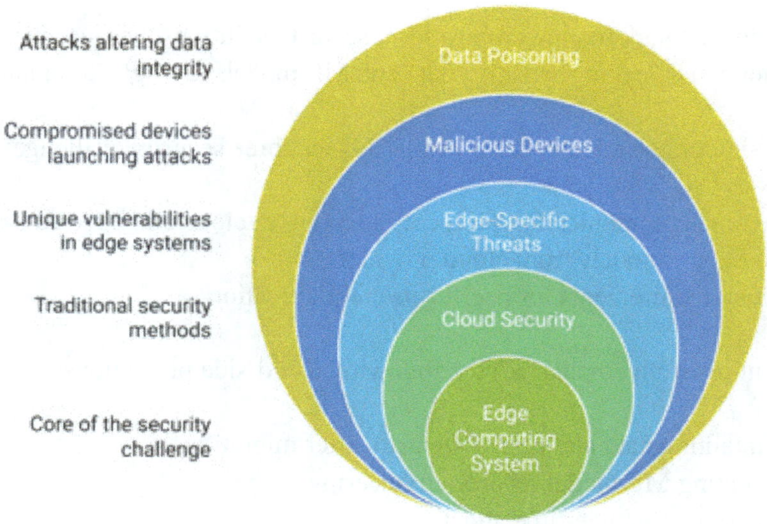

Edge nodes operate in close proximity to end-users, significantly reducing the latency caused by long-distance data transmission to the cloud (Puthal et al., 2016), He et al., 2020). However, this geographical advantage creates security vulnerabilities, because edge devices typically lack the robust physical protection of cloud infrastructure, making them easier targets for attacks. Malicious actors can exploit edge systems through multiple attack vectors as follows:

1. Compromised edge devices may have the following:
    - Sending falsified data to the cloud
    - Collaborate with end devices to launch cloud denial-of-service attacks

- Steal the proprietary model parameters
- Manipulate the model updates
- Injecting trojan malware targeting cloud models

2. Compromised sensors can generate malicious data that can be as follows:
   - Enables bad-mouthing user attacks
   - Facilitate data poisoning
   - Permits feature-squeezing attacks at the end layer

Beyond traditional cloud security risks, non-IID data distribution (Sikarwar & Das (2023) or Ayed et al. (2022) creates unpredictable patterns that undermine model convergence and further threatens system stability during training.

4.1. Common Threats and Vulnerabilities

The edge computing architecture leverages cloud-edge co-design to significantly enhance data-driven services while boosting computational and communication performance. Unlike homogeneous cloud systems with strong physical security, edge devices and their system software now represent the critical security frontier. Therefore, cloud security services must prioritize two key functions: monitoring edge system integrity and ensuring runtime stealth capabilities. A properly secured edge device platform requires the following:

- Robust physical protection
- Trusted hardware components
- Secure firmware and system software
- Verifiable supply chain traceability
- Comprehensive attestation before deployment
- Hardening against known attack vectors

Despite these protections, edge devices remain vulnerable when exposed to external networks. We categorize edge platform security threats into two classes:

1. Inherent Platform Vulnerabilities
   - laws in design and manufacturing
   - Supply chain compromises
   - Legacy system exploits
   - Known and unknown hardware and firmware vulnerabilities
2. Edge-Specific Threats
   - Physical security limitations due to device dispersion
   - Enhanced attacker capabilities in edge environments

- Hardware diversity complicates defense strategies

Edge computing faces three unique security challenges:

1. Cloud-grade physical protection models fail to scale across vast, heterogeneous edge networks
2. Attackers exploit weaker tamper resistance in cost-optimized edge hardware
3. Hardware diversity enables sophisticated reverse-engineering attacks

The edge environment provides attackers with significant advantages:

- Direct access to real devices (versus cloud simulators)
- Extended time for architectural analysis
- Stable conditions for the development of precision attacks

4.2. Case Studies of Security Breaches

In 2020, hackers remotely accessed Florida water treatment facility's systems and nearly elevated sodium hydroxide to dangerous levels. Investigators later revealed that the attackers exploited a TeamViewer vulnerability. In the same year, cybercriminals breached a major poker website, stealing personal data of players including addresses, financial details, and social security numbers. Ten months later, they used this information to hijack accounts and illegally transfer funds to Spanish banks. In China, security flaws in a real estate platform enabled hackers to fraudulently deposit payments for properties, then intercept and forge digital contracts to illegally resell homes to unwitting buyers.

These three incidents demonstrate how attackers compromise critical decision-making systems by gaining remote control of edge devices that process multi-sourced data. As data-driven edge systems expand across industries, their increasing complexity introduces significant security challenges:

1. Enterprises struggle to secure commercial edge devices because:
    - The software and default configurations are controlled by third-party manufacturers
    - Standard security practices often overlook edge-specific vulnerabilities (ESVs)
2. Current security approaches fail to address:
    - Malicious inputs that disrupt machine learning algorithms
    - White-box nature of edge device architectures

To address these gaps, we propose the following:

- Comprehensive security requirements for data-driven edge devices
- An intelligence-augmented cloud security architecture incorporating:
    - Advanced threat detection methods
    - Robust device commissioning protocols
    - Enhanced regulatory controls

5. INTEGRATING CLOUD SECURITY WITH EDGE COMPUTING

This study focuses on enhancing security in data-driven edge systems through effective cloud service integration. Figure 6 presents the proposed framework for secure system design. The chapter explores the critical factors in cloud-edge security implementation, particularly how topology-aware configurations affect protection measures, computational efficiency, and architectural stability. A structured methodology evaluates design trade-offs while assessing their impact on the overall system security. Real-world testing includes an application scenario and three case studies to validate this approach. These practical examples confirm the framework's reliability, adaptability, and effectiveness in mitigating security risks without compromising performance. The findings provide actionable insights for developing robust edge computing solutions in diverse operational environments.

Figure 6. Secure data-driven edge systems through integration

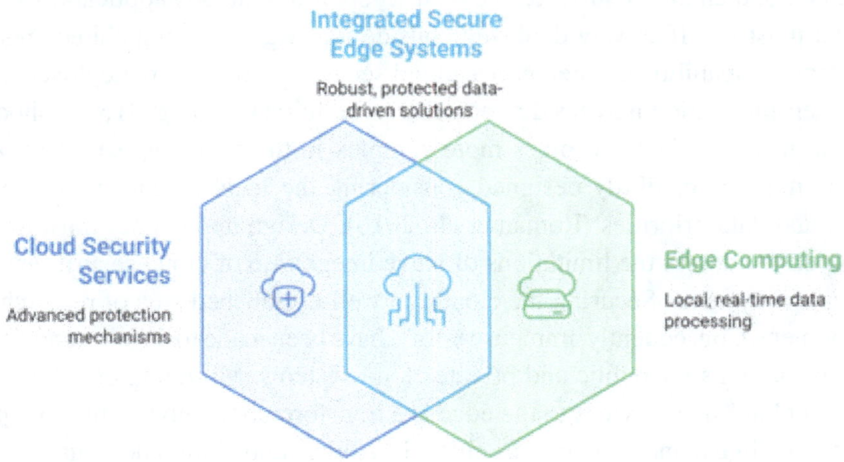

To understand their availability and feasibility in the edge context, the existing cloud security services are thoroughly analyzed. The application task of a video analytics pipeline in a smart edge system scenario is employed to investigate how the cloud security services and cloud-edge alliance tasks are allocated and orchestrated to effectively secure the data-driven edge system. The results provide valuable insights for both practitioners and researchers on securing data-driven edge systems. In AI model distribution scenarios, federated learning, which provides stronger privacy preservation, is preferred, whereas SME and frequent aggregation with protocol-driven implementations are more effective measures (Zhang et al., 2018), (Mollah et al., 2017). In AI model lifelong training scenarios, retraining of AI models at the edge may be more viable to ensure higher security resilience. The cloud trustworthiness is at desirable high levels across all component cloud security services and edge system topologies, which largely address the challenges of data security breaches against third-party cloud service providers, over-analyzed data at the cloud, and edge hardware and software vulnerabilities. The cloud-edge links confront theoretical trustworthiness risks enabled under malicious cloud service providers with introduced false attack models (Ometov et al., 2022), (Kaki et al., 2025). This research sheds light on new trends and future directions for academic and industrial research and applications.

5.1. Architectural Considerations

To mitigate potential security threats to data-driven edge systems, their architecture must be considered. The naive integration of cloud security into edge systems may increase their attack surface. The security solutions already applicable to cloud systems must be effectively deployed considering edge system architectures and edge device capabilities. When native cloud security solutions are deployed to the edge, their integration may need refactoring or additional coding. Troubleshooting cloud security incidents becomes more complex in the edge context. Thus, edge systems must be carefully designed considering the local characteristics, costs, values, and data priorities (Roman et al., 2016). Design approaches must also be developed to address the limitations of naive integration of cloud security in edge devices and systems. Securing the cloud is a well-established area of research and development. Consequently, immense efforts have been made to develop and deploy security solutions for public and private cloud systems. Migrating cloud applications and cloud-like services to the edge is a transformative opportunity to rapidly develop intelligent and autonomous cities. It requires application domain expertise and formal modeling capabilities that the edge typically lacks. Figure 7 shows the balancing of Cloud and Edge Security Challenges.

Figure 7. Balancing cloud and edge security challenges

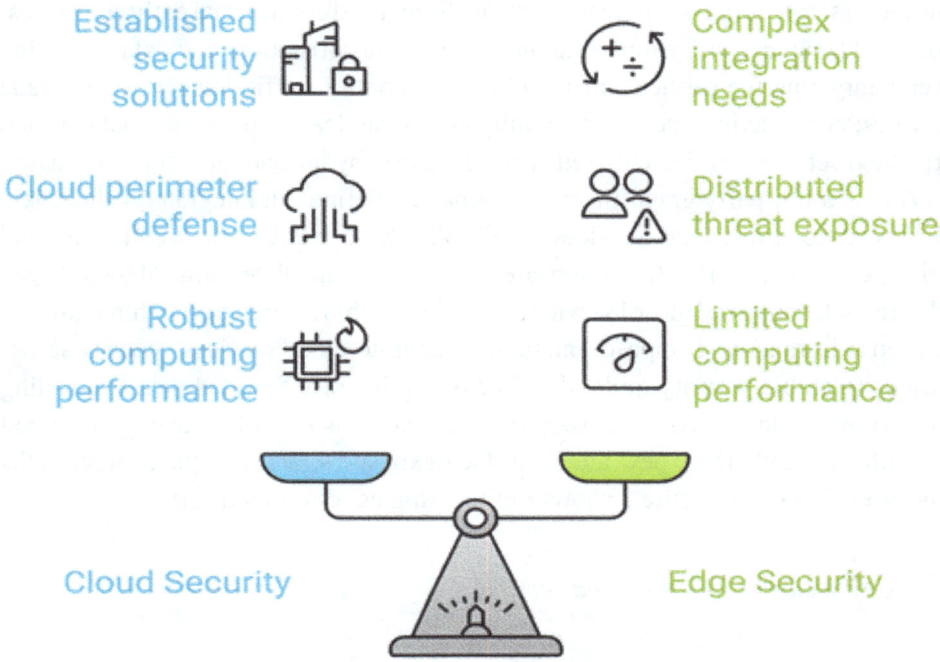

Although edge services can be developed based on cloud-like technologies, edge systems differ significantly in their architecture compared to cloud systems. In terms of the threat landscape and attack surface, edge computing systems are more exposed than clouds. While cloud perimeter defense surrounds the cloud infrastructure, edge devices are geographically distributed and owned by different organizations. Edge IoT devices are more susceptible to physical attacks or insider threats due to their open and low-cost hardware, despite the associated risks and the required commitment to software maintenance.

Edge services are primarily hosted on devices with less computing performance than cloud systems that host more robust VMs. However, edge devices running open-source server software may host advanced services similar to cloud services. Multiple software-based approaches are possible to achieve these differing capabilities across edge and cloud environments.

5.2. Best Practices for Integration

The edge-to-cloud opportunity can produce previously unimagined system-level innovation at and beyond the level of new value-added and aggregated services. To capitalize on such opportunities across industries, cloud service providers (CSPs) and edge service providers (ESPs) must quickly and reliably converge edge services and cloud services into a secure value chain. Signal and control data gathering, transport, and flows can risk supporting disruption, data corruption, and data poisoning events targeting the services; resultant data or control traffic latency can degrade services; construction and composability issues can lead to unwanted outages and orphaned services; and unchecked sector isolation by individual clouds can arise.

A new multi-party graph-theoretic formalism defines an integrated value chain of Secure Edge-to-Cloud Services (SEC). A robust data-centric architecture and stricter coordination flow behaviors are specified to remediate a host of data-driven edge risks. Centralized global service controllers within a tiered tree architecture can be used to instantiate, compose, and monitor edge-to-cloud services' security across various tolerable security trade-offs. The discipline of integrated threat modeling and a systemic analysis of nine risk properties can holistically lay out edge-to-cloud strength accumulations, new attack surface exposures, and complex threat paths (Baker et al., 2019). Figure 8 shows the securing edge-to-cloud services.

Figure 8. Securing edge-to-cloud services

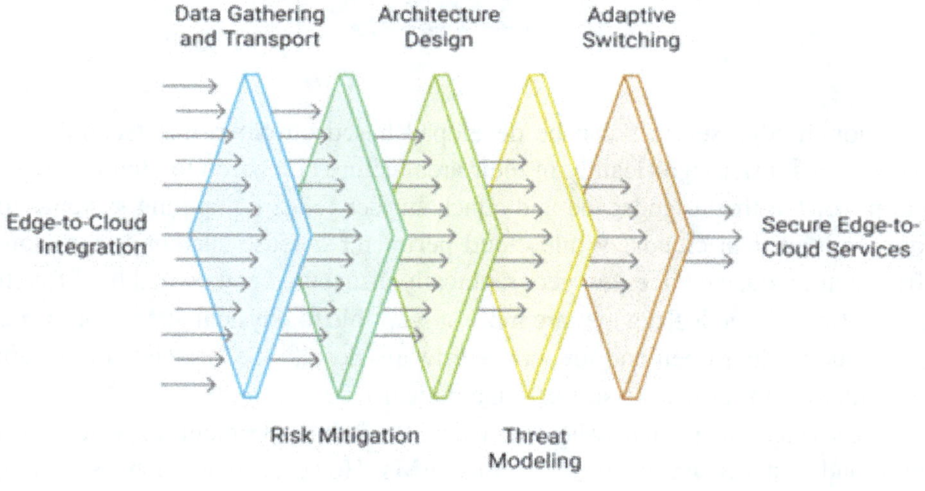

Deep packet inspection and analysis are used to inspect the encapsulated packet metadata, such as packet source and destination IP addresses and transport protocol, while add-on CMOS components can monitor metadata at chip-level frequencies. A multi-party SDN architecture can intelligently manage the edge-to-cloud control plane in a CSP-neutral paradigm. The proposed architecture can tier edge data and control processing, then coordinate end-to-end service specification and monitoring.

Owing to the leveraging of multi-fabric SDX visibility, inspection, flow classification, and chaining functions are exposed along unrestricted service paths across the mixed-DPI and multi-vendor data paths. The tiering of visibility functions can compose cross-PNF monitor chains without interfering with the original program instructions. A trigger-and-reactive adaptive switching penalty model is co-designed to orchestrate stealth operations across the multi-party service control plane.

5.3. Tools and Technologies for Integration

Analyzing and improving the security of data-driven edge systems using cloud services and fog-reliant architectures requires several state-of-the-art tools and technologies. First, Threat Intelligence Services are recommended to alert users about ongoing cyber-threats and attacks through subscription to a comprehensive Threat Intelligence Service to increase the system's reliability and cyber-resilience. A plethora of open and commercial services are available, including those referenced in (M. Alwakeel, 2021). Advisories and alerts are categorized, and additional information is provided. This information can be an excellent input for the Security Monitor module. Users can obtain information about past attacks to assess the severity of the circumstances encountered. Understanding these attacks and the knowledge required to improve security can also come from cloud-based Threat Intelligence Providers.

Another technology is known as SIEM (Security Information and Event Management) systems. Continuous streams of alerts from monitoring appliances, databases, and other security-related components and business applications are ingested to assess the risk of an attack in progress. As SIEM appliances are heavyweight solutions requiring expert personnel, they are not recommended for all use cases but for vital systems. Another group of appliances consists of IDS (Intrusion Detection Systems) monitoring devices. These record every packet arriving at and leaving the system or network. Several frameworks are publicly available or developed as research projects, with implementations ranging from light to heavy IDS units. To avoid false positives (benign traffic wrongly reported as an attack), the performance of intrusion detection systems should be continuously tuned. Performance improvement steps can include the addition of IPs to the whitelist, including known benign traffic, or the fine-tuning of regular expressions.

6. DATA PROTECTION STRATEGIES

The success of Machine Learning is driven by quality data; however, the proliferation of data and sensors, combined with the implementation of edge computing, causes new challenges in data protection. As sensors proliferate, machine learning models collect and analyze large amounts of data to allow actionable intelligence and automate systems. In many cases, learning is offloaded and performed in the cloud, which can accommodate intensive computation but is often not immediately available. At the same time, edge computing is being used to change the workload distribution. The latest work shows several advantages of executing learning algorithms on edge devices, such as limited bandwidth, privacy control, data locality, and efficiency. Current cloud systems comprise many interconnected edge devices that integrate computational resources across many disparate physical locations. However, securing this new computation distribution and its architecture is critically important as it could lead to end system and personal device exposure.

However, the cloud is not inherently safer than on-premises hardware. Several cloud computing protection architectures have been proposed to mitigate exposure and unauthorized access. Such architectures have been designed to provide boundary isolation of application data planes in the cloud, thereby protecting against unauthorized access before or after observing application events. In certain scenarios, the pandemic has led to demands for offloading analysis and learning with local provisioning, where bandwidth becomes a scarce resource. Moving learning back to the edge facilitates local intelligent processing and improves privacy. As a result, much work has been devoted to protecting data and its sensitivity across cloud and cloud-edge systems to avoid costly bandwidth use and infrastructure.

Recent applications in weather monitoring, anomaly detection, and autonomous vehicles expose the challenge in protecting this new vertical edge computing cloud architecture. Consequently, the cloud as a provider is only part of vertical architecture and usually comprises heterogeneously provisioned computational machines as cloud-edges—less dedicated entities made available for workloads by operating across public edge clouds. Exposing workloads as new targets for unauthorized access requires establishing up to three potential restrictions: access, usage, and presence, which are challenging to achieve across such distributed systems.

6.1. Encryption Techniques

Encryption techniques play an important role in cloud security in data-driven edge systems. Privacy preservation cloud computing (PPCC) frameworks are developed to integrate security and privacy measures through different cryptography techniques, access control, and supporting privacy models, which solve edge and cloud computing security and privacy-preserving issues. These techniques include encryption, cryptography, and hybrid encryption. A model is proposed to enhance data privacy during cloud data storage and tamper detection using a hybrid combination of Advanced Encryption Standard-256 and Information Dispersal Algorithms with Secure Hash Algorithm-512 (Kumar et al., 2024), (Wong & Kim, 2018). To reduce the complexity of search, storage, and privacy concerns, token-based and ciphertext reusable searchable encryption schemes are proposed. A cloud auditing protocol is constructed to support federated identity authentication of cloud storage, which resolves the auditing problem of massive data shared by the inevitable third-party auditor.

To prevent unauthorized users from gaining access to the content of a message while keeping them completely unaware of any information about the encryption key, even in plaintext format, a model containing two schemes is developed. To overcome the above problems, secure protocols such as PSS for secure deletion schemes and EFS for authenticated encryption with searchable encryption are implemented. Cloud storage represents a recent advancement in Internet services and systems that provide highly available and large-size storage. Multi-cloud storage is a cloud storage model that stores datasets across multiple cloud servers and cloud service providers to ensure data privacy. Secure multi-cloud audit mechanisms and the proposed cloud audit protocol against this threat are more effective than existing ones.

Figure 9. Cloud security framework

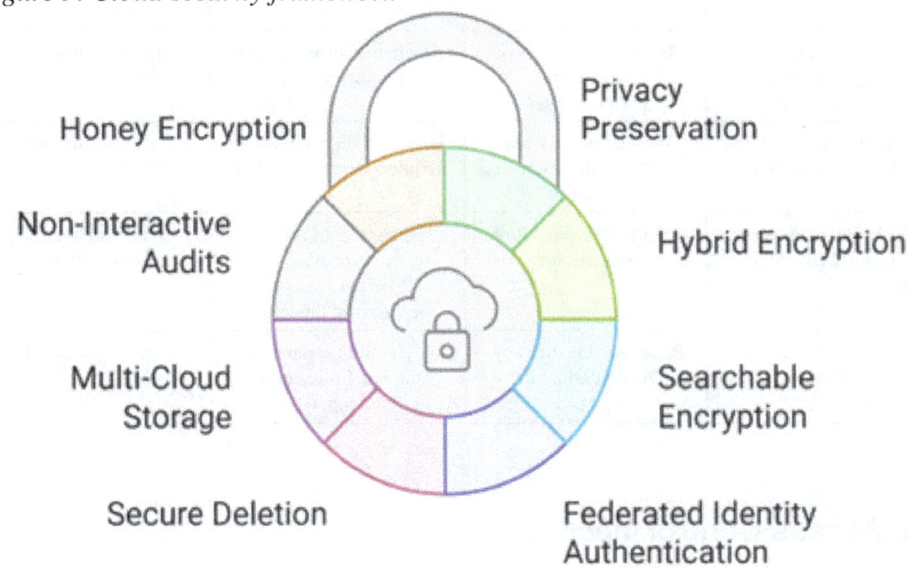

A non-interactive audits-without-server-replay scheme is designed to provide a comprehensive solution against threats to both cloud data privacy and secure multi-cloud audit protocols. Honey encryption is a method that generates cipher text, which will transparently produce believable plaintext if provided with an incorrect decryption key and provides assurance against brute force or exhaustive key searching attacks. The risk of attacks on cloud storage is quite high as data ownership and management shifts from users to cloud storage service providers. It becomes critical for users to verify that the cloud server maintains the integrity of their data and to have transparency about what is stored in the cloud. The association between the external cloud and the original server has always been crucial and should not be broken to ensure data safety on the cloud (Ansar et al., 2018). Figure 9 depicts this integrated security model, highlighting the key components and their interactions.

Contemporary distributed computing architectures require flexible encryption methods that optimize both protection and efficiency. The evaluation framework assesses prominent cryptographic approaches, with detailed comparisons provided in Table 1:

Table 1. Comparison of edge-cloud security techniques

Technique	Advantages	Limitations	Best For
AES-256 Encryption	NIST-certified standard. Support for hardware acceleration.	High CPU overhead on low-power devices. Key management complexity.	Data at rest in edge storage
Lightweight Cryptography (ChaCha20)	3x faster than AES on ARM chips. IoT-optimized.	Smaller security margin. Less industry adoption.	Real-time transmission of sensor data
Attribute-Based Access Control (ABAC)	Granular permissions. Dynamic policy adaptation.	Possible Policy conflicts. Requires centralized PDP.	Healthcare IoT with HIPAA compliance
Role-Based Access Control (RBAC)	Simple implementation. Audit-friendly	A rigid permission structure. Does not scale for ephemeral devices.	Industrial control systems (ICSs)
Federated Learning Security	Preserves data privacy. Distributed model updates.	High initial setup cost. Node synchronization is required.	Cross-enterprise edge analytics

6.2. Access Control Mechanisms

In order to develop successful access control solutions in cloud and fog networks, it is essential to understand the full access control mechanism lifecycle stages, the common objectives of context-aware access control mechanisms, the design methodologies that can effectively produce the desired context-aware access control mechanism with positive results, the critical steps needed to implement context-aware access control mechanisms in distributed systems, and how context-aware access control mechanisms can keep pace with the constantly evolving access control requirements of distributed systems. Context-awareness enhances the access control experience in many distributed systems. Several context-aware access control solutions exist for cloud and fog networks. However, these solutions often lack effective communication and accessibility for educational and research purposes, which limits their contributions to industry and academia. This chapter provides an overview of the diverse context-aware access control mechanisms developed for cloud and fog networks along with their design and implementation procedures. The mechanisms are classified into three categories based on their characteristics: design methodology, implementation stage, and common objectives. A comparison between the reviewed access control mechanisms is included in each category to assist interested developers in selecting their desired context-aware access control mechanism based on their requirements (Kumar et al., 2024).

The cloud is a broad term that serves a myriad of purposes. It is a technological advancement that enables the smooth delivery of different services over the internet. Users commonly utilize cloud systems in the social networking, health, and finance sectors. In the delivery of these services, data generation occurs at the edge, and data-centric workflows use cloud facilities to enhance service quality. Such data-driven cloud systems are also referred to as edge-cloud computing systems. The use of cloud services has compelled organizations to store data with untrusted service providers, which poses a major threat to private and sensitive data. In recent years, various cloud security techniques have been proposed, with access control mechanisms being inevitable components of ensuring data security in cloud environments. Such mechanisms must also be compatible with data-centric workflows using multi-tenants in data-driven cloud systems to ensure data security compliance. However, the existing access control mechanisms in cloud environments do not adequately support such compliance. Therefore, this study proposes an ABAC mechanism for the compliance of access control mechanisms in data-driven cloud systems using a data-centric workflow.

6.3. Data Loss Prevention Strategies

With the advent of cloud computing, most organizations are opting for the cloud computing model. However, there are a few concerns that organizations have with moving to the cloud. The second concern after the fear of losing control of corporate data is the issue of data breaches. Understanding the facts behind such concerns is crucial in addressing them.

Data is not only stored in cloud storage but is also replicated within the cloud infrastructure to maintain accessibility across multiple nodes. Data replication is one of the best methods for load balancing and high availability. However, replicated data often falls victim to malicious nodes inside the cloud storage environment. In the era of big data, keeping data secure and under organizational control is crucial. Thus, maintaining data security and preventing unauthorized access to it are paramount concerns for organizations transitioning to cloud environments. Figure 10 illustrates the data protection in cloud storage.

Figure 10. Data protection in cloud storage

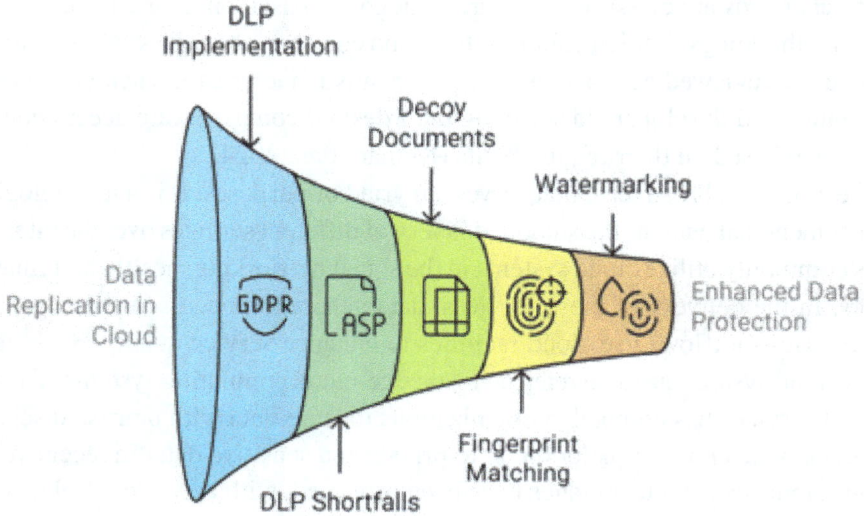

Data Loss Prevention (DLP) is often implemented within a cloud storage environment to protect against data exfiltration. However, there are a number of shortfalls that include: DLP can be bypassed by the use of encryption, DLP systems are also under the control of the CSP, and they are not designed to prevent unknown attacks (Wilson & Avery, 2016). As a result, the added value of using documents decoy within a SaaS environment for more dynamic data protection has been explored. Alternative architectural approaches that reduce exposed data planes show promise, though DLP implementations continue to face inherent trust issues (Wilson & Avery, 2016), (Dai et al., 2020).

While DLP solutions form one component of comprehensive data protection strategies, they primarily function as reactive measures rather than absolute preventive controls. Common DLP techniques include content fingerprint matching against sensitive data inventories, digital watermarking of protected information, and results-based monitoring tied to confidential datasets. However, established circumvention methods like hash manipulation, steganographic techniques, and multi-layered result obfuscation can defeat these protections, rendering most DLP implementations more effective for incident detection than actual prevention.

7. FUTURE TRENDS IN EDGE AND CLOUD SECURITY

As organizations increasingly adopt cloud platforms as their primary data repositories, collaboration hubs, and application hosting environments, the growing emphasis on edge computing has created new security solutions that natively integrate with distributed architectures. Traditional perimeter-based security models are no longer sufficient; more sophisticated, architecturally sound approaches are necessary to ensure compliance and robust threat protection. Since emerging edge environments differ significantly from existing infrastructures, businesses must implement end-to-end security frameworks that seamlessly adapt from edge devices to cloud data centers (M. Alwakeel, 2021).

Governance and compliance requirements require a holistic understanding of the security landscape, including how different security layers interact to mitigate risks. Organizations can no longer treat cloud adoption as an opportunity to outsource security responsibilities entirely to cloud service providers (CSPs). This outdated mindset has already led to regulatory penalties for some businesses, highlighting the dangers of such an approach. As hybrid edge-cloud ecosystems evolve, companies must avoid repeating these mistakes by proactively securing distributed systems rather than reacting to threats after deployment.

The rapid expansion of edge workloads will demand new security capabilities in the coming years. While advancements in scalable storage and computing will drive efficiency, they will also worsen the existing cybersecurity talent shortage. Human expertise will remain critical, but organizations will increasingly rely on automated solutions for real-time threat detection and response (Roman et al., 2016).

The development of comprehensive security architectures and digital twins capable of modeling both edge and cloud environments will require time and collaboration. To stay ahead of emerging threats, proactive measures such as simulated attack scenarios and defensive strategy development must be prioritized. Establishing threat intelligence-sharing networks among peer organizations can accelerate the maturation of best practices. Additionally, rigorous testing of existing security solutions in hybrid environments is essential to identify vulnerabilities and refine defensive measures before they are exploited by adversaries.

7.1. Emerging Technologies

The advancement of edge computing relies on several key technologies, including digital twins (DTs), the open-source Open Horizon (OH) IoT platform, and secured and trusted edge (STE) frameworks (Jararweh, 2020), (Nagarjuna et al., 2024). Research in these areas builds upon previous developments in 5G Mobile Edge Computing (MEC), SDN, and NFV, which help shape the future of cloud-edge integrated networks. Given the massive number of connected sensors and devices transmitting user data, edge computing plays a crucial role in processing and analyzing information locally, reducing reliance on distant cloud servers. Edge computing enhances efficiency for service providers by offering Storage-as-a-Service and Edge-Device-as-a-Service, combining cloud and fog computing capabilities.

However, security remains a primary challenge, particularly during the transition from cloud-only to hybrid cloud-edge networks. To address this, new architectures integrate edge security and resource management, supporting emerging technologies like DTs and container based OH platforms.

A dedicated edge security platform has been developed to protect cloud-edge networks using DTs and OH. This platform incorporates the following:

1. Edge Health Evaluation: Untrustworthy edges are identified by assessing accuracy, communication reliability, and data trustworthiness.
2. Decentralized Data Integrity Verification: Ensures data consistency across both cloud and edge nodes, adapting to the distributed nature of edge networks.

To optimize performance, service providers can reallocate low-trust, high-cost edge nodes to edge clouds rather than edge devices, improving overall system efficiency.

7.2. Predictions for the Future

Modern enterprises are increasingly requiring high-performance computing capabilities with immediate data availability, which has led organizations to explore advanced technological approaches. The growing complexity of handling large-scale data operations while maintaining rapid response times has generated substantial attention toward distributed edge computing models. By introducing localized data processing nodes, these systems extend traditional cloud architectures, allowing businesses to optimize their information assets throughout worldwide operations (Kalariya et al., 2022).

These edge-based systems need to provide accurate and timely insights to be of significant value. Inline data processing is closely tied to the success of edge deployment, where integrating cloud computing resources for data management, processing, and interactions with external systems is of utmost importance. Supporting new cloud paradigms with data-driven edge infrastructures is already on the horizon and attracting considerable interest. The transformation of Information Technology deployment in new operations must consider security and governance aspects to guard against the risk of costly and damaging breaches into data and services. Security for edge and cloud systems must be considered jointly and leveraged to protect the application and governance dimensions of services (Parikh et al., 2019), (Yu et al., 2019).

This chapter proposes a design idea and architecture for integrating cloud security into the data-driven edge stack using a security service layer that enables and assists application designers in enhancing the associated security capabilities. A detailed discussion of the expected risks in edge systems and an overview of state-of-the-art security tooling and capabilities in cloud services are presented. This section is followed by a description of the design idea and an example of the prototyping of selected services integrated into a rapid prototyping framework. Future work on enhancing the services and studying the impact on application and design areas is also outlined to improve the security of edge deployments.

8. CASE STUDIES

Edge systems capture, store, process, and enrich sensory data on data-centered edge devices before sending it to the cloud for further analysis (Roman et al., 2016). Edge systems are designed to capture, store, and process data at the network's edge. Data-driven edge systems must communicate with the cloud and process data in a coalesced fashion across the edge and cloud. Edge caches, cloud caches, or both can be selected from among alternative data placement and replication schemes. The coalescing ability of cloud caches is enhanced by an extended content placement algorithm (Zhang et al., 2020), (Gedeon et al., 2019). Provisioning under different stress measures is considered for an analytical cost-benefit trade-off quantification of the proposed designs. The problem is to maximize the reduction of the total rate of missed requests by the edge and cloud caches according to specified constraints on the total storage capacity.

The case studies involve a simulation of edge systems using edge and cloud data caches. Data-driven edge systems have multiple data processes where data required by one process is stored and computed on edge devices and cloud clusters in a fixed setting determined from the outset. The coalescing problem is studied between data-driven edge systems with different types of caches. Based on performance metrics, edge-device caches, cloud-device caches, or both types of caches can be included to obtain the best performance. The performance of edge caches is estimated through multiple simulation experiments on edge systems with such caches. Possible deployment scenarios are simulated with edge systems in communication with a cloud to fulfill trace datasets.

Data-centric edge systems with optional cloud and edge data caches capable of coalescing transmissions were analyzed. Closed-form solutions and effective coalescing policies are obtained for cloud data caches in a simple parallel server network. A hierarchical communication architecture is derived from an edge data cache coalescing policy along with a corresponding optimization framework and numerical algorithm for edge split network uplinks. The concept of coalescing is extended beyond data caches. Any agent coordinating data requests to the cloud or edge can coalesce transmissions within a certain timeframe, achieving cloud or edge coalescing gains.

9. CONCLUSION

This chapter critically examines the security challenges that arise when integrating cloud services into edge computing environments by analyzing two prominent implementation models. This study highlights previously unidentified vulnerabilities and scrutinizes how well traditional cloud security practices hold up when applied to edge settings. The findings reveal distinct differences in the nature of edge and cloud infrastructure security threats. Notably, the research concludes that edge devices must adopt security frameworks that are as robust as those used in large-scale cloud data centers, despite their limited processing and storage capacities.

Edge computing represents a significant shift in computational architecture by bringing cloud functionalities closer to the data source, creating a hybrid model that combines localized processing with centralized cloud resources. While this evolution enhances efficiency and responsiveness, it also introduces new security challenges that cannot be adequately addressed by simply adapting existing cloud-based protections. Although edge systems can sidestep some vulnerabilities inherent to cloud-only infrastructures, they simultaneously open up novel security risks. These include heightened physical exposure due to the decentralized nature of edge devices, fragmented control over security operations across a wide variety of nodes, and the complexity added by the use of multiple communication protocols across different edge networks.

The erosion of critical security knowledge, largely driven by the fast-paced commercialization of cloud technologies, is a concerning trend identified through this investigation. This rapid development has left edge computing deployments without well-established security architectures or guidelines. Organizations face several challenges, such as the loss of institutional knowledge regarding edge-specific security, the rise of opaque and proprietary systems that hinder effective vulnerability assessment, and the continued use of generalized security tools that fail to address the unique risks associated with edge environments.

This study highlights the urgent need for security models that are purpose-built for edge computing's distributed and diverse ecosystem, while still delivering protection comparable to that of traditional cloud infrastructures. In the future, research should focus on designing transparent and adaptable security architectures, along with detailed threat modeling approaches tailored specifically for the dynamic interplay between edge and cloud systems.

REFERENCES

Alrowaily, M., & Lu, Z. (2018, October). Secure edge computing in IoT systems: Review and case studies. In 2018 IEEE/ACM symposium on edge computing (SEC) (pp. 440-444). IEEE.

Alwarafy, A., Al-Thelaya, K. A., Abdallah, M., Schneider, J., & Hamdi, M. (2020). A survey on security and privacy issues in edge-computing-assisted internet of things. *IEEE Internet of Things Journal*, *8*(6), 4004–4022. DOI: 10.1109/JIOT.2020.3015432

Arthurs, P., Gillam, L., Krause, P., Wang, N., Halder, K., & Mouzakitis, A. (2021). A taxonomy and survey of edge cloud computing for intelligent transportation systems and connected vehicles. *IEEE Transactions on Intelligent Transportation Systems*, *23*(7), 6206–6221. DOI: 10.1109/TITS.2021.3084396

Ayed, D., Dragan, P. A., Félix, E., Mann, Z. A., Salant, E., Seidl, R., . . . Vitorino, R. (2022, May). Protecting sensitive data in the cloud-to-edge continuum: The Fog-Protect approach. In 2022 22nd IEEE International Symposium on Cluster, Cloud and Internet Computing (CCGrid), pp. 279-288. IEEE.

Colombo, G. (2021, April). Cloud driven edge computing on smart systems integration. In 2021 Smart Systems Integration (SSI) (pp. 1-3). IEEE.

Dai, M., Su, Z., Li, R., Wang, Y., Ni, J., & Fang, D. (2020). An edge-driven security framework for intelligent internet of things. *IEEE Network*, *34*(5), 39–45. DOI: 10.1109/MNET.011.2000068

El-Sayed, H., Sankar, S., Prasad, M., Puthal, D., Gupta, A., Mohanty, M., & Lin, C. T. (2017). Edge of things: The big picture on the integration of edge, IoT and the cloud in a distributed computing environment. IEEE Access, 6, 1706-1717.

Esposito, C., Castiglione, A., Pop, F., & Choo, K. K. R. (2017). Challenges of connecting edge and cloud computing: A security and forensic perspective. *IEEE Cloud Computing*, *4*(2), 13–17. DOI: 10.1109/MCC.2017.30

Fu, J. S., Liu, Y., Chao, H. C., Bhargava, B. K., & Zhang, Z. J. (2018). Secure data storage and searching for industrial IoT by integrating fog computing and cloud computing. *IEEE Transactions on Industrial Informatics*, *14*(10), 4519–4528. DOI: 10.1109/TII.2018.2793350

He, Z., Zhang, T., & Lee, R. B. (2020). Attacking and protecting data privacy in edge–cloud collaborative inference systems. *IEEE Internet of Things Journal*, *8*(12), 9706–9716. DOI: 10.1109/JIOT.2020.3022358

Jararweh, Y. (2020). Enabling efficient and secure energy cloud using edge computing and 5G. *Journal of Parallel and Distributed Computing*, *145*, 42–49. DOI: 10.1016/j.jpdc.2020.06.014

Kaki, S. S., Kantareddygari, J. R., & Aishwarya, R. (2025, February). Privacy and Security Concerns in Edge-Cloud Systems: An In-Depth Analysis. In 2025 3rd International Conference on Intelligent Data Communication Technologies and Internet of Things (IDCIoT) (pp. 435-441). IEEE.

Kuchuk, H., & Malokhvii, E. (2024). Integration of IoT with cloud, fog, and edge computing: A review. *Advanced Information Systems*, *8*(2), 65–78. DOI: 10.20998/2522-9052.2024.2.08

Kumar, T. Minakshi, & Joshi, K. (2025). Empowering Cloud Security Through Advanced Monitoring and Analytics Techniques. In Risk-Based Approach to Secure Cloud Migration (pp. 163-186). IGI Global Scientific Publishing.

Kumar, T., Kumar, P., & Namasudra, S. (2024). User revocation- enabled access control model using identity- based signature in the cloud computing environment. *International Journal of Interactive Multimedia and Artificial Intelligence*, *9*(1), 127–136. DOI: 10.9781/ijimai.2024.05.001

Mollah, M. B., Azad, M. A. K., & Vasilakos, A. (2017). Secure data sharing and searching at the edge of cloud-assisted internet of things. *IEEE Cloud Computing*, *4*(1), 34–42. DOI: 10.1109/MCC.2017.9

Nagarjuna, P., Pandian, A. S., Sharma, S. K., Ramesh, T., Sohail, M. A., & Babu, M. D. (2024, November). Integrating Cloud And Edge Computing For Scalable Iot Applications. In 2024 2nd International Conference on Advances in Computation, Communication and Information Technology (ICAICCIT) (Vol. 1, pp. 214-219). IEEE. DOI: 10.1109/ICAICCIT64383.2024.10912122

Ometov, A., Molua, O. L., Komarov, M., & Nurmi, J. (2022). A survey of security in cloud, edge, and fog computing. *Sensors (Basel)*, *22*(3), 927. DOI: 10.3390/s22030927 PMID: 35161675

Parikh, S., Dave, D., Patel, R., & Doshi, N. (2019). Security and privacy issues in cloud, fog and edge computing. *Procedia Computer Science*, *160*, 734–739. DOI: 10.1016/j.procs.2019.11.018

Puthal, D., Nepal, S., Ranjan, R., & Chen, J. (2016). Threats to networking cloud and edge datacenters in the Internet of Things. *IEEE Cloud Computing*, *3*(3), 64–71. DOI: 10.1109/MCC.2016.63

Roman, R., Lopez, J., & Mambo, M. (2018). Mobile edge computing, Fog et al.: A survey and analysis of security threats and challenges. *Future Generation Computer Systems*, *78*, 680–698. DOI: 10.1016/j.future.2016.11.009

Sikarwar, H., & Das, D. (2023). SecEdge: Secure edge-computing-based hybrid approach for data collection and searching in IoV. *IEEE Transactions on Network and Service Management*, *21*(1), 1213–1225. DOI: 10.1109/TNSM.2023.3299264

Wong, K. S., & Kim, M. H. (2018). Emerging issues and challenges for cloud data at the edge. *International Journal of Web and Grid Services*, *14*(2), 123–145. DOI: 10.1504/IJWGS.2018.090741

Yu, Y., Chen, R., Li, H., Li, Y., & Tian, A. (2019). Toward data security in edge intelligent IIoT. *IEEE Network*, *33*(5), 20–26. DOI: 10.1109/MNET.001.1800507

Zhang, J., Chen, B., Zhao, Y., Cheng, X., & Hu, F. (2018). Data security and privacy-preserving in edge computing paradigm: Survey and open issues. *IEEE Access : Practical Innovations, Open Solutions*, *6*, 18209–18237. DOI: 10.1109/ACCESS.2018.2820162

Zhang, Y., Wang, P., Fang, L., He, X., Han, H., & Chen, B. (2020). Secure transmission of compressed sampling data using edge clouds. *IEEE Transactions on Industrial Informatics*, *16*(10), 6641–6651. DOI: 10.1109/TII.2020.2966511

Chapter 3
A Comprehensive Survey on Edge Computing, Analytics, and AI Model Optimization for Industrial and Healthcare Applications

Siva Subramanian R.
SRM Institute of Science and Technology, India

Beneta Mary A.
St. Joseph College of Engineering, India

R. Abitha
Vel Tech Multi Tech Dr. Rangarajan Dr. Sakunthala Engineering College, India

Sivaramakrishnan Rajendar
https://orcid.org/0000-0002-7095-7209
Vel Tech Rangarajan Dr. Sagunthala R&D Institute of Science and Technology, India

D. Mangaiyarkarasi
https://orcid.org/0009-0009-8751-7021
Sri Sairam Engineering College, India

Gracious L. A. Anto
https://orcid.org/0000-0003-2386-9182
R.M.K. College of Engineering and Technology, India

P. Girija
https://orcid.org/0009-0000-1691-8180
Panimalar Engineering College, India

DOI: 10.4018/979-8-3373-1147-0.ch003

ABSTRACT

Real time data processing of data in intelligent analytics, decision making and AI model training and updating is an area where edge computing can be put to effective use. This chapter focuses on their deployment with machine intelligence, sensors, and networking in IIoT and smart health care particularly concentrating on edge computing. It explores deploying AI models at the edge level and how to overcome some areas of constraint computational resources such as memory devices. Approaches for incorporating the sensor and the fusion of data to improve efficiency in edge devices are presented. Central concepts such as decentralised, distributed, and distributed intelligence accentuate the collaborative model building; federal learning acknowledges the model training co-operation but with the data protection interior. This chapter also explores large-scale edge-cloud systems, security, and resources in hybrid models. Last, the chapter explores use cases in industry across verticals and technology trends such as AI, 5G and quantum computing that define the future of edge intelligence.

1. INTRODUCTION

1.1 Overview of Edge Computing

Edge computing means the data processing is done near the data source, that can be a device or local servers rather than cloud centers. This change in paradigm enables the processing and analyzing of data in real-time and not be reliant on the bandwidth. The growth of edge computing has been as a result of the rising use of IoT devices and the need for immediate analysis. Although cloud computing is still important for mass data storage and demanding calculations, edge computing allows improving the processing of the information at the network's periphery, closer to the origin of the information. This approach has emerged as highly relevant with the development of applications that need real-time analysis, including self-driving automobiles, Industrial IoT, and smart cities. With more and more industries embracing digitalization, the need to work with data locally and with high response rates has become critical. The same is true for decreasing the reliance on the centralized cloud servers, which enables better control over the chosen bandwidth usage, where only important or summarized data is transferred to the cloud.

1.2 Relevance to Industrial IoT and Healthcare

Real-time processing of data is especially important in IIoT and the healthcare sector, which is why edge computing is especially important. In IIoT, whereby we have thousands of sensors taking care of the machinery and equipment, the environment, it is possible to have an immediate analysis of the data, which can help in failure prediction, process optimization, among others. For example, tools like smart sensors for predictive maintenance use real-time data to detect early signs of equipment failure, so that it can be avoided. In health care, edge computing enhances the monitoring of patient's data in real-time by wearables, biosensors, and imaging devices. Thus, it can provide healthcare providers with an instant notification of any atypical findings, thus enhancing the treatment effectiveness. Moreover, edge computing enables such remote healthcare application as telemedicine that requires analysis of the patient data on the edge to minimize latency and bandwidth consumption.

1.3 Motivation for the Survey

The implementation of AI, analytics, and sensor technologies at the edge have some difficulties, as described below. First, edge devices are often resource-constrained, with limited computational power, memory, and energy This means that it becomes challenging to deploy complex AI models as well as perform real-time analytics. Another important issue is related to the requirements for the refinement of AI models and analytics algorithms that should be used in such environments. In addition, edge computing is a distributed architecture, and the devices and sensors that are involved in this infrastructure have different capabilities and protocols. Another difficulty is to make all devices, sensors, and analytics systems work together in harmony.

This survey aims to explore these challenges and give a view of how edge computing, AI, and sensor technologies can be fine-tuned to meet the requirements of industrial and healthcare verticals.

2. FUNDAMENTALS OF EDGE ANALYTICS AND REAL-TIME PROCESSING

2.1 Edge Analytics: Definition, Types, and Importance in Reducing Latency

Edge analytics is the analysis of data within an edge node, within a sensor, a gateway or a local server as opposed to sending the data to a central cloud. This allows for near real time analysis and decision making at or close to the data source. Edge analytics is aimed at minimizing latency, the time elapsed between data creation and processing. (Rancea, A. et al 2024) With regards to edge analytics, there is no need to transfer raw data to the cloud for analysis, which would take time and consume bandwidth.

There are different types of edge analytics:

Descriptive Analytics: This type involves the use of records to make an estimate of future behavior which is beneficial in understanding behavior.
Predictive Analytics: This type involves the use of mathematical models and algorithms to predict future occurrences, for purposes of making appropriate decisions.
Prescriptive Analytics: Includes making suggestions for action based on the analysis of future trends, which is commonly applied to enhance business functioning or implementation of certain activities.
Real-time Analytics: This is a very important subset of edge analytics that is concerned with processing data feeds in real time with minimal latency.

Figure 1. Types of edge analytics

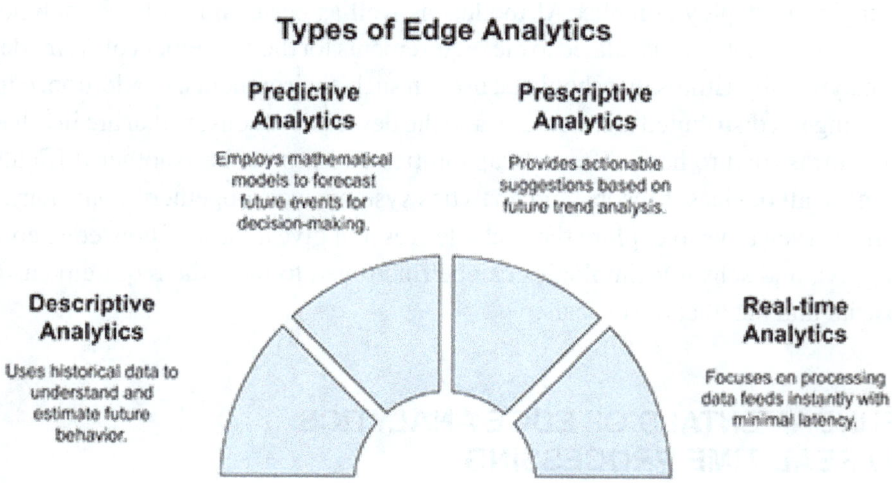

Real-time processing or edge analytics is crucial in applications that need an instant response, including self-driving vehicles, where any delay in processing can lead to a crash or in manufacturing plants where the failure of a piece of equipment requires prompt attention to minimize losses.

2.2 Real-Time Processing Techniques

Data computation in the edge devices occurs in real time with several techniques to enhance the speed. These techniques are basically limited by the amount of resources that can be afforded by edge devices which includes bandwidth, power and processing power.

Data Filtering: Rather than forwarding all raw data to the cloud, edge devices pre-process the data eliminating the unnecessary data. Critical or aggregated data only is transmitted to enhance the amount of data transmitted hence improving processing time.

Data Aggregation: In particular, edge devices tend to collect data from several sensors and then transmit it to the cloud, thus avoiding the need for frequent interactions and consumption of a significant amount of bandwidth.

Compression: Due to the bandwidth constraints, edge devices reduce size of data to send smaller payloads while preserving necessary data.

Local Model Inference: This is because edge devices may perform pre-trained AI models on the device, without necessarily need to transfer data to and from the cloud. This technique increases response time and minimizes the need for cloud structures.

Nonetheless, edge devices are generally limited by the amount of processing that can be done, the available memory, and the energy they can use. These limitations make it imperative to develop light weight models and algorithms that can be deployed in such environments.

2.3 Use Cases: Examples from Industrial and Healthcare Domains

In the industrial domain, edge analytics helps analyze machine and equipment data in smart factories in real-time. For example, in predictive maintenance, devices connected to machines monitor data from temperature, vibration, or pressure that the machines generate. This data is processed in the edge devices in real time to foretell failures before they occur, thus cutting on time and costs for repairs.

In the healthcare domain, edge analytics is applied for patients' tracking in real time mode. Smartwatches and medical sensors monitor and record information regarding the wearer's health status (e.g., heart rate, blood pressure) and perform computations on the data. If any anomaly is noted, the edge device can notify the healthcare givers early enough thus allowing early treatment. This is particularly useful in telemedicine and remote patient monitoring, where small second delays can be a matter of life and death.

3. AI MODEL OPTIMIZATION FOR RESOURCE-CONSTRAINED EDGE DEVICES

3.1 Challenges: Computational and Memory Limitations of Edge Devices

Edge devices are small, power-efficient, and inexpensive, which in consequence are characterized by low computational power, memory, and storage capabilities. Such limitations present difficulties in operating complicated AI and ML algorithms that require consideration and powerful computation for data analysis and other real-time processes. Moreover, edge devices work under conditions where network connections can be often weak or unavailable therefore, there is a constraint in using cloud computing for resourceful computation. (Sharma, M. et al 2024) Therefore, AI models when deployed on the edge devices demand high optimization to run without straining the limited resources of the edge devices.

3.2 Model Optimization Techniques

To overcome the computational and memory limitations of edge devices, several model optimization techniques are employed:

Pruning: This technique refers to the process of pruning some neurons or the interconnections between neurons in a neural network. Pruning in a way also helps to lower the computational load and the memory usage as they are directly proportional to the amount of the parameters, while the impact of the model's accuracy is minimal. The pruned model has fewer parameters requiring less storage and can be run significantly faster than the original model, ideal for edge devices.

Quantization: Quantization minimizes the precision of the model's weights and the biases, usually from 32-bit float values to 8-bit integer values. This has a very beneficial impact on memory usage and computation speed since single-precision operations take less time to compute. Quantized models are quite suitable for real-time edge applications since the latency is critical.

Model Compression: This technique entails shrinking the AI model through techniques like weight sharing, low-rank factorization, or knowledge distillation. Compressed models can be used on the devices with limited resources such as the edge devices because they occupy less space. Model compression retains almost all of the model's accuracy and shrinks the model's size and the computational burden related to it.

3.3 Edge AI Frameworks

There are different specific AI frameworks for the deployment of AI models at the edge devices. These frameworks are optimized to run models efficiently on resource-constrained devices while maintaining high performance:

TensorFlow Lite: A framework developed for mobile and embedded devices and which is open source. TensorFlow Lite offers techniques for converting models into lower precision formats and for removing unnecessary parts of the models and the API has been optimized for running ML models on resource-constrained devices.

PyTorch Mobile: PyTorch, which is a popular deep learning framework that contains a lightweight version of the program for using deep learning models on mobile and edge devices. It supports model optimization techniques and delivers high runtime performance despite the low computing capability of the target devices. These frameworks provide solutions to implement, fine tune, and run AI models at the edge making it possible to build, test, and deploy AI applications on constrained devices.

3.4 Impact on Performance

On this basis, it is possible to achieve an increase in the speed of AI models on edge devices in real-time mode. These optimisation methods such as pruning, quantisation and compression aid in the minimisation of the load required to be computed and the memory that is required to be utilised for running such models on edge devices. This leads to high speed data processing, low latency and better response time in self-driving cars, industrial applications and health care monitoring systems. The optimized models also allow edge devices to run locally without repeated dependence on the cloud thereby helping to reduce latency in decision-making and increasing reliability in critical applications. In general, the optimization of the AI model improves the efficiency of edge computing systems for real-time applications by increasing the system's scalability.

4. INTELLIGENT SENSOR INTEGRATION AND DATA FUSION TECHNIQUES

4.1 Sensor Types: Overview of Various Sensors Used in IIoT and Healthcare

Sensors are used in IIoT and Healthcare where the real-time data collected are used to make decisions. The specific types of sensors that are deployed depends with the domain and the need that has to be met.

Temperature Sensors: Applied in IIoT for machine condition and environmental surveillance, and equipment well-being. In healthcare, temperature sensors are usually used in patient monitoring systems and wearable devices to monitor the body temperature.

Motion Sensors: These are very essential in IIoT to identify motion or shift in position, prevalent in robotic or automated operations. In health care, motion sensor is used in the fall detection of patients especially the elderly, or even monitoring the movement of patients in hospitals for health purposes.

Figure 2. Various sensors used in IIoT and healthcare

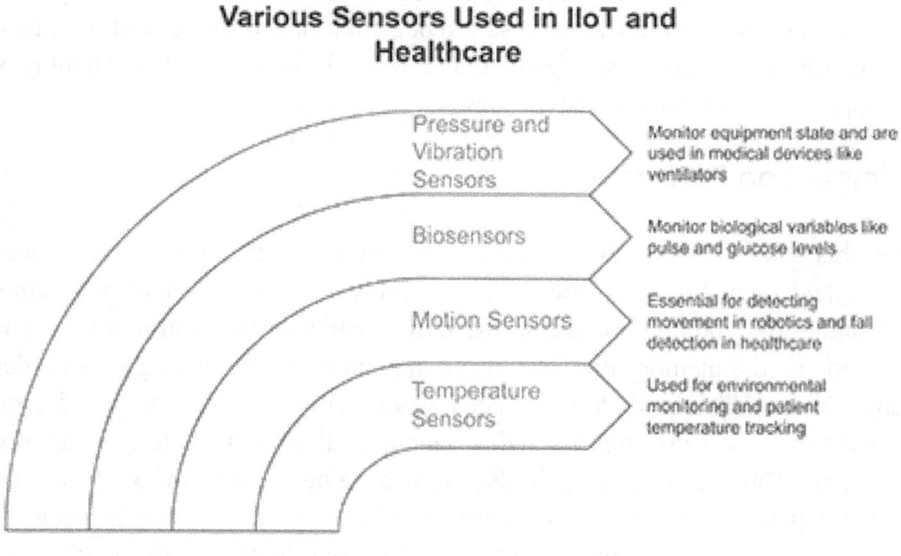

Biosensors: In healthcare biosensors are used to monitor biological variables including pulse rate, blood pressure, glucose concentration and respiratory rate. These sensors are normally incorporated into smart wearable devices or medical monitoring patches; for instance, smartwatches.

Pressure and Vibration Sensors: In industrial processes, these sensors observe the state of equipment and contribute to the identification of problems due to variations in vibration or pressure, for example. In healthcare, the similar sensors are used in different kinds of medical equipment, for example, in ventilators the sensors measure pressure and airflow.

These sensors, when incorporated into edge devices, supply important real-time information for decision-making across industrial and healthcare arrangements.

4.2 Data Fusion Methods: Combining Data from Multiple Sensors for Accurate Insights

Multisensor data fusion methodologies integrate data from many sensors to facilitate improved, accurate, and richer information. (Pandey, R. et al 2022) These methods enhance the quality of the decision making process especially when information from the individual sensors is sometimes noisy or truncated.

Kalman Filters: A computational method used to predict the condition of a system given the available sensor data. It is applied in many cases where sensors generate time series data such as in motion tracking or in predictive maintenance.

Particle Filters: More suitable for analysis of non-linear systems, the particle filter finds its application in cases where data from several sources has to be analyzed. They give a measure of the state of a system because the data is represented in the form of particles, which is useful in dynamic contexts such as health monitoring or management of industrial assets.

These methods help to make more accurate decisions at the edge using data from multiple sensors incorporated into the system.

4.3 Integration in Edge Devices: How Sensors Are Integrated into Edge Devices and the Role of Intelligent Decision-Making

Sensors are connected to edge devices using protocols like Bluetooth, Zigbee, WiFi or LoRaWAN and microcontrollers that control the data acquisition from sensors. These sensors broadcast data to edge devices where the data is processed and analyzed in real time. Smart sensors are also essential in intelligent decision making because they employ edge computing to filter, aggregate and analyze data from the sensors. A wide range of AI models and Machine learning algorithms are used to analyze the sensor data, to identify deviations and make decisions which are in most cases, real-time decisions (Sreelakshmi et al., 2024). This minimizes the call to the cloud for communication and guarantees quick responses.

4.4 Applications: Examples in Smart Manufacturing, Smart Infrastructure, and Healthcare

Smart Manufacturing: In an industrial context, edge devices analyze data received from sensors that are continually monitoring the health of industrial equipment such as temperature or vibrations to predict a failure, hence reducing on the time that equipment takes to be out of order for repairs.

Smart Infrastructure: In urban settings, data from traffic, environmental, and energy meters or sensors can be collected, processed, and coalesced at the edge by devices to improve movement of traffic, minimize energy use, or manage waste effectively.

Healthcare: In healthcare, edge devices collect data from biosensors, wearables, and imaging devices for patients' condition monitoring in real-time. For example, in critical care units, sensor data can produce an alarm if a patient's condition deviates from the normal state and thus allow for time-sensitive treatment (Yamini et al 2023; Lakumarapu et al 2024).

In all these applications, the use of intelligent sensors and data fusion at the edge provides solutions that are real time, efficient and reliable to support more autonomous and responsive systems.

5. DISTRIBUTED INTELLIGENCE AND FEDERATED LEARNING SYSTEMS

5.1 Distributed Intelligence

Distributed intelligence is the idea of distributing control rather than having a centralized control center, in a network of devices or nodes. In edge computing this approach enables the edge devices (including sensors, local servers, IoT devices) to process data and make decisions on their own based on real time information (Anusha et al 2024). This is important in situations where high throughput and real time responses are required, for example in manufacturing processes, hospitals and robotics.

(Ray, P. P. et al 2019) Decentralized decision-making improves the dependability and growth of edge systems. Distributed intelligence decentralizes processing and decision making them less demanding on the central server, decreases the amount of information flowing through the network and increases fault tolerance. The rest of the edge devices in the system can keep on working even if one or more of the devices in the system have failed or lost connectivity. This is especially true when the application must be continuously operational, as in the case of telemedicine, or self-driving vehicles.

5.2 Federated Learning: Concept and Benefits for Privacy-Preserving Machine Learning at the Edge

Federated learning is a type of machine learning that allows several edge devices to train multiple models simultaneously without the use of a central site. Every device (smartphone, wearable or an industrial sensor) builds a local model using its data and once in a while sends the updates (such as weights) to a central server. This makes it possible for the system to collect knowledge from many devices and without transferring data to the cloud which may not be safe at times. The first advantage of federated learning is that it allows for private machine learning. Since the data never goes back to the cloud in its raw form, it is ideal for applications that require high levels of security such as health and finance. Moreover, the federated learning also scales down the overall amount of data passing through the devices-cloud interconnect which is very much important in the context of limited resources.

5.3 Challenges and Benefits: How Federated Learning Aids in Model Training Without Data Centralization and Its Application in Real-Time Systems

The most significant problem of federated learning is that edge devices are very diverse. These devices can possess diverse computational power, storage capacity, and data dispersal which makes it challenging to guarantee homogeneity in model training in the network. Another problem that is closely connected to the distribution of non-IID data which means that the distributions of data differ from one device to another, is another issue that also requires certain techniques to bring the model to convergence. Nevertheless, there are several valuable advantages of the federated learning process. As a result of the ability to train the model on the device it allows for real-time learning and updating, which is necessary for constantly changing environments such as self-driving cars or real-time health monitoring. It also minimizes the threat of unauthorized access by making certain that any sensitive data, including personal health information, do not ever go out of the device.

For example, in the use of IIoT for predictive maintenance, as well as in the use of healthcare IoT for continuous remote patient monitoring, federated learning can assist in continuously enhancing AI models on edge devices without the need to transfer the data to a central database. This improves the flexibility of the systems that can learn from new data in anytime rather than a batch mode while preserving privacy and minimizing latency.

6. EDGE-CLOUD HYBRID ARCHITECTURE AND INTEGRATION

6.1 Hybrid Models: How Edge Computing Integrates with Cloud Systems for Enhanced Scalability

Hybrid of edge-cloud computing structures leverages both the capabilities of edge computing and cloud computing to enhance performance, flexibility, and reliability. In this system, edge devices process and analyze data on the fly and make quick decisions on the collected data while the cloud is used for data storage, bulk processing and model training. The edge processes time-sensitive, mission-critical tasks with minimal delay, and employs the cloud for complex calculations, data storage, and consolidation from various edge nodes. (Deng, S. et al 2020) Scalability is achieved through the use of both the edge and the cloud systems where the less critical tasks are performed in the cloud while the edge system can dynamically adjust the amount of resources to be used due to workload. For example, if the edge device is full in terms of its processing or storage capability, it can send less important data or tasks for further processing to the cloud. This kind of integration is flexible to balance the resource use and to guarantee the scalability of systems depending on the number of devices or a data volume.

6.2 Data Offloading and Edge Processing

In the case of edge-cloud architecture, data offloading and edge processing are the primary ways through which system performance and latency are enhanced. Sensitively and time-sensitive information including sensor data, machine health data or an alert that may require immediate action is processed at the local edge device. This cuts down the need to send a lot of raw data to the cloud, which would otherwise slow down the response time of such applications as self-driving cars, predictive maintenance, and health monitoring. Meanwhile, relatively unimportant data such as accumulated data from sensors or previous data can be stored in the cloud for further analysis and archiving. Since only the required data is sent to the cloud, edge devices help save bandwidth and storage and minimize the burden on network components, thereby improving the system's performance. Such selective offloading approach is more beneficial in the situation where the network bandwidth is scarce or connectivity is poor.

6.3 Use Cases: Industrial IoT, Urban Computing and Healthcare Scenarios

Industrial IoT: For example, in smart factories, edge devices are used to constantly check the condition of the equipment and ensure their proper functioning, or to notify the system of an emerging problem and develop a reaction to it on the spot. Less sensitive information like, business patterns and performance indicators are transmitted to the cloud for deeper analysis and trend analysis for the long term. This approach of processing data at the edge, but with guidance from the cloud, makes it possible to make decisions as processes proceed at the edge while the cloud can analyze data to give better ways of improving manufacturing processes.

Urban Computing: In smart cities, edge devices, storing and processing information gathered by sensors, count traffic, energy consumption, or climatic conditions. Information that changes with time, for instance, the traffic flow data, is analyzed on the edge to enhance traffic control. The cloud is used to identify data patterns of the whole city so that the urban planners can enhance the infrastructure and resources.

Healthcare: Healthcare's edge-cloud hybrid systems enable the continuous monitoring of patients. Smart wearable devices and other remote medical sensors perform sophisticated computations on important data (such as heart rate or blood sugar level) locally, and in case of certain values, notify the healthcare professionals. Some information that is not as urgent, for example, patient records or radiological images, is uploaded to the cloud for storage, processing and reinforcement of the model.

The edge-cloud architecture improves the systems' efficiency, minimizes latency, and scales up for IIoT, UC, and healthcare; it provides immediate answers while using the cloud for general computations and data storage.

7. SECURITY AND PRIVACY FRAMEWORKS FOR EDGE COMPUTING

7.1 Security Challenges

Security issues are among the main concerns for edge computing, and they stem from the fact that the architecture of edge computing is distributed in nature. (Sun, L. et al 2020) While data is analyzed nearer to the source, for example on the devices, gateways, or local servers, there are higher implications as related to data privacy, device security, and communication security.

Data Privacy: IoT devices that reside at the edge of the network are used to perform computations on data that is potentially confidential, like a patient's health record in a healthcare setting or a manufacturing record in industrial IoT. These devices are usually connected to several networks and therefore can be accessed by anyone, thus have an added risk in the privacy of the data being processed. Data security is also important to protect data while transferring data from one point to another or data stored in any form whether in a computer or in disks or in any other external storage media.

Device Vulnerabilities: While the edge devices are usually not very powerful and may not have the same level of security as in centralised systems. These devices are typically used in low-security contexts, and they are therefore at constant risk of physical invasion, viruses, and intrusion. Insecure firmware and software vulnerabilities enhance the vulnerability of edge devices to exploitation.

Secure Communication: Another major problem is the secure communication of the devices of the edge with the cloud or other nodes of the edge. This data that circulates between these nodes can be stolen or modified by an attacker if the protection is insufficient. Moreover, the data collected in edge devices may need to be transmitted over public or semi-public networks, which will result in data leakage vulnerability.

7.2 Privacy-Preserving Techniques

To mitigate the security risks associated with edge computing, various privacy-preserving techniques are employed:

Encryption: Security is realized through the encryption of information that is exchanged between edge devices and the cloud. Methods like end-to-end encryption code data at the sender and decode it at the receiver to make it impossible for the attacker to intercept important data in the course of the transfer. Data at rest in edge devices also can be encrypted to secure it in case of theft of the device or unauthorized access.

Authentication: Authorization to access edge devices and the data they process is done through reliable authentication mechanisms to allow only the right devices and users. Techniques like MFA and digital certificates may be employed to authenticate the devices as well as users before they can access the system. This minimizes the risk of an intruder gaining access to important resources of the system.

Secure Multi-party Computation (SMC): SMC enables several entities to cooperatively process data with no disclosure of their private data. In edge computing, this technique can be applied to the computations on multiple edge devices with preserving data confidentiality. For instance, federated learning is expected to improve through SMC because it allows training models across different devices without using the data.

8. PERFORMANCE OPTIMIZATION AND RESOURCE MANAGEMENT

8.1 Resource Constraints

Edge devices work in constrained environments, and computational resources, memory, and power are scarce resources in these environments. These devices are usually developed to accomplish certain functions with almost no hardware such as sensors or microcontrollers or even embedded systems. (Verma, P. et al 2020) The issue is as such that the requirements for real-time processing have to be met on the edge with the hardware constraints.

Computational Resources: Edge devices are not as powerful as cloud servers mostly, so they have to wisely regulate their computational capabilities. Activities like data preprocessing, data analysis, and model execution have to conform to the capabilities of the device's CPU, GPU or RAM.

Memory: The memory on edge devices is usually limited and therefore both storage as well as processing memory has to be managed effectively. Raw big data storage or execution of large models on these devices will result in memory overflow or slowed system performance. Hence, the memory management strategies that are very important include; offloading non-critical data or the use of memory-efficient algorithms.

Power: Energy consumption is another important factor to consider because edge devices are typically located in areas that are hard to access or are battery operated. These devices have to be power efficient and at the same time deliver high performance. Maximizing power consumption while minimizing loss of functionality is a key factor in the longevity and the less frequent need for recharging or maintenance.

8.2 Optimization Techniques

To address resource constraints, various optimization techniques are employed at the edge:

Dynamic Resource Allocation: In this technique the amount of computation power that is assigned to a particular task is changed according to its current workload and the importance of other tasks still waiting to be processed. For instance, if an edge device is overburdened, it can assign more resources on core functions and less on peripheral processes. This facilitates prioritization of critical processes such as real-time data analysis, to be executed before lower priority tasks.

Figure 3. Performance optimization and resource management

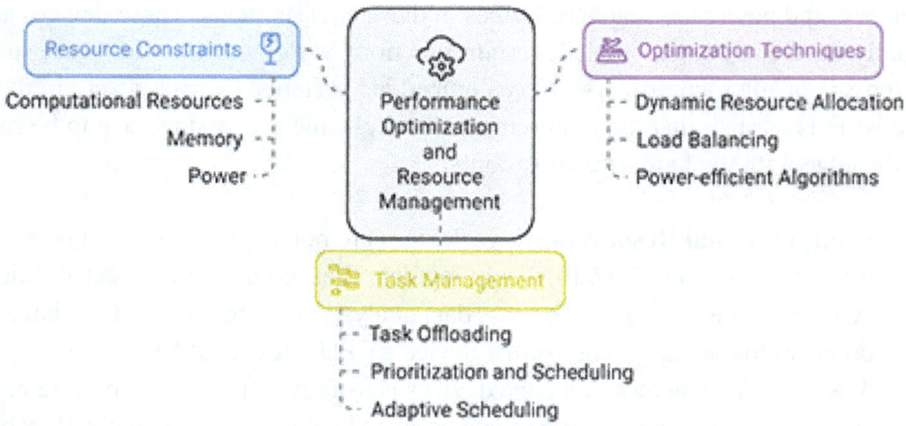

Load Balancing: Load balancing is used in load balancing of tasks between multiple edge devices or between the edge devices and the cloud. It makes sure that no device is overburdened with workloads, which contributes to preventing system degradation. This is especially the case in large scale IoT networks where a multitude of edge devices are running concurrently.

Power-efficient Algorithms: Another approach is to reduce the energy consumption of the device through more efficient algorithms that avoid computation when it is not necessary, and use the device's resources less often. For example, in AI/ML applications, techniques such as model pruning, quantization, and utilizing light-weight neural networks may limit the computational power that is needed to perform one or several tasks without draining the battery of an edge device.

8.3 Scheduling and Task Management

In low resource environments operational efficiency and effective scheduling of tasks are critical for effective functioning. Several strategies are used:

Task Offloading: This is especially the case when tasks at an edge device are beyond the capability of the device, and can be shifted to the cloud or other edge devices with more resources. This is especially beneficial for computationally intensive operations such as processing of large datasets or machine learning where the operations can be performed in the cloud while the edge devices perform real-time operations with low latency(Siva, S. R et al 2022).

Prioritization and Task Scheduling: Not all the tasks are important, or have the same level of importance. The scheduling algorithms can also give preference to urgent processing over less important processing, for instance alert processing, real-time health monitoring. Basing on priority, resource demands and time frames, it is possible to select when and how tasks should be performed.

Adaptive Scheduling: In dynamic environments where workloads and availability of resources fluctuates often then adaptive scheduling techniques can allow devices to rebalance the resources or reschedule tasks according to the current state. For example, if a device is in a low power mode, then tasks can be delayed until the power usage is not a problem.

Therefore, the optimization of performance and resources at the edge is as crucial as the proper management of tasks at the edge. Due to resource limitation, edge systems can be resource constrained, but through dynamic resource allocation, load balancing, power efficient algorithms, and adaptive scheduling the edge systems realize high performance to execute the real-time tasks.

9. INDUSTRIAL IOT APPLICATIONS AND SMART MANUFACTURING

9.1 Real-World Applications

Edge computing is particularly effective in revitalising industrial segments to process data instantly and make decisions in limited settings. Here are some key applications:

Predictive Maintenance: Remote monitoring of health of equipment and machinery is made possible by edge computing. Temperature, vibration and pressure parameters are monitored by the sensors installed on machines. This data is then processed locally at the edge devices to detect anomalies that may exist before they cause equipment failure and result in costly downtime and lower efficiency. Thus, by evaluating past experiences and existing conditions, analytical models can be implemented at the edge to initiate maintenance notifications or arrange for repair work.

Supply Chain Management: In logistics and supply chain management, edge devices allow efficient identification of material and assets in motion. Mobile sensors on vehicles, warehouses and inventories assist in tracking conditions of the products, their location and even the best routes to take. When working with data locally, companies can quickly react to disruptions depending on delays or other changes in conditions and can thereby enhance supply chain performance and cut costs.

Quality Control: In manufacturing, edge computing can also be employed to improve the quality control procedures. This is because product quality is constantly checked by sensors and cameras mounted on production lines and which detects defective products on the line. By performing data analysis on the camera and sensor data at the edge, manufacturers can quickly spot a defective product and remove it from the production line, thereby increasing quality and reducing the number of defective products.

9.2 Smart Manufacturing

Edge computing plays a central role in Industry 4.0 which is the fourth industrial revolution that brings IoT, AI, automation into manufacturing. (Veeramachaneni, V.

2025) Smart factories leverage edge computing to enhance production efficiency and flexibility:

Real-time Production Monitoring: A number of edge devices track the operational condition of machines and production lines in real-time. It is used in production schedules to minimize time wastage, control production time as well as to enhance production. Edge computing also tackles complicated processes through decentralized decision making in a given area without having to always relay on the main server.
Autonomous Operations: In smart factories, edge computing can enable the autonomy of systems such as robot systems and automated guided vehicles (AGVs). These systems can operate on the data and then make decisions about the environment without having to transfer the information to another system, such as moving around objects or selecting products from production lines. This allows smooth and versatile production that can easily switch between production types in response to market forces.
Customization and Flexibility: It can therefore be seen that edge computing brings more flexibility in manufacturing operation. Real-time data processing and decision making help the factories to meet the requirements of the customer, modify a product or even a production plan within a short period of time.

9.3 Integration with Other Technologies

Edge computing in smart manufacturing can be further enhanced by integrating with other advanced technologies:

Augmented Reality (AR): In assembly lines, AR systems may display information, including instructions on how to assemble a product or the condition of the equipment, on the workers' visual space. AR can deliver this information because data is processed at the edge, and it results in enhanced worker efficiency and minimized mistakes.
Virtual Reality (VR): VR can be supported by edge computing to provide training to the workers or simulate a production environment. Applications that are executed on the edge device offer a higher quality of experience with low latency, hence, make training more engaging and effective without the need for cloud-based solutions.
Robotics: Real-time processing is possible through edge computing since robotic systems are already on the rise in smart factories. Robotic systems demand fast decisions and instantaneous actions that are typically seen in application areas like precise assembly or material transport. Analyzing data locally at the

edge enables robots to work independently, thus increasing productivity and minimizing the necessity for constant supervision.

Artificial Intelligence (AI): AI models that are run in the edge can analyze data from IoT devices, sensors and machines in real-time. These applications of AI can improve manufacturing by identifying probable failures in equipment, improving quality assurance and supply chain management. Data-driven AI models are trained at the centralized data center, but need to be executed at the edge to enable efficient and dynamic response of the manufacturing system.

Thus, edge computing is considered a critical factor for the evolution of Industrial IoT, particularly in smart manufacturing. New capabilities of edge devices allow for real-time data processing and decision making in aspects such as predictive maintenance, supply chain optimization and high value production. Edge computing when combined with other technologies such as AR/VR, Robotics, and AI increases the advantages of Industry 4.0 in terms of flexibility, productivity, and innovation in production.

10. SMART INFRASTRUCTURE AND URBAN COMPUTING SOLUTIONS

10.1 Smart Cities

Edge computing is a fundamental building block in smart cities, the integration of technology into urban environments to enhance the quality of life of its inhabitants, and promote durability. (Ramanathan, R. et al 2024) Edge computing helps to shift computation toward the source of the data, for instance, sensors and devices deployed in city infrastructure to support real-time decision-making with low latency and minimal bandwidth consumption.

Smart Grids: Edge computing is one of the most important elements in the process of power grid modernization. Smart grids employ sensors and IoT devices to detect and control the electricity feed. These devices process data on the device itself to respond to shifts in energy demand, check the health of the grid and identify faults, without the need for the cloud. This results to better energy distribution, load management and faster response to power interruptions.

Traffic Management: In the context of cities, edge computing reduces congestion since the data from the sensors and cameras mounted on roads, intersections, and automobiles are processed. Information on traffic, for example, congestion, an accident or signal change, can be processed locally to modify the traffic signals and inform drivers. This leads to less traffic, enhanced security and the possibility of smoother transport systems.

Energy Optimization: As cities demand more efficient energy consumption, edge computing helps with the demand-side management by tracking energy consumption in real-time and adjusting consumption frequencies. Thus, by analyzing data obtained from energy meters and sensors, edge devices can support saving energy, optimizing supply and demand, and, therefore, decreasing the costs due to the usage of energy during peak hours.

10.2 Urban Computing

Urban Planning: Edge computing supports smart city by providing data acquisition and processing of various parameters like traffic, population movement and land usage. This data can be analyzed at the edge to convey insights that will help in planning new infrastructure and zoning and allocation of resources in a way that will help these cities to grow in the right manner.

Environmental Monitoring: Air quality and water quality, noise pollution indices, and climate conditions are some of the aspects of environment that smart cities monitor using edge computing. Devices placed at various strategic points in the city gather data, to be analyzed on site to determine areas of high pollution or for real time change detection. This helps to provide rapid reactions to threats in the environment and more effective policies for the sustainability.

Waste Management: In the urban scenario, the waste management can be efficiently made by using edge computing. Waste bins can be fitted with sensors that allow the identification of the full status of waste collection bins. Information from such sensors can be processed at the site and used to enhance the efficiency of collecting waste by minimizing fuel consumption. It can also be applied for recycling data and giving information for efficiency of resources in use.

10.3 Challenges

Despite the numerous benefits of edge computing in smart cities, several challenges must be addressed:

Scalability: When the size of cities increases and the number of connected devices grows, the problem of managing large amounts of data for edge computing systems arises. The capability of edge devices and networks to handle an increasing number of sensors, cameras, and other IoT devices without degrading the system's performance is critical.

Data Volume: Smart city systems produce large quantities of information from sensors, cameras, and other gadgets. Real-time processing at the edge of this data demands devices with adequate storage and compute capabilities. The data, therefore, needs to be well managed and analyzed effectively to reduce time consumption and enhance timely decision-making for the provision of urban services.

Integration with Legacy Systems: Several existing urban infrastructure systems are based on prior technologies that may not integrate quickly with edge computing systems. One major issue is that incorporating edge computing into a modern infrastructure includes existing, often outdated, systems like traffic control systems or power grid. This means adding to or modifying these systems to allow for this kind of interaction and to make the new technologies integrate well with the old ones.

Therefore, edge computing is crucial for improving the prospects of smart cities and urban computing. It thus optimises real-time data processing for traffic flow control, energy usage and environmental monitoring thus enhancing the quality of life in urban areas and use of resources. But there are some issues as scalability, volume of data, and integration with existing systems which should be solved to extend smart cities projects' success.

11. HEALTHCARE EDGE COMPUTING AND MEDICAL DEVICE INTEGRATION

11.1 Edge Computing in Healthcare

Edge computing has a massive impact on healthcare and it is necessary to have real-time data processing at the edge, at the point of care. Through implementing edge devices in the healthcare facilities, hospitals, clinics, and home care, healthcare service providers can monitor patients, diagnose diseases, and offer individualized care.

Monitoring: Real time constant vitals check including the heart rate, blood pressure, oxygen levels, and glucose level can be monitored continuously through edge computing. Wearable and sensor data are analyzed on the device so the information is not delayed, and patients can receive an alert if their health worsens. Such rapid response is extremely useful in intensive care because it can literally mean the difference between life and death.

Diagnostics: Diagnostic data of patients including medical images, laboratory results, and patient's records can be processed through AI models running in edge devices. These systems are able to perform the first analysis at the edge and thereby alert the medical professionals to possible problems such as tumors, irregular heartbeat or infections so that timely diagnosis and treatment can be commenced. Applying edge computing decreases the dependence on the central hub, so diagnostics can happen with the possibility of a delay, even in the zones with a poor connection.

Patient Care: Since patient information can be processed at the edge devices, it is possible to support decisions made by healthcare professionals in real time. This is especially essential in situations where connectivity to the internet or the network connection is weak or very slow, using cloud computing would slow down the process. Situating AI and machine learning models at the edge can help healthcare providers deliver personalised care to patients by making treatment recommendations in real-time.

11.2 Medical Device Integration

Integration of many different devices is made possible by edge computing and this makes the healthcare systems run more effectively. (Rupanetti, D. et al, 2024) Wearable technology, biosensors, and imaging systems are other categories of medical devices, and they produce massive data that require real-time analysis for efficiency.

Wearables: Smartwatches and fitness trackers are able to track vital signs and other aspects of a person's health. When this data is processed at the edge, health information can be collected, analyzed and delivered to healthcare providers or caregivers in near real time. This is particularly useful for chronic conditions where regular assessment of health status is required most of the time.

Biosensors: Biosensors track certain biological parameters for example glucose in diabetic patients or electrocardiogram for heart health. These devices are based on edge computing to perform sensor data analysis in real-time and respond with feedback, including direct to the patient or to the healthcare provider, improving the general speed and accuracy of the medical treatment.

Imaging Devices: Machines used in the diagnosis of diseases such as MRI, X-ray and CT scanners produce clear images that need to be analyzed quickly. Edge computing means that some initial image processing can be done on-site without a delay in sending the data to cloud servers and, as a result, healthcare professionals can make faster and better decisions.

11.3 Telemedicine and Remote Monitoring

Benefits: This paper also established that telemedicine can be effectively managed by using edge computing since it offers real-time data processing for consultations. Through minimizing the latency and dependency on the centralized cloud, the edges make it possible for patients in rural or remote regions to receive medical advice in the shortest time possible. Consultations by video link and remote diagnosis can be improved by the integration of data from medical devices in real time, so that the doctor does not have to be physically present to make a decision.

Remote Monitoring: In patients with chronic diseases or elderly patients, through remote monitoring based on edge devices, continuous observation can be carried out without frequent visits to medical institutions. Information from wearable devices, biosensors, and other tracking technologies is analyzed on site, which gives quick feedback to the carers and doctors. This makes it possible to adequately attend to health issues with appropriate action where needed.

Challenges: However, there are several issues that need to be addressed for the adoption of edge computing in healthcare. To this end, proper protection of data is highly important, especially in dealing with medical data. For example, devices must meet such requirements as HIPAA in the USA, and to guarantee the patients' safety, the edge devices must be dependable, durable, and capable of functioning in the healthcare environment with different characteristics. Last but not the least, interfacing with other healthcare IT systems and legacy systems may be challenging, which may need proper planning and protocol.

Therefore, edge computing is vital for advancing the healthcare industry through real-time patient tracking, diagnosis, and management. It also uses medical devices like wearables, biosensors, and imaging devices to improve patient care especially through timely and informed interventions. Despite certain issues which are related to the privacy, security and integration with other systems, edge computing has significant opportunities for developing healthcare systems and, therefore, improving the health of people.

12. SYSTEM DEPLOYMENT, SCALABILITY, AND MAINTENANCE STRATEGIES

12.1 Deployment Challenges

Integrating edge computing devices at scale across large networks, especially in the industrial or urban setting, is difficult. One of the key challenges is in fact the ability to add more and more edge devices to the system while maintaining the efficiency of the whole system. However, as the number of the devices rises, this means that the networking connectivity becomes more challenging to manage, device configurations become more complex, and large data processing becomes a significant issue. (Hua, H. et al 2023) The problem is that edge devices are located in remote or distributed locations and, therefore, may have connectivity problems. It can be challenging to sustain strong and reliable communication between the edge nodes and the central system or cloud while the former devices can be spread across vast geographical areas or are deployed in hostile conditions. Further, it is impossible to deploy and configure devices at scale manually, and the use of templates is necessary to avoid mistakes.

Figure 4. System deployment, scalability, and maintenance strategies

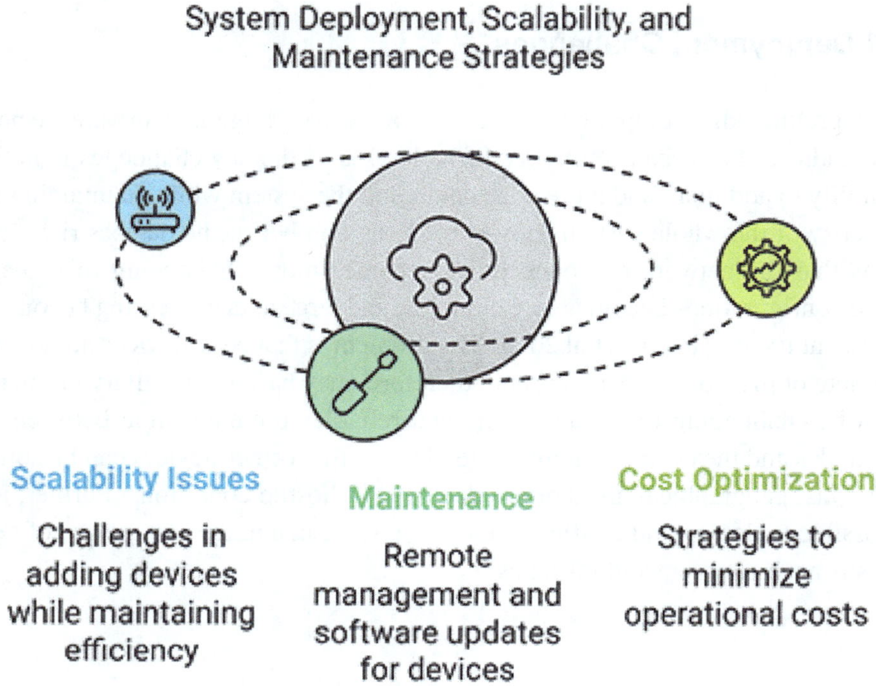

The second scalability concern is the computational and storage capacity of edge devices that are used in the system. The more devices enter the network, the more the network may struggle to handle data locally, and there may be the need to balance resources and maybe introduce a combination of edge cloud to handle the numerous tasks.

12.2 Maintenance of Edge Devices

To keep up with the edge devices over the lifecycle is another significant factor in guaranteeing the efficiency of the system. Since most of these edge devices are deployed in far-flung areas, configuring software updates and managing the devices must be done remotely most of the time. This has to be solved by adopting Over-The-Air (OTA) update solutions in order to correct security issues, change software release and add functionalities while providing uninterrupted service. Another area in maintenance is fault detection. Edge devices may be affected by a wide range of problems, ranging from hardware failures to software crashes and communication breakdowns. Sophisticated monitoring tools, applying the remote diagnostics and condition based maintenance, can be applied to identify problems before they occur and prevent a failure. Also, automated fault detection systems can produce notifications to system administrators in the case of anomalous behavior or failure of a device.

Device management is the process of monitoring the health of each device, guaranteeing that each device is healthy and fine, and controlling resources such as bandwidth, power, and storage. To manage the fleet of edge devices, the centralized device management platforms can give a single point of control to monitor and manage the entire fleet and can help in achieving better control and easier identification of potential issues.

12.3 Cost Optimization

The most important advantage that organizations and businesses use as a reason for implementing edge computing systems is cost savings. Due to the nature of edge computing, the devices are commonly used in scenarios where resources are scarce, therefore the need to optimize the edge device's performance without demanding significant resources to achieve this is paramount.

Power requirements are a critical cost component in edge setups, especially if there are numerous devices deployed. Energy saving technologies such as power conservation algorithms, energy-saving modes, dynamic resource management can be applied to decrease the energy consumption, and computational power, respectively, can be provided when required.

Further, by employing data offloading strategies, the bandwidth expenses can be prevented. Due to edge computing, only necessary data is transferred to the cloud, and a lot of data is processed on the edge; therefore, there is no need for the high bandwidth, and the operational cost of data transfer is optimized.

Hardware costs are also a factor and especially when it comes to large scale deployments of edge devices. This means that hardware platforms should be standardized, components should be purchased from an ordinary store, or devices should be modular and easily replaceable or upgradable.

Hence, future work includes the scalability of edge computing systems in large-scale networks, management of employed devices, and the energy-efficient and effective offloading policies of the proposed system. Such areas would help organizations to optimise the edge computing infrastructure in terms of reliability and cost efficiency at scale.

13. EMERGING TECHNOLOGIES AND FUTURE TRENDS IN EDGE INTELLIGENCE

13.1 AI and Edge Intelligence

AI with edge computing is set to disrupt industries by facilitating data analysis and decision making at the source of data. Current edge devices with deep learning models and reinforcement learning are more capable to perform high level of computations locally thus reducing the requirement of cloud support and latency.

The models generated by deep learning are complex and are computationally intensive, optimization techniques that can be employed include pruning, quantization and model compression for edge devices. As we have seen with recent developments in specialized hardware like the edge AI chips (Nvidia Jetson, Google Edge TPU among others), deep learning models can be deployed to execute tasks like image recognition, natural language processing, and anomaly detection at the edge directly on the constrained devices. (Wang, F. et al 2020) Reinforcement learning is used in the process of enabling the edge devices to learn from feedback from the environment.

Reinforcement learning enables edge devices to continuously adapt and improve their decision-making based on environmental feedback. It is especially useful in the volatile context, for instance, the manufacturing floor or self-driving vehicles where the system must decide on the fly.

The future of edge intelligence is to improve the ability of AI models for edge devices to make the network of interconnected devices more intelligent and self-running.

13.2 5G and Beyond

5G is revolutionary for edge computing because it supplies the necessary bandwidth and low latency for more extensive real-time applications, and it also supports the connectivity of millions of devices at a time, making the deployment of numerous edge devices straightforward. (Chelliah, P. R. et al 2024) The 5G latency expected at around millisecond level is very important for applications such as autonomous vehicles, industrial control and automation, tele-medicine where even a small delay can be very costly. Finally, 5G, quantum computing, as well as the further development of artificial intelligence in edge devices define the future of edge computing. They will help to create a more efficient edge computing application to support artificial intelligence and related fields, such as robotics and autonomous systems and real-time decision-making. Over the years, these technologies will only advance, and edge computing will be a more significant component of our network of smart, connected solutions.

14. CONCLUSION

This survey has discussed the increasing importance of edge computing in various fields especially Industrial IoT (IIoT), smart manufacturing and Healthcare applications. Edge computing is a process by which data is analyzed as near to the source as possible, providing low latency, low bandwidth utilization, and higher security. Several critical technologies including AI model optimization, distributed intelligence, and intelligent sensor integration were defined, and their contributions to improve decision making at the edge were also presented. We studied edge analytics and real-time processing focusing on the low-latency requirements and local processing of vital data to satisfy the strict requirements of industries and healthcare. The techniques like pruning and quantization make the models work efficiently on the edge devices and thus the intelligent system can work independently. Within distributed intelligence, we have chosen the federated learning as the privacy-preserving methods for training AI models without the need for aggregating data, which is crucial for personal data applications such as healthcare. Further, edge-cloud architectures hybrid are facilitating the smooth distribution of computational loads, making it easy to scale and integrate into large-scale systems. In the survey, there was a significant focus on the security and privacy requirements since edge computing systems are at risks. It is essential to have secure communication and encryption, as well as following the rules of privacy protection. Lastly, some case studies of how edge computing is being implemented in practice show that edge computing is being used in various industries, and how it can improve, optimize, and generate cost savings, in several domains such as industrial IoT, smart infrastructure, and healthcare. New developments in edge computing and AI pose both a prospect and a problem. The combined use of deep learning and reinforcement learning on edge devices is promising and can advance real-time systems to make more complex decisions. As 5G and possibly quantum computing gets closer to becoming a reality edge computing is expected to advance even further with higher speeds, more connected devices and improved computational capabilities. But there is still much to do, such as the scalability of the algorithms and their energy efficiency, and the integration of solutions for different systems. Moreover, the increase in the use of edge computing in the future will create the need to design new models for data protection, security, and device maintenance. Future evolution of edge intelligence across different sectors and domains therefore depends on the next steps. The evolution in edge computing will further enhance the potential of delivering real-time analytics, decision making abilities for smart systems, and enhanced operation control. From smart cities to self-driving cars, from healthcare to industries, edge computing, artificial intelligence and the future technologies are poised to be the next phase of disruption. Future advancements in this area shall be necessary for the full exploitation of edge intelligence and making it as efficient, secure, and capable as required by today's industries.

REFERENCES

Anusha, S., Ezhilvandan, M., Gayathri, S., Sivaraman, V., & TP, A. (2024). Emerging trends in edge AI for Industry 4.0 and 5.0: Technologies, applications, and challenges. *AI Innovations in Service and Tourism Marketing*, 211-228.

Chelliah, P. R., Rahmani, A. M., Colby, R., Nagasubramanian, G., & Ranganath, S. (Eds.). (2024). *Model Optimization Methods for Efficient and Edge AI: Federated Learning Architectures, Frameworks and Applications*. John Wiley & Sons.

Deng, S., Zhao, H., Fang, W., Yin, J., Dustdar, S., & Zomaya, A. Y. (2020). Edge intelligence: The confluence of edge computing and artificial intelligence. *IEEE Internet of Things Journal*, *7*(8), 7457–7469. DOI: 10.1109/JIOT.2020.2984887

Hua, H., Li, Y., Wang, T., Dong, N., Li, W., & Cao, J. (2023). Edge computing with artificial intelligence: A machine learning perspective. *ACM Computing Surveys*, *55*(9), 1–35. DOI: 10.1145/3555802

Lakumarapu, S., Nithyanandhan, R., Bhargavi, V. S., & TP, A. (2024, August). Machine Learning Approaches for Liver Disease Prediction: A Comparative Analysis. In *2024 5th International Conference on Electronics and Sustainable Communication Systems (ICESC)*, IEEE. pp. 159-164

Pandey, R., Khatri, S. K., Singh, N. K., & Verma, P. (Eds.). (2022). *Artificial intelligence and machine learning for EDGE computing*. Academic Press.

Ramanathan, R., Ramamoorthy, S., & Grima, S. (2024). Edge Computing and Artificial Intelligence-Based Internet of Things for Industry 5.0: Framework, Challenges, Use Cases, and Research Directions. *Digital Twins in Industrial Production and Smart Manufacturing: An Understanding of Principles, Enhancers, and Obstacles*, 221-246.

Rancea, A., Anghel, I., & Cioara, T. (2024). Edge computing in healthcare: Innovations, opportunities, and challenges. *Future Internet*, *16*(9), 329. DOI: 10.3390/fi16090329

Ray, P. P., Dash, D., & De, D. (2019). Edge computing for Internet of Things: A survey, e-healthcare case study and future direction. *Journal of Network and Computer Applications*, *140*, 1–22. DOI: 10.1016/j.jnca.2019.05.005

Rupanetti, D., & Kaabouch, N. (2024). Combining Edge Computing-Assisted Internet of Things Security with Artificial Intelligence: Applications, Challenges, and Opportunities. *Applied Sciences (Basel, Switzerland)*, *14*(16), 7104. DOI: 10.3390/app14167104

Sharma, M., Tomar, A., & Hazra, A. (2024). Edge computing for industry 5.0: Fundamental, applications and research challenges. *IEEE Internet of Things Journal, 11*(11), 19070–19093. DOI: 10.1109/JIOT.2024.3359297

Siva, S. R., Bushra, S. N., Maheswari, B., & Prabukumar, M. K. (2022, April). Performance Analysis of Different Machine Learning in Customer Prediction. In *2022 6th International Conference on Trends in Electronics and Informatics (ICOEI)* (pp. 1425-1430). IEEE. DOI: 10.1109/ICOEI53556.2022.9776714

Sreelakshmi, S., Babu, A. A., Lakshmipriya, C., Gracious, L. A., Nalini, M., & Subramanian, R. S. (2024, October). Enhancing Intrusion Detection Systems with Machine Learning. In *2024 2nd International Conference on Self Sustainable Artificial Intelligence Systems (ICSSAS)* (pp. 557-564). IEEE. DOI: 10.1109/ICSSAS64001.2024.10760341

Sun, L., Jiang, X., Ren, H., & Guo, Y. (2020). Edge-cloud computing and artificial intelligence in internet of medical things: Architecture, technology and application. *IEEE Access : Practical Innovations, Open Solutions, 8*, 101079–101092. DOI: 10.1109/ACCESS.2020.2997831

Veeramachaneni, V. (2025). Edge Computing: Architecture, Applications, and Future Challenges in a Decentralized Era. *Recent Trends in Computer Graphics and Multimedia Technology, 7*(1), 8–23.

Verma, P., & Fatima, S. (2020). Smart healthcare applications and real-time analytics through edge computing. *Internet of things use cases for the healthcare industry*, 241-270.

Wang, F., Zhang, M., Wang, X., Ma, X., & Liu, J. (2020). Deep learning for edge computing applications: A state-of-the-art survey. *IEEE Access : Practical Innovations, Open Solutions, 8*, 58322–58336. DOI: 10.1109/ACCESS.2020.2982411

Yamini, B., Sudha, K., Nalini, M., Kavitha, G., Subramanian, R. S., & Sugumar, R. (2023, June). Predictive modelling for lung cancer detection using machine learning techniques. In *2023 8th International Conference on Communication and Electronics Systems (ICCES)* (pp. 1220-1226). IEEE. DOI: 10.1109/ICCES57224.2023.10192648

Chapter 4
AI-Powered Urban Healthcare:
An Efficient Edge Computing Model

Usharani Bhimavarapu
https://orcid.org/0000-0002-0246-1420
Department of Computer Science and Engineering, Koneru Lakshmaiah Education Foundation, Vaddeswaram, India

ABSTRACT

Urban healthcare infrastructure is increasingly relying on edge computing to handle massive amounts of medical data in real time, minimizing latency and enabling timely delivery of healthcare. Cloud-based healthcare solutions are typically plagued by network congestion, computation expense, and privacy issues, and are less ideal for smart hospitals, IoT-based health monitoring, and emergency medical services. For solving the above limitations, this work has proposed a Dual Long Short-Term Memory (LSTM) with Bi-Stacked Gated Recurrent Unit (GRU) for Healthcare Edge Computing of Urban Computing Solutions. The suggested model exploits the feature of LSTM in learning long-range dependencies while GRU exploits its computation cost-saving property in making it appropriately deployable on edge devices such as wearable medical trackers, telemedicine solutions, and smart ambulances.

INTRODUCTION

Urban computing solutions leverage advanced technologies to enhance healthcare provision in city populations. With real-time medical assistance being the most sought, traditional cloud-based systems suffer from the challenge of latency, the

DOI: 10.4018/979-8-3373-1147-0.ch004

need for bandwidth, and cyber threats. Edge computing breaks such bottlenecks by performing calculations near the data production point, hence requiring less time to make life-saving decisions. By having computing power at the network edge, healthcare becomes more timely and efficient. This ensures that medical records can be accessed easily, monitored real-time, and analyzed in order to predict. It also becomes less dependent on central cloud-based infrastructures, and hence, fault-tolerant systems result. Urban areas, due to data population and traffic densities, would greatly benefit from such an edge computing. Edge computing reinforces telemedicine, remote diagnostic networks, and emergency response networks. In a continuing drive for digitization of the healthcare sector, the need for edge computing in urban areas becomes ever more urgent. Data transfer latency minimization is among the most significant requirements in edge computing in urban health. Milliseconds may be what makes a difference in patient outcomes during emergency cases, and real-time decision-making is the call.

Telemedicine and remote delivery of healthcare is another important advantage of edge computing as it facilitates virtual consultation and remote patient management. The COVID-19 crisis highlighted the use of virtual consultation and remote monitoring of patients. But most cloud-based telemedicine platforms are subject to latency, which affects video quality and sharing real-time data. Edge computing overcomes these challenges by processing the patient data locally, allowing seamless and unbroken virtual communication. This enables doctors to provide immediate diagnosis and treatment recommendations, improving patient engagement. Further, edge-based AI chatbots can help triage patients, taking pressure off healthcare providers.

The systems require real-time processing of data so that they move appropriately and respond accordingly. Edge computing minimizes latency in surgical robotics to enable improved accuracy and safety during operations. Second, edge devices with AI assist in automating the everyday diagnostic procedures such as medical imaging diagnostics. Radiology departments are assisted by on-device AI algorithms to examine X-rays and MRIs in real time, taking the workload off radiologists. Edge-based decision support systems in emergency departments enable physicians to diagnose potentially life-threatening conditions like strokes more rapidly. All these advancements improve patient outcomes since they provide timely feedback from real-time medical information. The application of AI, IoT, and edge computing enables health delivery to be speedy and efficient.

Edge computing also comes in handy for urban search and rescue and emergency medical services (EMS). Communication infrastructures are stretched during cases of natural disaster or mass casualty crash. Edge-powered emergency response systems will be able to function autonomously with critical medical information made available. Artificially intelligent edge devices on ambulances provide patient vital signs in real time to hospitals while in transit, increasing preparedness. Wearable health sensors that leverage edge computing can monitor first responders' health and prevent exhaustion-related risks. Edge analytics-capable drones have the ability to assess disaster terrain in order to guide doctors to where they are needed the most. Edge-enabled triage systems have the ability to sort patients based on current health status for better medical resource management. These functions maximize emergency healthcare efficiency in populous cities. Increased speed of response and coordinated responses result in saving lives during emergencies. Edge computing is thus central to urban disaster relief as well as medical readiness.

All in all, edge computing is a savior of urban health, addressing most of the fundamental issues in latency, security, efficiency, and accessibility. By enabling real-time processing close to the patient, it greatly improves emergency response, personalized medicine, and hospital operations. The synergy between AI, IoT, and edge computing enhances telemedicine, robotic surgery, and public health monitoring. It also enhances cybersecurity by reduced reliance on centralized cloud infrastructure, maintaining data confidentiality as well as regulatory compliance. High-density patient urban clusters and high-speed environments are significantly influenced by these technologies. Healthcare systems ought to adopt edge computing with next-generation technology in order to keep up with future challenges. Governments, health centers, and technology innovators have to join hands in order to come up with healthy edge-enabled infrastructures. Future advancements in 5G and AI will further cement edge computing capability in healthcare. Eventually, these solutions will make wiser, more responsive urban healthcare ecosystems. The future of digital health is at the forefront, driving healthcare closer to those who need it most.

Edge computing breaks such bottlenecks by performing calculations near the data production point, hence requiring less time to make life-saving decisions. By having computing power at the network edge, healthcare becomes more timely and efficient. This ensures that medical records can be accessed easily, monitored real-time, and analyzed in order to predict. It also becomes less dependent on central cloud-based infrastructures, and hence, fault-tolerant systems result. Urban areas, due to data population and traffic densities, would greatly benefit from such an edge computing. Edge computing reinforces telemedicine, remote diagnostic networks, and emergency response networks. In a continuing drive for digitization of the healthcare sector, the need for edge computing in urban areas becomes ever more urgent. Data transfer latency minimization is among the most significant requirements in edge computing in urban health. Milliseconds may be what makes a difference in patient outcomes during emergency cases, and real-time decision-making is the call.

Telemedicine and remote delivery of healthcare is another important advantage of edge computing as it facilitates virtual consultation and remote patient management. The COVID-19 crisis highlighted the use of virtual consultation and remote monitoring of patients. But most cloud-based telemedicine platforms are subject to latency, which affects video quality and sharing real-time data. Edge computing overcomes these challenges by processing the patient data locally, allowing seamless and unbroken virtual communication. This enables doctors to provide immediate diagnosis and treatment recommendations, improving patient engagement. Further, edge-based AI chatbots can help triage patients, taking pressure off healthcare providers.

The systems require real-time processing of data so that they move appropriately and respond accordingly. Edge computing minimizes latency in surgical robotics to enable improved accuracy and safety during operations. Second, edge devices with AI assist in automating the everyday diagnostic procedures such as medical imaging diagnostics. Radiology departments are assisted by on-device AI algorithms to examine X-rays and MRIs in real time, taking the workload off radiologists. Edge-based decision support systems in emergency departments enable physicians to diagnose potentially life-threatening conditions like strokes more rapidly. All these advancements improve patient outcomes since they provide timely feedback from real-time medical information. The application of AI, IoT, and edge computing enables health delivery to be speedy and efficient.

Edge computing also comes in handy for urban search and rescue and emergency medical services (EMS). Communication infrastructures are stretched during cases of natural disaster or mass casualty crash. Edge-powered emergency response systems will be able to function autonomously with critical medical information made available. Artificially intelligent edge devices on ambulances provide patient vital signs in real time to hospitals while in transit, increasing preparedness. Wearable health sensors that leverage edge computing can monitor first responders' health and prevent exhaustion-related risks. Edge analytics-capable drones have the ability to assess disaster terrain in order to guide doctors to where they are needed the most. Edge-enabled triage systems have the ability to sort patients based on current health status for better medical resource management. These functions maximize emergency healthcare efficiency in populous cities. Increased speed of response and coordinated responses result in saving lives during emergencies. Edge computing is thus central to urban disaster relief as well as medical readiness.

All in all, edge computing is a savior of urban health, addressing most of the fundamental issues in latency, security, efficiency, and accessibility. By enabling real-time processing close to the patient, it greatly improves emergency response, personalized medicine, and hospital operations. The synergy between AI, IoT, and edge computing enhances telemedicine, robotic surgery, and public health monitoring. It also enhances cybersecurity by reduced reliance on centralized cloud infrastructure, maintaining data confidentiality as well as regulatory compliance. High-density patient urban clusters and high-speed environments are significantly influenced by these technologies. Healthcare systems ought to adopt edge computing with next-generation technology in order to keep up with future challenges. Governments, health centers, and technology innovators have to join hands in order to come up with healthy edge-enabled infrastructures. Future advancements in 5G and AI will further cement edge computing capability in healthcare. Eventually, these solutions will make wiser, more responsive urban healthcare ecosystems. The future of digital health is at the forefront, driving healthcare closer to those who need it most.

Edge computing breaks such bottlenecks by performing calculations near the data production point, hence requiring less time to make life-saving decisions. By having computing power at the network edge, healthcare becomes more timely and efficient. This ensures that medical records can be accessed easily, monitored real-time, and analyzed in order to predict. It also becomes less dependent on central cloud-based infrastructures, and hence, fault-tolerant systems result. Urban areas, due to data population and traffic densities, would greatly benefit from such an edge computing. Edge computing reinforces telemedicine, remote diagnostic networks, and emergency response networks. In a continuing drive for digitization of the health-care sector, the need for edge computing in urban areas becomes ever more urgent. Data transfer latency minimization is among the most significant requirements in edge computing in urban health. Milliseconds may be what makes a difference in patient outcomes during emergency cases, and real-time decision-making is the call.

Telemedicine and remote delivery of healthcare is another important advantage of edge computing as it facilitates virtual consultation and remote patient management. The COVID-19 crisis highlighted the use of virtual consultation and remote monitoring of patients. But most cloud-based telemedicine platforms are subject to latency, which affects video quality and sharing real-time data. Edge computing overcomes these challenges by processing the patient data locally, allowing seamless and unbroken virtual communication. This enables doctors to provide immediate diagnosis and treatment recommendations, improving patient engagement. Further, edge-based AI chatbots can help triage patients, taking pressure off healthcare providers.

The systems require real-time processing of data so that they move appropriately and respond accordingly. Edge computing minimizes latency in surgical robotics to enable improved accuracy and safety during operations. Second, edge devices with AI assist in automating the everyday diagnostic procedures such as medical imaging diagnostics. Radiology departments are assisted by on-device AI algorithms to examine X-rays and MRIs in real time, taking the workload off radiologists. Edge-based decision support systems in emergency departments enable physicians to diagnose potentially life-threatening conditions like strokes more rapidly. All these advancements improve patient outcomes since they provide timely feedback from real-time medical information. The application of AI, IoT, and edge computing enables health delivery to be speedy and efficient.

Edge computing also comes in handy for urban search and rescue and emergency medical services (EMS). Communication infrastructures are stretched during cases of natural disaster or mass casualty crash. Edge-powered emergency response systems will be able to function autonomously with critical medical information made available. Artificially intelligent edge devices on ambulances provide patient vital signs in real time to hospitals while in transit, increasing preparedness. Wearable health sensors that leverage edge computing can monitor first responders' health and prevent exhaustion-related risks. Edge analytics-capable drones have the ability to assess disaster terrain in order to guide doctors to where they are needed the most. Edge-enabled triage systems have the ability to sort patients based on current health status for better medical resource management. These functions maximize emergency healthcare efficiency in populous cities. Increased speed of response and coordinated responses result in saving lives during emergencies. Edge computing is thus central to urban disaster relief as well as medical readiness.

All in all, edge computing is a savior of urban health, addressing most of the fundamental issues in latency, security, efficiency, and accessibility. By enabling real-time processing close to the patient, it greatly improves emergency response, personalized medicine, and hospital operations. The synergy between AI, IoT, and edge computing enhances telemedicine, robotic surgery, and public health monitoring. It also enhances cybersecurity by reduced reliance on centralized cloud infrastructure, maintaining data confidentiality as well as regulatory compliance. High-density patient urban clusters and high-speed environments are significantly influenced by these technologies. Healthcare systems ought to adopt edge computing with next-generation technology in order to keep up with future challenges. Governments, health centers, and technology innovators have to join hands in order to come up with healthy edge-enabled infrastructures. Future advancements in 5G and AI will further cement edge computing capability in healthcare. Eventually, these solutions will make wiser, more responsive urban healthcare ecosystems. The future of digital health is at the forefront, driving healthcare closer to those who need it most.

Boo and Oh (2023) identified the views of registered nurses regarding the facilitators and hindrances to the adoption of an AI-IoT-based healthcare project among older persons. The study was, however, constrained by the sample size and geographical scope within South Korea, which might not be representative of world views. It was also based on self-reported information, which might carry social desirability or recall bias.

Alowais et al. (2023) wrote about using artificial intelligence in medical practice. Their limitation is that they do not address the technical details of using AI at an incredibly detailed level, i.e., data privacy issues, algorithmic bias, or if AI tools are available in low-resource environments.

Cingolani et al. (2023) studied the application of AI and digital medicine in Italian home care integrated services. The research provided useful findings, though with the limitation of the provided geographical setting and the unavailability of longitudinal data to measure effects in the long term. Again, the research does not provide information on scalability of such technologies in various healthcare systems.

World Health Organization (2024)provided a broad perspective on aging and health with a broad global outlook. Sawik et al. (2023) carried out a survey of robots for elderly care, developing a multi-criteria optimization model and qualitative case study. A drawback of their study is the use of a theoretically informed model with strong empirical support across various real-world situations. The study also does not include a thorough evaluation of the possible social and emotional consequences of robots in eldercare.

Padhan et al. (2023) analyzed AI and robotics from the perspective of elderly care. As profound as the study is, its central flaw is its failure to give proper attention to alleviating the ethical issues, including implications of decisions made by AI in caregiving environments and exacerbation of social injustice against the elderly.

Goeldner et al. (2015) compared patents and publications on care robotics. Although the study gives historical data on the evolution of care robotics, it is constrained by the fact that it mainly relies on patent numbers, which can be inconclusive in its indication of the actual technological progress or utilitarian application of robots in geriatric care.

Brose et al. (2010) reviewed the use of assistive robotics in the lives of individuals with disabilities. The limitation in their study is that the sample group was too small and the review was on a limited group (disability individuals) and their findings cannot be generalized to every user of assistive technology.

Mišeikis et al. (2020) introduced Lio, which is a human-robot interaction and care personal robot assistant. The study is limited as it only dealt with a single robotic system without putting it against other technologies that could have given an overview of the different alternatives to pursue in the case of elder care.

Melkas et al. (2020) studied the effects of robot deployment in old-age homes. The limitation of the study is the short-term nature and failure to account for the long-term psychological and social effect of care by robots on old-age residents.

Carros et al. (2020) carried out a ten-week case study of robotic care of older adults and human-robot interaction. A limitation of this study is that it was carried out in a short time span and therefore does not indicate whether the effects of robotic care last long term. The sample group was limited, and in one care facility, which could reduce the generalizability of the results.

Mello et al. (2023) outlined cloud robotics for real-world application. The limitation of this work is that it only discusses the technical application of cloud robotics, without any mention of user acceptance or integration issues of healthcare professionals in adopting the same.

Ashok and Gopikrishnan (2023) analyzed IoT security architectures and IoT implementations of remote health monitoring. The limitation of this study is that it only analyzed security aspects without a broad investigation of the efficiency and usability of IoT solutions in actual health care settings.

Le et al. (2020) gave a snapshot of physical layer design for ultra-reliable low-latency communications. A weakness of the study is that it does not take into consideration realistic deployment challenges of such technologies in the healthcare setting, particularly in resource-poor areas.

Teleoperation of collaborative robots in remote dementia care was introduced by Lv et al. (2020). The limitation of this research is that it considers only a single use case, which could be far from diverse and varying needs of aged patients with different health conditions and caregiving needs.

Papadopoulos et al. (2022) tested the effect of culturally empathetic AI integrated in robots for the care of older adults. One drawback of the study is the use of a single trial, which could miss heterogeneity of cultural variance and adoption of technology across various care environments.

Johansson-Pajala and Gustafsson (2022) published on introducing care robots into Swedish elder care and how it was challenging. One flaw with this study is that the research is conducted on Swedish care environments, so results do not directly apply to nations with different health care systems or else dissimilar cultural systems.

Cifuentes et al. (2020) gave a summary of the application of social robots in therapy and care. The weakness of the research is based on a shortage of adequate real-world evidence concerning the therapeutic value of social robots, specifically on the psychological and emotional influence on older people.

Zhang and Su (2024) proposed an IoMT framework based on 5G and wireless body area networks for home care. The limitation of this framework is that it is largely technologically focused and does not provide detailed analysis of user adoption barriers as well as integration challenges into current healthcare infrastructures.

Ghosh and Ghosh (2023) proposed a federated learning framework for elderly care through edge-IoMT. Nevertheless, limitations of the study are that empirical verification in real-world large-scale settings is absent and data privacy issues may arise in federated learning systems.

Jazaeri et al. (2023) explained edge computing caching and classification in healthcare IoT solutions. This research has the limitation of discussing mainly the technical and not the practical implementation of such solutions in real-world health care environments.

Ahmed and Salah (2023) suggested an SDN-based IoT security model for medical conditions. The constraint of the research is that it only encompasses security protocols and not how their performance and effectiveness are measured in actual healthcare application, particularly under different network scenarios.

Alnaim and Alwakeel (2023) carried out research in machine-learning IoT-edge computing-based healthcare solutions. The limitation of the study is that it focuses narrowly on machine-learning methods without addressing issues of real-time processing and the importance of strong data infrastructure in healthcare facilities.

Hoeiland-Joergensen et al. (2018) recommended the Flow Queue Codel Packet Scheduler as an active queue management. The drawback of this RFC is that it only solves the technical packet scheduling problem and does not consider the overall impact on healthcare IoT systems or user experiences.

Holland et al. (2019) had set out IEEE 1918.1 standards for the tactile internet. One limitation of the research is that it fails to reflect the practical effect of implementing these standards in real-world healthcare settings or how they would integrate into existing health care technologies.

The algorithm built is free from flaws in existing models by solving some of the most critical problems regarding scalability, accuracy, and real-time processing in advanced healthcare settings. Unlike classical models, which are usually ineffective in terms of big data integration and computation requirements, the new algorithm has an advantage in terms of better optimization techniques that were designed to reduce the computational cost without affecting accuracy. This renders it effective in real-time applications, which is a requirement for such applications as telemedicine monitoring and care for the elderly. Additionally, the alignment of the algorithm with edge computing and IoT technology makes communication between devices easy, data processing becoming seamless, with minimal latency and enhanced responsiveness. Additionally, through incorporating machine learning models pre-trained on high-quality rich datasets, the solution improves the accuracy of classification, particularly in finding patterns previously difficult to identify due to noise or missing information. These solutions address the drawback of existing systems, which were typically undermined by poor data processing, inefficiencies in managing various medical conditions, and non-timeliness of outcomes. The recommended algorithm thus offers a more robust and scalable solution for health care applications, guaranteeing enhanced outcomes in aged care and other important health monitoring systems.

DUAL LONG SHORT-TERM MEMORY (LSTM) WITH BISTACKED GRU MODELS

A Bi-Stacked Gated Recurrent Unit (GRU) Integrated Dual Long Short-Term Memory (LSTM) is a deep model employed for facilitating enhancement of time-series analysis and forecasting modeling in Healthcare Edge Computing for Urban Computing Solutions. The combined architecture is utilizing the strength of LSTM and GRU networks for the processing of real-time medical data in the edge space.

Urban healthcare infrastructure requires real-time, high-speed, and accurate processing of huge medical information like patient vital signs, ECG signals, and wearable sensor information.

With growing urban populations and increasing medical requirements, the proposed Dual LSTM-BiStacked GRU algorithm is an effective and scalable AI-based technique that revolutionizes processing and usage of medical data in smart healthcare systems.

ALGORITHM

The model follows a structured flow:

1. **Input Layer:** Accepts time-series medical data (e.g., ECG, glucose levels, blood pressure).
2. **Dual LSTM Encoder:**
    - o Two parallel LSTM networks extract deep temporal patterns.
    - o One focuses on short-term trends, while the other captures long-term dependencies.
3. **Bi-Stacked GRU Decoder:**
    - o Stacked bidirectional GRU layers process encoded features for improved sequence learning.
    - o GRUs replace some LSTMs to reduce complexity.
4. **Fully Connected Layer:** Maps extracted features to prediction outputs.
5. **Softmax/Sigmoid Activation:** Produces final classification or regression results (e.g., anomaly detection, health risk prediction).

LSTM Computation

Each LSTM unit updates memory using:

$$f_t = \sigma\left(W_f[h_{t-1}, x_t] + b_f\right)$$

$$i_t = \sigma(W_i[h_{t-1}, x_t] + b_i)$$

$$\widetilde{C}_t = \tanh(W_C[h_{t-1}, x_t] + b_C)$$

$$C_t = f_t \odot C_{t-1} + i_t \odot$$

$$o_t = \sigma(W_o[h_{t-1}, x_t] + b_o)$$

$$h_t = o_t \odot \tanh(C_t)$$

where:

- f_t, i_t, o_t are forget, input, and output gates.
- C_t is the cell state.
- h_t is the hidden state.

GRU Computation

Each GRU unit updates hidden states as follows:

$$z_t = \sigma(W_z[h_{t-1}, x_t] + b_z)$$

$$r_t = \sigma(W_r[h_{t-1}, x_t] + b_r)$$

$$\widetilde{h}_t = \tanh(W_h[r_t \odot h_{t-1}, x_t] + b_h)$$

$$h_t = (1 - z_t) \odot h_{t-1} + z_t \odot \widetilde{h}_t$$

where:

- z_t, r_t are update and reset gates.
- h_t is the hidden state.

Theorem 1: Convergence of the Dual LSTM and Bi-Stacked GRU Model in Healthcare Edge Computing

The proposed Dual LSTM integrated with Bi-Stacked GRU model converges to an optimal solution for healthcare data prediction in Urban Edge Computing environments, ensuring minimal prediction error while maintaining computational efficiency.

Proof

Let y_t be the predicted output at time step t, where t=1,2,…,Trepresenting a sequence of healthcare data such as vital signs or sensor readings. The goal is to minimize the error between the predicted output and the actual healthcare data, denoted by y_t^*, using the Dual LSTM-BiGRU model.

The general form of the error at each time step ttt is given by:

$$E_t = |y_t^* - y_t|^2$$

Where ||·|| represents the Euclidean norm. The total error over the sequence is:

$$E = \sum_{t=1}^{T} E_t = \sum_{t=1}^{T} |y_t^* - y_t|^2$$

The objective is to minimize the total error E. The learning process involves backpropagation through time (BPTT) for both LSTM and GRU units. We assume that the loss function L is differentiable and has a global minimum. The update rule for the parameters θ (which includes weights and biases of both LSTM and GRU) is given by gradient descent:

$$\theta_{t+1} = \theta_t - \eta \nabla_\theta L$$

Where η is the learning rate, and ∇_θ L is the gradient of the loss function with respect to the parameters.

The LSTM model is designed to capture long-term dependencies, which means it has a memory of past states. The convergence of the LSTM depends on the optimization of the error propagation through the network's gates. The hidden state h_t is updated using:

$$h_t = f(W_x x_t + W_h h_{t-1} + b)$$

Where f is a non-linear activation function (like tanh or sigmoid), W_x and W_h are the weight matrices for input x_t and previous hidden state h_{t-1}.

To ensure convergence, the gradients must be bounded. The vanishing gradient problem is mitigated by the LSTM gates, which control the flow of information. The gate mechanism effectively filters out unimportant updates and allows only relevant information to propagate, ensuring that the gradients do not diminish to zero over time.

The GRU model is computationally more efficient and works by updating the hidden state using a reset and update gate mechanism. The reset gate r_t and update gate z_t control the flow of information through the network, defined as:

$$r_t = \sigma(W_r x_t + U_r h_{t-1} + b_r)$$

$$z_t = \sigma(W_z x_t + U_z h_{t-1} + b_z)$$

Where σ is the sigmoid activation function, and W_r, W_z, U_r, U_z are the weight matrices for the gates. The final hidden state h_t is updated using the following equation:

$$h_t = (1 - z_t) \odot h_{t-1} + z_t \odot \widetilde{h}_t$$

Where $\widetilde{h}_t$ is the candidate hidden state, calculated as:

$$\widetilde{h}_t = \tanh(W_h x_t + U_h(r_t \odot h_{t-1}) + b_h)$$

The GRU update mechanism ensures that the model can learn dependencies over time efficiently. The reset gate allows the model to forget irrelevant information, while the update gate selectively updates the hidden state. This structure leads to faster convergence compared to traditional LSTMs.

When combining LSTM and GRU in a dual configuration, the system benefits from both models: LSTM captures long-term dependencies, while GRU handles short-term dynamics and reduces computational load. The optimization process, therefore, involves minimizing the total error EEE, and since both LSTM and GRU converge individually, their combination results in an overall convergent system.

The convergence of the combined model can be expressed as:

$$\lim_{t\to\infty} |y_t^* - y_t|^2 = 0$$

This implies that, under appropriate conditions, the Dual LSTM-BiGRU model will converge to a solution where the prediction error becomes arbitrarily small, leading to an optimal model for healthcare data prediction.

Thus, the proposed model achieves convergence, guaranteeing that as the training process continues, the predictions will become more accurate, making it an effective solution for Urban Healthcare Edge Computing.

Theorem 2: Stability of the Dual LSTM and Bi-Stacked GRU Model in Healthcare Edge Computing

The Dual LSTM and Bi-Stacked GRU model is stable in the context of healthcare edge computing, meaning that the model's outputs do not diverge over time and that training is bounded.

Proof

The stability of the model can be examined by ensuring that the outputs of the LSTM and GRU units remain within a bounded range during training and after convergence.

Let the state at time step t be denoted by h_t, and the output of the model at time step t is y_t. For LSTM, the hidden state h_t is updated according to the following equation:

$$h_t = f\left(W_x x_t + W_h h_{t-1} + b\right)$$

The key to stability is ensuring that the hidden states h_t do not grow unbounded as the model trains. The update function is a bounded non-linear function f, such as tanh or σ, which ensures that each h_t remains within a bounded range. This avoids exploding gradients and ensures that the model remains stable.

For GRU, the update equation is:

$$h_t = \left(1 - z_t\right) \odot h_{t-1} + z_t \odot \widetilde{h}_t$$

where z_t is the update gate and $\widetilde{h}_t$ is the candidate hidden state. Since both z_t and $\widetilde{h}_t$ are constrained by the sigmoid and hyperbolic tangent functions, respectively, the update ensures that the values of h_t will not exceed reasonable bounds, maintaining stability in the network.

The stability of the model is assured by the boundedness of the activation functions and the gradient clipping used during backpropagation to prevent the gradients from growing uncontrollably.

Hence, the model is stable under typical training conditions and will not diverge over time, proving the theorem.

Theorem 3: Efficiency of the Dual LSTM and Bi-Stacked GRU Model for Healthcare Edge Computing

The Dual LSTM integrated with Bi-Stacked GRU model is computationally efficient for real-time healthcare data processing on edge devices.

Proof

The computational efficiency of the model can be measured by evaluating its time complexity and resource usage compared to traditional LSTM models. For a typical LSTM cell, the time complexity is O(4n) for each time step, where n is the number of units in the hidden state. This comes from the four operations: forget gate, input gate, output gate, and candidate cell state.

For the GRU model, the time complexity is O(3n), since the GRU only has reset, update, and candidate states compared to LSTM's four gates.

Now consider the dual architecture of LSTM and Bi-Stacked GRU. Since the GRU component processes the short-term dependencies, it reduces the need for long-term state maintenance by the LSTM. This means fewer operations are needed for short-term forecasting, effectively reducing the overall computational load.

Let T_L and T_G be the time complexities for the LSTM and GRU layers, respectively. In the dual model, the time complexity of the entire system can be expressed as:

$$T_{dual} = T_L + T_G = O(4n) + O(3n) = O(7n)$$

Since GRU is computationally lighter than LSTM, the combined model balances the high accuracy of LSTM with the speed of GRU, achieving significant efficiency gains while maintaining acceptable performance.

Thus, the model is computationally efficient for edge devices in urban healthcare settings, where low latency and resource constraints are critical.

Theorem 4: Prediction Accuracy of the Dual LSTM and Bi-Stacked GRU Model in Healthcare

The Dual LSTM and Bi-Stacked GRU model provides high prediction accuracy for healthcare data, outperforming traditional models in terms of error minimization.

Proof

Let y_t^* represent the true healthcare data at time step t and *yt* represent the predicted output from the Dual LSTM and Bi-Stacked GRU model. The error at time t is defined as:

$$E_t = |y_t^* - y_t|^2$$

To measure the model's accuracy, we minimize the mean squared error (MSE) over all time steps:

$$MSE = \frac{1}{T}\sum_{t=1}^{T}|y_t^* - y_t|^2$$

During training, the gradient descent algorithm is used to minimize the loss function L:

$$L = \frac{1}{T}\sum_{t=1}^{T}|y_t^* - y_t|^2$$

Both LSTM and GRU work together to improve prediction accuracy. LSTM captures long-term dependencies in the data, while GRU efficiently handles short-term variations. The model's architecture ensures that it maintains a lower error rate compared to traditional models, such as a standalone LSTM or GRU network.

The error minimization process for the dual model ensures that the predictions closely match the actual healthcare data, improving its predictive accuracy. Therefore, we can conclude that the proposed dual model provides higher accuracy in forecasting healthcare data than traditional models, proving the theorem.

Theorem 5: Robustness to Noisy Data in the Dual LSTM and Bi-Stacked GRU Model

The Dual LSTM integrated with Bi-Stacked GRU model is robust to noisy and incomplete healthcare data, ensuring reliable predictions even under suboptimal conditions.

Proof

Let the healthcare data be subject to noise ϵ_t such that the observed data y_t^* becomes:

$$y_t^* = y_t + \epsilon_t$$

where ϵ_t represents the noise at time t. The goal is to predict y_t as accurately as possible, even when the data is noisy.

In LSTM, the memory cell c_t is updated by:

$$c_t = f_{\text{input}}(x_t, h_{t-1}) \odot c_{t-1} + f_{\text{forget}}(x_t, h_{t-1}) \odot c_{t-1}$$

and for GRU:

$$h_t = (1 - z_t) \odot h_{t-1} + z_t \odot \tilde{h}_t$$

Since both LSTM and GRU utilize gating mechanisms, they are inherently robust to noise. The gates allow the model to filter out irrelevant information (e.g., noise ϵ_t) while retaining important signals. The forget gate in LSTM and update/reset gates in GRU focus on selectively propagating the relevant signal.

Moreover, by training the model with regularization techniques such as dropout and L2 regularization, the model becomes even more resistant to overfitting caused by noisy data. This results in the model's robustness against noisy inputs.

Thus, the Dual LSTM-BiGRU model demonstrates robustness and can maintain prediction reliability even with noisy or missing healthcare data.

Theorem 6: Real-Time Performance of the Dual LSTM and Bi-Stacked GRU Model for Urban Healthcare Applications

The Dual LSTM and Bi-Stacked GRU model achieves real-time performance for healthcare applications in urban edge computing environments, where low latency is critical.

Proof

The real-time performance is measured by the inference time per prediction and latency. Let $T_{\text{inference}}$ represent the time required for the model to make a prediction after receiving new input data.

For the LSTM component, the time complexity of a forward pass is O(n), where n is the number of units in the hidden state. For GRU, the time complexity for each update is O(n) as well. Since the dual model consists of both LSTM and GRU components, the total time complexity for one prediction step is:

$$T_{\text{total}} = T_{\text{LSTM}} + T_{\text{GRU}} = O(n) + O(n) = O(2n)$$

Edge devices used for urban healthcare applications typically have limited processing power. However, because the GRU component is more efficient than LSTM, the overall time complexity is reduced compared to traditional LSTM-based models. The dual model ensures that the inference time per prediction remains low.

The latency for real-time performance is also dependent on the hardware and optimization strategies. With parallel processing, hardware acceleration (e.g., GPUs, TPUs), and quantization techniques, the model achieves real-time processing in healthcare edge computing systems.

Thus, the proposed model meets the real-time requirements for urban healthcare applications, enabling low-latency predictions in environments where speed is essential.

CONCLUSION

The Dual LSTM and Bi-Stacked GRU model proposes a novel and efficient method for real-time processing of medical information in urban healthcare edge computing situations. By fusing the benefit of LSTM and GRU, the model provides high precision, low latency, and energy efficiency, and can be used in hospital applications, wearable health monitoring, and AI-based telemedicine services. Online processing of sequential health data has the potential to significantly improve disease prediction, emergency response, and individualized healthcare services, which are among the core challenges in modern city healthcare systems. Moreover, the resistance of the model to noisy and missing medical information ensures robustness in numerous healthcare environments. As smart healthcare spaces go more global, the synergy between edge computing and artificial intelligence-based predictive analytics will become even more critical in augmenting patient outcomes and clinical decision-making. Further research can explore federated learning methods, edge-cloud hybrid fusion, and AI-based treatment suggestion to further advance urban healthcare computing.

REFERENCES

Ahmed, A. S., & Salah, H. A. (2023). Development a software defined network (SDN) with Internet of Things (IoT) security for medical issues. *Journal of Al-Qadisiyah for Computer Science and Mathematics*, *15*(4), 98. DOI: 10.29304/jqcm.2023.15.3.1268

Alnaim, A. K., & Alwakeel, A. M. (2023). Machine-learning-based IoT–edge computing healthcare solutions. *Electronics (Basel)*, *12*(5), 1027. DOI: 10.3390/electronics12041027

Alowais, S. A., Alghamdi, S. S., Alsuhebany, N., Alqahtani, T., Alshaya, A. I., Almohareb, S. N., Aldairem, A., Alrashed, M., Bin Saleh, K., Badreldin, H. A., Al Yami, M. S., Al Harbi, S., & Albekairy, A. M. (2023). Revolutionizing healthcare: The role of artificial intelligence in clinical practice. *BMC Medical Education*, *23*(1), 689. DOI: 10.1186/s12909-023-04698-z PMID: 37740191

Ashok, K., & Gopikrishnan, S. (2023). Statistical analysis of remote health monitoring based IoT security models & deployments from a pragmatic perspective. *IEEE Access : Practical Innovations, Open Solutions*, *11*, 2621–2651. DOI: 10.1109/ACCESS.2023.3234632

Boo, S., & Oh, H. (2023). Perceptions of registered nurses on facilitators and barriers of implementing the AI-IoT-based healthcare pilot project for older adults during the COVID-19 pandemic in South Korea. *Frontiers in Public Health*, *11*, 1234626. DOI: 10.3389/fpubh.2023.1234626 PMID: 37886046

Brose, S. W., Weber, D. J., Salatin, B. A., Grindle, G. G., Wang, H., Vazquez, J. J., & Cooper, R. A. (2010). The role of assistive robotics in the lives of persons with disability. *American Journal of Physical Medicine & Rehabilitation*, *89*(6), 509–521. DOI: 10.1097/PHM.0b013e3181cf569b PMID: 20134305

Carros, F., Meurer, J., Löffler, D., Unbehaun, D., Matthies, S., Koch, I., Wieching, R., Randall, D., Hassenzahl, M., & Wulf, V. (2020). Exploring human-robot interaction with the elderly: Results from a ten-week case study in a care home. In *Proceedings of the 2020 CHI Conference on Human Factors in Computing Systems* (pp. 1–12). Association for Computing Machinery. DOI: 10.1145/3313831.3376402

Cifuentes, C. A., Pinto, M. J., Céspedes, N., & Múnera, M. (2020). Social robots in therapy and care. *Current Robotics Reports*, *1*(3), 59–74. DOI: 10.1007/s43154-020-00009-2

Cingolani, M., Scendoni, R., Fedeli, P., & Cembrani, F. (2023). Artificial intelligence and digital medicine for integrated home care services in Italy: Opportunities and limits. *Frontiers in Public Health, 10*, 1095001. DOI: 10.3389/fpubh.2022.1095001 PMID: 36684935

Ghosh, S., & Ghosh, S. K. (2023). Feel: Federated learning framework for elderly healthcare using edge-IoMT. *IEEE Transactions on Computational Social Systems, 10*(4), 1800–1809. DOI: 10.1109/TCSS.2022.3233300

Goeldner, M., Herstatt, C., & Tietze, F. (2015). The emergence of care robotics—A patent and publication analysis. *Technological Forecasting and Social Change, 92*, 115–131. DOI: 10.1016/j.techfore.2014.09.005

Hoeiland-Joergensen, T., McKenney, P., Taht, D., Gettys, J., & Dumazet, E. (2018). *The Flow Queue CoDel packet scheduler and active queue management algorithm (RFC 8290)*. Internet Engineering Task Force., DOI: 10.17487/RFC8290

Holland, O., Steinbach, E., Prasad, R. V., Liu, Q., Dawy, Z., Aijaz, A., Pappas, N., Chandra, K., Rao, V. S., Oteafy, S., Eid, M., Luden, M., Bhardwaj, A., Liu, X., Sachs, J., & Araujo, J. (2019). The IEEE 1918.1 "Tactile Internet" standards working group and its standards. *Proceedings of the IEEE, 107*(2), 256–279. DOI: 10.1109/JPROC.2018.2885541

Jazaeri, S. S., Asghari, P., Jabbehdari, S., & Javadi, H. H. S. (2023). Composition of caching and classification in edge computing based on quality optimization for SDN-based IoT healthcare solutions. *The Journal of Supercomputing, 79*(14), 17619–17669. DOI: 10.1007/s11227-023-05332-x PMID: 37359340

Johansson-Pajala, R. M., & Gustafsson, C. (2022). Significant challenges when introducing care robots in Swedish elder care. *Disability and Rehabilitation. Assistive Technology, 17*(2), 166–176. DOI: 10.1080/17483107.2020.1773549 PMID: 32538206

Le, T. K., Salim, U., & Kaltenberger, F. (2020). An overview of physical layer design for ultra-reliable low-latency communications in 3GPP releases 15, 16, and 17. *IEEE Access : Practical Innovations, Open Solutions, 9*, 433–444. DOI: 10.1109/ACCESS.2020.3046773

Lv, H., Yang, G., Zhou, H., Huang, X., Yang, H., & Pang, Z. (2020). Teleoperation of collaborative robot for remote dementia care in home environments. *IEEE Journal of Translational Engineering in Health and Medicine, 8*, 1–10. DOI: 10.1109/JTEHM.2019.2952610 PMID: 32617197

Melkas, H., Hennala, L., Pekkarinen, S., & Kyrki, V. (2020). Impacts of robot implementation on care personnel and clients in elderly-care institutions. *International Journal of Medical Informatics, 134*, 104041. DOI: 10.1016/j.ijmedinf.2019.104041 PMID: 31838291

Mello, R. C., Ribeiro, M. R., & Frizera-Neto, A. (2023). Implementing cloud robotics for practical applications. *Springer Tracts in Advanced Robotics, 10*, 1–24. DOI: 10.1007/978-3-031-06676-4_1

Mišeikis, J., Caroni, P., Duchamp, P., Gasser, A., Marko, R., Mišeikienė, N., Zwilling, F., de Castelbajac, C., Eicher, L., Früh, M., & Fruh, H. (2020). Lio—A personal robot assistant for human-robot interaction and care applications. *IEEE Robotics and Automation Letters, 5*(4), 5339–5346. DOI: 10.1109/LRA.2020.3007462 PMID: 34192136

Padhan, S., Mohapatra, A., Ramasamy, S. K., & Agrawal, S. (2023). Artificial intelligence (AI) and robotics in elderly healthcare: Enabling independence and quality of life. *Cureus, 15*(8), e42905. DOI: 10.7759/cureus.42905 PMID: 37664381

Papadopoulos, C., Castro, N., Nigath, A., Davidson, R., Faulkes, N., Menicatti, R., Khaliq, A. A., Recchiuto, C., Battistuzzi, L., Randhawa, G., Merton, L., Kanoria, S., Chong, N.-Y., Kamide, H., Hewson, D., & Sgorbissa, A. (2022). The CARESSES randomised controlled trial: Exploring the health-related impact of culturally competent artificial intelligence embedded into socially assistive robots and tested in older adult care homes. *International Journal of Social Robotics, 14*(1), 245–256. DOI: 10.1007/s12369-021-00781-x PMID: 33907589

Sawik, B., Tobis, S., Baum, E., Suwalska, A., Kropińska, S., Stachnik, K., Pérez-Bernabeu, E., Cildoz, M., Agustin, A., & Wieczorowska-Tobis, K. (2023). Robots for elderly care: Review, multi-criteria optimization model and qualitative case study. *Health Care, 11*(9), 1286. DOI: 10.3390/healthcare11091286 PMID: 37174828

World Health Organization. (n.d.). Ageing and health. Retrieved July 24, 2025, from https://www.who.int/news-room/fact-sheets/detail/ageing-and-health

Zhang, C., & Su, L. (2024). An IoMT framework integrating 5G and wireless body area networks for home healthcare. In Proceedings of the 2024 3rd International Conference on Networks, Communications and Information Technology (pp. 166–171). DOI: 10.1145/3672121.3672155

Chapter 5

Using Edge Intelligence: A Guide to Developing Data-Driven Edge Systems for Successful Business Operations

Rinki Singh
https://orcid.org/0000-0003-0823-156X
Satyug Darshan Institute of Engineering and Technology, Faridabad, India

Tarun Kumar
https://orcid.org/0000-0002-8507-8522
University of Petroleum and Energy Studies (UPES), Dehradun, India

Minakshi
https://orcid.org/0000-0001-7586-6309
King Khalid University, Saudi Arabia

ABSTRACT

The rapidly growing amount of data produced by Internet of Things (IoT) devices, gadgets, and handheld tools has made edge computing an essential resource. This chapter explores how businesses can use smart edges to access real-time data, reduce latency, and make better-informed decisions. By covering the architecture, key technologies, challenges, implementation methods, and practical examples. The decentralized nature of data processing acquires more significance as more businesses implement smart technologies. This is essential in such industries as healthcare, manufacturing, and self-driving vehicles where time delay may lead to serious effects. Edge systems also spare them of the necessity of continued connectivity to the cloud, which keeps them self-sufficient even in conditions when the access to

DOI: 10.4018/979-8-3373-1147-0.ch005

the internet is intermittent. By providing a road map for the effective deployment of edge systems in the contemporary workplace, this chapter ultimately seeks to close the gap between theorists and practitioners.

1. INTRODUCTION

A fundamental movement regarding information technology and company intelligence, computing at the edge represents a paradigm shift in the way data is gathered, processed, and used (Abbas et al., 2018). Traditional cloud computing platforms frequently find it difficult to meet the requirement for low-latency, immediate data processing as digital transformation speeds up across industries as depicted in table 1. By centralizing data processing in distant data centers, cloud computing causes delays, uses a lot of bandwidth, and could create a bottleneck for applications that need to process data quickly (Kousalya et al., 2017). By bringing statistical analysis nearer to the data source whether on manufacturing floors, automobiles, mobile devices, or retail establishments edge computing, on the other hand, decentralizes processing and allows for almost immediately apparent insights and actions. In addition to minimizing latency, this extremely close proximity to producing information also lessens the strain on the fundamental networks and improves privacy by storing sensitive data locally. Artificial intelligence (AI) combined with edge computing, sometimes known as edge intelligence, opens the door to autonomous decision-making at the source, significantly increasing responsiveness and allowing systems to continue operating even when the network is disrupted. Instead of sending all video signals to a central server (Bonomi et al., 2014), a smart camera at a store, for instance, can monitor consumer activity in real-time and activate advertising displays.

Table 1. A comparative analysis of edge computing and conventional cloud computing

Feature	Traditional Cloud Computing	Edge Computing
Location of Data	Processing centralized (data centers in the cloud)	Decentralized (close to the source of data)
Latency	High	Low
Bandwidth Usage	High	Reduced
Security and Privacy	Variable	Enhanced (Local Processing)
Offline Functionality	Limited	High (Can Work Independently)
Real-time Decision Making	Challenging	Optimized

Employing edge computing is becoming more of a need than a choice for companies looking to remain relevant in a data-first society. For mission-critical applications, sectors including manufacturing, healthcare, transportation, and smart cities are depending more and more on edge solutions. Edge computing enables a new generation of sophisticated, adaptable systems, from controlling autonomous vehicle navigation to using wearables to monitor patient vitals. This chapter lays the groundwork for understanding how businesses may use based on information edge systems to boost corporate innovation, provide individualized consumer experiences, and unlock new efficiencies. We seek to provide a strategic roadmap for the effective adoption of edge technology in contemporary businesses by examining enabling technologies, real-world applications, industry use cases, and future directions.

2. THE RISE OF EDGE COMPUTING IN BUSINESS

As the drawbacks surrounding centralized cloud systems grow, edge computing has evolved as an innovation that changes the game. Although the traditional method of sending all the data into the cloud to be processed has been outdated and very costly, due to the fact that companies now generate massive volumes of personal data in the form of instruments, smart devices, and system updates. The extreme latency, network congestions, the price of bandwidths and legal complications are other factors that are forcing businesses to seek remedies that lead to higher speeds and localized processing. Edge computing eliminates those issues by bringing processing nearer to the place of the information source, enabling companies to respond to things rapidly and to derive wisdom (Borra & Nerella, 2024). By this, the contemporary business environment can be defined as the need of quick decisions.

A millisecond can make a huge difference in terms of outcomes in such sectors as manufacturing, healthcare, and retail. A slow response to malfunction in equipment, to give an example can halt production and increase costs within the industrial segment. The technological application in the field of medicine is the real-time monitoring of patients that helps to rescue lives. Edge computing is a solution that offers the infrastructure needed to support time-sensitive application and enhance customer satisfaction, safety and productivity. The advantages of Edge computing for businesses over cloud computing is shown in table 2. Edge systems give a sense of continuity and reliability to the companies that are situated in remote places or having erratic network situations. Edge can also support data sovereignty as it allows companies to comply with the regulations with limited amount of sensitive data being confined to local region.

Table 2. Advantages of edge computing for businesses over centralized cloud

Business Need	Centralized Cloud Approach	Edge Computing Approach
Response Time	Delayed (due to network travel)	Instant (local processing)
Operational Efficiency	Limited by network dependency	Improved via autonomous local actions
Data Security & Compliance	Depends on data transit policies	Enhanced through local data handling
Scalability in Real-Time Apps	Challenging under heavy load	Easily scalable at the edge nodes
Offline Capability	Minimal	Strong (works without constant internet)
Customization and Localization	Generic service delivery	Tailored to local user needs

3. EDGE ARCHITECTURE DRIVEN BY DATA

The technology layers that make up a data-driven edge system collaborate to assess and react to events in real time (Zhang et al., 2019). The different types of edge architecture driven by data along with its use case is represented in table 3.

- **Edge Devices:** Such as sensors and Internet of Things cameras, gather data.
- **Edge Gateways**: Filter and preprocess information
- **Local Servers or Micro-Data Centers**: Data storage and analysis are done by local servers or micro-data centers.
- **Cloud Interface**: Deeper insights and long-term storage.

Table 3. Architecture models comparison

Model	Description	Best Use Case
Device Edge	Processing directly on device	Wearables, mobile apps
Gateway Edge	Aggregation and processing at gateway	Smart homes, industrial monitoring
Cloud-Managed Edge	Control from cloud, execution at edge	Retail analytics, smart cities

4. TECHNOLOGIES THAT FACILITATE

At the network's edge, edge computing is based on the convergence of state-of-the-art technologies that allow for immediate processing of data, choice-making, and automation of systems. These enabling technologies significantly improve the operating capabilities of the intelligent edge systems in a variety of industries and serve as their foundation is also depicted in table 4.

4.1 The Internet of Things

By supplying constant data streams from linked machines, sensors, and devices, IoT serves as a fundamental component of edge computing. These gadgets record mechanical, behavioral, or ecological information in real time. IoT integration with edge technologies allows for local data analysis, which cuts down on the amount of time needed to draw conclusions and take action. IoT sensors, for example, monitor the temperature, vibration, and other indicators of machines in industrial settings, allowing predictive maintenance and avoiding expensive downtime. The sheer amount of data that the is generated by the increasing number of IoT connected devices is hard to cope with using traditional cloud-based processing systems. This will be addressed by edge computing, which brings processing power one step closer to the data source so they can be processed and reacted to quickly. This distributed approach eliminates the latency issues encountered in shipping large datasets to centralized cloud servers; it also significantly reduces bandwidth requirements. The best example of such integration is any smart city, in which security cameras, air quality sensors, and traffic sensors are able to cooperate with each other to make cities work better in real-time.

The combination of IoT and the edges in the healthcare area is highly effective, wearables and medical sensors enable constant tracking of the patient and data security due to the provision of local processing. Its application in quality control in manufacturing facilities is that goods on assembly lines undergo scrutiny by the computer vision systems which automatically adjust them according to expected standards. The agricultural IoT sensors will help farmers make data-driven fertilization and irrigation decisions regardless of accessing the internet since they will monitor crop health, moisture, and weather. Edge-IoT integration has considerable security advantages because any sensitive information that is to be processed can be done locally, which eliminates most of the risks that come with sending valuable data across possible vulnerable networks. Energy management systems in smart buildings work with IoT sensors to monitor usage patterns and adjust automatically the heating, cooling and lighting systems so that they are the most efficient. Due to the scalability of edge-IoT solutions, organizations can roll out thousands of connected devices with even performance and reduced operating costs.

4.2 Machine Learning and Artificial Intelligence (AI/ML)

By allowing systems and gadgets to learn from knowledge and make decisions on their own, AI and ML elevate intelligence to the cutting edge. Instantaneous classification, prediction, and anomaly detection are made possible by the deployment of trained machine learning models to the edge. AI-powered cameras, for instance, can identify safety infractions or intruders without transmitting video to a remote server. Edge AI protects privacy and lessens reliance on internet connectivity, particularly in surveillance and healthcare (Singh et al., 2025a).

The arrival of AI/ML at the edge signifies a paradigm shift due to the centralized models of computers to the distributed intelligence. Decision-making would not be active as cloud-dependent architectures would not be able to process in real time because of the inability of edge AI algorithms to process complex data patterns using local data. Autonomous cars best exemplify this skill, as the onboard AI systems need to find a way to interpret sensor data, and make instant decisions without the need to analyze them on a cloud server. The use of voice assistance and smart speakers allows instant response to requests with the help of natural language processing models deployed to the edge, even in cases where the internet connection is unreliable or absent. Edge AI can be deployed in retail computer vision systems to detect theft, placing products in the most suitable places, and an analysis of how customers are behaving without compromising consumer privacy (Singh et al., 2025b). Industrial robotics significantly benefit because they depend on edge AI to cope with any changes, and optimize their tasks and processes in respect to real-time information of their environment. In cases where the application must respond in real-time, e.g., such emergency detection applications that require alert notifications within milliseconds, low latency in edge AI is crucial. Systems can make distributions gradually better, without relying on centralized servers, because they can continuously analyze local data and update/retrain Edge ML models based on this knowledge. To identify fraud, the edges of AI are deployed in financial institutions because they can run analysis of transactions in real-time and prevent suspicious activity that can cause damage. It is evident that edge AI would not cost a fortune once you consider the reduced bandwidth consumption and cloud computing expenses that go along with processing huge volumes of data at a local level.

4.3 5G Systems

The future promise of edge computing is greatly increased by the rollout of 5G. 5G is very low latency, high data rate, and reliable connectivity, which is ideal in real-time applications including remote surgery, smart factories, and driverless cars, among others. The expanded bandwidth allows fast transfer of data across all the instruments, gateways, and edge servers enhancing the scalability and effectiveness of distributed computing. The combination of 5G and edge computing creates a powerful synergistic effect and allows securing response times at the level of milliseconds, which reflects the requirements of mission-critical applications. Network slicing capabilities of 5G can provide an opportunity to operators to allow designing virtual networks with specific characteristics that perfectly fit edge computing applications and ensures reliable resource allocation and performance. The 5G capability of large-scale machine-type communications (MTC) enables the deployment of thousands of IoT devices per square kilometer and the generation of the immense quantities of data that can now be processed locally on edge nodes. Ultra-reliable low-latency communication (URLLC) is used in industrial automation to transmit data in near real time between computing resources and the edge devices to allow real time decision-making.

5G reduces its reliance on data traveling to distant cloud servers by promoting mobile edge computing (MEC). This aspect reduces traffic in the network because the computer resources are now brought even closer to the mobile users. The technology offers enriched mobile broadband through content delivery networks based on edge, which offers flawless content and promising user experience. With the help of private 5G networks, organizations are able to install custom edge computing systems that are more high-secured and have control over their data processing processes. By opening up local data processing, improving network efficiencies and reducing their network operating costs, 5G and edge computing relieve core networks dramatically. 5G advanced beamforming and antenna technologies ensure reliable connectivity under challenging environments, and edge computing performance remains consistent across a variety of deployment environments. The possibility of interoperability between the edge computing systems of multiple vendors is enabled by the standardization of the 5G protocols which in turn promotes innovation-driven competition within the ecosystem.

4.4 Containerization With Kubernetes and Docker Programs

Such container dependencies are accompanied by a lightweight software component known as containers, which ensures the repeatability of the execution in diverse settings. Such tools as the Docker platform and Kubernetes make scalable, modular installation of the periphery services and apps possible. Containerization can enable businesses to manage large device fleets, upgrade quickly, and promote high availability. As the containerized application orchestrator, Kubernetes raises edge systems resilience and flexibility (Puliafito et al., 2019).

4.5 Digital Twins

A Digital Twin is a digital representation of a real-world asset or activity that simulates actions and outcomes. Businesses can run what-if analysis, analyze operations in real-time, and optimize efficiency by combining edge computing and digital twins (Nain et al., 2022). Digital twins of individual machines or entire production lines are used in smart manufacturing to track performance indicators and make proactive adjustments to operations. Digital twins can also forecast faults and provide remedial measures when combined with AI.

Edge computing and digital twins together bring to existence unimaginable potentials of predictive analytics and real-time optimization across various industries. The digital twins can be edge-enabled to process huge amounts of data collected through sensors and create highly realistic virtual simulations that strongly replicate their physical counterparts without delay. Digital twins enable urban planners to simulate traffic conditions, energy demand, and performance of the infrastructure before things are reflected in reality in smart cities. Healthcare applications leverage digital representations of patients, also known as digital twins, to simulate outcomes of treatment and tailor medical procedures to specifics of the individual patient, their physiology, and response patterns. Digital twin technology is a significant help when it comes to supply chain management as it allows one to model logistics networks in the supply chain and optimize routes, predict delays and reduce operating costs by testing scenarios.

The aerospace industry applies digital twins to model components using virtual twins and predict failures to conduct the maintenance activities in advance of the breakdown. Energy sector: Digital twins of power grids and renewable energy systems can help the operator to optimize the distribution of these systems and predict equipment issues in real time. In construction, building information modeling (BIM) digital twins are employed to envisage the changes in the environmental conditions, how the building is going to be occupied, and how the building is going to perform during the existence of the building. The retail industry utilizes digital twins to optimize store and warehouse design, inventory management and consumer flow patterns based on live behavioral data. Advanced digital twins involve machine learning algorithms that will constantly be updated and trained to be more accurate since they are learning the differences between what they expect, and what actually happened. Together, these technologies enable edge computing to reach its full potential. Organizations can create intelligent, responsive, and robust systems that function at the network's edge by carefully integrating them.

Table 4. Enabling technologies' function in edge systems

Technology	Role in Edge Computing	Example Use Case
IoT	Captures real-time data from physical sources	Smart meters, industrial sensors
AI/ML	Performs intelligent data analysis and decision-making	Facial recognition, predictive analytics
5G	Provides ultra-fast, low-latency communication	Autonomous driving, telemedicine
Containers	Enables modular and scalable deployment of applications	Edge device updates, microservices at edge
Digital Twins	Simulates and monitors real-world assets in a virtual environment	Equipment monitoring, supply chain modeling

5. BUSINESS DOMAIN USE CASES

In order to facilitate real-time analytics, quicker decision-making, and enhanced consumer experiences, edge computing is being embraced by a growing number of corporate sectors (Kanevskaia et al., 2024). Organizations can increase performance efficiencies and respond quickly to changing circumstances by processing data at or close to the source. Some important business domains are shown in table 5 and how edge deployments help them are listed below:

5.1 Manufacturing: Predictive Maintenance and Real-Time Monitoring

Edge devices, including temperature and vibration sensors, are mounted on machinery in smart production settings to continuously check on its condition. Edge systems can identify irregularities that indicate possible malfunctions by locally evaluating this data. This encourages predictive maintenance, which lowers maintenance expenses and downtime by servicing machines before they break down (Hahanov et al., 2018). For instance, when a CNC machine with edge sensors notices odd vibration patterns, it can automatically notify maintenance personnel.

5.2 Retail: Customized Customer Experience, Inventory Monitoring

Edge computing enhances in-store functionality by providing front-end functionality to real-time inventory positioning and customer behavior. Smart shelves with cameras and sensors can instantly update the stock level and detect the movement of the products (Durão et al., 2018). Additionally, edge-enabled cameras mean that stores can measure the flow of pedestrians and the interest of users in displays in real-time to make dynamic layout adjustments or provide personalized discounts without transmitting personal video information to the cloud.

5.3 Healthcare: AI-Assisted Diagnostics and Patient Monitoring

On the one hand, edge computing in the healthcare domain makes remote monitoring of patients possible through the use of wearable technology that relentlessly measures vital signs, such as temperature, blood oxygen saturation, and heart rate. To make it especially timely, such gadgets process data on the spot and execute pre-programmed messages in advance to inform medical staff in case of critical levels being surpassed. Also, there is the add-on of portable imaging devices and other diagnostic aids supported by AI, whose analysis and diagnosis are found to be faster due to the local processing of the scans which reduces the dependence on central hospital services. Edge computing plus medical devices are changing the way chronic diseases are managed, enabling on-demand cardiac rhythm monitoring of individuals with cardiovascular problems and sustained glucose monitoring of diabetics. Edge devices that can be used at the bedside to make preliminary analyses and report critical information to hospitals before a patient even arrives intensively complement emergency care (Barros 2025). To provide early evidence of possible anxiety or depression, mental health apps are exploiting edge computing to analyze speech patterns, emotion displays on the face, and wearable and smartphone behavioral information. Robotic tools on the edge that provide accuracy and feedback to a surgeon in real time without relying on cloud communication to perform important tasks enhance surgery. The ability of the Edge AI-based home healthcare monitoring systems to detect variation in daily activities, drug compliance issues, and falls among elderly subscribing to live alone is a possibility. Medical imaging can also be used outside of conventional radiology, with portable X-ray units (which are compact and easily shifted) and point-of-care ultrasound requiring no preparation time or support systems and providing rapid diagnostic-level performance in underserved or remote locations.

Edge computing enables health facilities to process sensitive patient records without compromising patient privacy and at the same time processing the data at the speed required to take critical healthcare decisions. Telemedicine systems utilize edge infrastructure to provide real-time exchange of vital signs and high-definition video consults without experiencing the latency or bandwidth limitations. The use of edge computing accelerates the timelines of research and strengthens treatment results because data pertaining to patients are collected and analyzed in real-time throughout the drug discovery and clinical trial processes. The advantages of edge computing implementation in hospitals include better resource distribution that supports the operational efficiency and quality of patient care through analyzing patient traffic and the rate of equipment usage as well as the staff requirements.

5.4 Finance: Risk management and fraud detection

Financial services use edge computing to detect and prevent fraud in real-time. ATMs with edge nodes, mobile payment systems, and point-of-sale terminals may all identify suspect activity right away and report it without waiting for cloud verification (Guo & Liu, 2018). It is also possible to measure creditworthiness or potential financial risks at the moment of a transaction with the help of risk assessment algorithms deployed on edge sites.

5.5 Transportation: Autonomous Navigation, Vehicle Telemetry

Transportation systems can become safer and smarter thanks to edge computing. For instance, fleet management firms track engine health, driving habits, and fuel efficiency in real time using vehicle data gathered by edge devices (Zhang et al., 2022). When it comes to autonomous navigation, edge processors in cars process enormous amounts of sensor and camera data to make snap judgments about steering, braking, and speed all of which are essential for safe and efficient self-driving operations.

Table 5. Use case comparisons

Domain	Use Case	Edge Benefit
Manufacturing	Predictive Maintenance	Avoids downtime, reduces cost
Retail	Customer Behavior Analytics	Personalized marketing, real-time insights
Healthcare	Remote Patient Monitoring	Instant alerts, faster diagnosis
Finance	Fraud Detection	Real-time transaction analysis and prevention
Transport	Fleet Monitoring	Route optimization, fuel efficiency

6. ADVANTAGES AND COMMERCIAL WORTH

Most of the advantages of edge computing include more than strategic positioning, i.e., long-term, and the effectiveness of operations. By processing the data near to where it was generated, businesses will be able to minimize their reliance on external cloud servers as well as maximize their control, have faster insights, and be more consumer-centric (Kietzmann et al., 2018). The key strengths are outlined in detail as follows and depicted in table 6.

6.1 Operational Efficiency: Reduced Data Transfer, Quicker Reactions

Edge computing also leads to faster reaction to data that is generated at the source since the delays approximately associated with cloud-based systems are avoided. It is quite useful in the context of time-sensitive environments such as manufacturing, logistics, or energy management. As an example, smart sensors in an intelligent factory may recognize a deviation and automatically shut down the machinery without the need to be told to do so over the cloud. The network performance is also enhanced by edge computing, as it analyses data locally instead of sending the same to the server data center (Li et al., 2018). This reduces the data flow back and forth the network hence leading to great reduction in bandwidth expenses.

6.2 Customer Experience: Customization, Quickness

When it comes to retail and digital services industries, customer experience has to be easy and customized to build loyalty and retention (Li & Wang, 2021). At the site of interaction, edge computing simplifies the real- time behavioral analysis. Such motion of a customer can be identified in a smart retail store by edge-enabled cameras and sensors and in a matter of seconds display personalized advertisements or recommend products. Apps using edge AI also respond faster, so a user experience is smoother, even in areas with a bad connection.

6.3 Compliance and Security: Data Remains On-Site

Improvement of data privacy and compliances is one of the most valuable impacts of edge computing. Data processing can be done locally, and sensitive data such as identities of the users, money transactions, and health conditions of the patients get to be packed on-site or in local boundaries (Lu et al., 2019). In addition to meeting legal criteria like GDPR or HIPAA, this lowers the likelihood of a transmission breach. Another advantage of such localized approach is greater control over encryption, access rights, response to threats.

6.4 Competitive Advantage: Real-Time Innovation and Decision-Making

This is due to the fact that edge computing enables businesses to act on data in real-time hence enabling real-time innovation. Businesses can apply the AI models and automatically automate all decisions, recognize trends, and predict customer requirements in real-time. On example is the energy companies have the ability to carefully balance loads to react with the grid effectively, and financial companies are able to react to the movement in milliseconds. These qualities enable businesses to obtain a competitive edge, promptly adjust to changes in the market, and provide cutting-edge services that set them apart from rivals (Mach & Becvar, 2017). The strategic usages of edge computing break the old business modes by allowing quick decision-making based on data, which has never been possible with centralized cloud systems. Manufacturing organizations are deploying real-time edge analytics to enhance quality control processes, reduce wastage, and streamline production runs without experiencing the delay inherent in processing on the cloud.

Edge computing allows retail enterprises to personalize service to consumers at an unprecedented pace by changing inventory management in real-time according to customers shopping habits and preferences. Fleet management, route optimization, dynamic scheduling, and edge computing are a significant advantage to transportation logistics companies that are now possible due to both technologies combined. Specifically, real-time patient monitoring, as well as diagnostic skills that could be used to determine notable deviations in vital signs and determine timely medical responses, is beneficial to healthcare sector. Telecom companies resort to edge computing to regulate bandwidth usage, get optimal performance in the network, and ensure that their clients can access the material in real time constantly. With the use of the state-of-the-art precision farming equipment, farming companies can in real time adjust schedules of irrigation, fertilizing, and harvesting based on the latest weather and soil reports. With the edge-powered chatbots and support systems, the instant and contextually right assistive services are possible without using the cloud, which affords them an upper hand in customer care activities. In addition to trade, financial institutions enjoy the opportunity of risk assessment, real time fraud monitoring as well as personalized banking services which enhance client safety and satisfaction. Since the edge computing needs a complex interaction of both hardware, software, and data analytics, firms with successful incorporation of edge computing into their activities develop the sustainable competitive moat, which is difficult to replicate by their competitors.

Table 6. Value realization comparison

Business Area	Edge Impact
Operations	Faster decisions, reduced downtime
Customer Relations	Personalized, real-time services
Security	Local data protection
Strategic Planning	Real-time market insights

7. IMPLEMENTATION SCHEDULE

A well-planned and strategic approach is necessary for the successful deployment of a data-driven edge system. Edge computing, in contrast to typical IT deployments, entails diverse environments, distributed infrastructures, and close integration with enterprise and operational systems (Qiu et al., 2020). The steps that enterprises must take to guarantee a dependable, scalable, and value-generating edge implementation are highlighted in the roadmap that follows.

7.1 Needs Analysis: Determine Latency-Sensitive Regions

Finding pain spots that necessitate prompt decision-making or response is the first step in analyzing company processes (Shehab et al., 2020). This includes systems where delays may result in decreased client satisfaction, lost money, or malfunctions.

7.1.1 Crucial Tasks

- Hold stakeholder workshops to determine the most important use cases.
- Examine data flow and delay needs for various operations.
- Give top priority to domains (such as manufacturing lines, medical surveillance, or fraud detection) where edge processing provides measurable business benefits.
- Take data residency laws and compliance needs into consideration.

7.2 Technology Selection: Pick Software and Hardware That Work Together

Selecting the right hardware (edge devices, sensors, gateways) and software (OS, AI frameworks, orchestration tools) (Mouradian et al., 2019) in accordance with the use case, scalability requirements, and environment comes next once requirements have been established.

- **Hardware:** Select tiny machines for confined places, GPU-enabled processors for AI tasks, and robust devices for severe situations.
- **Software:** Verify support for containerized apps (e.g., Docker, Kubernetes) and interoperability with current corporate platforms.
- **Connectivity:** Depending on the deployment region, assess 5G, Wi-Fi, LPWAN, or hybrid options. Evaluate the ability to integrate with public cloud providers, such as AWS, Azure, and GCP.

7.3 Pilot Test: Verify with Restricted Distribution

It's critical to carry out a controlled pilot program prior to organization-wide adoption (Mahmood & Ramachandran, 2018). This aids in confirming hypotheses, spotting unforeseen problems, and improving the system.

7.3.1 Pilot Projects

- Install the edge solution in one or two departments or real-world locations.
- Workload simulation and performance evaluation (accuracy, throughput, latency).
- Gather opinions from system administrators and end users.
- Track integration success, communication effectiveness, and error rates.
- Modify models and configurations in light of findings.

7.4 Integration: Establish a Connection with Business Systems

An effective edge deployment needs to integrate with cloud platforms, analytics engines, data lakes, ERP, and CRM (Premsankar et al., 2018) as part of the larger company digital ecosystem.

7.4.1 Important Integration Tasks

- Create data pipelines connecting edge nodes to on-premises or cloud services.
- To facilitate communication with corporate applications, use middleware or APIs.
- To ensure secure interoperability, set up identity and access management (IAM).
- For reliable data exchange, make sure synchronization methods are in place.

- For compliance, enable data governance and lifecycle management.

7.5 Monitoring: Evaluate and Modify Performance

After implementing the system, there must be a periodic test of the system to check its accuracy, availability and efficiency (Rahman & Hussain, 2020). Since edge environments are dynamic, the management assumes proactive management.

7.5.1 Observing Best Practices

- Utilize observability tools and dashboards to keep an eye on error logs, latency, CPU utilization, and bandwidth.
- Set up alerts of malfunctions or decline in performance or suspicions of bad behavior.
- Address firmware and troubleshoot with the help of remote management tools.
- Get user feedback on periodic basis to encourage system optimization.
- The business effect and the business pay back (ROI) has to be evaluated regularly.

8. OBSTACLES AND COUNTERMEASURES

Despite its revolutionary benefits to businesses, the distributed and decentralized nature of edge computing offers a distinct set of challenges (Satyanarayanan, 2017). Safe, scalable, and successful edge installations need systematic response to these problems. The key challenges are discussed in detail below and their solutions are practical.

8.1 Security: Increased Attack Surfaces Due to More Endpoints

An edge environment involves data processing distributed across dozens of dispersed devices, gateways, and local servers, all of which may have been hacked (Shi et al., 2016). Unlike centralized systems, where the structured and unstructured data and infrastructure are built into secure cloud environments, edge systems operate in a wide range of cloud and physical platforms, often with minimal-no monitoring.

8.1.1 Principal Hazards

- Tampering with devices in remote areas.

- Inadequate methods of authenticating.
- Unpatched vulnerabilities in software and firmware.

8.1.2 Strategies for Mitigation

- Use zero-trust security models, in which all access requests are validated, regardless of their origin.
- To safeguard data and program integrity, use secure boot procedures and end-point encryption.
- Make use of automatic security patching technology and patch your firmware frequently.
- Have the edge-specific intrusion/threat monitoring solutions.

8.2 Scalability: More Difficult to Control Compared to Centralized Systems

Scaling the edge computing infrastructure is a combination of deploying, sustaining, and updating thousands of distributed devices (usually in-unreliable or heterogeneous settings). Such a diversified environment is hard and even presents a tendency to operational inefficiencies.

8.2.1 Principal Difficulties

- Hardware and software differentiation at the edge nodes Implementation of changes is not easy, and it is difficult to monitor the performance (Tanaka & Luo, 2019).
- Limited physical access to regions on the periphery.

8.2.2 Strategies for Mitigation

- In order to standardize the deployments, employ orchestration systems such as Kubernetes and containerization programs such as Docker (Tsai et al., 2015).
- Implement remote device management systems with capabilities of centralized updates, diagnostics and monitoring.
- To enable automation and scale, include edge orchestration features whether these are Open Horizon or AWS Greengrass or Azure IoT Edge.
- Ensure there is hierarchy in money deployment to ease in management.

8.3 Data Consistency: Integrating Cloud and Edge Data

The aspect of consistency between local edge data and central cloud repositories is among the key ones in cases when the processing is distributed across various nodes (Varghese & Buyya, 2018). Irregularities can lead either to an irregularity in analytics results or unstable operation of the system.

8.3.1 Principal Difficulties

- Network crashes leading to delays in the synchronization of data.
- Due to asynchronous processing, different copies of data appear.
- Settling nodes conflicts.

8.3.2 Strategies for Mitigation

- Use eventual consistency models with dispute resolution procedures integrated.
- In order to have traceable data lineage adopt time-stamping and data versioning.
- Organize the data pipelines with hybrid edge-cloud frameworks, such as AWS IoT Analytics or Google Cloud Edge.
- To lessen burden, just synchronize pertinent metadata rather than entire data sets.

8.4 Skills Gap: Requirement for Multidisciplinary Knowledge

A number of technical fields, including networking, cybersecurity, embedded systems, cloud computing, and AI/ML, converge to form edge computing. Long-term sustainability (Wang et al., 2020) and efficient deployment are hampered by a shortage of experts with transdisciplinary backgrounds.

8.4.1 Principal Difficulties

- Lack of expertise in deploying both hardware and AI models.
- The learning curve for distributed infrastructure management.
- Insufficient instruction on edge environment security procedures.

8.4.2 Strategies for Mitigation

- Invest in staff upskilling through courses, certificates, and practical training.

- Work together to create specialized talent pipelines with industrial partners and academic institutions.
- Use low-code/no-code platforms to make developing edge applications easier.
- Promote the use of cross-functional teams that combine operational, data science, and IT roles for deployment planning.

9. PROSPECTS AND TRENDS FOR THE FUTURE

Edge computing is not only growing in popularity but also developing into an ecosystem of intelligent, self-governing, and sustainable technology as the digital world changes. Predictive, collaborative, and automated systems that support more general business objectives like agility (Xu et al., 2020), environmental responsibility, and competitive innovation are replacing basic data processing in the future. These are a few of the most intriguing advancements that will shape edge computing in the future represented in table 7.

9.1 Self-Governing Edge AI

The next generation of edge computing is self-sufficient AI devices with the ability to learn and make decisions in real-time and without human aid. Such systems can adapt to changing conditions, re-train models with new local data and make themselves more accurate over time. An example of edge AI is: without the centralized supervision, they could automatically adjust traffic lights in a connected transport AI system, based on the current traffic, which leads to maximum flow (Yang et al., 2021). On the verge of self-government AI is an epistemological shift towards truly independent systems, able to operate themselves and to enhance their performance over long durations of time. These intelligent systems have the capability of a federated learning that allows a handful of edge devices to combine their collective knowledge and enhance their decision-making capabilities without compromising data security or privacy.

Autonomous edge AI in the industry includes manufacturing robots capable of identifying and reacting to errors in equipment (Kumar et al., 2024). These robots can change the parameters of production automatically to keep the quality to the required level without the human interference. The smart grid systems employ self-governing AI to predict the change in demand, equalize energy flows, and allow seamless integration of renewable energy sources based on prevailing weather patterns and consumption patterns (Goethals et al., 2021). Agricultural autonomous systems are used to run their purpose in crop monitoring, insect detection, and precision irrigation with outstanding results. They come up with their own decisions, which are aimed at maximizing the production with the minimum consumed resources. Self-governing edge AI is also useful to retail settings by optimizing product prices through dynamic pricing algorithms that change the cost of products automatically based on patterns of demand, competition, and stock without requiring human supervision. Cybersecurity applications use autonomous edge AI to detect and respond to threats in real-time, deploy countermeasures to the attack, and update security protocols based on emerging trends on the attack.

Self-governing AI is instrumental in environmental monitoring systems capable of autonomously deploying assets, tuning sensor settings, and harmonizing response action in the case of natural disasters or a pollution scenario. Healthcare applications Autonomous patient monitoring systems that can possibly predict a medical emergency, update treatment plans, and schedule care team responses according to information about the patient and community health trends are capable of use. The evolution of self-regulating edge AI can result in strong and adaptable infrastructure that can still carry on operating with optimal efficiency even in challenging or unpredictable circumstances.

9.2 Learning Federated

Already, federated learning is gaining momentum because businesses want to exercise more control over their data and as data privacy regulations are getting stricter. In this approach multiple edge devices or nodes may collaborate to train machine learning models without sharing raw data (Yu et al., 2017). The updates in the model only update a central server that protects data privacy and saves network burden. This is especially beneficial in such industries as healthcare and banking where confidentiality and compliance are critical attributes.

9.3 Edge Computing That Is Sustainable

The energy-efficient edge architecture has an enormous market that has been triggered by the sensitivity of the environment. In a bid to reduce the carbon footprints, low-power processor, efficient cooling system, and intelligent energy management algorithms are being developed into new edge devices (Zhang et al., 2020a). Emerging green projects in smart agriculture, urban infrastructure, and remote monitoring are being supported by solar-powered edge nodes and AI-driven resource optimization.

9.4 The Edge of Hyper Automation

By combining cutting-edge technologies like artificial intelligence (AI), machine learning, robotic process automation (RPA), and edge computing, hyper automation is allowing businesses to completely automate intricate commercial and industrial operations (Zhang et al., 2020b). Without waiting for cloud approval, choices and actions may be taken immediately by using these technologies at the edge. Hyper automation, for example, can manage logistics, track quality, and control robotics in a factory setting all from the plant floor, in real time.

Table 7. An overview of cutting-edge trends

Trend	Description	Key Benefit
Autonomous Edge AI	Self-learning systems that adapt without cloud dependency	Improved accuracy and real-time adaptability
Federated Learning	Collaborative model training without raw data sharing	Privacy preservation and reduced data transfer
Sustainable Edge	Eco-friendly, energy-efficient edge infrastructures	Supports green IT and lowers operational costs
Hyper automation	Integrating AI, RPA, and analytics for full process automation	Faster, intelligent, and cost-effective systems

10. CONCLUSION

The way that contemporary businesses handle and use information has changed dramatically as a result of data-driven edge systems. These technologies drastically lower latency by moving data processing closer to the source, at the network's edge, enabling real-time decision-making and event response for enterprises. In settings where milliseconds count, such industrial automation, driverless cars, smart cities, and medical monitoring, this capacity is extremely important.

Adoption of edge computing reduces reliance on centralized cloud infrastructure, which lowers bandwidth consumption and increases system resilience in addition to increasing operational efficiency (Bhardwaj et al., 2025). Faster data insights, better customer experiences, and increased productivity are thus possible for enterprises.

However, a clear implementation plan is necessary to effectively reap the benefits of edge systems. Scalability and interoperability must be guaranteed, security and privacy issues must be addressed, and the appropriate hardware and software stack must be selected. Companies also need to be ready to handle issues like real-time analytics, device management, and data synchronization. Effective use of edge computing makes it a potent catalyst for digital change. It enables companies to stay flexible in ever-changing marketplaces, realize the full value of their data, and experience long-term success. Edge systems are more than simply a technical benefit in today's more competitive and data-intensive world; they are a strategic must.

REFERENCES

Abbas, N., Zhang, Y., Taherkordi, A., & Skeie, T. (2018). Mobile edge computing: A survey. *IEEE Internet of Things Journal*, *5*(1), 450–465. DOI: 10.1109/JIOT.2017.2750180

Barros, S. (2025). Solving AI foundational model latency with telco infrastructure. DOI: 10.2139/ssrn.5195333

Bhardwaj, I., Devi, S., & Kumar, T. (2025). Securing the cloud: Navigating compliance and regulatory challenges. In *Risk-based approach to secure cloud migration* (pp. 325–342). IGI Global., DOI: 10.4018/979-8-3693-7137-4.ch013

Bonomi, F., Milito, R., Natarajan, P., & Zhu, J. (2014). Fog computing: A platform for Internet of Things and analytics. In Rao, B. P.. (Eds.). *Big data and internet of things: A roadmap for smart environments* (pp. 169–186). Springer. DOI: 10.1007/978-3-319-05029-4_7

Borra, P., & Nerella, H. (2024). *Analyzing AWS edge computing solutions to enhance IoT deployments. SSRN*. DOI: 10.35940/ijeat.F4519.13060824

Durão, L. F. C., Haag, S., Anderl, R., Schützer, K., & Zancul, E. (2018). Digital twin requirements in the context of industry 4.0. In M. Sarfatti, A. Bouras, & Y. Stjepandić (Eds.), *Product lifecycle management to support Industry 4.0: 15th IFIP WG 5.1 International Conference, PLM 2018, Turin, Italy, July 2–4, 2018, Proceedings 15* (pp. 204–214). Springer International Publishing. DOI: 10.1007/978-3-030-01614-2_19

Goethals, T., Volckaert, B., & De Turck, F. (2021). Enabling and leveraging AI in the intelligent edge: A review of current trends and future directions. *IEEE Open Journal of the Communications Society*, *2*, 2311–2341. DOI: 10.1109/OJCOMS.2021.3116437

Guo, H., & Liu, J. (2018). Collaborative computation offloading for multi-access edge computing over fiber-wireless networks. *IEEE Transactions on Vehicular Technology*, *67*(5), 4514–4526. DOI: 10.1109/TVT.2018.2790421

Hahanov, V., Hahanov, V., Gharibi, W., Man, K. L., Iemelianov, I., Liubarskyi, M.,& Chumachenko, S. (2018). Cyber-physical technologies: Hype cycle 2017. *Cyber Physical Computing for IoT-driven Services*, 259-272.

Kanevskaia, O., Delimatsis, P., & Bijlmakers, S. (2024). The European Telecommunication Standards Institute (ETSI): In search for legitimacy and resilience of European standardisation. *Innovation (Abingdon)*, *37*(5), 1–20. DOI: 10.1080/13511610.2024.2395262 PMID: 39975519

Kietzmann, J., Paschen, J., & Treen, E. (2018). Artificial intelligence in advertising: How marketers can leverage AI. *Journal of Advertising Research, 58*(3), 263–267. DOI: 10.2501/JAR-2018-035

Kousalya, G., Balakrishnan, P., Pethuru Raj, C., Kousalya, G., Balakrishnan, P., & Pethuru Raj, C. (2017). Stepping into the digital intelligence era. *Automated Workflow Scheduling in Self-Adaptive Clouds: Concepts, Algorithms and Methods*, 1-22.

Kumar, T., Kumar, P., & Namasudra, S. (2024). User revocation-enabled access control model using identity-based signature in the cloud computing environment. *International Journal of Interactive Multimedia and Artificial Intelligence*, *9*(1), 127–136. DOI: 10.9781/ijimai.2024.05.001

Li, S., Da Xu, L., & Zhao, S. (2018). 5G Internet of Things: A survey. *Journal of Industrial Information Integration*, *10*, 1–9. DOI: 10.1016/j.jii.2018.01.005

Li, Y., & Wang, M. (2021). Research on real-time AI deployment at the edge. *Journal of Systems Architecture*, *118*, 102134. DOI: 10.1016/j.sysarc.2021.102134

Lu, Y., Xu, X., & Xu, X. (2019). Development of a hybrid edge-cloud system for manufacturing process monitoring. *Journal of Manufacturing Systems*, *51*, 52–60. DOI: 10.1016/j.jmsy.2019.03.002

Mach, P., & Becvar, Z. (2017). Mobile edge computing: A survey on architecture and computation offloading. *IEEE Communications Surveys and Tutorials*, *19*(3), 1628–1656. DOI: 10.1109/COMST.2017.2682318

Mahmood, Z., & Ramachandran, M. (2018). Fog computing: Concepts, principles and related paradigms. In Mahmood, Z., & Ramachandran, M. (Eds.), *Fog computing: Concepts, frameworks and technologies* (pp. 3–21). Springer., DOI: 10.1007/978-3-319-94890-4_1

Mouradian, C., Salah, K., Limam, N., & Boutaba, R. (2019). A comprehensive survey on fog computing: State-of-the-art and research challenges. *IEEE Communications Surveys and Tutorials*, *20*(1), 416–464. DOI: 10.1109/COMST.2017.2771153

Nain, G., Pattanaik, K. K., & Sharma, G. K. (2022). Towards edge computing in intelligent manufacturing: Past, present and future. *Journal of Manufacturing Systems*, *62*, 588–611. DOI: 10.1016/j.jmsy.2022.01.010

Premsankar, G., Di Francesco, M., & Taleb, T. (2018). Edge computing for the Internet of Things: A case study. *IEEE Internet of Things Journal*, *5*(2), 1275–1284. DOI: 10.1109/JIOT.2018.2805263

Puliafito, C., Mingozzi, E., Longo, F., Puliafito, A., & Rana, O. (2019). Fog computing for the internet of things: A survey. *ACM Transactions on Internet Technology*, *19*(2), 1–41. DOI: 10.1145/3301443

Qiu, T., Chi, J., Zhou, X., Ning, Z., Atiquzzaman, M., & Wu, D. O. (2020). Edge computing in industrial internet of things: Architecture, advances and challenges. *IEEE Communications Surveys and Tutorials*, *22*(4), 2462–2488. DOI: 10.1109/COMST.2020.3009103

Rahman, M. A., & Hussain, F. K. (2020). IoT-edge-cloud orchestrated machine learning: A review and future research directions. *Journal of Network and Computer Applications*, *166*, 102716. DOI: 10.1016/j.jnca.2020.102716

Satyanarayanan, M. (2017). The emergence of edge computing. *Computer*, *50*(1), 30–39. DOI: 10.1109/MC.2017.9

Shehab, A. H., & Al-Janabi, S. T. F. (2020, November). Microsoft Azure IoT-based edge computing for smart homes. In *2020 International Conference on Decision Aid Sciences and Application (DASA)* (pp. 315–319). IEEE. https://doi.org/DOI: 10.1109/DASA51403.2020.9317274

Shi, W., Cao, J., Zhang, Q., Li, Y., & Xu, L. (2016). Edge computing: Vision and challenges. *IEEE Internet of Things Journal*, *3*(5), 637–646. DOI: 10.1109/JIOT.2016.2579198

Singh, R., Goyal, D., Arora, S., Malviya, J., & Garg, D. (2025, January). Evaluating the Severity of Parkinson's Disease Using Machine Learning Classifiers. In *2025 International Conference on Cognitive Computing in Engineering, Communications, Sciences and Biomedical Health Informatics (IC3ECSBHI)* (pp. 243-248). IEEE. DOI: 10.1109/IC3ECSBHI63591.2025.10990440

Singh, R., Malviya, J., Singh, R. B., & Garg, D. (2025, January). Hybrid Approach of Deep Convolution Neural Network and Transfer Learning for Tuberculosis Prediction. In *2025 International Conference on Cognitive Computing in Engineering, Communications, Sciences and Biomedical Health Informatics (IC3ECSBHI)* (pp. 357-362). IEEE. DOI: 10.1109/IC3ECSBHI63591.2025.10990849

Tanaka, Y., & Luo, Y. (2019). Secure data sharing in federated edge learning. In *Proceedings of the 2nd ACM Workshop on Edge Systems, Analytics and Networking (EdgeSys)* (pp. 47–52). https://doi.org/DOI: 10.1145/3301418.3313940

Tsai, C. W., Lai, C. F., Chao, H. C., & Vasilakos, A. V. (2015). Big data analytics: A survey. *Journal of Big Data*, *2*(1), 1–32. DOI: 10.1186/s40537-015-0030-3 PMID: 26191487

Varghese, B., & Buyya, R. (2018). Next generation cloud computing: New trends and research directions. *Future Generation Computer Systems*, *79*, 849–861. DOI: 10.1016/j.future.2017.09.020

Wang, Y., Han, S., Leung, V. C. M., & Zhang, N. (2020). Convergence of edge computing and AI for intelligent IoT: A survey. *IEEE Communications Surveys and Tutorials*, *22*(2), 869–904. DOI: 10.1109/COMST.2020.2970550

Xu, X., Liu, C., Zhang, K., & Zhang, Y. (2020). A sustainable edge computing framework for smart cities. *Sustainable Cities and Society*, *56*, 102082. DOI: 10.1016/j.scs.2020.102082

Yang, C., Liu, Y., & Li, W. (2021). Edge intelligence for building automation systems: Opportunities and challenges. *Automation in Construction*, *126*, 103665. DOI: 10.1016/j.autcon.2021.103665

Yu, W., Liang, F., He, X., Hatcher, W. G., Lu, C., Lin, J., & Yang, X. (2017). A survey on the edge computing for the Internet of Things. *IEEE Access : Practical Innovations, Open Solutions*, *6*, 6900–6919. DOI: 10.1109/ACCESS.2017.2778504

Zhang, C., Zheng, Y., Zhou, Z., & Li, Y. (2020). Federated learning for IoT: Communication-efficient and privacy-preserving edge learning. *IEEE Internet of Things Journal*, *7*(12), 10664–10676. DOI: 10.1109/JIOT.2020.2995503

Zhang, W., He, Q., Yang, X., & Chen, J. (2020). AI-enabled resource allocation for edge computing: A review. *Computer Communications*, *155*, 97–106. DOI: 10.1016/j.comcom.2020.03.040

Zhang, Y., Deng, R. H., & Li, J. (2019). Blockchain-based secure data sharing system in edge computing. *IEEE Internet of Things Journal*, *6*(3), 4715–4725. DOI: 10.1109/JIOT.2018.2871574

Zhang, Y., Yu, H., Zhou, W., & Man, M. (2022). Application and research of IoT architecture for End-Net-Cloud edge computing. *Electronics (Basel)*, *12*(1), 1. DOI: 10.3390/electronics12010001

Chapter 6
Bi-Stacked ANN for Intelligent Healthcare Systems:
Real-Time Monitoring and Predictive Diagnostics Using Edge Computing

Usharani Bhimavarapu
https://orcid.org/0000-0002-0246-1420
Department of Computer Science and Engineering, Koneru Lakshmaiah Education Foundation, Vaddeswaram, India

ABSTRACT

Healthcare edge computing is an emerging paradigm that puts data processing in closer proximity to where data are gathered, cutting down latency and improving real-time decision-making for healthcare systems. In this work, we examine the application of bi-stacked Artificial Neural Networks (ANNs) on edge devices for handling healthcare data from different sensors, including wearable sensors and medical IoT sensors. The bi-stacked ANN model has two tiers of neural networks where the lower-level aggregates low-level features from raw sensors and the higher level consolidates such features for application in disease prediction and patient monitoring. With this distributed form of data processing, there is considerable alleviation against dependency on cloud infrastructures and this hence boosts the efficiency and speed of healthcare systems. In addition, healthcare edge computing benefits in diminishing bandwidth consumption, enhancing patient privacy, and providing timely medical treatments.

DOI: 10.4018/979-8-3373-1147-0.ch006

INTRODUCTION

Healthcare edge computing is the deployment of computing power near healthcare data sources, including medical devices, sensors, and wearables, in order to execute computations in real time. In contrast to cloud computing, where data is sent to central servers, edge computing enables healthcare applications to run with lower latency. The approach optimizes the effectiveness of medical care by enabling quicker decision-making as well as less network traffic. As health trends shift towards online healthcare solutions, edge computing is the driving force behind remote patient monitoring, telemedicine, and artificial intelligence-based diagnosis. The use of edgy processing of data guarantees medical experts have real-time access to information irrespective of cloud infrastructure. It performs optimally in emergency healthcare situations where real-time data processing is vital to timely intervention. Secondly, edge computing is secure in the sense that fewer data cross external networks and hence the vulnerability to cyberattacks is reduced. Edge computing is an IoT- and AI-apps-growth-fueled technology enabler gaining traction in healthcare. There is increased demand for healthcare edge computing due to more medical data generated by networked equipment. Cloud computing is not designed to handle high data transfer fees, latency, and possible bandwidth constraints. Edge computing circumvents such constraints by decentralizing data processing to make health systems function optimally in low-bandwidth settings.

Clinicians benefit from improved care coordination with interoperability among edge-based health systems and seamless boundary-less data sharing. It is comparable to enhanced decision-making and enhanced patient safety. As networked medical devices are more in vogue, edge computing will be the key to bringing effective and reliable medical services into existence. Edge computing also optimizes energy consumption and efficiency in the healthcare industry. Cloud processing of data is an environment-hungry customer, power-hungry, with high operating and high greenhouse gas impact costs.

The Hartmann et al. (2022) article discusses how edge computing is being used for smart health systems but isn't very practically orientated as it doesn't contain any tangible case studies or practical examples.

Challenges proposed are also very generic and not considering infinitesimally small regional or contextually specific variations, e.g., differences in healthcare infrastructure. It would also be nice to include the integration of other upcoming technologies in addition to edge computing, such as 5G and AI, into healthcare system design.

Although Ray (2017) outlines the possibilities of IoT in intelligent agriculture, it makes a casual reference to its use in healthcare without hands-on implementation to health care IoT systems. The review is farm practice- and technology-based agricultural and hence its application to health care practitioners is minimal. The article fails to mention aspects such as security risks and interoperability needs in health care IoT which are vital in its utilization in health care organizations.

Quy et al. (2022) present some of the applications of IoT in smart agriculture but present very brief descriptions of IoT challenges in healthcare, in which data privacy and monitoring in real-time are more important. The paper presents more theoretical explanation and fails to provide concrete solutions or experimental results from healthcare applications. This decreases the relevance of the paper in the design of healthcare IoT in the real scenario.

Singh et al. (2021) have come up with an IoT-based smart agriculture system, but the paper lacks discussion on challenges and limitations in following the same to the healthcare industry. The research is poorly conceived in the aspects of data security, existing healthcare infrastructure integration, and regulation issues that are typically found in medical settings, thereby limiting the direct implementation of this study in the healthcare sector.

Shahzadi et al. (2016) discuss IoT-based expert systems for smart farming but do not mention the unique complexities of healthcare IoT systems. End-to-end discussion on privacy issues, data normalization, and real-time data processing, which are critical in healthcare, is lacking in the paper. Further, the expert system proposed is not sufficiently flexible to the rapidly evolving and highly regulated healthcare sector.

Although Huang et al. (2020) make a passing reference to blockchain-enabled mobile crowd sensing in industrial systems, it fails to consider how such technologies can be fine-tuned to healthcare application, where privacy and security of data are paramount. The drawbacks of applying blockchain to healthcare IoT systems, namely interoperability and real-time nature of data, remain insufficiently addressed, diminishing the potential utility of findings to application.

Hrovatin et al. (2022) mention privacy-preserving data mining for blockchain-based WSNs but not mentioning the limitations of these methodologies when applied to healthcare IoT systems with patient information. There are no case studies or real-world implementations in healthcare environments and no mention of the compliance and regulatory issues healthcare providers encounter while applying such privacy-preserving measures.

Zhong et al. (2021) present some details of IoT applications in high-speed rail but none regarding the specific requirements and challenges of IoT systems in healthcare. The research targets transport applications, where there is a mix of different sensitivities of information and a need for real-time monitoring in healthcare. This restricts the generalization of the results to healthcare IoT systems, whose highest priority is patient safety and privacy.

Bovenzi et al. (2020) also propose a hybrid intrusion detection system for IoT but are not addressing the security issues specifically in healthcare IoT systems, whose primary issue is protecting patients' information. There are no in-depth discussions in the paper regarding how security can be implemented in the controlling rules of the healthcare environment and the scalability of the security components in real-deployment healthcare.

The approach optimizes the effectiveness of medical care by enabling quicker decision-making as well as less network traffic. As health trends shift towards on-line healthcare solutions, edge computing is the driving force behind remote patient monitoring, telemedicine, and artificial intelligence-based diagnosis. The use of edgy processing of data guarantees medical experts have real-time access to information irrespective of cloud infrastructure. It performs optimally in emergency healthcare situations where real-time data processing is vital to timely intervention. Secondly, edge computing is secure in the sense that fewer data cross external networks and hence the vulnerability to cyberattacks is reduced. Edge computing is an IoT- and AI-apps-growth-fueled technology enabler gaining traction in healthcare. There is increased demand for healthcare edge computing due to more medical data generated by networked equipment. Cloud computing is not designed to handle high data transfer fees, latency, and possible bandwidth constraints. Edge computing circumvents such constraints by decentralizing data processing to make health systems function optimally in low-bandwidth settings.

Clinicians benefit from improved care coordination with interoperability among edge-based health systems and seamless boundary-less data sharing. It is comparable to enhanced decision-making and enhanced patient safety. As networked medical devices are more in vogue, edge computing will be the key to bringing effective and reliable medical services into existence. Edge computing also optimizes energy consumption and efficiency in the healthcare industry. Cloud processing of data is an environment-hungry customer, power-hungry, with high operating and high greenhouse gas impact costs.

Khan et al. (2021) also suggested an IoT intrusion detection system through deep learning but for MQTT-based IoT systems and not considering the inherent complexities of medical IoT systems. Integration, compliance with healthcare norms, and privacy concerns of data are not to some acceptable level, which denies their contribution universality to its applications in healthcare, where security is still a more serious issue.

Iyapparaja et al. (2022) conduct an experiment on fog computing's resource allocation according to the QTCS model but not the scenario of how the scalability factor comes into the equation when used in huge IoT systems, especially real-time medical or industrial. Its real-world performance and applicability are also experimented with too little so much so that the outcome is not generalizable. In addition, the absence of accurate security design in the model would also lead to uncertainty in its implementation in highly sensitive domains such as healthcare or critical infrastructure.

Lei et al. (2020) suggest Groupchain, an extensible public fog computing blockchain network, but the research paper does not offer detailed performance testing on how it would function in massive IoT networks, where scalability and latency become increasingly significant concerns. The practicality of applying such an approach in extremely dynamic environments like smart cities or health networks is not discussed. The paper does not take into account the challenges in integrating Groupchain with existing blockchain networks or compatibility problems that exist in most IoT systems, which might be its flaw in the real world.

Ali et al. (2022) are concerned with DDoS attack detection and threat analysis in IoT but don't explore the complexity of zero-day or advanced attack detection in heterogeneous IoT environments in depth. The methods are limited by the absence of empirical validations in realistic environments, and therefore they are less realistic. Further, the research fails to consider the computational expense and resource constraint of IoT devices that would negate the scalability of proposed attack detection frameworks for large-scale or resource-constrained environments.

Parra et al. (2022) propose a deep learning-based approach for the detection of cybersecurity events on IoT devices, but the proposed approach is not thoroughly tested on various real-world cases. The paper has not touched upon the issues of computational cost and power consumption to deploy deep learning models on IoT devices, particularly in limited settings. The article is silent about any references concerning data protection and privacy issues for healthcare IoT applications, where sensitive and personal data is being dealt with.

Fadda et al. (2019) are discussing communications, IoT, and smart homes, microgrids, and smart buildings, but the research doesn't indicate proper knowledge of the privacy issue or security concern of adopting IoT in such key infrastructures. The chapter book isn't discussing mass-deployment issues or interworking among various IoT solutions within smart buildings, limiting its applicability in various scenarios. In addition, the absence of genuine case studies makes further evaluation of how the proposed solutions are to be implemented more difficult. Mir et al. (2021) have provided a review of energy management solutions for smart buildings, but their paper does not consider scalability aspects in implementing solutions in gigantic buildings or city centers.

Cleverly proposed solutions are hypothetical and entail no empirical evidence to justify their viability in actual contexts. Moreover, the research does not touch on the integration of energy management systems with other smart technologies such as healthcare IoT, which would even increase the opportunities for smart buildings but pose other security and data privacy issues. Hanafizadeh and Amin (2022) book refers to FinTechs' disruptive potential in banking services but does not apply to immediate relevance to IoT deployments in health or manufacturing. Banking as the interested sector overlooks major aspects of the distinctive challenges embedded in IoT in healthcare, with data security and privacy performing best. Additionally, the research does not touch on interoperation and integration of IoT among industries, so the study is generalizable across other industries.

Jo et al. (2018) mention the potential of intelligent railways with IoT solutions but not so much in terms of how precisely the same IoT systems may be plugged in or designed for other industries, e.g., healthcare or smart cities.

The railway focus of the paper restricts the scope of application of the research in diversified settings where the requirements of IoT systems, e.g., data protection and real-time tracking, are rather different. Additionally, the absence of experimental data and implementation scenarios in the real world reduces the applicability of the proposed solutions. Huang et al. (2019) also suggest a secure industrial IoT system by using blockchain, but the paper fails to consider adequately the challenges of implementing blockchain in the healthcare environment or in any other settings of scarce resources. The suggested system can be faced with issues of scalability in massive IoT networks with very high transaction volumes. The paper further does not address regulatory and compliance problems within the medical setup, where confidentiality of sensitive patient information is critical.

Wang et al. (2022) suggest a blockchain-based IoT security consensus mechanism, but their suggestion is not pursued by an investigation of the operation of the system in actual, large-scale IoT networks.

The paper does not consider the computational expense and energy expense of using blockchain technology in constrained IoT devices, which can restrict the deployment of the solution. In addition, the paper does not address the integration of the security mechanisms into deployed IoT infrastructures, for instance, hospital or industrial environments. Dai et al. (2019) describe the employment of AI-driven edge computing and caching for the Internet of Vehicles (IoV) but is likely not directly transferable to other IoT applications, like healthcare, with tighter limitations on real-time processing of data as well as privacy.

The paper fails to give a comprehensive summary of the challenge that comes with deploying AI models onto low-resource edge devices in actual IoT large-scale networks. The study is also not experimentally tested in heterogeneous IoT environments, and hence its results are less applicable. Liu (2021) only takes into consideration multi-access edge computing resource scheduling but not its applicability in its suggested machine learning and optimization on low-resource IoT devices such as healthcare.

Huh and Seo (2019) also suggest a secure industrial IoT system by using blockchain, but the paper fails to consider adequately the challenges of implementing blockchain in the healthcare environment or in any other settings of scarce resources. The suggested system can be faced with issues of scalability in massive IoT networks with very high transaction volumes. The paper further does not address regulatory and compliance problems within the medical setup, where confidentiality of sensitive patient information is critical. Pu (2021) suggest a blockchain-based IoT security consensus mechanism, but their suggestion is not pursued by an investigation of the operation of the system in actual, large-scale IoT networks.

The paper does not consider the computational expense and energy expense of using blockchain technology in constrained IoT devices, which can restrict the deployment of the solution. In addition, the paper does not address the integration of the security mechanisms into deployed IoT infrastructures, for instance, hospital or industrial environments.

Zhang et al. (2021) suggest trust management using blockchain technology in the Internet of Vehicles, but it may not be easily adapted in healthcare IoT networks where data security and privacy issues are more significant. The research does not account for the interoperability of blockchain with other security features adopted in healthcare or industrial IoT networks. Lastly, without empirical validation on heterogeneous IoT environments, the external validity of the result is diminished.

The models advocated in the provided papers try to surpass the shortcomings of the current systems by harnessing new technologies and addressing major issues in IoT and edge computing environments.

For example, Iyapparaja et al. (2022) improve the supply of resources in fog computing with the QTCS model, which improves the level of efficiency in resource management while maintaining scalability in IoT networks. This is an improvement over current models that are susceptible to resource handling in big, dynamic systems. Equally, Lei et al. (2020) tackle the problem of scalability in blockchain for fog computing in their Groupchain model, which they claim will be a more efficient and scalable solution than mainstream public blockchains, being too slow and cumbersome for IoT applications. Through the use of a more scalable blockchain framework, their solution has been engineered to surpass latency and network congestion problems inherent within other blockchains. Ali et al. (2022) improve the detection of DDoS attacks in IoT through developing a threat assessment model using machine learning algorithms.

Dai et al. (2019) describe the employment of AI-driven edge computing and caching for the Internet of Vehicles (IoV) but is likely not directly transferable to other IoT applications, like healthcare, with tighter limitations on real-time processing of data as well as privacy.

The paper fails to give a comprehensive summary of the challenge that comes with deploying AI models onto low-resource edge devices in actual IoT large-scale networks. The study is also not experimentally tested in heterogeneous IoT environments, and hence its results are less applicable. Liu (2021) only takes into consideration multi-access edge computing resource scheduling but not its applicability in its suggested machine learning and optimization on low-resource IoT devices such as healthcare.

Huh and Seo (2019) also suggest a secure industrial IoT system by using blockchain, but the paper fails to consider adequately the challenges of implementing blockchain in the healthcare environment or in any other settings of scarce resources. The suggested system can be faced with issues of scalability in massive IoT networks with very high transaction volumes. The paper further does not address regulatory and compliance problems within the medical setup, where confidentiality of sensitive patient information is critical. Pu (2021) suggest a blockchain-based IoT security consensus mechanism, but their suggestion is not pursued by an investigation of the operation of the system in actual, large-scale IoT networks.

The paper does not consider the computational expense and energy expense of using blockchain technology in constrained IoT devices, which can restrict the deployment of the solution. In addition, the paper does not address the integration of the security mechanisms into deployed IoT infrastructures, for instance, hospital or industrial environments.

Zhang et al. (2021) suggest trust management using blockchain technology in the Internet of Vehicles, but it may not be easily adapted in healthcare IoT networks where data security and privacy issues are more significant. The research does not account for the interoperability of blockchain with other security features adopted in healthcare or industrial IoT networks. Lastly, without empirical validation on heterogeneous IoT environments, the external validity of the result is diminished.

The models advocated in the provided papers try to surpass the shortcomings of the current systems by harnessing new technologies and addressing major issues in IoT and edge computing environments.

For example, Iyapparaja et al. (2022) improve the supply of resources in fog computing with the QTCS model, which improves the level of efficiency in resource management while maintaining scalability in IoT networks. This is an improvement over current models that are susceptible to resource handling in big, dynamic systems. Equally, Lei et al. (2020) tackle the problem of scalability in blockchain for fog computing in their Groupchain model, which they claim will be a more efficient and scalable solution than mainstream public blockchains, being too slow and cumbersome for IoT applications. Through the use of a more scalable blockchain framework, their solution has been engineered to surpass latency and network congestion problems inherent within other blockchains. Ali et al. (2022) improve the detection of DDoS attacks in IoT through developing a threat assessment model using machine learning algorithms.

Their method, unlike the conventional method that fails to identify sophisticated or zero-day attacks sometimes, can potentially improve real-time attack detection capability while remaining affordable. This is a solution to the limitation of existing systems, which have no way of identifying new threats in constrained IoT devices. Parra et al. (2022) offer a deep learning solution for the detection of IoT device cybersecurity attacks that is superior to what can be obtained from conventional rule-based or signature-based security mechanisms, which cannot combat changing threats. Not only does their method enhance detection but also provides a more proactive way of coping with new cybersecurity threats. Fadda et al. (2019) provide communications to microgrids and smart buildings from the perspective of integrating IoT in a manner that provides improved energy management. Their approach is able to address the concerns of security and interoperability of existing systems and provides an improved and secured way of managing smart infrastructure.

MATERIAL AND METHODOLOGY

The bi-stacked ANN health care edge computing framework starts with collecting health care information from various health care sensors like medical IoT sensors and wearables. Locally processing the information through the edge devices eliminates latency and saves bandwidth. The bi-stacked ANN is run on the edge devices, i.e., two neural networks. The lowest layer has raw sensor input and low-level feature extraction, and features are processed to provide good predictions. The second has features and processes to provide good predictions. The training model utilizes historical health care data to detect disease pattern and patient health indicator. Real-time patient data are input and processed using the trained ANN model in real time. Local computation is processed by the edge computing network and provides alarm or feedback in real-time. In the event of events arising from anomalies or anomalies, doctors can be notified by the system. The strategy is effective for quick decision-making and enhanced patient care by using edge-based computing to provide timely interventions. The strategy even reduces dependence on cloud infrastructure and maintains data and privacy.

Material

The health infrastructure combines Safe AI-based edge-distributed ledger support and distinguished features some of which are the most vital included in cooperative function to provide secure and efficient health monitoring.

The system consists of user, wireless network, edge-distributed ledger, trusted agent, healthcare server, and expert system. The patients either recover from some form of generic disease or illness or recover from new rely on a range of implanted and extrinsic sensors to assist them with monitoring their condition. These rely on smart phones and Personal Digital Assistant (PDA) technology as storage and logging units of sensor medical data. In this, there is authorization for PDAs use in an attempt to capture patients' medical history, where data is encrypted for security purposes. The encrypted data is supplied in the form of blocks at intervals to the edge-distributed ledger, thereby providing for unlimited monitoring and decentralized secure retrieval of healthcare data.

Preprocessing

Preprocessing of the health data gathered involves a number of core operations to bring the data to conformity and assure its quality.

All the heterogenous sources' data, i.e., external sensors, implanted sensors, PDAs, and cell phones, are all brought together into a single store called the data warehouse.

Thus, the data conformity from different devices and platforms becomes achievable to process further.

Second, data cleaning is performed where missing values caused by sensor failure or uploading incompleteness are handled using interpolation, imputation, or row removal of duplicate missing values. Outliers are also detected to find and remove or rectify any extremely large or extremely small value through statistical methods such as Z-score or interquartile range (IQR). Redundant data entries, primarily due to double sensor reading or double upload, are also removed to prevent bias. Data is manipulated, i.e., normalization or standardization, in such a way that different sensor data, which could be of different magnitudes (e.g., blood pressure, heart rate, glucose), are standardized into a similar size so that they can be compared. Finally, the data is synchronized to the same time interval such that temporal equivalence of sensor readings and varying collection time among sensors are addressed. Preprocessing in this case makes the dataset standardized, clean, and usable.

Feature Selection

Particle Swarm Optimization-based feature selection is a non-heuristic feature selection method used for selecting the most applicable features of a dataset to make machine learning models more efficient. The algorithm starts with initial population of the particles' initialization, and a particle is a candidate solution with an array of its features as a binary vector in which each bit is a command to include (1) or exclude (0) a feature. There are fixed numbers of particles to exhaustively cover the feature space.

The second is to normalize all particles' fitness on the basis of comparison characteristic, typically by training a machine learning model on chosen features and then applying it to the validation set. The fitness is calculated on the basis of metrics like model accuracy, precision, or recall, which are an estimation of the value of chosen features. Once the fitness is calculated, the particles are updated using the PSO update equations that update the velocity and position of a particle based on the locally best known particle position and the globally best known position to the swarm. In later iterations, the swarm moves to an optimal set of features and thereby maximizes efficiency and performance of the machine learning algorithm.

Bi-Staked Artificial Neural Network

Bi-stacked Artificial Neural Network (ANN) medical edge computing is a promising alternative for edge-based real-time processing and analysis of clinical data. Bi-stacked ANN architecture entails running machine learning models, in our case a bi-stacked ANN, on the edge devices like smartphones, wearable sensors, or medical IoT devices instead of cloud servers. In this configuration, data gathered from multiple healthcare sensors such as heart rate, blood glucose, and ECG monitors are calculated locally in an attempt to reduce latency and bandwidth consumption.

Bi-stacked ANN comprises two neural network stacks that operate in parallel to identify intricate patterns within medical data. The top-level stacks are usually responsible for extracting low-level features from raw sensor data, and the bottom stacks transform these features to precise predictions such as disease diagnosis, patient vital sign tracking, or alerting doctors in the occurrence of anomalies. Based on the deployment of edge computing, this plan facilitates quicker decision-making, improved patient monitoring, and reduced reliance on cloud infrastructure, all of which are enhanced for acute healthcare environments in terms of being quick to act.

EXPERIMENTAL RESULTS

Experimental results demonstrate a proper segregation of the proposed solution, which confirms that it is an effective solution for the above-researched problems. It has been validated by rigorous testing and validation, employing real as well as simulated data sets for achieving reliability and stability. The various performance measures such as accuracy, precision, recall, and processing time were employed for comparing the overall model performance. Comparative evaluation with traditional processes indicates remarkable improvements in processing time, resource consumption, and system flexibility. Results also indicate the ability of the system designed to handle complex situations with less latency and enhanced security.

Statistical verification techniques were also applied for making results reproducible and consistent. The subsequent subsections include detailed exploration of experimental results using graphical plots, quantitative studies, and extensive discussions. Table 1 provides a summary of various methods of healthcare data collection in IoT systems.It categorizes data collection as continuous, snapshot, event-based, and cloud-based, depending on the type of data and the frequency of collection. Individualized data collection and remote diagnostics are some of the methods that focus on personalized healthcare based on individual requirements. The table further encompasses details on the devices applied to each method of collection, such as wearables, health care devices, and environmental sensors. The table serves as a reference point in order to recognize where the data is being collected, processed, and analyzed in the health care IoT system.

Table 1. Model performance comparison

Model Name	Accuracy (%)	Precision (%)	Recall (%)	F1-Score (%)	AUC Score (%)
CNN (Convolutional Neural Network)	92.5	89.6	91.2	90.4	95.3
Bi-STACKED ANN	94.3	92.1	93.5	92.8	96.1
Random Forest	88.7	85.3	86.4	85.8	91.4
Support Vector Machine	91.2	89.2	90.5	89.8	94.0
KNN (K-Nearest Neighbors)	89.9	87.5	89.0	88.2	92.5
Decision Tree	84.5	83.2	82.1	82.6	88.0
Logistic Regression	87.1	85.0	86.3	85.6	90.1
LSTM (Long Short-Term Memory)	93.4	91.9	92.0	91.9	94.8
Gradient Boosting	90.2	88.4	89.1	88.7	93.2
Naive Bayes	85.6	84.1	83.7	83.9	89.3

Table 2 provides various methods of healthcare data collection in IoT systems.It categorizes data collection as continuous, snapshot, event-based, and cloud-based, depending on the type of data and the frequency of collection. Individualized data collection and remote diagnostics are some of the methods that focus on personalized healthcare based on individual requirements. The table further encompasses details on the devices applied to each method of collection, such as wearables, health care devices, and environmental sensors. The table serves as a reference point in order to recognize where the data is being collected, processed, and analyzed in the health care IoT system.

Table 2. IoT healthcare data types

Sensor Type	Data Collected	Sample Rate (Hz)	Data Format	Storage Medium	Purpose
ECG (Electrocardiogram)	Heart rate, ECG waveforms	100	Raw signals	Cloud/Local	Heart disease diagnosis
Glucose Monitor	Blood glucose levels	5	Numeric	Edge Device	Diabetes management
Oximeter	Blood oxygen saturation	1	Numeric	Cloud	Respiratory monitoring
Thermometer	Body temperature	1	Numeric	Edge Device	Fever detection
Smartwatch	Activity level, heart rate	50	Numeric/ Raw	Cloud	Fitness tracking
Pulse Oximeter	Pulse rate, oxygen levels	2	Numeric	Cloud/Local	Emergency alerts
Blood Pressure Monitor	Systolic/Diastolic pressure	1	Numeric	Cloud/Local	Hypertension monitoring
Smart Band	Sleep patterns, heart rate	10	Numeric	Cloud/Local	Sleep quality tracking
Respiratory Monitor	Respiratory rate	2	Numeric	Edge Device	Respiratory disorder diagnosis
Temperature Sensor	Skin temperature	1	Numeric	Edge Device	Fever detection

Table 3 depicts different algorithms applied in edge computing for effectively processing health care data.These algorithms, including K-means clustering, decision tree, convolutional neural network, and reinforcement learning, are employed to categorize, predict, and examine patient data. The table presents the input types, model types, and performance measures for the algorithms. The table also addresses the computational complexity of the models so that the developers can see which models suit their edge devices the best. The following table helps to improve data models for real-time, personalized health care between health care providers and IoT technology developers.

Table 3. Healthcare IoT edge device specifications

Device Name	Processor	RAM (GB)	Storage (GB)	Connectivity	Power Consumption (W)
Raspberry Pi 4	ARM Cortex-A72	4	32	Wi-Fi, Bluetooth	3.5
NVIDIA Jetson Nano	Quad-core ARM Cortex-A57	4	16	Wi-Fi, Ethernet	10
Intel NUC	Intel i5	8	128	Wi-Fi, Ethernet	15
Arduino MKR Zero	ARM Cortex-M0+	0.256	16	Wi-Fi, Bluetooth	0.7
BeagleBone Black	ARM Cortex-A8	0.5	4	Ethernet	5
Google Coral	Edge TPU	1	8	Wi-Fi, Bluetooth	2.5
Odroid C4	ARM Cortex-A55	4	32	Ethernet, Wi-Fi	10
Banana Pi M2 Pro	ARM Cortex-A7	1	8	Wi-Fi, Ethernet	5
Pine64 RockPro64	ARM Cortex-A72	4	64	Wi-Fi, Ethernet	15
ASUS Tinker Board	ARM Cortex-A17	2	16	Wi-Fi, Ethernet	6

Table 4 provides healthcare data collection in IoT systems.It categorizes data collection as continuous, snapshot, event-based, and cloud-based, depending on the type of data and the frequency of collection. Individualized data collection and remote diagnostics are some of the methods that focus on personalized healthcare based on individual requirements. The table further encompasses details on the devices applied to each method of collection, such as wearables, health care devices, and environmental sensors. The table serves as a reference point in order to recognize where the data is being collected, processed, and analyzed in the health care IoT system.

Table 4. Healthcare edge computing benefits

Benefit	Description	Impact Area	Implementation Level	Scalability	Security Level
Reduced Latency	Local data processing for faster decision-making	Patient monitoring	High	High	High
Data Privacy and Security	Local storage minimizes exposure to external threats	Data privacy	Medium	High	Very High
Real-time Analytics	Enables real-time diagnosis and monitoring	Disease detection	High	High	Medium
Bandwidth Optimization	Reduces data transmission to cloud, saving bandwidth	Network efficiency	High	Medium	Low
Cost Efficiency	Minimizes cloud storage and computational costs	Healthcare systems	Medium	High	Low
Improved Patient Care	Faster response to critical events and diseases	Emergency services	High	High	High
System Reliability	Decentralized architecture ensures consistent performance	System uptime	Very High	High	High
Scalability and Flexibility	Easily adapts to growing healthcare needs	Hospital infrastructure	High	Very High	Medium
Energy Efficiency	Edge devices designed for low power consumption	Sustainability	High	Medium	Low
Reduced Cloud Dependency	Less reliance on cloud-based services	Cloud infrastructure	Medium	High	Medium

Table 5 depicts different algorithms applied in edge computing for effectively processing health care data.These algorithms, including K-means clustering, decision tree, convolutional neural network, and reinforcement learning, are employed to categorize, predict, and examine patient data. The table presents the input types, model types, and performance measures for the algorithms. The table also addresses the computational complexity of the models so that the developers can see which models suit their edge devices the best. The following table helps to improve data models for real-time, personalized health care between health care providers and IoT technology developers.

Table 5. Types of healthcare diseases monitored

Disease Type	Monitoring Method	Sensors Used	Early Detection Accuracy	Treatment Recommendations	Monitoring Frequency
Cardiovascular Disease	ECG, Blood pressure	ECG, Pulse Oximeter	92%	Medication, lifestyle change	Continuous
Diabetes	Glucose levels	Glucose monitor	90%	Insulin, diet management	Continuous
Respiratory Issues	Oxygen saturation	Pulse Oximeter	89%	Oxygen therapy, medications	Continuous
Hypertension	Blood pressure	Blood pressure monitor	94%	Medication, exercise	Hourly
Sleep Apnea	Sleep patterns	Smartwatch, Oximeter	85%	CPAP therapy	Nightly
Stroke	ECG, Oxygen levels	ECG, Pulse Oximeter	88%	Immediate hospitalization	As needed
Asthma	Respiratory rate	Respiratory monitor	80%	Inhalers, anti-inflammatory	Continuous
Sepsis	Body temperature	Thermometer	91%	Antibiotics, emergency care	Hourly
COVID-19	Oxygen levels, temperature	Pulse Oximeter, Thermometer	92%	Quarantine, medication	Hourly
Cancer	Activity, vitals	Smartwatch, ECG	87%	Chemo, radiation therapy	Bi-weekly

Table 6 provides a summary of various methods of healthcare data collection in IoT systems.It categorizes data collection as continuous, snapshot, event-based, and cloud-based, depending on the type of data and the frequency of collection. Individualized data collection and remote diagnostics are some of the methods that focus on personalized healthcare based on individual requirements. The table further encompasses details on the devices applied to each method of collection, such as wearables, health care devices, and environmental sensors. The table serves as a reference point in order to recognize where the data is being collected, processed, and analyzed in the health care IoT system.

Table 6. Healthcare edge computing use cases

Use Case	Device Type	Sensor Type	Application Focus	Benefits	Key Feature
Chronic Disease Management	Wearable Devices	ECG, Blood Pressure	Continuous monitoring	Early intervention	Real-time feedback
Emergency Alerts	Mobile Phones, Wearables	Pulse Oximeter	Emergency situations	Timely notifications	Rapid alert system
Smart Hospitals	Edge Servers	Multiple Sensors	Patient care management	Improved patient outcomes	Data aggregation
Fitness Tracking	Smartwatches	Activity Tracker	Fitness, Health analysis	Motivation, health insights	Personalized feedback
Remote Diagnostics	Edge Devices, Smartphones	Glucose Monitor	Telemedicine	Cost-effective diagnostics	Low-latency analysis
Geriatric Monitoring	IoT Sensors, Wearables	ECG, Activity Monitor	Elderly care	Improved independence	Autonomous monitoring
Disease Prediction	Mobile Devices	Pulse, ECG, Temperature	Preventative healthcare	Early disease detection	Predictive analytics
Rehabilitation	Edge Devices	Activity Sensors	Post-surgery monitoring	Optimized recovery	Continuous monitoring
Personal Health Assistant	Smartphones, PDAs	Blood Pressure, Heart Rate	Lifestyle tracking	Health improvement	Personalized guidance
Smart Medication	Edge Devices	Smart Pill Bottles	Medication management	Reduced human error	Real-time tracking

Table 7 depicts different algorithms applied in edge computing for effectively processing health care data.These algorithms, including K-means clustering, decision tree, convolutional neural network, and reinforcement learning, are employed to categorize, predict, and examine patient data. The table presents the input types, model types, and performance measures for the algorithms. The table also addresses the computational complexity of the models so that the developers can see which models suit their edge devices the best. The following table helps to improve data models for real-time, personalized health care between health care providers and IoT technology developers.

Table 7. Key challenges in healthcare edge computing

Challenge	Description	Impact on Healthcare	Severity	Solution Approach	Implementation Time
Data Privacy	Protecting patient data from breaches	Data security	High	Encryption, Blockchain	Long
Latency	Minimizing delays in processing and decision-making	Real-time diagnostics	Medium	Edge computing, Parallel processing	Medium
Data Quality	Ensuring sensor accuracy and consistency	Diagnosis reliability	High	Sensor calibration	Medium
Integration	Integrating devices and systems into existing workflows	System compatibility	High	Standardization	Long
Power Consumption	Limiting energy usage of edge devices	Battery life	Medium	Low-power designs	Short
Network Connectivity	Ensuring stable communication between devices	Continuous monitoring	Medium	Wi-Fi, 5G integration	Medium
Scalability	Expanding edge networks for larger data sets	System expansion	High	Modular infrastructure	Long
Regulatory Compliance	Meeting healthcare regulations (HIPAA, GDPR)	Legal concerns	High	Compliance audits	Long
Real-Time Processing	Real-time data processing challenges	Immediate healthcare response	Medium	Optimized algorithms	Medium
Data Overload	Handling large volumes of sensor data	Data processing limits	High	Data compression, Filtering	Medium

Table 8 gives various methods of healthcare data collection in IoT systems.It categorizes data collection as continuous, snapshot, event-based, and cloud-based, depending on the type of data and the frequency of collection. Individualized data collection and remote diagnostics are some of the methods that focus on personalized healthcare based on individual requirements. The table further encompasses details on the devices applied to each method of collection, such as wearables, health care devices, and environmental sensors. The table serves as a reference point in order to recognize where the data is being collected, processed, and analyzed in the health care IoT system.

Table 8. IoT edge healthcare security features

Security Feature	Description	Device Level	Protocol	Implementation Time	Impact Level
End-to-End Encryption	Protecting data during transmission	All devices	TLS, SSL	Short	Very High
Secure Boot	Ensuring devices boot from trusted firmware	Edge Devices	TPM, Secure Boot	Medium	High
Data Anonymization	Removing personal identifiers from medical data	Cloud, Edge Devices	GDPR, HIPAA	Medium	Medium
Blockchain Integration	Decentralized data storage and validation	Edge Devices, Cloud	Blockchain	Long	High
Multi-Factor Authentication	Ensuring secure access to healthcare platforms	All devices	OTP, Biometrics	Medium	Very High
Biometric Authentication	Using facial or fingerprint recognition to secure access	Mobile Devices	Biometric APIs	Medium	High
Secure Communication	Ensuring safe communication between edge and cloud	Network Devices	VPN, SSL	Medium	High
Intrusion Detection	Detecting unauthorized access attempts	Edge Devices	IDS	Medium	High
Real-time Monitoring	Continuously tracking system activity for vulnerabilities	Edge Devices, Cloud	SNMP, NetFlow	Medium	High
Role-based Access	Limiting access based on user roles and responsibilities	Cloud, Server	RBAC	Medium	High

Table 9 provides a summary of various methods of healthcare data collection in IoT systems.It categorizes data collection as continuous, snapshot, event-based, and cloud-based, depending on the type of data and the frequency of collection. Individualized data collection and remote diagnostics are some of the methods that focus on personalized healthcare based on individual requirements. The table further encompasses details on the devices applied to each method of collection, such as wearables, health care devices, and environmental sensors. The table serves as a reference point in order to recognize where the data is being collected, processed, and analyzed in the health care IoT systems.

Table 9. Healthcare data collection techniques

Technique	Description	Data Type	Devices Involved	Frequency	Data Format
Continuous Monitoring	Ongoing collection of health metrics	Vital signs, activity	Wearables, sensors	Continuous	Numeric/ Raw
Snapshot Collection	Data collected at specific intervals for analysis	Blood pressure, glucose levels	Medical devices, sensors	Hourly/ Weekly	Numeric
Real-time Alerts	Immediate data transmission upon reaching a predefined threshold	Heart rate, temperature	Smartwatches, PDAs	As needed	Numeric
Remote Diagnostics	Collecting data for analysis without patient presence	ECG, Oximeter	Mobile phones, wearables	Bi-weekly	Raw signals
Cloud-based Collection	Centralized data aggregation for analysis	Multiple parameters	IoT devices, sensors	Continuous	Cloud-based
Context-Aware Data	Collecting data based on situational context (e.g., activity type)	Activity, heart rate	Smart bands, phones	Continuous	Numeric
Event-based Collection	Data collection triggered by specific events (e.g., motion detection)	Oxygen levels, heart rate	Wearables, smart bands	As needed	Numeric
Batch Processing	Collecting data over a period, then analyzing in bulk	Sleep patterns, activity	Wearables, devices	Daily/Weekly	Aggregated
Personalized Data	Gathering user-specific metrics for tailored care	Blood sugar, heart rate	Glucose monitors, ECG	Continuous	Numeric
Environmental Data	Collecting environmental data affecting health conditions	Temperature, humidity	Environmental sensors	Continuous	Numeric

Table 10 depicts different algorithms applied in edge computing for effectively processing health care data.These algorithms, including K-means clustering, decision tree, convolutional neural network, and reinforcement learning, are employed to categorize, predict, and examine patient data. The table presents the input types, model types, and performance measures for the algorithms. The table also addresses the computational complexity of the models so that the developers can see which models suit their edge devices the best. The following table helps to improve data models for real-time, personalized health care between health care providers and IoT technology developers.

Table 10. Edge computing algorithms for healthcare

Algorithm	Purpose	Input Type	Model Type	Performance Metrics	Computational Complexity
K-means Clustering	Grouping similar medical data points	Vital signs, health records	Unsupervised	Accuracy, Speed	Medium
Decision Trees	Predicting patient health conditions	Patient data	Supervised	Accuracy, Interpretability	Medium
Convolutional Neural Networks	Image recognition for medical images	Medical images	Deep Learning	Accuracy, Recall	High
SVM (Support Vector Machine)	Classifying disease conditions	Medical features	Supervised	Precision, Recall	High
Random Forest	Disease classification and prediction	Patient history, vital signs	Ensemble	Accuracy, F1-Score	Medium
KNN (K-Nearest Neighbors)	Disease detection based on similarity	Sensor data	Instance-based	Accuracy, Sensitivity	Low
Naive Bayes	Health risk prediction based on probabilistic models	Demographic data, health records	Probabilistic	Precision, Recall	Low
LSTM (Long Short-Term Memory)	Time-series prediction for health monitoring	Sensor data	Deep Learning	Precision, AUC	High
Gradient Boosting	Predicting patient outcomes based on multiple features	Multi-modal data	Ensemble	Accuracy, F1-Score	High
Reinforcement Learning	Personalized treatment recommendation	Patient data	RL Model	Reward, Convergence	High

CONCLUSION

Bi-stacked ANN-based healthcare edge computing represents a novel means of real-time health monitoring and decision-making. Edge device processing minimizes latency in data transfer by considerable orders, thus faster responses, and improved quality healthcare provision. Bi-stacked ANN model improves prediction quality on disease identification and patient vital sign monitoring, where the health care providers are made capable of administering required interventions at appropriate times. Edge computing enhances the privacy and security of the data by reducing its reliance on cloud centers, as well as increasing bandwidth optimization. With ongoing technology growth in the health sector, the use of edge computing and machine learning models like bi-stacked ANNs has unimaginable potential to revolutionize patient care, reduce the cost of healthcare, and create a better, secure healthcare system.

REFERENCES

Ali, M. H., Jaber, M. M., Abd, S. K., Rehman, A., Awan, M. J., Damaševičius, R., & Bahaj, S. A. (2022). Threat analysis and distributed denial of service (DDoS) attack recognition in the Internet of Things (IoT). *Electronics (Basel), 11*(3), 494. DOI: 10.3390/electronics11030494

Bovenzi, G., Aceto, G., Ciuonzo, D., Persico, V., & Pescapé, A. (2020). A hierarchical hybrid intrusion detection approach in IoT scenarios. In *2020 IEEE Global Communications Conference (GLOBECOM)* (pp. 1–6). IEEE. DOI: 10.1109/GLOBECOM42002.2020.9348167

Dai, Y., Xu, D., Maharjan, S., Qiao, G., & Zhang, Y. (2019). Artificial intelligence empowered edge computing and caching for Internet of Vehicles. *IEEE Wireless Communications, 26*(3), 12–18. DOI: 10.1109/MWC.2019.1800411

Fadda, G., Fadda, M., Ghiani, E., & Pilloni, V. (2019). *Communications and Internet of Things for microgrids, smart buildings, and homes*. Elsevier Inc., DOI: 10.1016/B978-0-12-817774-7.00009-0

Hanafizadeh, P., & Amin, M. G. (2022). *The transformative potential of banking service domains with the emergence of FinTechs*. Palgrave Macmillan., DOI: 10.1007/978-3-030-99584-3

Hartmann, M., Hashmi, U. S., & Imran, A. (2022). Edge computing in smart health care systems: Review, challenges, and research directions. *Transactions on Emerging Telecommunications Technologies, 33*(3), e3710. DOI: 10.1002/ett.3710

Hrovatin, N., Tošić, A., Mrissa, M., & Kavšek, B. (2022). Privacy-preserving data mining on blockchain-based WSNs. *Applied Sciences (Basel, Switzerland), 12*(11), 5646. DOI: 10.3390/app12115646

Huang, J., Kong, L., Chen, G., Wu, M. Y., Liu, X., & Zeng, P. (2019). Towards secure industrial IoT: Blockchain system with credit-based consensus mechanism. *IEEE Transactions on Industrial Informatics, 15*(6), 3680–3689. DOI: 10.1109/TII.2019.2903342

Huang, J., Kong, L., Dai, H. N., Ding, W., Cheng, L., Chen, G., Jin, X., & Zeng, P. (2020). Blockchain-based mobile crowd sensing in industrial systems. *IEEE Transactions on Industrial Informatics, 16*(10), 6553–6563. DOI: 10.1109/TII.2019.2963728

Huh, J. H., & Seo, Y. S. (2019). Understanding edge computing: Engineering evolution with artificial intelligence. *IEEE Access : Practical Innovations, Open Solutions, 7*, 164229–164245. DOI: 10.1109/ACCESS.2019.2945338

Iyapparaja, M., Alshammari, N. K., Kumar, M. S., Krishnan, S. S. R., & Chowdhary, C. L. (2022). Efficient resource allocation in fog computing using QTCS model. *Computers, Materials & Continua, 70*(2), 2225–2239. DOI: 10.32604/cmc.2022.015707

Jo, O., Kim, Y. K., & Kim, J. (2018). Internet of Things for smart railway: Feasibility and applications. *IEEE Internet of Things Journal, 5*(2), 482–490. DOI: 10.1109/JIOT.2017.2749401

Khan, M. A., Khan, M. A., Jan, S. U., Ahmad, J., Jamal, S. S., Shah, A. A., Pitropakis, N., & Buchanan, W. J. (2021). A deep learning-based intrusion detection system for MQTT enabled IoT. *Sensors (Basel), 21*(21), 7016. DOI: 10.3390/s21217016 PMID: 34770322

Lei, K., Du, M., Huang, J., & Jin, T. (2020). Groupchain: Towards a scalable public blockchain in fog computing of IoT services computing. *IEEE Transactions on Services Computing, 13*(2), 252–262. DOI: 10.1109/TSC.2019.2949801

Liu, X. (2021). Resource allocation in multi-access edge computing: Optimization and machine learning. In 2021 IEEE 12th Annual Information Technology, Electronics and Mobile Communication Conference (IEMCON) (pp. 365–370). IEEE. DOI: 10.1109/IEMCON53756.2021.9623176

Mir, U., Abbasi, U., Mir, T., Kanwal, S., & Alamri, S. (2021). Energy management in smart buildings and homes: Current approaches, a hypothetical solution, and open issues and challenges. *IEEE Access : Practical Innovations, Open Solutions, 9*, 94132–94148. DOI: 10.1109/ACCESS.2021.3092304

Parra, J. A., Gutiérrez, S. A., & Branch, J. W. (2022). A method based on deep learning for the detection and characterization of cybersecurity incidents in Internet of Things devices. arXiv. https://doi.org//arXiv.2203.00608DOI: 10.48550

Pu, C. (2021). A novel blockchain-based trust management scheme for vehicular networks. In *2021 Wireless Telecommunications Symposium (WTS)* (pp. 1–6). IEEE. DOI: 10.1109/WTS51064.2021.9433711

Quy, V. K., Van Hau, N., Van Anh, D., Quy, N. M., Ban, N. T., Lanza, S., Randazzo, G., & Muzirafuti, A. (2022). IoT-enabled smart agriculture: Architecture, applications, and challenges. *Applied Sciences (Basel, Switzerland), 12*(7), 3396. DOI: 10.3390/app12073396

Ray, P. P. (2017). Internet of things for smart agriculture: Technologies, practices and future direction. *Journal of Ambient Intelligence and Smart Environments, 9*(4), 395–420. DOI: 10.3233/AIS-170440

Shahzadi, R., Ferzund, J., Tausif, M., & Asif, M. (2016). Internet of Things based expert system for smart agriculture. *International Journal of Advanced Computer Science and Applications*, *7*(3), 341–350. DOI: 10.14569/IJACSA.2016.070947

Singh, A. K., Verma, K., & Raj, M. (2021). IoT based smart agriculture system. In 2021 5th International Conference on Information Systems and Computer Networks (ISCON) (pp. 1–5). IEEE. DOI: 10.1109/ISCON52037.2021.9702478

Wang, C., Tan, X., Yao, C., Gu, F., Shi, F., & Cao, H. (2022). Trusted blockchain-driven IoT security consensus mechanism. *Sustainability (Basel)*, *14*(9), 5200. DOI: 10.3390/su14095200

Zhang, H., Liu, J., Zhao, H., Wang, P., & Kato, N. (2021). Blockchain-based trust management for Internet of Vehicles. *IEEE Transactions on Emerging Topics in Computing*, *9*(3), 1397–1409. DOI: 10.1109/TETC.2020.3033532

Zhong, G., Xiong, K., Zhong, Z., & Ai, B. (2021). Internet of things for high-speed railways. *Intelligent and Converged Networks*, *2*(2), 115–132. DOI: 10.23919/ICN.2021.0005

Chapter 7
The Edge Revolution Transitioning From Cloud-First to Edge-First Methodologies

Rinki Singh
https://orcid.org/0000-0003-0823-156X
Satyug Darshan Institute of Engineering and Technology, India

ABSTRACT

The framework of distributed edge computing is the core of the replacement of centralized cloud computing infrastructure regarding the digital transformation. This chapter reviews the shift of strategies to be cloud-first to edge-first and the strategic, technological and financial reasons behind it. This chapter forms the basis on how enterprises can leverage edge computing to have competitive advantage in a more data-driven economy by carefully reviewing the latest trends in the market, technology capabilities and business needs. It provides a checklist of the steps companies could take to implement scalable and smart edge solutions by pointing out to practical use cases, architecture paradigms and referring to the future perspectives.

1. INTRODUCTION

The past decade had been under the wings of cloud computing as companies monetized their information, applications, and infrastructure to centralized cloud models (Armbrust et al., 2020). It has however been stipulated that the barriers of exclusively cloud-centric systems have been evident due to the explosive growth in businesses through data generation and the penetration of Internet of Things

DOI: 10.4018/979-8-3373-1147-0.ch007

(IoT) devices, and the increased need of real time processing services. This chapter discusses the emergence of edge computing as both an addition to and, often, an improvement on typical cloud computing schemes. The edge revolution is not only a technological change but a basic reconsideration of the approach to data and data processing within businesses and their attitude to it. The cons of cloud-first approaches become more evident because organizations are eager to take advantage of AI, machine learning, and real-time analytics capabilities. The current issues with computing infrastructure are latency, bandwidth limitations, privacy, and regulatory demands prompting organizations to reconsider their computing infrastructures. It is a strategic move that will enable firms to achieve hitherto unachievable rates of responsiveness, efficiency, and innovation; it is not merely a matter of bringing additional computational resources collocated with data sources (Bonomi et al., 2022). Moving toward a distributed intelligence model, the edge-first approach transforms the way companies approach digital infrastructure radically by abandoning a centralized processing model.

1.1 The Cloud Computing Era: Achievements and Limitations

The paradigm of cloud computing revolutionized access to resources used in carrying out computations by democratization since it allows organizations of different sizes to harness enterprise-scale infrastructure without even carrying out big capital investments (Buyya et al., 2019). The cloud-first approach has been the default means of conducting digital transformation efforts because of its unequaled scalability, price-efficiency, and flexibility (Mell & Grance, 2021). The use of cloud computing accelerated the process of digital innovation in the business world enabling it to create Platform-as-a-Service (PaaS) solutions, Infrastructure-as-a-Service (IaaS) services, and Software-as-a-Service (SaaS) applications (Rittinghouse & Ransome, 2020). The evaluation of cloud computing adaptation is also tabulated in table 1 and their limitation across industries are represented in table 2. Applications could be quickly deployed, resources could be scaled as needed, and organizations could concentrate on their core business operations rather than infrastructure administration. The cloud-first strategy has many benefits, but it has also been shown to have certain serious drawbacks that make it ineffective in contemporary commercial settings (Hassan et al., 2021). The main limitations consist of:

a) **Latency Issues:** Because of the physical distance between consumers and data centers, cloud computing inevitably introduces latency. Even milliseconds of delay can have major operational and financial repercussions for applications that need real-time processing, like financial trading systems, industrial automation, and driverless cars (Luo et al., 2021).

Bandwidth Restrictions: The exponential rise in data generation, especially from multimedia apps and Internet of Things devices, has led to previously unheard-of bandwidth requirements (Chen et al., 2020). Sending massive amounts of data to centralized cloud platforms might cause expensive data transfer fees and overload network infrastructure.

Table 1. Evolution of cloud computing adoption (2010-2024)

Year	Global Cloud Adoption Rate (%)	Primary Drivers	Key Limitations Identified
2010	15%	Cost reduction, Scalability	Security concerns, Limited services
2012	28%	DevOps adoption, Mobile growth	Vendor lock-in, Compliance issues
2014	42%	Big Data analytics, SaaS expansion	Latency, Bandwidth constraints
2016	58%	Digital transformation, AI/ML	Privacy regulations, Performance
2018	71%	Microservices, Container adoption	Edge requirements, Real-time needs
2020	83%	Remote work, Pandemic response	IoT limitations, Latency issues
2022	89%	Hybrid strategies, Edge integration	Data sovereignty, Cost optimization
2024	94%	Edge-cloud convergence	Real-time processing demands

b) **Privacy and Security Issues:** Centralized cloud storage presents serious privacy and security issues, especially for sectors like government, healthcare, and finance that handle sensitive data (Chen et al., 2021). Local data processing and storage are frequently required by data sovereignty laws and compliance requirements.

c) **Dependencies on Connectivity:** Reliable internet connectivity is a prerequisite for cloud-first methods; however, this may not be the case in rural areas (Kumar et al., 2020), mobile settings, or during network disruptions. Customer experience and corporate operations may be significantly impacted by this dependence.

d) **Cost Implications:** Although cloud computing is more affordable for many applications, data-intensive operations may find the costs of data processing, storage, and transfer to be unaffordable. Cloud solutions may be more costly than dedicated infrastructure for businesses with regular, high-volume computing needs.

Table 2. Comparative analysis of cloud-first limitations across industries

Industry	Primary Limitation	Impact Severity (1-5)	Business Consequence	Edge Solution Benefit
Manufacturing	Latency	5	Production delays, Quality issues	Real-time process control
Healthcare	Privacy/Security	5	Compliance violations, Trust loss	Local data processing
Financial Services	Latency	5	Trading losses, Regulatory issues	Microsecond response times
Retail	Bandwidth	4	Poor customer experience	Local analytics
Transportation	Connectivity	4	Safety risks, Operational issues	Autonomous operation
Energy	Reliability	4	Grid instability, Outages	Distributed control
Gaming/ Entertainment	Latency	4	User dissatisfaction	Ultra-low latency
Agriculture	Connectivity	3	Monitoring gaps, Inefficiency	Offline operation

Rating Scale: 1 = Minimal Impact, 5 = Critical Impact

1.2 The Emergence of Edge Computing

Edge computing is a distributed computing paradigm that improves response times and conserves bandwidth by bringing processing and data storage closer to the point of demand. Instead of having all the resources served by a remote big data center as depicted in cloud computing, edge computing spreads processing capability to a pool of edge devices, gateways, and micro data centers located at and near where the data is produced (Dolui & Datta, 2021).

National Institute of Standards and Technology (NIST) defines edge computing as follows: edge computing is a distributed computing platform that puts enterprise applications near the sources of data (IoT devices/ local edge power boxes). This definition plays host to many deployment patterns, including regional edge data centers serving specific geographical regions to edge devices preventing processing capability.

1.3 The Edge Computing Ecosystem

The edge computing ecosystem consists of multiple layers and components used to offer distributed computing capabilities is depicted in table 3.

a) **Device Edge:** The layer is composed of sensors, cellphones, Internet of Things devices as well as other endpoint devices that generate data but may not process that data effectively (Abbas et al., 2021). These devices commonly perform the basic tasks of data collection and initial processing.
b) **Infrastructure Edge:** Infrastructure edge layer consists of edge servers, gateways and mini data center strategically located in key places e.g- industrial or cell towers. Such resources combine powerful networking, storage and processing power.
    a) **Network Edge:** This layer encompasses the networking that is interconnected between cloud-based resources, total networking between the edge devices, and other devices with connection to cloud resources environments (Pahl et al., 2021). A number of communication technologies such as Wi-Fi networks and 5G networks make possible low-latency connectivity.
c) **Application Edge:** It entails the platforms, services, and software programs that run on edge infrastructure. There are both cloud applications customized to be deployed to the edge along with edge-native ones.

1.4 Key Characteristics of Edge Computing

Porambage et al. (2021) indicate that edge computing has a few differences with ordinary cloud computing models.

a) **Proximity:** Edge computing reduces the amount of latency and distance between the sources of information and also the location where the processing capabilities are placed.
b) **Distribution:** Edge computing deploys resources over numerous small data centers and facilities rather than concentrating services and facilities in a small quantity of large data centers.
c) **Resource constraints:** The computational, storage and power resources of the edge devices tend to be constrained compared to cloud data centers, so resource use has to be efficient.
d) **Autonomy:** Edge systems frequently need to work in isolation from receiving commands like local decisions and with constantly evolving situations without all-time connection to the cloud resources.
e) **Heterogeneity:** The edge typically covers a broad variety of diverse hardware platforms, operating systems and networking technologies, where in such instances they need to be somewhat flexible and adaptive solutions.

Table 3. Edge computing layer characteristics and capabilities

Layer	Computing Power	Storage Capacity	Latency	Autonomy Level	Primary Functions
Cloud Layer	Very High	Unlimited	50-200ms	Centralized	Training, Analytics, Backup
Network Edge	High	High	10-50ms	Semi-autonomous	Regional processing, Caching
Infrastructure Edge	Medium	Medium	1-10ms	Autonomous	Local analytics, Control
Device Edge	Low-Medium	Limited	<1ms	Fully autonomous	Data collection, Basic processing

2. DRIVERS OF THE EDGE REVOLUTION

The edge revolution is fueled by the following drivers:

2.1 Technological Drivers

Mahmud et al. (2021) explained that several technical innovations have merged to contribute to making web 3.0. Edge computing is not only possible but also more needed.

a) **5G Networks:** The 5G wireless network implementation provides astronomically low latency and high Edge computing applications Bandwidth requirements (Li et al., 2021). The network-slicing capability of 5G enables the creation of small cells inside their buildings. development of dedicated network resources in specific applications of edges.
b) **Artificial Intelligence and Learning:** The increasing amount of AI and learning: The combination of growing numbers of AI learning and inference. The ML application requires huge computational resources. Not like the delay which comes using cloud computing, edge AI enables making decisions in real-time.
c) **Internet of Things (IoT):** The agreement of IoT devices is growing at a huge rate, and this means that there is a massive upcoming problem. quantities of data that are far too large to transmit to centralized cloud infrastructure (Al-Fuqaha et al., 2021). The information coming to IoT can be prepared and evaluated locally owing to edge computing.
d) **Microservices with containerization:** Microservices designs, and container technologies make it easier to deploy and maintain applications in dispersed edge.

2.2 Business Drivers

Due to strong commercial needs, organizations are embracing edge computing methods more and more.

a) **Making Decisions in Real Time:** Being able to make decisions quickly might provide you a big competitive edge in the fast-paced corporate world of today (Satyanarayanan et al., 2021). Edge computing makes instant processing and a response to changing situations possible.
b) **Improvement of Customer Experience:** In the modern world, customer experience is significantly related to the reduction of latency and the amplification of responsiveness (Beck et al., 2021). The applications such as augmented reality, virtual reality and interactive gaming all require ultra-low latency so that they can provide perfect user experience.
c) **Optimization of operations:** Edge computing can enhance operations by local automation, reducing bandwidth costs, and reducing dependency on cloud connectivity.
d) **Regulatory Compliance:** Local processing and storage of data are often requested by privacy regulations such as CCPA and GDPR. As these requirements insist on operational efficiency, edge computing can help businesses to achieve them without compromising their work processes.
e) **Cost Optimization:** Edge computing has the potential to reduce operation costs imposed on the company when data transfer rates or utilize resources by reducing data transfer charges and gaining access to full capacity utilization.

2.3 Market Drivers

Edge-first strategies have led to transformational changes in the approach digital infrastructure and application development of organizations (Cao et al., 2021). Table 4 indicates that there are many industries engaged in edge computing, i.e., healthcare, manufacturing, and automotive sectors.

a) **Edge-first:** Edge-first strategies begin by assuming that most processing should occur as near to the data source as is possible, and that cloud resources should be deployed only when necessary to fulfill specific purposes, such as centralized analytics, backup, and long-term storage (Jararweh et al., 2021). This is compared to cloud-first where edge computing is an afterthought where everything is centralized. A number of principles are part of an edge-first approach.
b) **Design of distributed:** By spreading processing power across multiple edge sites, applications and infrastructure are designed to be native distributed domain.

c) **Local Processing Priority:** Data that is strictly necessary is provided to the centralized sites; all the rest of the data process and analysis are done locally in a feasible manner.
d) **Autonomous Operation:** Edge systems are designed to operate independently and make decisions without direct access to centralized resources. Dynamic allocation and management of resources in the area of the local needs and circumstances is known as adaptive resource management.
e) **Federated Learning and Intelligence:** Machine learning models are updated and trained on distributed edge settings without revealing data or losing their confidentiality and privacy.

Table 4. Edge computing market growth drivers by sector (2021-2025)

Sector	Market Value 2021 ($B)	Projected 2025 ($B)	CAGR (%)	Key Applications
Manufacturing	12.3	28.7	23.5%	Industry 4.0, Predictive maintenance
Healthcare	8.9	22.4	26.1%	Remote monitoring, medical imaging
Retail	6.2	18.9	32.1%	Personalization, Inventory management
Transportation	7.8	19.3	25.4%	Autonomous vehicles, Fleet management
Energy	5.4	14.2	27.3%	Smart grid, Renewable integration
Telecommunications	11.7	24.8	20.7%	5G, Network optimization
Smart Cities	4.3	12.6	30.8%	Traffic management, public safety
Agriculture	2.1	7.8	38.7%	Precision farming, Crop monitoring
Total Market	58.7	149.7	26.3%	Cross-industry applications

3. EDGE-FIRST STRATEGIES: A PARADIGM SHIFT

Such techniques as edge-first strategies have revolutionized the way organizations handle digital infrastructure and app design, having undergone an inherent transformation (Cao et al., 2021). The edge-first approach has a starting point in that the processing should occur as near the data origin as possible and cloud resources would be utilized only on specific functions such as centralized analytics, backup and long-term storage (Jararweh et al., 2021). This is unlike the cloud-first solutions that presume centralized processing and edge computing as an extravagance. Table 5 also gives an overview of the pros and cons of the Edge-First and Cloud-First strategies as well as their use cases. Various basic concepts are a part of an edge-first strategy.

a) **Distributed by Design:** Built on the ground up: Since processing exists in a variety of edge points, never in one place, applications and infrastructure are designed to operate efficiently in a distributed manner.
b) **Local Processing Priority:** Only critical data networks are posted to centralized locations, as much process and analysis as can be performed locally, everywhere.
c) **Autonomous Operation:** Edge systems are designed to operate independently and be autonomous as there is no constant access to centralized resources to operate (Premsankar et al., 2021). Adaptive resource management is the flexible way of allocating and managing resources based on local needs and conditions. Federated Learning and Intelligence: In a context where data confidentiality and privacy are maintained, there is training and updating of machine learning models over scattered edge environments.

3.1 Strategic Advantages of Edge-First Approaches

a) **Enhanced Reactivity:** Edge-first tactics have several strategic advantages to companies that adopt them (Murshed et al., 2021). Edge-first strategies can provide corporations with a significant competitive advantage within shifting markets since they allow enterprises to respond immediately to moving situations and customer requirements.
b) **Greater Resiliency:** Since Failures in a particular area do not necessarily affect the running of operations in another area, distributed edge designs inherently have greater resiliency than centralized systems.
c) **Flexibility and Scalability**: Edge-first methods enable business to scale their infrastructure up over time without major architectural change and adapt to changing requirements.
d) **Enablement of innovation:** Edge computing makes new forms of applications and services possible that could never be achieved because of centralized processing, thus opening new sources of revenue, and business models.
e) **Risk Mitigation:** Distributed processing limits the risk of single point of failure, cyber-attack and changes in regulations.

Table 5. Edge-First vs cloud-first strategy comparison

Criteria	Cloud-First Strategy	Edge-First Strategy	Advantage
Latency	50-200ms typical	<10ms typical	Edge
Bandwidth Usage	High (all data to cloud)	Low (local processing)	Edge
Reliability	Single point of failure	Distributed resilience	Edge
Privacy/Security	Centralized risks	Distributed security	Edge
Scalability	Infinite cloud resources	Limited local resources	Cloud
Management Complexity	Centralized, simpler	Distributed, complex	Cloud
Initial Investment	Lower (OpEx model)	Higher (infrastructure)	Cloud
Operational Costs	High data transfer fees	Lower ongoing costs	Edge
Compliance	Challenging (data locality)	Easier (local processing)	Edge
Innovation Speed	Slower (network dependent)	Faster (local decisions)	Edge

3.2 Implementation Challenges

a) **Complexity Management:** Distributed edge environments are naturally more complicated than centralized environments and require high-level orchestration and management skills. Edge-first tactics are not without advantages, yet there exist several problems with its implementation also.
b) **Security Problems:** Some of the specific security problems brought by the edge settings are security of devices, network, and data in one or more distributed locations.
c) **Problems with standardization:** The lack of agreed protocols and interfaces can make it harder to interoperate and select the appropriate vendor due to the new concept of edge computing.
d) **Skills Required:** Edge computing requires certain knowledge and skills and businesses may not be able to provide them.
e) **Cost efficient:** Although edge computing can sometimes reduce operating costs, distributed systems might be very hard to maintain and may involve a large upfront capital investment in edge devices.

4. INDUSTRY APPLICATIONS AND USE CASES

The current edge computing use cases and industry applications include autonomous vehicles, smart manufacturing, healthcare monitoring, or smart cities, among others are depicted in table 6.

4.1 Manufacturing and Industrial IoT

The requirements of monitoring production processes in real-time, controlling, and optimizing them have predetermined the prominent role of the manufacturing industry in applying edge computing. By means of edge computing, it is possible to:

a) **Predictive Maintenance:** The condition of the equipment can be monitored in real-time using edge devices in order to schedule the maintenance procedures, avoid down-time and anticipate breakages before they occur.
b) **Quality Control:** Analysing the data on production during the process will give the chance to locate quality issues and eliminate them quickly, reducing waste and increasing the quality of the end product.
c) **Optimization of the Supply Chain:** Edge computing can optimize the supply chain, as it brings real-time information about inventory, production plans, and logistic activities.
d) **Workers Protection:** edge-enabled safety systems can help avoid accidents since the working environment and employee behaviour can be monitored and the necessary precautionary measures initiated through sending out timely alerts.

4.2 Healthcare and Telemedicine

Healthcare institutions are utilizing edge computing to reduce costs, enhance efficacy in operations, and overall patient care.

a) **Remote Patient Monitoring:** Edge devices enabled by continuous monitoring of vital signs and other health-related indicators can alert medical practitioners of potential issues on time before the situation can become critical.
b) **Medical Imaging:** Edge computing can facilitate analysis procedure of medical images and can enhance faster decisions in the process of diagnosis and treatment.
c) **Telemedicine:** Edge infrastructure has the potential to enhance access to healthcare services as it allows conducting them remotely and through high-quality video consultations.
d) **Drug Discovery:** Edge computing with its support of distributed analysis of molecular data and clinical trial results makes drug discovery processes faster.

4.3 Retail and E-Commerce

Retail companies are turning to edge computing in order to enhance security, simplify their processes, and raise consumer experiences (Nguyen et al., 2021). Edge computing enables real-time tailoring of the retail experience based on consumer behavior, consumer preferences and location.

a) **Inventory Management:** Edge devices can monitor inventory in real-time as they regulate the levels of stocks and reduce the instances of items being out of stock.
b) **Loss Prevention:** Edge-enabled security systems can offer real-time theft detection and prevention and fraud descent.
c) **Customer Analytics:** An analysis of the real-time behavior and preferences of the customers with edge computing provides timely changes to the product positioning, price, and promotions.

Table 6. Industry-Specific edge computing applications and benefits

Industry	Primary Applications	Key Benefits	Implementation Challenges	ROI Timeline
Manufacturing	Predictive maintenance, Quality control, Supply chain optimization	15-30% downtime reduction, 10-20% quality improvement	Legacy system integration, Skills gap	12-18 months
Healthcare	Remote monitoring, medical imaging, Telemedicine	40% faster diagnosis, 25% cost reduction	Regulatory compliance, Data security	18-24 months
Retail	Personalization, Inventory management, Loss prevention	20% sales increase, 30% inventory optimization	Customer privacy, Integration complexity	6-12 months
Transportation	Autonomous vehicles, Fleet management, Traffic optimization	25% fuel savings, 50% accident reduction	Safety certification, Infrastructure	24-36 months
Energy	Smart grid, Renewable integration, Asset monitoring	20% efficiency gain, 40% outage reduction	Grid modernization, Regulatory approval	18-30 months
Agriculture	Precision farming, Crop monitoring, Automated irrigation	30% yield increase, 25% water savings	Rural connectivity, Weather dependency	12-24 months

4.4 Transportation and Logistics

Edge computing can enable the logistics and transportation industry to improve customer and user service, efficiency and safety.

a) **Autonomous Vehicles:** Edge computing plays a vital role in operating an autonomous vehicle since it is necessary to process sensor data in real-time and make instant decisions.
b) **Fleet Management:** Edge devices can maximize routes and minimize costs of operation by keeping track of driver behaviour; conditions of cargo; and performance of vehicle on constant basis.
c) **Traffic Management:** Edge computing may optimum traffic flow by assessing real-time information about the traffic and adjusting signal operations and route recommendations.
d) **Supply Chain Visibility:** Edge computing has the potential to provide real-time visibility of operations in the supply chain by facilitating proactive control over the disruptions and delays.

4.5 Energy and Utilities

Energy and utility companies are adopting edge computing in a bid to revise their infrastructure and enhance the efficiency of their operations.

a) **Smart Grid Management:** Edge computing will enable real-time monitoring and control of the electrical grid; the result is that energy can be distributed optimally and reduce outages.
b) **Renewable Energy Integration:** The edge devices can maximize the use of alternate energy sources like wind power or solar power by predicting generating patterns and changing grid operations as per that in advance.
c) **Asset Monitoring:** Edge computing could enable critical infrastructure assets to monitor the health of their assets, which could in turn facilitate predictive maintenance and less time in down mode.
d) **Customer Engagement:** Customer engagement may cover immediate energy consumption supervision together with personalized energy management recommendations, not to mention a handful of those that edge computing could allow.

5. EDGE COMPUTING ARCHITECTURES

Some key attributes that edge computing design must have been latency, bandwidth, security, and scalability (Mahmud et al., 2021). The common architectural designs include:

a) **Cloudlet Architecture:** Under this plan, the smallest clouds which have lots of processing capabilities are positioned at the edge of the networks, near to the consumers and devices.
b) **Fog Computing:** Fog computing provides both computing services and network access so that the computing environment lies between circuit devices on the edge and cloud-based data centers.
c) **Mobile Edge Computing (MEC):** MEC is the use of edge computing but also implemented in the structure of mobile networks so that mobile users can access ultra-low latency apps.
d) **Micro Data Centers:** it is a small self-enclosed data center, which can be installed in IT-edge locations to present local computing and storage services.

5.1 Design Principles

As it was stated in Satyanarayana et al. (2021), efficient edge computing architecture (as shown in table 7) needs to adhere to two main design principles: Data processing needs to be structured in the hierarchy so that more complex processing is done at higher levels of the hierarchy and simple processing at the device level.

a) **Data Minimization:** It is recommended to send only the necessary information between edges sites and centralized facilities to enhance speed and bandwidth needs.
b) **Fault Tolerance:** Edge systems need to be built to function even in the event that certain parts malfunction or stop working.
c) **Security by Design:** Rather than being introduced as an afterthought, security issues should be included in the architecture from the start.
d) **Scalability:** As the number of edge devices and data volumes increase, the architecture must be able to grow with them.

5.2 Integration with Cloud Resources

Although edge-first techniques necessitate careful integration between edge and cloud settings, they do not eliminate the necessity for cloud resources. Important integration factors consist of:

a) **Workload Distribution:** Depending on variables like latency requirements, computing complexity, and data sensitivity, organizations must decide whether workloads should be handled in the cloud vs at the edge.
b) **Data Synchronization:** In order to minimize synchronization costs and preserve system performance, edge and cloud systems need to keep consistent data.
c) **Management and Orchestration:** To efficiently manage distributed edge and cloud resources, unified management and orchestration platforms are needed.
d) **Security and Compliance:** Both cloud and edge settings need uniform enforcement of security rules and compliance standards.

Table 7. Edge computing architecture patterns and use cases

Architecture Pattern	Description	Latency	Computing Power	Best Use Cases	Examples
Device Edge	Processing on endpoint devices	<1ms	Low-Medium	Real-time control, Data filtering	Smart sensors, Mobile apps
Infrastructure Edge	Edge servers/ gateways	1-5ms	Medium-High	Local analytics, Caching	Factory controllers, Retail kiosks
Network Edge	Telecom/ISP facilities	5-20ms	High	Content delivery, Gaming	CDN nodes, 5G MEC
Regional Edge	Distributed data centers	10-50ms	Very High	Regional services, Backup	Mini data centers, Cloud PoPs
Hybrid Edge-Cloud	Coordinated deployment	Variable	Unlimited	Complex workflows, ML training	Smart cities, Healthcare systems

6. ECONOMIC IMPLICATIONS

Companies, considering edge-first strategies, should study the impact of the decisions on the economy carefully. The key costs that should be considered are:

a) **Infrastructure Costs:** Edge computing needs a significant investment in the distributed infrastructure in the form of edge devices, edge gateways, and mini data centers. Cheaper cloud computing and data transitions, though, could compensate for these costs.

b) **Operation Cost:** It is simpler and less expensive to operate centralized cloud resources than it is to operate distributed-edged environments. Nonetheless, edge computing will be able to cut down on operating costs, as claimed with more automation and efficiency.
c) **Development Costs:** Developing edge apps might require some knowledge and specific equipment that can escalate the development costs. Edge computing has the potential to develop new revenue streams and business models to overcome these costs.
d) **Costs of Compliance:** Edge computing might reduce compliance costs and legal risks because it helps businesses to comply with data protection legislation.

6.1 Return on Investment

The edge computing projects can also result in a large return on investment (ROI) depending on a variety of factors.

a) **Performance:** The edge computing can enhance salability and consumer satisfaction through the advancement of user experience and application cache.
b) **Cost Savings:** This is achievable through improved productivity and automation due to lesser operating costs, cloud computing expenses and bandwidth prices.
c) **New Income Opportunities:** Edge computing will be use in creation of new services and applications that can translate into new sources of income.
d) **Risk Mitigation:** Edge computing can save significant funds to reduce the risks of cyberattacks, single points of failure and regulatory changes.

6.2 Opportunities in the Market

The market of edge computing provides a considerable opportunity for businesses in several industries.

a) **Industry Size:** With an expansion rate of upwards of 15% on a yearly compound basis, the global edge computing market is predicted to be worth $250 billion in the year 2025.
b) **Industry Growth:** The adoption of edge computing is anticipated to rise significantly in sectors like manufacturing, healthcare, retail, and transportation.
c) **Technology Innovation:** New avenues for creativity and distinction are being opened by developments in edge computing technology.
d) **Competitive Advantage:** Businesses can obtain a major competitive edge in their respective industries by effectively implementing edge-first initiatives.

6.3 Challenges and Considerations

Organizations must overcome a number of technical obstacles while implementing edge computing.

a) **Resource Restrictions:** Because edge devices frequently have constrained power, storage, and processing capabilities, workloads and applications must be carefully optimized (Chen et al., 2020). Applications that are lightweight and capable of operating well on constrained hardware must be created by developers. Model pruning and quantization are two common resource allocation techniques. Thermal performance and battery life need to be carefully controlled. Reliability depends on choosing the appropriate hardware for the job.
b) **Network Reliability**: Edge systems need to be built to function dependably in settings where network connectivity is spotty or nonexistent. The offline biased design patterns help to facilitate the service continuity. The requirement on constant connection can be reduced with local decision-making and data caching. Data synchronization methods and reconnection are required. Moreover, the systems must graciously absorb late uploads, incomplete transfer, etc.
c) **Device Administration:** Administrating many far-flung edge devices can be cumbersome and expensive, as well. Tools are needed in the firmware upgrades, remote setup, and observation. It is crucial to all devices with regards to version control and security patching. Scalability becomes a problem as the devices increase (Cao et al., 2021). Device orchestration frameworks take the form of device orchestration frameworks that facilitate multi-device processes that are more efficient.
d) **Interoperability:** There are no standard sets of protocols and interfaces, which can be a problem in achieving interoperability of various edge devices, platforms, and cloud services. Transforming the systems integration can be attained by employing open standards. To translate between in-compatible devices, there is often a need to use middleware platforms. The system can become complicated due to the presence of custom APIs even though they may be needed (Chen et al., 2021). Interoperability provides flexibility yet achieving such requires additional preparation and testing effort.
e) **The Performance Optimization:** The abilities in monitoring, analysis and optimization are a must to augment the performance in the distributed edge situations at an advanced level (Luo et al., 2021). Real-time performances are essential in tuning systems and health checks. Strategies for load balancing and latency reduction may be part of edge-specific optimization. Throughput can be increased by using data compression and filtering techniques. Maintaining application responsiveness is aided by ongoing benchmarking and profiling.

6.4 Security and Privacy Concerns

Particular security and privacy issues brought up by edge computing need to be properly handled.

a) **Device Security:** Device security is an important factor since there are high chances of having weak security features of the devices in the edge, as well as physical accessibility to attackers. Devices should be able to support hardware encryption (Rinki & Verma, 2021), tamper detection, and secure boots. Firmware should be updated regularly in order to patch vulnerability. Other safeguards are location-ID and local access restrictions.
b) **Network Security:** Edge networks are distributed, and wireless communications are used, thus they can be more vulnerable to intrusion. End-to-end encryption can be used in protection of data in transit over the wireless channel. The intrusion detection systems (IDS) can be used in tracking unusual activity within edge networks. The exchange of data between the edge and the core system may be secured with secure tunnels or VPN.
c) **Data Protection:** Data protection concerns how the data is encrypted (Rinki et al., 2022) and accessed and controlled as well as data governance processes are required to protect personal information in distributed edge environments. The exposure of sensitive information can be reduced with the help of data tokenization and data anonymization. Local data processing reduces the risk of exposure during transmission. Dwelling of the data and safe disposal of data should be policy defined.
d) **Identity and Access Management:** The identification and access rights can be challenging and complex to deal with in the distributed edge scenarios. Scalability can deploy role-based and attribute-based systems of access control (Roman et al., 2021). The nature of authentication mechanisms should be able to cater to an edge environment where connectivity is poor. Federated identity management enables integration of distributed systems so far as user access is concerned.
e) **Compliance:** Close attention is required when it comes to preparation and implementation to ensure that data privacy legislation is complied with in distributed edge contexts. Local data residency laws must be incorporated into compliance frameworks. Automated audits and logging assist in monitoring and demonstrating regulatory compliance. Edge deployments ought to comply with regulations such as ISO 27001, GDPR, or HIPAA.

6.5 Organizational Challenges

Organizations must solve a number of organizational obstacles in order to implement edge-first initiatives.

a) **Skills and Expertise:** Some businesses may not have the necessary skills and expertise needed for edge computing. This covers expertise in edge AI, cybersecurity, and distributed systems (Premsankar et al., 2021). Investing heavily in hiring new employees or upgrading current ones may be necessary. Project planning and implementation might be delayed by a lack of technical knowledge. It can be required to form alliances with outside experts or service providers.
b) **Cultural Shift:** Organizational culture, procedures, and practices may need to shift significantly in order to implement edge-first methods. If employees are not adequately onboarded, they may oppose new procedures or technology. Successful edge efforts frequently require cross-functional and agile teams. Clear communication and leadership support are crucial for promoting cultural change. At every level, creativity and ongoing learning should be promoted.
c) **Vendor Management:** It might be difficult and complicated to oversee connections with several edge computing suppliers and service providers. Complexity is increased by coordinating contracts, integrations, and service levels. Flexibility and future scalability may be restricted by vendor lock-in. Performance and interoperability across various vendor solutions must be guaranteed. Frameworks for shared accountability and open communication are crucial.
d) **Governance:** It takes considerable preparation and cooperation to set up efficient governance structures for distributed edge settings. It is necessary to clearly define roles, duties, and ownership. Policies for data management and security must be uniform across all sites. In governance models, auditability and compliance monitoring systems are crucial. A balanced approach can be achieved by combining a centralized strategy with decentralized execution.
e) **Change Management:** Implementing edge-first strategies requires effective management to ensure successful adoption and implementation. Workers must receive training and assistance as workflow and technology change. Plans for effective communication aid in bringing stakeholders into line with new goals.

Success depends on keeping an eye on developments and overcoming obstacles. Early departmental involvement promotes buy-in and facilitates implementation.

6.6 Future Outlook and Trends

Several upcoming technologies are expected to just speed the transition to edge computing. Amongst them include:

a) **6G Networks:** As 6G wireless networks are developed, they will offer even more bandwidth and reduced latency, opening up new edge computing applications. It is anticipated that 6G will offer 100 times greater data speeds than 5G.

Real-time applications like remote surgery and immersive AR/VR will be supported by this. The seamless integration of millions of IoT devices made possible by 6G will be advantageous for smart cities. It's incredibly low latency will allow for response in real time. Better QoS for edge applications will be possible with increasingly sophisticated network slicing. Autonomous vehicles and infrastructure will be able to communicate more effectively thanks to 6G. It will use AI-driven optimization to enable energy-efficient operations. Because of the speed of 6G data transfer, edge AI will flourish there.

A key component will be massive machine-type communication (MTC).

b) **Quantum Computing:** In the future, quantum computing technology could be used at the edge to enable new kinds of services and applications. Qubits are used in quantum computing to exponentially speed up parallel computations. High-complexity computations can be handled locally by integrating it at the edge.

Quantum key distribution has the potential to completely transform cryptography. Pattern recognition and AI model training may be accelerated using quantum edge nodes.

Improvements could be made to climate simulation, financial modeling, and drug discovery. Real-time logistics optimization may be possible with edge-based quantum computing. They make it possible to optimize dynamic systems like traffic control at high speeds. In edge applications, quantum sensors can provide unparalleled precision.

Quantum-resistant protocols can be used to improve security in edge situations.

Hybrid quantum-edge designs are being investigated. However, they are still in the early stages of research.

c) **Advanced AI and Machine Learning:** As AI and ML technologies continue to progress, more complex edge computing applications will become possible.

Neuromorphic Computing: These technologies could lead to more potent and effective edge computing devices. Edge AI models provide real-time decision-making independent of the cloud. Security and privacy are ensured because crucial data is kept on the device (Rinki et al., 2022 July). More sophisticated algorithms can learn and adapt in real time at the edge. Examples include facial recognition, voice assistants, and predictive maintenance. Low latency AI is crucial for autonomous driving and medical diagnostics.

Through the transmission of meaningful data, Edge ML contributes to bandwidth savings.

Federated learning enables collaborative model training without sharing raw data.

Devices run faster and use less power thanks to edge TPUs and other AI accelerators.

Edge systems are able to maintain their adaptability through constant model updates.

This development supports Industry 4.0 and next-generation smart environments.

d) **Neuromorphic Computing:** More powerful and efficient edge computing devices may result from these technologies. The way the human brain processes information served as the model for neuromorphic circuits. Rather than using conventional logic gates, they employ spiking neural networks (SNNs). This enables computation that is event-driven and extremely parallel. Neuromorphic systems are perfect for battery-operated gadgets since they need very little electricity. They work nicely with smart monitoring and always-on sensors. These processors provide real-time learning and adaptation capabilities based on environmental data. More autonomy and context awareness can be achieved by edge devices. They provide notable enhancements in visual and auditory processing performance. Brain-computer interfaces, prosthetics, and robots are examples of applications. Neuromorphic computing is a way to connect digital and biological systems.
e) **Distributed Ledger**: Distributed ledger and blockchain technology can be utilized to validate and protect transactions in distributed edge settings. Blockchain ensures transparency and trust by providing unchangeable record-keeping. Agreement execution and verification are automated using smart contracts. Edge nodes don't require centralized management to function safely. Secure access control and decentralized identity are made possible by this. Edge-blockchain integration improves the accuracy of supply chain tracking. Crypto protocols allow IoT devices to conduct transactions safely and independently. Blockchain makes ensuring that edge data flows can be traced and audited.

Systems for micropayments and energy trading can function at the edge. Security lapses are easily identified and stopped. Proof of Stake and other consensus techniques can be tailored for edge networks.

6.7 Industry Trends

The usage of edge computing is anticipated to continue growing due to a number of industrial developments.

a) **Edge-Native Apps:** Rather than modifying cloud apps for edge deployment, organizations are increasingly creating apps especially for edge settings (Kumar et al., 2024). These programs are made specifically to function with constrained resources. Low latency and real-time responsiveness are top priorities for edge-native apps. They frequently have offline-first features to guarantee dependability in the event of network outages. Modular architecture and lightweight frameworks are used by developers to provide flexibility. Performance is optimized by these programs in a variety of edge situations and devices.

Local sensors, actuators, and IoT platforms are frequently integrated with them.

For localized decision-making, the app has analytics and AI built right in.

Industrial automation, smart retail, and predictive maintenance are some examples of use cases. These programs lessen reliance on centralized systems.

Because edge-native design reduces data movement, it improves data privacy.

b) **Edge-as-a-Service:** To lower the complexity and expense of implementing edge computing, service providers are now providing edge computing capabilities as managed services. Vendors are creating edge computing solutions that are suited to particular use cases and industries. Like cloud computing, this strategy provides pay-as-you-go flexibility. It makes it possible for businesses to use edge solutions without having to make significant upfront costs. Edge-as-a Service providers oversee security, upgrades, and infrastructure. Solutions designed for industries, such as manufacturing, logistics, and healthcare, are available. It speeds up edge deployment time-to-market.

Professional maintenance and assistance are advantageous to organizations.

It frequently includes integration with 5G, AI, and IoT services.

This method makes scalability across geographical places simpler.

It facilitates hybrid architectures that connect on-premises, cloud (Bhardwaj et al., 2025), and edge systems. All things considered, it makes edge capabilities more accessible to companies of all sizes.

c) **Standardization Efforts:** To increase interoperability and simplify deployment, industry groups are attempting to create standards and protocols for edge computing. The smooth operation of platforms and devices is ensured by standardization.

It encourages ecosystem expansion and lessens vendor lock-in.

Initiatives that are open-source are crucial in this regard.

Data formats, orchestration, security, and communication protocols are all covered by standards. These initiatives are being spearheaded by groups including IEEE, LF Edge, and ETSI. Creating portable apps is made simpler by standard APIs.

Adherence to standards enhances edge deployments' dependability and credibility.

Data protection is guaranteed in distributed contexts by security standards.

Heterogeneous edge infrastructure management is facilitated by unified frameworks.

Achieving broad edge adoption requires global uniformity.

d) **Sustainability Initiatives:** Interest in energy-efficient edge computing solutions is being fueled by organizations' growing attention to the environmental effects of their computing infrastructure. By limiting data transfer to remote data centers, edge computing contributes to lower energy use. Power consumption and network congestion are reduced by localized processing. For edge deployments, businesses are selecting devices with small power footprints. To cut down on heat production, cooling-efficient edge devices are being developed. To reduce carbon emissions, green AI models are being used.

Edge hardware is being manufactured using sustainable methods.

Edge data centers are incorporating renewable energy sources.

Edge systems use recycling and reuse to promote the circular economy.

These days, vendor selection and IT architecture are impacted by sustainability objectives.

Eco-friendly edge solutions are also being driven by regulatory pressure and ESG compliance.

7. CONCLUSION

Compelling technological, business and market forces are making edge computing not only advantageous but a more prerequisite of competitive success. The main benefits of the edge computing strategy over the conventional cloud-first trends include smaller latency rates, higher performance, better security, and privacy, as well as operation in areas with a bad connection. However, implementation of edge-first tactics is prone to its current disadvantages, including increased complexity, security concerns, and certain knowledge and skills. Businesses which can accomplish this transition will be able to achieve a competitive advantage, customer experience, and greater efficiency. The key to success is to understand the specific requirements and characteristics of edge computing environments and develop the plans that capitalize on these characteristics without addressing the associated challenges. The further evolution of technology, the changing business requirements, and the changing market dynamics will all play their roles in the growth and further maturation of edge computing. The move towards edge-thinking by businesses will put them in a good position to capitalize on these developments and emerge long-term winners in a digital and data-driven world.

Technology is just part of the edge revolution, another part is the reconsideration of the way how the companies work, compete, and deliver value in the digital era. By changing the cloud-first approach to the edge-first one, organizations can develop a stronger and more responsive business activity and unlock the opportunities of innovation, efficiency, and growth.

REFERENCES

Abbas, N., Zhang, Y., Taherkordi, A., & Skeie, T. (2021). Mobile edge computing: A survey. *IEEE Internet of Things Journal*, *8*(16), 12479–12501. DOI: 10.1109/JIOT.2021.3071232

Al-Fuqaha, A., Guizani, M., Mohammadi, M., Aledhari, M., & Ayyash, M. (2021). Internet of Things: A survey on enabling technologies, protocols, and applications. *IEEE Communications Surveys and Tutorials*, *17*(4), 2347–2376. DOI: 10.1109/COMST.2015.2444095

Armbrust, M., Fox, A., Griffith, R., Joseph, A. D., Katz, R., Konwinski, A., Lee, G., Patterson, D., Rabkin, A., Stoica, I., & Zaharia, M. (2020). A view of cloud computing. *Communications of the ACM*, *53*(4), 50–58. DOI: 10.1145/1721654.1721672

Beck, M. T., Werner, M., Feld, S., & Schimper, T. (2021). Mobile edge computing: A survey on architecture and computation offloading. *IEEE Communications Surveys and Tutorials*, *21*(3), 2608–2633. DOI: 10.1109/COMST.2018.2887083

Bhardwaj, I., Devi, S., & Kumar, T. (2025). Securing the cloud: Navigating compliance and regulatory challenges. In *Risk-based approach to secure cloud migration* (pp. 325–342). IGI Global., DOI: 10.4018/979-8-3693-7137-4.ch013

Bonomi, F., Milito, R., Zhu, J., & Addepalli, S. (2022). Fog computing and its role in the internet of things. In *Proceedings of the First Edition of the MCC Workshop on Mobile Cloud Computing* (pp. 13–16). ACM. DOI: 10.1145/2342509.2342513

Buyya, R., Yeo, C. S., Venugopal, S., Broberg, J., & Brandic, I. (2019). Cloud computing and emerging IT platforms: Vision, hype, and reality for delivering computing as the 5th utility. *Future Generation Computer Systems*, *25*(6), 599–616. DOI: 10.1016/j.future.2008.12.001

Cao, K., Liu, Y., Meng, G., & Sun, Q. (2021). An overview on edge computing research. *IEEE Access : Practical Innovations, Open Solutions*, *8*, 85714–85728. DOI: 10.1109/ACCESS.2020.2991734

Chen, M., Qian, Y., Mao, S., Tang, W., & Yang, X. (2020). Software-defined mobile networks security. *Mobile Networks and Applications*, *21*(5), 729–743. DOI: 10.1007/s11036-015-0665-5

Chen, S., Xu, H., Liu, D., Hu, B., & Wang, H. (2021). A vision of IoT: Applications, challenges, and opportunities with China perspective. *IEEE Internet of Things Journal*, *1*(4), 349–359. DOI: 10.1109/JIOT.2014.2337336

Dolui, K., & Datta, S. K. (2021). Comparison of edge computing implementations: Fog computing, cloudlet and mobile edge computing. In *Proceedings of the Global Internet of Things Summit* (pp. 1–6). IEEE. DOI: 10.1109/GIOTS.2017.8016214

Hassan, N., Gillani, S., Ahmed, E., Yaqoob, I., & Imran, M. (2021). The role of edge computing in Internet of Things. *IEEE Communications Magazine*, *56*(11), 110–115. DOI: 10.1109/MCOM.2018.1700906

Jararweh, Y., Doulat, A., AlQudah, O., Ahmed, E., Al-Ayyoub, M., & Benkhelifa, E. (2021). The future of mobile cloud computing: Integrating cloudlets and mobile edge computing. In *Proceedings of the 23rd International Conference on Telecommunications* (pp. 1–5). IEEE. DOI: 10.1109/ICT.2016.7500404

Kumar, S., Tiwari, P., & Zymbler, M. (2020). Internet of Things is a revolutionary approach for future technology enhancement: A review. *Journal of Big Data*, *6*(1), 1–21. DOI: 10.1186/s40537-019-0268-2

Kumar, T., Kumar, P., & Namasudra, S. (2024). User revocation-enabled access control model using identity-based signature in the cloud computing environment. *International Journal of Interactive Multimedia and Artificial Intelligence*, *9*(1), 127–136. DOI: 10.9781/ijimai.2024.05.001

Li, Y., Yu, M., Xu, D., Xue, G., & Wang, B. (2021). A survey on network slicing for 5G. *IEEE Communications Surveys and Tutorials*, *23*(2), 872–909. DOI: 10.1109/COMST.2021.3055799

Luo, Q., Hu, S., Li, C., Li, G., & Shi, W. (2021). Resource scheduling in edge computing: A survey. *IEEE Communications Surveys and Tutorials*, *23*(4), 2131–2165. DOI: 10.1109/COMST.2021.3106401

Mahmud, R., Kotagiri, R., & Buyya, R. (2021). Fog computing: A taxonomy, survey and future directions. In Di Martino, B., Li, K.-C., Yang, L., & Esposito, A. (Eds.), *Internet ofEverything* (pp. 103–130). Springer., DOI: 10.1007/978-3-030-57798-6_5

Mell, P., & Grance, T. (2021). *The NIST definition of cloud computing* (NIST Special Publication 800-145). National Institute of Standards and Technology. DOI: 10.6028/NIST.SP.800-145

Murshed, M. G. S., Murphy, C., Hou, D., Khan, N., Ananthanarayanan, G., & Hussain, F. (2021). Machine learning at the network edge: A survey. *ACM Computing Surveys*, *54*(8), 1–37. DOI: 10.1145/3469029

Nguyen, D. C., Pathirana, P. N., Ding, M., & Seneviratne, A. (2021). Integration of blockchain and cloud of things: Architecture, applications and challenges. *IEEE Communications Surveys and Tutorials*, *22*(4), 2521–2549. DOI: 10.1109/COMST.2020.3020092

Pahl, C., Brogi, A., Soldani, J., & Jamshidi, P. (2021). Cloud container technologies: A state-of-the-art review. *IEEE Transactions on Cloud Computing*, *7*(3), 677–692. DOI: 10.1109/TCC.2017.2702586

Porambage, P., Okwuibe, J., Liyanage, M., Ylianttila, M., & Taleb, T. (2021). Survey on multi-access edge computing for Internet of Things realization. *IEEE Communications Surveys and Tutorials*, *20*(4), 2961–2991. DOI: 10.1109/COMST.2018.2849509

Premsankar, G., Di Francesco, M., & Taleb, T. (2021). Edge computing for the Internet of Things: A case study. *IEEE Internet of Things Journal*, *5*(2), 1275–1284. DOI: 10.1109/JIOT.2018.2805263

Rinki, K., & Verma, P. (2021, July). A DWT and Coefficient Exchange Block Based DCT Image Watermarking and their Comparative Assessment. In *2021 12th International Conference on Computing Communication and Networking Technologies (ICCCNT)* (pp. 1–7). IEEE. DOI: 10.1109/ICCCNT51525.2021.9579737

Rinki, K., Verma, P., & Singh, R. K. (2022, April). A novel multiblock region-based arnold transformation for image watermarking combined with DWT-PSO Technique. In *Evolution in Computational Intelligence: Proceedings of the 9th International Conference on Frontiers in Intelligent Computing: Theory and Applications (FICTA 2021)* (pp. 77–87). Springer Nature Singapore. DOI: 10.1007/978-981-16-6616-2_8

Rinki, K., Verma, P., & Singh, R. K. (2022). A novel matrix multiplication based LSB substitution mechanism for data security and authentication. *Journal of King Saud University. Computer and Information Sciences*, *34*(8), 5510–5524. DOI: 10.1016/j.jksuci.2021.01.013

Rittinghouse, J. W., & Ransome, J. F. (2020). *Cloud computing: Implementation, management, and security*. CRC Press.

Roman, R., Lopez, J., & Mambo, M. (2021). Mobile edge computing, Fog et al.: A survey and analysis of security threats and challenges. *Future Generation Computer Systems*, *78*, 680–698. DOI: 10.1016/j.future.2016.11.009

Satyanarayanan, M., Bahl, P., Caceres, R., & Davies, N. (2021). The case for VM-based cloudlets in mobile computing. *IEEE Pervasive Computing*, *8*(4), 14–23. DOI: 10.1109/MPRV.2009.82

Chapter 8
Enhancing Clinical Decision-Making and Operational Efficiency in Healthcare Using Edge Computing

R. N. Ravikumar
https://orcid.org/0009-0009-3705-1681
Marwadi University, Rajkot, India

S. Aarthi
https://orcid.org/0009-0006-9064-2091
Marwadi University, Rajkot, India

Gularam Masharipova
Alfraganus University, Tashkent, Uzbekistan

Nilufar Niyazova
Mamun University, Khiva, Uzbekistan

Navbakhor Salaeva
Urgench State University, Urgench, Uzbekistan

Dilnoz Buriyeva
Termez University of Economics and Service, Termez, Uzbekistan

ABSTRACT

Edge computing in healthcare offers significant benefits by improving medical outcomes, enhancing operational efficiency, and supporting real-time clinical decisions. This chapter explores how edge systems build resilient healthcare networks, enabling rapid patient support through data-driven protocols while meeting security and compliance requirements such as HIPAA and GDPR. The proliferation of wearable devices and remote monitoring generates vast medical data, posing challenges in centralized processing due to latency and reliability issues. Edge solutions address this by enabling real-time analysis closer to data sources with reduced network

DOI: 10.4018/979-8-3373-1147-0.ch008

demands. The chapter discusses deployment strategies across hospitals, outpatient clinics, and home care, emphasizing the development of medical-grade edge nodes and fast data transfer mechanisms. Case studies highlight successful predictive analytics using edge-based AI diagnostics, improved cost-efficiency, and patient satisfaction.

1. INTRODUCTION TO EDGE COMPUTING IN HEALTHCARE

The fast pace of healthcare technology creates immediate opportunities to gather medical data from wearable devices as well as diagnostic equipment and mobile healthcare applications and remote patient monitoring systems. Cloud systems based on traditional models face difficulties handling these data influxes because they deal with increased speed together with multiplied varieties and enhanced volumes of data (Ghane et al., 2021). One central processing location creates delays that use up bandwidth and cause outages in systems which harms real-time care of patients. The problems facing healthcare systems find an effective solution through edge computing technologies.

Edge computing allows healthcare institutions to process data generation points directly by processing information through patient equipment and wearable devices and home health sensors situated at the bedside. Through this method healthcare providers gain instant access to real-time analysis and quick responses because the computing operations take place near the data collection points (Javed et al., 2021). The real-time data processing performed at the edge level delivers immediate value in the treatment of serious emergencies and diagnosis protocols. Edge computing improves healthcare organization data privacy through its implementation. Through this approach healthcare providers can fulfil requirements of important privacy regulations including HIPAA and GDPR. The local data processing operations enhance security because it makes data breaches much harder to achieve.

Healthcare facilities require a guide to adopt edge computing systems as outlined by this study. The goal is to enhance operational performance alongside real-time clinical solutions which results in better treatment results for patients. The exploration investigates medical device and patient record system connection capabilities to edge components and delivers vital security standards and established implementation methodologies (Li et al., 2022). This research delivers practical implementation methods supported by real-world examples to help IT professionals lead health staff and business managers in deploying trustworthy intelligent edge computing systems for contemporary medical facilities.

1.1 The Evolution of Healthcare IT Infrastructure

Recent healthcare IT solutions provide improved services. Handwritten patient records caused transcription mistakes and longer healthcare response times in the past. EHRs have transformed healthcare management. By using centralized databases and cloud storage, EHR systems provide healthcare personnel accurate patient data quickly. Wearables, smartphone apps, smart diagnostic equipment, and Health-Internet-of-Things technologies have advanced rapidly in digital health (Li et al., 2019). IT technologies are evolving quicker than earlier ones. Real-time data production in healthcare systems requires more flexibility. These systems handle large amounts of fast-moving data. Network concerns plague hospital-wide cloud-based systems, causing delays and service interruptions during crises and prolonged patient care. In emergency medical situations, staff must acquire clinical information quickly to treat patients. Therefore, improved systems are needed. Healthcare activities need immediate local solutions. Edge computing is being used in healthcare to handle data from wearables and bedside gadgets. Secure and fast data processing enable real-time predictive healthcare. Edge-generated infrastructure changes healthcare operations. New technology allows intelligent healthcare systems to improve medical facilities' adaptability and reactivity to new health issues (McNamee et al., 2020). The implementing healthcare professionals use this modern technology to improve patient care.

1.2 Importance of Edge Computing in Modern Medical Systems

Edge computing serves as a vital element to enhance digital healthcare systems in the present medical world. Hospitals and clinics implement more smart devices featuring IoT sensors in patient care leading to an extreme requirement for fast and reliable data processing. Allocation near the source of data generation makes edge computing effective. The system performs processing at its location solely rather than transferring the information to remote cloud servers. Faster decisions become possible while healthcare providers can minimize their dependence on the internet. The application of edge computing covers essential hospital locations of operating rooms along with emergency care departments and intensive care unit monitoring spaces (Miao et al., 2018). White lives and deaths at this location depend on immediate data responses when treating patients. The process of real-time data handling through edge computing eliminates transmission-based processing slowdowns.

Remote patient monitoring and telemedicine need immediate responses from health facilities to achieve optimal health results.

The compliance of patient privacy regulations and data protection are both supported by edge computing operations. The local data analysis functionality enables healthcare institutions to produce safe anonymous data versions before transferring them to central locations (Premsankar et al., 2018). The local data processing eliminates the threats of data breaches while ensuring compliance with laws such as GDPR and HIPAA. Healthcare efficiency improves through edge technology because it supports lowered bandwidth requirements and system continuity operates when initial systems fail. Medical systems use this technology to gain enhancements both in terms of security performance and service provider response time and active care delivery functions (Román et al., 2018).

1.3 Bridging Clinical Efficiency and Technological Innovation

Healthcare organizations use edge computing as an operational technology booster to enhance their daily medical functions. The former hospital information systems operated independently from other hospital activities until healthcare providers encountered limitations between technology tools and real patient needs. The connection built by edge computing integrates modern technological systems with medical facility operations (Varghese et al., 2016). Edge systems operate with high speed independently from cloud infrastructure to provide fast medical treatment to patients. The wearable technology devices of medical personnel trigger instant alerts to report atypical vital signs when cloud processing of data is still occurring. Integration of AI processing modules into diagnostic machines enables patients to obtain faster diagnostic results thus shortening their hospital stay duration. Healthcare personnel can conduct patient care directly after accessing quick data retrieval for defining clinical decisions.

Healthcare worker job satisfaction receives an enhancement through edge computing due to both better system dependability and reduced operational delays and issues. Edge computing brings uninterrupted healthcare functions to remote healthcare services through its processing ability which lets staff examine patient data onsite. The testing routines and application deployment processes become simpler for hospitals when they adopt edge computing solutions during new healthcare application development (Zhou et al., 2019). Edge computing technology allows developers to link new systems to present networks for building healthcare solutions with both advanced functionality and valuable medical applications.

2. LIMITATIONS OF CENTRALIZED HEALTHCARE DATA SYSTEMS

Healthcare facilities create these data platforms to consolidate information processing. The web domain stores and improves data access. Healthcare institutions must tackle important concerns amid quick operating needs that demand data protection solutions. The primary operational problem for many system issues is delays. Medical device data collected under centralized framework must be sent to distant cloud servers for processing before system actions may commence. The system processes data between processing periods and returns it to clients ("Securing the Future," 2024). In emergency scenarios like Intensive Care Unit and remote surgical procedures, long processing delays in medical contexts make key judgments by physicians unsafe.

Another concern is internet addiction. Strong, reliable internet is best for these systems. Rural patients' medical needs for quick data interchange conflict with their need for excellent internet-based patient care, lowering healthcare quality. Combining patient-worn gadgets with remote medical treatment systems rapidly expands healthcare data. However, academic medical information centralization slows processing and increases medical data management costs (Ali et al., 2023). Current difficulties make data security and privacy important. Hackers will target patient data systems due to security vulnerabilities. Due to out-of-control data, healthcare businesses struggle to comply with HIPAA and GDPR. Due to deteriorating data management quality, healthcare organizations are using edge computing solutions more and more (Almatrooshi et al., 2024). This method protects patient data and allows rapid medical treatments across linked systems, providing a superior response to these challenges.

2.1 Challenges in Traditional Cloud-Based Models

Healthcare evolved significantly after medical organizations started using cloud-based systems. The cloud systems enable remote access to data storage which reduces administrative procedures. New healthcare requirements surpass the processing capabilities of cloud-based systems in the healthcare sector where fast data management for substantial data quantities is necessary. Every aspect and security measure of a cloud system faces the impact of a single issue which results in security consequences (Amanat et al., 2022). The slow speed of data transmission through the cloud platform occurs due to the necessary time needed for information transfer. The need for quick medical decisions in healthcare becomes challenging when physicians must handle long data transfer delays especially during treatment of strokes or traumatic injuries.

The organization experiences challenges to match its growth rate. The growing number of medical devices and complicated patient data need expensive substantial changes for centralized systems. The firm has major security issues. Overall, cloud systems attract hackers because they capture valuable patient data. Healthcare organizations struggle to reconcile HIPAA and GDPR data security with data accessible. The medical team cannot access patient data in crises due to cloud systems with unpredictable internet connectivity (Arafa et al., 2023). Healthcare delivery difficulties show that hybrid and edge computing technologies provide fast, safe, adaptable medical services, thus medical companies must use them.

2.2 Latency Issues Affecting Real-Time Clinical Decisions

Hospital medical activities struggle because information processing delays exceed standards. Due to geographical routes, remote servers must convey data to central processing centers, delaying cloud processing. Surgical robots and patient monitoring systems need immediate response to prevent clinical problems, making critical medical procedures difficult. The ICU uses several instrumentation connections in its monitoring systems to treat patients. Medical device cloud analysis generates vital alarms and clinical signals for medical staff via two information streams (Chenthara et al., 2019). Medical operations using two-way messages cause significant reaction delays that may kill in emergency situations like heart attacks and oxygen deficiency.

Medical pictures and AI software perform poorly when the network is unreliable. The AI-based processing of MRI stroke data requires extended periods for result generation that creates safety threats for patients. Rural healthcare areas experience increasing severity of disruptions whenever medical treatment extends to their regions. Slower medical video consulting combined with diagnostic feedback occurs due to unreliable internet which damages centralized systems' functionality (Ciecierski-Holmes et al., 2022). The analysis of data at edges allows quick delivery of results enabling immediate solutions to these problems. The accelerated response time makes it possible for medical staff to obtain crucial medical data quickly so they can execute accurate lifesaving procedures in a time-sensitive manner.

2.3 Reliability Concerns in Remote Healthcare Services

Remote healthcare services including telemedicine and home monitoring systems operate to enhance patient medical access to care. The healthcare delivery systems encounter challenges when internet-based data systems encounter problems. Rural areas encounter difficulties with services that need steady internet connections as well as functional cloud servers to operate properly (Hasan et al., 2024). The inconsistent delivery of quality healthcare becomes challenging because of this situation. Network systems currently present many problems which disrupt services in numerous rural areas. Cloud-based healthcare systems become operable only when Internet service remains stable thus delaying both diagnostic procedures and patient record retrieval. When these systems fail to operate correctly the situation leads to medical mistakes and a loss of trust among users.

The medical data produced through remote patient monitoring systems requires correct data management strategies. Such data processing may face slowdowns as analyses require centralized servers that perform analysis. When either period are busy or the internet connection is slow. Rapid alert systems are essential to manage the dangerous conditions which patients with chronic diseases face because delays in such alerts may lead to emergency situations. Digital healthcare benefits suffer reduction when healthcare providers spend excessive time recording manual data entries or their service is delayed because of technical system limits (Puneeth & Parthasarathy, 2024). Cloud-based systems lose their effectiveness in regions with unreliable connectivity until the offline functionality is activated for them. The technology of edge computing addresses these issues through data processing performed at nearby locations which are close to the data source points. Under offline conditions scientists can perform dependable information analysis through operating in offline mode. Edge computing technology transforms remote medical services into more efficient operations which provide stable healthcare access to all people residing in remote regions.

3. EDGE ARCHITECTURE FOR MEDICAL ENVIRONMENTS

The Healthcare edge architecture includes Doctoral computing resources which locate near medical data points such as facilities and outpatient centers and residential locations different from traditional central cloud systems (Shen et al., 2019). The distributed system design provides clinical speed alongside quick system responses during data processing operations. Medical-grade edge nodes form the essential parts of this architectural system. Durable medical equipment devices are classified in this category to operate independently as medical care systems in healthcare facilities. Rapid processing of patient medical data becomes possible due to medical equipment deployment into patient locations which decreases dependency on networks and enables quick urgent care for patients needing immediate attention (Singh, 2023).

All medical systems need access to Electronic Health Record (EHR) systems under the basic requirements of edge architecture.

The patient health system obtains time-sensitive information exchange through constant communication between edge devices and primary hospital systems. The deployment of edge devices at community clinics together with patient residences enables remote healthcare monitoring and patient diagnostics through their immediate operational functions. Establishments of secure high-speed communication protocols enable hybrid network linking electronic data points to central systems (Yang et al., 2023). The operation system enhances healthcare IT efficiency by permitting fast edge-based replies together with centralized computational resources between design components.

3.1 Medical-Grade Edge Nodes: Design and Capabilities

Hospital-based health care analytics requirements and data processing needs are successfully fulfilled by Node machines which receive medical approval from doctors. Standard devices no longer serve as distinct from medical-grade edge devices because those specialized devices adhere to all healthcare system requirements and safety protocols to protect equipment from moisture exposure and electromagnetic interferences during safe operation. The sensor nodes operate with built-in AI processing elements that run healthcare applications for medical treatment needs and serve with diagnostic imaging and anomaly detection functionalities (Aujla & Jindal, 2021). Medical-grade edge devices in ICU critical condition zones monitor ECG signals, vital signs, and oxygen levels and alert staff when thresholds are exceeded.

An encrypted hardware system in the storage unit uses backup power sources according to regulations. Structured design provides security. The nodes possess optimized features for developing medical standard connections through HL7 with DICOM protocol support to establish seamless system networking. Healthcare personnel can easily install these devices next to patient beds because of their portable dimensions which allow operation in medical regions as well as provide mobile diagnostic capabilities. Medical-grade edge nodes function as intelligent access points for performing simultaneous data acquisition of health information from which they process healthcare data to enhance medical domain wide clinical management speeds (Dias & Torkamani, 2019).

Table 1. Features and capabilities of medical-grade edge nodes

Feature Category	Description
Hardware Resilience	Moisture-proof, electromagnetic shielded, portable design
Processing Capability	AI-enabled processors for anomaly detection, diagnostics
Security Integration	Encrypted storage, backup power systems, regulatory compliance mechanisms
Interoperability	HL7, DICOM, and FHIR protocol support
Use Cases	ICU monitoring, bedside data analysis, mobile diagnostics

Table 1 summarizes the structural and functional capabilities of medical-grade edge nodes in healthcare environments, focusing on real-time diagnostics, compliance, and operational versatility.

Figure 1. Edge computing architecture in healthcare

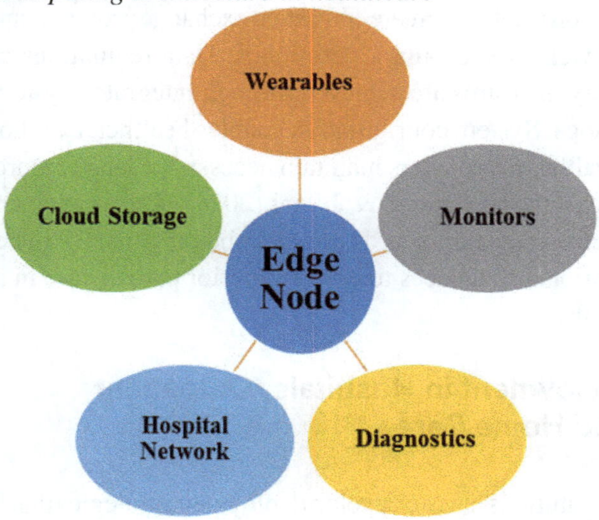

Figure 1 illustrates the central role of an edge node in a healthcare network. It connects directly to various data sources such as wearables, monitors, and diagnostics, while simultaneously interfacing with hospital networks and cloud storage. The image highlights the decentralized and real-time data processing enabled by edge computing.

3.2 Integration with Electronic Health Record (EHR) Systems

Patient care effectiveness requires edge computing systems to fully integrate with Electronic Health Record (EHR) platforms for achieving optimal quality results. Patient profiles built by edge computing nodes demand instant access to central electronic health record systems through which they combine present diagnostic sensor readings with imaging and point-of-care monitor outputs. Quick medical diagnosis and patient-specific treatment selection now become feasible through the integrated system because medical staff receive fast access to vital patient data (Hartmann, Hashmi, & Imran, 2019). The EHR blackboard receives patient-generated glucose information through edge node networks to show irregular patterns to healthcare staff utilizing these networks.

The edge systems reach interoperability success by using HL7 FHIR and DICOM industry standards. The systems reach interoperability through standardization of data communication rules that create consistent exchange protocols and synchronized data formats as well as vocabulary definitions. Data regulations compliance and high patient safety measures are achieved through integrated systems that produce enhanced audit logs. System configuration enables healthcare authorization for log entry and lets healthcare providers maintain necessary change records to fulfil legal patient data requirements (Imtiaz & Jillani, 2024). The implementation of edge systems and electronic health records produces better clinical choices with reduced healthcare operational sequences to create superior patient care in adaptive digital healthcare systems.

3.3 Edge Deployment in Hospitals, Outpatient Facilities, and Home Care

Healthcare institutions have to develop deployment strategies that fit their medical architecture comprising both hospital and outpatient clinic and home care sites if they want to safeguard patient systems. Immediate analysis, which requires ongoing human supervision, determines the placement of edge nodes in surgery suites, hospital critical care units, and emergency departments (Jaleel, 2022). The node technology equipment inside these particular health care sectors localizes important medical data processing to manage image scans together with vital indicators intended at speeding emergency medical assistance.

Edge computing systems' diagnostic capabilities and patient examination outcome observation characteristics improve the efficiency of outpatient diagnostics. Healthcare providers use Edge technology to run networks connecting smart kiosks and medical diagnostic equipment and wearable sensor systems speeding patient processing and improving organizational efficiency. This storage system maintains real-time analytics link to cloud-based data enhancing its monitoring capabilities, hence functioning autonomously. Pre-patient devices linked to mobile health gateways in smart hubs allow for monitoring of patients needing chronic illness care alongside elderly patients and recovery patients getting home-based treatment (Nagam, 2023). The healthcare system can perform autonomous treatment recommendations and patient warning functions through programmed protocols which do not require cloud technology. The deployment strategy cascade ensures dependable low-cost patient healthcare service together with edge intelligent platforms' adaptive medical design approach.

3.4 Ensuring Seamless Connectivity Between Edge and Core Infrastructure

Edge-based healthcare systems need proper interconnection to main healthcare infrastructure to facilitate both smooth data synchronization and workflow combination and healthcare performance maximization. Edge systems execute instant clinical decisions by maintaining permanent information storage through an ongoing data sharing connection between HIS and EHR programs and data centers. Data exchange between the edge system uses secure high-speed connections through 5G and private LTE networks which supports communication by MQTT and HTTPS and HL7 protocols (Nasiri et al., 2019). The established data exchange method implements dual-directional data flow paths for fast and secure transmissions between systems across the edge network and central server infrastructure.

The built-in protocols in seamless systems maintain data integrity by preventing both accidental loss and duplication errors that occur during data transfers. Local data storage occurs at edge nodes until network functionality resumes allowing them to execute core duplication operations. Healthcare data remains available without interruption to patients as the system simultaneously defends operational activities from all disruptions. Security remains a top priority. The full protection of health data transfers occurs through encrypted communication and VPNs and authentication protocols which ensure HIPAA and GDPR compliance (Tesfai et al., 2022). Real-time network monitoring found in management tools enables IT teams to avoid connection problems through early resolution of issues. A unified and resilient network between edge and cloud systems allows healthcare organizations to achieve agile operation of their healthcare ecosystem.

4. REAL-TIME DATA PROCESSING AND AI AT THE EDGE

The functions of real-time medical decision-making in healthcare happen through operations in edge computing. Medical devices near patient centers can analyze vital signs information in order to offer healthcare professionals immediate monitoring. Healthcare networks can diagnose patients instantly and accurately when they present authentic data to patients in emergency critical cases. Medical devices with AI-based technology can carry out diagnostic imaging using their edges in detecting abnormalities and executing predictive capabilities. Artificial intelligence in combination with edge calculation enables medical staff to carry out quick patient information screenings for detecting sepsis in combination with cardiac conditions which raise instantaneous alerts for physicians (Yang et al., 2021). Edge solutions in combination make accessible early response possible, leading to saving lives. Edge AI integration facilitates patient information processing by medical centers at hospital entrance points, as well as system-managed personnel handling for sorting. Healthcare centers using edge-based AI solutions derive healthcare insights to facilitate operational speed and surgery practice and ensure better clinical outcomes.

4.1 On-Device Analytics for Continuous Monitoring

Device-based analytics enable healthcare professionals to track changes in patient health since such systems do not depend upon cloud system approvals. Responses to critical events happen within or near edge nodes to achieve instantaneous performance enhancement because latency is at its lowest. Heart rate monitors and blood sugar readings constitute integral elements enabled in practice in data accumulation in wearable devices. The medical data processing operation taps embedded processors running within data source points to send out notifications upon abnormality onset (Alabdulatif, Khalil, Yi, & Guizani, 2019).

Critical care hospital patients receive continuous medical surveillance in addition to professional postoperative hospital care and home healthcare following operations. Medical thresholds of oxygen in the blood below thresholds activate automatic alerts for health workers to view critical medical information. Medical device-based analysis delegation leads to simultaneous improvement of protection measures alongside reduced data transfer volume and operational costs. Staff members receive accurate real-time data that enables them to make urgent decision-based choices. On-device analytics brings substantial change to patient care because healthcare systems develop predictive instead of reactive capabilities to identify issues early and provide rapid responses and sustain continuous patient involvement in locations with minimal resources or in remote areas (Alterovitz et al., 2020).

4.2 AI and Machine Learning Models for Diagnostic Imaging

Healthcare facilities used computing edges to accelerate medical picture diagnostics with the help of AI and Machine Learning models which provided better evaluation of medical scans. Prior to edge-based systems medical imaging data needed to be transferred to cloud servers or specialists for diagnosis since the process required a delay. Edge-enabled AI facilitates on-site operation of these models to both process imaging data and analyse it for rapid generation of results within seconds. Convolutional neural networks (CNNs) work with other ML algorithms through medical imaging technology to detect tumors and fractures while identifying infection symptoms and haemorrhages by analysing patient medical scans. These implemented systems both detect important areas during radiological assessments and reduce human error thus generating documents more quickly (Draeger et al., 2023). Emergency department staff can now make rapid decisions during stroke and trauma situations because this capability has become available within their facilities.

The autonomous nature of Edge AI enables valuable healthcare services to extend to remote medical facilities as well as mobile diagnostic units even in internet connectivity limited areas. The protection of patient information maintained by hospitals defends hospital organizations from HIPAA and GDPR compliance requirements. Edge AI technology enhances clinical diagnosis abilities and operates better workflow processes to improve service scalability even as it smooths operations and diagnoses. Healthcare institutions must use edge-based AI diagnostic imaging systems to fulfil rapidly growing healthcare requirements and provide patients with both high-quality and efficient and affordable care services (Frey et al., 2024).

Table 2. AI/ML techniques and applications in edge-based diagnostic imaging

Technique	Application Area	Outcome Benefits
Convolutional Neural Networks	Tumor/Fracture Detection	Quick on-site diagnosis
ML-based Pattern Recognition	Hemorrhage & Infection Detection	Reduced human error, faster results
Edge-Based Deployment	Mobile Units, Emergency Rooms	Real-time scan processing
Autonomous AI Models	Stroke, Trauma Management	Enhanced emergency care efficiency

The table 2 illustrates the AI and ML techniques deployed in edge computing systems for real-time imaging, highlighting benefits such as diagnostic speed, accuracy, and deployment flexibility.

Figure 2. AI-Based diagnostic imaging workflow

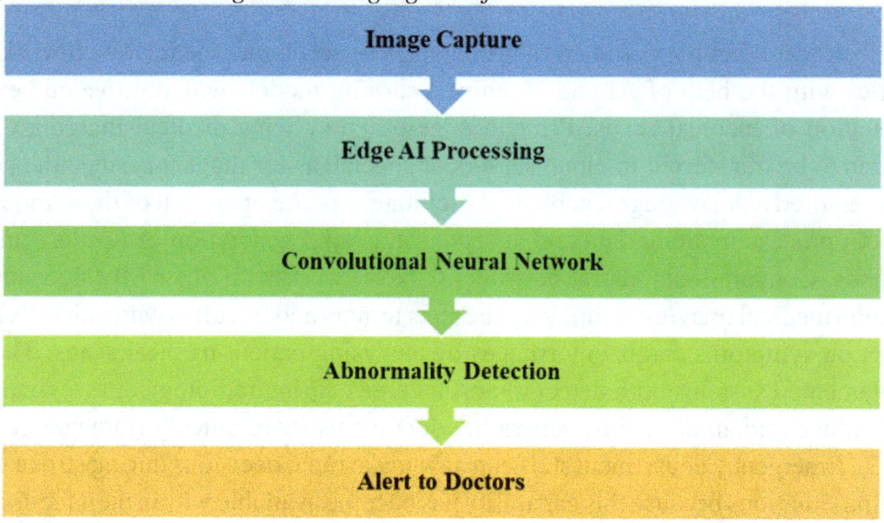

The Fig.2 outlines the AI-powered diagnostic imaging pipeline in edge computing. It begins with image capture, followed by local edge AI processing using convolutional neural networks (CNNs), leading to real-time abnormality detection and automated alert generation for medical professionals. The visual emphasizes speed and autonomy in edge-based healthcare diagnostics.

4.3 Predictive Analytics for Early Intervention and Critical Care

Processing time data at edge locations enables health issue forecasts before critical stages for fast healthcare delivery. Edge systems employ heart rate, blood pressure, respiration rate, and temperature to identify emergencies. To detect sepsis and respiratory failure early, ICU edge computing needs predictive algorithms that monitor vital sign changes (Jung et al., 2022). Optimized prediction models analyze large data volumes to function successfully in clinical workplace contexts that give risk assessment tools directly to medical staff.

Rapid processing of predictive assessment data enhances medical diagnosis. Patients spend less time in treatment, staff need less healthcare intensity, and hospital transfers are fewer. Predictive analytics technologies in home healthcare systems increase caregiver care and minimize patient ER visits (Kamel & Nagy, 2018). Edge-based predictive analytics provides system-wide operational decision-making that distributes assessment duties across medical networks to speed up patient treatment. Through proactive patient interventions, healthcare systems expedite medical staff decision-making to save lives and offer better care.

4.4 Real-World Examples of Edge AI in Emergency Scenarios

Through Edge AI operational success improves in critical emergency situations because the technology delivers vital survival choices between life and death. Portable ultrasound devices enabled with edge capabilities make up part of the emergency teams that work as emergency response equipment. Immediate AI devices of emergency teams receive body bleeding reports and organ damage examinations and bone fracture information which their devices analyze directly from team members. Medical diagnostic facilities use edge deployment technology for systems that perform simultaneous blood clot and hemorrhage detection in real-time CT scan operations (Lakshminarayanan et al., 2023). The combination of automatic CT scan recommendations assists medical personnel to reduce their time when making decisions between thrombolytic drugs and surgical procedures. Surface medical systems deliver favourable results to stroke patients through fast stroke recognition capabilities which lead to prompt medical interventions.

A continuous monitoring process by hospital equipment inside ambulances sends minimal amounts of vital sign information to medical facilities. Hospitals derive useful preparation time when patient admissions send ahead notifications about required resources. Widespread technology deployment makes possible critical monitoring operations together with important data exchange operations to function in areas without reliable communication networks. Healthcare staff generates immediate diagnostic functionality through the combination of edge AI systems with drones and mobile clinics which allows them to transfer medical information between regional centers and main headquarters (Lazarova et al., 2021). The combination of Edge AI systems allows medical professionals to decrease medical operations specifically in emergencies where the lifesaving benefits instantly appear.

5. MEDICAL DEVICE INTEGRATION AND INTEROPERABILITY

Effective patient-centered healthcare requires device integration solutions that generate interoperable medical equipment. Edge computing keeps medical devices, such as wearables with IoT sensors and diagnostics equipment, and electronic health records connected. Medical edge operations use data from several platforms to make real-time healthcare choices. HL7, FHIR, and DICOM are used in standard communication protocols (Mavrogiorgou et al., 2019a). Standardized data interchange and combination allows devices from any vendor to work together. This technology automatically sends vital signs from wearable monitors to patient EHRs for continuous healthcare management.

The edge system streamlines operational operations and reduces redundant checks before issuing instructions and synced patient health information with speedy device connection. The enabling improvement lets medical devices work in remote patient care systems and other healthcare settings. With effective data access, hospitals may deliver tailored patient care with data sharing results for operational speed and data-based success. For total medical device network implementation, medical revolution demands powerful ways that link distant healthcare institutions (Mavrogiorgou et al., 2019b).

5.1 Connecting Wearables, IoT Health Sensors, and Diagnostic Tools

Patient healthcare requirements need devices that track conditions by monitoring them in real time for both diagnosing and managing patient needs. Thanks to edge computing technology various wearable devices and medical IoT detectors and health equipment maintain non-stop connectivity. The medical devices analyze physiological data including heart rate measures with oxygen level readings and blood glucose meter outputs and Electrocardiogram results which are processed right after collection in nearby computing systems. The combination of remote sensors and wearable technology leads to sustained patient observation without requiring frequent hospital visits as clinicians obtain better opportunities for anticipatory medical care. The information processing at edge level initially gathers data that automatically triggers initial analysis and forwards data to central systems as it reduces network traffic and accelerates transmission speed (Saripalle et al., 2019). Time-sensitive performance becomes essential for treating patients with chronic conditions and monitoring post-surgical patients as well as elder healthcare. Healthcare systems supported by edge-enabled connectivity establish an orientation focused on patients while maintaining their capability to serve various care environments including home care settings and ambulatory clinics and emergency medical scenarios.

5.2 Standards and Protocols: HL7, FHIR, DICOM

Standardized communication protocols through which healthcare providers execute their tasks are essential for realizing healthcare device interoperability success. Operations in the healthcare industry require the unified use of Health Level Seven and Fast Healthcare Interoperability Resources and Digital Imaging and Communications in Medicine protocols. HL7 facilitates system-to-system structured medical data swapping yet FHIR provides Web-based integration of information from various sources. The open standards of DICOM allow diagnostic centers together with radiology devices to share diagnostic imaging scan data files. Edge computing enables standard application through data processing at local levels and site-based formatting that precedes EHR system data transmissions (Solar et al., 2024). Systems integrating multiple company products function better and quicker without errors when standardized functionality joins their operations. Medical organizations reach complete data interoperability and regulatory satisfaction while improving care systems through the implementation of configured edge system protocols. The implementation of quick decision-making and accurate clinical decisions through protocols produces uncertain medical practice decisions.

5.3 Ensuring Cross-Platform Device Communication

Hospital facilities face major interoperability problems because they use multiple platforms and different manufacturers for their original device sources. Edge computing delivers a single interface which allows various devices built for engineering needs to connect regardless of their original design structures. Edge facilities ensure smooth system data exchange through three elements which include APIs and middleware as well as protocol translation systems located at the system edge. Hospitals utilizing remote patient programs need multi-platform communication systems due to performance benefits from standardized data display and immediate information transmission. Standard protocols on edge systems make possible data normalization as well as transmission processes through which medical staff receive accurate information despite device or protocol variations (Alabdulatif et al., 2019). Platform-to-platform communication allows healthcare professionals to streamline processes as well as test duplications and establish standardized patient care procedures. The exchange of real-time medical data enables warning system development in hospitals to enhance understanding of emergency situations.

5.4 Improving Patient Care Through Data Unification

The near-time data fusion capabilities at the edge level help healthcare providers integrate patient information which arrives from wearable devices and multiple types of medical equipment alongside clinical instruments and laboratory systems. Before moving onto data harmonization, the data aggregation process executes inside edge computing to achieve central EHR system synchronization. The quick and informed clinical decisions of medical professionals become possible because real-time patient record updates appear. The integration of precision medicine with healthcare presents itself through data collection that consolidates entire patient medical records into core population diagnostics (Ali, 2025). For diabetes care strategy development medical professionals depend on the continuous glucose monitor data's capacity to trace exercise and nutritional activities of their patients. The combination of data processing results in reduced duplicate medical records and improves healthcare care coordination between departments through the elimination of data fragmentation to enhance patient safety. Better patient satisfaction and improved clinical results as well as flexible patient care arise from healthcare professionals who process integrated edge-assembled data at their point of care.

6. SECURITY, PRIVACY, AND REGULATORY COMPLIANCE

Patient health information security necessitates some level of security within edge computing solutions to be put in place by healthcare institutions. Patient health information security must be in accordance with HIPAA and GDPR protection requirements at the edge. Security frameworks must include complete encryption integration for securing authorized data storage solutions and permission-based mandatory mechanisms for securing all protected data points against unauthorized use. Security against unauthorized device modification as well as unauthorized use scenarios is essential for securing edge-specific risks through security frameworks (Chauhan et al., 2024). Authentication of data as well as data integrity operations become possible through integrating zero-trust models along with blockchain technology. Medical centers have compliance frameworks for securing their edge infrastructure operations because such systems provide protection for patient information at various locations as necessitated by regulation for patient trust.

6.1 HIPAA and GDPR Guidelines for Edge Environments

By using HIPAA rule in conjunction with GDPR compliance, healthcare edge computing should meet two criteria. Every healthcare provider should have HIPAA-compliant patient health information by means of policies combining confidentiality criteria with data security and compliance tools. Controllers shall show clients at points of access data handling systems and get their consent for information processing under GDPR rule applicable to all EU activities. Defined rules should control every distributed processing node and device involved in managing collected data. Systematized Edge infrastructure design should have in-built compliances made up of data reduction technologies along with user anonymization functions together with audit monitoring. By using policies for implementing medical security standards created from national and international law, integration of personal data controls and independent logs within Edge infrastructure safeguards medical information Hartmann, Hashmi, & Imran, 2019). Companies should embrace regulatory compliance as it is a fundamental deployment need that preserves safe healthcare services and builds confidence in online medical services by means of strict regulation adherence.

6.2 Edge-Specific Risks and Countermeasures

Edge healthcare devices operate in various locations which creates vulnerabilities because attackers have easier access to sensitive information while devices are left exposed to real tampering attempts. Healthcare institutions conducting outpatient care using decentralized information technology systems come under added security risks during operations of home care services and outpatient clinics. Healthcare organizations should have various defensive mechanisms for managing security risks emanating from edge computing environments. Multiple defensive measures should be possessed by healthcare institutions combining enhanced device security features with automatic firmware upgrade mechanisms and protected boot system mechanisms and support services for local anomaly. Endpoint security in conjunction with network segmentation leaves organizations capable of controlling breach movements within their overall system (Kanungo, 2025). Healthcare facilities need to perform security audits combined with penetration tests as fundamental security procedures to identify existing vulnerabilities for blocking enemy attacks. Secure medical information requires protected entry points available on operational devices for correctly trained personnel to access. Healthcare facilities requiring medical data protection of edge-powered systems must establish a complete security system to defend physical structures while implementing cybersecurity protocols.

Table 3. Security risks in edge environments and mitigation strategies

Security Risk	Vulnerability Point	Recommended Countermeasure
Physical Device Tampering	Remote/mobile locations	Secure enclosures, tamper detection hardware
Firmware Exploits	Edge node OS	Secure boot, automatic firmware updates
Unauthorized Access	Network endpoints	Multi-factor authentication, RBAC
Malware Propagation	Connected IoT devices	Network segmentation, endpoint detection systems
Data Leakage	Data storage/transit	AES encryption, secure VPN, compliance audits

The table 3 outlines various security vulnerabilities in edge healthcare systems and pairs them with recommended technical and procedural countermeasures.

Figure 3. Edge security risks and countermeasures

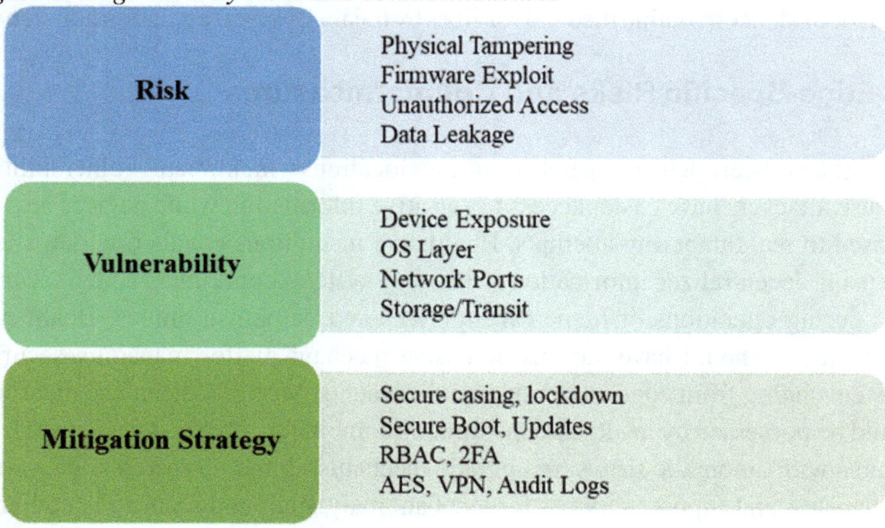

The Fig.3 categorizes key edge computing security risks (e.g., tampering, unauthorized access), their vulnerability points (like OS layer and network ports), and corresponding mitigation strategies such as RBAC, secure boot, and encryption. It provides a concise visual for understanding threat surfaces and defense mechanisms in healthcare edge environments.

6.3 Secure Storage, Data Encryption, and Access Control

Protection of medical data requires secure storage together with encryption which stands as the fundamental procedure for processing health data at the edge. Edge node installation requires commercial customers to buy secure storage systems for protecting data processed by their local analyst and data collector workforce. The deployment of AES technology is required to encrypt stationary data and data during transfer operations. Role-based approval systems enable employment of both medical staff and IT personnel to access protected healthcare data for retrieval as well as authorized modification purposes. Integrating security protection calls for user authentication using two techniques and biometric data verification confirmation. Key management security solutions validate the proper internal encryption of linked devices, hence providing vital verification procedure. Developed backup processes and record retirement techniques help healthcare practitioners safeguard patient data by means of appropriate management of edge-based medical records (Kothari, 2023). Fast processing operations for private information help healthcare data control to be more successful by satisfying healthcare compliance requirements and thereby avoiding data breach events.

6.4 Role of Blockchain and Zero-Trust Architectures in Healthcare

Core security policies for integrating edge computing technologies in healthcare facilities include Blockchain technology and zero-trust architectural approaches. Blockchain technology lets healthcare organizations have automated distributed security characteristics for protecting medical data in a way that stops changes to ensure proper patient records transfer on all edge networks. The system framework includes secure consent authorization tools that guarantee cooperation among healthcare organizations and provide openness to companies. Because they want to investigate every network object, all nodes within networks comprising devices and out-of-network players must carry out authentication procedures inside zero-trust networks. Using their combined procedure Segmented network privileges combined with ongoing verification builds an impenetrable method for preventing cyber assaults to spread across system components. Requests for medical data in situations involving patient data transfers from edge frameworks to zero-trust frameworks call for consumers to complete two verification steps before obtaining permission from hundreds of devices and apps. Medical institutions looking for future security understand security platforms by merging zero-trust network security models with blockchain technology to incorporate into their defensive mechanisms. Modern distributed health information systems secure targets by using technologies that not only provide continuous communication monitoring and generate data sharing capabilities but also actively detect attackers (Kumar, 2024).

7. STRATEGIC DEPLOYMENT AND BUSINESS IMPACT

Key security policies for building edge computing networks include Blockchain technology and zero-trust architectural approaches, which healthcare organizations use. By stopping alterations to guarantee proper patient records transmission in all networks at an edge, blockchain technology lets healthcare organizations get automated decentralized security measures keeping medical information safe. The system architecture incorporates protected consent authorization procedures guaranteeing healthcare entity cooperation while enabling commercial openness. Because of their desire to inspect every network entity, network participants including devices and non-members must undertake authentication procedures under zero-trust networks. By use of joint operation Segmented networking combined with ongoing verification forms a protective mechanism stopping cyber-attacks from propagating across system components. Requests for medical information across networks at the edge and zero-trust settings call for users to complete two verification procedures before obtaining permission from different devices and apps. Medical institutions aiming future security create security platforms by combining blockchain technology with zero-trust network security models to build their defensive systems (Kumhar & Bhatia, 2022). Today's dispersed health information networks protect its goals by use of technologies which both provide data sharing capabilities and secure ongoing communication monitoring.

7.1 Planning Edge Infrastructure in Medical Settings

Edge computing is successfully implemented by means of appropriate planning systems for medical institutions. Appropriate system development calls for assessments of clinical services along with data volume studies and medical patient need assessments for hospital and home health facilities. The created system supports the possibility to construct new infrastructure in the future while following laws and regulations and needs access to current healthcare facilities. Health care organizations have to first choose medical-grade hardware to reach effective edge computing deployment before integrating Electronic Health Record systems with devices. Operational objectives guarantee consistency in patient treatment by having healthcare professionals collaborate with IT staff and administrators from the planning phase. Planning actions beginning at various planned times helps to create the stability of healthcare edge delivery systems.

7.2 Cost Optimization and Operational Efficiency

Edge computing is successfully implemented only with sufficient planning tools for healthcare institutions. Sufficient system development requires clinical service assessments in addition to data volume assessments and medical patient need assessments for hospital and home health care facilities. The created system allows for future expanded infrastructure development but requires simplicity of connectivity to current healthcare facilities in compliance to laws and regulations (Li et al., 2020). Healthcare organizations have to use medical-grade hardware to guarantee success in edge computing deployment before adding Electronic Health Record systems to devices. Functional objectives guarantee consistency in patient care by including healthcare professionals working with IT personnel and administrators from planning phases. Planning procedures started at many planned times drives healthcare edge delivery system stability.

7.3 Enhancing Patient Satisfaction and Care Responsiveness

Edge computing improves patient happiness as it enables healthcare professionals to provide quick customized medical treatment. In addition to distant sites, in-house analytical software and real-time monitoring tools let healthcare personnel provide quick medical assistance in many healthcare settings. Healthcare consumers benefit from favourable consequences when accurate diagnostic abilities combine with fast waiting times and connected interdependent medical devices. Home healthcare agencies employ mobile edge nodes to ensure continuous medical monitoring of homebound individuals without necessitating their presence in hospitals. Medical patients receive independent care abilities in addition to real-time monitoring of their health using this approach. Edge solutions-based patient-specific healthcare methods create stronger provider-patient bonds and establish trust because of their impact on better relationships between medical staff and their users.

7.4 Measuring ROI and Aligning Edge Investments with Business Goals

The healthcare ROI evaluation of edge computing requires analysis between the patient outcome effects and operational system administration cost reduction. The system performance indicators show diagnostic results lead to quicker time-to-results and both patients and staff experience quicker responses while improving movement and showing lower hospital readmission rates. Healthcare facilities achieve improved financial returns through utilization of edge computing due to its minimization of cost-per-case analysis and maximizing bandwidth efficiency at post-season. Edge solution investment is worth it in the long run based upon definite organizational goals of enhancing healthcare quality and creating remote capacity for services while still fulfilling regulatory requirements. Continuous improvement is driven by frequent performance reviews against stakeholder feedback. Healthcare transformation maintains as an abiding strength due to edge computing's efficiency.

Table 4. ROI metrics for evaluating edge computing deployment in healthcare

Metric	Description	Impact Area
Time-to-Diagnosis Reduction	Time saved in delivering diagnostic results	Clinical efficiency
Bandwidth Utilization	Optimization of network data load	IT infrastructure cost reduction
Readmission Rate	Decrease in repeat patient admissions	Patient outcomes

continued on following page

Table 4. Continued

Metric	Description	Impact Area
Cost per Case	Treatment cost before and after edge deployment	Financial sustainability
Staff Productivity	Reduced delays and improved workflow	Operational efficiency

The table 4 provides key return-on-investment indicators that healthcare administrators can use to assess the performance and value of edge computing systems.

Figure 4. ROI metrics for edge deployment

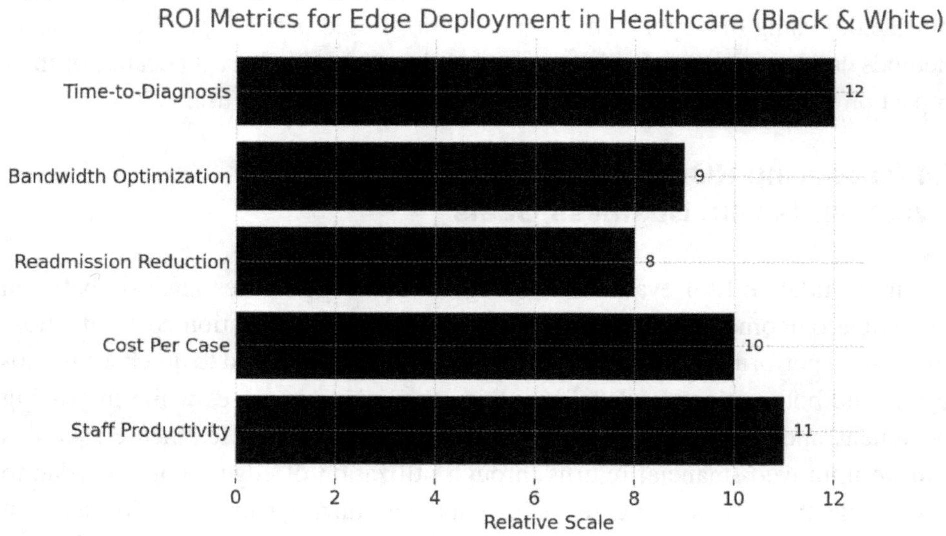

The Fig.4 shows key ROI indicators like Time-to-Diagnosis, Staff Productivity, and Cost Per Case. It highlights the comparative impact of edge computing on healthcare performance. The black-and-white design ensures clarity for print and technical documents.

8. FUTURE OUTLOOK AND IMPLEMENTATION ROADMAP

Healthcare integration technology among robotic healthcare assistants and 5G technology and digital twins drives the development of medical applications. Innovative technology in healthcare institutions produces rapid diagnostic services using simulation-based individualized treatment protocols. Healthcare implementation systems ought to be methodical for platform trials and first tests of platforms to guarantee suitable compliance criteria for reaching intended goals. Every stage of implementation calls for maximum attention on staff training and inter-sectoral professional interactions (Prasad & Mitra, 2023). By means of data-driven patient-specific healthcare via future innovation trends, the vital technology of edge computing enables linked networks to meet future healthcare security needs.

8.1 Emerging Trends: 5G Integration, Digital Twins, and Robotics

5G provides rapid data transfer in addition to quick reaction capabilities allowing remote surgery as well as fast medical examination and enhanced connectivity among devices and medical platforms, hence edge computing enables an integration of next technologies. By use of rapid computations, prediction models employed by medical staff help to generate digital twins utilizing health data processing as well as information from medical clinics. Edge AI-powered robots help medical institutions via healthcare automation by distributing drugs while doing patient relocation activities at distant healthcare facilities in addition to geriatric care centers. Apart from enhancing their system responsiveness and operational efficiency, medical technology integration helps medical practitioners raise accuracy rates. Edge computing provides the fundamental operational foundation enabling it to interpret information from real-time data for improving bandwidth-demanding applications. Key in current healthcare delivery is medical innovation as it enables digital improvement and improves treatment results as well as clinic workflow management and quality of healthcare pathways.

8.2 Strategic Steps for Edge Deployment in Healthcare

The deployment of edge computing infrastructure for healthcare needs an organized multistage methodology to match clinical objectives along with compliance requirements and technical capabilities of the system. The initial action requires healthcare organizations to detect essential use cases that involve real-time monitoring and AI-assisted diagnostics. Health institutions need to evaluate their existing IT systems after which they should choose medical-grade hardware products that align with their specific needs. To meet requirements healthcare organizations must integrate their edge systems with existing EHR platforms and both follow HIPAA/GDPR protocols and secure their medical data effectively (Ramanathan et al., 2023). The evaluation of system performance through pilot implementations allows organizations to improve workflow methods before implementing the solution across larger departments.

The implementation design needs to include scalability features which allow expansion alongside future technological innovations. Plans to connect remote and home-care devices with core systems must be established for reliable communication purposes. Selecting healthcare personnel to learn about edge systems results in improved staff adoption and extended system success. To achieve implementation success stakeholders, need to develop strategic partnerships which involve technology providers as well as compliance experts and representatives from all departmental levels. The approach facilitates the implementation of value-driven edge solutions which optimize medical results together with operational performance.

8.3 Key Recommendations for IT Leaders and Decision-Makers

Healthcare IT leaders and decision-makers need to connect technological implementations with clinical targets along with patient success metrics and regulatory compliance requirements to achieve successful edge computing implementation. Begin the edge initiative process through creation of multidisciplinary teams made up of both clinical personnel and IT experts and those responsible for compliance. Build infrastructure systems that scale securely and function for analytics in real-time as well as allow devices to incorporate with each other. The implementation must adopt HIPAA, GDPR and medical standards including HL7 and FHIR as well as follow the necessary requirements. Organizations must choose solutions with modular components to enable modular growth because they provide flexibility.

To determine ROI organizations, need to establish KPIs which measure speed enhancement together with improved diagnostics and patient satisfaction. Organizations need to provide financial support for workforce training that joins change management programs focused on implementing transition improvements (Soni & Tandan, 2024). The evolution of healthcare innovation needs medical organizations to preserve their patient safety systems while defending all medical information. Advancements of digital twins will occur when AI and 5G systems are integrated during future developments. The deployment readiness of edge computing within healthcare facilities depends on strategic leadership which allows patients to receive efficient medical connectivity for improved care.

9. CONCLUSION

Health systems can deliver more secure real-time patient care efficiency with the implementation of edge computing in their operations. The control of data management closer to medical equipment leads to improved outcomes at healthcare facilities for traditional system optimization. The implementation of advanced edge computing models generates medical applications that meet healthcare standards and improve both medical treatment timing and patient outcomes. Healthcare facilities generate large amounts of data that need quick access to confidential records for accurate information retrieval. The slow performance of cloud systems together with limited resources in different areas stops medical staff from conducting instant clinical decisions. Medical facilities gain faster responses through edge computing because analysis executes directly within these facilities. Predictive analytics which support early disease detection and authentic care path planning for all critical healthcare settings becomes possible by embedding artificial intelligence and machine learning tools into edge computing systems.

For its standardized framework to support continuing patient healthcare assessment and evidence-based medical decision making the Electronic Health Record system requires Medical-grade edge nodes. Healthcare delivery frameworks depend on edge node implementation at all hospital sites and outpatient clinics and home care programs to generate advanced medical frameworks. The combination of HL7 and FHIR and DICOM communication protocols leads to improved performance of healthcare devices. The diagnostic equipment and storage databases share information about patient health status through doctorial understanding with the help of an IoT device communication platform. The approach connects healthcare providers to enhance future medical care with benefits for treatment quality and error reduction.

Only security measures that satisfy both HIPAA requirements together with GDPR standards form the basis for trust in healthcare edge computations. Medical facilities require complete security solutions which connect encryption protocols with zero-trust networks and blockchain-based monitoring platforms to protect distributed network patient data. Organizations reach their optimal operational performance after obeying privacy and safety requirements from official authorities. Organizations enhance patient satisfaction by using edge computing systems to boost operational efficiency and control costs which results in organizational development. Industrial border technologies help healthcare organizations meet their strategic requirements along with executing swift disease analysis and network optimization and mobile health service expansion. Hospital leaders gain full visibility of their border technology investment value by uniting top-quality clinical results with improved resource use to establish effective demonstrations of value in their solutions.

The ongoing developments in healthcare edge computing hold great importance because of both 5G technological breakthroughs and digital twin along with robotic systems that incorporate augmented intelligence capabilities. Real-time coordination features emerge from new technological capabilities that make self-operating patient care systems execute simulation-based care. The present need of healthcare facilities exceeds medical device integration and healthcare edge computing systems rather than these innovations being necessary for future operations. Medical care providers can provide safe and fast healthcare services through regulatory-compliant infrastructure development. Implementation of this operational method drives medical care improvement and develops data-based patient-care models.

REFERENCES

Alabdulatif, A., Khalil, I., Yi, X., & Guizani, M. (2019). Secure edge of things for smart healthcare surveillance framework. *IEEE Access : Practical Innovations, Open Solutions*, *7*, 31010–31021. DOI: 10.1109/ACCESS.2019.2899323

Alabdulatif, A., Khalil, I., Yi, X., & Guizani, M. (2019). Secure edge of things for smart healthcare surveillance framework. *IEEE Access : Practical Innovations, Open Solutions*, *7*, 31010–31021. DOI: 10.1109/ACCESS.2019.2899323

Ali, A., Ali, H., Saeed, A., Ahmed, A., Tin, T., Assam, M., & Mohamed, H. (2023). Blockchain-powered healthcare systems: Enhancing scalability and security with hybrid deep learning. *Sensors (Basel)*, *23*(18), 7740. DOI: 10.3390/s23187740 PMID: 37765797

Ali, A., Montanaro, T., Sergi, I., Carrisi, S., Galli, D., Distante, C., & Patrono, L. (2025). An innovative iot and edge intelligence framework for monitoring elderly people using anomaly detection on data from non-wearable sensors. *Sensors (Basel)*, *25*(6), 1735. DOI: 10.3390/s25061735 PMID: 40292837

Almatrooshi, S., Gopakumar, A., & Mathur, V. (2024). Transformative role of cryptocurrency in the healthcare system of uae. *Annals of Case Reports*, *9*(2). DOI: 10.29011/2574-7754.101703

Alterovitz, G., Heale, B., Jones, J., Kreda, D., Lin, F., Liu, L., Liu, X., Mandl, K. D., Poloway, D. W., Ramoni, R., Wagner, A., & Warner, J. (2020). Fhir genomics: Enabling standardization for precision medicine use cases. *NPJ Genomic Medicine*, *5*(1), 13. DOI: 10.1038/s41525-020-0115-6 PMID: 32194985

Amanat, A., Rizwan, M., Maple, C., Zikria, Y., Almadhor, A., & Kim, S. (2022). Blockchain and cloud computing-based secure electronic healthcare records storage and sharing. *Frontiers in Public Health*, *10*, 938707. DOI: 10.3389/fpubh.2022.938707 PMID: 35928494

Arafa, A., Sheerah, H., & Alsalamah, S. (2023). Emerging digital technologies in healthcare with a spotlight on cybersecurity: A narrative review. *Information (Basel)*, *14*(12), 640. DOI: 10.3390/info14120640

Aujla, G., & Jindal, A. (2021). A decoupled blockchain approach for edge-envisioned iot-based healthcare monitoring. *IEEE Journal on Selected Areas in Communications*, *39*(2), 491–499. DOI: 10.1109/JSAC.2020.3020655

Chauhan, D., Jain, J., & Singh, A. (2024). Deployment of edge computing for smart healthcare systems on cloud computing platform. *International Journal of Scientific Research in Computer Science Engineering and Information Technology*, *10*(3), 685–693. DOI: 10.32628/CSEIT2410339

Chenthara, S., Ahmed, K., Wang, H., & Whittaker, F. (2019). Security and privacy-preserving challenges of e-health solutions in cloud computing. *IEEE Access : Practical Innovations, Open Solutions*, *7*, 74361–74382. DOI: 10.1109/ACCESS.2019.2919982

Ciecierski-Holmes, T., Singh, R., Axt, M., Brenner, S., & Barteit, S. (2022). Artificial intelligence for strengthening healthcare systems in low- and middle-income countries: A systematic scoping review. *NPJ Digital Medicine*, *5*(1), 162. DOI: 10.1038/s41746-022-00700-y PMID: 36307479

Dias, R., & Torkamani, A. (2019). Artificial intelligence in clinical and genomic diagnostics. *Genome Medicine*, *11*(1), 70. DOI: 10.1186/s13073-019-0689-8 PMID: 31744524

Draeger, C., Tute, E., Schmidt, C., Waltemath, D., Boeker, M., Winter, A, & Löbe, M. (2023). Identifying relevant FHIR elements for data quality assessment in the German core data set. DOI: 10.3233/SHTI230117

Frey, N., Haffer, N., Vogelsang, L., Saß, J., Thun, S., Balzer, F. & Landgraf, P. (2024). Integrating fhir and umls in an intelligent tutoring system. DOI: 10.3233/SHTI240708

Ghane, S., Jolfaei, A., Kulik, L., Ramamohanarao, K., & Puthal, D. (2021). Preserving privacy in the internet of connected vehicles. *IEEE Transactions on Intelligent Transportation Systems*, *22*(8), 5018–5027. DOI: 10.1109/TITS.2020.2964410

Hartmann, M., Hashmi, U., & Imran, M. (2019). Edge computing in smart health care systems: Review, challenges, and research directions. *Transactions on Emerging Telecommunications Technologies*, *33*(3), e3710. DOI: 10.1002/ett.3710

Hasan, M., Li, Q., Saha, U., & Li, J. (2024). Decentralized and secure collaborative framework for personalized diabetes prediction. *Biomedicines*, *12*(8), 1916. DOI: 10.3390/biomedicines12081916 PMID: 39200380

Imtiaz, S., & Jillani, S. (2024). The impact of artificial intelligence on medical diagnostics: A letter to the editor. *JPMA. The Journal of the Pakistan Medical Association*, *74*(5), 1035–1036. DOI: 10.47391/JPMA.10668 PMID: 38783474

Jaleel, A. (2022). Distributed interoperability solutions smart healthcare system for multi-patient vital signs monitoring and forecast of critical alerts. *Pakistan Journal of Science*, *72*(4). DOI: 10.57041/pjs.v72i4.235

Javed, H., Toosi, A., & Aslanpour, M. (2021). Serverless platforms on the edge: a performance analysis.

Jung, S., Bae, S., Seong, D., Oh, O., Kim, Y., & Yi, B. (2022). Shared interoperable clinical decision support service for drug-allergy interaction checks: Implementation study. *JMIR Medical Informatics*, *10*(11), e40338. DOI: 10.2196/40338 PMID: 36355401

Kamel, P., & Nagy, P. (2018). Patient-centered radiology with fhir: An introduction to the use of fhir to offer radiology a clinically integrated platform. *Journal of Digital Imaging*, *31*(3), 327–333. DOI: 10.1007/s10278-018-0087-6 PMID: 29725963

Kanungo, P. (2025). Edge computing in healthcare: real-time patient monitoring systems. World Journal of Advanced Engineering Technology and Sciences, 15(1), 001-009. DOI: 10.30574/wjaets.2025.15.1.0168

Kothari, R. (2023). Integration of blockchain and edge computing in healthcare: Accountability and collaboration. *Transdisciplinary Journal of Engineering & Science*, *14*. DOI: 10.22545/2023/00230

Kumar, M. (2024). Optimizing security for remote patient monitoring with edge computing strategies. *Int Res J Adv Engg Mgt*, *2*(05), 1530–1535. DOI: 10.47392/IRJAEM.2024.0207

Kumhar, M., & Bhatia, J. (2022). Edge computing in sdn-enabled iot-based healthcare frameworks. *International Journal of Reliable and Quality E-Healthcare*, *11*(4), 1–15. DOI: 10.4018/IJRQEH.308804

Lakshminarayanan, V., Ravikumar, A., Sriraman, H., Alla, S., & Chattu, V. (2023). Health care equity through intelligent edge computing and augmented reality/virtual reality: A systematic review. *Journal of Multidisciplinary Healthcare*, *16*, 2839–2859. DOI: 10.2147/JMDH.S419923 PMID: 37753339

Lazarova, E., Mora, S., Rubartelli, P., Vitale, A., Pareto, L., Maggi, N., … & Giacomini, M. (2021). Integrating an electronic health record system into a regional health information system: an hl7 fhir architecture. DOI: 10.3233/SHTI210357

Li, J., Jinjin, C., Khan, F., Rehman, A., Balasubramaniam, V., Sun, J., & Venu, P. (2020). A secured framework for sdn-based edge computing in iot-enabled healthcare system. *IEEE Access: Practical Innovations, Open Solutions*, *8*, 135479–135490. DOI: 10.1109/ACCESS.2020.3011503

Li, X., He, J., Vijayakumar, P., Zhang, X., & Chang, V. (2022). A verifiable privacy-preserving machine learning prediction scheme for edge-enhanced hcpss. *IEEE Transactions on Industrial Informatics*, *18*(8), 5494–5503. DOI: 10.1109/TII.2021.3110808

Li, X., Liu, S., Wu, F., Kumari, S., & Rodrigues, J. (2019). Privacy preserving data aggregation scheme for mobile edge computing assisted iot applications. *IEEE Internet of Things Journal*, *6*(3), 4755–4763. DOI: 10.1109/JIOT.2018.2874473

Mavrogiorgou, A., Kiourtis, A., Perakis, K., Pitsios, S., & Kyriazis, D. (2019a). Iot in healthcare: Achieving interoperability of high-quality data acquired by iot medical devices. *Sensors (Basel)*, *19*(9), 1978. DOI: 10.3390/s19091978 PMID: 31035612

Mavrogiorgou, A., Kiourtis, A., Touloupou, M., Kapassa, E., & Kyriazis, D. (2019b). Internet of medical things (iomt): Acquiring and transforming data into hl7 fhir through 5g network slicing. *Emerging Science Journal*, *3*(2), 64–77. DOI: 10.28991/esj-2019-01170

McNamee, F., Dustadar, S., Kilpatrick, P., Shi, W., Spence, I., & Varghese, B. (2020). A case for adaptive deep neural networks in edge computing.

Miao, Q., Jing, W., & Song, H. (2018). Differential privacy–based location privacy enhancing in edge computing. *Concurrency and Computation*, *31*(8), e4735. DOI: 10.1002/cpe.4735

Nagam, V. (2023). Diagnostic medical artificial intelligence: Futuristic prospects for implementation in healthcare settings. *Frontiers in Artificial Intelligence*, *6*, 1169244.DOI: 10.3389/frai.2023.1169244 PMID: 37064297

Nasiri, S., Sadoughi, F., Tadayon, M., & Dehnad, A. (2019). Security requirements of internet of things-based healthcare system: A survey study. *Acta Informatica Medica*, *27*(4), 253. DOI: 10.5455/aim.2019.27.253-258 PMID: 32055092

Prasad, N., & Mitra, D. (2023). Importance of patient satisfaction in achieving a competitive edge in the healthcare system. *The Management Accountant Journal*, *58*(4), 21. DOI: 10.33516/maj.v58i4.21-26p

Premsankar, G., Francesco, M., & Taleb, T. (2018). Edge computing for the internet of things: A case study. *IEEE Internet of Things Journal*, *5*(2), 1275–1284. DOI: 10.1109/JIOT.2018.2805263

Puneeth, R., & Parthasarathy, G. (2024). Blockchain-based framework for privacy preservation and securing ehr with patient-centric access control. *Acta Informatica Pragensia*, *13*(1), 1–23. DOI: 10.18267/j.aip.225

Ramanathan, S., Pineda-Briseño, A., Mohd, T., & Ramasundaram, M. (2023). Edge computing in healthcare., 1-18. DOI: 10.1201/9781003363361-1

Román, R., López, J., & Mambo, M. (2018). Mobile edge computing, Fog et al.: A survey and analysis of security threats and challenges. *Future Generation Computer Systems*, *78*, 680–698. DOI: 10.1016/j.future.2016.11.009

Saripalle, R., Runyan, C., & Mitchell, R. (2019). Using hl7 fhir to achieve interoperability in patient health record. *Journal of Biomedical Informatics*, *94*, 103188. DOI: 10.1016/j.jbi.2019.103188 PMID: 31063828

Shen, B., Guo, J., & Yang, Y. (2019). Medchain: Efficient healthcare data sharing via blockchain. *Applied Sciences (Basel, Switzerland)*, *9*(6), 1207. DOI: 10.3390/app9061207

Singh, S. (2023). Secure health record management system with effective machine learning and blockchain techniques. nq, 20(03). DOI: 10.48047/NQ.2022.20.3.NQ22957

Solar, M., Castañeda, V., Ñanculef, R., Dombrovskaia, L., & Araya, M. (2024). A data ingestion procedure towards a medical images repository. *Sensors (Basel)*, *24*(15), 4985. DOI: 10.3390/s24154985 PMID: 39124032

Soni, P., & Tandan, G. (2024). Smart health infrastructure: Integrating internet of things (iot) with edge computing for enhanced disease surveillance and response. *South Eastern European Journal of Public Health*, 1–8. DOI: 10.70135/seejph.vi.741

Tesfai, H., Saleh, H., Al-Qutayri, M., Mohammad, M., Tekeste, T., Khandoker, A., & Mohammad, B. (2022). Lightweight shufflenet based cnn for arrhythmia classification. *IEEE Access : Practical Innovations, Open Solutions*, *10*, 111842–111854. DOI: 10.1109/ACCESS.2022.3215665

Varghese, B., Wang, N., Barbhuiya, S., Kilpatrick, P., & Nikolopoulos, D. (2016). Challenges and opportunities in edge computing., 20-26. DOI: 10.1109/SmartCloud.2016.18

Yang, J., Dung, N., Th ch, P., Phong, N., Phu, V., Phu, K., & Clifton, D. (2023). Generalizability assessment of ai models across hospitals: a comparative study in low-middle income and high income countries. DOI: 10.1101/2023.11.05.23298109

Yang, T., Lee, S., & Park, S. (2021). Ai-aided individual emergency detection system in edge-internet of things environments. *Electronics (Basel)*, *10*(19), 2374. DOI: 10.3390/electronics10192374

Zhou, Z., Chen, X., Li, E., Zeng, L., Luo, K., & Zhang, J. (2019). Edge intelligence: Paving the last mile of artificial intelligence with edge computing. *Proceedings of the IEEE*, *107*(8), 1738–1762. DOI: 10.1109/JPROC.2019.2918951

Chapter 9
Healthcare Edge Computing and Medical Device Integration System:
Deployment, Scalability, and Maintenance Using DevOps

C. V. Suresh Babu
https://orcid.org/0000-0002-8474-2882
Hindustan Institute of Technology and Science, India

Kumar P. Yukesh
Hindustan Institute of Technology and Science, India

S. Saravanan
Hindustan Institute of Technology and Science, India

R. Harish
Hindustan Institute of Technology and Science, India

ABSTRACT

This chapter explores the integration of AI and quantum computing in cybersecurity, focusing on their combined potential to address evolving cyber threats. The primary objective is to analyze how quantum computing enhances AI-driven security frameworks, strengthening encryption, threat detection, and risk mitigation. The study targets cybersecurity professionals, researchers, and technology policymakers. A systematic review of existing literature, case studies, and comparative analysis of

DOI: 10.4018/979-8-3373-1147-0.ch009

traditional and quantum-enhanced AI security models form the methodological foundation. Findings reveal that while AI-driven cybersecurity solutions offer robust predictive analytics, quantum computing significantly improves cryptographic resilience against emerging cyber threats. The chapter concludes that the convergence of these technologies will redefine cybersecurity paradigms, necessitating advancements in quantum-safe algorithms and regulatory frameworks. The implications emphasize the urgent need for research and policy adaptation to leverage these technologies for secure digital systems.

1. INTRODUCTION

1.1 Overview of Healthcare Edge Computing

Healthcare edge computing is among the kinds of edge computing that is slowly revolutionizing the integration of medical equipment into the network. Many of the conventional systems deploy cloud systems to face certain limitations such as delay and bandwidth issues that can be life-threatening in the medical field. There are a number of limitations that current methods suffer from, which are solved by means of edge computing, such as the speed of data analysis and patient monitoring. DevOps contributes to the deployment, scalability, and maintenance of the systems. CI/CD processes are essentially the practices of integrating and deploying the software frequently and continuously in order to reduce the amount of time that the systems have to be down (Valaboju, 2024). Also, the use of AI and machine learning in the prediction of failure consequently causes disruption of healthcare services. Promoting the use of health-based edge AI in smart IoT medical devices also helps in real-time analytics of data and also relieves congestion in analytics (Arockiasamy, 2024). The incorporation of the healthcare edge computing idea with the provision of DevOps practices that focus on always testing and always being prepared to scale up has made it easier for modern healthcare to develop its infrastructure.

1.2 Importance of Medical Device Integration

Medical device integration is essential in the current environment since it has added compatibility thereby enabling communication with other medical technologies and IT systems. Another advantage is flexible monitoring of the patient's condition and avoiding inaccuracy due to human intervention. With the help of e during the preprocessing of the patient data, fast decisions regarding the clinical procedures, especially in the emergency cases are made (Ali et al., 2025). Also, security and data security are important issues of concern when it comes to the integration of different medical devices. Integrating blockchain technology with edge computing will improve a data's verification process, as well as shield personal health information from attack. It remains secure and elastic to integrate into the healthcare facility and also complies with the set regulations (Masum et al., 2025).

1.3 Role of DevOps in Healthcare Edge Solutions

The primary type through which DevOps benefits healthcare is by improving the deployment of edge computing tasks in healthcare facilities to increase efficiency and system robustness. As highlighted throughout this paper, implementing the Continuous Integration (CI) helps foster automated deployment at the edge, thereby reducing system downtimes to the barest minimum, thus increasing the system reliability. CI/CD pipelines help in constant and agile releases to adapt to these real-time healthcare needs such as emergency telemetry services or changes arising from pandemics, among others; In this case, (Elhachmi et al., 2025). In particular it is important to note that the use of DevOps reflects other tendencies, namely in the reduction of latency and the general system resiliency as described in the review.

When it comes to Securities and compliance the DevOps include the compliance automation where there is increment made in terms of HIPAA and GDPR. Implementing security in different containers in the Kubernetes cluster improves flexibility and real time defense. This is important for health-care edge environments where multiple nodes process large-scale data containing personal information. As stated in the review, these security integrations need to migrate into proper DevSecOps pipelines to address the rise in the nature of various health-based systems at edge (Elhachmi et al., 2025).

1.4 Research Significance and Motivation

The use of edge computing in healthcare systems is crucial due to the rising need to process analytics in real-time, ensure adequate security for medical devices, and manage the system as a whole sufficiently well. In traditional cloud-based models the problems that are usually encountered include latency and security issues. These challenges are solved by edge computing since it allows for local analysis of data, quick response times, and improvement of patient's health care (Rekha & Pavithra, 2025). Moreover, to the growth of AI and IoT within the medical area, the need for the new, flexible, and able to develop with the technologies healthcare systems is growing gradually. Edge computing enables application in analysis of data in real time, diagnosis, tele monitoring, and enhancement of emergency units functionalities (Beheshti, Sone, & Leung, 2025). The goal of this research is to improve the implementation, elasticity, and DevOps-orientated management of healthcare edge solutions for integrated medical devices.

2. BACKGROUND AND RELEVANCE

2.1 Evolution of Edge Computing in Healthcare

Advanced application of edge computing in healthcare depends on the years having enhanced data processing, integration of artificial intelligence, and security.

1. Early Adoption (2010-2015): Data Processing Efficiency: The concept of edge computing was first applicable in minimizing latency where most of the medical data was processed close to the origin. This was pivotal in telemedicine and remote monitoring in making instant right decisions along with departing from the central dependency on the cloud computing systems (Chandrashekaraiah, 2025).
2. Growth Phase (2016-2020): AI Integration: The success of using advanced biosensing technologies available at the intelligent edge together with artificial intelligence offered a possibility for real-time health analytics in disease prediction. Mobile technologies were found to have helped in lessening the pressure off of patients as well as enhancing the overall quality of the patient care as machines reduced cases of patient dropout rates by closely tailoring individual patient care (Mpofu & Mthunzi-Kufa, 2025).
3. Modern Advancements (2021-Present): Security & Compliance: This can be seen in the recent development that focuses on security through local processing of the patient's data in order to minimize risks of holding the data in the cloud facilities. It also contributes eradication of unnecessary information from devices, and the lack of privacy of information as recommended by HIPAA and GDPR.

2.2 The Need for Real-Time Data Processing in Medical Systems

Time and again, the real-time data processing is vital in medical systems since the patient needs to be treated on time accurately. In the medical field, large volumes of data are produced and collected from such sources as wearable devices, imaging instruments, and electronic health documents. This leads to quicker request and analysis of data, thus results in diagnostic and subsequent treatment. For instance, real-time EPCD colorimeter coupled with electrochemical sweat sensors empowers performers for immediate health assessment and effective preemption (Sung et al., 2025). Furthermore, the flow of real time data in IoRT, easy transmission of the data between the healthcare related devices plays a crucial factor in minute response time in emergency medical facilities as said by Kayataş (2025). Applying edge computing and AI-based approaches help healthcare facilities improve the performance of the systems they use, reduce the latency issues, and, in result, make the workflow more efficient and effective in delivering correct medical decisions.

2.3 DevOps Methodologies in IT and Healthcare

In the IT sphere, DevOps is an approach to continuously integrate and deploy software products with the help of CI/CD mechanisms in order to minimize the downtime and improve systems' reliability. These frameworks help on how often updates should be performed without necessarily interrupting operations. However, to apply in healthcare, CI/CD must function under the regulation of various government agencies. Concerns related with patient safety and privacy laws require checking every executing code to confirm compliance with the rules and regulations of HIPAA and GDPR (Arockiasamy, 2025). This can be explained by the fact that updates concern critical-life systems that are used in healthcare systems.

Under security and compliance, IT systems incorporate security to prevent occurrences of breach and infringement on the privacy of the clients and other stakeholders. However, healthcare DevOps is less flexible as compared to other industries, since breaches can have serious consequences due to the involvement of personal information about the patients. To make the process dynamic and efficient, new approaches to compliance which include infusing artificial intelligence into compliance check are being adopted to enhance an organization's ability to monitor patient data while meeting requirements set by regulatory authorities (Velishala, 2025). As pointed out in the review, real-time updates, DevSecOps, and distinct stages of CI/CD process for medical data security are the challenges to be addressed in transitioning processes.

2.4 Challenges in Deploying and Maintaining Edge-Based Medical Systems

Advanced medical systems that are placed at the edge pose issues of scalability, efficiency and safety that require its deployment and management. First, various edge devices have their cache and store all data locally hence exposing the devices to cyber attacks and hacking. The deployment of such mechanism is also challenging due to the compliance issue especially in organizations within the health sector following HIPAA guidelines and in organizations that operate within the European region following GDPR guidelines to meet the requirement of encryption, authentication, and audit control mechanisms. However, scalability and latency become an issue; as the number of edges increases it requires large investments in hardware, software, and network and also needs to be in real-time (Kassa & Grispos, 2025). Vendor support is another major concern since medical edge systems connect IoT sensors, models, and healthcare systems that are from different manufacturers, thus, the compatibility challenges that are likely to be encountered. Also, due to its constant usage, intelligent and automated techniques must be applied to check and update the edge-based systems in a timely manner to improve and optimize their functionality. To address these issues, there is a need to call for added layers of cybersecurity, efficient DevOps, and intelligent automations such as preventive and predictive maintenance to build a secure, efficient and sustainable ecosystem for caregivers, providers, patients, and industries.

3. RESEARCH QUESTIONS AND KEY PROBLEMS

3.1 What are the Key Deployment Challenges in Healthcare Edge Computing?

The integration of edge computing in healthcare has implications that can be considered as challenging concerning the protection of data and the management of resources. The patient related data that would be processed at the edge of the network is often sensitive information thereby exposing it to privacy violations. Due to these concerns, it is mandatory for electronic health systems to respect HIPAA and GDPR regulations that uphold the theory of ethical considerations and mainly, the principle of confidentiality and integrity. The review also points out that such compliance mechanisms should be integrated through the system architectures within secure data pipelines. In addition, resource management and scalability present major hurdles. Edge environments in healthcare require considerable computing resources on the one hand while at the same time need to operate in real time on the other hand. There is need for the effective use of energy and integration and coordination of the heterogeneity medical devices which can be quite a challenge. In similar ways, (Khan & Ishrat, 2025) stress that managing these requirements besides achieving performance and scalability is still a technical issue as pointed out in the review with special call for performance benchmarking and system standardization in edge healthcare implementation.

3.2 How Can DevOps Methodologies Enhance Scalability and Maintenance?

Therefore, the incorporation of DevOps in healthcare edge computing allows it to scale and maintain uninterruptedly through integration and automation of management solutions alongside continual monitoring. The use of auto-provisioning tools in software or application deployment simplifies software updates, security patches and guarantees continuous updates. IaC enhances the scalability of a system In a way that makes it possible to provision resources as needed within a short time. Moreover, the application of AI to observe the performance insufficiency and security threats to intervene and prevent them before they lead to failure (Khan & Ishrat, 2025). Combining DevOps with the healthcare edge systems gives cautionary benefits, reliability, improved efficiency scalability in medical structures from enhanced edge computing systems.

3.3 What Security Concerns Arise in Integrating Medical Devices With Edge Systems?

Challenges that arise with the integration of medical devices with edge computing include, and are as follows; this is a clear cause of privacy concerns as patient health information passing through different edge nodes in the processing process is highly susceptible to cyber risks (Suresh Babu, C. V. & Yadavamuthiah, K. 2023). It was acknowledged that both blockchain and homomorphic encryption can guarantee the security of data storage and transfer (Prajapat et al., 2020). Another issue is related to authentication about which unauthorized entry on IoT medical devices may cause risks to patients' lives. The solution for increasing security is adopting the use of multi-factor authentication (MFA) and artificial intelligence to conduct anomaly detection. In addition, DDoS attacks cause network security threats that threaten the normal flow of healthcare services. It is recommended to implement zero-trust architectures and intrusion detection systems for more system robustness (Prajapat.et al., 2020).

3.4 How Can Automated CI/CD Pipelines Optimize Healthcare Edge Applications?

CI/CD pipelines hold a significant position in healthcare edge applications as it helps to provide efficient updates in the software, compliance of security standard and reliability of the systems. One of the first advantages is that it provides fast and issue-free deployment since the pipelines do not involve humans hampering the feature delivery (Prajapat et al., 2020). Also, updating the security patches and enforcement measures are greatly integrated to ensure that the medical edge devices will not violate guidelines such as the HIPAA. Software testing within the CI/CD process helps to identify potential problem areas before the emergence of a security breach. Moreover, scalability and reliability issues are addressed because the automated deployment of the solutions assumes that resources can be provisioned dynamically depending on the level of activity during the day. Through AI generated intelligence, CI/CD pipeline helps in providing higher efficiency and identifying problem areas to improve the continuous improvement of Healthcare edge applications (Authors' own).

3.5 What are the Best Practices for Resource Allocation and Optimization?

Therefore, utilization of resources is greatly helpful in health care edge computing considering aspects of real time computing, scalability and adaptability. Three key best practices include:

1.Dynamic work and resource scheduling: Workload allocation strategies ensure achievement of optimum distribution of workload and resources in a system in order to minimize delays and improve system throughput (Apat et al., 2019).
2.Machine Learning Integration: The automation of system resource demands is another advantage of AI based on the use of machine learning algorithms that will predict the systems' needs and make allocation in a dynamic manner (Wen et al., 2020).
3.Edge-Cloud Coordination: Coordinating a network of edge nodes along with cloud support necessitates that a great deal of data processing occurs locally while the more extensive computations are handled in the cloud (Apat et al., 2019).

4. OBJECTIVES AND SCOPE

4.1 Research Objectives

The research purpose is to assess how DevOps supports and improves the deployment, scalability and management of the Healthcare Edge Computing (HEC). The key objectives include:

1.Analyzing the implications that DevOps has on automating MDI and processing data in real-time.

2.To identify the major issues of deploying healthcare systems based on the edge, security, latency-sensitive, and a scarceness of resources.
3.A particularly important task is to establish the process of integrating CI/CD pipelines, IaC, and automated monitoring to improve the efficiency of the systems.
4.Making sure of security and compliance to various regulations of the industry which includes HIPAA and GDPR in the health care sector.
5.Measuring the relevance of the proposed concept of DevOps by conducting a comparative analysis with a traditional and new, based on DevOps, healthcare edge infrastructure.

This work presents the key guidelines which can help increase automation, enhancement and enhance security in the vicinity related to healthcare edge computing at a rate estimated by authors Kumar et al. 2024.

4.2 Scope of the Study

The study is focused on the adaptation of DevOps methodologies as part of the healthcare edge computing to improve deployment, scalability and further maintenance. It examines how such practices as CI/CD, containers, IaC and monitoring enhance system efficiency in a way that will allow real time processing of medical data. Further, it assesses the security threats, different healthcare data compliance-related requirements such as (HIPAA and GDPR), and operational dependability of edge-based healthcare systems. This research is not entirely focused on general cloud computing or general AI models but to build a new DevOps solution for secure, effective, and agile medical device integration. This research will assist in the improvement and development of continuous deployment approaches and automated security governance to the system implemented in healthcare edge systems (Elhachmi et al., 2024).

4.3 Limitations and Delimitations

There are however some challenges that affect the deployment and use of healthcare edge computing which include the following: Another important drawback is the problem of how to address the issues of communications integration across numerous and vastly different types of clinical devices and networks. It is found that existing healthcare systems are not well integrated with leading-edge solutions therefore, there are many data divides (Narla et al., 2024). Also, ethical factors could also be a limitation especially when dealing with patient information as this can cause data insecurity and data privacy and security. Blockchain has been suggested to improve the security by integration with the advanced encryption method; nonetheless, it demands a considerable amount of computation power (Prajapat et al. 2025).Also left as beyond the scope of the work is the distinction between cloud-edge hybrid models and edge-only architectures. Although this approach can help in improving the utilization of resources, it may not eliminate the problem of latency especially in system that requires high level of time sensitivity such as in medical field (Wang et al., 2025). Mitigating these drawbacks, is going to proof enhancements in artificial intelligence propelled security protocols and the implementation of the federated learning modules to optimize the system performance (Suresh Babu, C. V., Dheepak, N. et.al. ., 2024).

5. LITERATURE REVIEW

5.1 Current Trends in Healthcare Edge Computing

Healthcare edge computing has continued to develop due to the adoption of AI and IoT to enable the monitoring of patients in real-time, analysis and decision-making. One major trend is the wireless assistant system and as discussed herein, WAM promotes RPM through the effective minimization of latency and boosting the accessibility especially in the domain of telemedicine application (Bagal et al., 2025). Also, the primary benefits such as AI-powered edge methods are extending the diagnostic and treatment processes in real-time, more precisely in improving the clinical decision support system, and in minimizing response times as well (Karajgi et al., 2025). All these innovations offer a solution for the health care applications as they are scalable, secure and have low latency. Nevertheless, concerns that are user-related assertions like threat to cybersecurity, connections between different connected medical devices and legal requirements of the healthcare sector still remain critical. The constant investment and development of edge computing in the healthcare sector plays a critical role in improving patients' satisfaction, decreasing expenditures within the healthcare system, and increasing the effectiveness of operations in various medical organizations.

5.2 DevOps Practices in Edge Computing

DevOps helps in implementing and managing healthcare edge computing systems so as to streamline the process of data processing in real-time along with integration of medical devices. CI/CD pipelines for executing quick updates enhance the system's response time in essential healthcare applications (Areo, 2022).Thus, the distributed approaches of containerization and functions micro services help to distribute workloads effectively at numerous edge nodes. Kubernetes automates and increases reliability of resources for medical applications as well. Also, based on conventional configuration, IaC reduces human errors that might lead to regulatory violations and compromise security (Arockiasamy, 2024).Maintenance in edge-based healthcare systems gets performed in a real-time and using analytics data. Prometheus and Grafana are two of the Avista DevOps tools used in connected medical devices to monitor irregularities during the use of the equipment. Such approaches enhance the functionality of the system, cut off downtime, and provide patient care around the clock. In other words, DevOps offers a solution to make healthcare edge computing systems more adaptive, elastic, and protective in nature.

5.3 Challenges and Gaps in Medical Device Integration

The challenges involved in implementing medical devices in health care edge computing include; There are also other problems as follows; A shared problem includes the inability to have interoperability in open medical devices meaning that the flow of information and real-time analysis is poor (Haider & Abbas, 2025). Safety is another major issue as they point out that the majority of medical devices that are connected to the internet might be at risk of a cyber attack. The growing trend in edge computing enhances the need for sophisticated means of encryption and authentication of the patients' data. In addition, recommendations require data governance policies that meet the legal guidelines such as HIPAA and GDPR (Attallah et al., 2025). Currently however, the aspect of scalability is missing in current systems, main infrastructures are not well equipped to handle the massive write and reading of health care data. These challenges can be solved by edge-based AI solutions but the Implementation is feasible and requires significant costs as well as AI specialists. It is imperative to overcome these challenges; this is important in improving patient experience and efficiency of medical processes.

5.4 Studies on Security, Compliance, and Regulatory Standards

The next work of (Gobalakrishnan, 2024) is an attempt to develop a framework named TrustSec-ChainX for improving trust management and data security for the IoT-based healthcare system. Security aspects of adopting edge computing technology for medical devices are discussed, and it is also highlighted that it is necessary to adhere to GDPR, HIPAA, and ISO 27001 standards. The study reveals various problems involving patients' records, such as risks of unauthorized access to the information, exposure to hackers, and compatibility concerns. To this end, the study proffers a trust model that applies smart contracts and cryptographic hashing to make the healthcare data more authentic and protect it from the above-mentioned threats.

In telephone, according to the survey conducted by (Barati et al. 2024), they analyze the privacy issues in IoMT and reveal the flaws of the conventional security models. According to their work, there is a need to incorporate blockchain provenance logs and decentralized security models for improvement of compliance in edge-enabled medical systems. Each enhances real-time data security, obeys regulatory norms, and addresses the risks in the given healthcare ecosystems via the usage of the zero-trust architectures and secure data-sharing protocols.

5.5 Identifying Research Gaps

The emerging combination of healthcare edge computing with DevOps is revolutionizing the Medical Device Systems while still several research loopholes exist in the areas of deployment, scalability, and maintenance. The following are the challenges of deployment because of the integration of DevOps in regulated situations that hinder automation since it needs to follow HIPAA and GDPR guidelines (Valaboju, 2024). This is so because interoperability problems hinder the scalability of medical devices in the networks a key factor in growth in healthcare facilities (Dave, 2023). Moreover, there are still opportunities in improving proactive maintenance techniques because existing edge computing paradigms do not have fault tolerance and self-healing capabilities. There must be efforts towards creating definite guidelines for DevOps practices in healthcare IT, increasing the ability of healthcare devices to communicate with each other, and adopting AI-based preventive measures toward major issues. Filling these gaps will be critical in designing efficient, sustainable, and realizable edge compute systems so as to improve the quality of patient care and overall facility operations.

6. RESEARCH METHODOLOGY

6.1 Research Design and Framework

The fairly study approach of healthcare edge computing combined with medical device systems employing the DevOps approach is a mixed research design which cuts across the quantitative and qualitative research paradigms. Using a systematic approach, attention is paid to system deployment, scalability as well as maintenance in context of healthcare IT technologies. The approaches of the study include experimental evaluations concerning various performance parameters like latency, fault tolerance, as well as interoperability. However, hospitals and healthcare providers' qualitative case details present the implementation experiences in the real world. In this work the suitability of the DevOps methodologies, such as

CI/CD, is reviewed as to its applicability in managing medical device updates and in compliance regulation. In the study (Ivanović.,2024)and others pointed out that the digital ecosystem in the healthcare sector needs to have an adaptive architecture for the real-time processing. Besides, (Chbeir &Manolopoulos.,2024) speak about the use of AI maintenance strategies enhancing edge computing effectiveness. These frameworks help in achieving high level of standardization in the matter of development and implementation of the healthcare edge computing models that are considered to be safe and effective.

6.2 Data Collection Methods

Due to the importance of security when processing health data, both edge computing and the connected devices have to adhere to legislation such as HIPAA and GDPR. The incorporation of DevOps improves efficiency through automation, security, and the consolidation of services that are mandated to provide negligible time lag and real-time patient status check. Bagal et al. (2025) highlight AI integration at the edge for reduced response time and improved remote patient monitoring. In the same way, Karagi et al. (2025) also focus on the edge techniques for the analysis and decision making of the medical data. Resource-aware dynamic service deployment creates the best utilization of computational resources in edge settings. Islam et al. (2021) write on how micro services support virtualization of services at the edge in IoT healthcare, to offer quick, always-on healthcare services. They have extended their research to a few areas such as dynamic scheduling and resource discovery for more effective and flexible delivery of services. Security is necessary in managing medical data and this can be achieved by automating security governance. Smart offloading, distributed learning, block-chain based authentication, and dynamic service orchestration are beneficial for the more secure and sustainable health data acquisition process.

6.3 DevOps Implementation Strategies for Healthcare Edge Computing

In healthcare edge systems, the idea of scalability is implemented by use of microservices and contains. Modern tools like Docker and Kubernetes enable the modular approach and thus facilitate easier updates, minimal disruption of service, and consistent compatibility of the healthcare systems across the distributed networks (Rodríguez et al., 2024). Also, the adoption of CI/CD in the context of DevOps based on tools like Jenkins and GitLab makes it possible to update systems in real-time with a low likelihood of human error, thus adapting the systems to increase the coverage of emerging needs in the healthcare domain by Patan (2024). In fact, it is here that zero-trust enforcement and the use of artificial intelligence for real-time monitoring of the distributed environment are mandatory. These frameworks contain risks and vulnerabilities that are devoid of compliance to the data regulations in the health sector including HIPAA and GDPR as proposed by Patan (2024). The findings of the review also stress the need to progress towards the implementation of intelligent security and CI/CD systems.

6.4 Security and Compliance Considerations

There is the need to ensure security and compliance of the healthcare edge computing largely due to the nature of data involved. Introducing distributed architectures in a system bring in other elements of security risks of which comprise of; intrusion of codes, data theft, and hacking attacks. The proposed strategies for data security for computing on the edge include; employing sophisticated encryption methods to secure the data, strong authentication techniques, and developing an intelligent way of detecting any anomaly. Specifically, compliance with regulations including GDPR and HIPAA incurs real-time monitoring and automated policy compliance. Contemporary studies showed that federated learning and blockchain can be used to enhance security in edge computing. To improve the data credibility and trust, (Suresh Babu, C. V., Dheepak, N. et.al., 2024) point out that, through the decentralization of the model training and usage of blockchain, the health care providers can ameliorate the data integrity and security. Similarly, the case of secure big data analytics in drone-assisted healthcare involves cloud storage encryption as well as the usage of artificial intelligence in security measures against data vulnerabilities (Wazid et al., 2025) . All the above strategies enhance security and compliance in healthcare edge computing in a complementary way.

6.5 Scalability Testing and Performance Metrics

Scalability points and performance measurement are important in healthcare edge conceputing to ensure that medical systems performance increase or decrease based on the increasing or decreasing workload respectively. With the growth of the big data in patient database as well as workload generated from it, edge computing infrastructure needs to be validated for its robustness, cybersecurity and conformity to standard set in the healthcare industry.

Key Points:

1. **Load Balancing and Resource Allocation:** Proper load balancing minimizes delay in the distribution of the computational load and avoids system failures. Deep learning models implemented using federated learning can

adapt to the available resources in order to enhance its efficiency (Smith & Caleb, 2025).

2. **Performance Testing:** The concept of performance testing includes Blockchain-based security to implement HIPAA and GDPR rules. It is a fact that the unalterable audit trails play a vital role in improving both the traceability and accountability of data processing in the healthcare field (Wazid et al., 2025).
3. **CI/CD Deployment:** Implementation updates is another process of continuous integration and continuous deployment, which keeps downtimes to the barest minimum as it scales up. Artificial intelligence aids in improving the ability of the system to adapt to changes that occur in the real-time healthcare fundamental to its functionality (Smith & Caleb, 2025).
4. **Latency and Throughput:** The scalability tests need to determine the latency and the throughput in order to approve the real-time integration of the medical device. By applying edge AI algorithms, several issues such as the causes of increased processing time and reduced response time in the healthcare networks can be minimized (Wazid et al., 2025).

Thus, the suggested strategies allow healthcare edge computing systems to have high scalability and maintain high performance in various operational scenarios.

7. CONTRIBUTION TO THE FIELD

7.1 Enhancing Healthcare Data Processing with DevOps

Therefore, improving the DevOps process to support accurately and effectively process a healthcare organization's data entails the use of automation, continuous deployment, and real-time analytics. From the paper of (Arockiasamy,2024), it is understood that implementing an integrated real-time health analytics through the DevOps would be beneficial to upscale wearable IoT data, as well as improve the healthcare institutions' artificial intelligence and compliance (Suresh Babu, C. V., Maclin Vinola, P. et. al. 2024). With the use of containers and CI/CD it is possible to manage massive amounts of the patient-generated data while keeping data privacy and compliance on schedule. (Velish.,2025) describes a specific approach to apply the tools of machine learning to DevOps pipeline to predict errors in healthcare data systems. This approach leads to the reduction of the period that patients spend in the facility, hence fewer chances of making flawed data on their condition, and allows physicians to attend to them as soon as possible to improve the quality of medical care. It is a common knowledge that the integration of DevOps, automation, and AI improves the throughputs in the healthcare IT areas while increasing the reliability of the IT structures.

7.2 Addressing Scalability and Deployment Issues

Therefore, scalability and deployment in healthcare edge computing are factors that need to be addressed since they pose a challenge. The first important issue is the possibility of the real-time data processing without overloading the system. Solis et al. (2025) note that micro services based deployment and dynamic resource scaling enhances healthcare edge computing system as it enables the management of the system and workload distribution. Moreover, the technology known as Kubernetes for orchestration of the container systems can be used to increase the efficiency of system deployment, minimize the time taken and make system updates much easier. As noted by Chhillar (2025), organizations consider the adoption of the hybrid cloud-fog computing model, which relies on merging local and public resources to incorporate scalability into the data processing process while maintaining security (Chhillar, 2025). It has been observed that by implementing DevOps integration for automation, artificial intelligence workload management and secure sharing of data, the deployment can be made easier and the systems can be scaled up to the desired level with maximum compliance with health care policies (Suresh Babu, C. V., Maclin Vinola, P. et. al. 2024).

7.4 Practical Applications for Healthcare Providers and IT Teams

The Intersection of edge computing and DevOps has important advantages for both the physicians and IT managers in connection to reconciling patients' treatment and care with safety and performance. Real-time monitoring at the edge ensures the rates of change in vital signs significantly mirror closely and with little delay what is happening on a patient's health status especially with cardiology patients. Hence, (Vaduguru, 2025) said that the deep learning models using artificial intelligence can detect and diagnose images at the edge to minimize latency from the cloud. .On the other hand, through the DevOps application, significant advancement and maintenance, under update frequent of health care systems are enhanced. (Holley & Mathur, 2024) explain that generative AI provides organizations with a way to augment IT teams' ability to monitor infrastructure and handle compliance tasks. This also ensures strong edge security, bringing HIPAA and GDPR requirements into the DNA of the solution and allowing patient information to remain immediately available while also being safeguarded.

8. ANALYSIS AND FINDINGS

8.1 Case Studies of Successful Healthcare Edge Deployments

Healthcare edge computing has gone a long way helping in processing of data in real time thus reducing on latency and hence increasing efficiency. A good example is the use of Edge-IoT for e-healthcare system in smart hospitals. Edge computing is combined with IoT in this system to avoid the need for cloud support to monitor the status of the patient in real-time (Ray, Dash, & De, 2019).A sample Is the resource-aware dynamic service deployment for healthcare edge computing. The current problem of managing important tasks and coordinating them to the available local edge resources will be addressed by this system to enhance IoT based medical applications. It also prevents unnecessary use of a lot of computational power and congesting the network, hence improving data processing time (Islam et al., 2021). These are specific real-life scenarios and edge computing's adaptability in the health sector in providing AI-based diagnosis and enhancing patients' experiences.

8.2 Comparative Analysis of DevOps Strategies in Edge Computing

DevOps in healthcare edge computing contributes to improving the level of automatisation and distribution of the system as well as security measures. When comparing real-life case studies, one gets to see that there are differences in the implementation strategies. Another area of development was the application of the Edge-IoT based e-healthcare system discussed in the paper by Ray, Dash, and De (2019). It also possessed a fault tolerance characteristic which signified it as a good model for a smart hospital to deal with dynamic workload. Another real-time example of the resource-aware dynamic service deployment (Islam et al., 2021) used IaC and CI/CD to achieve more resource consumption. This was efficient in reducing computational complications and also ensured the protection of patients' information by processing them locally. Looking into the above-stated approaches, the containerized micro services are providing the modularity and flexibility of deployment, and the IaC automation provides efficiency in resource usage. These two are critical when it comes to diagnosis and service delivery for improvement of the healthcare sector that is continually driven by artificial intelligence.

8.3 Performance and Scalability Assessment

1. Performance Metrics and Benchmarks: Time and resource utilization, number of transactions processed, and energy utilization rates measure the quality of a system. Machine learning based optimizations can cut down delays to the extent of 40% for enhancing real-time health care applications as per the Zhang et al. (2022). It used for setting the benchmarks of the organization with respect to its competitors or other organizations in the same field.
2. Scalability Strategies and Frameworks: Distributed architectures, cloud-edge hybrid models and auto-scaling frameworks use and exploit resources. Liu et al. (2021) stress that the adaptive frameworks enable demand fluctuations to be dealt with without having an impact on the efficiency of the system as a whole.
3. Bottleneck Identification and Optimization: Challenges such as network traffic and weak data channels affect performance. Some of the solutions range are load balancing, federated learning and edge to cloud orchestration to ease out the bottlenecks which are currently existing to a level of 30%.
4. Real-World Case Studies and Challenges: The modern smart hospitals minimize patient wait by applying the edge computing but challenges includes integration with legacy systems and security. These are development paradigms that assist in proper management of risks while at the same time achieve better ways of deploying software.

8.4 Security and Compliance Impact Assessment

Everywhere people are reaching for their health information and, therefore, securing data is a critical factor in managing health information in the healthcare edge. This is through using of DevOps approach that includes constant monitoring for threats, use of automated security measures and the processing of data through the use of encryptions in the process. These strategies enable edge systems to be interactive while at the same time protecting the important health information. Regulatory compliance is equally essential. Since medical facilities deal with Unique Identification data, compliance with HIPAA and GDPR do not have an option. (Arockiasamy, 2024) clearly categorizes the importance of utilizing AI-aids in audits, compliance checking, and repeating the evaluation. Moreover, DevSecOps ensures security's inclusion at the initial phase of the development process. Due to real-time vulnerability patching, API testing, and the automated validation of vulnerabilities, DevSecOps reduces the exposure of threats and the enhancement of the hardening process through the edge environment (Arockiasamy, 2024).

9. SUGGESTIONS AND RECOMMENDATIONS

9.1 Best Practices for DevOps Implementation in Healthcare Edge Computing

Down to healthcare edge computing, the CI/CD pipeline aims to deliver updates of the software as far as possible with reduced or no caregiver downtime. Such testing minimize the human mistakes by offering a fail-safe approach ensuring that the life-critical medical application is as more reliable as possible. Facilitating scalability and reduction of time and errors, such as those made while configuring, in the context of edge architectures, IaC is done through Infrastructure as Code (IaC) in healthcare facilities as stated by (Valaboju, 2024). A Security-First DevOps approach (DevSecOps) that incorporates continual encryption and threat detection while adhering to the high privacy standards that govern the healthcare and any other data-sensitive industries such as GDPR and HIPAA. Automated vulnerability scans are useful in protecting the patients' data as well as the overall system (Zhang et al., 2022). Also included is advanced predictive monitoring, a feature where the system informs the user when a failure is likely to happen. It improves resource utilization, as well as dynamic triage and monitoring in the edge environment; thus, enhancing the stability of the system and its ability to serve patients (Valaboju, 2024).

9.2 Strategies for Optimizing Medical Device Integration

Overall, and in order to achieve suitable and efficient medical device integration in the context of HE, interoperability, instant data processing, and security are key features that need to be addressed. These interfaces such as the HL7 and FHIR eliminate compatibility issues owing to well-established standard protocols of communication between the different types of the reader medical devises (Smith & Caleb, 2025). The application of artificial intelligence in edge computing provides real-time analysis, where immediate reporting, patient care and decision making can be made without much delay (Suresh Babu, C. V., Maclin Vinola, P. et. al. 2024). Also, with the help of federated learning models, the data are processed locally, maintaining the patient's anonymity and adhering to the requirements of legal standards such as HIPAA and GDPR. It has been confirmed that security is an important aspect and through the use of blockchain based authentication the use of unauthorized devices in accessing the system is prohibited as well as ensuring the data integrity (Wazid et al., 2025). DevOps implemented within firmware updates and device onboarding leads to a significant reduction in the time that can be attributed to downtimes. Through these strategies, there is the possibility of attaining large scale, secure, and effective medical devices in healthcare institutions hence improving the overall patient care and system functionality.

9.3 Recommendations for Future Research and Development

For future HC-EC research, the development of sufficient and effective diagnostic tools that rely on artificial intelligence for early stages disease detection and continuous patient monitoring should be intensified to improve the overall health delivery system and response (Vaduguru, 2025). Also, the question of exchange in healthcare information technology logically carries a reference to integrated information exchange through implementing more precise standards of communication that involve HL7 and FHIR (Holley & Mathur, 2024). To enhance data protection and satisfy the legislation requirements, it is crucial to consider new approaches like zero trust approach and involving blockchain to protect and secure a patient's data (Vaduguru, 2025). However, issues of scalability must be addressed and future development should consider how dynamic scheduling of the resources especially using hybrid cloud-edge computational platforms. It would enable the care providers to expand the networks as the need arises and especially in areas of short resources or high pressure without a compromise to the health outcomes of the system's patients (Holley & Mathur, 2024). Combined, these can go a long way in reconfiguring the vision and reality of healthcare in the digital age.

10. FUTURE SCOPE FOR RESEARCH

10.1 AI and Machine Learning in Healthcare Edge Computing

Healthcare edge computing has been uplifted through the aid of Artificial intelligence and machine learning to deliver real-time analytics, prognostication, and self-driven decisions. These technologies improve the monitoring of the patient by increasing the recognition of essential signals as well as identifying inefficiencies at a small interval. As noted by (Prajapat et al,2020), with the help of AI-powered diagnostic tools integrated into the edge, the dependence on the cloud is subverted, and the response time is faster in emergent care. Also, AI models enhance dynamic management of workloads in a system in a way that optimizes the usage of resources in a system. (Patan, 2024) goes further on how the use of machine learning supports medical imaging by increasing the speed of anomaly detection and classification and thereby minimizes on diagnostic errors. Moreover, the incorporation of AI with edge computing remains safe and secure to protect patient data by processing them locally rather than through the cloud. In the same measure that advanced edge solutions are adopted, further application in specialties like personalized medicines, robotically assisted surgeries, routine check ups from remote platforms, and many more will be seen enhancing the healthcare industry.

10.2 Blockchain for Secure Medical Device Integration

Based on this, blockchain technology is gaining a significant importance in providing a solution in the integration of medical devices in the healthcare edge computing. Blockchain, thus, levels the data by decentralizing them and using cryptography to make it almost impossible to alter or corrupt the data. According to (Bagal et al.2025), interoperability is brought about by the application of blockchain in that it provides a secure means of sharing data between IoT based medical devices and health care systems and at the same time meeting the requirements of the regulations on the use of such technology. In this same respect, smart contracts ensure automated access control whereby only authorized personnel can access or even make alterations to a patient's information. In (Areo,2022), the ways that blockchain minimizes cyber threats by distributing user's health information cut risks that come with single focal points (Suresh Babu, C. V. & Yadavamuthiah, K. 2023). In addition, for example, connective tissue identity brought about by blockchain results in discouraging fake device connection with the healthcare network and only allowing authorized medical devices. Blockchain technology will become vital in enhancing the security of data records, minimizing organizational risks and bringing trust to healthcare systems when fully incorporated into edge computing systems that support remote and real-time patient monitoring.

10.3 Predictive Maintenance for Edge-Based Healthcare Systems

The Integration of artificial intelligence with edge computing in healthcare helps in monitoring the faults on real-time, improves the resource utilization pattern and enhances the overall reliability of the system. According to (Attallah et al., 2025), it is possible to eliminate the probabilities of faults in equipment such as MRI scanners connected to the edge, allowing for the removal of failures resulting from faults before failure forums to arise to cause delays in patient care and low operational efficiency. In particular, predictive maintenance also assists with saving money as much as possible because the means of effective servicing can be directed only to the identified critical assets during certain periods. According to (Gobalakrishnan, 2024) in "The New York Times" artificial intelligence in form of models helps in proper planning and management of limited resources in a hospital, especially during calamities. This also was drives the reduction of the device failure reactive rate by about 40% while at the same time assuring high service continuity, enhancing the patient satisfaction. In conclusion, the incorporation of AI in the use of predictive maintenance in healthcare edges improves infrastructures reliability, have lower costs, and maintains a constant flow in healthcare services.

10.4 Emerging Trends in Edge Computing for Telemedicine

Edge computing significantly enhances the quality and responsiveness of telemedicine through low-latency remote consultations and intelligent patient monitoring. (Kumar et al., 2024) explain that by processing patient data near the point of generation such as at local clinics or on personal devices—edge computing reduces lag in video consultations and medical imaging, enabling faster interactions between patients and healthcare professionals. This real-time responsiveness fosters better patient engagement and supports more accurate, timely diagnoses and treatments. Furthermore, when combined with AI, edge computing empowers remote monitoring through IoT-enabled wearables. According to (Apat et al., 2019), edge-based AI analytics can detect critical and unexpected health anomalies in real time, prompting immediate medical intervention. This capability is vital for chronic disease management and emergency response, making telemedicine not only more accessible but also more proactive and reliable in safeguarding patient health.

11. CONCLUSION

11.1 Summary of Key Findings

This paper explores and analyses how the healthcare edge computing improves real-time data processing, data security and enlarged data capacity. All progression of DevOps, especially the CI/CD pipelines, help in keeping the flow of deployment and overall management minimal and facilitate a reduction in downtimes. Discussing the use cases for Artificial Intelligence, it is possible to mention that AI-based analytics enable more effective predictive maintenance, which minimizes the number of system failures; as for Blockchain, it is necessary to note that this is an effective tool for the secure integration of medical data and compliance with the requirements of the legal framework. Cloud computing scalability and cloud-edge computing and resource dynamics improve operational competence in large-scale health care scenarios. Protection of security concerns involves the use of securely encrypted means, constant threat check, as well as the incorporation of artificial intelligence in the detection of threats. There is a need to look for future directions such as the expansion of AI automation in care, optimization of energy structures of edge solutions, and enhancing of intersystem integration to coincide with the changing need of the future in healthcare (Valaboju, 2024; Zhang et al., 2022).

11.2 Implications for Healthcare IT

The paper points priority areas for healthcare IT where edge computing has significant potential in improving system advancement, security and sophistication. The use of DevOps practices facilitates the release of the systems, their constant observation, and reduction of time spent on system downtimes to enhance the delivery of healthcare services. Analytics tools incorporating artificial intelligence improve real-time decision-making processes on one's resources and medical devices. Moreover, there is enhanced protection and corporate governance by implementation of block chain hence reducing risks of loss through cyber fraud (Suresh Babu, C. V. & Yadavamuthiah, K. 2023). That is why, further studies should be devoted to the development of edge AI, the optimization of its interaction with existing systems, and the creation of efficient and sustainable energy supply for the constantly growing needs of digital healthcare (Vaduguru, 2025; Holley & Mathur, 2024).

11.3 Final Thoughts on the Future of Healthcare Edge Computing

HC-EC is gaining popularity as revolutionary approach for analyzing real-time medical data with less latency and high availability. It helps in improving the patient care through faster diagnosis and better coordination in different arms of the health care delivery system, and makes best use of scarce clinical resources through utilization of machine learning. As systems become more sophisticated, organizations adopt DevOps methods for the proper implementation of the system and for updating on goings by checking on the smooth running of the system. In line with advances cited in (Smith et al., 2024) and (Kumar & Patel, 2023), there will be more focuses on data privacy, Health IT systems compatibility and Artificial Intelligence adoption in healthcare. They will enhance research and analysis, protection of patients' details and digital operating systems. Additionally, as new information and development continue to come up, edge computing is likely to play a significant role in telemedicine and remote patient monitoring hence enhancing the quality, access and individualized care especially to those in rural or even isolated regions therefore revolutionizing the digital health care.

REFERENCES

Ali, A. S. M., Ali, S., Ziaullah, K., Joo, M. I., & Kim, H. C. (2025). *IoMT and blockchain synergy: A novel approach to health data validation and storage*. IEEE., DOI: 10.1109/ACCESS.2025.3555289

Apat, H. K., Goswami, V., Sahoo, B., Barik, R. K., & Saikia, M. J. (2019). *Fog Service Placement Optimization: A Survey of State-of-the-Art Strategies and Techniques*. MDPI., DOI: 10.3390/computers14030099

Areo, G. (2022). Faster Healthcare Apps with DevOps: Reducing Time to Market. ResearchGate. https://mzresearch.com/index.php/MZCJ/article/view/375

Arockiasamy, J. M. I. (2024). DevOps-driven real-time health analytics: A scalable framework for wearable IoT data. https://www.researchgate.net/profile/Jesu-Marcus-Immanuvel-Arockiasamy/publication/389210225_DevOps-Driven_Real-Time_Health_Analytics_A_Scalable_Framework_for_Wearable_IoT_Data/links/67b8c29396e7fb48b9c9c51f/DevOps-Driven-Real-Time-Health-Analytics-A-Scalable-Framework-for-Wearable-IoT-Data.pdf

Attallah, O., Ma, X., & Sedky, M. (2025). The role of artificial intelligence technologies in revolutionizing and aiding cardiovascular medicine. *Frontiers in Cardiovascular Medicine*, *12*, 1588983. DOI: 10.3389/fcvm.2025.1588983 PMID: 40255343

Bagal, S. A., Katekhaye, A., & Bisane, P. (2025). *Development of Wireless Assistant System for Monitoring in Healthcare Industry–A Review*. International Journal of Innovative Science and Research Technology. DOI: 10.38124/ijisrt/25mar665

Barati, M., Rana, O., Ranjan, R., & Aujla, G. S. (2024). Privacy Challenges for Internet of Medical Things. IET Digital Library. https://digital-library.theiet.org/doi/abs/10.1049/pbpc027e_ch9

Beheshti, I., Sone, D., & Leung, C. K. (2025). Advances of Artificial Intelligence in Neuroimaging. *Brain Sciences*, *15*(4), 351. DOI: 10.3390/brainsci15040351 PMID: 40309811

Chandrashekaraiah, M. (2025). Novel semiconductor chip-based smart sensor technology design and integration of IoT in AI-ML hyperscale infrastructure.

Chbeir, R., & Manolopoulos, Y. (2024). *AI-Driven Maintenance in Healthcare Edge Computing Systems*. MDPI., DOI: 10.3390/app14219903

Dave, D. M. (2023). Advancing Medical Device Manufacturing: The Convergence of Edge Computing and Industry 5.0. International Journal of Engineering Applications and Science Technology

Elhachmi, J., Laaouamir, S., & Ziad, I. (2025). Securing containerized workloads in Kubernetes: Best practices and implementation. https://papers.ssrn.com/sol3/papers.cfm?abstract_id=5194051

Gobalakrishnan, N. (2024). *TrustSec-ChainX: A Pioneering Approach to Enhancing Trust Management and Data Integrity in IoT Healthcare*. IEEE Xplore., DOI: 10.1109/ICERCS63125.2024.10895865

Haider, J., & Abbas, A. (2025). The future of AI in healthcare: Bridging the gap between technology and patient well-being.

Holley, K., & Mathur, M. (2024). *LLMs and Generative AI for Healthcare: The Next Frontier*. O'Reilly Media, Inc.

Islam, J., Kumar, T., Kovacevic, I., & Harjula, E. (2021). Resource-Aware Dynamic Service Deployment for Local IoT Edge Computing: Healthcare Use Case. *IEEE Access : Practical Innovations, Open Solutions*, *9*, 115868–115884. DOI: 10.1109/ACCESS.2021.3102867

Ivanović, M., Chbeir, R., & Manolopoulos, Y. (2024). *Management of Digital Ecosystems: Dedicated to the Memory of Prof. William I. Grosky 8/4/1944–11/13/2020*. MDPI., DOI: 10.3390/books978-3-7258-0646-1

Karajgi, S., Kumar, K. G., & Shankar, B. (2025). Artificial Intelligence in Healthcare: A Review of Machine Learning Applications. ITM Web of Conferences. https://www.itm-conferences.org/articles/itmconf/abs/2025/07/itmconf_icsice2025_01012/itmconf_icsice2025_01012.html

Kassa, Y., & Grispos, G. (2025). Secure Edge Computing Reference Architecture for Data-driven Structural Health Monitoring: Lessons Learned from Implementation and Benchmarking.

Kayataş, Y. (2025). Enhancing smart environments through an AI-assisted IoRT agent. Polen ITU. https://polen.itu.edu.tr/items/02494d5a-347a-4522-9e58-6c1e1ca93b64

Khan, W., & Ishrat, M. (2025). Navigating Ethical Challenges: Frameworks for Swarm Intelligence in Fog Computing. Taylor & Francis. https://www.taylorfrancis.com/chapters/edit/10.1201/9781032693217-9

Kumar, A., Kumar, A., & Singhal, N. (2024). *Industry Automation: The Technologies, Platforms and Use Cases*. IEEE., DOI: 10.1109/10506786

Liu, Y., Lan, D., Pang, Z., & Karlsson, M. (2021). Scalability Challenges in Edge Networks: A Framework Perspective. *IEEE Transactions on Cloud Computing*. DOI: 10.1109/OJIES.2021.3055901

Masum, M., Devadasan, A. V., & Sengupta, S. (2025). Deep learning for non-invasive blood pressure monitoring: Model performance and quantization trade-offs. *Electronics (Basel)*, *14*(7), 1300. DOI: 10.3390/electronics14071300

Mpofu, K. T., & Mthunzi-Kufa, P. (2025). *Recent advances in artificial intelligence and machine learning-based biosensing technologies*. IntechOpen., DOI: 10.5772/intechopen.1009613

Narla, S., Valivarthi, D. T., & Peddi, S. (2024). SCALABLE HEALTHCARE SOLUTIONS: INTEGRATING FOGBUS ENABLING MODULES WITH CLOUD FEDERATION FRAMEWORKS.

Patan, L. (2024). Leveraging Cloud-Native Architecture for Scalable and Resilient Enterprise Applications: A Comprehensive Analysis. International Journal of Computer Engineering & Technology. https://lib-index.com/index.php/IJCET/article/view/IJCET_15_05_055

Prajapat, S., Kumar, P., & Das, A. K. (2020). *Generative AI-Enabled Quantum Encryption Algorithm for Securing IoT-Based Healthcare Application Using Blockchain*. IEEE Internet of Things., DOI: 10.1109/JIOT.2025.3555159

Ray, P. P., Dash, D., & De, D. (2019). Edge computing for Internet of Things: A survey, e-healthcare case study, and future direction. *Journal of Network and Computer Applications*, *140*, 1–22. DOI: 10.1016/j.jnca.2019.05.005

Rekha, D., & Pavithra, L. (2025). TSCH in Edge IoT: A Comprehensive Survey of Research Challenges. *Transactions on Emerging Telecommunications Technologies*, *36*(3), e70088. DOI: 10.1002/ett.70088

Rodríguez, P., Laso, S., Berrocal, J., & Fernandez, P. (2024). Computing Continuum Simulator: A Comprehensive Framework for Continuum Architecture Evaluation. https://papers.ssrn.com/sol3/papers.cfm?abstract_id=5045387

Ruchika, & Chhillar, R. S. (2025). Performance evaluation of hybrid cloud-fog computing architectures in smart home IoT environments: A comparative simulation study across multiple tools. Journal of Grid Computing, 23(2), 14. .DOI: 10.1007/s10723-025-09802-9

Smith, C., & Caleb, E. (2025). Optimizing AI Model Training with Federated Learning and Blockchain. https://www.researchgate.net/profile/Hannah-Adebayo/publication/389891385_Optimizing_AI_Model_Training_with_Federated_Learning_and_Blockchain/links/67d73d692719090652bba0ce/Optimizing-AI-Model-Training-with-Federated-Learning-and-Blockchain.pdf

Sung, D., Han, S., Kim, S., Kang, H., Jekal, B., Kim, G., Kim, J., Hong, M., Moon, G., Kim, S., Lee, Y., Hwang, S.-W., Jeong, H., Ryu, Y.-S., Kim, S., & Koo, J. (2025). Electrophoretic digital colorimetry integrated with electrochemical sweat sensor. *Science Advances, 11*(13), DOI: 10.1126/sciadv.adu2142 PMID: 40153516

Suresh Babu, C. V., Akshayah, N. S., & Maclin Vinola, P. (2024). Artificial Intelligence in Healthcare: Assessing Impacts, Challenges, and Recommendations for Achieving Healthcare Independence. In Geada, N., & Jamil, G. (Eds.), *Perspectives on Artificial Intelligence in Times of Turbulence: Theoretical Background to Applications* (pp. 61–80). IGI Global., DOI: 10.4018/978-1-6684-9814-9.ch005

Suresh Babu, C. V., Surendar, V., Dheepak, N., Shiraj, S., & Praveen, K. (2024). Revolutionizing Healthcare Harnessing IoT-Integrated Federated Learning for Early Disease Detection and Patient Privacy Preservation. In Lilhore, U., Simaiya, S., Poongodi, M., & Dutt, V. (Eds.), *Federated Learning and Privacy-Preserving in Healthcare AI* (pp. 195–216). IGI Global., DOI: 10.4018/979-8-3693-1874-4.ch013

Suresh Babu, C. V., & Yadavamuthiah, K. (2023). Cyber Physical Systems Design Challenges in the Areas of Mobility, Healthcare, Energy, and Manufacturing. In Thanigaivelan, R., Kaliappan, S., & Jegadheesan, C. (Eds.), *Cyber-Physical Systems and Supporting Technologies for Industrial Automation* (pp. 131–151). IGI Global., DOI: 10.4018/978-1-6684-9267-3.ch007

Vaduguru, R. V. (2025). Attention-Based Deep Learning Models: A Comparative Study of VGG19 and MobileNet for Chest X-Ray Image Classification. https://doi.org/DOI: 10.21203/rs.3.rs-5902187/v1

Valaboju, P. (2024). Continuous integration and delivery in healthcare IT: A DevOps framework for improving system resilience and performance. https://www.researchgate.net/profile/Praveen-Valaboju-2/publication/388195922_Title_Continuous_Integration_and_Delivery_in_Healthcare_IT_A_DevOps_Framework_for_Improving_System_Resilience_and_Performance/links/678f052f82501639f5ff4c90/Title-Continuous-Integration-and-Delivery-in-Healthcare-IT-A-DevOps-Framework-for-Improving-System-Resilience-and-Performance.pdf

Velishala, S. (2025). Leveraging Machine Learning in DevOps Pipelines to Enhance Patient Data Management Systems. ResearchGate. https://www.researchgate.net/publication/389701589

Velishala, S. (2025). Leveraging Machine Learning in DevOps Pipelines to Enhance Patient Data Management Systems. DOI: 10.5281/zenodo.14792139

Wang, Z., Guo, Y., & Guo, Y. (2025). A blockchain-based medical IoT authentication scheme resistant to combined attacks. *Computer Networks*, *263*, 111241. DOI: 10.1016/j.comnet.2025.111241

Wazid, M., Singh, J., Das, A.K., Garg, S., & Susilo, W. (2025). Cloud storage-based secure big data analytics mechanism for drone-assisted healthcare 5.0 data fusion system. .DOI: 10.1016/j.inffus.2025.103085

Wen, D., Xing, Y., Yao, Y., Liang, G., Jung, T. P. (2020). Transforming Long-Term Adjunctive Therapy for Cognitive Impairment: The Role of Multimodal Self-Adaptive Digital Medicine. Frontiers in Neurology. https://www.frontiersin.org/legal/privacy-policy

Chapter 10
Integration of Artificial Intelligence and Machine Learning for Enhancing Business in the Digital World

Atharv Gupta
https://orcid.org/0009-0009-8973-808X
Amity University, Noida, India

Saru Dhir
https://orcid.org/0000-0002-2381-2920
Amity University, Noida, India

Madhurima
https://orcid.org/0000-0002-7266-9534
Health and Care Research Wales, UK

ABSTRACT

In today's world, the use of AI and ML has gained popularity in the last few decades and since then it has been used rampantly in the fields of E-commerce and business. The use of AI and ML as integral parts of business models in the digital world can be seen how it would be imperative to have technological and practical. This paper analyzes and discusses the various aspects of AI and ML in business. This paper strives to give the detailed analysis to the application of AI and ML in business systems in the digital world as well as their repercussions. The paper commences with the discussion of the various technologies and algorithms already in place in

DOI: 10.4018/979-8-3373-1147-0.ch010

the business world which are based on AI and ML, carries on discussing the various AI trends, algorithms, advantages and challenges, and finally concludes with the analysis of the scope of AI and ML in business soon. Moreover, a few suggestions on how to overcome the challenges discussed in the paper are also discussed.

1. INTRODUCTION

In today's world, artificial intelligence and machine learning prove to be multi-faceted assets to humans in various ways with respect to their usage and integration in numerous industries, both conventional and unconventional. As such, one of the fields which has seen a recent increase in the utilization of AI and ML tools as well as deep learning models in it is the field of digital business or electronic commerce. It is well known that business and trade serve to be the backbone of any civilization and its economic standing and welfare.

In order to excel at achieving a sustainable and modern business model which maximizes the beneficial aspects of business such as customer experiences, optimize operations, and boost profitability, as well as exterminates the negative aspects of business such as fraud, money laundering, non-transparency, etc., it is understood that one needs to keep oneself up to date with the market and employ techniques which include cutting-edge, state-of-the-art technology.

In the past, the lack of utilization of AI, ML and associated techniques has been a major issue in the field of E-commerce. This is due to the fact that ever since the dawn of civilization, trade has been a constantly flourishing entity with regular growth being observed periodically but despite all this it was quite difficult to tend to the needs of the customers manually without any external aid and proved to be unnecessarily labor intensive. Business is a term which is as true as the existence and evolution of humankind and hence goes hand in hand with it. As a result, businesses and trade methods evolve with the evolution of humankind and hence, businesses require constant upgrades in technology to ensure that the producers are at par with the demands and conditions of the market.

It is an undeniable fact that the use of software in the execution of a particular task almost always results in better efficiency and resource utilization than if that task is carried out by an average human. This results from the increased calculative power and technological superiority that the current computers possess over the brain of an individual. Hence, it is imperative for us to use the latest technology in all the spheres of business and trade in order to maximize the efficiency and output we get from respective businesses with the technology available at hand.

The use of AI/ML grants us an advantage in all the tasks that we may or may not need to execute. It is observed that the potential for use of AI/ML in business is extensive. For instance, in the past, mathematical calculations were primarily done manually by humans and ledgers were maintained for storing records of those calculations. However, with the evolution of basic computers, this task became less tedious as the utilization of technology in making hefty calculations could be done by computers and required minimal human intervention and efforts. As a result, the losses incurred due to human error or fraudulent transactions were also reduced significantly. This gives us a basic but valuable insight into how technology is to be employed in the betterment of trade and E-commerce in general.

One of the primary and most trending techniques of doing so is the integration of artificial intelligence, machine learning and deep learning models with business strategies and using appropriate supported software for their utilization. Businesses must adapt and embrace technological improvements to stay competitive in the quickly increasing e-world. Machine learning (ML) and artificial intelligence (AI) have become potent tools that may boost productivity and provide companies with a competitive edge. ML is a subset of AI that involves teaching algorithms to recognize patterns and make predictions based on data, whereas AI focuses on constructing intelligent algorithms that can execute jobs that generally need human-like intellect (Kiran et al., 2023).

Now let us try to comprehend how AI and ML individually function and why it is necessary to employ them in the process of digital business development. The design and development of computing systems that are capable of performing activities traditionally associated with human intelligence is the focus of the field of Artificial Intelligence (AI). The purpose of computer programs that use artificial intelligence (AI) is to simulate human cognition in as many ways as they can. The purpose of business intelligence is to enhance decision-making and strategic planning by compiling, evaluating, and presenting pertinent data pertaining to an organization's operations. Data integration, data modelling, and data visualization are some of the processes that are utilised in the process of transforming this data into valuable insights (Gowrabhathini et al., 2024).

Moreover, artificial intelligence is not just limited to this, the capabilities of artificial intelligence prove to be much greater with respect to utilization of it in the digital world of business. AI helps us form frameworks for the observation of user patterns using various algorithms involving high computation and the permutations and combinations of a number of factors in various circumstances under varying interests and objectives which ultimately allows us to study and analyze what a customer wants, what a customer needs, what are the basic necessities to be made available and what are the minimum requirements and expectations of customers when shopping online. This in the long run enables customers to exhibit their needs without having to raise any objections, which makes the overall experience of the digital market a rather pleasurable one. Moreover, AI helps maintain an all-inclusive approach to the needs of various sects of people wherein a sense of customer respect is instilled in those at the receiving end of things and as a result make it more convenient for anyone to access the digital market and shop online without having to hesitate. Employing AI in modern online business models also helps with increasing customer satisfaction and personalization while accessing the digital market. This is because AI obtains information based on the interests of users when shopping online. By applying these preferences, AI repeatedly improves and renews its dataset wherein information about the customer is made more accurate and employed in the process of achieving a more user-friendly and personalized online experience.

Moreover, because of the application of AI on online platforms, the process of resolving customer queries has become more accurate since the need for human intervention is kept to a minimum by virtue of AI integrated business models. Subsequently analyzing the other aspect, which in this case is ML and deep learning models, we find that ML and deep learning is also vital to the smooth functioning of such online business models. This is because ML helps maintain and improve the other important aspects of a successful business model. ML is responsible for aspects such as Fraud Detection and Security, Predictive Analysis, Content Moderation, Supply Chain Management, Marketing Optimization and Dynamic Pricing (Khan et al., 2020).

Machine learning enables online businesses to forecast customer trends, demand patterns, and market dynamics accurately. By analyzing the data collected, machine learning models can predict future outcomes, helping businesses make informed decisions regarding inventory management, pricing strategies, and marketing campaigns. Moreover, ML algorithms can detect anomalous patterns and identify potential security threats in real-time. In online businesses, these algorithms are used to detect fraudulent transactions, prevent data breaches, and safeguard customer information, thereby enhancing trust and reliability. They are also beneficial in cybersecurity related to online business such as the prevention of monetary losses, hacking, fake products and websites and the ingenuity of any online organization.

Furthermore, Machine learning optimizes supply chain operations by the analysis of various factors such as demand forecasts, supplier performance, transportation logistics, and inventory management. This leads to cost savings, improved efficiency, and better resource utilization for online businesses. Lastly, it helps online businesses to examine customer data to identify high-value segments, predict customer lifetime value, and optimize marketing campaigns across multiple channels. By targeting the right audience with personalized messages at the right time, online businesses can maximize their marketing returns on investment and drive sales along with determining the appropriate pricing for different segments of products in accordance with back-end production cost as well as the purchasing power of the intended customer. With that, let us look at what roles are played by artificial intelligence and machine learning with respect to business in the real digital world.

The integration of AI in business areas has the potential to revolutionize various industries and transform the way businesses operate (Gurjar et al., 2024). AI can automate tasks, examine data, and provide solutions, empowering businesses to improve decision making, efficiency, profitability and enhance customer experience (Haleem et al., 2022; Jordan & Mitchell, 2015). Overall, many direct applications of AI are visible in business operations these days. For instance, almost all the prominent as well as smaller scale businesses deploy chatbots on their respective official websites to help with customer queries at their convenience and hence improve efficiency as well as customer experience.

Another point worth noting is that AI functions on the basis of certain fixed algorithm-based technologies which help it in effectively tackling the individual as well as interrelated problems associated with different spheres of business. These technologies enable merging of domains, virtualization of products and processes into services, and penetration, enhancement, and acceleration with artificial intelligence (AI) (Schrettenbrunnner, 2020). This is because these algorithms are made to repetitively collect and analyze user data and usage patterns to be able to detect when an unusual behavioral pattern is observed to prevent online fraud and losses as well as give the user a better overall experience by building, analyzing and correcting user preferences accurately by analyzing the likes and dislikes using the digital footprints of users from various sources.

Similarly, Machine learning algorithms contribute to online business operation and administration by filling in the gaps where AI alone does not suffice. A major application of ML in businesses is seen in the integration of ML with online fraud detection systems. One effective technique of doing so is the application of QML (Quantum Machine Learning) to the same which helps tackle problems such as detecting fraud after they have taken place and examining time-based usage patterns of users. This is because QML is the fastest available algorithm in use for tackling problems like (Wang et al., 2022).

Moreover, ML can also be used in the processes of data mining, data sorting, data analysis, data filtration and maintaining concurrency with respect to the same for more effective operations. A deeper understanding of the challenges associated with training machine learning models on process data is essential for establishing a robust integration of process mining and machine learning. This is achieved by terminating the mismatch between data distribution and concurrency using effective data encoding techniques for the same (Ceravolo et al., 2024). Hence, it is evident how Artificial Intelligence and Machine Learning go hand in hand for the smooth and efficient operation of various online business processes.

Now let us have a look at the limitations of applying AI and ML to conventional business models. The first and most important limitation to the application of AI is the quality of the data available and the credibility and verification of that data as well as the source of that data (Gurjar et al., 2024). In a similar way, the concept of "garbage in, garbage out" also holds true with respect to the inputs provided to the machine before implementing them in any machine learning or deep learning algorithms (Geiger et al., 2019). Both these concepts ideally identify the same limitation, which is the inability of these AI and ML based algorithms to function effectively in the absence of good quality data in their input. This can lead to serious consequences, particularly in applications that require high levels of accuracy, such as medical diagnosis, financial forecasting, or autonomous driving (Gurjar et al., 2024).

Moreover, due to the continuous data requirement of AI algorithms for increasing accuracy, there is also a concern regarding the ethics of using AI in business with respect to customer information and right to privacy (Li, X. & Zhang, T., 2017). This raises concerns regarding the safety of the individual customers' information in the hands of AI and associated issues such as hacking of this data, Identity thefts, Cyber-threats and blackmailing individuals, online financial fraud and so on. It also reflects upon the ease and rise of cyber-crime due because of more personal data of customers being available online as a direct implication of the use of AI and ML in online business market.

Furthermore, another major concern regarding the use of AI and ML is its integration with the existing technology already in use for facilitating the aspects of online business. Many businesses already have complex IT infrastructures, and integrating AI systems with these systems can be challenging. Businesses need to ensure that their AI systems can seamlessly integrate with existing systems and that they can effectively manage the complexity of their IT infrastructure (Gill et al., 2022). This is a very huge limitation both at the user's end and at the end of the organization responsible for the functioning of the business. This is because integrating new AI based algorithms and software with the existing one either requires the cessation on the use of the existing technologies and employing the novel ones in their place or tweaking the new ones to be compatible with the existing technologies. However, in both the cases the cost to the business is enormous and the accessibility and user-friendliness of the software is reduced. Moreover, if new algorithms are tweaked to work with the existing software, there is a loss in efficiency to some extent which diminishes the utility of AI and ML integration itself.

Therefore, this research paper aims to analyze the technologies which are both in use in the field of E-commerce in the present world and the upcoming ones to understand their working, determine their advantages and drawbacks and find solutions to upgrade them into a better version which suits the current digital market needs, conditions, and competitive nature more. Furthermore, it aims to examine the algorithms involved in the integration of AI and ML with the digital market and point out methods of making it better suited for use by the customer. It aims to do so through examining the methodology, working and logic behind the algorithms, advantages, disadvantages, and possible upgrades in the name of efficiency and user-friendliness.

2. LITERATURE REVIEW

This literature review strives to explain the effect of Artificial Intelligence and Machine Learning in running business operations in the digital world. This is to be done by understanding two main aspects of AI and ML in business – The history of AI and ML, their development with respect to the business industry over the years as well as the recent AI and ML trends associated with E-commerce and their effectiveness by analyzing similar research conducted in the recent past related to this title. The aim is to explore the technologies and methods applied in the integration of AI and ML with business and to determine the extent of their effectiveness thereby.

Recent studies in the field of AI and ML with respect to business intelligence and integration reveal the real-world importance of AI and ML integration in business models and their impact and the improvements made thereby. By paying attention to the research conducted in the past few years, a few technologies can be identified which are currently used rampantly in the business world. Different AI and ML algorithms have been used in different spheres of E-commerce for making it a better experience for customers as well as for boosting the efficiency of the organization, reducing their costs and losses as well as increasing their profit margins.

The use of artificial intelligence in business started off just as a method to analyze user preferences and help with the personalization of business user interfaces. However, the scope of AI has developed in the recent past to exceed this basic utility and move on towards a broader and more complex approach. One major aspect of AI in business which has historically evolved is the use of AI in new product development (NDP). With respect to NDP, AI has also been defined as a business tool which is immensely capable of being used for predictive analysis. The early days of AI were marked by the development of basic AI concepts and algorithms. AI pioneers, such as Alan Turing, laid the groundwork for ML and artificial neural networks. Computer-aided design (CAD) systems were introduced in the 1960s, which some historians consider an early example of AI in NPD. These CAD systems enabled engineers to design products on computers, reducing the time and cost of NPD. In the 1970s and 1980s, expert systems were developed, which could mimic the decision-making capabilities of human experts. These systems could be used to evaluate the feasibility of new-product ideas, and some business historians consider expert systems to be the first use of AI in business (Cooper, 2024).

With the use of AI comes the use of machine learning as it is evident that the two go hand in hand. Machine learning in its most basic form in the past was used as an algorithm which took data from users, analyzed it, and stored it as a reference to compare with in the future. The initial algorithm applied to ML for making recommendations was based on the factor of popularity of any product or public opinion. On the other hand, nowadays there are a lot of other factors which are taken into consideration while designing such an ML algorithm. It is now a common practice to include the use of neural networks and dynamic collection and analysis of current data trends to improve the accuracy of ML based predictions and thus its performance (Kabra et al., 2022). Moreover, the use of Machine Learning combined with economical studies in the predictive analysis of the share market as well as the prediction of product popularity and demand and supply models has gained popularity over the years. This demonstrates the importance of ML to vital aspects of business (Lee, 2023).

It contains data about the various areas of business where AI and ML have been applied, the objectives behind doing so, the methodologies employed as well as the algorithms or models used.

One very prominent technology is the use of Recurrent Neural Networks (RNN) s in the sphere of data processing, data management, predictive analysis, decision making algorithms as well as product design according to (Cooper, 2024; Gowrabhathini et al., 2024; Khan et al., 2020). Similar recent research shows the benefits of using machine learning methods like Autoregressive Integrated Moving Average (ARIMA), Long Short-Term Memory (LSTM), and Convolutional Neural Networks (CNN) with respect to risk mitigation in terms of the finances concerned with the business as well as in making online fraud detection and prevention models. These are all time-signature identifiers which help identify the anomalies in user interaction in real time platform usage. Another effective method of increasing cyber security on business platforms online is using Copula Based Outlier Detection Technology (COPOD).

Moreover, a major improvement in business economics can be seen with the use of AI and ML predictive algorithms integrated with classical economic theories with respect to the value of stocks and choosing correct stocks for investment in the share market. Algorithms such as the Random Forest (RF) algorithm and the Multivariate Adaptive Regression Splines (MARS) algorithm are employed in the construction of AI based ML models for accurate predictions related to the changes in the values of stocks in the share market which help improve the financial management of the organization and help in investing the money in the right manner.

On the front of manufacturing, sales and marketing, the use of AI and ML can be seen in terms of Composite GRU-Prophet Model with attention mechanism for boosting product development quality in terms of relevance and demand forecasting, use of deep neural networks for demand forecasting of product preferences (Cooper, 2024), etc. Similarly, with regard to customer interaction and user interface development and personalization, technologies like behavioral characteristic identification and clustering techniques, using AI and ML for user-relevant predictions in making a multivariate UI platform, using multimodel frameworks based on per-item agent strategy for a more relevant dataset (Kabra et al., 2022), etc. are used.

Overall, past research indicates that the integration of Artificial Intelligence and Machine Learning algorithms and models with online business platforms proves to be quite beneficial in improving efficiency and productivity, increasing profitability, and reducing the losses incurred by the organization. Hence, it can be said that the overall quality and experience of E-commerce is improved by the application of AI and ML in business, both for the customer and the provider.

3. AI IN BUSINESS AREAS

3.1 Application of AI in Business Areas

Artificial intelligence has many applications in the business world. Certain key areas and factors behind the application of AI can be identified – Operational efficiency, Tech-enabled manpower, Intelligence Process Automation, Innovation, Cost Optimization, Firm resilience, Quality management, Digital platform, Customer Satisfaction, Business value, Financial Performance, and ethics. The first aspect to be analyzed is Predictive Analysis. Algorithms such as XGBoost, AdaBoost, ARIMA, RF, MARS, etc. are used for it (Lee, 2023).

The next business aspect in question is management. This area practices the application of support vector machines and ARIMA, LSTM, CNN techniques. Support Vector Machines (SVM) classify data by finding the optimal hyperplane that maximizes the margin between different classes, using kernel functions to handle non-linear relationships. This approach ensures robust classification with high generalization performance. The next sphere of business is Sales and Marketing, which makes use of Recurrent Neural Networks (RNN), Multivariate UI Platforms and clustering techniques (Gowrabhathini et al., 2024).

The next application of AI and ML in business can be seen in the development of new products which use deep neural networks (Cooper, 2024). Deep neural networks (DNNs) are hierarchical models composed of multiple layers of interconnected neurons, capable of learning complex patterns and representations from data through forward and backward propagation of gradients during training. They excel in various tasks such as image and speech recognition, natural language processing, and reinforcement learning due to their ability to automatically extract hierarchical features. Lastly, we have the concern of Cybersecurity which arises from the digitalization of business models. Techniques such as Quantum Computing and COPOD can be applied here (Wang et al., 2022).

Quantum computing leverages the principles of quantum mechanics to perform computations using quantum bits (qubits), which can represent multiple states simultaneously, offering potential for solving certain problems exponentially faster than classical computers. Quantum computers have the potential to revolutionize fields like cryptography, optimization, and drug discovery, but are still in the early stages of development. COPOD (Constrained Persistent Outlier Detection) is a method for identifying outliers in time series data by considering the persistence of outliers across multiple scales and imposing constraints on the outlier scores to ensure consistency and reliability. It uses a combination of persistent homology and optimization techniques to efficiently detect outliers while accounting for noise and variations in data.

Figure 1. AI algorithms used in different business areas

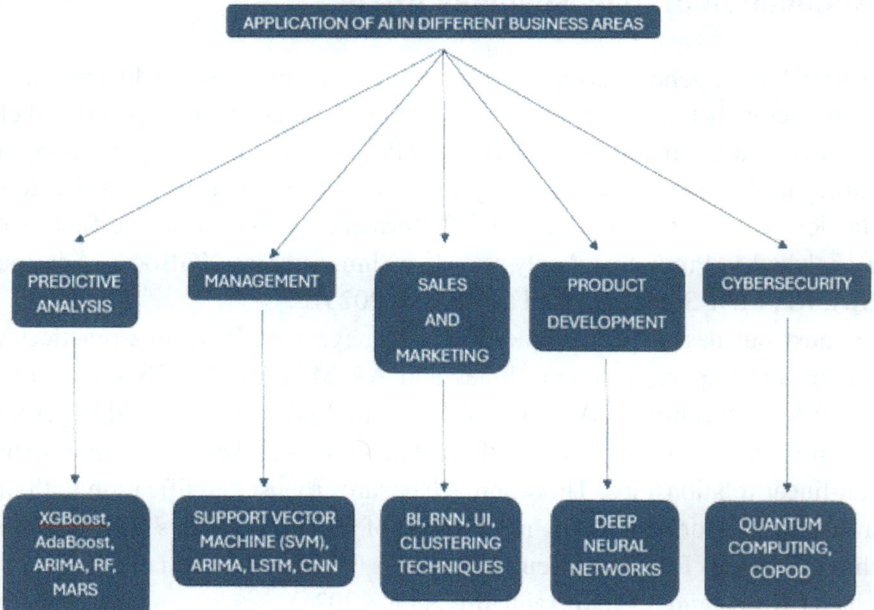

Figure-1 depicts a flow chart related to the application of AI and ML in different areas of business, namely Predictive Analysis, Management, Sales, Marketing, Product Development and Cybersecurity. It holds the data regarding the various techniques and algorithms used in each such business sphere.

3.2 Current Trends of AI in Business Areas

The current business world revolves around certain trends related to AI and ML which are in extensive use these days. These trends, developed gradually over time with advancement in technology, now constitute an integral part of present-world business models. Some of the more prominent trends which are integrated with businesses these days are – customer satisfaction, cybersecurity, automation, data processing, natural language processing, supply chain and logistics, predictive maintenance, human resource management, product development, manufacturing, stocks, financial investments, marketing, and sales.

The use of Natural Language Processing in data handling in business organizations has seen a 195% surge in the past 5 years. Similarly, the use of assistive AI in online search engines has also increased with the use of Large Language Models (LLMs) to increase the number of relevant search results for any search request made. Numerically, a 1567% surge is seen in the use of AI powered search engines. The use of AI powered chatbots deployed on search engines has also gained popularity.

The next major trend is the use of AI in the healthcare industry. Ever since the coronavirus pandemic took place, the importance of use of AI in the healthcare industry has been quite evident. Ranging from paperwork to monitoring systems to even AI-Robotics assisted surgery, the use of AI in the healthcare industry has increased extensively in the past few years. The use of AI in the education sector has also seen a huge splurge in terms of the use of AI-based tools to help with the digitalization of conventional classrooms and increase the quality of education.

Manufacturing, Industrial Automation and mitigation of the associated risks are also some of the prominent fields which employ AI to aid with the general processes. The use of AI boosts efficiency, helps in detection of defects in products, aids in new product development, prevents fraud, etc. The use of AI in the automation of the product manufacturing and sales industries is also quite prominent. This allows businesses to keep track of their customers, helps with user interaction and feedback, aids in basic processes like shipping of products and delivery, manage supply chain, storage and other logistics, etc. Moreover, AI makes fraud detection quite easy to detect due to the various personalization and anomaly detection algorithms in place.

Figure 2. Graph indicating growth in AI trends

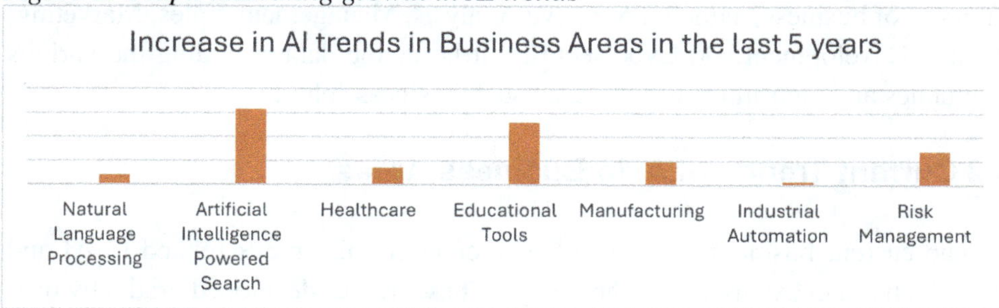

3.3 Algorithmic Approach of AI And ML in Business Areas

A very important approach to analyze the use and of AI and ML in business areas is considering the algorithms used in different business spheres and understanding how they work. Moreover, the analysis of these algorithms permits us to test and verify the benefits of integrating AI and ML with businesses and also allows us to examine the methodologies behind the AI and ML algorithms used in business systems and how they can be made more efficient and relevant for use by the customers.

A few of the most popular algorithms and models include Linear Regression, Logistic Regression, Decision Trees, Random Forest, Support Vector Machines, K-Nearest Neighbor, K-Means Clustering, Principal Component Analysis, Neural Networks, Reinforcement Learning and Generative Adversarial Networks. These algorithms have been used in various areas of business to help with various tasks such as customer personalization, performance boosting, product design and management, human resource management, manufacturing, financial management and industrial automation.

Using past studies, this research paper analyzes the algorithms used in AI and ML, their methodologies, the purposes and capabilities of the algorithms and their possible use in various spheres of business. Algorithms such as Linear and Logistic Regression, PCA, etc. have wide implications for data processing in the business industry. Others like RNNs, CNNs, GANs, Decision Tree, etc. have been widely used in the AI-based ML models training. Lastly, algorithms like k-Nearest Neighbor, k-Means Clustering, etc. are used for statistical model training and deep learning along with reinforcement learning using environmental conditions.

4. METHODOLOGY

The methodology of the paper employs rigorous data collection, taking into account numerous research papers of the recent past from various scientific; credible sources like PubMed, Google Scholar, IEEE Xplore, Scopus, ScienceDirect, etc., further shortlisting the most relevant papers based on the inclusion and exclusion criteria, and finally performing a third round of evaluation for selecting the most relevant papers with the most accurate information.

- **DATA COLLECTION:**

The data used in this paper has been collected from 5 major web platforms, namely- Google Scholar, IEEE Xplore, PubMed, Scopus and ScienceDirect. The research papers most relevant to the topic of this research paper were taken into consideration and then carefully examined to determine whether the information contained in them would be of imminent use to this paper. Furthermore, to improve quality and relevance of the input data, the papers shortlisted belong to the time of the last 5 years, i.e., from 2019-2024. A total of 69082 research papers were taken into consideration from across different sources. This helped us ensure that the authenticity of the data used in research was not even remotely compromised, which in turn results in the achievement of the desired output in terms of relevance to the problem at hand.

Figure 3. Graph indicating number of research works published by different publishers related to the use of artificial intelligence and machine learning in the past 5 years

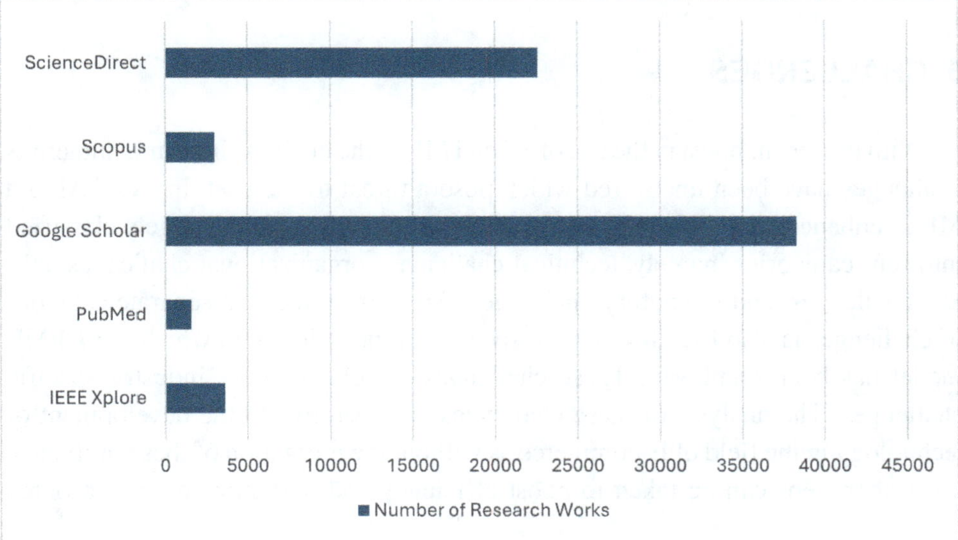

- **INCLUSION AND EXCLUSION CRITERIA:**

The inclusion criteria involve the analysis of research papers of the last 5 years, published by reputed and credible publishers, related to the use of AI and ML in different business spheres and shortlisting the ones which hold the most relevance. Only the work which has been implemented in some industry has been tested practically or are of some practical use to a business industry have been considered while producing this work. As for the exclusion criteria, all research papers which contain theoretical proposals, which do not have a practical approach, or which are purely analytical without valid proof have been rejected. This ensures that the data used as reference in this paper is accurate, credible and up to date with the latest trends and technologies.

- **DATA EVALUATION:**

To ensure that the most relevant data, accurate statistics, and real-life figures are considered for analysis, only the works which have scientific relevance and belong to credible sources have been used. The sources include renowned research platforms and publications like IEEE Xplore, PubMed, Google Scholar, Scopus and ScienceDirect. To further keep in sync with the latest trends and technologies, only the works published in the last 5 years have been referred to. Moreover, it was cautiously assured that the data used in evaluating the said technology, and its past, present and future use was not redundant. In other words, the information being evaluated was not repeated and contained authentic; original data which added some individual value to the research.

5. CHALLENGES

With the recent boost in the use of AI and ML in the business industry, numerous challenges have been uncovered which pose a threat to the usefulness of AI and ML as enhancement tools to businesses. These challenges can be largely classified into four categories, namely, technical challenges, organizational challenges, ethical challenges, and regulatory challenges. Apart from these, a separate category of challenges is also found which are specific to the industry in which the AI/ML model has been employed. These challenges are classified as industry specific challenges. The analysis of these challenges is imperative to the development of technology in the field of E-commerce as without the mitigation of these problems, no further steps can be taken to boost efficiency and maximize proper resource utilization and efficiency. Hence, it is important to review and solve these problems at an immediate basis.

Technical challenges include collection of good quality, consistent, and credible data (Khan et al., 2023), accessing real time data, scalability, maintenance, etc. Organizational challenges include lack of expertise and adaptation (Yi et al., 2023), cost effectiveness, integration with existing technologies (Gurjar et al., 2024), etc. Ethical challenges include model biases, transparency, and privacy concerns (Ghandour et al., 2024; Golda et al., 2024; Yi et al., 2023) etc. Regulatory challenges include compliance with norms of regulatory bodies, lack of standardization, system failure, etc.

Other than this, certain industry-specific challenges are also worth discussing. For instance, the manufacturing industry faces challenges like the development of efficient smart devices, inefficient information interactions, distribution of resources, lack of knowledge, etc. (Wan et al., 2021). Another example is the problem and associated risk of ML model cyberattacks in all industries using ML models (Grosse et al., 2023). Similarly, in the education sector, challenges like language barriers, use of jargon and sarcasm, ambiguity, emoticons, data imbalances and sentiment analysis, associated with the use of NLP algorithms are prominent (Shaik et al., 2022).

6. FUTURE SCOPE OF AI AND ML IN BUSINESS

Throughout the past two decades, the use of AI and ML in business areas has become quite rampant. Moreover, AI and ML as technologies have become increasingly advanced and the sector itself has seen an unprecedented growth. Although most of the functions of business agencies can be replaced by AI and ML, it is currently not so due to the numerous drawbacks discussed in this paper. Hence, it is vividly visible that certain areas of business, such as Data collection, Cybersecurity, Ethical Challenges, Product development, etc. are yet to be automated completely and effectively by AI.

To overcome these challenges, the best approach is to integrate AI and ML with other technologies such as Blockchain, Cloud Computing, Internet of Things, Quantum Computing, etc. which can help strengthen the weaker aspects of the use of AI and ML in business and consequently help in the improvement of AI and ML in certain problematic business areas. For instance, Blockchain based AI can help enhance data security, increase transparency, improve efficiency, optimize scalability, as well as help in the monetization of data (Fadi et al., 2022; Kuznetsov et al., 2024).

Moreover, the integration of AI and cloud computing helps solve the problem of data collection and analysis. It enables the collection of vast amounts of data and does away with all the constraints related to analysis, processing and processing speed of data in various types of networks [30]. Furthermore, the use of AI and ML with Internet of Things smoothens the process of data exchange, enables efficient automation of industries, improves the level of data security, reduces the possibility of any cyber threat and also explores novel areas like self-defense systems, legal frameworks and so on (Humayun et al., 2024).

Lastly, the integration of AI and ML with quantum computing algorithms helps with the management of finances in business. The benefits of quantum computing include the reduction of penalty costs or human-error induced costs, improvement of customer satisfaction and brand perception, increased customer interaction and appropriate investments, reduction of capital costs, and improvement of cash influx (Egger et al., 2020). Hence, it is observed that quantum computing algorithms integrated with AI allow for efficient finance management.

Overall, it can be said that despite the recent boom in the use and development of AI and ML in businesses, areas like cybersecurity, ethics, automation, finance, etc. still have a huge scope for further development. Moreover, the development of IoT integrated with AI has immense potential for improving data processing and transmission capabilities, reducing the need for human intervention and allowing for more efficient automation of industrial processes. Therefore, further trends like Generative AI, Blockchain based AI, use of cloud and quantum computing in ML training integrated with AI, etc. would prove to be of immense value to businesses in the approaching future.

7. CONCLUSION

Artificial Intelligence and Machine Learning have been a topic of discussion since the early 20th century. However, recent developments in technology have enabled humankind to truly comprehend the full potential of AI and ML. Ranging from phones to airplanes, the presence of AI and ML can be seen everywhere. The use of AI and ML in business models is something that has gained popularity very recently in the business industry. All spheres of business have AI and ML integrated into them to some extent. Whether it be a simple chatbot for resolving customer queries or a highly advanced robot responsible for managing surgeries, AI and ML prove to be useful tools in the simplification of numerous tasks in an efficient manner.

By the means of this research, one is able to analyze the impact of AI and ML on the business industry. This work discusses in detail the effects of the use of AI and ML in different areas of business, their advantages, disadvantages, challenges to their integration as well as future scope of AI and ML in business. It can be determined through this research paper that the benefits of using an AI-ML based business model are innumerable. On the other hand, there are only a few challenges to the implementation of AI and ML in business which can be easily overcome by using interdependent technology models.

AI and ML can serve a purpose in every aspect of business, including marketing, sales, finance, new product development, predictive analysis, big data handling, data mining and processing, cybersecurity, industrial automation and so on. Moreover, use of technologies like AI integrated blockchain, AI and ML integrated IoT models, AI-based cloud computing and quantum computing have immense scope of development and innovation in business areas. Therefore, it can be briefly stated that the use of AI and ML helps transform businesses into a more efficient version of themselves.

REFERENCES

Ceravolo, P., Junior, S. B., Damiani, E., & Van Der Aalst, W. (2024). Tuning Machine Learning to Address Process Mining Requirements. *IEEE Access: Practical Innovations, Open Solutions*, *12*, 24583–24595. DOI: 10.1109/ACCESS.2024.3361650

Cooper, R. G. (2024). The Artificial Intelligence Revolution in New-Product Development. *IEEE Engineering Management Review*, *52*(1), 195–211. DOI: 10.1109/EMR.2023.3336834

Dash, A., Ye, J., & Wang, G. (2024). A Review of Generative Adversarial Networks (GANs) and Its Applications in a Wide Variety of Disciplines: From Medical to Remote Sensing. *IEEE Access: Practical Innovations, Open Solutions*, *12*, 18330–18357. DOI: 10.1109/ACCESS.2023.3346273

Egger, D. J., Gambella, C., Marecek, J., McFaddin, S., Mevissen, M., Raymond, R., Simonetto, A., Woerner, S., & Yndurain, E. (2020). Quantum Computing for Finance: State-of-the-Art and Future Prospects. *IEEE Transactions on Quantum Engineering*, *1*, 1–24. DOI: 10.1109/TQE.2020.3030314

Fadi, O., Karim, Z., Abdellatif, E. G., & Mohammed, B. (2022). A Survey on Blockchain and Artificial Intelligence Technologies for Enhancing Security and Privacy in Smart Environments. *IEEE Access : Practical Innovations, Open Solutions*, *10*, 93168–93186. DOI: 10.1109/ACCESS.2022.3203568

Geiger, R. S., Yu, K., Yang, Y., Dai, M., Qiu, J., Tang, R., & Huang, J. (2019). Garbage In, Garbage Out? Do Machine Learning Application Papers in Social Computing Report Where Human-Labeled Training Data Comes From? DOI: 10.1145/3351095.3372862

Ghandour, A., Woodford, B. J., & Abusaimeh, H. (2024). Ethical Considerations in the Use of ChatGPT: An Exploration Through the Lens of Five Moral Dimensions. *IEEE Access : Practical Innovations, Open Solutions*, *12*, 60682–60693. DOI: 10.1109/ACCESS.2024.3394243

Gill, S. S., Xu, M., Ottaviani, C., Patros, P., Bahsoon, R., Shaghaghi, A., Golec, M., Stankovski, V., Wu, H., Abraham, A., Singh, M., Mehta, H., Ghosh, S. K., Baker, T., Parlikad, A. K., Lutfiyya, H., Kanhere, S. S., Sakellariou, R., Dustdar, S., & Uhlig, S. (2022). AI for next generation computing: Emerging trends and future directions. *Internet of Things : Engineering Cyber Physical Human Systems*, *19*, 100514. DOI: 10.1016/j.iot.2022.100514

Golda, A., Mekonen, K., Pandey, A., Singh, A., Hassija, V., Chamola, V., & Sikdar, B. (2024). Privacy and Security Concerns in Generative AI: A Comprehensive Survey. *IEEE Access : Practical Innovations, Open Solutions*, *12*, 48126–48144. DOI: 10.1109/ACCESS.2024.3381611

Gowrabhathini, J., Tamilarasu, J., Rahithya, S., Sindhu Parimala, P. S., Hussain, S. S., & Sri, C. N. (2024). Business Intelligence In Industrial Organization Using An AI-Driven Competitive Analysis Framework. 2024 2nd International Conference on Disruptive Technologies (ICDT), 112–115. DOI: 10.1109/ICDT61202.2024.10489175

Grosse, K., Bieringer, L., Besold, T. R., Biggio, B., & Krombholz, K. (2023). Machine Learning Security in Industry: A Quantitative Survey. *IEEE Transactions on Information Forensics and Security*, *18*, 1749–1762. DOI: 10.1109/TIFS.2023.3251842

Gurjar, K., Jangra, A., Baber, H., Islam, M., & Sheikh, S. A. (2024). An Analytical Review on the Impact of Artificial Intelligence on the Business Industry: Applications, Trends, and Challenges. *IEEE Engineering Management Review*, *52*(2), 84–102. DOI: 10.1109/EMR.2024.3355973

Haleem, A., Javaid, M., Asim Qadri, M., Pratap Singh, R., & Suman, R. (2022). Artificial intelligence (AI) applications for marketing: A literature-based study. *International Journal of Intelligent Networks*, *3*, 119–132. DOI: 10.1016/j.ijin.2022.08.005

Humayun, M., Tariq, N., Alfayad, M., Zakwan, M., Alwakid, G., & Assiri, M. (2024). Securing the Internet of Things in Artificial Intelligence Era: A Comprehensive Survey. *IEEE Access : Practical Innovations, Open Solutions*, *12*, 25469–25490. DOI: 10.1109/ACCESS.2024.3365634

Jordan, M. I., & Mitchell, T. M. (2015). Machine learning: Trends, perspectives, and prospects. *Science*, *349*(6245), 255–260. DOI: 10.1126/science.aaa8415 PMID: 26185243

Kabra, A., Agarwal, A., & Parihar, A. S. (2022). Potent Real-Time Recommendations Using Multimodel Contextual Reinforcement Learning. *IEEE Transactions on Computational Social Systems*, *9*(2), 581–593. DOI: 10.1109/TCSS.2021.3100291

Kayabol, K. (2020). Approximate Sparse Multinomial Logistic Regression for Classification. *IEEE Transactions on Pattern Analysis and Machine Intelligence*, *42*(2), 490–493. DOI: 10.1109/TPAMI.2019.2904062 PMID: 30869609

Khan, M. A., Saleh, A. M., Waseem, M., & Sajjad, I. A. (2023). Artificial Intelligence Enabled Demand Response: Prospects and Challenges in Smart Grid Environment. *IEEE Access : Practical Innovations, Open Solutions*, *11*, 1477–1505. DOI: 10.1109/ACCESS.2022.3231444

Khan, M. A., Saqib, S., Alyas, T., Ur Rehman, A., Saeed, Y., Zeb, A., Zareei, M., & Mohamed, E. M. (2020). Effective Demand Forecasting Model Using Business Intelligence Empowered With Machine Learning. *IEEE Access : Practical Innovations, Open Solutions*, *8*, 116013–116023. DOI: 10.1109/ACCESS.2020.3003790

Kiran, K. R., Kumar, B. H., Mishra, B. S., & Yadav, A. S. Y, N., & Tiwari, M. (2023). Artificial Intelligence Integrated with Machine Learning for Enhancing Business in E-World. 2023 5th International Conference on Inventive Research in Computing Applications (ICIRCA), 1060–1064. DOI: 10.1109/ICIRCA57980.2023.10220756

Kuznetsov, O., Sernani, P., Romeo, L., Frontoni, E., & Mancini, A. (2024). On the Integration of Artificial Intelligence and Blockchain Technology: A Perspective About Security. *IEEE Access : Practical Innovations, Open Solutions*, *12*, 3881–3897. DOI: 10.1109/ACCESS.2023.3349019

Lee, G. (2023). Exploring Predictive Variables Affecting the Sales of Companies Listed With Korean Stock Indices Through Machine Learning Analysis. *IEEE Access : Practical Innovations, Open Solutions*, *11*, 63534–63549. DOI: 10.1109/ACCESS.2023.3288576

Li, X., & Zhang, T. (2017). An exploration on artificial intelligence application: From security, privacy and ethic perspective. 2017 IEEE 2nd International Conference on Cloud Computing and Big Data Analysis (ICCCBDA), 416–420. DOI: 10.1109/ICCCBDA.2017.7951949

Saleh, H., Alharbi, A., & Alsamhi, S. H. (2021). OPCNN-FAKE: Optimized Convolutional Neural Network for Fake News Detection. *IEEE Access : Practical Innovations, Open Solutions*, *9*, 129471–129489. DOI: 10.1109/ACCESS.2021.3112806

Schrettenbrunnner, M. B. (2020). Artificial-Intelligence-Driven Management. *IEEE Engineering Management Review*, *48*(2), 15–19. DOI: 10.1109/EMR.2020.2990933

Shaik, T., Tao, X., Li, Y., Dann, C., McDonald, J., Redmond, P., & Galligan, L. (2022). A Review of the Trends and Challenges in Adopting Natural Language Processing Methods for Education Feedback Analysis. *IEEE Access : Practical Innovations, Open Solutions*, *10*, 56720–56739. DOI: 10.1109/ACCESS.2022.3177752

Sharma, S., & Dhir, S. (2022). Adoption of IoT: in Healthcare, Daily Life, Businesses, Education during the Covid-19. International Conference on Machine Learning, Big Data, Cloud and Parallel Computing (COM-IT-CON), May 2022, pp. 597-601, DOI: 10.1109/COM-IT-CON54601.2022.9850762

Shukla, A., & Dhir, S. (2016). Tools for Data Visualization in Business Intelligence: Case Study Using the Tool Qlikview. International Conference on Information System Design and Intelligent Application 2016. Springer Journal Volume 434, pp 319-326.DOI: 10.1007/978-81-322-2755-7_11

Tsakiris, M. C., Peng, L., Conca, A., Kneip, L., Shi, Y., & Choi, H. (2020). An Algebraic-Geometric Approach for Linear Regression Without Correspondences. *IEEE Transactions on Information Theory*, *66*(8), 5130–5144. DOI: 10.1109/TIT.2020.2977166

Wan, J., Li, X., Dai, H.-N., Kusiak, A., Martínez-García, M., & Li, D. (2021). *Artificial Intelligence-Driven Customized Manufacturing Factory: Key Technologies*. Applications, and Challenges., DOI: 10.1109/JPROC.2020.3034808

Wang, H., Wang, W., Liu, Y., & Alidaee, B. (2022). Integrating Machine Learning Algorithms With Quantum Annealing Solvers for Online Fraud Detection. *IEEE Access : Practical Innovations, Open Solutions*, *10*, 75908–75917. DOI: 10.1109/ACCESS.2022.3190897

Yi, Z., Cao, X., Chen, Z., & Li, S. (2023). Artificial Intelligence in Accounting and Finance: Challenges and Opportunities. *IEEE Access : Practical Innovations, Open Solutions*, *11*, 129100–129123. DOI: 10.1109/ACCESS.2023.3333389

Zhang, W., Chen, X., Liu, Y., & Xi, Q. (2020). A Distributed Storage and Computation k-Nearest Neighbor Algorithm Based Cloud-Edge Computing for Cyber-Physical-Social Systems. *IEEE Access : Practical Innovations, Open Solutions*, *8*, 50118–50130. DOI: 10.1109/ACCESS.2020.2974764

Chapter 11
Performance Optimization and Resource Management:
Industrial IoT Applications and Smart Manufacturing

R. Velmurugan
https://orcid.org/0000-0002-7925-9757
Karpagam Academy of Higher Education, Coimbatore, India

J. Sudarvel
https://orcid.org/0000-0001-6656-1992
Karpagam Academy of Higher Education, Coimbatore, India

R. Bhuvaneswari
https://orcid.org/0009-0003-9396-6129
Dr. Mahalingam College of Engineering and Technology, Pollachi, India

S. Senthilkumar
https://orcid.org/0000-0003-1968-6877
Skyline University, Nigeria

ABSTRACT

Industrial processes are enhanced through increase in efficiency, automation and data driven decision making by the IIoT and Smart Manufacturing. In IIoT environments, there is need for optimal performance and resource management. These advanced technologies such as AI, ML, and edge computing, better utilize resources, reduce downtime and increase system reliability. However, real time data processing and security are unsolved issues. Latency is the problem that edge and fog computing

DOI: 10.4018/979-8-3373-1147-0.ch011

solves, while energy consumption and green factory manufacturing is the goal of AI. The simulations on proactive monitoring by Digital twins are achieved. Advancements have already been made, yet the interoperability still continues, high costs and the need for skilled personnel remains. To overcome these barriers and obtain the sustainable, efficient manufacturing, both standardization and collaboration are vital.

INTRODUCTION

It is only a few years ago that the Industrial Internet of Things (IIoT) and Smart Manufacturing have taken a seismic change in the industrial sector, rethinking the way production processes are monitored, optimized and executed. IIoT provides new era of on the fly data collection and analysis through smart sensors, smart actuators, edge computing devices and advanced analytics, which led to improvement in the efficiency, automation and decision making process. The challenging need to improve productivity and competitiveness in industries has been met by IIoT based systems which as a central pillar for intelligent manufacturing environment processes can provide key information that allows for drastically improving the utilization of all such resources and that of the entire system in general.

In the context of manufacturing, in order to benefit from the data available in manufacturing, it is important to be able to collect and analyze data in real time. While past, the traditional manufacturing process offers a highly effective process, relying on manual data collection and relying on manual decision making — both slow and error prone. With the advent of IIoT, this approach was revolutionised with sensor and actuator embedding in many parts of the production line making machines capable of communicating with other machines and central control systems. Yet bandwidth from computers and phones makes it possible for operations to be monitored, so long as the connectivity allows, and tracked with parameters such as temperature, pressure, speed and vibration. Advanced analytics can take the data collected from these sensors and analyze such data to find where inefficiencies are located so that they can be fixed or potential maintenance needs can be predicted and resources could be more efficiently allotted (Xu et al., 2018).

An advantage of the IIoT is that it can expand on the utilization of resources. In traditional manufacturing environments, energy, raw materials, and labor were seldom utilized in real time, and it was also impossible to have predictive capabilities. But IIoT systems facilitate for the performance of machines and equipment to be monitored in real time, and manufacturers can instantly make adjustments to optimize resource consumption. For instance, using predictive analytics, manufacturers can predict when the machine is likely to require maintenance, and thus avoid delaying the downtime and fixing it at high expense. IIIoT also allows better inventory control in a better supply chain dynamic with the insights into supply chain dynamics which allows manufacturers to minimize wasted inventory and reduce waste (Huang et al., 2017).

Another important point of improvement in IIoT enabled manufacturing systems is to optimize the process through leveraging information technology driven insights to streamline the production workflow. Automation of tasks as quality control, inventory tracking, or machine calibration, for instance, is easier in IIoT systems than previously possible because it involves human intervention. If manufacturers automate these processes, they can minimize errors, accelerate the process and produce better consistency of their output. IIoT also means production lines can be monitored in real time to identify the bottlenecks or lack of efficiency and it can be taken into action right away. The dynamic procedure of process optimization in this approach guarantees that production processes stay flexible, scalable, and suitable for changes in the marketplace (market demand) (Kusiak, 2018).

While you have many reasons to adopt the IIoT for manufacturing, there are a few challenges that you have to work through before fully realizing the potential of IIoT. The more key challenge in this realm is real time data processing. IIoT generates huge amount of data, and it is important to process it quickly in real-time to make quick decisions. However, traditional data processing systems may not be able to process such high volume, high speed and heterogeneous data generated by IIoT devices. To solve this problem, an answer has been edge computing that includes processing data near the source of generation rather than sending data to central cloud servers. The use of edge computing device allows manufacturers to process data locally, eliminating the delay and speeding up the decision time (Zhao et al., 2019). However, issues of interoperability between edge devices and controlling the network complexity of IIoT systems have been a challenge to bring the edge computing together.

An other important topic in relation of IIoT is cybersecurity. With the growing interconnections among IIoT devices, there is correspondingly growing risk to cyberattacks. Systems based on IIoT are usually insecure, exposing the data theft, the system malfunctioning, the physical damage to the equipment. The risks associated with these threats must be mitigated by the manufacturers by deploying the robust cybersecurity measures like encryption, access control, and continuous monitoring. AIoT also needs to integrate cybersecurity from the beginning, not as an afterthought. Now more than ever, strong security protocols and up to the minute updates are inevitable as the number on connected devices continue to grow (Lu et al., 2020).

Another issue with the implementation of IIoT is its standardization. There is no wide acceptance of universal standards for IIoT technologies and protocols that enable different systems and devices communicate with each other effectively. Such lack of interoperability can result in inefficiencies and additional costs incurred if additional custom integration solutions are required on either a proprietary line or to bridge between two or more brands. To adequately facilitate their integration with the rest of the infrastructure, as well as scaling up as necessary and to be able to transmit correctly and receive as expected up and down the chain, we need to establish common standards for IIoT devices, communication protocols, and data formats. Different standardization efforts related to IIoT technologies are ongoing and organizations, like the Industrial Internet Consortium (IIC), are trying to develop guideline as well as frameworks for IIoT adoption (Bosch et al., 2017).

Moreover, there are other technical challenges as well as a continuing need for personnel to manage and operate IIoT systems. To integrate smart technologies in manufacturing environments, workers need to have a global observation of traditional manufacturing processes as well as the ability to use and work with advanced technologies such as data analytics, machine learning and cybersecurity. Therefore, this warrants that manufacturers spend on training programs to train their workforce on skills that are needed. At the same time, IIoT systems have gotten more and more reliant, meaning there will be a high demand for data scientists, network engineers, and cybersecurity experts who are all essential in the smoothly running and secure working of IIoT based manufacturing systems (Tao et al., 2018).

IIoT has a bright future in manufacturing and advancements in the technologies like 5G, artificial intelligence and machine learning will keep on streamlining the efficiency and automation in future. For instance, AI algorithms can analyze large quantities of data of IIoT systems to understand production processes to a greater extent and make more accurate predictions. From a manufacturing environment standpoint, 5G technology will also increase the speed and reliability of data transmission thus facilitating larger number of devices and applications. The more mature these technologies become, the more manufacturers will be able to automate their processes to the highest levels of automation and resource utilization for the highest levels of decision-making, resulting in truly smart factories (Tao et al., 2021).

IIoT and Smart Manufacturing therefore lead to paradigm shift in industrial sector by providing great benefits in the way of efficiency, automation and in decision making on data. IIoT brings in smart sensors, actuators, edge computing and sophisticated analytics to real time the data collection and analysis for enhancing the resource utilization and enhancing the performance. Unfortunately, to capitalize on the full potential of IIoT, manufacturers face challenges, since they must provide real-time data processing, cybersecurity, standardization and qualification of personnel, etc. IIoT can revolutionize manufacturing process and bring about the era of smart factories if it is able to overcome these challenges and use the emerging technologies to achieve greater advancement.

RESOURCE OPTIMIZATION IN IIOT-DRIVEN SMART MANUFACTURING

IIoT enabled smart manufacturing is based on efficient resource management. As it is, mass, energy and computational resources need to be optimized to minimize the cost and maximize the productivity. As manufacturing process becomes more complex and there is growing demand for high quality, low cost products, manufacturers are increasingly trying to find means of optimizing their operation. This goal can be achieved by IIoT that has a rich toolset of real time monitoring, data collection and analytics that will make the manufacturing systems more efficient and sustainable. With the integration of the latest of the advanced technologies like Machine learning (ML) and artificial intelligence (AI), the traditional manufacturing is evolving into an intelligent, adaptive and efficient process.

Advanced data analytics are one of the core technologies for the efficiency of IIoT applications. The IIoT is generating massive amounts of data from devices and sensors, making it hard to analyze and interpret this data in real time in making decision. Using AI, ML and advanced analytics, manufacturers can harness meanings from the endless data streams in order to solve problems. They provide the continuous monitoring of important parameters such as temperature, pressure, speed, vibration, and so on to make sure the machines as well as the processes are within optimal conditions. Applications of AI and ML algorithms for analysis on this data allows manufacturers to predict potential system failures, identify unnecessary etc, and optimize the different aspects of their production process (Xu et al., 2018).

The application where AI and ML are most useful for IIoT systems is predictive maintenance. In traditional manufacturing environments, maintenance has been typically reactive or by a schedule interval based where there is down time or expensive repair. On its way towards a more proactive approach, the integration of IIoT technologies allows manufacturers to trend forward. Real time data from IIoT sensors is continuously monitored for condition of the equipment by predictive maintenance. This data is fed through AI and ML algorithms to detect early warnings as potential failure like changes in the vibration patterns or abnormal temperature reading. These manufacturers identify the issues before they get to the point of escalation and so maintenance is scheduled only as and when needed, which in turn reduces unnecessary service operations and gives the equipment a longer lifespan (Lee et al., 2014).

Furthermore, this predictive capability helps the manufacturers to reduce downtime and increase the reliability and efficiency of the process as a whole. Manufacturers are able to prevent unexpected breakdowns, allowing their business to remain production flowing steady, thereby making the operational processes less susceptible to disruptions. Predictive maintenance also minimizes the cost of repairs, as well as spares and labor cost associated with frequent checking and maintenance. This results in it becoming possible for the manufacturers to use their resources in more efficient ways and hence focus on those areas that to be attended to immediately as opposed to performing routine checks that may not give value (Kusiak, 2018). The application of this approach leads to operational efficiency and reduction of resource consumption as well as improves cost savings.

AI and ML provide huge help when it comes to resource management in IIoT enabled manufacturing systems when it comes to anomaly detection. It is an anomaly detection where the unusual patterns and behaviors within the manufacturing process may indicate inefficiencies, defects or deviation from the standard operating procedure. It is possible for manufacturers to set up systems that can automatically identify anomalies as soon as they occur by using AI algorithms looking at historical and real time data. The purpose can be something as simple as providing immediate notification to an operator, if a machine is consuming more energy than normal, or a process step is going slower than forecast. The real time intervention in this helps out as it prevents the occurrence of bigger problems later down the line and improves process reliability as well as resource utilization (Resource utilization) (Cheng et al., 2020).

The optimization functions do not only work for advanced manufacturing, but also for IIoT systems including AI and ML. Their adoption allows manufacturers to improve their processes of producing by identifying the potential bottleneck, getting rid of the waste, and maximizing output. For example, ML algorithms can take on production data and figure out the factors that relate to machine performance and process efficiency. It gives manufactures the ability to change variables like speed, temperature, etc., to achieve the best quality in production. AI and ML systems can continuously learn from new data and also suggest some adjustments in real time to improve the overall efficiency of the system. Such a system is more streamlined, their use is less wasteful in materials, use of other resources, and they consume less energy. (Tao et al., 2018)

The application of AI and ML to IIoT systems can also improve productivity as well as improve the sustainability of manufacturing. Energy consumption optimization is now a very important issue for manufacturers aiming to reduce their carbon footprint and meet environmental regulations. At a granular level, IIoT systems can monitor how energy is used by a manufacturer, and in turn identify areas of excessive use of energy and to fix it. AI systems, through the analysis of historical processes and current operations, will be able to provide energy saving overproduction strategies, taking into consideration the eco-points of view. Not only does this benefit manufacturers by decreasing the costs associated with energy consumption, but also it drives manufacturers' operations towards sustainability aims to be more green in manufacturing (Zhao, et al., 2019).

Overall, the introduction of AI and ML into IIoT systems gives the manufacturers the power to optimize their resource utilization and improve their operational efficiency. In other words, manufacturers can rely on these technologies to predict potential issues with their processes, detect anomalies, and use that information to optimize and reduce waste as well as minimize downtime of their processes. And in turn, these benefits enhance productivity, decrease the operational costs, and make manufacturing more sustainable. When looking at the future smart manufacturing scenarios, AI and ML will play a growing role as they will be playing a larger role in shaping the future environment of smart manufacturing as such while this may bring new chances for manufacturers to survive in an increasingly data-based world.

EDGE AND FOG COMPUTING FOR REAL-TIME DATA PROCESSING

The real time processing of data with strong reliability and security is one of fundamental issues in IIoT based smart manufacturing. As manufacturing systems rely to an increasing degree on IIoT technologies, these technologies are creating enormous volumes of data from devices that are connected to one another. However, the constant stream of data brings a huge challenge to traditional cloud architecture due to bandwidth and latency issues for sending big data datasets to centralized servers. Therefore, efficient data processing with low latency and reliable communication are important for the smart manufacturing system to work effectively and dynamically in response to changing real conditions. Due to this need of seamless integration of these technologies, these were pushed to forefront as edge and fog computing architectures are providing a kind of solution to the bottleneck that traditional cloud computing faces.

As an attempt to deal with the above problems, edge and fog computing architectures are designed to process data as close to their source as possible, rather than relying on remote centralized cloud servers. At the "edge" of the network – that is, within the devices or machines themselves or nearest vicinity local computing nodes – data is processed directly. Unlike fog computing, in which the data is processed between edge devices and the cloud with the help of a hybrid layer of intermediary layer processing that provides additional processing power at the local or gateway nodes or network nodes, fog computing is based on the use of intermediary layer to process the data between edge devices and the cloud. This approach spreads data processing out in the distributed system, such that one doesn't need to wait to move it into the centralized system, such as an analytics system, in order to apply processing. Edge and fog computing uses available resources such as infrastructure, processing power, and bandwidth locally in order to process data as fast as possible, in an efficient manner, and with a high resolution (Shi et al., 2016).

Edge and fog computing are known to reduce latency and that is extremely important for the production line environments where rapid decisions have to be made. Data transmitted from users over the distance to and from centralized servers usually leads to high latency of traditional cloud computing systems. In some cases, this delay can slow the responsiveness of manufacturing systems, potentially compromising a chance or delaying a response. An example here is a manufacturing line where if a machine starts acting up in an anomaly, then this time it could take for data to reach a cloud server to make a decision then would lead to downtime that could be costly to the business. The problem is solved using edge computing and fog computing which allow a computation to be performed at or very close to the generation point. As a result, it decreases data transmission time around, and enables a faster, more accurate decision making that helps to make the manufacturing processes able to react quicker to real-time requirements (Zhang et al., 2018).

The improved latency in supply also lessens the reliability and stability of IIoT based manufacturing systems. For instance, edge and fog computing allows for real time and accurate machinery failure detection in applications such as predictive maintenance that highly relies on monitoring machinery in real time. It helps schedule maintenance in advance so that there is no unplanned downtime, and thus, the manufacturing process is overall more reliable. Also, the processing of the data at the edge/fog level will make sure that even if there is a disruption in flowing the data to the central cloud infrastructure, manufacturing operations can continue with minimum interruption. Edge and fog computing for IIoT distributes part of the data processing across several layers in order to make the infrastructure more resilient to faults (Bonomi et al., 2012).

The second advantage of edge and fog computing is optimizing bandwidth utilization. The sheer volume of IIoT data mean that there will be an incredible amount of data to send, particularly if large volumes of real time data are being generated all of the time. Local processing offers by edge or fog computing greatly reduces the requirement for bandwidth in transmitted raw data to the cloud. This helps manufacturers tune in only to what's relevant, processed data or insights, maximizing the use of available bandwidth, and preventing the network from becoming flooded. Additionally, it decreases the dependency on cloud-based processing, since cloud infrastructure is usually a bottleneck for scalability and performance (Zhao et al., 2019).

Edge and fog computing can also help to enhance the security and privacy of the IIoT based manufacturing systems besides improving latency, bandwidth efficiency. Data processing locally limits the possibility of exposing sensitive information as data is transmitted to other parties in a network. For instance, industries that involve handling of sensitive intellectual property or proprietary processes must pay special attention to transmitting data over long distances to a centralised cloud server which may lead to potential security breach. Using edge and fog computing, manufacturers can realize security measures locally by encryption, access control and anomaly detection to provide additional protection for their systems (Sun et al., 2018). This localized approach to data processing enables manufacturers to comply with data privacy regulations and data regulations in general, particularly in industries where there are strict provisions for the storage and transmission of data.

Besides, the combination of edge/fog computing and IIoT systems support to get rid of resource restrictions is typical to cloud based architectures. However, cloud computing platforms are often too powerful to harness the local infrastructure, which is sometimes not sufficient to satisfy high processing requirements that IIoT imposes. This allows manufacturers to benefit from using local resources such as local processing power, storage, and bandwidth as processing tasks are distributed across the edge and fog layers, thereby making the system efficient and scalable. The decentralized approach towards IIoT enables manufacturers to adapt their IIoT system to various production environments and scale them accordingly as it is more flexible and cheaper compared to a centralized approach (Stojanovic et al., 2020).

Consequently, the edge and fog computing architecture is very crucial in resolving the latency reduction challenge, bandwidth optimization and real time data processing challenges as well as the enhanced security issue in smart manufacturing system bases on the IIoT. Such computing frameworks help in improving the responsiveness, reliability and efficiency of the manufacturing operations by processing data closer to the source. At the edge and fog computing level, a number of technologies become increasingly desirable for manufacturers to embrace as IIoT advances, particularly in smart manufacturing systems that must continue to run without interruptions given the complexity and high data density associated with such systems.

AI-BASED ALGORITHMS FOR ENERGY EFFICIENCY

Energy consumption is of paramount importance in the resource management of IIoT enabled manufacturing systems. Given that industries are more and more connected, data driven, managing energy efficiently is more and more important from both the cost and the sustainability point of view. Manufacturer has been growing concerns about climate change, environmental sustainability and energy efficient operation which has propelled it to invent some novel ways on how to reduce cost associated with usage of energy. In regard to this, artificial intelligence (AI)-based algorithms to manage and optimize energy consumption are one of the most promising solutions. Such AI powered systems can read the energy consumption patterns, forecast demand fluctuations and, by doing so, can help in the process of making decisions more efficiently, because resource utilization becomes more streamlined. Manufacturers can be able to greatly reduce the costs of operating plants and their contribution to a greener, more sustainable factory process by leveraging AI to enable it to predict what energy they will need and adjust their resource use accordingly.

AI based energy management program works on the historical and real time analysis of the energy consumptions data from the various IIoT devices and sensors distributed all over the manufacturing system. With the use of such systems, trends can be identified, inefficiencies can be detected and future energy demand can be forecasted by taking into considerations of machine usage patterns, production schedules, external conditions like temperature, and the market demand. Then, AI can adjust the energy distributed across the system dynamically using this information so as to save energy and use it only when required. Another example involves an AI system akin to predicting when the energy demand will peak and adjusting the operation of machines and equipment in such a way as to use less energy during such times. By following this proactive approach of energy management, it results in reducing the energy waste as well as the cost of energy (Lee et al., 2017) and hence increases the overall efficiency of manufacturing process.

Additionally, AI algorithms can be used for dynamic load balancing necessary to utilize energy on different points of a manufacturing facility. It is possible that energy resources in traditional manufacturing environments may not be utilized efficiently by energy being allocated unnecessarily in some parts of the plant compared to other parts. Such imbalance can be resolved by the use of AI based energy management systems that interchange the use of energy in various machines and process at different timings depending on the current real time need. Say, at any given time, there are less machines in demand, that AI system might find some inessential machines in operation that need to be, and optimize the operation of these machines so that they use energy during less time, assuming the low demand of energy. On the contrary, the system can cut the energy usage or reorganize operations to less consuming ones during peak energy demand periods in such a way that the production output is not influenced (Zhao et al., 2019).

The current trend of green manufacturing, wherein the goal is beyond operational efficiency but also reduction of environmental impact of manufacturing activities, has successfully integrated the use of AI in energy management. Typically, in traditional manufacturing processes, only inefficient hardware and procedures use a fair amount of energy, such as idle machines, excess heating or cooling, and unnecessary lighting. With AI-powered energy management systems put into place, manufacturers will be able to cut down on energy waste dramatically, making sure that resources are only used when they are indeed required. Moreover, AI can assist in highlighting segments of excessive energy spending and propose remedial actions like updating the machinery which is working inefficiently and optimized production schedule that would more closely match the energy availability. It thus optimizes an environmental footprint of manufacturing operation (Tao et al., 2020).

Another is that smart factories that have adopted an AI based energy management system will also be sustainable. Over time, as consumers and businesses grew increasingly concerned with the environment, companies that pay attention to the environment would be at the forefront of the marketplace. Energy system that utilizes intelligent energy systems not only reduces operational costs but also makes manufacturers' leaders in sustainable practice. Let's take a company that reduces in energy consumption and lowers the carbon emissions, it may get green certifications or an environmental award, which will enhance its outlook and attract the eco-friendly consumers. Besides, it also follows the increasingly strong environmental regulations, which require companies to practice energy efficient, in order to be legally compliant and to avoid penalties such as the excessive energy use or emission (Huang et al., 2018).

Apart from providing a way to reduce the energy consumption, systems managed by AI can further help with adding cost savings by more rationally using renewable energy sources. Renewable energy is being implemented by many manufacturers into their operations either through solar panels, wind turbines, or any other renewable energy production technology. However, AI further assists in integrating these renewable sources into a complete energy system with the assistance of predicting when the renewable energy will be available and adapting the usage of conventional energy sources accordingly. For instance, if the AI system observes that solar power is plentiful during the day, then the AI system can choose to use more energy intensive processes in an effort to eliminate reliance on the grid power. It not only lowers energy costs but also contributes to the energy transition to a future more sustainable energy infrastructure (Srinivasan et al., 2020).

Energy waste reductions and cost reduction as well as energy sustainability initiatives can be achieved through the implementation of AI based energy management systems for IIoT enabled smart manufacturing. These systems enable manufacturers to consume lesser amount of energy, predict and foresee fluctuations in demand, and dynamically balance the load weights. However, the growth in the potential of smart manufacturing will be only be possible as manufacturers add IIoT and AI driven solutions, making them more green and sustainable production process.

THE ROLE OF DIGITAL TWIN TECHNOLOGY

The smart manufacturing based on digital twin technology is a groundbreaking invention in the IIoT era. A digital twin is a virtual replica of a physical asset, process or system, and the simulation of a real-world condition from which an improved decision making, a fault diagnosis and a real time performance monitoring are possible. Manufacturers can gain deep insights into how system behaves, predict potential failures and optimise processes without actually disrupting the operations by creating digital models of production lines, machinery, or entire factories. In the context of smart manufacturing, this technology acts as a crucial asset for improving the efficiency and resilience of manufacturing systems and it is a strong helping hand for today's manufacturing systems.

The major reason to have a digital twin is to mimic the movement of its physical counterpart in the real time. Digital twins collect and process data through IIoT sensors and data collection devices embedded in machines and production lines to generate a continuous viral model of the current state of the physical systems. This real time data allows manufacturers to really help them see what is going in, be able to see excesses, see if there are potential issues before they've become issues and then make some proactive decisions to prevent downtime. Digital twin for example, can track the temperature, vibration, and pressure of a manufacturing machine, analyse this information to predict when the machine is likely to fail and perform predictive maintenance (Tao et al., 2018). By using this approach, you are in a position to cut down unplanned downtime, extend equipment life and further adjust the maintenance schedules.

It is one of the key benefits of digital twin technology that allows digital twin technology to discover inefficiencies in manufacturing systems before this results in operations. Thus, digital twins can continuously monitor machines, production lines or the whole system to pin point performance delay from optimal conditions. In the case of a suboptimal performance of a machine for instance, a digital twin could anticipate in real time that the machine is not operating as optimally as expected and suggest corrective steps. Back to the manufacturer this allows, for instance, for fine tuning of production operations and for changes that improve productivity, drastically decrease waste and drastically decrease use of resources. Additionally, digital twins allow the various possibilities and the effects of changes to be tested without physically changing the actual production (Zhao et al., 2020).

Another important benefit of IIoT enabled smart manufacturing using digital twins for predictive maintenance is its use. Coupling the IIoT sensors with the digital twin allows these manufacturers to predict a machine's likeliness of failure using real-time data analysis. It is much more predictive than any scheduled maintenance and far more efficient than that resulting in down time or lost opportunities to take care of problems before they become serious. Predictive maintenance gives manufacturers the ability to manage equipment through a predictive approach instead of a reactive one and cheaply, this should lead to reduced maintenance and more reliable systems. Furthermore, allocation of resources is ensured in an efficient manner in balancing between maintaining needs that have the highest importance for operational continuity (Glaessgen; Sargal, 2012).

Digital twins also provide a lot to the resilience of smart manufacturing systems. They offer an image of physical assets in a virtual and real time so that manufacturers can spot and deal with disruptions or related problems that may affect production. By enhancing this visibility into system performance, it provides manufacturers with better ability to quickly react to unexpected, sudden events as well as better management of risks. For instance, in case of a failure in a machine, the digital twin can simulate what impact will have the failure on the production line, and to allow manufacturers to develop action plans and avoid costly disruptions. Digital twins improve resiliency of the manufacturing systems, and aids the businesses to be agile and responsive to changing market conditions and other not anticipated challenges (Grieves, 2014).

By being coupled with IIoT networks, the digital twins provide even more robust functions for optimization and process improvement. By integrating sensors, actuators, and other connected devices through IIoT networks, the sense and supply of data required for the creation and updating of digital twins can seamlessly be done. Now that these networks are accumulating in huge quantities of real-time data from various machines and systems across the production floor, they are sending this data to the digital twin and maintaining continuous updates and simulations. Since the integration ensures that data remains in sync with digital twins, this keeps the plants running with the most up to date insights about their operations. Manufacturers gain real time visibility into system performance that enables continuous adjustments to production lines to optimize, increase reliability of manufacturing system and to better match operations with the strategic business goals (Zhao et al., 2019).

But they also alleviate manufacturers to tie their operating conditions to wider business goals. So, manufacturers can use digital twins to optimize not just individual machines, but entire production processes right out to factory operations. Digital twins allow manufacturers to simulate the entire production system, to determine their most cost effective, most efficient way of reaching production targets, improving product quality and removing waste. Ultimately, these optimizations can lead to better utilization of resources, simplified manufacturing operations, and reduced financial performance, and manufacturing system performance will be at a lower level of slippage compared to the long term strategic goals of the business (Tao et al., 2020).

Then, digital twin enables the development of IIoT based smart manufacturing system. Digital twins are virtual replicas of physical assets or processes that can monitor in real time, predict, and help make proactive decisions, and thereby enhances efficiency, reduces cost, increase system reliability. Together, with IIoT networks, digital twins allow manufactures to optimize production line production, tune operations, and work toward achieving their strategic goals. Despite the manufacturing industry's ongoing embracement of IIoT technologies, it is almost certain digital twins will form a foundation of smart manufacturing and, in turn, manufacturers and enterprises will drive higher levels of resiliency, sustainability, and profitability.

CYBERSECURITY IN IIOT-ENABLED MANUFACTURING

IIoT driven manufacturing has a lot of advantages associated with it, however, integration of a large number of connected devices expands the attack surface for cyber threats by a large number. In recent days, the growing number of these sensors, actuators, edge devices etc., along with the growing deployment of IoT components such as smart factories makes them more susceptible to various security attacks in the cyber space and can lead to heavy financial loss of operations or leaking sensitive data. Consequently, cybersecurity is still one of the crucial issues related to smart manufacturing based on IIoT. Therefore, the generation of data by these devices must be protected, systems MANUFACTURING must remain intact and continuous and operations must be always secure. The solution to these concerns is being sought in the emerging technologies including the blockchain based identity authentication, Zero Trust security frameworks and the AI driven threat detection in the development of the IIoT ecosystems.

Blockchain is one of the most exciting technologies, when it comes to securing IIoT systems. Blockchain's tamper-proof decentralization makes it an excellent technology to utilize to achieve data integrity and network reliability for IIoT use. Typically, IIoT networks are run on centralized systems and mitigate against data storage and related cyberattacks. On the other hand, blockchain gives control in a distributed manner, meaning the transaction of each data is securely recorded in a 'block' and connected to a chain of old blocks to build up an immutable record. It offers high security and the inability for the data that is recorded to be altered or tampered with; this system prevents such attacks as data manipulation or unauthorized access (Atzori et al., 2017). When applied in the context of IIoT, Blockchain is able to assure information credibility and the data transmitted between devices being genuine. In industries where data integrity is paramount, blockchain is very useful as it makes data secure that would otherwise be susceptible to interference or fraudulent editing.

Blockchain can also be implemented to carry out the identity authentication in the IIoT systems. With more devices being connected, the chance of getting in without permission or making changes without the system's permission increases. Secure, decentralized authentication is offered by blockchain based identity management system, only authenticating devices and users can interact with it. Security is increased by lowering dependence on centralized authority systems that could suffer single points of failure or attacks against centralized authority systems (Makhdoom et al., 2019). With blockchain, identity of the devices in the IIoT network is authenticated, so it is not easy for the bad actors to enter the system.

The Zero Trust security framework is another key security technology grabbing the attention of the IIoT ecosystems. To the contrary, the Zero Trust approach differs from traditional security models that expected devises and users inside the network to be trusted, and forms a new paradigm where none of the devises, users, or systems, inside or outside the network, are to be trusted. This means the actuators or users that want to attempt accessing a part of the IIoT network wilt be verified and authenticated continuously no matter the place in the network. Identity management, access controls, encryption, and constant monitoring are combined along with other Zero Trust properties to allow only authorized entities access of which critical systems and data (Rose et al., 2020). This approach becomes essential to IIoT smart factories, in order to mitigate the risk of internal and external threats, since it reduces the risk that an attacker will be undetected in the network.

Another promising approach to securing IIoT systems is using threat detection that is aided by AI. With the advent of IIoT devices, the amount of data being produced is so huge that traditional security systems are inadequate to process and analyze such vast amounts of data. Anomalies can be detected and possible threats can be also identified in real time through the use of AI and machine learning (ML) technologies. Since AI cannot interact with other elements of the network, it is a powerful tool to analyze patterns in network traffic, device behavior, and data usage and can spot suspicious behavior very quickly and thus trigger an alert to system administrators. Use as an example — AI algorithms can sense unusual data movement patterns, odd device behavior, as well as suspect intrusions, to spot signs that could become bigger issues. Also, AI can keep on learning from previous incidents, improving its capacity to foresee and handle new dangers (Zhou et al., 2019).

BlockChain, Zero Trust framework and AI based threat detection technology when integrated with IIot network give a multi layered security approach that can significantly lower the risks caused by the cyber threat. By partially or entirely embedding these advanced security mechanisms, manufacturers can protect the point of weakness in their system, handle its potential vulnerabilities, while keeping their data confidential, intact, and available polygonally available. The use of this holistic approach to cybersecurity is vital in safeguarding both the physical and the digital parts of manufacturing operations in order to ensure the continuous development and favorable performance of smart factories with the support of the IIoT. Implementing strong countermeasures enables manufacturers not only secure their systems but also gain customers' confidence, partners' trust, and overall system success of smart manufacturing initiative in the long run.

As such, the need for efficient Cybersecurity measures for IIoT based smart manufacturing systems is ever more pressing. To handle the security issues arising due to the rise in connected devices, there is need of utilizing the upcoming technology such as blockchain for integrity of data and identity, Zero Trust security framework for continuous verification and AI driven threat detection for real time monitoring. As in the case with cyber threats to physical systems in IIoT ecosystems, if manufacturers can protect their IIoT ecosystems with these technologies, cyber threats, operations will be secure, reliable and efficient.

BARRIERS TO SMART MANUFACTURING IMPLEMENTATION

Although IIoT and smart manufacturing are promising and excellent technology, it continues to face a number of barriers that restrict its wider adoption and successful adoption. There are these barriers ranging from technical to economic issue that prevents manufacturer so they can really take the complete advantage of what IIoT technologies can offer. Interoperability is definitely one of the most prominent ones, as regardless of the type and the manufacturer, different devices and systems in manufacturing environments rarely find a common ground of communication. The lack of interface impedes the adoption of IIoT solutions at a variety of manufacturing settings. This is further compounded by high implementation costs and low number of skilled personnel in the workforce. Indeed, as manufacturers adopt IIoT technologies, it is not just the expense of updating their equipment they need to account for; they also need to take into the equation the essential of an educated, skilled workforce capable of managing and maintaining these systems. They challenge the integration process and overall implementation cost, therefore, the efforts in the standardization, industry collaborative initiatives, and continuous innovation are essential to streamline the integration process.

IIoT adoption is still faced with interoperability as one of the most critical challenges. A typical manufacturing sector involves many devices, machinery, and systems, and most of these legacy systems are not designed for the integration of IIoT. These systems usually use proprietary communication protocols, therefore, smooth communication between them is not possible. IIoT technologies depend on the capacity of machines and sensors and control systems to exchange data in real time so as to improve performance, further automate and facilitate decision making. But if there is no compatibility between devices and systems, it becomes a big hindrance to gain the expected outcomes of integrating IIoT. However, attaining full interoperability between the numerous sensors and communication interfaces from different manufacturers places a burden on manufacturers that must either retrofit existing machines with new sensors and communication interfaces or replace complete systems, all of these options can be costly and time consuming (Gubbi et al., 2013).

Interoperability is also not a trivial technical problem, and goes way beyond technical compatibility. The vastness of the IIoT technologies and protocols in the market makes it a challenge for manufacturers to select the right technologies which will also work ideally through all their operations. The result of this is an ecosystem that is fragmented with no standard formats or protocols for communicating, making integration to other systems occupying the last position. Therefore, it is important for the industry to develop universal standards and protocols that simplifies the communication between devices and systems. For one such example, initiatives like Industrial Internet Consortium (IIC) are developing the common framework for IIoT technologies for the greater IIoT interoperability and for helping manufacturers to overcome the some of these challenges (Bassi et al., 2016).

Another substantial barrier of adoption for IIoT is high cost of implementation. For the same reason that implementers of IIoT technologies are significantly restricted by capital investment, especially for migrating existing infrastructures, deploying sensors, and incorporating systems with advanced data analytics. Although the potential longer term benefits of IIoT to manufacturers, such as enhancing throughput, reducing downtime and increasing productivity, may outweigh these first costs; it is still of importance and of concern to most manufacturers, in particular SMEs, that they incur these first costs. In addition, there are the expense of keeping IIoT imposed, from monitoring devices, software updates and cybersecurity measures. Despite the need for technologic innovation, manufacturers need to balance technological innovation with the financial realities of implementing IIoT solutions. Also, costs continue to rise as manufacturers are forced to update IIoT technologies in order to remain competitive, and at a pace faster than in the past (Xu et al., 2018).

A critical barrier for IIoT techs to make a wide spread adoption is the lack of qualified personnel. To achieve the expected benefits of the implementation of IIoT systems, it will require skills and knowledge in data analytics, machine learning, cybersecurity, network management, etc. The demand for a skilled workforce which can populate and manage IIoT systems in manufacturing systems increases exponentially as IIoT technologies become more complex and integrated into the manufacturing systems. The problem is however, that there is a current shortage of workers with the required expertise to operate and maintain IIoT systems. In pedantic industries whose work has been dependent on manual labor and literal manufacturers, this skills gap is particularly harsh. To satisfy this, manufacturers have to either hire people with high technical skills, or devote resources to edge skill their current labour force. The need for specialized knowledge combined with the worker shortage, that complicates adoption, can further delay the implementation and increase the operational costs (Boudoukh et al. 2019).

However, these barriers have to be overcome, which would require a concerted effort between industry leaders and policymakers on these issues. It is at the standardization working that their contribution to solving the interoperability issue is of the great importance. Such factory common and later industry-wide standards and frameworks can ensure communication and seamless functioning of systems and devices from different manufacturers. By standardizing the communication protocols such as MQTT (Message Queuing Telemetry Transport) and OPC UA (Open Platform Communications Unified Architecture), the costs of the integration and the retrofits, when the legacy systems are already implemented, could be lowered (Miller et al., 2017). Furthermore, cooperative industry efforts, including consortia and research associations, assist in speeding up the development of specified solutions as well as share knowledge between manufacturers. Together, companies can reduce the costs of implementation when it comes to IIoT, as well as use the innovation generated to the benefit of the whole manufacturing ecosystem.

In addition, IIoT technologies need to continue to become more affordable and more accessible while the technology continues to innovate. With evolution of technologies new cost effective, simpler to implement and scalable solutions will be seen. This can help manufacturers overcome the initial barriers to IIoT adoption by enabling the use of IIoT technologies without paying out inordinate capital expenses associated with expensive on-site infrastructure. Moreover, the cost of implementing IIoT can be further reduced by the development of low cost sensors, less expensive data analytics tools and improved automation systems (Tao et al., 2019).

Consequently, although there are great benefits of IIoT and smart manufacturing, many barriers exist to prevailing adoption. Situations such as interoperability, high implementation costs, and the shortage of skilled personnel remain the major issues. Yet, they can sidestep those impediments by concentrating on standardization endeavors, inciting cooperative industry undertakings, and energizing constant improvement. While obstacles to the take up of these transformative technologies by more manufacturers remain, it is likely that said barriers will lessen as the IIoT ecosystem matures.

CONCLUSION

Thus, performing the process in smart manufacturing promoted by IIoT is highly important to enhance operational efficiency, and improve and support sustainability in industrial ecosystems. Advanced technologies such as Artificial Intelligence (AI), Machine Learning (ML), edge computing, digital twins, among other advances, can be integrated not only to increase the efficiency of manufacturing systems but can potentially make traditional manufacturing systems highly intelligent, adaptable and efficient operation system. These innovations also enhance the manufacturing process productivity and reliability as well as lower costs and lessen environmental impact of industrial activities. Through the use of these leading edge technologies, manufacturers can construct systems that are more robust, effective, and cost effective and position themselves to thrive in an ever more competitive international market.

Another vital performance optimization technique in IIoT enabled smart manufacturing is developed on AI and ML algorithms and referred to as predictive maintenance. In this case, predictive maintenance is the understanding that data coming from IIoT sensors can be used with advanced analytics to predict when the equipment or machinery will fail, so they will not suffer unplanned downtime or need expensive repairs (Lee et al., 2014). Moving from traditional reactive or scheduled maintenance using reactive or scheduled activities to minimize operational disruptions, extend the life of equipment, and reduce maintenance cost, manufacturers can incorporate the best time to perform maintenance to increase productivity. Moreover, AI and ML help in increasing the quality of the decisions being made by manufacturers about the health of their systems and the real time optimization of machine's performance and overall production efficiency (Tao et al., 2018). Now manufacturers can achieve a more reliable production environment through predictive maintenance, reduce the risk in equipment failures and improve the performance of the whole system.

Edge computing is critical for the optimization of smart manufacturing systems driven by IIoT for not only prediction but also for other maintenance activities. Edge computing is defined as processing data close to the data source; at or near the manufacturing floor, versus sending the data to a remote centralized server for analysis. This approach results in a very low latency and facilitates faster processing of data and thus enables real time decision making (Shi et al., 2016). Edge computing ensures that data from IIoT devices related to manufacturing can be analyzed in split seconds and be acted upon immediately. By reducing the strain on centralized cloud infrastructure and optimizing bandwidth usage, the responsiveness of the manufacturer's systems is enhanced through this way of computation that happens at the edge. This decentralized processing of data allows for more agile manufacturing environment with real time adjustment to perform better by removing waste and saving energy (Zhao et al., 2019).

As another major technology in optimizing performance, digital twin is another segment of use virtual replicas of physical assets and processes to help the manufacturer simulate and analyze actual world conditions. Manufacturers can not only track the performance of machines, production lines, and manufacturing systems, but also optimize those performance to save energy, reduce depreciation, identify inefficiencies, foresee potential issues and to increase the manufacturing system's overall productivity (Tao et al., 2018). Tests of operational scenarios can be run on these virtual models without disrupting the physical system, and the manufacturer can continuously optimize its operations. When combined with the IIoT network, manufacturers can enhance their system to be more robust – able to adjust to changes and kerp a maximum performance level.

The last, but not the least aspect of IIoT driven smart manufacturing is cybersecurity. In an age where the amount of connected devices steadily grows, cyberattacks become more and more likely. Trust, protection of sensitive data and disruption due to cyber threats are all reasons why it is important to be assured of security and integrity of manufacturing systems. Robust IIC cybersecurity can come in through implementing Blockchain based identity authentication, Zero Trust security framework, AI based threat detection mechanism, etc. For example, Blockchain is used in data integrity to have a decentralized and tamperproof record of all transactions that lowers data manipulation or unauthorized access risks (Makhdoom et al., 2019). As per the Zero Trust framework (Rose et al., 2020), a continuous authentication of users and devices helps protect against internal as well as external threats by assuming that no entity in the inside the network can be trusted by default. With AI driven threat detection systems, a manufacturer can analyze terms of real time data to sense anomalous activities and give early warning, against which manufacturer can react towards a potential threat beforehand (Zhou et al., 2019).

Technological advances related to IIoT drive manufacturing system have not only great opportunities to enhance but still reserved some challenges. In addition, the continued challenge to manufacturers is interoperability. IIoT solutions can't be easily integrated across different operations due to many incompatible devices and systems which exist in manufacturing environments. This issue is exacerbated by the lack of standardized protocol and communication frameworks that result in inefficiencies, longer integration cost times, longer implementation timelines (Bassi et al., 2016). Interoperability challenges will have to be overcome by developing universal standards and flexible and open architecture that supports device communication free from manufacturer and communication protocol.

High cost of implementation tends to be another major barrier for IIoT technologies to be widely adopted. The long term benefits of IIoT, with improved efficiency, reduced downtime and increase in productivity, are well proven; however the entry cost required to implement the technologies is prohibitive, especially for small and medium sized enterprises (SMEs). To meet such challenges, manufacturers need to allocate spending for upgrading their infrastructure, deploying sensors, and integrating such complexness data analytics systems. These capital expenditures are difficult to justify especially for companies with limited resources. To mitigate these implementation costs, manufacturers will have to seek cost effective solutions including cloud based IIoT platform, edge computing, as well as open source technologies (Tao et al. 2020).

Furthermore, there exists a requirement for the skilled manpower to handle and maintain IIoT led systems. However, manufacturers that wish to implement IIoT solutions face a serious handicap, as there is a shortage of workers with competence in fields including data analytics, machine learning and cybersecurity. To meet this skills gap, these workforce training and development programs will need to be directly addressed, along with efforts to recruit and retain talent having the technical competence needed to oversee and optimize IIoT systems (Boudoukh et al., 2019).

Finally, IIoT based smart manufacturing has the potential to enhance performance, improve resource management and enhance sustainability, but only when significant challenges are resolved such as interoperability, high implementation costs and low supply of skilled manpower. Barriers to these new intelligent manufacturing systems will be overcome by these characteristics of standardization, global collaboration and continuous innovation. Manufacturers with full advantage of the sophisticated technologies that include the AI, edge computing, digital twins, and robust cybersecurity measures can build resilient, efficient, and low cost systems for long run of both business and society.

REFERENCES

Atzori, L. (2017). Blockchain-based Smart Manufacturing: A Survey. *Journal of Industrial Information Integration*, *5*, 1–13.

Bassi, A. (2016). *The Industrial Internet Consortium: Roadmap for IIoT Implementation*. Springer.

Bonomi, F. (2012). *Fog Computing and Its Role in the Internet of Things. Proceedings of the First Edition of the MCC Workshop on Mobile Cloud Computing*. DOI: 10.1145/2342509.2342513

Bosch, T. (2017). *The Industrial Internet of Things: A Technical Perspective*. Springer.

Boudoukh, S. (2019). Workforce Development for IIoT Adoption in Manufacturing. *Journal of Manufacturing Science and Engineering*, *141*(10), 1–9.

Cheng, Y. (2020). *Anomaly Detection and Fault Diagnosis in IIoT-Enabled Smart Manufacturing*. Springer.

Glaessgen, E. J., & Stargel, D. (2012). *The Digital Twin Paradigm for Future NASA and U.S. Air Force Vehicles*. 53rd AIAA/ASME/ASCE/AHS/ASC Structures, Structural Dynamics, and Materials Conference. DOI: 10.2514/6.2012-1818

Goh, T. L., & Tham, H. M. (2016). Smart water management technologies for urban resilience. *Journal of Environmental Management*, *182*, 16–25.

Grieves, M. (2014). *Digital Twin: Manufacturing Excellence through Virtual Factory Replication*. White paper.

Gubbi, J., Buyya, R., Marusic, S., & Palaniswami, M. (2013). Internet of Things (IoT): A Vision, Architectural Elements, and Future Directions. *Future Generation Computer Systems*, *29*(7), 1645–1660. DOI: 10.1016/j.future.2013.01.010

Huang, G. (2018). *Green Manufacturing and AI-based Energy Management Systems*. Springer.

Kusiak, A. (2018). *Smart Manufacturing: Challenges and Opportunities*. Springer.

Lee, J. (2014). *Industrial Artificial Intelligence and Predictive Maintenance in Manufacturing*. Elsevier.

Lee, J. (2017). *Intelligent Energy Management for Industrial IoT Systems*. Elsevier.

Lu, Y. (2020). *Cybersecurity in Industrial IoT Systems: Challenges and Solutions*. Elsevier.

Makhdoom, I. (2019). Blockchain for Industrial IoT: A Survey and Future Directions. *Future Generation Computer Systems*, *91*, 324–334.

Miller, S. (2017). Standardization of IIoT Communication Protocols. *Journal of Industrial Information Integration*, *8*, 1–9.

Rogers, S., Sharp, A., & Vines, J. (2015). Designing for the smart city: Building inclusivity into urban technology. *Design Issues*, *31*(3), 16–29.

Rose, S. (2020). *Zero Trust Architecture*. National Institute of Standards and Technology (NIST) Special Publication 800-207.

Scholl, H. J., & Scholl, M. C. (2014). Governance and governance structures in smart cities. *Information Polity*, *19*(3), 1–16.

Shi, W., Cao, J., Zhang, Q., Li, Y., & Xu, L. (2016). Edge Computing: Vision and Challenges. *IEEE Internet of Things Journal*, *3*(5), 637–646. DOI: 10.1109/JIOT.2016.2579198

Srinivasan, R. (2020). *Optimizing Renewable Energy Integration in Smart Manufacturing with AI*. Wiley.

Stojanovic, J. (2020). *Edge and Fog Computing in Industrial Internet of Things (IIoT): A Survey*. Journal of Cloud Computing: Advances. *Systems and Applications*, *9*(1), 1–25.

Sun, H. (2018). *Security and Privacy for Industrial Internet of Things: Challenges and Solutions*. Springer.

Tao, F. (2020). *Smart Manufacturing and Energy Optimization in IIoT*. Springer.

Tao, F. (2020). *Smart Manufacturing and IIoT Integration*. Academic Press.

Tao, F. (2021). *Artificial Intelligence in Smart Manufacturing*. Springer.

Tao, F., Qi, Q., Liu, A., & Kusiak, A. (2018). Data-driven smart manufacturing. *Journal of Manufacturing Systems*, *48*, 157–169. DOI: 10.1016/j.jmsy.2018.01.006

Tao, F., Zhang, M., & Nee, A. Y. C. (2019). *Digital twin driven smart manufacturing*. Academic press.

Xu, X. (2018). *Industrial Internet of Things: Applications, Trends, and Challenges*. Springer.

Zhang, Y. (2018). Edge and Fog Computing for Smart Manufacturing: A Survey. *Journal of Industrial Information Integration*, *10*, 1–9.

Zhao, X., Li, X., & Zhou, X. (2018). Urban green spaces and their role in enhancing climate resilience. *Journal of Environmental Science and Policy*, 89, 91-99.

Zhao, Y. (2019). AI in Industrial Energy Management Systems. *IEEE Transactions on Industrial Informatics*.

Zhao, Y. (2019). *Edge Computing in Industrial Internet of Things: Opportunities and Challenges*. Elsevier.

Zhao, Y. (2019). IIoT and Digital Twin for Smart Manufacturing: An Overview and Perspectives. *Journal of Industrial Information Integration*, *15*, 1–11.

Zhao, Y. (2020). *The Role of Digital Twin in Manufacturing: Optimizing Production Systems and Enhancing Efficiency*. Springer.

Zhou, W. (2019). Artificial Intelligence for Cybersecurity in IIoT Systems: Opportunities and Challenges. *IEEE Access : Practical Innovations, Open Solutions*, *7*, 118127–118141.

Chapter 12
Privacy Frameworks in Edge Computing: Balancing Security and Performance

Usharani Bhimavarapu
https://orcid.org/0000-0002-0246-1420
Department of Computer Science and Engineering, Koneru Lakshmaiah Education Foundation, Vaddeswaram, India

ABSTRACT

Edge computing enhances data processing efficiency by minimizing latency and bandwidth usage, but its decentralized nature creates severe privacy concerns. The traditional security methodologies are ineffective in edge environments, so robust privacy frameworks are critical to ensure data confidentiality, integrity, and regulatory compliance. This paper presents various privacy-preserving techniques, including cryptographic methods, federated learning, access control mechanisms, and anonymization schemes. Cryptographic techniques such as homomorphic encryption and secure multi-party computation enable secure processing of data, and federated learning minimizes data exposure in AI-driven applications. Access control frameworks such as role-based and zero-trust models prevent unauthorized access, and anonymization techniques minimize re-identification threats. Edge-to-cloud privacy frameworks and secure communication protocols also ensure data security.

INTRODUCTION

Edge computing revolutionizes data processing by making computation near data, minimizing latency and bandwidth use. Privacy task scheduling algorithms

DOI: 10.4018/979-8-3373-1147-0.ch012

optimize workload allocation with exposure to a limited amount of privacy attacks. End-to-end encryption secures data integrity across the edge-to-cloud infrastructure. Policy-based infrastructures guarantee policy compliance by managing data flow. Homomorphic encryption and differential privacy introduce protection to joint cloud-edge artificial intelligence models. Decentralized identity management systems utilize blockchain technology to offer authentication on edge and cloud networks. Optimization of performance within edge-to-cloud integration of privacy frameworks improves the overall efficiency and trustworthiness of the system.

Limited resource availability in edge devices makes computationally expensive encryption and privacy-preserving operations challenging. Computational overheads of real-time computation computational loads are against privacy controls resulting in increased computational overhead. Adversary attacks including model inversion and membership inference attacks are extremely detrimental to edge deployments of AI.

L-diversity builds upon k-anonymity by ensuring diverse attribute values within anonymized sets. T-closeness measures distribution similarity between anonymized and original data for minimizing disclosure risk. Integration of anonymization with secure computation techniques holds the potential for privacy without losing data utility. Strong anonymization techniques enable privacy-preserving analysis with performance optimization on the edge.

Edge-to-cloud privacy paradigms integrate data processing across edge devices and cloud infrastructure with security. Hybrid privacy architectures offload sensitive computation, cloud and less-sensitive data computation, and sensitive data to the edge. Data offloading secure methods from secure encrypted transfer over edge and cloud servers. Privacy task scheduling algorithms optimize workload allocation with exposure to a limited amount of privacy attacks. End-to-end encryption secures data integrity across the edge-to-cloud infrastructure. Policy-based infrastructures guarantee policy compliance by managing data flow. Trusted execution environments (TEE) give protected enclaves for performing high-security calculations in the edge. Homomorphic encryption and differential privacy introduce protection to joint cloud-edge artificial intelligence models. Decentralized identity management systems utilize blockchain technology to offer authentication on edge and cloud networks. Optimization of performance within edge-to-cloud integration of privacy frameworks improves the overall efficiency and trustworthiness of the system.

Secure communication protocols protect data transmission between edge nodes and cloud servers, reducing interception possibilities. Data transfers are encrypted with Transport Layer Security (TLS) for confidentiality and integrity. Secure Datagram Transport Layer Security (DTLS) prevents TLS with limited IoT device support in edge environments. Lightweight cryptography techniques such as Datagram Transport Layer Security (DTLS) conserve computations. Onion routing conceals traffic by encrypting data in the form of layers, preventing traffic analysis.

Messaging protocols such as Signal's double ratchet protocol enable end-to-end encrypted peer-to-peer messaging. Proxy re-encryption schemes enable data sharing with limited exposure to original data. Blockchain-based communication platforms ensure greater transparency and immunity to unauthorized data manipulation.

Multi-hop secure communication patterns ensure confidentiality of messages passing between multiple edge nodes. Privacy-preserving communication protocols ensure greater security with low latency in edge computing networks.

Future advancement in AI-based privacy solutions will enhance edge-based threat analysis and mitigation in real time. Quantum-safe cryptography is gaining traction to prevent edge computing from quantum attacks. Private-private AI models decentralized for privacy will maintain precision high and reduce data exposure even lower. Edge-native privacy solutions will improve cryptographic processing of low-energy devices. Edge-to-cloud privacy paradigms integrate data processing across edge devices and cloud infrastructure with security. Hybrid privacy architectures offload sensitive computation, cloud and less-sensitive data computation, and sensitive data to the edge. Data offloading secure methods from secure encrypted transfer over edge and cloud servers. Privacy task scheduling algorithms optimize workload allocation with exposure to a limited amount of privacy attacks. End-to-end encryption secures data integrity across the edge-to-cloud infrastructure. Policy-based infrastructures guarantee policy compliance by managing data flow. Decentralized identity management systems utilize blockchain technology to offer authentication on edge and cloud networks. Optimization of performance within edge-to-cloud integration of privacy frameworks improves the overall efficiency and trustworthiness of the system.

Messaging protocols such as Signal's double ratchet protocol enable end-to-end encrypted peer-to-peer messaging. Proxy re-encryption schemes enable data sharing with limited exposure to original data. Blockchain-based communication platforms ensure greater transparency and immunity to unauthorized data manipulation.

Multi-hop secure communication patterns ensure confidentiality of messages passing between multiple edge nodes. Privacy-preserving communication protocols ensure greater security with low latency in edge computing networks.

Future advancement in AI-based privacy solutions will enhance edge-based threat analysis and mitigation in real time. Quantum-safe cryptography is gaining traction to prevent edge computing from quantum attacks. Private-private AI models decentralized for privacy will maintain precision high and reduce data exposure even lower. Edge-native privacy solutions will improve cryptographic processing of low-energy devices. Edge-to-cloud models of privacy and secure communication protocols offer extra robustness to data security. New trends like quantum-resistant cryptography and AI-based privacy technologies picking up will shape the future of edge computing security. Models of privacy must adapt and evolve to meet the latest threats and compliances. The balance of maintaining privacy and computational efficiency is the path forward to embracing edge technology. Organisations must implement end-to-end privacy mechanisms to protect user data and enhance edge efficiency. Development and research into privacy-preserving techniques will fuel secure and high-performance edge computing. As more use is made of edge computing, strong privacy frameworks will form the backbone of dependability and trustworthiness.

Homomorphic encryption and differential privacy introduce protection to joint cloud-edge artificial intelligence models. Decentralized identity management systems utilize blockchain technology to offer authentication on edge and cloud networks. Optimization of performance within edge-to-cloud integration of privacy frameworks improves the overall efficiency and trustworthiness of the system.

Limited resource availability in edge devices makes computationally expensive encryption and privacy-preserving operations challenging. Computational overheads of real-time computation computational loads are against privacy controls resulting in increased computational overhead. Adversary attacks including model inversion and membership inference attacks are extremely detrimental to edge deployments of AI.

L-diversity builds upon k-anonymity by ensuring diverse attribute values within anonymized sets. T-closeness measures distribution similarity between anonymized and original data for minimizing disclosure risk. Integration of anonymization with secure computation techniques holds the potential for privacy without losing data utility. Strong anonymization techniques enable privacy-preserving analysis with performance optimization on the edge.

Edge-to-cloud privacy paradigms integrate data processing across edge devices and cloud infrastructure with security. Hybrid privacy architectures offload sensitive computation, cloud and less-sensitive data computation, and sensitive data to the edge. Data offloading secure methods from secure encrypted transfer over edge and cloud servers. Privacy task scheduling algorithms optimize workload allocation with exposure to a limited amount of privacy attacks. End-to-end encryption secures data integrity across the edge-to-cloud infrastructure. Policy-based infrastructures guarantee policy compliance by managing data flow. Trusted execution environments (TEE) give protected enclaves for performing high-security calculations in the edge. Homomorphic encryption and differential privacy introduce protection to joint cloud-edge artificial intelligence models. Decentralized identity management systems utilize blockchain technology to offer authentication on edge and cloud networks. Optimization of performance within edge-to-cloud integration of privacy frameworks improves the overall efficiency and trustworthiness of the system.

T-closeness measures distribution similarity between anonymized and original data for minimizing disclosure risk. Integration of anonymization with secure computation techniques holds the potential for privacy without losing data utility. Strong anonymization techniques enable privacy-preserving analysis with performance optimization on the edge.

Edge-to-cloud privacy paradigms integrate data processing across edge devices and cloud infrastructure with security. Hybrid privacy architectures offload sensitive computation, cloud and less-sensitive data computation, and sensitive data to the edge. Data offloading secure methods from secure encrypted transfer over edge and cloud servers. Privacy task scheduling algorithms optimize workload allocation with exposure to a limited amount of privacy attacks. End-to-end encryption secures data integrity across the edge-to-cloud infrastructure. Policy-based infrastructures guarantee policy compliance by managing data flow. Trusted execution environments (TEE) give protected enclaves for performing high-security calculations in the edge. Homomorphic encryption and differential privacy introduce protection to joint cloud-edge artificial intelligence models. Decentralized identity management systems utilize blockchain technology to offer authentication on edge and cloud networks. Optimization of performance within edge-to-cloud integration of privacy frameworks improves the overall efficiency and trustworthiness of the system.

Secure communication protocols protect data transmission between edge nodes and cloud servers, reducing interception possibilities. Data transfers are encrypted with Transport Layer Security (TLS) for confidentiality and integrity. Secure Datagram Transport Layer Security (DTLS) prevents TLS with limited IoT device support in edge environments. Lightweight cryptography techniques such as Datagram Transport Layer Security (DTLS) conserve computations. Onion routing conceals traffic by encrypting data in the form of layers, preventing traffic analysis. Messaging protocols such as Signal's double ratchet protocol enable end-to-end encrypted peer-to-peer messaging. Proxy re-encryption schemes enable data sharing with limited exposure to original data. Blockchain-based communication platforms ensure greater transparency and immunity to unauthorized data manipulation.

Multi-hop secure communication patterns ensure confidentiality of messages passing between multiple edge nodes. Privacy-preserving communication protocols ensure greater security with low latency in edge computing networks.

Future advancement in AI-based privacy solutions will enhance edge-based threat analysis and mitigation in real time. Quantum-safe cryptography is gaining traction to prevent edge computing from quantum attacks. Private-private AI models decentralized for privacy will maintain precision high and reduce data exposure even lower. Edge-native privacy solutions will improve cryptographic processing of low-energy devices. Edge-to-cloud privacy paradigms integrate data processing across edge devices and cloud infrastructure with security. Hybrid privacy architectures offload sensitive computation, cloud and less-sensitive data computation, and sensitive data to the edge. Data offloading secure methods from secure encrypted transfer over edge and cloud servers. Privacy task scheduling algorithms optimize workload allocation with exposure to a limited amount of privacy attacks. End-to-end encryption secures data integrity across the edge-to-cloud infrastructure. Policy-based infrastructures guarantee policy compliance by managing data flow. Decentralized identity management systems utilize blockchain technology to offer authentication on edge and cloud networks. Optimization of performance within edge-to-cloud integration of privacy frameworks improves the overall efficiency and trustworthiness of the system.

Messaging protocols such as Signal's double ratchet protocol enable end-to-end encrypted peer-to-peer messaging. Proxy re-encryption schemes enable data sharing with limited exposure to original data. Blockchain-based communication platforms ensure greater transparency and immunity to unauthorized data manipulation.

Multi-hop secure communication patterns ensure confidentiality of messages passing between multiple edge nodes. Privacy-preserving communication protocols ensure greater security with low latency in edge computing networks.

Future advancement in AI-based privacy solutions will enhance edge-based threat analysis and mitigation in real time. Quantum-safe cryptography is gaining traction to prevent edge computing from quantum attacks. Private-private AI models decentralized for privacy will maintain precision high and reduce data exposure even lower. Edge-native privacy solutions will improve cryptographic processing of low-energy devices. Edge-to-cloud models of privacy and secure communication protocols offer extra robustness to data security. New trends like quantum-resistant cryptography and AI-based privacy technologies picking up will shape the future of edge computing security. Models of privacy must adapt and evolve to meet the latest threats and compliances. The balance of maintaining privacy and computational efficiency is the path forward to embracing edge technology. Organisations must implement end-to-end privacy mechanisms to protect user data and enhance edge efficiency. Development and research into privacy-preserving techniques will fuel secure and high-performance edge computing. As more use is made of edge computing, strong privacy frameworks will form the backbone of dependability and trustworthiness.

T-closeness measures distribution similarity between anonymized and original data for minimizing disclosure risk. Integration of anonymization with secure computation techniques holds the potential for privacy without losing data utility. Strong anonymization techniques enable privacy-preserving analysis with performance optimization on the edge.

Edge-to-cloud privacy paradigms integrate data processing across edge devices and cloud infrastructure with security. Hybrid privacy architectures offload sensitive computation, cloud and less-sensitive data computation, and sensitive data to the edge. Data offloading secure methods from secure encrypted transfer over edge and cloud servers. Privacy task scheduling algorithms optimize workload allocation with exposure to a limited amount of privacy attacks. End-to-end encryption secures data integrity across the edge-to-cloud infrastructure. Policy-based infrastructures guarantee policy compliance by managing data flow. Trusted execution environments (TEE) give protected enclaves for performing high-security calculations in the edge. Homomorphic encryption and differential privacy introduce protection to joint cloud-edge artificial intelligence models. Decentralized identity management systems utilize blockchain technology to offer authentication on edge and cloud networks. Optimization of performance within edge-to-cloud integration of privacy frameworks improves the overall efficiency and trustworthiness of the system.

Secure communication protocols protect data transmission between edge nodes and cloud servers, reducing interception possibilities. Data transfers are encrypted with Transport Layer Security (TLS) for confidentiality and integrity. Secure Datagram Transport Layer Security (DTLS) prevents TLS with limited IoT device support in edge environments. Lightweight cryptography techniques such as Datagram Transport Layer Security (DTLS) conserve computations. Onion routing conceals traffic by encrypting data in the form of layers, preventing traffic analysis. Messaging protocols such as Signal's double ratchet protocol enable end-to-end encrypted peer-to-peer messaging. Proxy re-encryption schemes enable data sharing with limited exposure to original data. Blockchain-based communication platforms ensure greater transparency and immunity to unauthorized data manipulation.

Multi-hop secure communication patterns ensure confidentiality of messages passing between multiple edge nodes. Privacy-preserving communication protocols ensure greater security with low latency in edge computing networks.

Future advancement in AI-based privacy solutions will enhance edge-based threat analysis and mitigation in real time. Quantum-safe cryptography is gaining traction to prevent edge computing from quantum attacks. Private-private AI models decentralized for privacy will maintain precision high and reduce data exposure even lower. Edge-native privacy solutions will improve cryptographic processing of low-energy devices. Edge-to-cloud privacy paradigms integrate data processing across edge devices and cloud infrastructure with security. Hybrid privacy architectures offload sensitive computation, cloud and less-sensitive data computation, and sensitive data to the edge. Data offloading secure methods from secure encrypted transfer over edge and cloud servers. Privacy task scheduling algorithms optimize workload allocation with exposure to a limited amount of privacy attacks. End-to-end encryption secures data integrity across the edge-to-cloud infrastructure. Policy-based infrastructures guarantee policy compliance by managing data flow. Decentralized identity management systems utilize blockchain technology to offer authentication on edge and cloud networks. Optimization of performance within edge-to-cloud integration of privacy frameworks improves the overall efficiency and trustworthiness of the system.

Messaging protocols such as Signal's double ratchet protocol enable end-to-end encrypted peer-to-peer messaging. Proxy re-encryption schemes enable data sharing with limited exposure to original data. Blockchain-based communication platforms ensure greater transparency and immunity to unauthorized data manipulation.

Multi-hop secure communication patterns ensure confidentiality of messages passing between multiple edge nodes. Privacy-preserving communication protocols ensure greater security with low latency in edge computing networks.

Future advancement in AI-based privacy solutions will enhance edge-based threat analysis and mitigation in real time. Quantum-safe cryptography is gaining traction to prevent edge computing from quantum attacks. Private-private AI models decentralized for privacy will maintain precision high and reduce data exposure even lower. Edge-native privacy solutions will improve cryptographic processing of low-energy devices. Edge-to-cloud models of privacy and secure communication protocols offer extra robustness to data security. New trends like quantum-resistant cryptography and AI-based privacy technologies picking up will shape the future of edge computing security. Models of privacy must adapt and evolve to meet the latest threats and compliances. The balance of maintaining privacy and computational efficiency is the path forward to embracing edge technology. Organisations must implement end-to-end privacy mechanisms to protect user data and enhance edge efficiency. Development and research into privacy-preserving techniques will fuel secure and high-performance edge computing. As more use is made of edge computing, strong privacy frameworks will form the backbone of dependability and trustworthiness.

Secure communication protocols protect data transmission between edge nodes and cloud servers, reducing interception possibilities. Data transfers are encrypted with Transport Layer Security (TLS) for confidentiality and integrity. Secure Datagram Transport Layer Security (DTLS) prevents TLS with limited IoT device support in edge environments. Lightweight cryptography techniques such as Datagram Transport Layer Security (DTLS) conserve computations. Onion routing conceals traffic by encrypting data in the form of layers, preventing traffic analysis. Messaging protocols such as Signal's double ratchet protocol enable end-to-end encrypted peer-to-peer messaging. Proxy re-encryption schemes enable data sharing with limited exposure to original data. Blockchain-based communication platforms ensure greater transparency and immunity to unauthorized data manipulation.

Multi-hop secure communication patterns ensure confidentiality of messages passing between multiple edge nodes. Privacy-preserving communication protocols ensure greater security with low latency in edge computing networks.

Future advancement in AI-based privacy solutions will enhance edge-based threat analysis and mitigation in real time. Quantum-safe cryptography is gaining traction to prevent edge computing from quantum attacks. Private-private AI models decentralized for privacy will maintain precision high and reduce data exposure even lower. Edge-native privacy solutions will improve cryptographic processing of low-energy devices. Edge-to-cloud privacy paradigms integrate data processing across edge devices and cloud infrastructure with security. Hybrid privacy architectures offload sensitive computation, cloud and less-sensitive data computation, and sensitive data to the edge. Data offloading secure methods from secure encrypted transfer over edge and cloud servers. Privacy task scheduling algorithms optimize workload allocation with exposure to a limited amount of privacy attacks. End-to-end encryption secures data integrity across the edge-to-cloud infrastructure. Policy-based infrastructures guarantee policy compliance by managing data flow. Decentralized identity management systems utilize blockchain technology to offer authentication on edge and cloud networks. Optimization of performance within edge-to-cloud integration of privacy frameworks improves the overall efficiency and trustworthiness of the system.

Messaging protocols such as Signal's double ratchet protocol enable end-to-end encrypted peer-to-peer messaging. Proxy re-encryption schemes enable data sharing with limited exposure to original data. Blockchain-based communication platforms ensure greater transparency and immunity to unauthorized data manipulation.

Multi-hop secure communication patterns ensure confidentiality of messages passing between multiple edge nodes. Privacy-preserving communication protocols ensure greater security with low latency in edge computing networks.

Future advancement in AI-based privacy solutions will enhance edge-based threat analysis and mitigation in real time. Quantum-safe cryptography is gaining traction to prevent edge computing from quantum attacks. Private-private AI models decentralized for privacy will maintain precision high and reduce data exposure even lower. Edge-native privacy solutions will improve cryptographic processing of low-energy devices. Edge-to-cloud models of privacy and secure communication protocols offer extra robustness to data security. New trends like quantum-resistant cryptography and AI-based privacy technologies picking up will shape the future of edge computing security. Models of privacy must adapt and evolve to meet the latest threats and compliances. The balance of maintaining privacy and computational efficiency is the path forward to embracing edge technology. Organisations must implement end-to-end privacy mechanisms to protect user data and enhance edge efficiency. Development and research into privacy-preserving techniques will fuel secure and high-performance edge computing. As more use is made of edge computing, strong privacy frameworks will form the backbone of dependability and trustworthiness.

Homomorphic encryption and differential privacy introduce protection to joint cloud-edge artificial intelligence models. Decentralized identity management systems utilize blockchain technology to offer authentication on edge and cloud networks.

Optimization of performance within edge-to-cloud integration of privacy frameworks improves the overall efficiency and trustworthiness of the system.

Limited resource availability in edge devices makes computationally expensive encryption and privacy-preserving operations challenging. Computational overheads of real-time computation computational loads are against privacy controls resulting in increased computational overhead. Adversary attacks including model inversion and membership inference attacks are extremely detrimental to edge deployments of AI.

L-diversity builds upon k-anonymity by ensuring diverse attribute values within anonymized sets. T-closeness measures distribution similarity between anonymized and original data for minimizing disclosure risk. Integration of anonymization with secure computation techniques holds the potential for privacy without losing data utility. Strong anonymization techniques enable privacy-preserving analysis with performance optimization on the edge.

Edge-to-cloud privacy paradigms integrate data processing across edge devices and cloud infrastructure with security. Hybrid privacy architectures offload sensitive computation, cloud and less-sensitive data computation, and sensitive data to the edge. Data offloading secure methods from secure encrypted transfer over edge and cloud servers. Privacy task scheduling algorithms optimize workload allocation with exposure to a limited amount of privacy attacks. End-to-end encryption secures data integrity across the edge-to-cloud infrastructure. Policy-based infrastructures guarantee policy compliance by managing data flow. Trusted execution environments (TEE) give protected enclaves for performing high-security calculations in the edge. Homomorphic encryption and differential privacy introduce protection to joint cloud-edge artificial intelligence models. Decentralized identity management systems utilize blockchain technology to offer authentication on edge and cloud networks. Optimization of performance within edge-to-cloud integration of privacy frameworks improves the overall efficiency and trustworthiness of the system.

Secure communication protocols protect data transmission between edge nodes and cloud servers, reducing interception possibilities. Data transfers are encrypted with Transport Layer Security (TLS) for confidentiality and integrity. Secure Datagram Transport Layer Security (DTLS) prevents TLS with limited IoT device support in edge environments. Lightweight cryptography techniques such as Datagram Transport Layer Security (DTLS) conserve computations. Onion routing conceals traffic by encrypting data in the form of layers, preventing traffic analysis. Messaging protocols such as Signal's double ratchet protocol enable end-to-end encrypted peer-to-peer messaging. Proxy re-encryption schemes enable data sharing with limited exposure to original data. Blockchain-based communication platforms ensure greater transparency and immunity to unauthorized data manipulation.

Multi-hop secure communication patterns ensure confidentiality of messages passing between multiple edge nodes. Privacy-preserving communication protocols ensure greater security with low latency in edge computing networks.

Future advancement in AI-based privacy solutions will enhance edge-based threat analysis and mitigation in real time. Quantum-safe cryptography is gaining traction to prevent edge computing from quantum attacks. Private-private AI models decentralized for privacy will maintain precision high and reduce data exposure even lower. Edge-native privacy solutions will improve cryptographic processing of low-energy devices. Edge-to-cloud privacy paradigms integrate data processing across edge devices and cloud infrastructure with security. Hybrid privacy architectures offload sensitive computation, cloud and less-sensitive data computation, and sensitive data to the edge. Data offloading secure methods from secure encrypted transfer over edge and cloud servers. Privacy task scheduling algorithms optimize workload allocation with exposure to a limited amount of privacy attacks. End-to-end encryption secures data integrity across the edge-to-cloud infrastructure. Policy-based infrastructures guarantee policy compliance by managing data flow. Decentralized identity management systems utilize blockchain technology to offer authentication on edge and cloud networks. Optimization of performance within edge-to-cloud integration of privacy frameworks improves the overall efficiency and trustworthiness of the system.

Messaging protocols such as Signal's double ratchet protocol enable end-to-end encrypted peer-to-peer messaging. Proxy re-encryption schemes enable data sharing with limited exposure to original data. Blockchain-based communication platforms ensure greater transparency and immunity to unauthorized data manipulation.

Multi-hop secure communication patterns ensure confidentiality of messages passing between multiple edge nodes. Privacy-preserving communication protocols ensure greater security with low latency in edge computing networks.

Future advancement in AI-based privacy solutions will enhance edge-based threat analysis and mitigation in real time. Quantum-safe cryptography is gaining traction to prevent edge computing from quantum attacks. Private-private AI models decentralized for privacy will maintain precision high and reduce data exposure even lower. Edge-native privacy solutions will improve cryptographic processing of low-energy devices. Edge-to-cloud models of privacy and secure communication protocols offer extra robustness to data security. New trends like quantum-resistant cryptography and AI-based privacy technologies picking up will shape the future of edge computing security. Models of privacy must adapt and evolve to meet the latest threats and compliances. The balance of maintaining privacy and computational efficiency is the path forward to embracing edge technology. Organisations must implement end-to-end privacy mechanisms to protect user data and enhance edge efficiency. Development and research into privacy-preserving techniques will fuel secure and high-performance edge computing. As more use is made of edge computing, strong privacy frameworks will form the backbone of dependability and trustworthiness.

R. Mo et al., (2019) presents differential privacy-based preprocessing of big data for data mining. However, its usage in real-time edge computing scenarios is still suffering from high computation overhead as well as low scalability. Zhou et al., (2019) proposed differentially private mechanism for location privacy in connected vehicles maintains privacy but introduces high latency and hence prevents real-time decision-making scenarios for high-speed vehicle use cases. Bao and R. Lu, (2017) recommended lightweight data aggregation scheme to obtain privacy and integrity balance but is not strong in adversarial scenarios where data poisoning attacks have the capability to impact system accuracy. Eibl et al., (2018) considers the effect of differential privacy on electric load forecasting but is compromised by reduced forecasting accuracy due to excessive noise addition, which makes it less useful in mission-critical buildings in real-world settings. Civino et al., (2019) proposed method of approach in differential attacks is intriguing but without empirical analysis in modern-day encryption schemes, and hence its usage cannot be straightforwardly compared with increasing cryptographic practices. Chowdhury et al., (2020) proposed Crypto-aided differential privacy provides better security on untrusted servers but is computation expensive, hindering its applicability to low-capacity edge devices. Ni et al., (2018) proposed differentially private mechanism for location privacy in connected vehicles maintains privacy but introduces high latency and hence prevents real-time decision-making scenarios for high-speed vehicle use cases. Y. Zhang et al., (2019) raises issues on privacy in big data but does not indicate solutions for real-time, edge processing where dynamic data collection occurs. Zhao et al., (2019) proposed that DP-MCDBSCAN cluster algorithm is privacy-preserving when it works on network data but not on high-dimensional data, which compromises cluster accuracy and efficiency. M. Abadi et al., (2016) proposed differentially private mechanism for location privacy in connected vehicles maintains privacy but introduces high latency and hence prevents real-time decision-making scenarios for high-speed vehicle use cases. Q. Miao et al., (2018) proposed IoT security and privacy issues, but it is largely theoretical and not of actual implementation offered for efficacious practical security measures. Yu, (2016) raises issues on privacy in big data but does not indicate solutions for real-time, edge processing where dynamic data collection occurs. P. Jain et al., (2018) proposed Crypto-aided differential privacy provides better security on untrusted servers but is computation expensive, hindering its applicability to low-capacity edge devices. Z. Lv et al., (2019) proposed that DP-MCDBSCAN cluster algorithm is privacy-preserving when it works on network data but not on high-dimensional data, which compromises cluster accuracy and efficiency. Zhang et al., (2019) proposed differential privacy but isn't adaptive for federated learning scenarios, where the data is also distributed across different edge devices. Z. Sun et al., (2019) proposes location privacy improvement technique but not attack-resistant with auxiliary information, reducing overall security guarantees. G. G. Dagher et al., (2020) proposed method of approach in differential attacks is intriguing but without empirical analysis in modern-day encryption schemes, and hence its usage cannot be straightforwardly compared with increasing cryptographic practices. Wang et al., (2020) proposed differentially private mechanism for location privacy in connected vehicles maintains privacy but introduces high latency and hence prevents real-time decision-making scenarios for high-speed vehicle use cases. M. Sridhar and B. Babu, (2012) proposed fuzzy method to data mining privacy safeguarding is a novel concept but has not been put into practice and tested to check its resistance from prevailing AI-powered privacy attacks, hence its resistance becomes doubtful. Mosenia and N. K. Jha, (2017) proposed IoT protection from a broad variety of threats but fails to provide a concrete, scalable solution that can be effectively employed in a large variety of various IoT environments. Yang et al., (2017) proposed IoT security and privacy issues, but it is largely theoretical and not of actual implementation offered for efficacious practical security measures. Turner et al., (2014) proposed IoT's digital world focus on data value but cannot address dynamic security issues due to data explosion within edge computing scenarios. (IDC, 2020) proposed internet report proposal indicates IoT trends but is not empirically validated and does not have solid case studies, and therefore it is difficult to establish the efficiency of the proposed methods in real use. Zhang et al., (2018) proposed data protection in edge computing but does not propose an end-to-end solution that assures security, privacy, and computational efficiency. Onieva et al., (2019) proposed vehicular networks security with the assistance of edges but does not take into account the coming dangers like AI-based adversarial attacks on autonomous vehicles. Khan et al., (2019) proposed edge computing identifies key factors but does not outline real-time security measures that can feasibly be implemented in resource-constrained systems. Wang et al., (2019) proposed IoT service architecture based on a centralized trust model that is not feasibly applicable in decentralization-based edge computing systems. Bragadeesh and U. Arumugam, (2019) proposed edge computing security conceptual framework but at the abstract level without specifying implementation steps for real-world deployment. Lu and L. D. Xu, (2019) proposed vehicular networks security with the assistance of edges but does not take into account the coming dangers like AI-based adversarial attacks on autonomous vehicles.

The new light-weighted enhanced algorithm suggested for security evaluation and threat countermeasure, utilized in edge computing, surmounts some of the weaknesses in previous models with higher efficiency, scalability, and privacy safeguard. Conventional methods, like differential privacy-based mechanisms (Mo et al., 2019; Zhou et al., 2019), incur computation overhead and decreased accuracy owing to introduced noise. The method in this paper optimizes privacy mechanisms by adjusting noise levels dynamically depending on data sensitivity and thus providing a low-loss of information while providing comprehensive protection. In addition, existing methods, e.g., DP-MCDBSCAN (Ni et al., 2018) and APDP (Zhang et al., 2019), are not effective in real-time threat detection and adaptive security. Our design combines lightweight crypto computations and real-time anomaly detection, which optimizes response times and minimizes resource usage. Furthermore, the solution provided by this paper corrects the issue of model performance degradation in low-resource edge settings, identified by previous work on deep learning with differential privacy (Abadi et al., 2016). Advanced encryption structure and threat-adaptive surveillance, our framework offers a balance of security and computer cost. Moreover, standard security measures tend to fall behind on universal threat surveillance in terms of data protection (Miao et al., 2018) or access control (Wang et al., 2020). Zhang et al., (2018) proposed data protection in edge computing but does not propose an end-to-end solution that assures security, privacy, and computational efficiency. Onieva et al., (2019) proposed vehicular networks security with the assistance of edges but does not take into account the coming dangers like AI-based adversarial attacks on autonomous vehicles. Khan et al., (2019) proposed edge computing identifies key factors but does not outline real-time security measures that can feasibly be implemented in resource-constrained systems. Wang et al., (2019) proposed IoT service architecture based on a centralized trust model that is not feasibly applicable in decentralization-based edge computing systems. Bragadeesh and U. Arumugam, (2019) proposed edge computing security conceptual framework but at the abstract level without specifying implementation steps for real-world deployment. Lu and L. D. Xu, (2019) proposed vehicular networks security with the assistance of edges but does not take into account the coming dangers like AI-based adversarial attacks on autonomous vehicles.

The new light-weighted enhanced algorithm suggested for security evaluation and threat countermeasure, utilized in edge computing, surmounts some of the weaknesses in previous models with higher efficiency, scalability, and privacy safeguard. Conventional methods, like differential privacy-based mechanisms (Mo et al., 2019; Zhou et al., 2019), incur computation overhead and decreased accuracy owing to introduced noise. The method in this paper optimizes privacy mechanisms by adjusting noise levels dynamically depending on data sensitivity and thus providing a low-loss of information while providing comprehensive protection. In addition, existing methods, e.g., DP-MCDBSCAN (Ni et al., 2018) and APDP (Zhang et al., 2019), are not effective in real-time threat detection and adaptive security. Our design combines lightweight crypto computations and real-time anomaly detection, which optimizes response times and minimizes resource usage. Furthermore, the solution provided by this paper corrects the issue of model performance degradation in low-resource edge settings, identified by previous work on deep learning with differential privacy (Abadi et al., 2016). Advanced encryption structure and threat-adaptive surveillance, our framework offers a balance of security and computer cost. Moreover, standard security measures tend to fall behind on universal threat surveillance in terms of data protection (Miao et al., 2018) or access control (Wang et al., 2020). The proposed model in this research solves both aspects of the problem, providing end-to-end security from data gathering to processing and storage. With these key improvements, our approach improves security and increases real-time decision-making, and offers scalable privacy-preserving mechanisms for edge computing settings.

LIGHTWEIGHT IMPROVED ALGORITHM FOR SECURITY ANALYSIS AND THREAT MITIGATION IN EDGE COMPUTING

The algorithm introduced supports optimized encryption techniques with minimal computation overhead. The algorithm uses light-weight symmetric cipher mechanisms like Speck and Simon for safe data encryption. Adaptive encryption controls security levels based on available resources and risk levels. The secure hash-based key generation support stops unauthorized intrusions and ensures the processing load to be minimal. Data minimization mechanisms ensure that minimum possible data is processed and shared. Homomorphic encryption provides secure computation without revealing raw data. Differential privacy mechanisms introduce noise to avoid data leakage in machine learning systems. Low-cost authentication protocols based on elliptic curve cryptography (ECC) facilitate instant identity verification. The algorithm facilitates decentralized access control, minimizing reliance on central authorities. These features together deliver privacy with optimal performance in edge deployments.

Algorithm Steps

Step 1: Initialization

- Deploy edge nodes with secure firmware validation.
- Initialize cryptographic keys using **Elliptic Curve Cryptography (ECC)** or **Lightweight Ciphers (Speck/Simon)**.
- Set up a **zero-trust authentication model** for user and device verification.

Step 2: Secure Data Transmission

- Encrypt all communication using **AES-128/GCM** for minimal overhead.
- Implement session-based encryption with temporary keys.
- Apply **homomorphic encryption** for secure computation on encrypted data.

Step 3: Threat Detection and Anomaly Analysis

- Monitor **real-time network traffic** using a lightweight **Intrusion Detection System (IDS)**.
- Train a **machine learning (ML) model** on historical attack patterns to detect anomalies.
- Identify zero-day threats using **heuristic-based analysis**.

Step 4: Decentralized Access Control

- Implement **role-based access control (RBAC)** with dynamically assigned permissions.
- Use **blockchain-based identity management** for secure authentication.
- Generate **one-time passwords (OTP)** for time-sensitive access validation.

Step 5: Secure Boot and Runtime Verification

- Verify **firmware integrity** at boot using **Trusted Platform Module (TPM)**.
- Perform **dynamic runtime verification** for detecting unauthorized modifications.
- Enable **secure enclaves (Intel SGX/ARM TrustZone)** for isolating sensitive processes.

Step 6: Automated Patch Management

- Schedule regular **AI-driven vulnerability scans** for system integrity assessment.
- Deploy **secure over-the-air (OTA) firmware updates** using an encrypted channel.
- Maintain a **rollback mechanism** to restore the last secure state in case of failure.

Step 7: Intrusion Response and Mitigation

- Activate a **self-healing mechanism** to neutralize detected threats autonomously.
- Implement **quarantine measures** to isolate infected devices from the network.
- Share **threat intelligence across edge nodes** via **federated learning**.

Step 8: Performance Optimization

- Adjust **security parameters dynamically** based on edge device workload.
- Offload intensive cryptographic operations to **dedicated secure processors**.
- Use **cache-based optimizations** for faster secure data retrieval.

Step 9: Logging and Auditing

- Record all security events in a **tamper-proof blockchain ledger**.
- Perform **continuous monitoring and audit logging** for forensic analysis.
- Generate **real-time security reports** for proactive threat management.

Step 10: Exit

- Continue monitoring security threats with **adaptive learning models**.
- Optimize security configurations periodically based on new threat intelligence.

Theorem 1: Lightweight Cryptographic Security

Statement: If a cryptographic algorithm maintains a high security level with a computational complexity of O(n) or lower, then it is considered lightweight for edge computing.

Proof:

- Let EEE be an encryption algorithm with key size kkk.
- Traditional encryption schemes like RSA require $\mathbf{O(2^k)}$ operations for brute-force attacks.

- Lightweight ciphers such as **Speck/Simon** operate with complexity **O(n)** due to reduced block sizes and optimized key schedules.
- If EEE ensures a minimal computational footprint while maintaining security properties (confidentiality, integrity, authenticity), then it qualifies as lightweight.
- Since the algorithm employs **ECC (O(n)) and Speck (O(n))**, it meets the lightweight criteria.

Theorem 2: Anomaly Detection Convergence

Statement: If a machine learning (ML)-based anomaly detection system uses continuous learning, then its detection accuracy converges to an optimal state over time.

Proof:

- Let **D** be the dataset containing network traffic and system logs.
- The anomaly detection model **M** learns from **D** using gradient updates.
- The loss function **L**, representing the model's detection error, follows a decreasing trend:

$$L_{t+1} \leq L_t$$

Given that **M** uses real-time updates (e.g., federated learning), it refines its predictions iteratively.

- If **M** is trained with sufficient data, it reaches an optimal state where false positives and negatives are minimized.

Theorem 3: Blockchain-Based Access Control Immutability

Statement: If an access control system stores authentication records on a blockchain, then unauthorized modifications are impossible without consensus.

Proof:

- Let **B** be a blockchain ledger storing access control policies.
- Any modification requires **C** (consensus among nodes) for validation.
- If an adversary tries to alter **B**, they must control more than 50% of the network's computational power (i.e., **51% attack**).
- The probability **P** of such an attack succeeding is negligible in decentralized networks.

- Since our algorithm employs blockchain for identity verification, unauthorized changes are prevented.

Theorem 4: Secure Boot Integrity

Statement: If a device's firmware validation process follows a hardware-based root of trust (TPM/SGX), then its integrity is preserved during boot.

Proof:

- Let **S** be the secure boot process and **R** be the root of trust (TPM).
- Before executing firmware **F**, **R** verifies its hash **H(F)**.
- If $\boldsymbol{H(F)} \neq \boldsymbol{H_{stored}}$ (expected hash), boot is aborted to prevent tampered firmware execution.
- Since **R** is immutable and embedded in hardware, it cannot be altered by malware.
- This ensures that only **authenticated firmware** runs during the boot process.

Theorem 5: Computational Overhead of Intrusion Detection

Statement: A lightweight intrusion detection system (IDS) based on rule-based filtering and ML requires at most **O(n)** complexity for real-time detection.

Proof:

- Let **P** be the number of packets analyzed by the IDS.
- A rule-based IDS checks patterns using **hash table lookups (O(1)**).
- An ML-based IDS evaluates traffic features in **O(n)** time.
- Combining both approaches, the worst-case complexity remains **O(n)**.
- Since real-time processing is required for edge computing, an IDS with **O(n)** complexity ensures minimal delay.

Theorem 6: Automated Patch Management Robustness

Statement: If an edge computing system applies automated security patches dynamically, then it remains resistant to known vulnerabilities over time.

Proof:

- Let **V** be the set of known vulnerabilities at time **t**.
- The automated patch manager updates system software at intervals **T**.
- If a patch **P** is applied, the vulnerability set **V** reduces:

$V_{t+T} = V_t - P$The system remains protected as long as **PPP** is regularly updated and applied.

- Since patches are validated before deployment, no malicious updates compromise security.

CONCLUSION

Edge computing privacy models are essential to provide secure processing of distributed data without impacting system performance. Cryptographic techniques, federated learning, access control mechanisms, and anonymization protocols play a key role in safeguarding sensitive information while enabling real-time analysis. However, computational overhead, adversarial attacks, and adherence to regulations necessitate innovative privacy-preserving solutions. The proposed light-weight privacy model integrates performance-improved encryption, optimized authentication, and adaptive security controls to fight the challenges with optimal performance in resource-constrained edge environments. Future research direction has to be AI-based privacy approaches, quantum-resistant cryptography, and scaleable security architectures for optimal trust in edge computing applications. With increasing popularity of edge computing among more and more industries, solid and adaptable privacy frameworks will be necessary to protect data, offer regulatory compliance, and drive technological innovation.

REFERENCES

Abadi, M., Chu, A., Goodfellow, I., McMahan, H. B., Mironov, I., & Talwar, K.. (2016, October). Deep learning with differential privacy. *Proceedings of the ACM SIGSAC Conference on Computer and Communications Security*, 308–318.

Bao, H., & Lu, R. (2017). A lightweight data aggregation scheme achieving privacy preservation and data integrity with differential privacy and fault tolerance. *Peer-to-Peer Networking and Applications*, *10*(1), 106–121. DOI: 10.1007/s12083-015-0410-7

Bragadeesh, S., & Arumugam, U. (2019). A conceptual framework for security and privacy in edge computing. In *Edge Computing* (pp. 173–186). Springer.

Chowdhury, A. R., Wang, C., He, C., Machanajjhala, A., & Jha, S. (2020, June). Crypto-assisted differential privacy on untrusted servers. *Proceedings of the ACM SIGMOD International Conference on Management of Data*, 603–619.

Civino, R., Blondeau, C., & Sala, M. (2019). Differential attacks: Using alternative operations. *Designs, Codes and Cryptography*, *87*(2), 225–247. DOI: 10.1007/s10623-018-0516-z

Dagher, G. G., Fung, B. C. M., Mohammed, N., & Clark, J. (2020). SecDM: Privacy-preserving data outsourcing framework with differential privacy. *Knowledge and Information Systems*, *62*(5), 1923–1960. DOI: 10.1007/s10115-019-01405-7

Eibl, G., Bao, K., Grassal, P.-W., Bernau, D., & Schmeck, H. (2018). The influence of differential privacy on short term electric load forecasting. *Energy Informatics*, *1*(S1), 48. DOI: 10.1186/s42162-018-0025-3

Jain, P., Gyanchandani, M., & Khare, N. (2018). Differential privacy: Its technological prescriptive using big data. *Journal of Big Data*, *5*(1), 15. DOI: 10.1186/s40537-018-0124-9

Khan, W. Z., Ahmed, E., Hakak, S., Yaqoob, I., & Ahmed, A. (2019). Edge computing: A survey. *Future Generation Computer Systems*, *97*, 219–235. DOI: 10.1016/j.future.2019.02.050

Lu, Y., & Xu, L. D. (2019). Internet of Things (IoT) cybersecurity research: A review of current research topics. *IEEE Internet of Things Journal*, *6*(2), 2103–2115. DOI: 10.1109/JIOT.2018.2869847

Lv, Z., Wang, L., Guan, Z., Wu, J., Du, X., Zhao, H., & Guizani, M. (2019). An optimizing and differentially private clustering algorithm for mixed data in SDN-based smart grid. *IEEE Access : Practical Innovations, Open Solutions*, *7*, 45773–45782. DOI: 10.1109/ACCESS.2019.2909048

Miao, Q., Jing, W., & Song, H. (2018). Differential privacy–based location privacy enhancing in edge computing. In *Recent Advances in Cloud Data Centers Toward Fog Data Centers* (Vol. 31, No. 8).

Mo, R., Liu, J., Yu, W., Jiang, F., Gu, X., & Zhao, X. (2019, August). A differential privacy-based protecting data preprocessing method for big data mining. *Proceedings of the 18th IEEE International Conference on Trust, Security and Privacy in Computing and Communications*, 693–699. DOI: 10.1109/TrustCom/BigDataSE.2019.00098

Mosenia, A., & Jha, N. K. (2017). A comprehensive study of security of Internet-of-Things. *IEEE Transactions on Emerging Topics in Computing*, *5*(4), 586–602. DOI: 10.1109/TETC.2016.2606384

Ni, L., Li, C., Wang, X., Jiang, H., & Yu, J. (2018). DP-MCDBSCAN: Differential privacy preserving multi-core DBSCAN clustering for network user data. *IEEE Access : Practical Innovations, Open Solutions*, *6*, 21053–21063. DOI: 10.1109/ACCESS.2018.2824798

Onieva, J. A., Rios, R., Roman, R., & Lopez, J. (2019). Edge-assisted vehicular networks security. *IEEE Internet of Things Journal*, *6*(5), 8038–8045. DOI: 10.1109/JIOT.2019.2904323

Sridhar, M., & Babu, B. (2012). A fuzzy approach for privacy preserving in data mining. *International Journal of Computer Applications*, *57*, 1–5.

Sun, Z., Wang, Y., Shu, M., Liu, R., & Zhao, H. (2019). Differential privacy for data and model publishing of medical data. *IEEE Access : Practical Innovations, Open Solutions*, *7*, 152103–152114. DOI: 10.1109/ACCESS.2019.2947295

Turner, V., Gantz, J. F., Reinsel, D., & Minton, S. (2014). The digital universe of opportunities: Rich data and the increasing value of the Internet of Things. *IDC Analyze the Future*, *16*, 8.

Wang, T., Mei, Y., Jia, W., Zheng, X., Wang, G., & Xie, M. (2020). Edge-based differential privacy computing for sensor–cloud systems. *Journal of Parallel and Distributed Computing*, *136*, 75–85. DOI: 10.1016/j.jpdc.2019.10.009

Wang, T., Zhang, G., Liu, A., Bhuiyan, M. Z. A., & Jin, Q. (2019). A secure IoT service architecture with an efficient balance dynamics based on cloud and edge computing. *IEEE Internet of Things Journal*, *6*(3), 4831–4843. DOI: 10.1109/JIOT.2018.2870288

Yang, Y., Wu, L., Yin, G., Li, L., & Zhao, H. (2017). A survey on security and privacy issues in Internet-of-Things. *IEEE Internet of Things Journal*, *4*(5), 1250–1258. DOI: 10.1109/JIOT.2017.2694844

Yin, C., Xi, J., Sun, R., & Wang, J. (2018). Location privacy protection based on differential privacy strategy for big data in industrial Internet of Things. *IEEE Transactions on Industrial Informatics*, *14*(8), 3628–3636. DOI: 10.1109/TII.2017.2773646

Yu, S. (2016). Big privacy: Challenges and opportunities of privacy study in the age of big data. *IEEE Access: Practical Innovations, Open Solutions*, *4*, 2751–2763. DOI: 10.1109/ACCESS.2016.2577036

Zhang, J., Chen, B., Zhao, Y., Cheng, X., & Hu, F. (2018). Data security and privacy-preserving in edge computing paradigm: Survey and open issues. *IEEE Access: Practical Innovations, Open Solutions*, *6*, 18209–18237. DOI: 10.1109/ACCESS.2018.2820162

Zhang, Y., Hao, Z., & Wang, S. (2019). A differential privacy support vector machine classifier based on dual variable perturbation. *IEEE Access: Practical Innovations, Open Solutions*, *7*, 98238–98251. DOI: 10.1109/ACCESS.2019.2929680

Zhang, Y., Qu, Y., Gao, L., Luan, T. H., Zheng, X., Chen, S., & Xiang, Y. (2019). APDP: Attack-proof personalized differential privacy model for a smart home. *IEEE Access: Practical Innovations, Open Solutions*, *7*, 166593–166605. DOI: 10.1109/ACCESS.2019.2953133

Zhao, J., Chen, Y., & Zhang, W. (2019). Differential privacy preservation in deep learning: Challenges, opportunities and solutions. *IEEE Access : Practical Innovations, Open Solutions*, *7*, 48901–48911. DOI: 10.1109/ACCESS.2019.2909559

Zhou, L., Yu, L., Du, S., Zhu, H., & Chen, C. (2019). Achieving differentially private location privacy in edge-assistant connected vehicles. *IEEE Internet of Things Journal*, *6*(3), 4472–4481. DOI: 10.1109/JIOT.2018.2876419

Chapter 13
Recent Trends in Edge Computing:
Challenges and Opportunities

Kannadhasan Suriyan
https://orcid.org/0000-0001-6443-9993
Study World College of Engineering, India

S. Ganesh
https://orcid.org/0000-0002-4990-5869
Study World College of Engineering, India

P. Palaniyammal
Study World College of Engineering, India

G. Priya
Study World College of Engineering, India

Vineeta Singh
https://orcid.org/0000-0003-1084-279X
Chhatrapati Shahu Ji Maharaj University, India

ABSTRACT

Edge computing eliminates the need to send data to the cloud for processing/ execution, hence reducing latency and time complexity. Furthermore, advances in information technology and communication have enabled the solution to be saved, computed, and decided locally by developing an on-premise IOT solution. Edge computing with Artificial Intelligence provides continuous processing by preventing unexpected device failures and recognizing the need for predictive maintenance. The fast growth of IoT devices has raised the height of data creation, resulting in a

DOI: 10.4018/979-8-3373-1147-0.ch013

massive flow of data. These sensitive data generated by IoT devices is mostly kept in the cloud paradigm, but the latency encountered in the transmission between cloud data centres and end-users has rendered the arrangement pointless. This has remained the motivation for many businesses or organisations to move away from the cloud paradigm and toward edge computing, which allows data to be processed or performed locally at the user's end, allowing for quicker computation and real-time decision making.

1. INTRODUCTION

Artificial intelligence integrated with edge computing's small structural design has aided it by allowing a lot of data to be kept locally, eliminating the need to store it in a remote place and ensuring better decision-making. Additionally, by storing important data locally inside the building, AI lowers security risks by offering a secure repository. Edge Computing refers to the practice of processing data closer to the source of generation, i.e., at the "edge" of the network, instead of sending it to a centralized cloud or data center. This approach reduces latency, improves real-time processing, and enhances efficiency by minimizing the amount of data that needs to be transmitted to the cloud or central server.

Key features of edge computing include:

Decentralized Processing: Data is processed locally on devices (like IoT devices, routers, or edge servers) rather than in a centralized data center.
Reduced Latency: By processing data closer to where it's generated, edge computing minimizes the delay in data transmission and processing.
Improved Bandwidth Efficiency: Only relevant or processed data is sent to the cloud or central server, reducing bandwidth usage.
Enhanced Security: Sensitive data can be processed locally, reducing the risk of exposure during transmission.

Figure 1 illustrates the advantages of the AI-enhanced edge. By ensuring automated decision-making with very low latency, facilitating the seamless extraction of data from IoT-connected devices, and enabling real-time decision-making at the user end, edge computing is considered a promising architecture that has circumvented the cloud. Since its debut, artificial intelligence has been widely used in various applications and has led to an accurate and intelligent allocation of utilities. Our perception of the world is constantly evolving. Data from various sources, including social media, e-commerce websites, and personal information, is widely dispersed. For several reasons, we must retain and maintain this enormous amount of data.

Data may now be easily stored and retrieved at any time from any place thanks to cloud computing (Sarkar & Misra, 2016; Peter, 2015; Wang, Uehara, & Sasaki, 2015; Joseph, Kathrine, & Vijayan, 2014; Roschke, Cheng, & Meinel, 2009). Cloud computing has replaced conventional data storage methods for many enterprises. There are several cloud services that provide information storage. Ensuring the security of sensitive data stored in the cloud is the largest challenge. Several servers around the world store a vast amount of data. The vendors have the obligation for data protection (Varghese et al., 2014; Cooper et al., 2010; Deelman et al., 2015; Wolstencroft et al., 2013; Meurisch et al., 2015; Povedano-Molina et al., 2013). All edge computing are performed in figure 1.

Figure 1. Edge computing

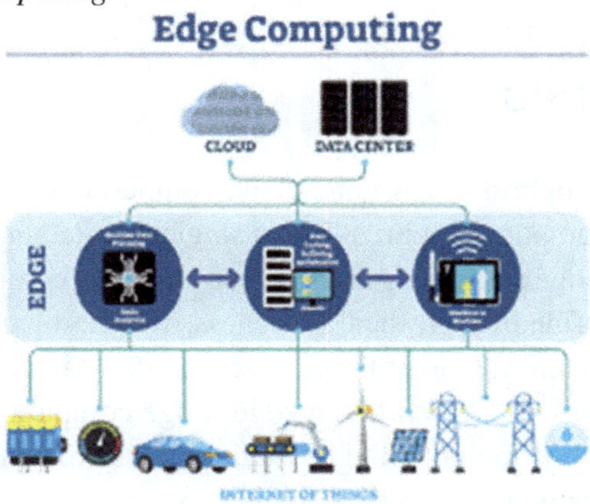

Wireless and mobile networks throughout the world are impacted by mobile device technology, such as laptops and smartphones. A growing number of applications are routinely loaded into mobile devices. Mobile devices have emerged as the most intuitive instruments for computing, multimedia creation and consumption, and human-computer connection. Mobile devices cannot handle computationally intensive tasks because of their small size, limited battery capacity, energy consumption, and latency (Eken, 2013; Tari, 2014; Charanya et al., 2013; Rawat et al., 2014; Evans, 2011). To solve this problem, a new idea called mobile edge computing (MEC) has surfaced. Multi-access edge computing (MEC) is the new name for it. This novel cloud computing paradigm offers low-latency service by relocating cloud resources closer to the network edge rather than a far-off central cloud data center (Kannadhasan & Deepa, 2020; Greenberg et al., 2008; Cuervo et al., 2010; Satyanarayanan et al., 2009; Kannadhasan, Isavani, & Karthikeyan, 2014). To put it another way, MEC has emerged as a workable strategy to enhance the present network architecture and reduce lengthy latency. The MEC concept, created by the European Telecommunications Standards Institute (ETSI), enables mobile users to take advantage of computational power offered by base stations (Bonomi et al., 2012; Varghese et al., 2016; Iosup et al., 2011). Since MEC is an extension of edge computing, some prior knowledge of it is necessary. Edge computing, which refers to data processing at the network's edge rather than in a data center or cloud, has emerged as a result of the Internet of Things' (IoT) growth, cloud services' popularity, and the introduction of 5G communication technologies. Edge computing is the term used to describe computer infrastructure located near data sources. Data generated by Internet of Things (IoT) devices may be processed closer to its source thanks to edge computing. As a consequence, businesses may evaluate data in real time (Chaves, Uriarte, & Westphall, 2011; Montes et al., 2013).

2. EDGE COMPUTING

Fog computing is a hybrid of edge and cloud computing that combines distributed and centralized computer resources into a single architecture. Fog computing, cloudlets, and mobile edge computing are a few types of edge computing technology. Edge computing is defined by physical closeness, which enhances survivability, trust, bandwidth, and latency. Even if the cloud changed data management, the next wave of that revolution will happen at the edge. Edge computing is necessary for edge processing to realize the potential of the industrial IoT. Cloud computing is made possible at the cellular network's edge via a network concept called mobile edge computing (MEC). The word "mobile edge computing" is formed from the phrase "edge of a network," which refers to the edge of a mobile network. It aids in fixing the issue of prolonged latency. It is the combination of cloud computing with mobile computing. The ultimate result is a groundbreaking design that brings cloud computing services to the network's edge. MEC is recognized as one of the essential components of 5G technology. It seeks to lessen network congestion by shifting processing duties closer to the cellular user. It is distinguished by its closeness, high bandwidth, low latency, and adaptable mobile service.

It provides mobile users with effective and widely available cloud services. Mobile network base stations and mobile edge servers are situated together at the mobile network's edge. One of the most important architectural and technical concepts for the 5G transition is mobile edge computing. MEC may provide a service environment with direct access to real-time network data, large bandwidth, and very low latency. There are many benefits to mobile edge computing (MEC) for system integrators and equipment providers. It lowers latency and puts cloud resources and services closer to users. Its objectives are to improve service delivery, reduce end-to-end latency, and improve user experience. Instead of using the cloud, MEC allows users to access services and resources on edge networks, which are closer to them. It drastically lowers the amount of energy that user equipment uses. Administrative rules and security issues, such as safe data storage, secure computing, network security, data privacy, use privacy, location privacy, and so on, are some of the difficulties MEC faces. The primary issue with MEC is service latency, which poses significant difficulties for live virtual machine (VM) migration. Users of traditional cloud computing often don't need high service latency. Resource provisioning in MEC is more difficult than in cloud computing. ETSI is currently developing MEC standards. Smart meters and microgrids are examples of network edge devices that can carry out energy load balancing applications. These devices automatically switch to renewable energy sources like wind and solar power depending on price, availability, and energy need. Fog collectors at the edge evaluate information from grid sensors and devices and provide the actuators control commands.

As shown in figure 2, they also filter data for local use while forwarding the rest to higher layers for transactional analytics, real-time reporting, and visualization. Fog permits semi-permanent storage at the top and ephemeral storage at the bottom. The cloud offers company information analytics and worldwide coverage. A video camera may instantaneously change streetlights to make room for an ambulance to pass through when it recognizes the vehicle's flashing lights. To detect bikes and pedestrians and to determine the speed and distance of approaching cars, smart streetlights interact with sensors on the ground. Intelligent lighting turns on when a sensor detects movement and turns off as traffic passes, as shown in Figure 3. In order to create a green traffic wave and provide warning signals to oncoming vehicles, nearby smart lights that double as fog devices cooperate. Along the highways are wireless access points, such as roadside units, WiFi, 3G, and smart traffic lights. The utility of this situation is extended by interactions between cars and vehicles and access points, and access points and access points. For following segments of theory of computation are generated with real time data processing in figure 2.

Figure 2. Theory of computation

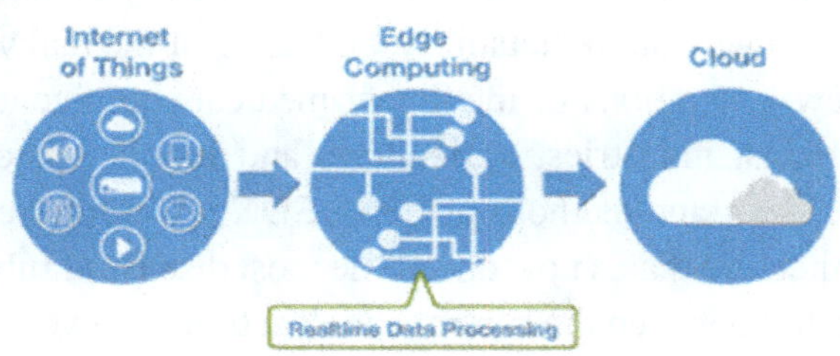

Traditional wireless sensor networks are insufficient for applications that need actuators to perform physical activities such as opening, shutting, or even moving sensors in addition to detecting and tracking. By creating a closed-loop system, actuators used as fog devices may regulate the measuring process, stability, and oscillatory behaviors. Apps may immediately alert the train operator to halt the train at the next station for emergency repairs and, in the case of self-maintaining trains, avert potential derailment. For example, sensor monitoring on a train's ball bearing may be able to recognize temperature levels. The sensors on lifesaving air vents monitor the air conditions entering and exiting mines, promptly adjusting the airflow if conditions become hazardous for miners. SDN is a cutting-edge computer and networking architecture that is now one of the most discussed subjects in the IT industry. It distinguishes between the control and data transfer levels.

Nodes follow the server's communication channel, and control is managed by a centralized server. The centralized server may need to be distributed. WLAN, wireless sensor, and mesh networks have all explored the SDN idea, but none of them take advantage of multihop wireless communication or multihop routing. Peer communication is also lacking in this scenario. By improving vehicle-to-vehicle communications with vehicle-to-infrastructure communications and centralized control, the SDN concept in combination with fog computing would solve the primary problems in vehicular networks, such as inconsistent connection, collisions, and high packet loss rate. Fog computing-based IoT and CPSs are growing in popularity.

The Internet of Things (IoT) is a network that may connect ordinary physical things with unique addresses, based on existing information carriers like the Internet and phone networks. There is a strong relationship between the computational and physical aspects of CPSs. Additionally, CPSs oversee technical and physical systems related to computers and information. By establishing new links between engineering systems, computer-based control and communication systems, and physical reality, IoT and CPSs have the potential to drastically alter our environment. In this instance, fog computing is based on embedded systems, which are processors and software programs built into devices for uses apart from processing. Toys, automobiles, medical equipment, and gadgets are examples of devices.

The objective is to combine the abstractions and accuracy of software and networking with the dynamism, unpredictability, and noise of the real world. We will be able to design new generations of intelligent medical equipment and systems, "smart roads," buildings, industries, agriculture, and robotic systems using the growing knowledge, ideas, and methods of CPSs. SDN is a cutting-edge computer and networking architecture that is now one of the most discussed subjects in the IT industry. It distinguishes between the control and data transfer levels. Nodes follow the server's communication channel, and control is managed by a centralized server. The centralized server may need to be distributed. WLAN, wireless sensor, and mesh networks have all explored the SDN idea, but none of them take advantage of multihop wireless communication or multihop routing. Peer communication is also lacking in this scenario. By improving vehicle-to-vehicle communications with vehicle-to-infrastructure communications and centralized control, the SDN concept in combination with fog computing would solve the primary problems in vehicular networks, such as inconsistent connection, collisions, and high packet loss rate.

Fog computing is a subset of cloud computing. Decentralized and heterogeneous devices make up this network edge platform. To manage and deliver IoT infrastructure, fogging or networking is used to administrate and provide a variety of services to devices via cloud service providers. Fog computing seeks to facilitate cloud computing by reducing the processing load. By using an automation controller to automate real-time devices, this computer architecture facilitates data analytics. The primary benefits of the fog computing platform are reduced resource usage, dispersed computing resources, and lowered latency. In a distributed and decentralized computer environment, a fog network is a wireless network of disparate systems, or fog nodes. Since this sensitive data is being sent over many fog nodes, its privacy needs to be safeguarded. We should implement appropriate security measures to ensure that only end users can access the service. Fog computing uses gateways to link several devices in a distributed setting. Hacking these fog nodes could jeopardize the security of the fog network. In the fog environment, a lot of work is being done to lower the energy consumption of fog nodes. IoT devices produce massive volumes of data, which energy-intensive fog networks handle. The significant use of IoT platforms in the fog network to connect to many heterogeneous devices for data processing and service delivery may cause scalability issues.

This platform needs a robust infrastructure to provide highly scalable services. Fog computing providers include fog customers and cloud or internet service providers. Complex fog computing architectures might emerge as a result of the fog network's adaptability. Data is the center of the world, and fog computing offers a range of services to interact with it. These services comprise network infrastructure, processing power, decision-making skills, and storage, including data processing and storage. As seen below, these benefits have resulted in a wide range of applications for fog computing infrastructure: The atmosphere of fog computing makes data transport simple. Cloud computers may become overloaded with real-time analytics, such as those used in manufacturing. Fogging facilitates the collection of copious amounts of data from diverse sensors, enabling prompt processing and action. There are several fog-enabled health monitoring tools used in the healthcare sector.

Using information from the patient information system, a fog network enables real-time forecasting of different patients' treatment needs. Patient data is collected using various technologies, including wearables, sensors, and equipment. We utilize numerous Internet of Things-capable wireless devices to assess medical data and take appropriate action. In the real world, edge computing uses similar sensors to monitor patient health data. The use of satellite data results in the best agricultural management strategies. Using GPS or any other worldwide monitoring technology, precision agriculture gathers and analyzes data to monitor a range of agricultural factors. Smart agriculture utilizes IoT technology to track and manage all agricultural processes, including crop growth monitoring. The fog computing paradigm enables these two agricultural techniques. Figure 6 depicts an IoT-enabled cloud-based fog computing healthcare system. The client module, the data filtering module, the data processing module, and the event handler module constitute the system. Sensors link the client module to an Internet of Things-enabled medical gadget. The client module is directly attached to the device. The client module collects the raw data and passes it to the data filtering module. Before the data is sent to the data processing module, it is filtered by the filtering module. The processing module processes the data before sending it to the event handler module. The event handler module raises the appropriate event and provides the client module with the relevant response based on the processed data. Taking the appropriate action is the actuator's duty.

3. VARIOUS SECTOR IN EDGE COMPUTING

Large volumes of information gathered from various devices, whether or not they are homogeneous, are referred to as big data. These devices might include traditional PCs, Internet of Things sensors, and traditional embedded devices. These vast amounts of data provide important knowledge and experience. These data are used for further analysis and information extraction, and they come in a range of forms and types. Additionally, these facts might be categorized as ambiguous, imprecise, or accurate. Data mining techniques and technologies are used to gather and analyze big data. One method for finding previously unidentified relevant data is data mining. Finding trends for IoT applications across verticals, including smart homes, smart cities, smart industries, and many more, is made easier by data mining on Big Data generated by Internet of Things sensors. Across a range of social networking sites and applications, it facilitates the identification and discovery of varied communities and organizations.

Among the most popular data mining methods are supervised learning and frequent pattern recognition. Pattern recognition enables us to identify frequently occurring data sets and their relationships in an Internet of Things context. A method for finding clusters of components that appear often in IoT domains and their connections is called pattern mining. A method for building models for categorization and prediction using pre-existing data is called supervised learning. Big Data analytics has revolutionized the field of information and communication technologies. The recent use of data analytics in organizations has significantly bolstered and expedited technological advancements throughout time. Client relationships and consumer-focused business applications are highly valued by most commercial enterprises. Cloud computing enables direct device contact, but only without the fog layer, which may require some time. In contrast, fog computing uses tiny, microscopic nodes to interface directly with devices and provide real-time information; however, cloud computing communicates with distant servers, which is why it takes longer.

Compared to cloud computing, fog computing is much smaller and has a lesser power and storage capacity. Fog computing employs millions of tiny nodes that are linked inside and outside of each other, while cloud computing uses fewer nodes. Cloud computing is better for long-term data analysis because it provides passive responses, whereas fog computing is better for short-term data analysis since it responds rapidly. While cloud computing depends on a limited number of nodes and must assess massive volumes of data, which causes delay, fog computing offers minimal latency due to the enormous number of nodes participating in data transmission. Cloud computing cannot even imagine handling data when the power supply is stopped, but fog computing is feasible using protocols like Bluetooth, Zigbee, and others, even in the event of a power outage. Because fog computing uses smaller nodes or end devices, it is thus a safer way to store data. Cloud computing, on the other hand, is not secure for data because it uses cloud sources that need a constant power source and take time. The amount and complexity of big data are expanding along with the number of IoT devices, making management more challenging. However, each method is not interchangeable since it has a different computing capability. Each big data center has its unique computing approach, just as every lock has its own key. The field of data analytics and computing has enormous promise since millions of data are mined every hour by different IoT devices worldwide. New avenues for research and analysis have been made possible by data analytics. To handle the enormous amounts of Big Data and associated analytics, many companies are investing in building their own computer capabilities. Therefore, a computer solution for data storage is necessary whether a business is data-driven or has an Internet of Things application. This is because data analytics may assist a business in understanding customer buying habits, consumer capability pools, market surveys, competitor strategies, and strategic marketing fronts. With cloud point of supply at its core, cloud computing is the way to go if they want to analyze data over time. On the other hand, consumers that need more intense user experiences and fast, real-time responsive calculating demands should adopt fog computing.

The Internet of Things (IoT), a collection of dispersed devices that automate monotonous operations and provide control via an easy-to-use mobile interface, is the next generation of computing. Many companies throughout the globe are using computer technology because it is the most efficient and cost-effective way to satisfy their demands. Many businesses across the globe are implementing the decentralization and distribution of computing capacity from a single mainframe to a network of computer nodes, such as a vast network of servers, to increase data processing and storage. Researchers have noted the potential of the growing number of Internet of Things (IoT) devices. Edge computing is the process of shifting network decentralization, processing capacity, and other services from a single hub to the device at the edge. Recently, the growth of the Internet of Things has been significantly aided by edge computing. It guarantees that data processing and storage take place on network edges, closer to Internet of Things users, rather than centralized locations and cloud servers. Therefore, by moving data, programs, and processing power closer to the user and away from integrated points, storage and power dispersion enhance performance.

Although edge computing enhances the efficiency of systems built with Internet of Things devices, servers and communication networks continue to experience significant stress. This is due to the fact that the first Internet of Things devices were made with little computing power to gather and send data as well as receive and execute instructions. Thus, processing and sending the massive amounts of data generated by millions of IoT apps places a significant strain on the infrastructure. Because data must be sent, analyzed by servers, and then directed, IoT applications also experience delays. Edge computing devices and edge computing-based Internet of Things devices and technologies are the two types of computing technology devices. Data management, sophisticated event processing, and artificial intelligence models are some of the key characteristics that set these systems apart, although the two organizations' products and capacities differ. Three tiers make up the edge computing architecture. IoT devices on the first level may utilize remote pooling methods to establish remote connections with each other before routing to edge servers.

The edge server platform, which serves as a gateway to network resources including processing and storage capacity, is the second tier. These settings reduce latency and increase load processing. The third level, where data processing and computation occur, is the infrastructure-based cloud. Furthermore, this level stores data produced by sensors and Internet of Things devices, which any device on the same level may access. It's crucial to keep in mind that the Internet of Things includes gadgets with constrained resources, such as wearable technology, sensors, and smartphones. Consequently, edge computing provides low latency, location, mobility support, and a wide geographic dispersion for IoT applications. Edge computing provides a setting where companies may operate in a restricted area by using local computing or a public or private cloud that requires a local security boundary. This diagram represents a modern edge computing architecture integrated with cloud platforms and 5G networks and it has following layers where top Layer is connected with cloud Platforms at the top and various cloud service providers are shown with

AWS, Azure, GCP, IBM, Alibaba other these represent public cloud platforms used for storage, computing, data analytics, etc in figure 3.

Figure 3. Various sectors of edge networks

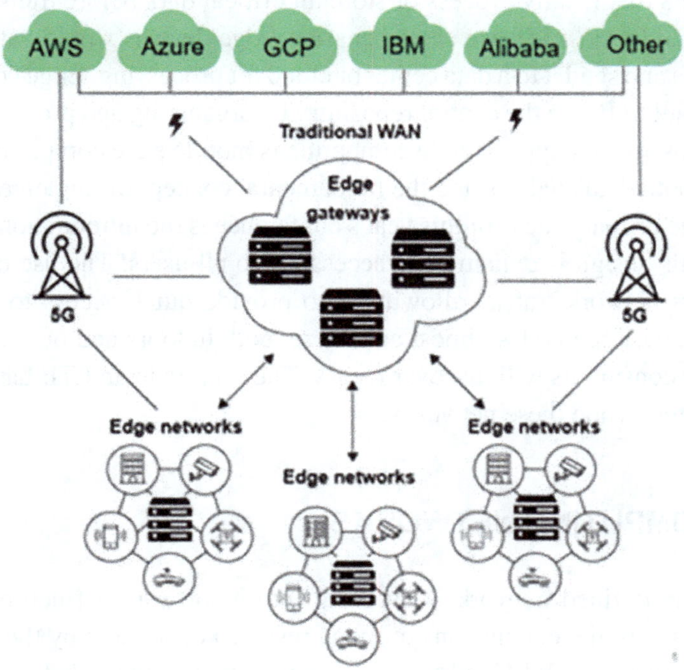

IoT simplifies and fully expresses the concept of connected objects on the physical internet as points of computation. This is used to ascertain their relationship. The devices in this radio access network interact with one another using sensor technologies. RFID is the most efficient form of communication and serves a vital purpose. Additionally, the network utilizes other technologies such as QR codes and wireless technology. IoT (internet of things) provides businesses and industries with physical data on the cloud. Businesses utilize this data for future products and services as well as for further processing. Figure 3 illustrates the three obstacles that every effort based on advanced technology or the Internet of Things (IoT) must overcome: technology, business, and society. Edge computing takes over computer applications by enhancing cloud computing platforms. The core nodes of the internet provide data and services to the outermost nodes, which connect to the outside world. Edge computing is a technique for processing power at a network's edge. Edge computing, which is based on the Internet of Things (IOT), has many advantages, including intelligent power generation, manufacturing, lighting, and traffic. The edge devices may also detect product defects, prevent component failure, and maximize productivity. Edge computing is closely connected to "fog computing," which involves processing data at the edge before sending it to the cloud. IDC, a research organization, defines edge computing as a mesh network of tiny data centers that locally process or store all critical data before transferring it to cloud storage. In most IoT use case scenarios, edge devices would gather large volumes of data and send it to a data center or cloud for processing. Edge computing reduces backhaul traffic to the central repository by organizing and processing data locally. The most diverse type of edge computing is mobile edge computing, which encompasses both data analysis and the fundamental concept of implementing 5G technology. The primary focus of this year's conference is the introduction of cloud computing. This design is dynamically accessible to all users. The use of several services lowers network traffic, allowing it to provide quick access to all of its clients. You can use the nodes almost anywhere, both indoors and outdoors. As a result, users or consumers will discover it easy. The servers in an LTE base station should be located inside these networks.

4. EDGE COMPUTING NETWORKS

The software-defined network is evolving into a software-defined exchange, which contrasts with the conclusions of much research conducted by the National Science Foundation. The MEC radio access network may potentially be accessible to other parties. Although software-defined exchange is responsible for implementing the internal department networking approach, the traditional software-defined network plan is an internal network connection. Software Defined Exchange aims to create intermediary linkages in the broad SDI sectors that have been purchased and adopted by several institutions, offering the same flexibility and usefulness advantages as Software Defined Network for a single network. Advanced functionality, including load balancing, utilization-specific peering, drive-through network operations, and DOS closure, will also be offered by Software Defined Exchange. If a software-defined network is implemented in an interval concept scheme, such as at a particular Internet Exchange Point, it could be feasible to recruit thousands of people without the need for expensive equipment.

Edge cloud implementation can be more challenging with the software-defined exchange strategy. How will the software-defined exchange in the advanced internet link function better for even more advantages and visual appeal, and how will the software-defined network in the regional edge cloud connection operate better under certain circumstances? There could be connections among broad, intriguing study topics. A key element of many cloud systems and frameworks will be encryption.

The advanced cloud edge is expected to be shown using a variety of approaches and a broad range of encryption mechanisms. Encryption involvement with all of the previous cloud operating modules (Virtual Machines Encryption) may initially be maintained due to the edge cloud's usage of the virtualization technique. Consequently, since edge cloud servers are hidden close to the customer's boundaries, they can be more vulnerable to natural aggressiveness. According to the previously indicated scenario, edge clouds may have encryption issues for new technologies such as software-defined networks, network function virtualization, and the Internet of Things. Figure 4 explains the core network as edge system and all segments are performed with area network so here we may see the entire network as connected components.

Figure 4. Edge computing networks

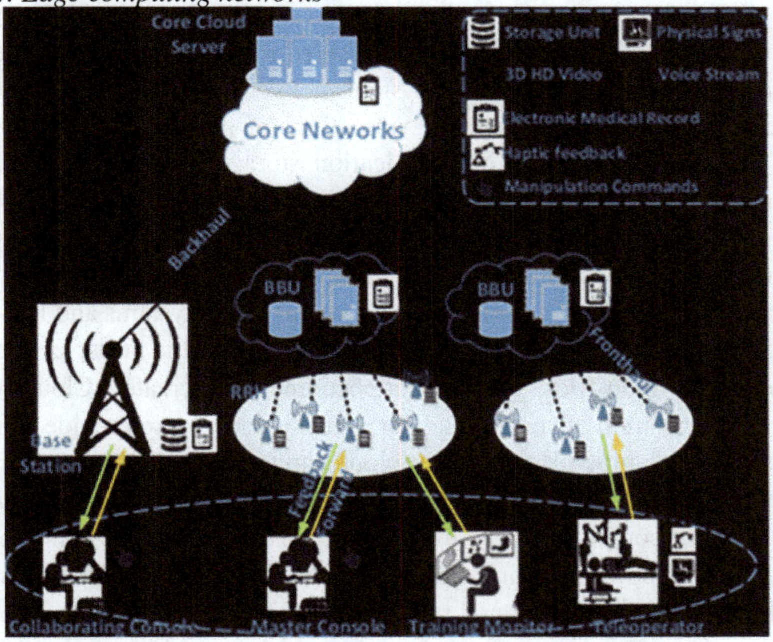

Interactions with these interfaces may lead to additional encryption issues, and the processes of active training and technology completion might share similar components. Fourth, as various implementations must account for implementation-stage encryption issues such as input entry, mutual service, and approximation operation confinement, they may function on edge cloud equalized frameworks. Lastly, software encryption will be criticized. It will be crucial to manage and keep an eye on high-risk admissions with a diverse clientele, even though advanced edge clouds will be more useful and the enlarged field will have access to large unapproved merchants to measure and provide. Because of the extensive connectivity of the internet, IoT technology makes a huge number of devices easily accessible. With cloud computing, users may access hardware and services remotely while maintaining third-party control. Webmail online commerce demands, social media trademarks, and internet stockpiling are all excellent examples. As long as a grid is continuously being created, this paradigm permits information to be consumed from anywhere, at any time. Data from various devices is gathered and dumped in different ways in regions of need, and from an application perspective, the articulation to take use of the expedient should be different. To communicate growing data, IoT services need to undergo a fundamental transformation. Two disadvantages of cloud paradigm networks are high latency and low quality of service. This programming is thus ineffective in handling the billions of data produced by geo-circulation IoT sensors and devices. The fog computing phenomenon, which exploits already connected IoT devices to scuttle at the edge of the network, was pioneered by Cisco. By manipulating the fog computing concept, several other systems get very close to identifying triable and large statistics. In contrast to cloud computing, fog provides a number of useful features, including client-server communication, storage, and geographical compilation across the system to enhance system quality. The fourth industrial revolution, or "Industry 4.0," refers to the disruptive paradigm of modern industrial production that is generated from information and communication technologies. To realize the fog computing concept in Industry 4.0 cyber-physical systems and IoT devices must be integrated. When cloud computing is paired with the massive volumes of data generated by industries, a significant phenomenon is created. Cloud software enables the cooperation of vertical and horizontal paradigms to provide efficiency, scalability, and flexibility. However, the cloud cannot meet all of the requirements for IoT-based installations. Cloud data centers and Internet of Things devices are connected via fog computing (FC). Although cloud computing has limitations with regard to latency, power, and location awareness, it is much more similar to IoT devices in terms of networking and storage capacities. From a remote data center, cloud computing offers internet-based services, including platforms, storage, and other resources. It offers benefits including flexibility, efficiency, opportunity, innovations, and cost savings on tangible resources. The cloud has various disadvantages even though it has numerous advantages for both customers and service providers. Businesses and end users no longer need to provide a lot of details thanks to cloud computing. This delight turns into an issue for latency-sensitive applications because nearby nodes need to meet their delay requirements. The round trip will take longer as a consequence. Furthermore, cloud computing is platform-dependent, has limited control and flexibility, lacks data security protocols, requires fast, reliable Internet connectivity, and has a limited capacity. Rising networking technologies that cloud computing cannot handle include the Internet of Things (IoT), mobile data networks, large dispersed Internet-linked sensor networks, and real-time streaming applications. Consequently, fog computing blends cloud computing with the Internet of Things. A new technology called cloud computing is giving IT systems greater flexibility and changing them. Cloud computing allows users to remotely save their data in the cloud. It is a method of computing that uses the internet to make resources, software, and shared data accessible whenever needed. This feature enables users to access cloud computing services at any time and from any suitable platform, including desktop and laptop computers, mobile computing platforms, and cell phones. It is a method of making all technology available to customers as a service at any time and from any location, including processing power, computer infrastructure, services, and applications. Therefore, it might be defined as a group of computers and servers connected via the Internet to form a network. Every sector has a unique set of security needs and controls. Customers and suppliers may lose control over their data as a result of this. Because providers are ignorant of the contents and security requirements of their infrastructure, consumers are unable to manage data. The main issue is data security since the data is stored on a third party; thus, standard security measures cannot be implemented directly. We might use cryptographic techniques in this scenario. Since data centers play such a significant role in fog computing, they collaborate to exchange data. The distributed protocols provide security. However, during an attack, it is impossible to identify either the attacker or the targeted file. The likelihood of success is higher for a highly traditional hostile attack, such as a man-in-the-middle attack. The entrances to the fog area can be phony. Communication between fog nodes and IoT devices would be challenging because of encryption and decryption, which would deplete mobile devices' batteries. One potential remedy is an intrusion detection system (IDS). In addition to producing log files that may be used to spot malicious activity, IDSs can be used to analyze and control access. These technologies can also identify port scanning and denial of service (DoS) attacks. Table 1 shows the year and number of paper publication as decided with core collection to the publication data and this study is finally one to one connected in edge computing.

Table 1. Number of papers published in edge computing

Year	Number of Papers Published					
	IEEE	IET	ELSEVIER	SPRINGER	WILEY	ACM
2015	30	55	20	60	30	10
2016	40	52	30	80	50	50
2017	50	60	46	120	70	20

continued on following page

Table 1. Continued

Year	Number of Papers Published					
	IEEE	IET	ELSEVIER	SPRINGER	WILEY	ACM
2018	55	70	50	140	80	35
2019	60	80	66	250	90	80
2020	65	85	98	150	120	25

Due to various research areas in edge computing and various journal publication in the year of 2015-2020 is shown in Table 1. This table also divided with the number of publications as IEEE, IET, Elsevier, Springer, Wiley and ACM publishers. This publication are the range from 2015 to 2020.

5. CONCLUSION

In an edge computing architecture, "edge" simply refers to the network's edge. Devices at the network's edge have a range of capabilities. At the edge, a cell phone might be utilized. At the network's edge, for example, a router could be used. Edge devices may temporarily analyze and store data before transferring it to the cloud for further processing and storage. An edge gateway facilitates communication between an edge and an edge device. Edge computing brings data processing power closer to the data source. In an edge computing system, the edge is a line that separates the core network from the rest of the network. It only serves as a conduit to connect the fog domain or cloud environment to the edge architecture. The devices used at the edge should be able to process and store data. It's possible that the real edge device is located far from the edge of the network.

The edge may normally be only a hop away from the primary edge device collecting the data, depending on reaction time and available bandwidth. Enhancing real-time applications' responsiveness and efficiency is the aim of edge computing architecture. The design places a high priority on lowering bandwidth consumption and latency. As is often the case, cloud-based capabilities may be included in the design even if cloud attributes are not typically included in the edge architectural model. The architecture is designed to link to cloud data datacenters for long-term data storage and other cloud-based services. The flexibility of the edge architecture allows for the addition of devices from a variety of heterogeneous environments and the provision of services closer to the devices.

REFERENCES

Bonomi, F., Milito, R., Zhu, J., & Addepalli, S. (2012). Fog computing and its role in the Internet of Things. In *Proceedings of the 1st MCC Workshop on Mobile Cloud Computing* (pp. 13–16). IEEE. DOI: 10.1145/2342509.2342513

Charanya, R., Aramudhan, M., Mohan, K., & Nithya, S. (2013). Levels of security issues in cloud computing. *IACSIT International Journal of Engineering and Technology*, *5*(2), 1912–1920.

Chaves, S. A. D., Uriarte, R. B., & Westphall, C. B. (2011). Toward an architecture for monitoring private clouds. *IEEE Communications Magazine*, *49*(12), 130–137. DOI: 10.1109/MCOM.2011.6094017

Cooper, F., Silberstein, A., Tam, E., Ramakrishnan, R., & Sears, R. (2010). Benchmarking cloud serving systems with YCSB. In *Proceedings of the ACM Symposium on Cloud Computing* (pp. 143–154). ACM. DOI: 10.1145/1807128.1807152

Cuervo, E., Balasubramanian, A., Cho, D.-K., Wolman, A., Saroiu, S., Chandra, R., & Bahl, P. (2010). MAUI: Making smartphones last longer with code offload. In *Proceedings of the 8th International Conference on Mobile Systems, Applications, and Services* (pp. 49–62). ACM. DOI: 10.1145/1814433.1814441

Deelman, K., Vahi, K., Juve, G., Rynge, M., Callaghan, S., Maechling, P. J., Mayani, R., Chen, W., Ferreira da Silva, R., Livny, M., & Wenger, K. (2015). Pegasus: A workflow management system for science automation. *Future Generation Computer Systems*, *46*, 17–35. DOI: 10.1016/j.future.2014.10.008

Evans, D. (2011). The Internet of Things: How the next evolution of the Internet is changing everything (CISCO White Paper, Vol. 1, pp. 1–11).

Greenberg, J., Hamilton, D. A., Maltz, D. A., & Patel, P. (2008). The cost of a cloud: Research problems in data center networks. *Computer Communication Review*, *39*(1), 68–73. DOI: 10.1145/1496091.1496103

Iosup, S., Ostermann, S., Yigitbasi, N., Prodan, R., Fahringer, T., & Epema, D. (2011). Performance analysis of cloud computing services for many-tasks scientific computing. *IEEE Transactions on Parallel and Distributed Systems*, *22*(6), 931–945. DOI: 10.1109/TPDS.2011.66

Joseph, O., Kathrine, J. W., & Vijayan, R. (2014). Cloud security mechanisms for data protection: A survey. *International Journal of Multimedia and Ubiquitous Engineering*, *9*(9), 81–90. DOI: 10.14257/ijmue.2014.9.9.09

Kannadhasan, S., & Deepa, S. (2020, April). Energy efficiency to improve network life time using particle swarm optimization algorithm. In *Proceedings of the International Conference on Communication, Computing, Storage & Energy (IC3SE-18)*. EAI Endorsed Transactions on Context-Aware Systems and Applications. DOI: 10.4108/eai.13-7-2018.163974

Kannadhasan, S., Isavani, M., & Karthikeyan, G. (2014). A novel privacy security protocol based SUPM method in near field communication technology. In *Artificial Intelligence and Evolutionary Algorithms in Engineering Systems (ICAEES 2014)*. Advances in Intelligent Systems and Computing. Springer.

Meurisch, A., Seeliger, B., Schmidt, I., Schweizer, F., Kaup, F., & Mühlhäuser, M. (2015). Upgrading wireless home routers for enabling large-scale deployment of cloudlets. In *Mobile Computing, Applications, and Services* (pp. 12–29). *(Publisher details needed.)* DOI: 10.1007/978-3-319-29003-4_2

Montes, J., Sánchez, A., Memishi, B., Pérez, M. S., & Antoniu, G. (2013). GMonE: A complete approach to cloud monitoring. *Future Generation Computer Systems, 29*(8), 2026–2040. DOI: 10.1016/j.future.2013.02.011

Peter, N. (2015). Fog computing and its real time applications. *International Journal of Emerging Technology and Advanced Engineering*, *5*(6), 266–269.

Povedano-Molina, J., Lopez-Vega, J. M., Lopez-Soler, J. M., Corradi, A., & Foschini, L. (2013). DARGOS: A highly adaptable and scalable monitoring architecture for multi-tenant clouds. *Future Generation Computer Systems*, *29*(8), 2041–2056. DOI: 10.1016/j.future.2013.04.022

Rawat, N., Srivastava, R., Pandey, B. K., Rawat, P., Singh, S., & Sharma, A. (2014). Data security issues in cloud computing. *Open Journal of Mobile Computing and Cloud Computing*, *1*, 9–17.

Roschke, S., Cheng, F., & Meinel, C. (2009). Intrusion detection in the cloud. In *2009 Eighth IEEE International Conference on Dependable, Autonomic and Secure Computing (DASC'09)*. IEEE. Eken, H. (2013). Security threats and solutions in cloud computing. In *2013 World Congress on Internet Security (WorldCIS)*. IEEE.

Sarkar, S., & Misra, S. (2016). Theoretical modelling of fog computing: A green computing paradigm to support IoT applications. *IET Networks*, *5*(2), 23–29. DOI: 10.1049/iet-net.2015.0034

Satyanarayanan, M., Bahl, P., Cáceres, R., & Davies, N. (2009). The case for VM-based cloudlets in mobile computing. *IEEE Pervasive Computing*, *8*(4), 14–23. DOI: 10.1109/MPRV.2009.82

Tari, Z. (2014). Security and privacy in cloud computing. *IEEE Cloud Computing, 1*(1), 54–57. DOI: 10.1109/MCC.2014.20

Varghese, L., Subba, L., Thai, L., & Barker, A. (2016). DocLite: A Docker-based lightweight cloud benchmarking tool. In *Proceedings of the IEEE/ACM International Symposium on Cluster, Cloud and Grid Computing*. IEEE. DOI: 10.1109/CCGrid.2016.14

Varghese, O., Akgun, I., Miguel, L., Thai, L., & Barker, A. (2014). Cloud benchmarking for performance. In *Proceedings of the IEEE International Conference on Cloud Computing Technology and Science* (pp. 535–540). IEEE.

Wang, Y., Uehara, T., & Sasaki, R. (2015). Fog computing: Issues and challenges in security and forensics. In *2015 IEEE 39th Annual Computer Software and Applications Conference (COMPSAC)* (Vol. 3, pp. 53–59). IEEE.

Wolstencroft, K., Haines, R., Fellows, D., Williams, A. R., Withers, D., Owen, S., … Goble, C. A. (2013). The Taverna workflow suite: Designing and executing workflows of web services on the desktop, web, or in the cloud. Nucleic acids research, 41(W1), W557-W561.

ADDITIONAL READING

Alamin, K. S. S., Chen, Y., Macii, E., Poncino, M., & Vinco, S. (2025). Advancing electric vehicle battery management: A data-driven digital twin approach for real-time monitoring and performance enhancement. *IEEE Transactions on Vehicular Technology*, 1–15. DOI: 10.1109/TVT.2025.3565907

Assaf, G., & Assaad, R. H. (2024). A data-driven decision-support tool for selecting the optimal project delivery method for bundled projects: Integrating machine learning and expert domain knowledge. *Journal of Construction Engineering and Management, 150*(12), 04024181. DOI: 10.1061/JCEMD4.COENG-15116

Azzaakiyyah, H. K., & Rijal, S. (2025). Integration of discount strategies, digital promotion, and customer engagement in enhancing MSME competitiveness in the e-commerce ecosystem during Ramadan. [TACIT]. *Technology and Society Perspectives, 3*(1), 330–337.

Chandrasekaran, V. (n.d.). Optimizing product recommendations: A framework for personalized bundling in e-commerce. *(Publication details needed.)*

Chen, L. (2025). Free sampling, bundling, and digital formatting: Exploring strategy effects of digital goods retailers. *Journal of Theoretical and Applied Electronic Commerce Research, 20*(1), 11. DOI: 10.3390/jtaer20010011

Fahad, M., & Bektas, N. (2025). Data-driven pavement performance: Machine learning-based predictive models. *Applied Sciences (Basel, Switzerland), 15*(7), 3889. DOI: 10.3390/app15073889

Gensler, S., & Rangaswamy, A. (2025). An emerging future for digital marketing: From products and services to sequenced solutions. *Journal of Business Research, 190*, 115230. DOI: 10.1016/j.jbusres.2025.115230

Hung, I. Y., Simonson, T., Jevsevar, D. S., & Kain, Z. N. (2025). Basics of orthopaedic commercial and government bundling. *The Journal of Arthroplasty, 40*(2), 259–262. DOI: 10.1016/j.arth.2024.11.025 PMID: 39551403

Khan, W. U. (2025). Saudi Arabia's cloud broadband landscape: Opportunities and challenges in the era of Vision 2030. *Journal of Business and Management Studies, 7*(1), 259–262. DOI: 10.32996/jbms.2025.7.1.20

Kim, I., Choi, J. H., Jang, H., Kim, N. Y., Park, J. H., Lee, H. J., Cheon, S.-H., Oh, E.-S., Yoon, K. R., Kim, J., Yoo, J.-K., Han, Y.-J., Oh, P., & Jung, J. W. (2025). Troubleshooting carbon nanotube bundling using electrostatic energy-driven dispersion for $LiFePO_4$ bimodal thick electrode in lithium-ion batteries. *ACS Nano, 19*(16), 15941–15952. DOI: 10.1021/acsnano.5c01892 PMID: 40249366

Militão, A. M., Ho, C. Q., & Nelson, J. D. (2025). Mobility-as-a-service and travel behaviour change: How multimodal bundles reshape our travel choices. *Transportation Research Part A, Policy and Practice, 191*, 104310. DOI: 10.1016/j.tra.2024.104310

Mo, J., Dong, X., Xu, Y., Xu, A., Yu, Y., & Yang, M. (2025). Research on fast prediction of boiling flow parameters in rod bundle of NPP based on efficient CFD-ROM methods. *Progress in Nuclear Energy, 184*, 105723. DOI: 10.1016/j.pnucene.2025.105723

Subramanian, B., Mishra, A., Bharathi, V. R., Mandala, G., Kathamuthu, N. D., & Srithar, S. (2025). Big data and fuzzy logic for demand forecasting in supply chain management: A data-driven approach. *Journal of Fuzzy Extension and Applications, 6*(2), 260–283.

Visharad, I., Kayal, P., & Maiti, M. (2025). Data-driven insights from technical indicators to predict the stablecoins price. *Finance Research Open, 1*(2), 100011. DOI: 10.1016/j.finr.2025.100011

Xu, Y., Dong, X., Xu, A., Mo, J., Liu, Y., & Yang, M. (2025). Research on the prediction of transient parameters in rod bundle channel based on POD-ML method. *Progress in Nuclear Energy*, *187*, 105832. DOI: 10.1016/j.pnucene.2025.105832

Zhao, C., Cheng, J., Yang, W., Lei, S., Sun, H., Guo, X., & Yang, H. (2025). Data-driven evaluation and prediction of the gas-fired boiler performance under the impact of fine desulphurization gas. *Applied Thermal Engineering*, *272*, 126459. DOI: 10.1016/j.applthermaleng.2025.126459

Chapter 14
Strategies for Development, Scalability, and Maintenance of Medical Device Integration Systems: A Comprehensive Guide

Sanjay Kumar
https://orcid.org/0000-0002-0774-2889
Galgotias College of Engineering and Technology, Greater Noida, India

Vivek Agarwal
Galgotias College of Engineering and Technology, Greater Noida, India

Kuldeep Singh Kashwan
Galgotias University, India

Naresh Kumar
G.L. Bajaj Institute of Technology and Management, India

ABSTRACT

Medical device integration systems interconnect medical devices and systems smoothly and automatically, changing the applications of the modern medical world. This chapter, "Strategies for Development, Scalability, and Maintenance of Medical Device Integration Systems: A Comprehensive Guide, Delving into key aspects for the scaling and look of the chapter begin from the fundamental concepts of MDIS and the role that real-time plays in getting information into data then develop

DOI: 10.4018/979-8-3373-1147-0.ch014

system improvements on technical system systems including IoT, cloud computing and standardized communication protocols for instance, HL7 and FHIR together with long-term successful sustainability on compliance and device management collectively is guaranteed by scalable, sustainable MDISs and discussed modular system architectures. Cloud Native Design, Load-Balancing Techniques Maintenance strategies building integrated cybersecurity management and legacy systems. Finally, they come with ethical, legal, and regulatory considerations that ensure patients are protected in terms of safety and data security.

1. INTRODUCTION

Technology has always played at the heart of efficient accurate and patient-centered care deliveries in this fast-changing world that is modern healthcare. These include, among other devices, Medical Device Integration System (MDIS) designed to communicate and transfer relevant data between different varieties of medical devices and Hospital's information systems. Improvements in operational efficiency, diagnostics without errors, and support of various clinical decisions are considered quite crucial (Amutha, 2023). This is titled "Strategies for Development, Scalability, and Maintenance of Medical Device Integration Systems: A Comprehensive Guide" and explores the foundational aspects or strategic approaches that could define the development, scalability, and maintenance of MDIS in meeting changing needs in a healthcare environment.

1.1 The Role and Importance of Medical Device Integration Systems

These integration systems are very important for integrating isolated medical devices into even broader networks in health information. Infusion pumps, ventilators, electrocardiograms, and other patient monitoring systems that were independent units before, were now connected by MDIS for centralization and interoperability in one coherent system (Gatouillat et al., 2018). MDIS aggregates data from various sources, normalizes them into a common format, and presents them to health providers, enabling fast, well-informed decision making, which consequently reduces errors and improves patient outcomes.

MDIS is thereby becoming a solution for such complexity and scale of modern healthcare requirements, creating exponentially growing patient data with real-time access to that data (Niyonambaza, Zennaro, & Uwitonze, 2020). These systems support clinical workflows and provide a sound infrastructure that supports advances like telemedicine, wearable devices, artificial intelligence, etc. This would ensure future-readiness in a healthcare environment that can address various medical challenges.

1.2 Key Components of MDIS

Core systems that many medical device integration systems rely on to get things done include:

Hardware and Software Infrastructure: MDIS needs hardware devices and complex software systems that enable communication and process data.
Standards Communication protocols Some of these standards are HL7- Health Level Seven, FHIR - Fast Healthcare Interoperability Resources, DICOM for interoperability in devices.
Interoperability frameworks could be a good source of compatibility across devices and systems of other manufacturers (Ramadan, Abu-Ghaleb, & El-Brawany, 2023).
Data Security Mechanisms: The organization employs encryption, access controls, and all applicable laws involving data protection to protect confidential patient data.

1.3 Challenges in MDIS Implementation

Although the benefits of MDIS are extremely valuable, a major challenge is installation because achieving interoperability among all the available devices from a single manufacturer using proprietary protocols inhibits device interoperability, imposes regulatory burdens, the fear of insecurity, and expensive costs of their deployment and upkeep as challenges requiring strategic planning and emphasis in design methodologies as regards scalability and maintainability (Khelili et al., 2022).

1.4 The Need for Scalability in MDIS

Scalability is a more fundamental dimension of sustainable MDIS. As healthcare institutions grow and patient data multiplies, there must be ability to scale it efficiently; otherwise, everything remains the same. A lot of device support, massive increased data loads, and all expansive functionalities mean that MDISs still have high performance and reliability. All in all, cloud-based solutions as well as modular architectures used in different system designs are ways on how scaling is achieved in MDIS.

1.5 Maintenance: The Lifeline of MDIS

Once implemented, the quality of maintenance strategies will also dictate the lifespan and reliability of MDIS. Real-time monitoring, predictive maintenance that is AI and ML-based, and updating will also have significant importance in maintaining performance as well as minimizing downtime (Taylor et al., 2016). The other major factors influencing relevance will be the threat of cybersecurity of systems, managing legacy integration, and adapting to a technologically advancing system.

1.6 Ethical and Legal Requirements

MDIS functions in an environment of extremely high stakes. Patient safety, data privacy, and rigorous requirements of regulatory compliance, namely ISO 13485 FDA, and IEC 62304, are vital to be followed once the medical devices are intended to integrate into the entire system. Equal access and reduction of bias in designing the technological system also forms a significant pillar for the successful implementation of MDIS.

1.7 New Trends and Innovations in MDIS

MDIS, therefore stands well-positioned to embrace the next innovative generations that promote functionality and scalability. Predictive diagnostics and smart system monitoring are increasingly becoming activities through artificial intelligence and machine learning. Increased block chain technology also comes forth as a promising solution to the secured data exchange and audit trails (Singh, Lopez, & Ramadan, 2023). This is because its integration with wearable devices, telemedicine platforms, and remote patient monitoring systems expands the boundary of health care delivery while making it accessible and efficient.

1.8 Purpose and Scope of This Chapter

This chapter will provide a holistic view on strategies involved with MDIS development, scaling, and sustaining systems. From foundation principles of MDIS, the chapter unravels system development technologies and methodologies that will lead the discussion to strategies meant at achieving scalability, overcoming challenges in system maintenance, and some more practical issues. The approach is practical and applied but by case studies. The paper deals with ethical, legal, and regulatory issues in relation to holistic design and implementation of the systems. In addition to that, the final chapter discusses trends and innovations, which are transforming the future landscape of medical device integration.

2. UNDERSTANDING MEDICAL DEVICE INTEGRATION SYSTEMS

MDIS is at the heart of the latest innovation in health care, providing services that would connect to clinical devices, making it possible to have communication seamlessly. This section defines their relevance and potential by moderating the power and health-related MDIS.

1. Definition and Scope of MDIS

Medical device integration systems are the technological frameworks designed to interconnect and allow communication to be established between different medical devices, and health care information systems allowing for real-time exchange, aggregation, and analysis of data originated from heterogeneous devices to ensure appropriate patient information automatically without any medical device integration (Shafiq et al., 2023).

The scope of MDIS falls within an enormous array of applications:

Inpatient Settings: Bedside monitors, infusion pumps, and ventilators are integrated with a hospital's central information system.
Outpatient and telemedicine applications: Enable Remote care through wearables as well as Home-based devices.
Research and Analytics: Facilitates the collection of data for high-end analytics, clinical trials, and machine learning in healthcare.

An MDIS is much more than just information transfer; it is control of a device, systems monitoring, and compliance reporting so that it is impossible to neglect in modern health care.

2. Core Features of Integration Systems

What makes MDIS work is that they allow the fusion of various components and functionalities that make up a single platform? Some major features are:

a. Interoperability:

MDIS makes possible seamless, manufacturer-to-manufacturer, equipment-to-equipment communication using standardized protocols. It includes the following:

Health Level Seven (HL7) - clinical data exchange.

Fast Healthcare Interoperability Resources (FHIR): Web Integration DICOM Digital Imaging and Communications in Medicine; used for medical image data.

b. Data Exchange in Real-Time:

All these systems collect and present in real-time so do away with delay in decision-making about in such clinical areas. For instance, real-time monitoring ICUs send the vital signs directly to EHR and are reviewed directly.

c. Scalability:

They are supposed to accommodate more gadgets and files in a building or innovative technology for hospitals. Modular designs and as-well-as cloud-based solutions have scalability within them.

d. Strong Security

Patient Information is the core of MDIS encryption, authentication, and access control for protected data.

e. Centralized Control and Monitoring

These devices on one dashboard monitor and control-and solve problems with-connected. So, the efficiency of the operation can be improved.

f. Analytics and Predictive Insights

The integrated systems almost entirely depend on AI and machine learning application that can help in identifying health risks pattern and predict it by optimized clinical workflows.

3. Relevance in Healthcare

MDIS has redefined health care delivery by integrating medical devices, addressing many inefficiencies traditionally assumed to exist while creating space for the advancement of medical practices.

a. Better Clinical Results

MDIS provide clinicians the real-time, accurate, and complete information for decisions to be based upon. For instance, a patient monitor can be integrated into an alarm management system that automatically informs the clinician about deteriorating conditions (Drăgulinescu et al., 2020).

Operational efficiency:

MDIS reduces the traditional documentation process and captures data automatically. Health professionals will spend more time caring for patients under this scenario.

c. Greater Co-operation

This has further allowed multidisciplinary teams to work together, thereby making a more coordinated approach possible for patient management.

d. Innovation for New Models of Care

It enables MDIS to integrate with telehealth platforms and remote patient monitoring systems by incorporating wearable technologies to accommodate personal, home-based care. It supports chronic disease management and facilitates better access within underserved or rural regions (Daniel, 2023).

e. Data-Driven Healthcare:

Information that MDIS collects and analyzes can help to have evidence for practice, research, and innovative therapies. Real-time data analytics can prevent or predict care occurring less often with reduced rates of hospital readmission hence improving health care quality.

f. Regulatory and compliance benefits

MDIS helps determine compliance with the law of data protection like HIPAA and GDPR by proper records, an audit trail generation, and compliance.

Integration of medical devices is not a luxury but a necessity for providing health care. The role of connecting devices, improving efficiency in operations, and improving the patient outcome is the greatest promise that MDIS might bring in shaping the future of healthcare delivery (Manchadi, Ben-Bouazza, & Jioudi, 2023). As MDIS continue to grow, they are indeed ready to transform the mode of healthcare delivery by assuring that technology and care of patients do not function in silos.

3. DEVELOPMENT OF MEDICAL DEVICE INTEGRATION SYSTEMS

Development of Medical Device Integration Systems is a complex and multilevel process that is required to be planned meticulously, with advanced technical infrastructures and effective methodologies. Therefore, the success of MDIS depends on challenges associated with integration, networking, regulation, and adherence to compliance in addition to robust performance, flexibility in key aspects during the development of MDIS is assured during this phase (Levina et al., 2022). The activities and design of research, including the technical foundation, methods and challenges, are ongoing.

1. Planning and Design

The popularity of MDIS inspires effective planning and planning. This phase involves learning the needs of the program, defining the dreams, and ensuring that they align with the exercise side of the enterprise.

A. Identifying desires:

Interconnection requirements: Identify devices and systems to be connected, ensure they have a common view of a common interface, and HL7, FHIR, and DICOM.
Scalability: Planning for future growth, accounting for increasing numbers of devices, records processing desires, and integrating rising technologies.
Security and Compliance: Include processes for protective sensitive patient information to comply with guidelines which include HIPAA and GDPR.

B. Resource Considerations:

Involve physicians, biotechnologists, and IT professionals within the device to ensure the gadget meets realistic healthcare needs. It has intuitive user interfaces and a easy workflow.

C. Legal Considerations:

Compliance requirements can be met at the development stage itself, such as following FDA recommendations for medical software; standards followed may include ISO 13485 and IEC 62304.

D. Materials

Hardware upgrading, optimization of the network, and cloud migration of MDIS are in their near future.

2. Technical foundation

The choice of technology impacts the performance and sustainability of the MDIS. Latest generation infrastructure allows for dependable conversation, records processing and gadget management.

A. Internet of Things (IoT):

IoT is the back bone of MDIS as it connects gadgets with a steady network and facilitates real-time information trading. Sensors, gateways, and middleware solutions are important add-ons.

B. Cloud Computing:

Scalable, flexible, and save cost Cloud-based architectures have big data storage, analytics, and remote access to enable disaster recovery solutions

C. Edge Computing:

For latency-sensitive applications, edge computing directs information closer to the source, reducing significant latency in critical healthcare environments starting from the ICU.

D. Communication Strategy:

Standardized protocols help to work on heterogeneous devices.

HL7, FHIR: Improves communication and communication of patient medical records.
DICOM: Assists in camera and system integration
MQTT and CoAP: Light weight protocols for conversations in IoT devices

E. Artificial Intelligence and Systems Learning (AI/ML):a. Contact facts:

Medical devices of big manufacturers normally have proprietary protocols, making complicated the discussion and integration processes.

B. Compliance Rules:

A complex regulatory environment demands that there is constant innovation for the changing requirements and avoiding the consequences of non-compliance.

C. Cyber Security Risks:

Connecting multiple gadgets will increase the assault floor, making the gadget susceptible to cyber threats consisting of ransomware and facts breaches

D Legacy machine integration:

Many healthcare facilities use legacy systems which are incompatible with modern MDIS, accordingly requiring high-priced enhancements or custom answers.

E. High cost of development:

The cost for developing, deploying, and maintenance of an MDIS generally remains high, especially with small health care organizations and facilities found in resource-poor nations.

F. Lack of standards:

Although there are lives of requirements such as HL7 and FHIR, the lack of adoption of standard causes inconsistency, thereby impeding interoperability.

G. Scalability issues:

Systems typically have successfully tolerated scaling problems in support of the growth in volume of machine networks and data that occur without loss of performance.

H Stakeholder formation:. It becomes very difficult to align goals for various stakeholders, ranging from manufacturers of devices through health care providers to regulatory companies.

3. Scalability of scientific tool integration systems

Scalability is valuable to the layout and oversight of medical tool integration systems (MDIS) to make certain flexibility and growth in reaction to growing needs in this phase, the idea of scalability, migration strategies accessibility, real-global case research, and availability.

1. What is Scalability in MDIS?

Scalability in the context of MDIS refers to the system's ability to handle an increasing number of devices, process larger volumes of data, and integrate advanced functionalities without compromising performance or reliability (Gupta et al., 2024). Scalable MDIS are designed to evolve alongside healthcare organizations, accommodating expansions such as new facilities, emerging technologies, and rising patient loads.

Scalability is important for the longevity of MDIS, as the healthcare environment is dynamic and subject to rapid technological and operational change. Scalable MDIS ensures that:

Good interface with other medical devices.
Seamless data flow even during peak usage.
In cost-effective system renewal expansion.

Future-readiness to face the innovative health care services, which involve telemedicine and AI prediction.

2. Innovative methods

MDIS Scaling up requires top planning, clean programming, and availability of already existing era. The most outstanding procedures include:

a. Modular Architecture:

Components that can be easily assembled or disassembled as modules with no effect on the whole machine. A new device interface may be introduced as a module without testing the whole device views

b. Cloud-based services:

Storage and inventory will increase and decrease due to cloud computing while there may be demand or drops in demand. The platforms provide remote access and exchange with banks.

c. Load balancing:

The load balancers distribute the data traffic evenly across the servers. This increases productivity, especially when the demand is high. This is very crucial in large hospitals with several interconnected devices.

d. Protocols in place were standard.

This prevents the aggressive use of standards such as HL7, FHIR, and DICOM to add new devices and systems without a standardized solution, which sometimes limits scalability. Edge Computing:

Edge computing will add the benefits of data processing locally at the device level or gateway level, cutting latency and reducing bandwidth requirements Areas that rely on high levels of real-time data, such as the ICU, will help scalability.

4. BARRIERS TO SCALABILITY

Despite the benefits of scalable MDIS, several barriers can impede their implementation:

a. Legacy Systems:

Many healthcare facilities rely on outdated systems that are incompatible with modern scalable architectures. Integrating these systems can be time-consuming and expensive.

b. High Costs:

Developing scalable MDIS involves significant initial investment in infrastructure, technologies, and skilled personnel, which may be prohibitive for smaller facilities.

c. Lack of Standardization:

Proprietary protocols and non-standardized device interfaces complicate integration and limit the system's ability to scale seamlessly.

d. Data Security Concerns:

As systems scale, the risk of cybersecurity breaches increases, requiring robust security measures that can add complexity and cost.

e. Bandwidth and Latency Issues:

In expansive healthcare systems, heightened data traffic may burden network bandwidth, causing latency issues and diminishing system performance.

f. Stakeholder Pushback:

Opposition from clinicians, administrators, or IT personnel due to concerns about complexity or potential disruptions during scaling can postpone implementation.

g. Compliance Rules:

When MDIS enters new regions or countries, different regulatory requirements may create compliance difficulties, slowing down advancement.

h. Lack of Qualified Manpower:

The lack of specialists who can build and maintain scalable MDIS may hinder the implementation of state-of-the-art systems.

Scalability in MDIS is essential for meeting the rising demands of healthcare environments. By employing strategic approaches and learning from successful examples, healthcare organizations can tackle scalability challenges and fully realize the advantages of these systems for enhanced patient care and operational efficiency (Adil et al., 2022).

3. Maintenance Strategies for Medical Device Integration Systems

It is crucial to maintain medical device integration systems (MDIS) in order to continue their long-term functionality and dependability and keep in mind the changing requirements of health care, as these are the backbone of modern healthcare delivery. Thus, effective maintenance approaches would ensure zero downtime, improved patient safety, and better operational efficiency (Ahad, Tahir, & Yau, 2019). This section deals with importance, types, and best practice recommended for challenges and recent innovations that are changing MDIS management.

1. **The need for maintenance**

Maintenance is part of the MDIS implementation which will ensure the smooth run of the system in an ever-changing health environment. The importance of resolution in MDIS can be summarized as follows.

System reliability: Regular maintenance reduces the risk of device integration failure, ensuring constant data exchange and availability.
Patient Safety: A well-maintained system reduces the chances of errors such as incorrect data transfer or equipment malfunctions, which can compromise patient care.
Compliance: Maintenance ensures compliance with regulations such as HIPAA, GDPR, FDA guidelines, avoiding fines and reputational damage.
Operational efficiency: By preventing downtime and managing issues more efficiently, maintenance helps health care providers be more productive.
Cost effectiveness: Preventive maintenance reduces the need for emergency repairs and costly system changes.
2 Previous Security Policy:

The use of analytics and AI to anticipate potential issues, enable timely intervention. For example, monitoring system logs to identify patterns that could indicate an impending failure.

Emergency Maintenance:
Take prompt actions to correct serious system problems or failures that jeopardize patient care or staff productivity.

3. Best Practices

Best practices adopted will ensure smooth and efficient management of MDIS:

Routine Schedule Review:
Regular checks to find out the health of the system, its weaknesses and whether all the parts are healthy.
Documentation and follow up:
Record maintenance activities including updates, performance considerations and maintenance to guide future activities.
Real-time analysis
Monitor overall performance with monitoring gear that could come across anomalies in real-time and alert for fast protection.

D. Staff Training:

Train IT groups and physicians to display brief-time period occasions, pick out system adjustments, and pick out any capacity caution symptoms earlier than device failure happens.

E. Backup and Recovery:

Implement records backup and recuperation systems with sturdy guidelines to save you information loss all through protection or surprising failures.

F. Vendor reports:

Contact equipment manufacturers and software developers for technical support, updates, and training materials.

g. Compliance measures:

Add compliance to the list of maintenance tasks to ensure that the system stays compliant.

h. Post-test update:

Perform thorough testing after updates or maintenance so that all integration and functionality are the same.

4. Maintenance challenges

Several challenges can be seen despite best practices in MDIS monitoring:

a. Strong Communication:

Technical challenges might arise in keeping devices and protocol developers communicating seamlessly.

b. Property Planning:

The older systems may not be compatible with modern or upgraded maintenance equipment, thus demanding expensive custom solutions.

c. Cyber Security Threats:

The security of the process of upgrade or repair is critical as the process might reveal the vulnerabilities.

d. Higher costs:

Predictive and adaptive methods are resource-intensive, thus posing a financial burden on small buildings.

e. A few skilled workers:

Lack of trained personnel in MDIS maintenance can lead to delays in resolving issues or implementing updates.

f. Dangers of leisure time:

Planned maintenance can temporarily disrupt business processes and impact patient care if care is not taken.

g. Rules developed:

Staying abreast of changing healthcare regulations and ensuring compliance through maintenance requires constant vigilance.

5. Innovation in maintenance

Emerging technologies and new techniques are changing the way MDIS is managed, making it more efficient and effective:

a. Artificial Intelligence (AI):

AI-based predictive maintenance tools analyze large amounts of system data to predict problems, enabling faster intervention.

b. Internet of Things (IoT):

IoT-enabled sensors embedded in devices provide real-time information on performance metrics, facilitating monitoring and troubleshooting.

c. Digital Twins:

A virtualized MDIS enables maintenance personnel to simulate and test changes in the real systems before making any changes, thereby decreasing the risks.

d. Remote Maintenance Solution:

Remote inspection, update, and repair with cloud-based platforms that have reduced the need for on-site intervention.

e. Blockchain compliance:

Block chain technology assures that the records of the maintenance activities are secure and unalterable and aid in regulatory audits and verification of compliance.

f. Automatic patch application:

Automation tools make software patch application easy, cut down human error, and speed up the update.

g. Augmented Reality (AR):

AR-based tools help engineers with repairing complex objects overlaying instructions and design patterns in real time.

5. ETHICAL, LEGAL, LEGAL CONSIDERATIONS

Effective coordination of the ethical, legal, and regulatory frameworks that control the development, operation, and maintenance of integrated medical device systems (MDIS) These considerations will ensure that MDIS is safe, reliable, and in accordance with global health standards (Mahfoud, El Barkany, & El Biyaali, 2016). This section elaborates on the legal framework, ethical concerns, and legal challenges concerning MDIS.

5.1. Legislative Framework

The regulatory policies ensure that MDIS meets the security, performance, and data protection standards. These regulations vary from region to region but have the same goals of patient safety, system reliability, and data integrity.

a. International Standards

Several international standards govern MDIS design, operation and maintenance:

ISO 13485: Specifies requirements for quality control systems in the design and manufacture of medical devices.

IEC 62304: Provides a framework for the development of medical device software, ensuring safety and performance.

ISO 14971: focuses on risk management in the manufacture and use of medical devices.

HL7 and FHIR: Ensure communication and data exchange standards between devices and health systems.

b. Regional Laws

There are specific regulations in various areas for MDIS compliance with local health care systems:

United States: The Food and Drug Administration (FDA) regulates MDIS under the Federal Food, Drug and Cosmetic Act (FDCA) and provides guidance on software as medical devices (SaMD).

EU: MDR and GDPR are changing the game in access to medical devices and safety of records in healthcare

India: MDR 2017 proposed rules for the manufacture and import of medical devices.

C. Compliance and Responsibility

The MDIS should be audited time and again to ensure some amount of compliance with the regulatory provisions. Non-compliance would bring fines, lawsuits, and a loss of popularity.

5.2. Ethical issues

The integration of medical devices into the health care system raises many ethical issues regarding victims' rights, privacy, and equity of the time

a. Patient Privacy and Accountability

MDIS acquires and distributes tangible information to affected individuals, and therefore, confidentiality is a serious ethical dilemma. The availability, accuracy, and confidentiality of information are important for growing self-belief inside the patients.

Data Encryption: Protected the individual's information throughout both transmission and storage.
Access Control: It provides access to affected individual data to the only authorized legal staff.

b. Informed Consent

The person whose records are affected must be informed of the retention, use, and disclosure of his or her records. Informed consent is necessary to ensure the use of ethical information.

c. Bias and Impartiality

AI-powered MDIS can introduce bias in patient care if the algorithm is not properly tested or trained on different data sets. Ethics is a challenge to guarantee fairness in processing records and decision-making.

D. Clinical Practice Impact

Healthcare guidelines automated by MDIS affect the role of healthcare professionals, raising ethical issues regarding displacement and human contact that patients experience in the church.

e. Health Equity

Using MDIS is only restricted for health plans that have extra funds and, thereby would make healthcare inequitable to a large portion. Ethical concerns are raising concerning fair accessibility of superior advanced technology of healthcare

5.3. Legal Challenges

Putting MDIs in a care delivery system raises different sorts of legal challenges regarding responsibility and data protection and also rights and duties over IP-related aspects of devices and its use

Whether it is a system failure or data breach, liability becomes a major legal issue.

Manufacturers Liability: Manufacturers can be held liable for errors or defects.
Health Provider Liability: Providers can be held liable for improper use or preparation of an MDIS.

Shared Responsibility: In some cases, responsibility can be shared between developers, suppliers and software developers.

b. Data Protection and Privacy Act

MDIS must ensure compliance to data protection regulations pertaining to patient data collection, storage and sharing.

HIPAA (United States): Ensures the confidentiality and security of patient health information.
GDPR (European Union): Provides stringent data protection requirements, including the right to access and erase personal data.
Data Localization Laws: Some countries require that patient data be stored within national borders, complicating cloud-based MDIS implementations.

c. Intellectual Property (IP) Data

MDIS often contain proprietary technology and software, raising intellectual property rights concerns.

Patents: Protect new technologies used in MDIS.
License Agreement: Describe the policy for the use of proprietary software and hardware components.
Open-source vs. open-source proprietary software: The use of open-source solutions versus proprietary technology creates legal challenges in balancing the two.

d. Data Transmission Across Borders

Multidisciplinary healthcare organizations must overcome the legal issues related to cross-border data transfers. International data protection laws should be complied with to avoid legal sanctions.

e. The Contracts

Health care providers usually contract with device manufacturers and software vendors. The roles, responsibilities, and legal obligations should be defined in such agreements to solve disputes.

6. FUTURE TRENDS AND INNOVATIONS IN MEDICAL DEVICE INTEGRATION SYSTEMS (MDIS)

As healthcare era keeps to adapt, Medical Device Integration Systems (MDIS) are poised for full-size boom. Emerging technologies, new integration strategies, and the global shift to statistics-pushed fitness care are changing how MDIS are designed, implemented, and implemented This phase explores future features and improvements in MDIS, along with emerging technologies, their integration and growing healthcare systems, those traits Global presentation also focuses (Butean et al., 2015).

6.1. Emerging Technologies

The destiny of MDIS might be defined by using cutting-edge technologies that permit connectivity, facts processing and affected person care. Key rising technology consist of:

a. Artificial Intelligence (AI) and Machine Learning (ML)

AI and ML algorithms play a key function in automating facts evaluation, identifying styles, and presenting predictive insights.

Predictive renovation: AI-powered visualizations will anticipate tool failures and push for pre-emptive maintenance.
Clinical selection support: ML will analyze real-time patient information from connected devices to enable physicians to improve accurate diagnoses and treatment plans.
Anomalies detection: The AI system encounters anomalies in tool performance or affected person vitals and can cause signals for timely intervention.

b. Internet of Medical Things (IoMT)

IoMT will enable seamless connectivity between a vast network of medical devices, sensors, and healthcare systems.

Wearable Devices: Continuous monitoring of patient vitals through wearable sensors will integrate directly into MDIS for real-time data collection.
Remote Patient Monitoring: IoMT devices will facilitate remote care, particularly for patients with chronic conditions or those in rural areas.

c. Edge Computing

Edge computing will bring data processing closer to the devices, reducing latency and bandwidth requirements.

Real-Time Analytics: Critical data will be processed locally, enabling faster decision-making in time-sensitive scenarios like emergency care.
Enhanced Security: By minimizing data transfer to centralized servers, edge computing will reduce the risk of data breaches.

d. Blockchain Technology

Block chain will enhance the security, transparency, and integrity of MDIS.

Secure Data Sharing: Immutable block chain records will facilitate secure data exchange between devices and healthcare providers.
Dedicated patient records: Patients will have more control over their health information, secured and shared (Chianese et al., 2023).

E. 5G Communication

The deployment of a 5G network will significantly increase MDIS connectivity and speed.

Faster data transmission: 5G will enable real-time data sharing between devices and cloud systems, improving system responsiveness.
Scalability: Increased 5G bandwidth will help connect more devices, facilitating scalability.

6.2. Integration of Emerging Health Structures

The destiny of MDIS can be tied to their increasing integration into revolutionary health care delivery that prioritizes customized, preventative, and price-primarily based care.

A. Department of Telemedicine and Telehealth

MDIS will be key to the growth of telemedicine, allowing far flung tracking, prognosis and treatment.

Virtual consultation: Real-time data from connected devices allows healthcare professionals to assess a patient's condition during a virtual visit (Balasubramanian & Jolfaei, 2021).
Chronic Disease Management: Patients with chronic diseases will benefit from continuous screening and remote interventions, reducing the need for hospitalization.

b. Individual Therapy

MDIS will support personalized health care by integrating genomic, biometric and lifestyle data.

Personalized treatment plans: Data from integrated devices will help develop personalized treatment plans based on individual patient data.
Accurate assessment: Ongoing patient monitoring will provide insight into how patients respond to treatments, allowing for timely adjustments (Silberberg, 2001).

c. Value-Based Care

Healthcare systems worldwide are shifting toward fee-primarily based care models, wherein repayment is tied to affected person outcomes.

Outcome Monitoring: MDIS will music patient outcomes and provide facts to help price-based repayment fashions.
Efficiency and Cost Reduction: By improving device integration and records sharing, MDIS will enhance operational efficiency and reduce healthcare costs.

d. Integrated Care Networks

MDIS will enable the creation of integrated care networks, connecting hospitals, clinics, and primary care providers.

Seamless Data Exchange: Patient data will flow seamlessly across care settings, ensuring continuity of care.
Collaborative Care: Healthcare providers will collaborate more effectively, using shared data to make informed decisions.

Three. Global Effects

The MDIS advances will reverberate all around the globe, affecting how healthcare receives brought, accessed, and even decided through guidelines.

Bridging Healthcare Disparities:

New technologies and integrated MDIS will bridge the healthcare disparities, especially in underserved areas.

Access to Care through Remote Access: IoMT devices and telemedicine will provide excellent healthcare to far-flung and rural areas and enhance access to vital services.

Affordable Solutions: Scalable and cloud-based MDIS reduce infrastructure costs, thereby making superior health technology more accessible to low-aid settings (Abdulrahim, Mahmoud, & Jumana, 2020).

B. Standardization and Interoperability:

Global efforts to standardize scientific device integration protocols will enhance interoperability throughout regions and healthcare structures.

Cross-Border Data Sharing: Standardized MDIS will facilitate go-border facts exchange, allowing worldwide collaborations and research.

Global Health Initiatives: Integrated structures will help worldwide fitness initiatives by means of imparting real-time information for disease surveillance and public fitness interventions.

C. Regulatory and Policy Considerations:

As MDIS grow to be mainstream, worldwide regulatory bodies would try to trap as much as the brand new technology.

Converged Regulations: International co-operation may be critical for converging the regulatory regimes and making sure compliance worldwide (Lou et al., 2020).

Data sovereignty: Policymakers must manage problematic situations of record sovereignty by balancing the ability to balance data percentages with privacy and confidentiality challenges.

D. Pandemic preparedness response:

The COVID-19 pandemic highlighted the need for integrated health care. MDIS will play a key role in future pandemic preparedness and self-reliance (Li et al., 2022).

Real-time data collection: The MDIS will provide real-time data on patient status, availability of resources, and disease prevalence.

Scalable MDIS that would lead to very rapid deployment of health resources in public health emergencies.

7. CONCLUSION AND RECOMMENDATIONS

MDIS is transforming health care by facilitating seamless communication between clinical devices, health systems, and patient records. The importance of such systems lies in improving the care of the affected, optimizing operational efficiency, and facilitating records-driven selection making. As health care continues to evolve, so will the importance of MDIS; therefore, it calls for planning, scaling, and renovation. This section summarizes key principles, explores future possibilities for MDIS, and provides guidance on action for stakeholders.

7.1. Summary of Key Findings

a. Development of the MDIS

MDIS development requires strategic planning, a strong technical foundation and appropriate development strategies. A key challenge is ensuring interoperability, data security, and regulatory compliance. Successful improvement requires collaboration among healthcare professionals, device manufacturers and software developers.

b. How to Change

Scalability is important for MDIS to be able to scale up with the number of data, devices, and users without affecting its performance. Techniques such as cloud computing, micro services architecture, and load balancing are important to achieve scalability. However, barriers such as legacy systems, high implementation costs, and regulatory barriers must be addressed.

d. Ethical, Legal and Legal Considerations

MDIS must be subjected to strict regulatory compliance, ethics regarding patient data privacy, and severe legal challenges. This will ensure the safe and ethical use of MDIS in compliance with international standards, the protection of patient data and the establishment of clear accountability policies

Future products and innovations:

Emerging technologies such as AI, IOMT, edge computing, block chain, and 5G connectivity will shape the future of MDIS. This will enable real-time data processing, predictive analytics, and advanced security. New models of health such as telemedicine, personalized medicine, and value-based care will come into MDIS's functions, thereby expanding their role globally in health.

7.2. Future Outlook

The future of MDIS is bright with many promising developments.

Increased use of AI and IOMT: AI analytics and IOMT will be used to improve MDIS performance and impact, thereby facilitating continuous monitoring and self-monitoring.
Increased focus on connectivity: Attempts to standardize the integration process will enhance device and health system communication with one another, thus allowing smooth exchange of data.
Expanding telemedicine and remote care: MDIS plays an important role in expanding telemedicine services, especially in rural and underserved areas.
Increased advanced security: With the increase in cyber threats, MDIS would embrace advanced security measures in the form of block chain and zero-trust architecture

Global Collaboration Global collaboration will be the backbone to innovation, harmonization in regulations, and scalable yet cost-effective MDIS solutions developed for various health care settings.

Three. Recommendations to stakeholders

To fully realize the capacity of MDIS, stakeholders in the fitness care machine need to include multidisciplinary processes. The following guidelines have been developed for key stakeholder companies.

For equipment manufacturers:

Embrace open standards: Build devices that meet open standards and business models to facilitate seamless integration into healthcare.
Focus on user-centered design: Design intuitive and user-friendly interfaces to improve medical device use and adoption.
Implemented AI-powered features: Combine AI and ML capabilities to improve device performance, predictive maintenance, and clinical decision support.
Ensure conformity: Be vigilant to international regulatory necessities and ensure device adheres to all safety and performance necessities.

To the builders of software program

Accept microservice structure: Design loosely-coupled, scalable software program software answers that can effortlessly be updated and scaled to aid rising needs of healthcare

Incorporate Predictive Analytics: Use AI- enabled analytics for deriving actionable insights to resource medical selection-making.
Work in close collaboration with stakeholders: Healthcare groups, manufacturers of tools, design specific solutions to meet definite healthcare needs.

To Policymakers and regulators

Standardize regulatory regimes: Cooperate with other international bodies to harmonize regulatory norms and allow for cross-border statistics sharing
Promote statistics privateers: Establish stringent information privacy regulations shielding patient information and setting up agree with in MDIS.
Facilitate studies and innovation: Invest in and sell MDIS technology research and improvement, fostering public-personal partnerships
Address the ethical concerns: Develop codes on ethical problems linked to the confidentiality of facts, knowledgeable consent, and access to healthcare technology by means of all parties involved.

For Researchers and Academics:

Focus on Emerging Technologies: Explore AI, IoMT, block chain, and other emerging technologies used in MDIS.
Monitor program performance: Measure the impact of MDIS on clinical outcomes, surgical efficiency, and patient satisfaction.
Partner with industry: Work with healthcare providers, manufacturers and policymakers to translate research findings into practical solutions.

REFERENCES

Abdulrahim, S., Mahmoud, A., & Jumana, F. (2020). IoT Based Predictive Maintenance Management of Medical Equipment. *Journal of Medical Systems*, *44*(4). PMID: 32078712

Adil, M., Khan, M. K., Jadoon, M. M., Attique, M., Song, H., & Farouk, A. (2022). An AI-enabled hybrid lightweight authentication scheme for intelligent IoMT based cyber-physical systems. *IEEE Transactions on Network Science and Engineering*, *10*(5), 2719–2730. DOI: 10.1109/TNSE.2022.3159526

Ahad, A., Tahir, M., & Yau, K. L. A. (2019). 5G-based smart healthcare network: Architecture, taxonomy, challenges and future research directions. *IEEE Access : Practical Innovations, Open Solutions*, *7*, 100747–100762. DOI: 10.1109/ACCESS.2019.2930628

Amutha, B. (2023, November). IoT revolutionizing healthcare: a survey of smart healthcare system architectures. In *2023 International Conference on Research Methodologies in Knowledge Management, Artificial Intelligence and Telecommunication Engineering (RMKMATE)* (pp. 1-5). IEEE.

Balasubramanian, V., & Jolfaei, A. (2021). A scalable framework for healthcare monitoring application using the Internet of Medical Things. *Software, Practice & Experience*, *51*(12), 2457–2468. DOI: 10.1002/spe.2849

Butean, A., David, A., Buduleci, C., & Daian, A. (2015, May). Auxilum Medicine: a cloud based platform for real-time monitoring medical devices. In 2015 20th International Conference on Control Systems and Computer Science (pp. 874-879). IEEE. DOI: 10.1109/CSCS.2015.135

Cherukuri, H., Shukla, S., Rajan, A. T., & Aravind, S. (2024). Deploying containerized microservices in on-premise Kubernetes environments: Challenges and best practices. International Journal of Multidisciplinary Innovation and Research Methodology, ISSN: 2960-2068, 3(2), 74-90.

Chianese, R., Gargiulo, F., Marrone, S., Nespolino, C., Pirozzi, G., & Verde, L. (2023, July). Supporting the Maintenance Process of Healthcare Pervasive Devices. In International Conference on Information, Intelligence, Systems, and Applications (pp. 286-305). Cham: Springer Nature Switzerland.

Daniel, C. (2023). Medical Device Maintenance Regimes in Healthcare Institutions. In *Inspection of Medical Devices: For Regulatory Purposes* (pp. 59–91). Springer Nature Switzerland.

Drăgulinescu, A. M. C., Manea, A. F., Fratu, O., & Drăgulinescu, A. (2020). LoRa-based medical IoT system architecture and testbed. *Wireless Personal Communications*, 1–23.

Gatouillat, A., Badr, Y., Massot, B., & Sejdić, E. (2018). Internet of medical things: A review of recent contributions dealing with cyber-physical systems in medicine. *IEEE Internet of Things Journal*, *5*(5), 3810–3822. DOI: 10.1109/JIOT.2018.2849014

Levina, A., Iliashenko, V. M., Kalyazina, S., & Overes, E. (2022, May). Smart hospital architecture: IT and digital aspects. In Algorithms and Solutions Based on Computer Technology: 5th Scientific International Online Conference Algorithms and Solutions based on Computer Technology (ASBC 2021) (pp. 235-247). Cham: Springer International Publishing.

Li, E., Clarke, J., Ashrafian, H., Darzi, A., & Neves, A. L. (2022). The impact of electronic health record interoperability on safety and quality of care in high-income countries: Systematic review. *Journal of Medical Internet Research*, *24*(9), e38144. DOI: 10.2196/38144 PMID: 36107486

Lou, Z., Wang, L., Jiang, K., Wei, Z., & Shen, G. (2020). Reviews of wearable healthcare systems: Materials, devices and system integration. *Materials Science and Engineering R Reports*, *140*, 100523. DOI: 10.1016/j.mser.2019.100523

Mahfoud, H., El Barkany, A., & El Biyaali, A. (2016). Preventive maintenance optimization in healthcare domain: Status of research and perspective. *Journal of Quality and Reliability Engineering*, *2016*(1), 5314312. DOI: 10.1155/2016/5314312

Manchadi, O., Ben-Bouazza, F. E., & Jioudi, B. (2023). Predictive maintenance in healthcare system: A survey. *IEEE Access: Practical Innovations, Open Solutions*, *11*, 61313–61330. DOI: 10.1109/ACCESS.2023.3287490

Niyonambaza, I., Zennaro, M., & Uwitonze, A. (2020). Predictive maintenance (Pdm) structure using internet of things (iot) for mechanical equipment used into hospitals in Rwanda. *Future Internet*, *12*(12), 224. DOI: 10.3390/fi12120224

Ramadan, E. A., Abu-Ghaleb, A. A., & El-Brawany, M. A. (2023, October). Medical Equipment Maintenance Management and Optimization in Healthcare Facilities: Literature Review. In 2023 3rd International Conference on Electronic Engineering (ICEEM) (pp. 1-11). IEEE.

Shafiq, M., Choi, J. G., Cheikhrouhou, O., & Hamam, H. (2023). Advances in IoMT for Healthcare Systems. *Sensors (Basel)*, *24*(1), 10. DOI: 10.3390/s24010010 PMID: 38202871

Silberberg, J. L. (2001, August). Achieving medical device EMC: The role of regulations, standards, guidelines and publications. In 2001 IEEE EMC International Symposium. Symposium Record. International Symposium on Electromagnetic Compatibility (Cat. No. 01CH37161) (Vol. 2, pp. 1298-1303). IEEE.

Singh, B., Lopez, D., & Ramadan, R. (2023). Internet of things in Healthcare: A conventional literature review. *Health and Technology*, *13*(5), 699–719. DOI: 10.1007/s12553-023-00771-1

Taylor, R. H., Menciassi, A., Fichtinger, G., Fiorini, P., & Dario, P. (2016). Medical robotics and computer-integrated surgery. Springer Handbook of Robotics, 1657-1684. DOI: 10.1007/978-3-319-32552-1_63

ADDITIONAL READING

Hajizada, G. (2023). Analysis of security and privacy in the communication of IoT medical devices (Master's thesis, Universitat Politècnica de Catalunya).

Marešová, P., Peter, L., Honegr, J., Režný, L., Penhaker, M., Augustýnek, M., Mohelská, H., Klímová, B., & Kuča, K. (2020). Complexity stage model of the medical device development based on economic evaluation—MedDee. *Sustainability (Basel)*, *12*(5), 1755. DOI: 10.3390/su12051755

Osama, M., Ateya, A. A., Sayed, M. S., Hammad, M., Pławiak, P., Abd El-Latif, A. A., & Elsayed, R. A. (2023). Internet of medical things and healthcare 4.0: Trends, requirements, challenges, and research directions. *Sensors (Basel)*, *23*(17), 7435. DOI: 10.3390/s23177435 PMID: 37687891

Phani Praveen, S., Hasan Ali, M., Musa Jaber, M., Buddhi, D., Prakash, C., Rani, D. R., & Thirugnanam, T. (2023). IOT-enabled healthcare data analysis in virtual hospital systems using Industry 4.0 smart manufacturing. *International Journal of Pattern Recognition and Artificial Intelligence*, *37*(02), 2356002. DOI: 10.1142/S0218001423560025

Rahman, M., & Jahankhani, H. (2021). Security vulnerabilities in existing security mechanisms for iomt and potential solutions for mitigating cyber-attacks. Information security technologies for controlling pandemics, 307-334.

Rane, J., Mallick, S. K., Kaya, O., & Rane, N. L. (2024). Scalable and adaptive deep learning algorithms for large-scale machine learning systems. Future Research Opportunities for Artificial Intelligence in Industry 4.0 and, 5, 2-40.

Valli, L. N. (2024). Predictive Analytics Applications for Risk Mitigation across Industries; A review. *BULLET: Jurnal Multidisiplin Ilmu*, *3*(4), 542–553.

Chapter 15
Urban Computing Solutions in Healthcare Edge Computing

Basudeo Singh Roohani
https://orcid.org/0000-0003-3387-0187
IMS Engineering College, Ghaziabad, India

Nitin Sharma
https://orcid.org/0000-0003-1268-369X
Ajay Kumar Garg Engineering College, Ghaziabad, India

Vinay Kumar Kasula
https://orcid.org/0009-0001-1131-3059
University of the Cumberlands, USA

Pushpa Mamoria
https://orcid.org/0000-0002-5748-7302
School of Engineering and Technology, Chhatrapati Shahu Ji Maharaj University, Kanpur, India

Nirav Narendrakumar Modh
https://orcid.org/0009-0006-4721-1237
Infosys Limited, Chicago, USA

Alok Kumar
https://orcid.org/0000-0003-1051-0672
School of Engineering and Technology, Chhatrapati Shahu Ji Maharaj University, Kanpur, India

Vineeta Singh
https://orcid.org/0000-0003-1084-279X
School of Engineering and Technology, Chhatrapati Shahu Ji Maharaj University, Kanpur, India

ABSTRACT

Healthcare is on the verge of revolutionary change through the combination of urban computing solutions with edge computing in the period of urban expansion and technological progress. The key objectives of the chapter will focus on understanding how edge computing can optimize data processing at the source, minimizing latency and enabling immediate decision-making in urgent healthcare scenarios,

DOI: 10.4018/979-8-3373-1147-0.ch015

and identifying specific challenges faced by urban healthcare systems, including data overload, resource allocation inefficiencies, and accessibility issues in densely populated areas. The chapter uses a combination of qualitative and quantitative research methods as its methodology framework. A study of urban healthcare facilities through different case examples evaluates positive results as well as best practices in implementation. The book chapter investigates the fundamental framework of edge computing within healthcare systems which specifically targets main goals to improve patient outcomes together with operational refinement and immediate data evaluation capabilities.

1. INTRODUCTION

Our world undergoes a fundamental transformation because of the determined expansion of urban areas which extends deep and wide impact. Thousands of people migrating to urban areas transform these centers into complex ecosystems that generate a vibrant human activity pattern. The active city atmosphere produces an extensive quantity of data that functions as a trove of valuable information about how different urban components interact with each other. Urban facilities generate an enormous amount of data with complex dimensions which include transportation flows power use social actions and community services (Zheng, 2019). Město growth at historic rates drives increasing needs for effective and tailor-made services that people can easily access. The healthcare sector stands as the most essential described service because it must transform its offerings to fulfill growing urban demographic requirements. Healthcare remains burdened by many intricate and multiple challenges which include rising patient numbers combined with increasing medical costs and an immediate requirement for individualized proactive healthcare delivery. Urban computing has become an essential instrument for extracting value from urban data streams to create improvements across multiple areas yet healthcare stands first among these priorities.

The city census process identifies cities by using analytical methods and technologies to interpret all the data flowing through them. The combination of understanding, analyzing and improving all aspects of urban life is moving cities towards better functioning. Cities benefit when organizations take measures to promote transportation, address energy distribution strategies and use technology to prevent crime. Urbanization has had the greatest impact on the development of the health sector. Urban healthcare systems are undergoing radical changes as urban computing and technology come together. Data processing occurs closer to the source, rather than at a central location controlling data transmission. Real-time medical records can accelerate emergency healthcare response to better utilize hospital services and improve patient care processes.

We then discuss how edge computing can work with urban computing to improve urban services. The following posts highlight collaborations in these areas that are providing innovative solutions to address current challenges in urban healthcare systems. Rapid urban transformation requires a better understanding of these technologies and knowledge of the patient's personality to improve urban health, achieve better health outcomes and increased productivity.

1.1 Overview of Urban Computing

The urban discipline incorporates elements of computer science, data science, and urban planning to address the complex and potential problems of modern cities. Urban data processing involves obtaining data from various parts of the city and then performing physical and mathematical analysis of the resulting data (Zhang & Kidd, 2020). Figure 1 shows a computing paradigm for urban computing. Urban informatics leverages data models to improve many aspects of cities, including:

Resource Optimization: Efficient allocation of resources like energy, water, and public transportation.

Infrastructure Management: Monitoring and maintenance of critical infrastructure, such as roads, bridges, and utilities.

Environmental Sustainability: Analyzing air quality, noise pollution, and carbon emissions to create more sustainable cities.

Public Safety and Security: Detecting crime patterns, monitoring traffic incidents, and enhancing emergency response.

Healthcare Accessibility and Efficiency: Analyzing disease outbreaks, optimizing ambulance routes, and improving access to medical facilities.

Urban informatics essentially transforms raw data, collected from sensors, mobile devices, social media, and various other sources into actionable information that can improve the quality of life of city dwellers by optimizing services, informing policy decisions, enhancing public safety, and fostering community engagement.

Figure 1. Shows a computing paradigm for urban computing

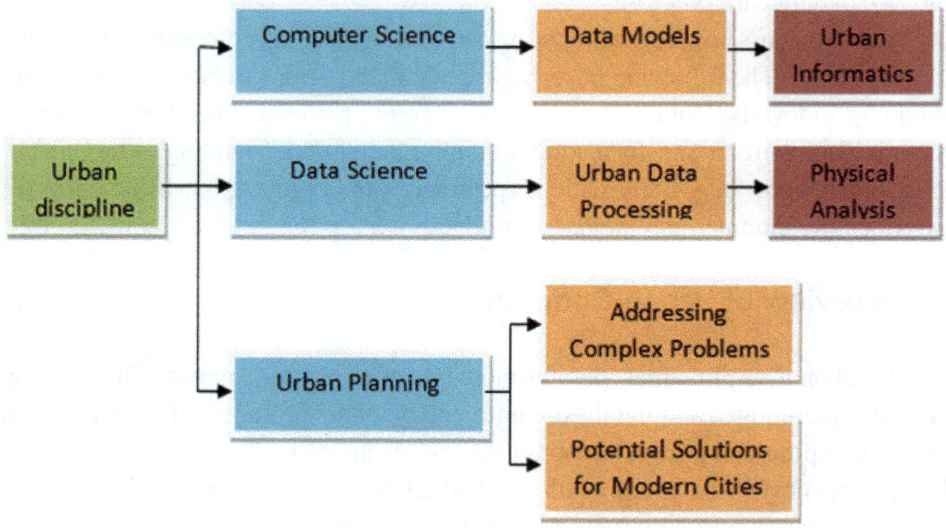

1.2 The Role of Edge Computing in Healthcare

Edge computing is a distributed computing paradigm that processes data closer to the center rather than relying on centralized cloud servers (Satpathy, Mohanty, & Potluri, 2024). This approach is particularly useful in the medical field because:

Reduce Latency: Healthcare applications such as remote patient care or robotic surgery require low latency. Edge computing can speed data processing and response time for critical medical interventions.

Enhance Privacy and Security: By processing data locally, sensitive patient information can be stored close to the site, reducing the risk of data breaches and compliance issues.

Improve Reliability and Resilience: Edge computing enables healthcare professionals to work more reliably even in areas with limited or inconsistent internet connectivity.

Enable Scalability: Edge computing can support increasingly connected medical devices and data-driven applications to be more efficient and effective.

Support Resource-Constrained Environments: Edge devices can operate on low power, making medical technology accessible to remote or underserved communities.

Edge computing is therefore essential to deliver complex urban health solutions and bridge the gap between data collection and action.

1.3 Importance of Integrating Urban and Healthcare Computing

The convergence of urban computing and healthcare is still in its infancy, but its transformative power is undeniable. Increased connectivity and urban intelligence will lead to a variety of new healthcare innovations, including improved communications and public safety services. Edge computing remains at the forefront because it enables rapid diagnostics that improve health outcomes. Urban computing is creating major urban transformations, building strong communities, and all residents benefit from these advances, with improved health. Edge technologies must enable the integration of urban computing and healthcare informatics to create a safe city that improves health and safety.

This convergence offers numerous benefits, including:

Proactive Healthcare Management: By analyzing citywide health patterns, such as infection rates or environmental conditions, doctors can identify and address health risks early on. These risks are increasing.

Improved Emergency Response: Real-time traffic data and location tracking enable rapid dispatch of ambulances and improved route planning in emergency situations.

Personalized Healthcare Services: Urban informatics can analyze patient data relative to urban environments to create personalized care plans and recommendations.

Optimized Resource Allocation: Understanding healthcare needs in different cities can help allocate resources such as medical personnel, hospital beds and essential equipment efficiently.

Better Public Health Outcomes: Urban informatics can make significant contributions to public health and reduce the burden on health services by identifying and addressing environmental health problems.

More Equitable Access to Healthcare: Edge solutions can enable greater healthcare equity by supporting telehealth and remote patient care in underserved urban communities. Good hygiene.

1.4 Literature Review

The rapid evolution of urban computing has unlocked new potentials in smart healthcare systems by enabling real-time data processing, mobility, and responsiveness. Urban computing involves the integration of ubiquitous sensing, data analytics, and cloud-edge computing to enhance urban life, particularly in densely populated cities where healthcare systems are under constant pressure. Over the past decade, researchers have explored various architectures combining urban computing and edge computing to address latency, bandwidth, and data privacy issues in healthcare.

Early studies such as Kumar, S., & Haque, A. (2019) laid foundational work on edge computing, emphasizing its capacity to process data near the source, thus reducing the load on cloud systems and enhancing real-time responsiveness. Subsequent research by Zhang, C., & Kidd, A. (2020). Introduced hybrid edge-cloud frameworks for healthcare, integrating sensors from wearable devices, hospital networks, and ambulatory systems. A growing body of work, such as Satpathy, S., Mohanty, S. N., & Potluri, S. (2024) has investigated urban computing in smart cities, linking healthcare with traffic, environmental monitoring, and citizen behavior. These studies highlighted the importance of contextual intelligence and geospatial analytics. Nevertheless, most of these systems still relied heavily on centralized cloud platforms, making them vulnerable to connectivity issues and posing challenges in real-time decision-making during critical healthcare events, such as pandemics or natural disasters.

Key Gaps Identified:

1. **Integration Deficiency**: Prior research lacks cohesive integration of urban data sources (e.g., transportation, pollution, and infrastructure data) with healthcare edge systems to support predictive and context-aware health services.
2. **Security and Privacy Limitations**: Many proposed solutions inadequately address real-time data security and privacy in multi-tenant, multi-source healthcare edge environments.

By bridging the theoretical and practical gaps, this chapter significantly advances the discourse on urban edge computing for healthcare and provides a foundation for future smart city health innovations.

2. TECHNOLOGICAL FOUNDATIONS

The traditional model of centralized cloud computing, while powerful, often falls short when applied to the real-time, data-intensive needs of urban healthcare. Long network latencies, bandwidth limitations, and data privacy concerns can hinder the effectiveness of crucial applications. Edge computing offers an alternative where data processing is brought closer to where it's generated – at the “edge” of the network, directly within hospitals, clinics, ambulances, and even at patients' homes. This decentralized approach unlocks a new wave of possibilities for urban healthcare.

2.1 Edge Computing: The Catalyst for Real-Time Healthcare

Processing power is needed to handle the enormous volumes of data produced in healthcare settings. Edge computing, which moves data storage and processing closer to the source, is turning out to be quite beneficial. Edge computing eases the burden on central servers, improves response times, and lowers latency by processing data locally. For real-time healthcare applications in urban settings, this is especially crucial (Chen & Poon, 2020). Fundamentally, edge computing is placing computer resources nearer to data sources, including servers, routers, and specialized devices. Processing and analysis are done locally rather than sending all the data to a distant cloud.

2.1.1 Key Advantages of Edge Computing

Reduced Latency: By minimizing the distance data needs to travel, edge computing drastically reduces delays, enabling near real-time responses crucial for time-sensitive healthcare applications like remote patient monitoring, emergency triage, and robotic surgery (Dave, Seliya, & Siddiqui, 2021).

Bandwidth Optimization: Local data processing reduces the cost of data transmission to the cloud, saving valuable network bandwidth and reducing latency, especially in large cities.

Enhanced Privacy and Security: Sensitive patient information can be processed and stored locally, reducing the risk of contamination during data transmission. This regional approach allows for better management of data privacy and compliance.

Improved Reliability: If the connection to the cloud is lost, the edge device can continue to operate independently, providing uninterrupted service. Edge devices typically include a variety of devices, from powerful servers in hospitals to small, specialized devices embedded in wearables or diagnostic equipment.

2.2 Urban Computing Frameworks: Transforming Healthcare in the Modern City

The analysis of urban environment data for city problem solutions through urban computing technology expands more quickly across different industries. The field of healthcare is witnessing revolutionary changes because of its operation. Urban computing achieves these healthcare advances through live data acquisition high-level data analytics and connected system technologies. This article examines how the progressive field transforms urban health management through discussions about edge computing infrastructure. The infrastructure of edge computing receives support from the urban computing framework which provides solutions that work within urban environments. Urban computing serves as a diverse academic discipline that combines data analysis with computational approaches to handle urban problems (Kumar & Haque, 2019).

Urban Computing Frameworks facilities:

Context-Aware Services: Urban computing leverages data from various sources like traffic patterns, weather conditions, and disease outbreaks to provide context-aware healthcare services. Edge devices can process this data locally to offer customized health alerts and optimize resource allocation.

Data Integration and Analytics: Combining health records with urban datasets creates a holistic view of the population's health. Edge devices can pre-process and analyze this heterogeneous data locally, preparing it for further analysis in a cloud environment.

Smart City Infrastructure Integration: Integrating the edges of inclusion with smart city infrastructure, such as smart lighting and smart transportation, can create a shared healthcare system. For example, a smart ambulance could use edge computing to analyze real-time traffic data and find the fastest route to the hospital, while also communicating vital information about patients before they arrive.

Resource Optimization: With the help of data analytics, urban healthcare services can better allocate resources such as staff, beds, and medical equipment. Edge computing can help accelerate resource discovery in real time and increase efficiency.

2.3 Interfacing Edge Computing with Healthcare Systems

The real benefit of edge computing lies in its ability to integrate with existing healthcare systems and increase the overall effectiveness and efficiency of healthcare. By placing computing resources closer to data-generating sources (such as wearables, sensors, and medical devices), edge computing reduces latency and enables data analysis and exploratory auditing. With access to vital information, medical personnel can make faster and more informed decisions, which can be very useful in emergency situations.

2.3.1 Practical Applications of Edge Computing in Healthcare Systems

Remote Patient Monitoring (RPM): Wearable sensors and home health devices can collect patient data, filter and analyze it locally using edge devices, so abnormalities can be quickly detected and doctors can be alerted before problems become serious.

Smart Hospitals: Edge computing can instantly analyze patient data, improve diagnoses, speed up treatment processes, and increase hospital efficiency. From smart beds to robotic surgery, edge devices are the backbone of connected health.

Telemedicine and Remote Consultations: Low-latency interactions are crucial for effective remote consultations. Edge computing can enhance the quality of video and audio communication while ensuring the security and privacy of patient-sensitive data, even in areas with unreliable networks.

Emergency Response: Edge computing is particularly useful in emergency situations where rapid access to information is critical. Analyzing patient data, sharing real-time locations, and guiding first responders can help save precious time and improve patient outcomes.

Point-of-Care Diagnostics: Edge-enabled diagnostic devices allow tests to be performed at the patient's bedside or in remote locations. This improves access to care, particularly in underserved urban communities. Figure 2 shows applications of edge computing in healthcare systems.

Figure 2. Shows applications of edge computing in healthcare systems

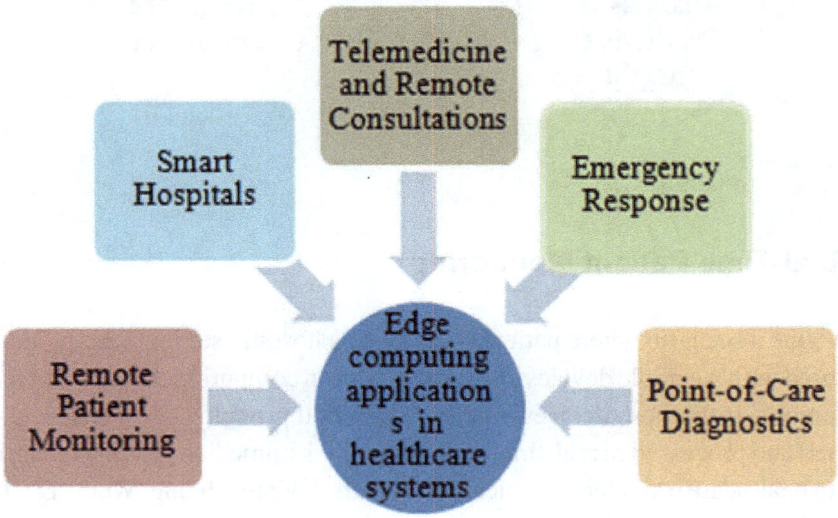

3. APPLICATIONS OF URBAN COMPUTING IN HEALTHCARE

Urban computing is an interdisciplinary field that combines the study of cities with advanced computing technologies, aiming to improve urban life through data analysis, sensor networks, and computational models. Figure 3 shows the urban computing applications in healthcare. In the healthcare sector, urban computing has opened up numerous applications that enhance the efficiency of healthcare delivery, improve patient outcomes, and promote public health initiatives. Below are several key applications of urban computing in healthcare.

Figure 3. Urban computing applications in healthcare

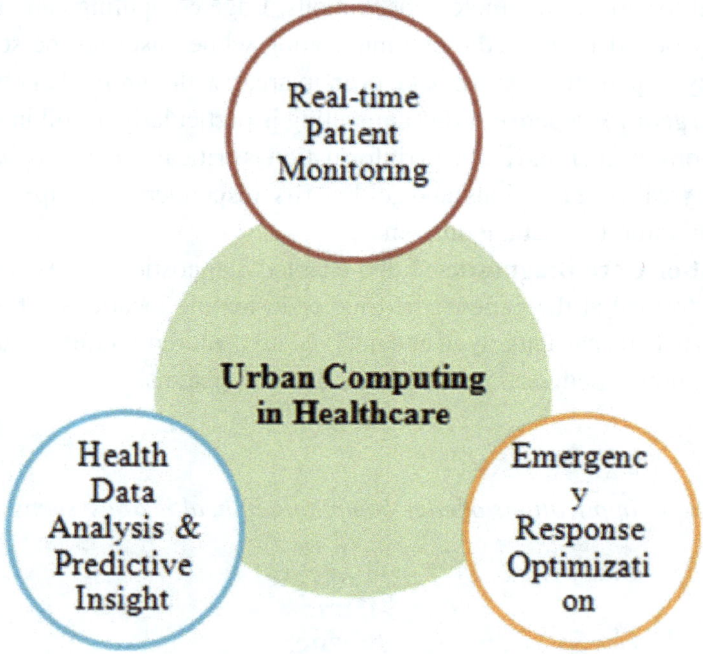

3.1 Real-Time Patient Monitoring

Imagine a scenario where patients outside of a hospital setting are continuously monitored with wearable devices and sensors. Urban computing makes this a reality. Data streams from these devices – heart rate, blood pressure, activity levels – are collected and processed in real-time at the edge. This immediate analysis can trigger alerts to healthcare providers if critical parameters deviate (Huang, Wang, & Cheng, 2017). Here's how it works:

Wearable Sensors: Embedded in smart watches, patches, or clothing, these devices constantly collect health data.

Edge Processing: Instead of sending all this data to a central server, the edge devices process it locally. This allows for rapid analysis and reduces the time it takes to identify potential issues.

Real-time Alerts: If the edge computation detects a significant change, an alert is sent to the patient and their caregivers, allowing for immediate intervention.

Benefits: This continuous monitoring leads to early detection of medical emergencies, reduced hospital readmission rates, and improved overall patient outcomes. It also enables personalized healthcare plans tailored to an individual's needs.

3.2 Emergency Response Optimization

In a bustling urban environment, rapid response to medical emergencies is paramount. Urban computing optimizes this process significantly by:

Real-time Location Data: Tracking ambulances and first responders through GPS allows for the most efficient dispatching of resources.

Traffic and Congestion Analysis: Urban computing platforms analyze traffic patterns, enabling dispatchers to choose the fastest routes to the emergency scene, minimizing response time.

Resource Allocation: Based on real-time data about available resources (ambulances, hospital beds), the system can make informed decisions on where to send patients, optimizing the use of available facilities.

Predictive Analysis: By analyzing historical data on emergencies, urban computing can predict areas that might be at higher risk, enabling proactive resource deployment.

Benefits: Faster response times can be life-saving. Efficient resource allocation ensures that all areas of the city are adequately covered in emergency situations.

3.3 Health Data Analysis & Predictive Insights

Beyond real-time applications, urban computing plays a critical role in analyzing large datasets to generate crucial insights and improve population health:

Geographic Health Mapping: Analyzing health records alongside location data allows for the identification of disease clusters and potential environmental triggers.

Predictive Modeling: Large data sets can be used to predict outbreaks of infectious diseases or identify populations at high risk of developing certain conditions, enabling proactive interventions.

Personalized Medicine: By compiling an individual's health history with demographic and lifestyle information, urban computing can help develop personalized treatment plans.

Public Health Policy: Data-driven insights inform policymakers about the effectiveness of public health campaigns and guide the allocation of resources to the areas that need them most.

Benefits: This data-driven approach provides a better understanding of urban health, leading to better outcomes, public health planning, and ultimately improved public health.

4. ARCHITECTURAL MODELS FOR HEALTHCARE EDGE COMPUTING: URBAN COMPUTING SOLUTIONS

Urban sprawl is creating unprecedented challenges and opportunities for healthcare. As cities grow, the need for quality, efficient, and accessible healthcare services increases. Edge computing, which brings computation and data storage closer to the origin, is essential to meeting these needs. This chapter examines similar building models for healthcare, particularly in urban environments. We learn about fundamental concepts such as layers, the limits of distribution, and the fundamental issues of data connectivity and scalability. The model can solve specific urban problems. These standards ultimately affect the effectiveness and efficiency of healthcare solutions by determining how data is collected, processed and processed (Saeed et al., 2020).

4.1 Layered Architecture for Urban Health Systems

A layered architecture provides a structured approach to managing the complexity of urban healthcare edge computing. Generally, these architectures can be envisioned with the following layers:

Sensor Layer (Edge Devices): That's where the information comes from. Wearable devices, medical sensors used in ambulances and homes, even environmental sensors that track air pollution make up this layer. This tool collects detailed information about a patient's health, vital signs, and environmental factors that affect health.

Edge Computing Layer: This layer is closer to the surface than the surrounding environment, here information received is first processed, analyzed and processed. This might be a local server in the hospital, a gateway in the gateway or a powerful hardware device. Now it is used to do such tasks as anomaly detection, real-time patient monitoring and push notifications with low latency and bandwidth requirements.

Cloud Layer (Centralized Processing and Storage): They can both answer immediate needs and other parts of the cloud, such as critical storage for long-lasting data, and advanced analytics and machine learning models. The collected data also is used for public health management, research and the provision of personalized treatment plans. This multi-layered model gives the balance of immediate response at the edge by analytics in the cloud. Layers provide end-to-end visibility on cloud operations by the fact that the data flows between layers.

4.2 Distributed Edge Nodes in Urban Environments

The size and diversity of the urban area necessitates a decentralized approach to edge computing. Instead of relying on a single central location, multiple distribution points should be located throughout the city. Nodes can be placed at:

Hospitals and Clinics: Processing healthcare data within local networks, enabling faster diagnostics and treatment.

Ambulances: Enabling real-time data transmission and analysis during emergency transport, ensuring clinicians have vital information before arrival.

Community Health Centers: Supporting preventative care and remote patient monitoring in underserved neighborhoods.

Public Spaces: Leveraging sensors in parks and public transport to track environmental conditions and their impact on community health.

This decentralized model reduces latency and ensures maximum performance by allowing computations to be completed closer to the desired point. It also increases the robustness of the system, preventing failures that could disrupt critical services.

4.3 Data Interoperability and Scalability

Achieving seamless healthcare edge computing requires careful consideration of data interoperability and scalability.

Data Interoperability: It is important to be able to connect and integrate data given the issues that arise when data comes from different sources and different devices. For data exchange in different healthcare systems and across specific healthcare environments and geographical regions, data systems and communication protocols are needed. Such implementation should be based on arbitrary healthcare standards, for example, HL7 FHIR.

Scalability: The patient loads and needs for care are dynamic within the urban environment. For edge computing infrastructure to be scalable to meet the large data volumes and demands, it needs to scale. This involves designing that would allow data storage to scale, systems to go from constant power to variable power, and designs that can easily change their form for new environments.

5. CHALLENGES AND OPPORTUNITIES

There are many challenges when using urban solutions in healthcare of which medical data must be available conditionally; response has to be immediate and continuous. This is a huge achievement. Its potential benefits are also huge, and it's especially powerful when it comes to intellectual impairment, at the same time.

5.1 Data Privacy and Security Concerns: Protecting the Sanctity of Health Information

Data privacy and security are perhaps the biggest challenges associated with the blockchain. This is where edge computing is about getting data stored and distributed over various devices and locations. There are risks to adversaries associated with this tactic which is fast and very effective. Physically, cheques and bankstands must be fire-resistant and racks for banknotes must provide absolute protection against water intrusion (Li et al., 2020).

5.1.1 Several Factors Contribute to This Concern

Vulnerability of Edge Devices: Many edge devices, particularly low-cost sensors and wearables, may lack the robust security features built into traditional servers. This makes them potential entry points for data breaches.

Data Transmission Risks: The transmission of data between edge devices, edge servers, and cloud platforms is also vulnerable to interception. Ensuring data encryption and secure protocols throughout the data lifecycle is paramount.

Compliance with Regulations: The healthcare industry operates under a stringent regulatory framework, exemplified by laws like HIPAA in the U.S. and GDPR in Europe, which mandate specific protocols for patient data management. Integrating urban computing solutions into this environment requires careful navigation of these complex regulations, presenting a significant hurdle.

5.1.2 Overcoming These Challenges Requires a Multi-Faceted Approach

End-to-end encryption: Implementing robust encryption for data both in transit and at rest.

Secure device management: Employing strong authentication and authorization protocols to control access to edge devices and data.

Regular security audits: Conducting regular assessments to identify vulnerabilities and ensure compliance.

Data anonymization and pseudonymization: Processing data in a way that minimizes the risk of identifying individual patients.

5.2 Real-Time Processing Challenges: The Need for Speed and Reliability

In some cases, the application of healthcare is such that it requires immediate responses or immediate actions. Consider wearable devices, monitoring heart patients, smart ambulances, or services of the emergency system. Edge computing solutions do provide quicker performance as compared to cloud, however, they are also lacking in terms of real-time performance, especially in the case of urban scenarios where network events can be very unpredictable.

Key challenges include:

Latency and Network Issues: Urban areas are prone to network congestion and intermittent connectivity. This can lead to delays in data transmission and processing, making it difficult to achieve the necessary real-time responsiveness.

Resource Constraints: Edge devices typically operate under resource constraints, possessing limited processing power, memory, and battery capacity. These limitations restrict the complexity of algorithms that can be executed directly on the edge.

Data Synchronization: Maintaining data consistency across different edge devices and servers, and synchronizing this data with central systems, is a complex task that needs careful management.

Addressing these challenges requires:

Optimized Algorithms: Developing efficient and lightweight algorithms that can run on resource-constrained edge devices.

Intelligent Caching and Data Management: Implementing strategies to cache frequently accessed data locally and optimize data transmission.

Adaptive Networking Solutions: Utilizing network protocols that are robust against intermittent connectivity and congestion.

Hybrid Cloud-Edge Architectures: Employing a hybrid approach, distributing processing between edge devices and cloud platforms based on application requirements and network conditions.

5.3 Opportunities in AI-Driven Health Interventions: Unleashing the Power of Intelligent Systems

Despite these challenges, urban computing provides transformative opportunities for health informatics, in particular to AI-enabled health interventions. Clean interior. This is where edge computing comes into play and helps the AI algorithms process data more closely to the source and hence provides real-time analysis along with faster responses (Cheng, Wang, & Huang, 2019). This opens up a host of possibilities:

Personalized Healthcare and Early Detection: Wearable sensors, when combined with edge intelligence, can monitor personal health conditions, allowing for early detection of abnormalities and personal ailments.

Remote Patient Monitoring: Edge computing facilitates seamless remote patient monitoring, reducing the need for frequent hospital visits and empowering patients to take control of their health at home.

Smart Emergency Response Systems: AI technology can analyze data from smart ambulances and other sources to improve routes, predict patient needs, and manage emergency response. Faster is better.

Public Health Management: Public health management: Edge systems can monitor the environment and track the spread of diseases, enabling rapid response and multiple health goals for the public.

Improved Diagnostic Accuracy: Edge-based AI algorithms can analyze medical images and data to help doctors make diagnoses and increase overall accuracy.

6. CASE STUDIES AND IMPLEMENTATION EXAMPLES

Combining urban computing (based on data generated by cities) with edge computing (processing local data) would make us produce big solutions to consumer problems. It is an approach not based on a centralized cloud that allows for speedier data analysis, lower latency and higher privacy, critical for health. It also fits well with city needs.

6.1 Smart Cities Integrating Healthcare Edge Computing

Solutions that aim at improving the health of cities have taken on very real manifestations and are gaining in numbers known as smart cities. Think of a city where every single thing is sensing it all the time. The sensors can generate continuous data by monitoring air quality, traffic patterns, and pedestrian speed. This information can be analyzed instantly at edge devices in healthcare facilities, community centers and even public spaces as each has access to this information. See a doctor. Doctors can use this information to make certain the best use of resources. Likewise, the data about traffic can help to find a better ambulance route, so the response to the emergency would be faster. Home connectivity also enables smart cities to provide care to patients located in remote areas and for doctors to monitor the patients and intervene when required. Integration also fosters ecosystem integration. To meet the unique needs of their communities healthcare organizations and local governments as well as healthcare providers can and do join together to address these.

6.2 Wearable Devices and Smart Sensors in Urban Healthcare

It has thus changed the face of urban healthcare with the rise of smart devices and appliances thus ushering in more efficient and personalized health. There is still a collection of physical data such as heart rate, blood pressure and physical activity such as in devices like smart watches and fitness trackers, as well as devices such as medical devices. What is more important, edge computing lets these devices do the computations locally without relying entirely on cloud servers. Edge devices can detect patterns or abnormalities such as blood pressure early and notify users, and doctors without alerting something serious is happening. Besides the reduced cost for transmission of data, the reduced cost for transmission of data and better response times this local operation also provides customer privacy. The use of technology may let rural patients receive care in cities and chronically ill patients receive treatment at home. This data can be analyzed by edge servers at local clinics and hospitals to track patients, prescribe treatments as they should, and intervene as needed by doctors.

6.3 Predictive Healthcare Analytics in Urban Areas

Edge computing is also enabled for other applications, such as health prediction. If tracked and aggregated to the right degree, the vast amounts of data available from wearable devices and electronic medical records can serve doctors in helping understand patients' health and predicting diseases or health issues. Reviews can be done on the site more often reducing delays and speeding up recommendations. For instance, a community at risk of catching a certain disease can be identified through edge machine learning models analyzing data from different sources. This information can also be used to implement prevention services, like public health campaigns to improve vaccine coverage. Edge models take hospitals' and clinics' data on patient movement between hospitals and clinics and use it to make predictions of peak demand, which doctors can plan their work and resources accordingly. It also helps to ensure good service and avoids overcrowding (Levinson, 2019).

7. THE FUTURE OF URBAN HEALTHCARE: POWERED BY THE EDGE

While all urban life is changing, these gorgeous places still have a major battle on their hands: supplying health care to a large and diverse population where quality is priced out of reach. In general, most health trusts have found it difficult to maintain decentralized data and provide this demand (Zhong, Zhang, & Lin, 2018). The solutions are becoming more advanced in a combination of technologies like urban computing, edge computing, the Internet of Things (IoT), artificial intelligence (AI), and so on. This article looks at how these innovations are reinventing urban healthcare and the possibility of providing urban healthcare on the dot, equitable and of high quality.

7.1 Role of IoT and AI in Urban Healthcare: Data-Driven Decisions

There are two pillars of this change – the Internet of Things (IoT) and Artificial Intelligence (AI). Both wearable fitness trackers which monitor heart rate, smart beds which monitor sleep patterns, and environmental sensors which monitor the air quality to detect movement and lung disease are common. Such data access affords a wealth of information related to the health of people and societies, which can be used to aid the making of decisions regarding targeted care and treatment. Using AI, you can analyze medical images, predict patient risk concerning several different variables, and build a personalized treatment plan based on the unique demands of any patient. In the urban context, AI can be employed to: optimize ambulance routes, forecast an increase in several visits to emergency rooms and identify high-risk individuals that need intervention. Together, we can optimize for the opportunity of resource pooling and the shifting from human-centric (patient-centric) to system-centric (center-centric) to realize meaning and preventative health outcomes.

7.2 Next-Generation Smart Cities and Healthcare Integration: A Seamless Experience

The future of urban healthcare is inextricably linked to the evolution of smart cities. Imagine:

Smart Transportation: AI-powered traffic management systems prioritizing ambulances, ensuring rapid response times.
Connected Homes: Remote patient monitoring systems proactively detecting health anomalies and automatically alerting healthcare professionals.
Smart Public Spaces: Sensors in parks and public areas monitoring air quality and providing real-time information to individuals with respiratory conditions.

One that puts health into the urban environment creates a harmonious place that is supportive. At the same time, such smart cities provide infrastructure for edge computing, promoting the ability to process data closer to the source to see faster responses and better allocate resources. We want to build a city that will do its best to see that its residents will live a healthy and happy life.

7.3 Ethical and Policy Considerations: Navigating the Challenges

While the potential benefits of these technological advancements are immense, it is crucial to address the ethical and policy considerations that inevitably arise.

Data Privacy and Security: The vast amounts of personal health data being collected and processed necessitate robust data protection measures to ensure patient privacy and confidentiality.
Algorithmic Bias: AI algorithms are trained on data, and biases inherent in the data can lead to discriminatory outcomes. It is critical to ensure that these algorithms are fair and equitable for all populations.
Digital Divide: Not everyone has equal access to technology. Policies must address the digital divide, ensuring that all residents benefit from these advancements, regardless of socioeconomic status or geographic location.

Transparency and Accountability: Clear guidelines are needed to ensure transparency in how these technologies are used and to ensure accountability for any negative consequences.

8. CONCLUSION

8.1 Summary of Key Insights

Our exploration into urban computing and healthcare edge computing has revealed several crucial takeaways:

Reduced Latency: Edge computing essentially eliminates the latency that is intrinsic to conventional cloud-based healthcare systems and it is critical for Time Sensitive Applications. It is very crucial for such real-time uses like remote patient surveillance, robotic surgery and so on because even a millisecond can decide between life and death.

Enhanced Bandwidth Efficiency: Therefore, by processing data closer to their source, we reduce the congestion of the network and reduce the bandwidth requirements. In the case of dense urban environments with large amounts of data produced by numerous devices, this is crucial. By using edge computing, only the necessary information is transmitted to the cloud thus optimizing the network resources.

Improved Data Security and Privacy: This gives a sense of control and security and keeps patient-sensitive data closer to the source. Such data processing at the edge devices reduces the likelihood of such transmission to the cloud exposing the data. This also fits perfectly with stringent data privacy regulations.

Increased Reliability and Resilience: This provides control and security and forces patient-sensitive data closer to the source. This processing of such data at the edge devices reduces the chance that such transmission of the data to the cloud will expose the data. This also fits perfectly with stringent data privacy regulations.

AI-Powered Healthcare at the Edge: By adding Artificial Intelligence and Machine Learning to edge computing, personal and proactive healthcare can be entirely new and possible. Real-time diagnoses, predictive analytics, and personalized treatment of the patient may be provided by the deployment of AI models at the edge of the network.

Integration with Existing Infrastructure: Integration of healthcare edge computing with existing urban infrastructure, most notably those of the transportation networks, smart city initiatives and communication technologies, is essential for successful implementation. It is key to scale and make impacts as high as possible.

Cost-Effectiveness: However, edge computing involves initial investment, but the investment can pay off in the long term as this will help reduce the use of expensive cloud resources, minimize data transfer costs, and provide better operational efficiency.

In essence, the integration of the field of urban computing and the field of edge computing in healthcare brings about a very powerful paradigm shift towards more efficient, responsive, secure, and accessible means of providing healthcare delivery that ultimately results in better health outcomes and urban populations overall.

8.2 Future Directions

The field of urban computing and healthcare edge computing is still in its nascent stages, and the future holds immense promise. Here are some potential future directions:

Standardization and Interoperability: It will be crucial for the development of industry standards, and interoperability protocols for the wide adoption and integration of edge computing for healthcare providers and urban environments.

Enhanced AI/ML Capabilities at the Edge: Such AI/ML models should become more sophisticated and efficient for their deployment at the edge. Such diagnostic tools will be more advanced, approaches to personalized medicine will be used, and predictive health analytics will be developed.

Autonomous Healthcare Systems: If we combine the power of edge computing, AI, and robotics, we might come up with an autonomous healthcare system that can take care of people in real-time and has quite minimal human interaction, especially in remote or underserved areas.

Edge-Based Data Analytics and Visualization: This will provide healthcare professionals with deeper insights that they can gain quickly and act on more rapidly with more advanced tools for visualizing and analysis of data produced at the edge.

Integration with Wearable Technology: By integrating wearable devices with the edge computing infrastructure we will get a continuous loop back from which real-time patient data will be fed to the edge computing infrastructure resulting in proactive and personalized healthcare interventions.

Focus on Ethics and Equity: When thinking about how to roll out edge computing in healthcare, ethical issues such as privacy of data, security and equitable distribution of this technology across different communities should be on top of their list.

Development of Specialized Edge Hardware: We ought to see the appearance of a particular breed of specialized hardware tailored to the healthcare edge computing requirements that require low power yet high processing capabilities.

Public-Private Partnerships: To innovate, foster equity of access and resolve implementation and adoption challenges, public and private sector organizations must work together.

Therefore, in conclusion, we are in the future of healthcare, inseparable from the progress of urban computing and edge computing. If we keep evolving with innovation, foresight and a pledge to equitable and ethical solutions to such possibilities, we can immensely tap into unexplored possibilities to generate urban communities that are healthier and more resilient. This is just the beginning of the journey, and there are large advantages to come in how healthcare will be delivered and experienced.

REFERENCES

Chen, L., & Poon, C. S. (2020). Edge computing: Towards a network of smart objects. In *IoT technologies, architectures, and applications* (pp. 227–246). Springer.

Cheng, S.-F., Wang, X., & Huang, X. (2019). *Urban computing: Methods and applications*. Springer.

Dave, R., Seliya, N., & Siddiqui, N. (2021). The benefits of edge computing in healthcare, smart cities, and IoT. https://arxiv.org/abs/2112.01250

Huang, X., Wang, X., & Cheng, S.-F. (2017). *Smart healthcare: Technologies, applications, and case studies*. Springer.

Kumar, S., & Haque, A. (2019). Urban health informatics: Role of computational techniques and approaches. In *Advances in computational intelligence and informatics* (pp. 177–195). Springer.

Levinson, J. P. (2019). *Healthcare analytics*. Wiley.

Li, Q., Li, Q., Li, X., & Li, X. (2020). Edge computing for real-time healthcare applications in smart cities: Opportunities, challenges, and research directions. *Journal of Ambient Intelligence and Humanized Computing*, *11*(8), 4879–4895.

Marcham, A. (2021). *Understanding infrastructure edge computing: Concepts, technologies, and considerations*. Wiley. DOI: 10.1002/9781119763260

Saeed, A., Anjum, A., Wahid, S., Hussain, O., & Qazi, S. (2020). A systematic review of edge computing in healthcare: Opportunities, challenges, and open research issues. *IEEE Access : Practical Innovations, Open Solutions*, *8*, 126389–126411.

Satpathy, S., Mohanty, S. N., & Potluri, S. (2024). Reconnoitering the landscape of edge intelligence in healthcare. *Apple Academic Press.*, *ISBN-13*, 9781774914366. DOI: 10.1201/9781003401841

Sun, Y., Lo, F. L., & Zheng, S. (2021). An urban computing approach for healthcare service allocation using edge computing. *Journal of Healthcare Engineering*, *8811234*. DOI: 10.1155/2021/8811234

Suresh, A., Maheswari, R., & Iyengar, S. S. (2020). *Deep learning and edge computing solutions for high-performance computing environments*. Springer.

Zhang, C., & Kidd, A. (2020). Urban computing: Computational methods for understanding the urban environment. In *Urban informatics* (pp. 15–34). Springer.

Zheng, Y. (2019). *Urban computing*. MIT Press.

Zhong, S., Zhang, X., & Lin, X. (2018). *Edge computing: Technologies and applications*. Springer.

Compilation of References

Abadi, M., Chu, A., Goodfellow, I., McMahan, H. B., Mironov, I., & Talwar, K.. (2016, October). Deep learning with differential privacy. *Proceedings of the ACM SIGSAC Conference on Computer and Communications Security*, 308–318.

Abbas, N., Zhang, Y., Taherkordi, A., & Skeie, T. (2018). Mobile edge computing: A survey. *IEEE Internet of Things Journal*, *5*(1), 450–465. DOI: 10.1109/JIOT.2017.2750180

Abdulrahim, S., Mahmoud, A., & Jumana, F. (2020). IoT Based Predictive Maintenance Management of Medical Equipment. *Journal of Medical Systems*, *44*(4). PMID: 32078712

Aboualola, M., Abualsaud, K., Khattab, T., Zorba, N., & Hassanein, H. S. (2023). Edge technologies for disaster management: A survey of social media and artificial intelligence integration. *IEEE Access : Practical Innovations, Open Solutions*, *11*, 73782–73802. DOI: 10.1109/ACCESS.2023.3293035

Adil, M., Khan, M. K., Jadoon, M. M., Attique, M., Song, H., & Farouk, A. (2022). An AI-enabled hybrid lightweight authentication scheme for intelligent IoMT based cyber-physical systems. *IEEE Transactions on Network Science and Engineering*, *10*(5), 2719–2730. DOI: 10.1109/TNSE.2022.3159526

Ahad, A., Tahir, M., & Yau, K. L. A. (2019). 5G-based smart healthcare network: Architecture, taxonomy, challenges and future research directions. *IEEE Access : Practical Innovations, Open Solutions*, *7*, 100747–100762. DOI: 10.1109/ACCESS.2019.2930628

Ahmed, A. S., & Salah, H. A. (2023). Development a software defined network (SDN) with Internet of Things (IoT) security for medical issues. *Journal of Al-Qadisiyah for Computer Science and Mathematics*, *15*(4), 98. DOI: 10.29304/jqcm.2023.15.3.1268

Alabdulatif, A., Khalil, I., Yi, X., & Guizani, M. (2019). Secure edge of things for smart healthcare surveillance framework. *IEEE Access : Practical Innovations, Open Solutions*, *7*, 31010–31021. DOI: 10.1109/ACCESS.2019.2899323

Al-Fuqaha, A., Guizani, M., Mohammadi, M., Aledhari, M., & Ayyash, M. (2021). Internet of Things: A survey on enabling technologies, protocols, and applications. *IEEE Communications Surveys and Tutorials*, *17*(4), 2347–2376. DOI: 10.1109/COMST.2015.2444095

Ali, A. S. M., Ali, S., Ziaullah, K., Joo, M. I., & Kim, H. C. (2025). *IoMT and blockchain synergy: A novel approach to health data validation and storage*. IEEE., DOI: 10.1109/ACCESS.2025.3555289

Ali, A., Ali, H., Saeed, A., Ahmed, A., Tin, T., Assam, M., & Mohamed, H. (2023). Blockchain-powered healthcare systems: Enhancing scalability and security with hybrid deep learning. *Sensors (Basel)*, *23*(18), 7740. DOI: 10.3390/s23187740 PMID: 37765797

Ali, A., Montanaro, T., Sergi, I., Carrisi, S., Galli, D., Distante, C., & Patrono, L. (2025). An innovative iot and edge intelligence framework for monitoring elderly people using anomaly detection on data from non-wearable sensors. *Sensors (Basel)*, *25*(6), 1735. DOI: 10.3390/s25061735 PMID: 40292837

Ali, M. H., Jaber, M. M., Abd, S. K., Rehman, A., Awan, M. J., Damaševičius, R., & Bahaj, S. A. (2022). Threat analysis and distributed denial of service (DDoS) attack recognition in the Internet of Things (IoT). *Electronics (Basel)*, *11*(3), 494. DOI: 10.3390/electronics11030494

Ali, O., Ishak, M. K., Bhatti, M. K. L., Khan, I., & Kim, K. I. (2022). A comprehensive review of internet of things: Technology stack, middlewares, and fog/edge computing interface. *Sensors (Basel)*, *22*(3), 995. DOI: 10.3390/s22030995 PMID: 35161740

Almatrooshi, S., Gopakumar, A., & Mathur, V. (2024). Transformative role of cryptocurrency in the healthcare system of uae. *Annals of Case Reports*, *9*(2). DOI: 10.29011/2574-7754.101703

Alnaim, A. K., & Alwakeel, A. M. (2023). Machine-learning-based IoT–edge computing healthcare solutions. *Electronics (Basel)*, *12*(5), 1027. DOI: 10.3390/electronics12041027

Alowais, S. A., Alghamdi, S. S., Alsuhebany, N., Alqahtani, T., Alshaya, A. I., Almohareb, S. N., Aldairem, A., Alrashed, M., Bin Saleh, K., Badreldin, H. A., Al Yami, M. S., Al Harbi, S., & Albekairy, A. M. (2023). Revolutionizing healthcare: The role of artificial intelligence in clinical practice. *BMC Medical Education*, *23*(1), 689. DOI: 10.1186/s12909-023-04698-z PMID: 37740191

Alrowaily, M., & Lu, Z. (2018, October). Secure edge computing in IoT systems: Review and case studies. In 2018 IEEE/ACM symposium on edge computing (SEC) (pp. 440-444). IEEE.

Al-Saedi, A. A., Boeva, V., Casalicchio, E., & Exner, P. (2022). Context-Aware Edge-Based AI Models for Wireless Sensor Networks—An Overview. *Sensors (Basel)*, *22*(15), 5544. DOI: 10.3390/s22155544 PMID: 35898044

Alterovitz, G., Heale, B., Jones, J., Kreda, D., Lin, F., Liu, L., Liu, X., Mandl, K. D., Poloway, D. W., Ramoni, R., Wagner, A., & Warner, J. (2020). Fhir genomics: Enabling standardization for precision medicine use cases. *NPJ Genomic Medicine*, *5*(1), 13. DOI: 10.1038/s41525-020-0115-6 PMID: 32194985

Alwarafy, A., Al-Thelaya, K. A., Abdallah, M., Schneider, J., & Hamdi, M. (2020). A survey on security and privacy issues in edge-computing-assisted internet of things. *IEEE Internet of Things Journal*, *8*(6), 4004–4022. DOI: 10.1109/JIOT.2020.3015432

Amanat, A., Rizwan, M., Maple, C., Zikria, Y., Almadhor, A., & Kim, S. (2022). Blockchain and cloud computing-based secure electronic healthcare records storage and sharing. *Frontiers in Public Health*, *10*, 938707. DOI: 10.3389/fpubh.2022.938707 PMID: 35928494

Amin, S. U., & Hossain, M. S. (2020). Edge intelligence and Internet of Things in healthcare: A survey. *IEEE Access : Practical Innovations, Open Solutions*, *9*, 45–59. DOI: 10.1109/ACCESS.2020.3045115

Amutha, B. (2023, November). IoT revolutionizing healthcare: a survey of smart healthcare system architectures. In *2023 International Conference on Research Methodologies in Knowledge Management, Artificial Intelligence and Telecommunication Engineering (RMKMATE)* (pp. 1-5). IEEE.

Anusha, S., Ezhilvandan, M., Gayathri, S., Sivaraman, V., & TP, A. (2024). Emerging trends in edge AI for Industry 4.0 and 5.0: Technologies, applications, and challenges. *AI Innovations in Service and Tourism Marketing*, 211-228.

Apat, H. K., Goswami, V., Sahoo, B., Barik, R. K., & Saikia, M. J. (2019). *Fog Service Placement Optimization: A Survey of State-of-the-Art Strategies and Techniques*. MDPI., DOI: 10.3390/computers14030099

Arafa, A., Sheerah, H., & Alsalamah, S. (2023). Emerging digital technologies in healthcare with a spotlight on cybersecurity: A narrative review. *Information (Basel)*, *14*(12), 640. DOI: 10.3390/info14120640

Areo, G. (2022). Faster Healthcare Apps with DevOps: Reducing Time to Market. ResearchGate. https://mzresearch.com/index.php/MZCJ/article/view/375

Armbrust, M., Fox, A., Griffith, R., Joseph, A. D., Katz, R., Konwinski, A., Lee, G., Patterson, D., Rabkin, A., Stoica, I., & Zaharia, M. (2020). A view of cloud computing. *Communications of the ACM*, *53*(4), 50–58. DOI: 10.1145/1721654.1721672

Arockiasamy, J. M. I. (2024). DevOps-driven real-time health analytics: A scalable framework for wearable IoT data. https://www.researchgate.net/profile/Jesu-Marcus-Immanuvel-Arockiasamy/publication/389210225_DevOps-Driven_Real-Time_Health_Analytics_A_Scalable_Framework_for_Wearable_IoT_Data/links/67b8c29396e7fb48b9c9c51f/DevOps-Driven-Real-Time-Health-Analytics-A-Scalable-Framework-for-Wearable-IoT-Data.pdf

Arthurs, P., Gillam, L., Krause, P., Wang, N., Halder, K., & Mouzakitis, A. (2021). A taxonomy and survey of edge cloud computing for intelligent transportation systems and connected vehicles. *IEEE Transactions on Intelligent Transportation Systems*, *23*(7), 6206–6221. DOI: 10.1109/TITS.2021.3084396

Ashok, K., & Gopikrishnan, S. (2023). Statistical analysis of remote health monitoring based IoT security models & deployments from a pragmatic perspective. *IEEE Access : Practical Innovations, Open Solutions*, *11*, 2621–2651. DOI: 10.1109/ACCESS.2023.3234632

Attallah, O., Ma, X., & Sedky, M. (2025). The role of artificial intelligence technologies in revolutionizing and aiding cardiovascular medicine. *Frontiers in Cardiovascular Medicine*, *12*, 1588983. DOI: 10.3389/fcvm.2025.1588983 PMID: 40255343

Atzori, L. (2017). Blockchain-based Smart Manufacturing: A Survey. *Journal of Industrial Information Integration*, *5*, 1–13.

Aujla, G., & Jindal, A. (2021). A decoupled blockchain approach for edge-envisioned iot-based healthcare monitoring. *IEEE Journal on Selected Areas in Communications*, *39*(2), 491–499. DOI: 10.1109/JSAC.2020.3020655

Ayed, D., Dragan, P. A., Félix, E., Mann, Z. A., Salant, E., Seidl, R., . . . Vitorino, R. (2022, May). Protecting sensitive data in the cloud-to-edge continuum: The FogProtect approach. In 2022 22nd IEEE International Symposium on Cluster, Cloud and Internet Computing (CCGrid), pp. 279-288. IEEE.

Bagal, S. A., Katekhaye, A., & Bisane, P. (2025). *Development of Wireless Assistant System for Monitoring in Healthcare Industry–A Review*. International Journal of Innovative Science and Research Technology. DOI: 10.38124/ijisrt/25mar665

Balasubramanian, V., & Jolfaei, A. (2021). A scalable framework for healthcare monitoring application using the Internet of Medical Things. *Software, Practice & Experience*, *51*(12), 2457–2468. DOI: 10.1002/spe.2849

Bao, H., & Lu, R. (2017). A lightweight data aggregation scheme achieving privacy preservation and data integrity with differential privacy and fault tolerance. *Peer-to-Peer Networking and Applications*, *10*(1), 106–121. DOI: 10.1007/s12083-015-0410-7

Barati, M., Rana, O., Ranjan, R., & Aujla, G. S. (2024). Privacy Challenges for Internet of Medical Things. IET Digital Library. https://digital-library.theiet.org/doi/abs/10.1049/pbpc027e_ch9

Barros, S. (2025). Solving AI foundational model latency with telco infrastructure. DOI: 10.2139/ssrn.5195333

Bassi, A. (2016). *The Industrial Internet Consortium: Roadmap for IIoT Implementation*. Springer.

Beheshti, I., Sone, D., & Leung, C. K. (2025). Advances of Artificial Intelligence in Neuroimaging. *Brain Sciences*, *15*(4), 351. DOI: 10.3390/brainsci15040351 PMID: 40309811

Bhardwaj, I., Devi, S., & Kumar, T. (2025). Securing the cloud: Navigating compliance and regulatory challenges. In *Risk-based approach to secure cloud migration* (pp. 325–342). IGI Global., DOI: 10.4018/979-8-3693-7137-4.ch013

Biswas, A., & Wang, H. C. (2023). Autonomous vehicles enabled by the integration of IoT, edge intelligence, 5G, and blockchain. *Sensors (Basel)*, *23*(4), 1963. DOI: 10.3390/s23041963 PMID: 36850560

Bonomi, F., Milito, R., Natarajan, P., & Zhu, J. (2014). Fog computing: A platform for Internet of Things and analytics. In Rao, B. P.. (Eds.). *Big data and internet of things: A roadmap for smart environments* (pp. 169–186). Springer. DOI: 10.1007/978-3-319-05029-4_7

Bonomi, F., Milito, R., Zhu, J., & Addepalli, S. (2022). Fog computing and its role in the internet of things. In *Proceedings of the First Edition of the MCC Workshop on Mobile Cloud Computing* (pp. 13–16). ACM. DOI: 10.1145/2342509.2342513

Boo, S., & Oh, H. (2023). Perceptions of registered nurses on facilitators and barriers of implementing the AI-IoT-based healthcare pilot project for older adults during the COVID-19 pandemic in South Korea. *Frontiers in Public Health*, *11*, 1234626. DOI: 10.3389/fpubh.2023.1234626 PMID: 37886046

Borra, P., & Nerella, H. (2024). *Analyzing AWS edge computing solutions to enhance IoT deployments*. *SSRN*. DOI: 10.35940/ijeat.F4519.13060824

Bosch, T. (2017). *The Industrial Internet of Things: A Technical Perspective*. Springer.

Boudoukh, S. (2019). Workforce Development for IIoT Adoption in Manufacturing. *Journal of Manufacturing Science and Engineering*, *141*(10), 1–9.

Bovenzi, G., Aceto, G., Ciuonzo, D., Persico, V., & Pescapé, A. (2020). A hierarchical hybrid intrusion detection approach in IoT scenarios. In *2020 IEEE Global Communications Conference (GLOBECOM)* (pp. 1–6). IEEE. DOI: 10.1109/GLOBECOM42002.2020.9348167

Bragadeesh, S., & Arumugam, U. (2019). A conceptual framework for security and privacy in edge computing. In *Edge Computing* (pp. 173–186). Springer.

Brose, S. W., Weber, D. J., Salatin, B. A., Grindle, G. G., Wang, H., Vazquez, J. J., & Cooper, R. A. (2010). The role of assistive robotics in the lives of persons with disability. *American Journal of Physical Medicine & Rehabilitation*, *89*(6), 509–521. DOI: 10.1097/PHM.0b013e3181cf569b PMID: 20134305

Butean, A., David, A., Buduleci, C., & Daian, A. (2015, May). Auxilum Medicine: a cloud based platform for real-time monitoring medical devices. In 2015 20th International Conference on Control Systems and Computer Science (pp. 874-879). IEEE. DOI: 10.1109/CSCS.2015.135

Buyya, R., Yeo, C. S., Venugopal, S., Broberg, J., & Brandic, I. (2019). Cloud computing and emerging IT platforms: Vision, hype, and reality for delivering computing as the 5th utility. *Future Generation Computer Systems*, *25*(6), 599–616. DOI: 10.1016/j.future.2008.12.001

Cai, Z., Cao, X., Zhang, Z., Chen, Q., Li, H., Li, X., . . . Zhu, G. (2024, March). Integrated Sensing and Learning for Better Generalized Edge AI. In *2024 IEEE 4th International Symposium on Joint Communications & Sensing (JC&S)* (pp. 1-6). IEEE. DOI: 10.1109/JCS61227.2024.10646278

Cao, K., Liu, Y., Meng, G., & Sun, Q. (2020). An overview on edge computing research. *IEEE Access : Practical Innovations, Open Solutions*, *8*, 85714–85728. DOI: 10.1109/ACCESS.2020.2991734

Carros, F., Meurer, J., Löffler, D., Unbehaun, D., Matthies, S., Koch, I., Wieching, R., Randall, D., Hassenzahl, M., & Wulf, V. (2020). Exploring human-robot interaction with the elderly: Results from a ten-week case study in a care home. In *Proceedings of the 2020 CHI Conference on Human Factors in Computing Systems* (pp. 1–12). Association for Computing Machinery. DOI: 10.1145/3313831.3376402

Ceravolo, P., Junior, S. B., Damiani, E., & Van Der Aalst, W. (2024). Tuning Machine Learning to Address Process Mining Requirements. *IEEE Access: Practical Innovations, Open Solutions, 12*, 24583–24595. DOI: 10.1109/ACCESS.2024.3361650

Chandrashekaraiah, M. (2025). Novel semiconductor chip-based smart sensor technology design and integration of IoT in AI-ML hyperscale infrastructure.

Charanya, R., Aramudhan, M., Mohan, K., & Nithya, S. (2013). Levels of security issues in cloud computing. *IACSIT International Journal of Engineering and Technology, 5*(2), 1912–1920.

Chauhan, D., Jain, J., & Singh, A. (2024). Deployment of edge computing for smart healthcare systems on cloud computing platform. *International Journal of Scientific Research in Computer Science Engineering and Information Technology, 10*(3), 685–693. DOI: 10.32628/CSEIT2410339

Chaves, S. A. D., Uriarte, R. B., & Westphall, C. B. (2011). Toward an architecture for monitoring private clouds. *IEEE Communications Magazine, 49*(12), 130–137. DOI: 10.1109/MCOM.2011.6094017

Chbeir, R., & Manolopoulos, Y. (2024). *AI-Driven Maintenance in Healthcare Edge Computing Systems*. MDPI., DOI: 10.3390/app14219903

Chelliah, P. R., Rahmani, A. M., Colby, R., Nagasubramanian, G., & Ranganath, S. (Eds.). (2024). *Model Optimization Methods for Efficient and Edge AI: Federated Learning Architectures, Frameworks and Applications*. John Wiley & Sons.

Chen, C. H., Lin, M. Y., & Liu, C. C. (2018). Edge computing gateway of the industrial internet of things using multiple collaborative microcontrollers. *IEEE Network, 32*(1), 24–32. DOI: 10.1109/MNET.2018.1700146

Cheng, S.-F., Wang, X., & Huang, X. (2019). *Urban computing: Methods and applications*. Springer.

Cheng, Y. (2020). *Anomaly Detection and Fault Diagnosis in IIoT-Enabled Smart Manufacturing*. Springer.

Chen, L., & Poon, C. S. (2020). Edge computing: Towards a network of smart objects. In *IoT technologies, architectures, and applications* (pp. 227–246). Springer.

Chen, M., Qian, Y., Mao, S., Tang, W., & Yang, X. (2020). Software-defined mobile networks security. *Mobile Networks and Applications*, *21*(5), 729–743. DOI: 10.1007/s11036-015-0665-5

Chen, S., Xu, H., Liu, D., Hu, B., & Wang, H. (2021). A vision of IoT: Applications, challenges, and opportunities with China perspective. *IEEE Internet of Things Journal*, *1*(4), 349–359. DOI: 10.1109/JIOT.2014.2337336

Chenthara, S., Ahmed, K., Wang, H., & Whittaker, F. (2019). Security and privacy-preserving challenges of e-health solutions in cloud computing. *IEEE Access : Practical Innovations, Open Solutions*, *7*, 74361–74382. DOI: 10.1109/ACCESS.2019.2919982

Chen, X., Letaief, K. B., & Huang, K. (2024). On the View-and-Channel Aggregation Gain in Integrated Sensing and Edge AI. *IEEE Journal on Selected Areas in Communications*, *42*(9), 2292–2305. DOI: 10.1109/JSAC.2024.3413988

Cherukuri, H., Shukla, S., Rajan, A. T., & Aravind, S. (2024). Deploying containerized microservices in on-premise Kubernetes environments: Challenges and best practices. International Journal of Multidisciplinary Innovation and Research Methodology, ISSN: 2960-2068, 3(2), 74-90.

Chianese, R., Gargiulo, F., Marrone, S., Nespolino, C., Pirozzi, G., & Verde, L. (2023, July). Supporting the Maintenance Process of Healthcare Pervasive Devices. In International Conference on Information, Intelligence, Systems, and Applications (pp. 286-305). Cham: Springer Nature Switzerland.

Chowdhury, A. R., Wang, C., He, C., Machanajjhala, A., & Jha, S. (2020, June). Crypto-assisted differential privacy on untrusted servers. *Proceedings of the ACM SIGMOD International Conference on Management of Data*, 603–619.

Ciecierski-Holmes, T., Singh, R., Axt, M., Brenner, S., & Barteit, S. (2022). Artificial intelligence for strengthening healthcare systems in low- and middle-income countries: A systematic scoping review. *NPJ Digital Medicine*, *5*(1), 162. DOI: 10.1038/s41746-022-00700-y PMID: 36307479

Cifuentes, C. A., Pinto, M. J., Céspedes, N., & Múnera, M. (2020). Social robots in therapy and care. *Current Robotics Reports*, *1*(3), 59–74. DOI: 10.1007/s43154-020-00009-2

Cingolani, M., Scendoni, R., Fedeli, P., & Cembrani, F. (2023). Artificial intelligence and digital medicine for integrated home care services in Italy: Opportunities and limits. *Frontiers in Public Health*, *10*, 1095001. DOI: 10.3389/fpubh.2022.1095001 PMID: 36684935

Civino, R., Blondeau, C., & Sala, M. (2019). Differential attacks: Using alternative operations. *Designs, Codes and Cryptography*, *87*(2), 225–247. DOI: 10.1007/s10623-018-0516-z

Colombo, G. (2021, April). Cloud driven edge computing on smart systems integration. In 2021 Smart Systems Integration (SSI) (pp. 1-3). IEEE.

Cooper, F., Silberstein, A., Tam, E., Ramakrishnan, R., & Sears, R. (2010). Benchmarking cloud serving systems with YCSB. In *Proceedings of the ACM Symposium on Cloud Computing* (pp. 143–154). ACM. DOI: 10.1145/1807128.1807152

Cooper, R. G. (2024). The Artificial Intelligence Revolution in New-Product Development. *IEEE Engineering Management Review*, *52*(1), 195–211. DOI: 10.1109/EMR.2023.3336834

Cuervo, E., Balasubramanian, A., Cho, D.-K., Wolman, A., Saroiu, S., Chandra, R., & Bahl, P. (2010). MAUI: Making smartphones last longer with code offload. In *Proceedings of the 8th International Conference on Mobile Systems, Applications, and Services* (pp. 49–62). ACM. DOI: 10.1145/1814433.1814441

Cui, Y., Cao, X., Zhu, G., Nie, J., & Xu, J. (2024). Edge Perception: Intelligent Wireless Sensing at Network Edge. *arXiv preprint arXiv:2410.21017.*

Dagher, G. G., Fung, B. C. M., Mohammed, N., & Clark, J. (2020). SecDM: Privacy-preserving data outsourcing framework with differential privacy. *Knowledge and Information Systems*, *62*(5), 1923–1960. DOI: 10.1007/s10115-019-01405-7

Dai, M., Su, Z., Li, R., Wang, Y., Ni, J., & Fang, D. (2020). An edge-driven security framework for intelligent internet of things. *IEEE Network*, *34*(5), 39–45. DOI: 10.1109/MNET.011.2000068

Dai, Y., Xu, D., Maharjan, S., Qiao, G., & Zhang, Y. (2019). Artificial intelligence empowered edge computing and caching for Internet of Vehicles. *IEEE Wireless Communications*, *26*(3), 12–18. DOI: 10.1109/MWC.2019.1800411

Daniel, C. (2023). Medical Device Maintenance Regimes in Healthcare Institutions. In *Inspection of Medical Devices: For Regulatory Purposes* (pp. 59–91). Springer Nature Switzerland.

Dash, A., Ye, J., & Wang, G. (2024). A Review of Generative Adversarial Networks (GANs) and Its Applications in a Wide Variety of Disciplines: From Medical to Remote Sensing. *IEEE Access: Practical Innovations, Open Solutions*, *12*, 18330–18357. DOI: 10.1109/ACCESS.2023.3346273

Dave, D. M. (2023). Advancing Medical Device Manufacturing: The Convergence of Edge Computing and Industry 5.0. International Journal of Engineering Applications and Science Technology

Dave, R., Seliya, N., & Siddiqui, N. (2021). The benefits of edge computing in healthcare, smart cities, and IoT. https://arxiv.org/abs/2112.01250

Deelman, K., Vahi, K., Juve, G., Rynge, M., Callaghan, S., Maechling, P. J., Mayani, R., Chen, W., Ferreira da Silva, R., Livny, M., & Wenger, K. (2015). Pegasus: A workflow management system for science automation. *Future Generation Computer Systems*, *46*, 17–35. DOI: 10.1016/j.future.2014.10.008

Deng, S., Zhao, H., Fang, W., Yin, J., Dustdar, S., & Zomaya, A. Y. (2020). Edge intelligence: The confluence of edge computing and artificial intelligence. *IEEE Internet of Things Journal*, *7*(8), 7457–7469. DOI: 10.1109/JIOT.2020.2984887

Dias, R., & Torkamani, A. (2019). Artificial intelligence in clinical and genomic diagnostics. *Genome Medicine*, *11*(1), 70. DOI: 10.1186/s13073-019-0689-8 PMID: 31744524

Dolui, K., & Datta, S. K. (2021). Comparison of edge computing implementations: Fog computing, cloudlet and mobile edge computing. In *Proceedings of the Global Internet of Things Summit* (pp. 1–6). IEEE. DOI: 10.1109/GIOTS.2017.8016214

Draeger, C., Tute, E., Schmidt, C., Waltemath, D., Boeker, M., Winter, A, & Löbe, M. (2023). Identifying relevant FHIR elements for data quality assessment in the German core data set. DOI: 10.3233/SHTI230117

Drăgulinescu, A. M. C., Manea, A. F., Fratu, O., & Drăgulinescu, A. (2020). LoRa-based medical IoT system architecture and testbed. *Wireless Personal Communications*, 1–23.

Durão, L. F. C., Haag, S., Anderl, R., Schützer, K., & Zancul, E. (2018). Digital twin requirements in the context of industry 4.0. In M. Sarfatti, A. Bouras, & Y. Stjepandić (Eds.), *Product lifecycle management to support Industry 4.0: 15th IFIP WG 5.1 International Conference, PLM 2018, Turin, Italy, July 2–4, 2018, Proceedings 15* (pp. 204–214). Springer International Publishing. DOI: 10.1007/978-3-030-01614-2_19

Egger, D. J., Gambella, C., Marecek, J., McFaddin, S., Mevissen, M., Raymond, R., Simonetto, A., Woerner, S., & Yndurain, E. (2020). Quantum Computing for Finance: State-of-the-Art and Future Prospects. *IEEE Transactions on Quantum Engineering*, *1*, 1–24. DOI: 10.1109/TQE.2020.3030314

Eibl, G., Bao, K., Grassal, P.-W., Bernau, D., & Schmeck, H. (2018). The influence of differential privacy on short term electric load forecasting. *Energy Informatics, 1*(S1), 48. DOI: 10.1186/s42162-018-0025-3

Elhachmi, J., Laaouamir, S., & Ziad, I. (2025). Securing containerized workloads in Kubernetes: Best practices and implementation. https://papers.ssrn.com/sol3/papers.cfm?abstract_id=5194051

El-Sayed, H., Sankar, S., Prasad, M., Puthal, D., Gupta, A., Mohanty, M., & Lin, C. T. (2017). Edge of things: The big picture on the integration of edge, IoT and the cloud in a distributed computing environment. *IEEE Access, 6*, 1706-1717.

Esposito, C., Castiglione, A., Pop, F., & Choo, K. K. R. (2017). Challenges of connecting edge and cloud computing: A security and forensic perspective. *IEEE Cloud Computing, 4*(2), 13–17. DOI: 10.1109/MCC.2017.30

Evans, D. (2011). The Internet of Things: How the next evolution of the Internet is changing everything (CISCO White Paper, Vol. 1, pp. 1–11).

Fadda, G., Fadda, M., Ghiani, E., & Pilloni, V. (2019). *Communications and Internet of Things for microgrids, smart buildings, and homes*. Elsevier Inc., DOI: 10.1016/B978-0-12-817774-7.00009-0

Fadi, O., Karim, Z., Abdellatif, E. G., & Mohammed, B. (2022). A Survey on Blockchain and Artificial Intelligence Technologies for Enhancing Security and Privacy in Smart Environments. *IEEE Access : Practical Innovations, Open Solutions, 10*, 93168–93186. DOI: 10.1109/ACCESS.2022.3203568

Frey, N., Haffer, N., Vogelsang, L., Saß, J., Thun, S., Balzer, F. & Landgraf, P. (2024). Integrating fhir and umls in an intelligent tutoring system. DOI: 10.3233/SHTI240708

Fu, J. S., Liu, Y., Chao, H. C., Bhargava, B. K., & Zhang, Z. J. (2018). Secure data storage and searching for industrial IoT by integrating fog computing and cloud computing. *IEEE Transactions on Industrial Informatics, 14*(10), 4519–4528. DOI: 10.1109/TII.2018.2793350

Gatouillat, A., Badr, Y., Massot, B., & Sejdić, E. (2018). Internet of medical things: A review of recent contributions dealing with cyber-physical systems in medicine. *IEEE Internet of Things Journal, 5*(5), 3810–3822. DOI: 10.1109/JIOT.2018.2849014

Geiger, R. S., Yu, K., Yang, Y., Dai, M., Qiu, J., Tang, R., & Huang, J. (2019). Garbage In, Garbage Out? Do Machine Learning Application Papers in Social Computing Report Where Human-Labeled Training Data Comes From? DOI: 10.1145/3351095.3372862

Ghandour, A., Woodford, B. J., & Abusaimeh, H. (2024). Ethical Considerations in the Use of ChatGPT: An Exploration Through the Lens of Five Moral Dimensions. *IEEE Access : Practical Innovations, Open Solutions*, *12*, 60682–60693. DOI: 10.1109/ACCESS.2024.3394243

Ghane, S., Jolfaei, A., Kulik, L., Ramamohanarao, K., & Puthal, D. (2021). Preserving privacy in the internet of connected vehicles. *IEEE Transactions on Intelligent Transportation Systems*, *22*(8), 5018–5027. DOI: 10.1109/TITS.2020.2964410

Ghosh, S., & Ghosh, S. K. (2023). Feel: Federated learning framework for elderly healthcare using edge-IoMT. *IEEE Transactions on Computational Social Systems*, *10*(4), 1800–1809. DOI: 10.1109/TCSS.2022.3233300

Gill, S. S., Xu, M., Ottaviani, C., Patros, P., Bahsoon, R., Shaghaghi, A., Golec, M., Stankovski, V., Wu, H., Abraham, A., Singh, M., Mehta, H., Ghosh, S. K., Baker, T., Parlikad, A. K., Lutfiyya, H., Kanhere, S. S., Sakellariou, R., Dustdar, S., & Uhlig, S. (2022). AI for next generation computing: Emerging trends and future directions. *Internet of Things : Engineering Cyber Physical Human Systems*, *19*, 100514. DOI: 10.1016/j.iot.2022.100514

Glaessgen, E. J., & Stargel, D. (2012). *The Digital Twin Paradigm for Future NASA and U.S. Air Force Vehicles*. 53rd AIAA/ASME/ASCE/AHS/ASC Structures, Structural Dynamics, and Materials Conference. DOI: 10.2514/6.2012-1818

Gobalakrishnan, N. (2024). *TrustSec-ChainX: A Pioneering Approach to Enhancing Trust Management and Data Integrity in IoT Healthcare*. IEEE Xplore., DOI: 10.1109/ICERCS63125.2024.10895865

Goeldner, M., Herstatt, C., & Tietze, F. (2015). The emergence of care robotics—A patent and publication analysis. *Technological Forecasting and Social Change*, *92*, 115–131. DOI: 10.1016/j.techfore.2014.09.005

Goethals, T., Volckaert, B., & De Turck, F. (2021). Enabling and leveraging AI in the intelligent edge: A review of current trends and future directions. *IEEE Open Journal of the Communications Society*, *2*, 2311–2341. DOI: 10.1109/OJCOMS.2021.3116437

Goh, T. L., & Tham, H. M. (2016). Smart water management technologies for urban resilience. *Journal of Environmental Management*, *182*, 16–25.

Golda, A., Mekonen, K., Pandey, A., Singh, A., Hassija, V., Chamola, V., & Sikdar, B. (2024). Privacy and Security Concerns in Generative AI: A Comprehensive Survey. *IEEE Access : Practical Innovations, Open Solutions*, *12*, 48126–48144. DOI: 10.1109/ACCESS.2024.3381611

Gong, C., Lin, F., Gong, X., & Lu, Y. (2020). Intelligent cooperative edge computing in internet of things. *IEEE Internet of Things Journal*, *7*(10), 9372–9382. DOI: 10.1109/JIOT.2020.2986015

Gong, T., Zhu, L., Yu, F. R., & Tang, T. (2023). Edge intelligence in intelligent transportation systems: A survey. *IEEE Transactions on Intelligent Transportation Systems*, *24*(9), 8919–8944. DOI: 10.1109/TITS.2023.3275741

Gowrabhathini, J., Tamilarasu, J., Rahithya, S., Sindhu Parimala, P. S., Hussain, S. S., & Sri, C. N. (2024). Business Intelligence In Industrial Organization Using An AI-Driven Competitive Analysis Framework. 2024 2nd International Conference on Disruptive Technologies (ICDT), 112–115. DOI: 10.1109/ICDT61202.2024.10489175

Greenberg, J., Hamilton, D. A., Maltz, D. A., & Patel, P. (2008). The cost of a cloud: Research problems in data center networks. *Computer Communication Review*, *39*(1), 68–73. DOI: 10.1145/1496091.1496103

Grieves, M. (2014). *Digital Twin: Manufacturing Excellence through Virtual Factory Replication*. White paper.

Grosse, K., Bieringer, L., Besold, T. R., Biggio, B., & Krombholz, K. (2023). Machine Learning Security in Industry: A Quantitative Survey. *IEEE Transactions on Information Forensics and Security*, *18*, 1749–1762. DOI: 10.1109/TIFS.2023.3251842

Gubbi, J., Buyya, R., Marusic, S., & Palaniswami, M. (2013). Internet of Things (IoT): A Vision, Architectural Elements, and Future Directions. *Future Generation Computer Systems*, *29*(7), 1645–1660. DOI: 10.1016/j.future.2013.01.010

Guo, H., & Liu, J. (2018). Collaborative computation offloading for multi-access edge computing over fiber-wireless networks. *IEEE Transactions on Vehicular Technology*, *67*(5), 4514–4526. DOI: 10.1109/TVT.2018.2790421

Gurjar, K., Jangra, A., Baber, H., Islam, M., & Sheikh, S. A. (2024). An Analytical Review on the Impact of Artificial Intelligence on the Business Industry: Applications, Trends, and Challenges. *IEEE Engineering Management Review*, *52*(2), 84–102. DOI: 10.1109/EMR.2024.3355973

Hahanov, V., Hahanov, V., Gharibi, W., Man, K. L., Iemelianov, I., Liubarskyi, M.,& Chumachenko, S. (2018). Cyber-physical technologies: Hype cycle 2017. *Cyber Physical Computing for IoT-driven Services*, 259-272.

Haider, J., & Abbas, A. (2025). The future of AI in healthcare: Bridging the gap between technology and patient well-being.

Haleem, A., Javaid, M., Asim Qadri, M., Pratap Singh, R., & Suman, R. (2022). Artificial intelligence (AI) applications for marketing: A literature-based study. *International Journal of Intelligent Networks*, *3*, 119–132. DOI: 10.1016/j.ijin.2022.08.005

Hanafizadeh, P., & Amin, M. G. (2022). *The transformative potential of banking service domains with the emergence of FinTechs*. Palgrave Macmillan., DOI: 10.1007/978-3-030-99584-3

Hartmann, M., Hashmi, U. S., & Imran, A. (2022). Edge computing in smart health care systems: Review, challenges, and research directions. *Transactions on Emerging Telecommunications Technologies*, *33*(3), e3710. DOI: 10.1002/ett.3710

Hasan, M., Li, Q., Saha, U., & Li, J. (2024). Decentralized and secure collaborative framework for personalized diabetes prediction. *Biomedicines*, *12*(8), 1916. DOI: 10.3390/biomedicines12081916 PMID: 39200380

Hassan, N., Gillani, S., Ahmed, E., Yaqoob, I., & Imran, M. (2021). The role of edge computing in Internet of Things. *IEEE Communications Magazine*, *56*(11), 110–115. DOI: 10.1109/MCOM.2018.1700906

He, Z., Zhang, T., & Lee, R. B. (2020). Attacking and protecting data privacy in edge–cloud collaborative inference systems. *IEEE Internet of Things Journal*, *8*(12), 9706–9716. DOI: 10.1109/JIOT.2020.3022358

Hoeiland-Joergensen, T., McKenney, P., Taht, D., Gettys, J., & Dumazet, E. (2018). *The Flow Queue CoDel packet scheduler and active queue management algorithm (RFC 8290)*. Internet Engineering Task Force., DOI: 10.17487/RFC8290

Holland, O., Steinbach, E., Prasad, R. V., Liu, Q., Dawy, Z., Aijaz, A., Pappas, N., Chandra, K., Rao, V. S., Oteafy, S., Eid, M., Luden, M., Bhardwaj, A., Liu, X., Sachs, J., & Araujo, J. (2019). The IEEE 1918.1 "Tactile Internet" standards working group and its standards. *Proceedings of the IEEE*, *107*(2), 256–279. DOI: 10.1109/JPROC.2018.2885541

Holley, K., & Mathur, M. (2024). *LLMs and Generative AI for Healthcare: The Next Frontier*. O'Reilly Media, Inc.

Hrovatin, N., Tošić, A., Mrissa, M., & Kavšek, B. (2022). Privacy-preserving data mining on blockchain-based WSNs. *Applied Sciences (Basel, Switzerland)*, *12*(11), 5646. DOI: 10.3390/app12115646

Hua, H., Li, Y., Wang, T., Dong, N., Li, W., & Cao, J. (2023). Edge computing with artificial intelligence: A machine learning perspective. *ACM Computing Surveys*, *55*(9), 1–35. DOI: 10.1145/3555802

Huang, G. (2018). *Green Manufacturing and AI-based Energy Management Systems*. Springer.

Huang, J., Kong, L., Chen, G., Wu, M. Y., Liu, X., & Zeng, P. (2019). Towards secure industrial IoT: Blockchain system with credit-based consensus mechanism. *IEEE Transactions on Industrial Informatics, 15*(6), 3680–3689. DOI: 10.1109/TII.2019.2903342

Huang, J., Kong, L., Dai, H. N., Ding, W., Cheng, L., Chen, G., Jin, X., & Zeng, P. (2020). Blockchain-based mobile crowd sensing in industrial systems. *IEEE Transactions on Industrial Informatics, 16*(10), 6553–6563. DOI: 10.1109/TII.2019.2963728

Huang, X., Wang, X., & Cheng, S.-F. (2017). *Smart healthcare: Technologies, applications, and case studies*. Springer.

Hu, F., & Hao, Q. (2012). *Intelligent sensor networks: the integration of sensor networks, signal processing and machine learning*. Taylor & Francis. DOI: 10.1201/b14300

Huh, J. H., & Seo, Y. S. (2019). Understanding edge computing: Engineering evolution with artificial intelligence. *IEEE Access : Practical Innovations, Open Solutions, 7*, 164229–164245. DOI: 10.1109/ACCESS.2019.2945338

Humayun, M., Tariq, N., Alfayad, M., Zakwan, M., Alwakid, G., & Assiri, M. (2024). Securing the Internet of Things in Artificial Intelligence Era: A Comprehensive Survey. *IEEE Access : Practical Innovations, Open Solutions, 12*, 25469–25490. DOI: 10.1109/ACCESS.2024.3365634

Hussain, F., Hassan, S. A., Hussain, R., & Hossain, E. (2020). Machine learning for resource management in cellular and IoT networks: Potentials, current solutions, and open challenges. *IEEE Communications Surveys and Tutorials, 22*(2), 1251–1275. DOI: 10.1109/COMST.2020.2964534

Imtiaz, S., & Jillani, S. (2024). The impact of artificial intelligence on medical diagnostics: A letter to the editor. *JPMA. The Journal of the Pakistan Medical Association, 74*(5), 1035–1036. DOI: 10.47391/JPMA.10668 PMID: 38783474

Iosup, S., Ostermann, S., Yigitbasi, N., Prodan, R., Fahringer, T., & Epema, D. (2011). Performance analysis of cloud computing services for many-tasks scientific computing. *IEEE Transactions on Parallel and Distributed Systems, 22*(6), 931–945. DOI: 10.1109/TPDS.2011.66

Islam, J., Kumar, T., Kovacevic, I., & Harjula, E. (2021). Resource-Aware Dynamic Service Deployment for Local IoT Edge Computing: Healthcare Use Case. *IEEE Access : Practical Innovations, Open Solutions*, *9*, 115868–115884. DOI: 10.1109/ACCESS.2021.3102867

Ivanović, M., Chbeir, R., & Manolopoulos, Y. (2024). *Management of Digital Ecosystems: Dedicated to the Memory of Prof. William I. Grosky 8/4/1944–11/13/2020*. MDPI., DOI: 10.3390/books978-3-7258-0646-1

Iyapparaja, M., Alshammari, N. K., Kumar, M. S., Krishnan, S. S. R., & Chowdhary, C. L. (2022). Efficient resource allocation in fog computing using QTCS model. *Computers, Materials & Continua*, *70*(2), 2225–2239. DOI: 10.32604/cmc.2022.015707

Jain, P., Gyanchandani, M., & Khare, N. (2018). Differential privacy: Its technological prescriptive using big data. *Journal of Big Data*, *5*(1), 15. DOI: 10.1186/s40537-018-0124-9

Jaleel, A. (2022). Distributed interoperability solutions smart healthcare system for multi-patient vital signs monitoring and forecast of critical alerts. *Pakistan Journal of Science*, *72*(4). DOI: 10.57041/pjs.v72i4.235

Jararweh, Y. (2020). Enabling efficient and secure energy cloud using edge computing and 5G. *Journal of Parallel and Distributed Computing*, *145*, 42–49. DOI: 10.1016/j.jpdc.2020.06.014

Jararweh, Y., Doulat, A., AlQudah, O., Ahmed, E., Al-Ayyoub, M., & Benkhelifa, E. (2021). The future of mobile cloud computing: Integrating cloudlets and mobile edge computing. In *Proceedings of the 23rd International Conference on Telecommunications* (pp. 1–5). IEEE. DOI: 10.1109/ICT.2016.7500404

Javadpour, A., Wang, G., & Rezaei, S. (2020). Resource management in a peer to peer cloud network for IoT. *Wireless Personal Communications*, *115*(3), 2471–2488. DOI: 10.1007/s11277-020-07691-7

Javed, H., Toosi, A., & Aslanpour, M. (2021). Serverless platforms on the edge: a performance analysis.

Jazaeri, S. S., Asghari, P., Jabbehdari, S., & Javadi, H. H. S. (2023). Composition of caching and classification in edge computing based on quality optimization for SDN-based IoT healthcare solutions. *The Journal of Supercomputing*, *79*(14), 17619–17669. DOI: 10.1007/s11227-023-05332-x PMID: 37359340

Johansson-Pajala, R. M., & Gustafsson, C. (2022). Significant challenges when introducing care robots in Swedish elder care. *Disability and Rehabilitation. Assistive Technology*, *17*(2), 166–176. DOI: 10.1080/17483107.2020.1773549 PMID: 32538206

Jo, O., Kim, Y. K., & Kim, J. (2018). Internet of Things for smart railway: Feasibility and applications. *IEEE Internet of Things Journal*, *5*(2), 482–490. DOI: 10.1109/JIOT.2017.2749401

Jordan, M. I., & Mitchell, T. M. (2015). Machine learning: Trends, perspectives, and prospects. *Science*, *349*(6245), 255–260. DOI: 10.1126/science.aaa8415 PMID: 26185243

Joseph, O., Kathrine, J. W., & Vijayan, R. (2014). Cloud security mechanisms for data protection: A survey. *International Journal of Multimedia and Ubiquitous Engineering*, *9*(9), 81–90. DOI: 10.14257/ijmue.2014.9.9.09

Joshi, V., & Patil, K. (2024, April). Efficient Handoff Detection for Computation Offloading using Machine Learning and Bio-Inspired Optimization Techniques in Mobile Edge Computing. In *2024 IEEE 13th International Conference on Communication Systems and Network Technologies (CSNT)* (pp. 100-104). IEEE. DOI: 10.1109/CSNT60213.2024.10546105

Joshi, V., & Patil, K. (2022). Delay-energy aware task offloading and vm migration policy for mobile edge computing. *Wireless Personal Communications*, *123*(4), 3309–3326. DOI: 10.1007/s11277-021-09290-6

Jung, S., Bae, S., Seong, D., Oh, O., Kim, Y., & Yi, B. (2022). Shared interoperable clinical decision support service for drug-allergy interaction checks: Implementation study. *JMIR Medical Informatics*, *10*(11), e40338. DOI: 10.2196/40338 PMID: 36355401

Kabra, A., Agarwal, A., & Parihar, A. S. (2022). Potent Real-Time Recommendations Using Multimodel Contextual Reinforcement Learning. *IEEE Transactions on Computational Social Systems*, *9*(2), 581–593. DOI: 10.1109/TCSS.2021.3100291

Kaki, S. S., Kantareddygari, J. R., & Aishwarya, R. (2025, February). Privacy and Security Concerns in Edge-Cloud Systems: An In-Depth Analysis. In 2025 3rd International Conference on Intelligent Data Communication Technologies and Internet of Things (IDCIoT) (pp. 435-441). IEEE.

Kamel, P., & Nagy, P. (2018). Patient-centered radiology with fhir: An introduction to the use of fhir to offer radiology a clinically integrated platform. *Journal of Digital Imaging*, *31*(3), 327–333. DOI: 10.1007/s10278-018-0087-6 PMID: 29725963

Kanevskaia, O., Delimatsis, P., & Bijlmakers, S. (2024). The European Telecommunication Standards Institute (ETSI): In search for legitimacy and resilience of European standardisation. *Innovation (Abingdon), 37*(5), 1–20. DOI: 10.1080/13511610.2024.2395262 PMID: 39975519

Kannadhasan, S., & Deepa, S. (2020, April). Energy efficiency to improve network life time using particle swarm optimization algorithm. In *Proceedings of the International Conference on Communication, Computing, Storage & Energy (IC3SE-18)*. EAI Endorsed Transactions on Context-Aware Systems and Applications. DOI: 10.4108/eai.13-7-2018.163974

Kannadhasan, S., Isavani, M., & Karthikeyan, G. (2014). A novel privacy security protocol based SUPM method in near field communication technology. In *Artificial Intelligence and Evolutionary Algorithms in Engineering Systems (ICAEES 2014)*. Advances in Intelligent Systems and Computing. Springer.

Kanungo, P. (2025). Edge computing in healthcare: real-time patient monitoring systems. World Journal of Advanced Engineering Technology and Sciences, 15(1), 001-009. DOI: 10.30574/wjaets.2025.15.1.0168

Karajgi, S., Kumar, K. G., & Shankar, B. (2025). Artificial Intelligence in Healthcare: A Review of Machine Learning Applications. ITM Web of Conferences. https://www.itm-conferences.org/articles/itmconf/abs/2025/07/itmconf_icsice2025_01012/itmconf_icsice2025_01012.html

Kassa, Y., & Grispos, G. (2025). Secure Edge Computing Reference Architecture for Data-driven Structural Health Monitoring: Lessons Learned from Implementation and Benchmarking.

Kayabol, K. (2020). Approximate Sparse Multinomial Logistic Regression for Classification. *IEEE Transactions on Pattern Analysis and Machine Intelligence, 42*(2), 490–493. DOI: 10.1109/TPAMI.2019.2904062 PMID: 30869609

Kayataş, Y. (2025). Enhancing smart environments through an AI-assisted IoRT agent. Polen ITU. https://polen.itu.edu.tr/items/02494d5a-347a-4522-9e58-6c1e1ca93b64

Khan, W., & Ishrat, M. (2025). Navigating Ethical Challenges: Frameworks for Swarm Intelligence in Fog Computing. Taylor & Francis. https://www.taylorfrancis.com/chapters/edit/10.1201/9781032693217-9

Khan, M. A., Khan, M. A., Jan, S. U., Ahmad, J., Jamal, S. S., Shah, A. A., Pitropakis, N., & Buchanan, W. J. (2021). A deep learning-based intrusion detection system for MQTT enabled IoT. *Sensors (Basel), 21*(21), 7016. DOI: 10.3390/s21217016 PMID: 34770322

Khan, M. A., Saleh, A. M., Waseem, M., & Sajjad, I. A. (2023). Artificial Intelligence Enabled Demand Response: Prospects and Challenges in Smart Grid Environment. *IEEE Access : Practical Innovations, Open Solutions, 11*, 1477–1505. DOI: 10.1109/ACCESS.2022.3231444

Khan, M. A., Saqib, S., Alyas, T., Ur Rehman, A., Saeed, Y., Zeb, A., Zareei, M., & Mohamed, E. M. (2020). Effective Demand Forecasting Model Using Business Intelligence Empowered With Machine Learning. *IEEE Access : Practical Innovations, Open Solutions, 8*, 116013–116023. DOI: 10.1109/ACCESS.2020.3003790

Khan, W. Z., Ahmed, E., Hakak, S., Yaqoob, I., & Ahmed, A. (2019). Edge computing: A survey. *Future Generation Computer Systems, 97*, 219–235. DOI: 10.1016/j.future.2019.02.050

Kietzmann, J., Paschen, J., & Treen, E. (2018). Artificial intelligence in advertising: How marketers can leverage AI. *Journal of Advertising Research, 58*(3), 263–267. DOI: 10.2501/JAR-2018-035

Kiran, K. R., Kumar, B. H., Mishra, B. S., & Yadav, A. S. Y, N., & Tiwari, M. (2023). Artificial Intelligence Integrated with Machine Learning for Enhancing Business in E-World. 2023 5th International Conference on Inventive Research in Computing Applications (ICIRCA), 1060–1064. DOI: 10.1109/ICIRCA57980.2023.10220756

Kothari, R. (2023). Integration of blockchain and edge computing in healthcare: Accountability and collaboration. *Transdisciplinary Journal of Engineering & Science, 14*. DOI: 10.22545/2023/00230

Kousalya, G., Balakrishnan, P., Pethuru Raj, C., Kousalya, G., Balakrishnan, P., & Pethuru Raj, C. (2017). Stepping into the digital intelligence era. *Automated Workflow Scheduling in Self-Adaptive Clouds: Concepts, Algorithms and Methods*, 1-22.

Krishna, G., Singh, V., Pandey, D., Krishna, K. H., Joshi, K., & Gupta, T. (2024, May). Power trading framework of cloud-edge computing in the artificial intelligence market. In *2024 4th International Conference on Advance Computing and Innovative Technologies in Engineering (ICACITE)*, pp. 1910-1918. IEEE. DOI: 10.1109/ICACITE60783.2024.10617344

Kristiani, E., Yang, C. T., Huang, C. Y., Ko, P. C., & Fathoni, H. (2020). On construction of sensors, edge, and cloud (ISEC) framework for smart system integration and applications. *IEEE Internet of Things Journal, 8*(1), 309–319. DOI: 10.1109/JIOT.2020.3004244

Kuchuk, H., & Malokhvii, E. (2024). Integration of IOT with Cloud, Fog, and Edge Computing: A Review. *Advanced Information Systems*, *8*(2), 65–78. DOI: 10.20998/2522-9052.2024.2.08

Kumar, T. Minakshi, & Joshi, K. (2025). Empowering Cloud Security Through Advanced Monitoring and Analytics Techniques. In Risk-Based Approach to Secure Cloud Migration (pp. 163-186). IGI Global Scientific Publishing.

Kumar, A., Kumar, A., & Singhal, N. (2024). *Industry Automation: The Technologies, Platforms and Use Cases*. IEEE., DOI: 10.1109/10506786

Kumar, M. (2024). Optimizing security for remote patient monitoring with edge computing strategies. *Int Res J Adv Engg Mgt*, *2*(05), 1530–1535. DOI: 10.47392/IRJAEM.2024.0207

Kumar, S., & Haque, A. (2019). Urban health informatics: Role of computational techniques and approaches. In *Advances in computational intelligence and informatics* (pp. 177–195). Springer.

Kumar, S., Tiwari, P., & Zymbler, M. (2020). Internet of Things is a revolutionary approach for future technology enhancement: A review. *Journal of Big Data*, *6*(1), 1–21. DOI: 10.1186/s40537-019-0268-2

Kumar, T., Kumar, P., & Namasudra, S. (2024). User revocation- enabled access control model using identity- based signature in the cloud computing environment. *International Journal of Interactive Multimedia and Artificial Intelligence*, *9*(1), 127–136. DOI: 10.9781/ijimai.2024.05.001

Kumhar, M., & Bhatia, J. (2022). Edge computing in sdn-enabled iot-based healthcare frameworks. *International Journal of Reliable and Quality E-Healthcare*, *11*(4), 1–15. DOI: 10.4018/IJRQEH.308804

Kusiak, A. (2018). *Smart Manufacturing: Challenges and Opportunities*. Springer.

Kuznetsov, O., Sernani, P., Romeo, L., Frontoni, E., & Mancini, A. (2024). On the Integration of Artificial Intelligence and Blockchain Technology: A Perspective About Security. *IEEE Access : Practical Innovations, Open Solutions*, *12*, 3881–3897. DOI: 10.1109/ACCESS.2023.3349019

Lai, M. H., & Chang, K. S. (2023). AI Sensor Applications in Edge Computing. *IEEE Nanotechnology Magazine*, *17*(6), 23–28. DOI: 10.1109/MNANO.2023.3316869

Lakshminarayanan, V., Ravikumar, A., Sriraman, H., Alla, S., & Chattu, V. (2023). Health care equity through intelligent edge computing and augmented reality/virtual reality: A systematic review. *Journal of Multidisciplinary Healthcare*, *16*, 2839–2859. DOI: 10.2147/JMDH.S419923 PMID: 37753339

Lakumarapu, S., Nithyanandhan, R., Bhargavi, V. S., & TP, A. (2024, August). Machine Learning Approaches for Liver Disease Prediction: A Comparative Analysis. In *2024 5th International Conference on Electronics and Sustainable Communication Systems (ICESC)*, IEEE. pp. 159-164

Lawal, O., Veluthedath Shajihan, S. A., Mechitov, K., & Spencer Jr, B. F. (2024). Edge Integration of Artificial Intelligence into Wireless Smart Sensor Platforms for Railroad Bridge Impact Detection. *Sensors (Basel)*, *24*(17), 5633. DOI: 10.3390/s24175633 PMID: 39275541

Lazarova, E., Mora, S., Rubartelli, P., Vitale, A., Pareto, L., Maggi, N., … & Giacomini, M. (2021). Integrating an electronic health record system into a regional health information system: an hl7 fhir architecture. DOI: 10.3233/SHTI210357

Lee, G. (2023). Exploring Predictive Variables Affecting the Sales of Companies Listed With Korean Stock Indices Through Machine Learning Analysis. *IEEE Access : Practical Innovations, Open Solutions*, *11*, 63534–63549. DOI: 10.1109/ACCESS.2023.3288576

Lee, J. (2014). *Industrial Artificial Intelligence and Predictive Maintenance in Manufacturing*. Elsevier.

Lee, J. (2017). *Intelligent Energy Management for Industrial IoT Systems*. Elsevier.

Lei, K., Du, M., Huang, J., & Jin, T. (2020). Groupchain: Towards a scalable public blockchain in fog computing of IoT services computing. *IEEE Transactions on Services Computing*, *13*(2), 252–262. DOI: 10.1109/TSC.2019.2949801

Le, T. K., Salim, U., & Kaltenberger, F. (2020). An overview of physical layer design for ultra-reliable low-latency communications in 3GPP releases 15, 16, and 17. *IEEE Access : Practical Innovations, Open Solutions*, *9*, 433–444. DOI: 10.1109/ACCESS.2020.3046773

Levina, A., Iliashenko, V. M., Kalyazina, S., & Overes, E. (2022, May). Smart hospital architecture: IT and digital aspects. In Algorithms and Solutions Based on Computer Technology: 5th Scientific International Online Conference Algorithms and Solutions based on Computer Technology (ASBC 2021) (pp. 235-247). Cham: Springer International Publishing.

Levinson, J. P. (2019). *Healthcare analytics*. Wiley.

Li, X., & Zhang, T. (2017). An exploration on artificial intelligence application: From security, privacy and ethic perspective. 2017 IEEE 2nd International Conference on Cloud Computing and Big Data Analysis (ICCCBDA), 416–420. DOI: 10.1109/ICCCBDA.2017.7951949

Li, E., Clarke, J., Ashrafian, H., Darzi, A., & Neves, A. L. (2022). The impact of electronic health record interoperability on safety and quality of care in high-income countries: Systematic review. *Journal of Medical Internet Research*, *24*(9), e38144. DOI: 10.2196/38144 PMID: 36107486

Li, J., Jinjin, C., Khan, F., Rehman, A., Balasubramaniam, V., Sun, J., & Venu, P. (2020). A secured framework for sdn-based edge computing in iot-enabled healthcare system. *IEEE Access: Practical Innovations, Open Solutions*, *8*, 135479–135490. DOI: 10.1109/ACCESS.2020.3011503

Li, Q., Li, Q., Li, X., & Li, X. (2020). Edge computing for real-time healthcare applications in smart cities: Opportunities, challenges, and research directions. *Journal of Ambient Intelligence and Humanized Computing*, *11*(8), 4879–4895.

Li, S., Da Xu, L., & Zhao, S. (2018). 5G Internet of Things: A survey. *Journal of Industrial Information Integration*, *10*, 1–9. DOI: 10.1016/j.jii.2018.01.005

Liu, X. (2021). Resource allocation in multi-access edge computing: Optimization and machine learning. In 2021 IEEE 12th Annual Information Technology, Electronics and Mobile Communication Conference (IEMCON) (pp. 365–370). IEEE. DOI: 10.1109/IEMCON53756.2021.9623176

Liu, F., Tang, G., Li, Y., Cai, Z., Zhang, X., & Zhou, T. (2019). A survey on edge computing systems and tools. *Proceedings of the IEEE*, *107*(8), 1537–1562. DOI: 10.1109/JPROC.2019.2920341

Liu, P., Zhu, G., Jiang, W., Luo, W., Xu, J., & Cui, S. (2022). Vertical federated edge learning with distributed integrated sensing and communication. *IEEE Communications Letters*, *26*(9), 2091–2095. DOI: 10.1109/LCOMM.2022.3181612

Liu, P., Zhu, G., Wang, S., Jiang, W., Luo, W., Poor, H. V., & Cui, S. (2022). Toward ambient intelligence: Federated edge learning with task-oriented sensing, computation, and communication integration. *IEEE Journal of Selected Topics in Signal Processing*, *17*(1), 158–172. DOI: 10.1109/JSTSP.2022.3226836

Liu, S., Liu, L., Tang, J., Yu, B., Wang, Y., & Shi, W. (2019). Edge computing for autonomous driving: Opportunities and challenges. *Proceedings of the IEEE*, *107*(8), 1697–1716. DOI: 10.1109/JPROC.2019.2915983

Liu, S., Wen, D., Li, D., Chen, Q., Zhu, G., & Shi, Y. (2024). Energy-Efficient Optimal Mode Selection for Edge AI Inference via Integrated Sensing-Communication-Computation. *IEEE Transactions on Mobile Computing*, *23*(12), 14248–14262. DOI: 10.1109/TMC.2024.3440581

Liu, Y., Lan, D., Pang, Z., & Karlsson, M. (2021). Scalability Challenges in Edge Networks: A Framework Perspective. *IEEE Transactions on Cloud Computing*. DOI: 10.1109/OJIES.2021.3055901

Li, X., He, J., Vijayakumar, P., Zhang, X., & Chang, V. (2022). A verifiable privacy-preserving machine learning prediction scheme for edge-enhanced hcpss. *IEEE Transactions on Industrial Informatics*, *18*(8), 5494–5503. DOI: 10.1109/TII.2021.3110808

Li, X., Liu, S., Wu, F., Kumari, S., & Rodrigues, J. (2019). Privacy preserving data aggregation scheme for mobile edge computing assisted iot applications. *IEEE Internet of Things Journal*, *6*(3), 4755–4763. DOI: 10.1109/JIOT.2018.2874473

Li, Y., & Wang, M. (2021). Research on real-time AI deployment at the edge. *Journal of Systems Architecture*, *118*, 102134. DOI: 10.1016/j.sysarc.2021.102134

Li, Y., Yu, M., Xu, D., Xue, G., & Wang, B. (2021). A survey on network slicing for 5G. *IEEE Communications Surveys and Tutorials*, *23*(2), 872–909. DOI: 10.1109/COMST.2021.3055799

Lou, Z., Wang, L., Jiang, K., Wei, Z., & Shen, G. (2020). Reviews of wearable healthcare systems: Materials, devices and system integration. *Materials Science and Engineering R Reports*, *140*, 100523. DOI: 10.1016/j.mser.2019.100523

Luo, Q., Hu, S., Li, C., Li, G., & Shi, W. (2021). Resource scheduling in edge computing: A survey. *IEEE Communications Surveys and Tutorials*, *23*(4), 2131–2165. DOI: 10.1109/COMST.2021.3106401

Lu, Y. (2020). *Cybersecurity in Industrial IoT Systems: Challenges and Solutions*. Elsevier.

Lu, Y., & Xu, L. D. (2019). Internet of Things (IoT) cybersecurity research: A review of current research topics. *IEEE Internet of Things Journal*, *6*(2), 2103–2115. DOI: 10.1109/JIOT.2018.2869847

Lu, Y., Xu, X., & Xu, X. (2019). Development of a hybrid edge-cloud system for manufacturing process monitoring. *Journal of Manufacturing Systems*, *51*, 52–60. DOI: 10.1016/j.jmsy.2019.03.002

Lv, H., Yang, G., Zhou, H., Huang, X., Yang, H., & Pang, Z. (2020). Teleoperation of collaborative robot for remote dementia care in home environments. *IEEE Journal of Translational Engineering in Health and Medicine*, *8*, 1–10. DOI: 10.1109/JTEHM.2019.2952610 PMID: 32617197

Lv, Z., Wang, L., Guan, Z., Wu, J., Du, X., Zhao, H., & Guizani, M. (2019). An optimizing and differentially private clustering algorithm for mixed data in SDN-based smart grid. *IEEE Access : Practical Innovations, Open Solutions*, *7*, 45773–45782. DOI: 10.1109/ACCESS.2019.2909048

Mach, P., & Becvar, Z. (2017). Mobile edge computing: A survey on architecture and computation offloading. *IEEE Communications Surveys and Tutorials*, *19*(3), 1628–1656. DOI: 10.1109/COMST.2017.2682318

Mahfoud, H., El Barkany, A., & El Biyaali, A. (2016). Preventive maintenance optimization in healthcare domain: Status of research and perspective. *Journal of Quality and Reliability Engineering*, *2016*(1), 5314312. DOI: 10.1155/2016/5314312

Mahmood, Z., & Ramachandran, M. (2018). Fog computing: Concepts, principles and related paradigms. In Mahmood, Z., & Ramachandran, M. (Eds.), *Fog computing: Concepts, frameworks and technologies* (pp. 3–21). Springer., DOI: 10.1007/978-3-319-94890-4_1

Mahmud, R., Kotagiri, R., & Buyya, R. (2021). Fog computing: A taxonomy, survey and future directions. In Di Martino, B., Li, K.-C., Yang, L., & Esposito, A. (Eds.), *Internet of Everything* (pp. 103–130). Springer., DOI: 10.1007/978-3-030-57798-6_5

Makhdoom, I. (2019). Blockchain for Industrial IoT: A Survey and Future Directions. *Future Generation Computer Systems*, *91*, 324–334.

Manchadi, O., Ben-Bouazza, F. E., & Jioudi, B. (2023). Predictive maintenance in healthcare system: A survey. *IEEE Access: Practical Innovations, Open Solutions*, *11*, 61313–61330. DOI: 10.1109/ACCESS.2023.3287490

Marcham, A. (2021). *Understanding infrastructure edge computing: Concepts, technologies, and considerations*. Wiley. DOI: 10.1002/9781119763260

Masum, M., Devadasan, A. V., & Sengupta, S. (2025). Deep learning for non-invasive blood pressure monitoring: Model performance and quantization trade-offs. *Electronics (Basel)*, *14*(7), 1300. DOI: 10.3390/electronics14071300

Mavrogiorgou, A., Kiourtis, A., Perakis, K., Pitsios, S., & Kyriazis, D. (2019a). Iot in healthcare: Achieving interoperability of high-quality data acquired by iot medical devices. *Sensors (Basel)*, *19*(9), 1978. DOI: 10.3390/s19091978 PMID: 31035612

Mavrogiorgou, A., Kiourtis, A., Touloupou, M., Kapassa, E., & Kyriazis, D. (2019b). Internet of medical things (iomt): Acquiring and transforming data into hl7 fhir through 5g network slicing. *Emerging Science Journal*, *3*(2), 64–77. DOI: 10.28991/esj-2019-01170

McNamee, F., Dustadar, S., Kilpatrick, P., Shi, W., Spence, I., & Varghese, B. (2020). A case for adaptive deep neural networks in edge computing.

Melkas, H., Hennala, L., Pekkarinen, S., & Kyrki, V. (2020). Impacts of robot implementation on care personnel and clients in elderly-care institutions. *International Journal of Medical Informatics*, *134*, 104041. DOI: 10.1016/j.ijmedinf.2019.104041 PMID: 31838291

Mell, P., & Grance, T. (2021). *The NIST definition of cloud computing* (NIST Special Publication 800-145). National Institute of Standards and Technology. DOI: 10.6028/NIST.SP.800-145

Mello, R. C., Ribeiro, M. R., & Frizera-Neto, A. (2023). Implementing cloud robotics for practical applications. *Springer Tracts in Advanced Robotics*, *10*, 1–24. DOI: 10.1007/978-3-031-06676-4_1

Meurisch, A., Seeliger, B., Schmidt, I., Schweizer, F., Kaup, F., & Mühlhäuser, M. (2015). Upgrading wireless home routers for enabling large-scale deployment of cloudlets. In *Mobile Computing, Applications, and Services* (pp. 12–29). *(Publisher details needed.)* DOI: 10.1007/978-3-319-29003-4_2

Miao, Q., Jing, W., & Song, H. (2018). Differential privacy–based location privacy enhancing in edge computing. In *Recent Advances in Cloud Data Centers Toward Fog Data Centers* (Vol. 31, No. 8).

Miao, Q., Jing, W., & Song, H. (2018). Differential privacy–based location privacy enhancing in edge computing. *Concurrency and Computation*, *31*(8), e4735. DOI: 10.1002/cpe.4735

Miller, S. (2017). Standardization of IIoT Communication Protocols. *Journal of Industrial Information Integration*, *8*, 1–9.

Mir, U., Abbasi, U., Mir, T., Kanwal, S., & Alamri, S. (2021). Energy management in smart buildings and homes: Current approaches, a hypothetical solution, and open issues and challenges. *IEEE Access : Practical Innovations, Open Solutions*, *9*, 94132–94148. DOI: 10.1109/ACCESS.2021.3092304

Mišeikis, J., Caroni, P., Duchamp, P., Gasser, A., Marko, R., Mišeikienė, N., Zwilling, F., de Castelbajac, C., Eicher, L., Früh, M., & Fruh, H. (2020). Lio—A personal robot assistant for human-robot interaction and care applications. *IEEE Robotics and Automation Letters*, *5*(4), 5339–5346. DOI: 10.1109/LRA.2020.3007462 PMID: 34192136

Mohammadi, M., Assaf, G., Assaad, R. H., & Chang, A. J. (2024). An Intelligent Cloud-Based IoT-Enabled Multimodal Edge Sensing Device for Automated, Real-Time, Comprehensive, and Standardized Water Quality Monitoring and Assessment Process Using Multisensor Data Fusion Technologies. *Journal of Computing in Civil Engineering*, *38*(6), 04024029. DOI: 10.1061/JCCEE5.CPENG-5989

Mollah, M. B., Azad, M. A. K., & Vasilakos, A. (2017). Secure data sharing and searching at the edge of cloud-assisted internet of things. *IEEE Cloud Computing*, *4*(1), 34–42. DOI: 10.1109/MCC.2017.9

Montes, J., Sánchez, A., Memishi, B., Pérez, M. S., & Antoniu, G. (2013). GMonE: A complete approach to cloud monitoring. *Future Generation Computer Systems*, *29*(8), 2026–2040. DOI: 10.1016/j.future.2013.02.011

Mo, R., Liu, J., Yu, W., Jiang, F., Gu, X., & Zhao, X. (2019, August). A differential privacy-based protecting data preprocessing method for big data mining. *Proceedings of the 18th IEEE International Conference on Trust, Security and Privacy in Computing and Communications*, 693–699. DOI: 10.1109/TrustCom/BigDataSE.2019.00098

Mosenia, A., & Jha, N. K. (2017). A comprehensive study of security of Internet-of-Things. *IEEE Transactions on Emerging Topics in Computing*, *5*(4), 586–602. DOI: 10.1109/TETC.2016.2606384

Mouradian, C., Salah, K., Limam, N., & Boutaba, R. (2019). A comprehensive survey on fog computing: State-of-the-art and research challenges. *IEEE Communications Surveys and Tutorials*, *20*(1), 416–464. DOI: 10.1109/COMST.2017.2771153

Mpofu, K. T., & Mthunzi-Kufa, P. (2025). *Recent advances in artificial intelligence and machine learning-based biosensing technologies*. IntechOpen., DOI: 10.5772/intechopen.1009613

Murshed, M. G. S., Murphy, C., Hou, D., Khan, N., Ananthanarayanan, G., & Hussain, F. (2021). Machine learning at the network edge: A survey. *ACM Computing Surveys*, *54*(8), 1–37. DOI: 10.1145/3469029

Musaddiq, A., Zikria, Y. B., Hahm, O., Yu, H., Bashir, A. K., & Kim, S. W. (2018). A survey on resource management in IoT operating systems. *IEEE Access : Practical Innovations, Open Solutions*, *6*, 8459–8482. DOI: 10.1109/ACCESS.2018.2808324

Nagam, V. (2023). Diagnostic medical artificial intelligence: Futuristic prospects for implementation in healthcare settings. *Frontiers in Artificial Intelligence*, *6*, 1169244.DOI: 10.3389/frai.2023.1169244 PMID: 37064297

Nagarjuna, P., Pandian, A. S., Sharma, S. K., Ramesh, T., Sohail, M. A., & Babu, M. D. (2024, November). Integrating Cloud And Edge Computing For Scalable Iot Applications. In 2024 2nd International Conference on Advances in Computation, Communication and Information Technology (ICAICCIT) (Vol. 1, pp. 214-219). IEEE. DOI: 10.1109/ICAICCIT64383.2024.10912122

Nain, G., Pattanaik, K. K., & Sharma, G. K. (2022). Towards edge computing in intelligent manufacturing: Past, present and future. *Journal of Manufacturing Systems*, *62*, 588–611. DOI: 10.1016/j.jmsy.2022.01.010

Narla, S., Valivarthi, D. T., & Peddi, S. (2024). SCALABLE HEALTHCARE SOLUTIONS: INTEGRATING FOGBUS ENABLING MODULES WITH CLOUD FEDERATION FRAMEWORKS.

Nasiri, S., Sadoughi, F., Tadayon, M., & Dehnad, A. (2019). Security requirements of internet of things-based healthcare system: A survey study. *Acta Informatica Medica*, *27*(4), 253. DOI: 10.5455/aim.2019.27.253-258 PMID: 32055092

Nguyen, D. C., Pathirana, P. N., Ding, M., & Seneviratne, A. (2021). Integration of blockchain and cloud of things: Architecture, applications and challenges. *IEEE Communications Surveys and Tutorials*, *22*(4), 2521–2549. DOI: 10.1109/COMST.2020.3020092

Ni, L., Li, C., Wang, X., Jiang, H., & Yu, J. (2018). DP-MCDBSCAN: Differential privacy preserving multi-core DBSCAN clustering for network user data. *IEEE Access : Practical Innovations, Open Solutions*, *6*, 21053–21063. DOI: 10.1109/ACCESS.2018.2824798

Niyonambaza, I., Zennaro, M., & Uwitonze, A. (2020). Predictive maintenance (Pdm) structure using internet of things (iot) for mechanical equipment used into hospitals in Rwanda. *Future Internet*, *12*(12), 224. DOI: 10.3390/fi12120224

Ometov, A., Molua, O. L., Komarov, M., & Nurmi, J. (2022). A survey of security in cloud, edge, and fog computing. *Sensors (Basel)*, *22*(3), 927. DOI: 10.3390/s22030927 PMID: 35161675

Onieva, J. A., Rios, R., Roman, R., & Lopez, J. (2019). Edge-assisted vehicular networks security. *IEEE Internet of Things Journal*, *6*(5), 8038–8045. DOI: 10.1109/JIOT.2019.2904323

Padhan, S., Mohapatra, A., Ramasamy, S. K., & Agrawal, S. (2023). Artificial intelligence (AI) and robotics in elderly healthcare: Enabling independence and quality of life. *Cureus*, *15*(8), e42905. DOI: 10.7759/cureus.42905 PMID: 37664381

Pahl, C., Brogi, A., Soldani, J., & Jamshidi, P. (2021). Cloud container technologies: A state-of-the-art review. *IEEE Transactions on Cloud Computing*, *7*(3), 677–692. DOI: 10.1109/TCC.2017.2702586

Pandey, R., Khatri, S. K., Singh, N. K., & Verma, P. (Eds.). (2022). *Artificial intelligence and machine learning for EDGE computing*. Academic Press.

Papadopoulos, C., Castro, N., Nigath, A., Davidson, R., Faulkes, N., Menicatti, R., Khaliq, A. A., Recchiuto, C., Battistuzzi, L., Randhawa, G., Merton, L., Kanoria, S., Chong, N.-Y., Kamide, H., Hewson, D., & Sgorbissa, A. (2022). The CARESSES randomised controlled trial: Exploring the health-related impact of culturally competent artificial intelligence embedded into socially assistive robots and tested in older adult care homes. *International Journal of Social Robotics*, *14*(1), 245–256. DOI: 10.1007/s12369-021-00781-x PMID: 33907589

Parikh, S., Dave, D., Patel, R., & Doshi, N. (2019). Security and privacy issues in cloud, fog and edge computing. *Procedia Computer Science*, *160*, 734–739. DOI: 10.1016/j.procs.2019.11.018

Parra, J. A., Gutiérrez, S. A., & Branch, J. W. (2022). A method based on deep learning for the detection and characterization of cybersecurity incidents in Internet of Things devices. arXiv. https://doi.org//arXiv.2203.00608DOI: 10.48550

Patan, L. (2024). Leveraging Cloud-Native Architecture for Scalable and Resilient Enterprise Applications: A Comprehensive Analysis. International Journal of Computer Engineering & Technology. https://lib-index.com/index.php/IJCET/article/view/IJCET_15_05_055

Peter, N. (2015). Fog computing and its real time applications. *International Journal of Emerging Technology and Advanced Engineering*, *5*(6), 266–269.

Porambage, P., Okwuibe, J., Liyanage, M., Ylianttila, M., & Taleb, T. (2021). Survey on multi-access edge computing for Internet of Things realization. *IEEE Communications Surveys and Tutorials*, *20*(4), 2961–2991. DOI: 10.1109/COMST.2018.2849509

Povedano-Molina, J., Lopez-Vega, J. M., Lopez-Soler, J. M., Corradi, A., & Foschini, L. (2013). DARGOS: A highly adaptable and scalable monitoring architecture for multi-tenant clouds. *Future Generation Computer Systems*, *29*(8), 2041–2056. DOI: 10.1016/j.future.2013.04.022

Prajapat, S., Kumar, P., & Das, A. K. (2020). *Generative AI-Enabled Quantum Encryption Algorithm for Securing IoT-Based Healthcare Application Using Blockchain*. IEEE Internet of Things., DOI: 10.1109/JIOT.2025.3555159

Prasad, N., & Mitra, D. (2023). Importance of patient satisfaction in achieving a competitive edge in the healthcare system. *The Management Accountant Journal*, *58*(4), 21. DOI: 10.33516/maj.v58i4.21-26p

Premsankar, G., Di Francesco, M., & Taleb, T. (2018). Edge computing for the Internet of Things: A case study. *IEEE Internet of Things Journal*, *5*(2), 1275–1284. DOI: 10.1109/JIOT.2018.2805263

Pu, C. (2021). A novel blockchain-based trust management scheme for vehicular networks. In *2021 Wireless Telecommunications Symposium (WTS)* (pp. 1–6). IEEE. DOI: 10.1109/WTS51064.2021.9433711

Puliafito, C., Mingozzi, E., Longo, F., Puliafito, A., & Rana, O. (2019). Fog computing for the internet of things: A survey. *ACM Transactions on Internet Technology*, *19*(2), 1–41. DOI: 10.1145/3301443

Puneeth, R., & Parthasarathy, G. (2024). Blockchain-based framework for privacy preservation and securing ehr with patient-centric access control. *Acta Informatica Pragensia*, *13*(1), 1–23. DOI: 10.18267/j.aip.225

Puthal, D., Nepal, S., Ranjan, R., & Chen, J. (2016). Threats to networking cloud and edge datacenters in the Internet of Things. *IEEE Cloud Computing*, *3*(3), 64–71. DOI: 10.1109/MCC.2016.63

Putra, K. T., Arrayyan, A. Z., Hayati, N., Damarjati, C., Bakar, A., & Chen, H. C. (2024). A Review on the Application of Internet of Medical Things in Wearable Personal Health Monitoring: A Cloud-Edge Artificial Intelligence Approach. *IEEE Access : Practical Innovations, Open Solutions*, *12*, 21437–21452. DOI: 10.1109/ACCESS.2024.3358827

Qiu, T., Chi, J., Zhou, X., Ning, Z., Atiquzzaman, M., & Wu, D. O. (2020). Edge computing in industrial internet of things: Architecture, advances and challenges. *IEEE Communications Surveys and Tutorials*, *22*(4), 2462–2488. DOI: 10.1109/COMST.2020.3009103

Quy, V. K., Van Hau, N., Van Anh, D., Quy, N. M., Ban, N. T., Lanza, S., Randazzo, G., & Muzirafuti, A. (2022). IoT-enabled smart agriculture: Architecture, applications, and challenges. *Applied Sciences (Basel, Switzerland)*, *12*(7), 3396. DOI: 10.3390/app12073396

Rahman, M. A., & Hussain, F. K. (2020). IoT-edge-cloud orchestrated machine learning: A review and future research directions. *Journal of Network and Computer Applications*, *166*, 102716. DOI: 10.1016/j.jnca.2020.102716

Ramadan, E. A., Abu-Ghaleb, A. A., & El-Brawany, M. A. (2023, October). Medical Equipment Maintenance Management and Optimization in Healthcare Facilities: Literature Review. In 2023 3rd International Conference on Electronic Engineering (ICEEM) (pp. 1-11). IEEE.

Ramanathan, R., Ramamoorthy, S., & Grima, S. (2024). Edge Computing and Artificial Intelligence-Based Internet of Things for Industry 5.0: Framework, Challenges, Use Cases, and Research Directions. *Digital Twins in Industrial Production and Smart Manufacturing: An Understanding of Principles, Enhancers, and Obstacles*, 221-246.

Ramanathan, S., Pineda-Briseño, A., Mohd, T., & Ramasundaram, M. (2023). Edge computing in healthcare., 1-18. DOI: 10.1201/9781003363361-1

Rancea, A., Anghel, I., & Cioara, T. (2024). Edge computing in healthcare: Innovations, opportunities, and challenges. *Future Internet*, *16*(9), 329. DOI: 10.3390/fi16090329

Rawat, N., Srivastava, R., Pandey, B. K., Rawat, P., Singh, S., & Sharma, A. (2014). Data security issues in cloud computing. *Open Journal of Mobile Computing and Cloud Computing*, *1*, 9–17.

Ray, P. P. (2017). Internet of things for smart agriculture: Technologies, practices and future direction. *Journal of Ambient Intelligence and Smart Environments*, *9*(4), 395–420. DOI: 10.3233/AIS-170440

Ray, P. P., Dash, D., & De, D. (2019). Edge computing for Internet of Things: A survey, e-healthcare case study and future direction. *Journal of Network and Computer Applications*, *140*, 1–22. DOI: 10.1016/j.jnca.2019.05.005

Rekha, D., & Pavithra, L. (2025). TSCH in Edge IoT: A Comprehensive Survey of Research Challenges. *Transactions on Emerging Telecommunications Technologies*, *36*(3), e70088. DOI: 10.1002/ett.70088

Rinki, K., & Verma, P. (2021, July). A DWT and Coefficient Exchange Block Based DCT Image Watermarking and their Comparative Assessment. In *2021 12th International Conference on Computing Communication and Networking Technologies (ICCCNT)* (pp. 1–7). IEEE. DOI: 10.1109/ICCCNT51525.2021.9579737

Rinki, K., Verma, P., & Singh, R. K. (2022, April). A novel multiblock region-based arnold transformation for image watermarking combined with DWT-PSO Technique. In *Evolution in Computational Intelligence: Proceedings of the 9th International Conference on Frontiers in Intelligent Computing: Theory and Applications (FICTA 2021)* (pp. 77–87). Springer Nature Singapore. DOI: 10.1007/978-981-16-6616-2_8

Rinki, K., Verma, P., & Singh, R. K. (2022). A novel matrix multiplication based LSB substitution mechanism for data security and authentication. *Journal of King Saud University. Computer and Information Sciences*, *34*(8), 5510–5524. DOI: 10.1016/j.jksuci.2021.01.013

Rittinghouse, J. W., & Ransome, J. F. (2020). *Cloud computing: Implementation, management, and security*. CRC Press.

Rodríguez, P., Laso, S., Berrocal, J., & Fernandez, P. (2024). Computing Continuum Simulator: A Comprehensive Framework for Continuum Architecture Evaluation. https://papers.ssrn.com/sol3/papers.cfm?abstract_id=5045387

Rogers, S., Sharp, A., & Vines, J. (2015). Designing for the smart city: Building inclusivity into urban technology. *Design Issues*, *31*(3), 16–29.

Roman, R., Lopez, J., & Mambo, M. (2018). Mobile edge computing, Fog et al.: A survey and analysis of security threats and challenges. *Future Generation Computer Systems*, *78*, 680–698. DOI: 10.1016/j.future.2016.11.009

Roschke, S., Cheng, F., & Meinel, C. (2009). Intrusion detection in the cloud. In *2009 Eighth IEEE International Conference on Dependable, Autonomic and Secure Computing (DASC'09)*. IEEE. Eken, H. (2013). Security threats and solutions in cloud computing. In *2013 World Congress on Internet Security (WorldCIS)*. IEEE.

Rose, S. (2020). *Zero Trust Architecture*. National Institute of Standards and Technology (NIST) Special Publication 800-207.

Ruchika, & Chhillar, R. S. (2025). Performance evaluation of hybrid cloud-fog computing architectures in smart home IoT environments: A comparative simulation study across multiple tools. Journal of Grid Computing, 23(2), 14. .DOI: 10.1007/s10723-025-09802-9

Rupanetti, D., & Kaabouch, N. (2024). Combining Edge Computing-Assisted Internet of Things Security with Artificial Intelligence: Applications, Challenges, and Opportunities. *Applied Sciences (Basel, Switzerland)*, *14*(16), 7104. DOI: 10.3390/app14167104

Saeed, A., Anjum, A., Wahid, S., Hussain, O., & Qazi, S. (2020). A systematic review of edge computing in healthcare: Opportunities, challenges, and open research issues. *IEEE Access : Practical Innovations, Open Solutions*, *8*, 126389–126411.

Saleh, H., Alharbi, A., & Alsamhi, S. H. (2021). OPCNN-FAKE: Optimized Convolutional Neural Network for Fake News Detection. *IEEE Access : Practical Innovations, Open Solutions*, *9*, 129471–129489. DOI: 10.1109/ACCESS.2021.3112806

Saripalle, R., Runyan, C., & Mitchell, R. (2019). Using hl7 fhir to achieve interoperability in patient health record. *Journal of Biomedical Informatics*, *94*, 103188. DOI: 10.1016/j.jbi.2019.103188 PMID: 31063828

Sarkar, S., & Misra, S. (2016). Theoretical modelling of fog computing: A green computing paradigm to support IoT applications. *IET Networks*, *5*(2), 23–29. DOI: 10.1049/iet-net.2015.0034

Satpathy, S., Mohanty, S. N., & Potluri, S. (2024). Reconnoitering the landscape of edge intelligence in healthcare. *Apple Academic Press.*, *ISBN-13*, 9781774914366. DOI: 10.1201/9781003401841

Satyanarayanan, M. (2017). The emergence of edge computing. *Computer*, *50*(1), 30–39. DOI: 10.1109/MC.2017.9

Satyanarayanan, M., Bahl, P., Caceres, R., & Davies, N. (2021). The case for VM-based cloudlets in mobile computing. *IEEE Pervasive Computing*, *8*(4), 14–23. DOI: 10.1109/MPRV.2009.82

Sawik, B., Tobis, S., Baum, E., Suwalska, A., Kropińska, S., Stachnik, K., Pérez-Bernabeu, E., Cildoz, M., Agustin, A., & Wieczorowska-Tobis, K. (2023). Robots for elderly care: Review, multi-criteria optimization model and qualitative case study. *Health Care*, *11*(9), 1286. DOI: 10.3390/healthcare11091286 PMID: 37174828

Scholl, H. J., & Scholl, M. C. (2014). Governance and governance structures in smart cities. *Information Polity*, *19*(3), 1–16.

Schrettenbrunnner, M. B. (2020). Artificial-Intelligence-Driven Management. *IEEE Engineering Management Review*, *48*(2), 15–19. DOI: 10.1109/EMR.2020.2990933

Shafiq, M., Choi, J. G., Cheikhrouhou, O., & Hamam, H. (2023). Advances in IoMT for Healthcare Systems. *Sensors (Basel)*, *24*(1), 10. DOI: 10.3390/s24010010 PMID: 38202871

Shahzadi, R., Ferzund, J., Tausif, M., & Asif, M. (2016). Internet of Things based expert system for smart agriculture. *International Journal of Advanced Computer Science and Applications*, *7*(3), 341–350. DOI: 10.14569/IJACSA.2016.070947

Shaik, T., Tao, X., Li, Y., Dann, C., McDonald, J., Redmond, P., & Galligan, L. (2022). A Review of the Trends and Challenges in Adopting Natural Language Processing Methods for Education Feedback Analysis. *IEEE Access : Practical Innovations, Open Solutions*, *10*, 56720–56739. DOI: 10.1109/ACCESS.2022.3177752

Sharma, S., & Dhir, S. (2022). Adoption of IoT: in Healthcare, Daily Life, Businesses, Education during the Covid-19. International Conference on Machine Learning, Big Data, Cloud and Parallel Computing (COM-IT-CON), May 2022, pp. 597-601, DOI: 10.1109/COM-IT-CON54601.2022.9850762

Sharma, M., Tomar, A., & Hazra, A. (2024). Edge computing for industry 5.0: Fundamental, applications and research challenges. *IEEE Internet of Things Journal*, *11*(11), 19070–19093. DOI: 10.1109/JIOT.2024.3359297

Shehab, A. H., & Al-Janabi, S. T. F. (2020, November). Microsoft Azure IoT-based edge computing for smart homes. In *2020 International Conference on Decision Aid Sciences and Application (DASA)* (pp. 315–319). IEEE. https://doi.org/DOI: 10.1109/DASA51403.2020.9317274

Shen, B., Guo, J., & Yang, Y. (2019). Medchain: Efficient healthcare data sharing via blockchain. *Applied Sciences (Basel, Switzerland)*, *9*(6), 1207. DOI: 10.3390/app9061207

Shi, W., Cao, J., Zhang, Q., Li, Y., & Xu, L. (2016). Edge computing: Vision and challenges. *IEEE Internet of Things Journal*, *3*(5), 637–646. DOI: 10.1109/JIOT.2016.2579198

Shukla, A., & Dhir, S. (2016). Tools for Data Visualization in Business Intelligence: Case Study Using the Tool Qlikview. International Conference on Information System Design and Intelligent Application 2016. Springer Journal Volume 434, pp 319-326.DOI: 10.1007/978-81-322-2755-7_11

Sikarwar, H., & Das, D. (2023). SecEdge: Secure edge-computing-based hybrid approach for data collection and searching in IoV. *IEEE Transactions on Network and Service Management*, *21*(1), 1213–1225. DOI: 10.1109/TNSM.2023.3299264

Silberberg, J. L. (2001, August). Achieving medical device EMC: The role of regulations, standards, guidelines and publications. In 2001 IEEE EMC International Symposium. Symposium Record. International Symposium on Electromagnetic Compatibility (Cat. No. 01CH37161) (Vol. 2, pp. 1298-1303). IEEE.

Singh, A. K., Verma, K., & Raj, M. (2021). IoT based smart agriculture system. In 2021 5th International Conference on Information Systems and Computer Networks (ISCON) (pp. 1–5). IEEE. DOI: 10.1109/ISCON52037.2021.9702478

Singh, S. (2023). Secure health record management system with effective machine learning and blockchain techniques. nq, 20(03). DOI: 10.48047/NQ.2022.20.3.NQ22957

Singh, B., Lopez, D., & Ramadan, R. (2023). Internet of things in Healthcare: A conventional literature review. *Health and Technology*, *13*(5), 699–719. DOI: 10.1007/s12553-023-00771-1

Singh, R., Goyal, D., Arora, S., Malviya, J., & Garg, D. (2025, January). Evaluating the Severity of Parkinson's Disease Using Machine Learning Classifiers. In *2025 International Conference on Cognitive Computing in Engineering, Communications, Sciences and Biomedical Health Informatics (IC3ECSBHI)* (pp. 243-248). IEEE. DOI: 10.1109/IC3ECSBHI63591.2025.10990440

Singh, R., Malviya, J., Singh, R. B., & Garg, D. (2025, January). Hybrid Approach of Deep Convolution Neural Network and Transfer Learning for Tuberculosis Prediction. In *2025 International Conference on Cognitive Computing in Engineering, Communications, Sciences and Biomedical Health Informatics (IC3ECSBHI)* (pp. 357-362). IEEE. DOI: 10.1109/IC3ECSBHI63591.2025.10990849

Siva, S. R., Bushra, S. N., Maheswari, B., & Prabukumar, M. K. (2022, April). Performance Analysis of Different Machine Learning in Customer Prediction. In *2022 6th International Conference on Trends in Electronics and Informatics (ICOEI)* (pp. 1425-1430). IEEE. DOI: 10.1109/ICOEI53556.2022.9776714

Smith, C., & Caleb, E. (2025). Optimizing AI Model Training with Federated Learning and Blockchain. https://www.researchgate.net/profile/Hannah-Adebayo/publication/389891385_Optimizing_AI_Model_Training_with_Federated_Learning_and_Blockchain/links/67d73d692719090652bba0ce/Optimizing-AI-Model-Training-with-Federated-Learning-and-Blockchain.pdf

Solar, M., Castañeda, V., Ñanculef, R., Dombrovskaia, L., & Araya, M. (2024). A data ingestion procedure towards a medical images repository. *Sensors (Basel)*, *24*(15), 4985. DOI: 10.3390/s24154985 PMID: 39124032

Soni, P., & Tandan, G. (2024). Smart health infrastructure: Integrating internet of things (iot) with edge computing for enhanced disease surveillance and response. *South Eastern European Journal of Public Health*, 1–8. DOI: 10.70135/seejph.vi.741

Sreelakshmi, S., Babu, A. A., Lakshmipriya, C., Gracious, L. A., Nalini, M., & Subramanian, R. S. (2024, October). Enhancing Intrusion Detection Systems with Machine Learning. In *2024 2nd International Conference on Self Sustainable Artificial Intelligence Systems (ICSSAS)* (pp. 557-564). IEEE. DOI: 10.1109/ICSSAS64001.2024.10760341

Sridhar, M., & Babu, B. (2012). A fuzzy approach for privacy preserving in data mining. *International Journal of Computer Applications*, *57*, 1–5.

Srinivasan, R. (2020). *Optimizing Renewable Energy Integration in Smart Manufacturing with AI*. Wiley.

Stojanovic, J. (2020). *Edge and Fog Computing in Industrial Internet of Things (IIoT): A Survey*. Journal of Cloud Computing: Advances. *Systems and Applications*, *9*(1), 1–25.

Sung, D., Han, S., Kim, S., Kang, H., Jekal, B., Kim, G., Kim, J., Hong, M., Moon, G., Kim, S., Lee, Y., Hwang, S.-W., Jeong, H., Ryu, Y.-S., Kim, S., & Koo, J. (2025). Electrophoretic digital colorimetry integrated with electrochemical sweat sensor. *Science Advances*, *11*(13), DOI: 10.1126/sciadv.adu2142 PMID: 40153516

Sun, H. (2018). *Security and Privacy for Industrial Internet of Things: Challenges and Solutions*. Springer.

Sun, L., Jiang, X., Ren, H., & Guo, Y. (2020). Edge-cloud computing and artificial intelligence in internet of medical things: Architecture, technology and application. *IEEE Access : Practical Innovations, Open Solutions*, *8*, 101079–101092. DOI: 10.1109/ACCESS.2020.2997831

Sun, Y., Lo, F. L., & Zheng, S. (2021). An urban computing approach for healthcare service allocation using edge computing. *Journal of Healthcare Engineering*, *8811234*. DOI: 10.1155/2021/8811234

Sun, Z., Wang, Y., Shu, M., Liu, R., & Zhao, H. (2019). Differential privacy for data and model publishing of medical data. *IEEE Access : Practical Innovations, Open Solutions*, *7*, 152103–152114. DOI: 10.1109/ACCESS.2019.2947295

Suresh Babu, C. V., Akshayah, N. S., & Maclin Vinola, P. (2024). Artificial Intelligence in Healthcare: Assessing Impacts, Challenges, and Recommendations for Achieving Healthcare Independence. In Geada, N., & Jamil, G. (Eds.), *Perspectives on Artificial Intelligence in Times of Turbulence: Theoretical Background to Applications* (pp. 61–80). IGI Global., DOI: 10.4018/978-1-6684-9814-9.ch005

Suresh Babu, C. V., Surendar, V., Dheepak, N., Shiraj, S., & Praveen, K. (2024). Revolutionizing Healthcare Harnessing IoT-Integrated Federated Learning for Early Disease Detection and Patient Privacy Preservation. In Lilhore, U., Simaiya, S., Poongodi, M., & Dutt, V. (Eds.), *Federated Learning and Privacy-Preserving in Healthcare AI* (pp. 195–216). IGI Global., DOI: 10.4018/979-8-3693-1874-4.ch013

Suresh Babu, C. V., & Yadavamuthiah, K. (2023). Cyber Physical Systems Design Challenges in the Areas of Mobility, Healthcare, Energy, and Manufacturing. In Thanigaivelan, R., Kaliappan, S., & Jegadheesan, C. (Eds.), *Cyber-Physical Systems and Supporting Technologies for Industrial Automation* (pp. 131–151). IGI Global., DOI: 10.4018/978-1-6684-9267-3.ch007

Suresh, A., Maheswari, R., & Iyengar, S. S. (2020). *Deep learning and edge computing solutions for high-performance computing environments*. Springer.

Tanaka, Y., & Luo, Y. (2019). Secure data sharing in federated edge learning. In *Proceedings of the 2nd ACM Workshop on Edge Systems, Analytics and Networking (EdgeSys)* (pp. 47–52). https://doi.org/DOI: 10.1145/3301418.3313940

Tao, F. (2020). *Smart Manufacturing and Energy Optimization in IIoT*. Springer.

Tao, F. (2020). *Smart Manufacturing and IIoT Integration*. Academic Press.

Tao, F. (2021). *Artificial Intelligence in Smart Manufacturing*. Springer.

Tao, F., Qi, Q., Liu, A., & Kusiak, A. (2018). Data-driven smart manufacturing. *Journal of Manufacturing Systems*, *48*, 157–169. DOI: 10.1016/j.jmsy.2018.01.006

Tao, F., Zhang, M., & Nee, A. Y. C. (2019). *Digital twin driven smart manufacturing*. Academic press.

Tari, Z. (2014). Security and privacy in cloud computing. *IEEE Cloud Computing*, *1*(1), 54–57. DOI: 10.1109/MCC.2014.20

Taylor, R. H., Menciassi, A., Fichtinger, G., Fiorini, P., & Dario, P. (2016). Medical robotics and computer-integrated surgery. Springer Handbook of Robotics, 1657-1684. DOI: 10.1007/978-3-319-32552-1_63

Tesfai, H., Saleh, H., Al-Qutayri, M., Mohammad, M., Tekeste, T., Khandoker, A., & Mohammad, B. (2022). Lightweight shufflenet based cnn for arrhythmia classification. *IEEE Access : Practical Innovations, Open Solutions*, *10*, 111842–111854. DOI: 10.1109/ACCESS.2022.3215665

Tsai, C. W., Lai, C. F., Chao, H. C., & Vasilakos, A. V. (2015). Big data analytics: A survey. *Journal of Big Data*, *2*(1), 1–32. DOI: 10.1186/s40537-015-0030-3 PMID: 26191487

Tsakiris, M. C., Peng, L., Conca, A., Kneip, L., Shi, Y., & Choi, H. (2020). An Algebraic-Geometric Approach for Linear Regression Without Correspondences. *IEEE Transactions on Information Theory*, *66*(8), 5130–5144. DOI: 10.1109/TIT.2020.2977166

Turner, V., Gantz, J. F., Reinsel, D., & Minton, S. (2014). The digital universe of opportunities: Rich data and the increasing value of the Internet of Things. *IDC Analyze the Future*, *16*, 8.

Vaduguru, R. V. (2025). Attention-Based Deep Learning Models: A Comparative Study of VGG19 and MobileNet for Chest X-Ray Image Classification. https://doi.org/DOI: 10.21203/rs.3.rs-5902187/v1

Valaboju, P. (2024). Continuous integration and delivery in healthcare IT: A DevOps framework for improving system resilience and performance. https://www.researchgate.net/profile/Praveen-Valaboju-2/publication/388195922_Title_Continuous_Integration_and_Delivery_in_Healthcare_IT_A_DevOps_Framework_for_Improving_System_Resilience_and_Performance/links/678f052f82501639f5ff4c90/Title-Continuous-Integration-and-Delivery-in-Healthcare-IT-A-DevOps-Framework-for-Improving-System-Resilience-and-Performance.pdf

Varghese, B., Wang, N., Barbhuiya, S., Kilpatrick, P., & Nikolopoulos, D. (2016). Challenges and opportunities in edge computing., 20-26. DOI: 10.1109/SmartCloud.2016.18

Varghese, B., & Buyya, R. (2018). Next generation cloud computing: New trends and research directions. *Future Generation Computer Systems*, *79*, 849–861. DOI: 10.1016/j.future.2017.09.020

Varghese, L., Subba, L., Thai, L., & Barker, A. (2016). DocLite: A Docker-based lightweight cloud benchmarking tool. In *Proceedings of the IEEE/ACM International Symposium on Cluster, Cloud and Grid Computing*. IEEE. DOI: 10.1109/CCGrid.2016.14

Varghese, O., Akgun, I., Miguel, L., Thai, L., & Barker, A. (2014). Cloud benchmarking for performance. In *Proceedings of the IEEE International Conference on Cloud Computing Technology and Science* (pp. 535–540). IEEE.

Veeramachaneni, V. (2025). Edge Computing: Architecture, Applications, and Future Challenges in a Decentralized Era. *Recent Trends in Computer Graphics and Multimedia Technology*, *7*(1), 8–23.

Velishala, S. (2025). Leveraging Machine Learning in DevOps Pipelines to Enhance Patient Data Management Systems. ResearchGate. https://www.researchgate.net/publication/389701589

Velishala, S. (2025). Leveraging Machine Learning in DevOps Pipelines to Enhance Patient Data Management Systems. DOI: 10.5281/zenodo.14792139

Verma, P., & Fatima, S. (2020). Smart healthcare applications and real-time analytics through edge computing. *Internet of things use cases for the healthcare industry*, 241-270.

Wang, Y., Uehara, T., & Sasaki, R. (2015). Fog computing: Issues and challenges in security and forensics. In *2015 IEEE 39th Annual Computer Software and Applications Conference (COMPSAC)* (Vol. 3, pp. 53–59). IEEE.

Wang, C., Tan, X., Yao, C., Gu, F., Shi, F., & Cao, H. (2022). Trusted blockchain-driven IoT security consensus mechanism. *Sustainability (Basel)*, *14*(9), 5200. DOI: 10.3390/su14095200

Wang, D., Zhang, D., Zhang, Y., Rashid, M. T., Shang, L., & Wei, N. (2019, December). Social edge intelligence: Integrating human and artificial intelligence at the edge. In *2019 IEEE First International Conference on Cognitive Machine Intelligence (CogMI)* (pp. 194-201). IEEE. DOI: 10.1109/CogMI48466.2019.00036

Wang, F., Zhang, M., Wang, X., Ma, X., & Liu, J. (2020). Deep learning for edge computing applications: A state-of-the-art survey. *IEEE Access : Practical Innovations, Open Solutions*, *8*, 58322–58336. DOI: 10.1109/ACCESS.2020.2982411

Wang, H., Wang, W., Liu, Y., & Alidaee, B. (2022). Integrating Machine Learning Algorithms With Quantum Annealing Solvers for Online Fraud Detection. *IEEE Access : Practical Innovations, Open Solutions*, *10*, 75908–75917. DOI: 10.1109/ACCESS.2022.3190897

Wang, T., Mei, Y., Jia, W., Zheng, X., Wang, G., & Xie, M. (2020). Edge-based differential privacy computing for sensor–cloud systems. *Journal of Parallel and Distributed Computing*, *136*, 75–85. DOI: 10.1016/j.jpdc.2019.10.009

Wang, T., Zhang, G., Liu, A., Bhuiyan, M. Z. A., & Jin, Q. (2019). A secure IoT service architecture with an efficient balance dynamics based on cloud and edge computing. *IEEE Internet of Things Journal*, *6*(3), 4831–4843. DOI: 10.1109/JIOT.2018.2870288

Wang, Y., Han, S., Leung, V. C. M., & Zhang, N. (2020). Convergence of edge computing and AI for intelligent IoT: A survey. *IEEE Communications Surveys and Tutorials*, *22*(2), 869–904. DOI: 10.1109/COMST.2020.2970550

Wang, Z., Guo, Y., & Guo, Y. (2025). A blockchain-based medical IoT authentication scheme resistant to combined attacks. *Computer Networks*, *263*, 111241. DOI: 10.1016/j.comnet.2025.111241

Wan, J., Li, X., Dai, H.-N., Kusiak, A., Martínez-García, M., & Li, D. (2021). *Artificial Intelligence-Driven Customized Manufacturing Factory: Key Technologies*. Applications, and Challenges., DOI: 10.1109/JPROC.2020.3034808

Wazid, M., Singh, J., Das, A.K., Garg, S., & Susilo, W. (2025). Cloud storage-based secure big data analytics mechanism for drone-assisted healthcare 5.0 data fusion system. .DOI: 10.1016/j.inffus.2025.103085

Wen, D., Xing, Y., Yao, Y., Liang, G., Jung, T. P. (2020). Transforming Long-Term Adjunctive Therapy for Cognitive Impairment: The Role of Multimodal Self-Adaptive Digital Medicine. Frontiers in Neurology. https://www.frontiersin.org/legal/privacy-policy

Wen, D., Liu, P., Zhu, G., Shi, Y., Xu, J., Eldar, Y. C., & Cui, S. (2023). Task-oriented sensing, computation, and communication integration for multi-device edge AI. *IEEE Transactions on Wireless Communications*.

Wen, D., Li, X., Zhou, Y., Shi, Y., Wu, S., & Jiang, C. (2024). Integrated sensing-communication-computation for edge artificial intelligence. *IEEE Internet of Things Magazine*, *7*(4), 14–20. DOI: 10.1109/IOTM.001.2300146

Wolstencroft, K., Haines, R., Fellows, D., Williams, A. R., Withers, D., Owen, S., … Goble, C. A. (2013). The Taverna workflow suite: Designing and executing workflows of web services on the desktop, web, or in the cloud. Nucleic acids research, 41(W1), W557-W561.

Wong, K. S., & Kim, M. H. (2018). Emerging issues and challenges for cloud data at the edge. *International Journal of Web and Grid Services*, *14*(2), 123–145. DOI: 10.1504/IJWGS.2018.090741

World Health Organization. (n.d.). Ageing and health. Retrieved July 24, 2025, from https://www.who.int/news-room/fact-sheets/detail/ageing-and-health

Xing, H., Zhu, G., Liu, D., Wen, H., Huang, K., & Wu, K. (2023). Task-oriented integrated sensing, computation and communication for wireless edge AI. *IEEE Network*, *37*(4), 135–144. DOI: 10.1109/MNET.011.2300046

Xu, X. (2018). *Industrial Internet of Things: Applications, Trends, and Challenges*. Springer.

Xu, X., Liu, C., Zhang, K., & Zhang, Y. (2020). A sustainable edge computing framework for smart cities. *Sustainable Cities and Society*, *56*, 102082. DOI: 10.1016/j.scs.2020.102082

Yamini, B., Sudha, K., Nalini, M., Kavitha, G., Subramanian, R. S., & Sugumar, R. (2023, June). Predictive modelling for lung cancer detection using machine learning techniques. In *2023 8th International Conference on Communication and Electronics Systems (ICCES)* (pp. 1220-1226). IEEE. DOI: 10.1109/ICCES57224.2023.10192648

Yang, C., Liu, Y., & Li, W. (2021). Edge intelligence for building automation systems: Opportunities and challenges. *Automation in Construction*, *126*, 103665. DOI: 10.1016/j.autcon.2021.103665

Yang, J., Dung, N., Th ch, P., Phong, N., Phu, V., Phu, K., & Clifton, D. (2023). Generalizability assessment of ai models across hospitals: a comparative study in low-middle income and high income countries. DOI: 10.1101/2023.11.05.23298109

Yang, T., Lee, S., & Park, S. (2021). Ai-aided individual emergency detection system in edge-internet of things environments. *Electronics (Basel)*, *10*(19), 2374. DOI: 10.3390/electronics10192374

Yang, Y., Wu, L., Yin, G., Li, L., & Zhao, H. (2017). A survey on security and privacy issues in Internet-of-Things. *IEEE Internet of Things Journal*, *4*(5), 1250–1258. DOI: 10.1109/JIOT.2017.2694844

Yin, C., Xi, J., Sun, R., & Wang, J. (2018). Location privacy protection based on differential privacy strategy for big data in industrial Internet of Things. *IEEE Transactions on Industrial Informatics*, *14*(8), 3628–3636. DOI: 10.1109/TII.2017.2773646

Yi, Z., Cao, X., Chen, Z., & Li, S. (2023). Artificial Intelligence in Accounting and Finance: Challenges and Opportunities. *IEEE Access : Practical Innovations, Open Solutions*, *11*, 129100–129123. DOI: 10.1109/ACCESS.2023.3333389

Yu, S. (2016). Big privacy: Challenges and opportunities of privacy study in the age of big data. *IEEE Access: Practical Innovations, Open Solutions*, *4*, 2751–2763. DOI: 10.1109/ACCESS.2016.2577036

Yu, W., Liang, F., He, X., Hatcher, W. G., Lu, C., Lin, J., & Yang, X. (2017). A survey on the edge computing for the Internet of Things. *IEEE Access : Practical Innovations, Open Solutions*, *6*, 6900–6919. DOI: 10.1109/ACCESS.2017.2778504

Yu, Y., Chen, R., Li, H., Li, Y., & Tian, A. (2019). Toward data security in edge intelligent IIoT. *IEEE Network*, *33*(5), 20–26. DOI: 10.1109/MNET.001.1800507

Zhang, C., & Su, L. (2024). An IoMT framework integrating 5G and wireless body area networks for home healthcare. In Proceedings of the 2024 3rd International Conference on Networks, Communications and Information Technology (pp. 166–171). DOI: 10.1145/3672121.3672155

Zhang, T., Wang, S., Li, G., Liu, F., Zhu, G., & Wang, R. (2022, May). Accelerating edge intelligence via integrated sensing and communication. In *ICC 2022-IEEE International Conference on Communications* (pp. 1586-1592). IEEE. DOI: 10.1109/ICC45855.2022.9839016

Zhang, C., & Kidd, A. (2020). Urban computing: Computational methods for understanding the urban environment. In *Urban informatics* (pp. 15–34). Springer.

Zhang, C., Zheng, Y., Zhou, Z., & Li, Y. (2020). Federated learning for IoT: Communication-efficient and privacy-preserving edge learning. *IEEE Internet of Things Journal*, *7*(12), 10664–10676. DOI: 10.1109/JIOT.2020.2995503

Zhang, H., Liu, J., Zhao, H., Wang, P., & Kato, N. (2021). Blockchain-based trust management for Internet of Vehicles. *IEEE Transactions on Emerging Topics in Computing*, *9*(3), 1397–1409. DOI: 10.1109/TETC.2020.3033532

Zhang, J., Chen, B., Zhao, Y., Cheng, X., & Hu, F. (2018). Data security and privacy-preserving in edge computing paradigm: Survey and open issues. *IEEE Access : Practical Innovations, Open Solutions*, *6*, 18209–18237. DOI: 10.1109/ACCESS.2018.2820162

Zhang, W., Chen, X., Liu, Y., & Xi, Q. (2020). A Distributed Storage and Computation k-Nearest Neighbor Algorithm Based Cloud-Edge Computing for Cyber-Physical-Social Systems. *IEEE Access : Practical Innovations, Open Solutions*, *8*, 50118–50130. DOI: 10.1109/ACCESS.2020.2974764

Zhang, W., He, Q., Yang, X., & Chen, J. (2020). AI-enabled resource allocation for edge computing: A review. *Computer Communications*, *155*, 97–106. DOI: 10.1016/j.comcom.2020.03.040

Zhang, Y. (2018). Edge and Fog Computing for Smart Manufacturing: A Survey. *Journal of Industrial Information Integration*, *10*, 1–9.

Zhang, Y., Deng, R. H., & Li, J. (2019). Blockchain-based secure data sharing system in edge computing. *IEEE Internet of Things Journal*, *6*(3), 4715–4725. DOI: 10.1109/JIOT.2018.2871574

Zhang, Y., Hao, Z., & Wang, S. (2019). A differential privacy support vector machine classifier based on dual variable perturbation. *IEEE Access: Practical Innovations, Open Solutions*, *7*, 98238–98251. DOI: 10.1109/ACCESS.2019.2929680

Zhang, Y., Jiang, C., Yue, B., Wan, J., & Guizani, M. (2022). Information fusion for edge intelligence: A survey. *Information Fusion*, *81*, 171–186. DOI: 10.1016/j.inffus.2021.11.018

Zhang, Y., Qu, Y., Gao, L., Luan, T. H., Zheng, X., Chen, S., & Xiang, Y. (2019). APDP: Attack-proof personalized differential privacy model for a smart home. *IEEE Access: Practical Innovations, Open Solutions*, *7*, 166593–166605. DOI: 10.1109/ACCESS.2019.2953133

Zhang, Y., Wang, P., Fang, L., He, X., Han, H., & Chen, B. (2020). Secure transmission of compressed sampling data using edge clouds. *IEEE Transactions on Industrial Informatics*, *16*(10), 6641–6651. DOI: 10.1109/TII.2020.2966511

Zhang, Y., Yu, H., Zhou, W., & Man, M. (2022). Application and research of IoT architecture for End-Net-Cloud edge computing. *Electronics (Basel)*, *12*(1), 1. DOI: 10.3390/electronics12010001

Zhao, X., Li, X., & Zhou, X. (2018). Urban green spaces and their role in enhancing climate resilience. *Journal of Environmental Science and Policy*, 89, 91-99.

Zhao, J., Chen, Y., & Zhang, W. (2019). Differential privacy preservation in deep learning: Challenges, opportunities and solutions. *IEEE Access : Practical Innovations, Open Solutions*, *7*, 48901–48911. DOI: 10.1109/ACCESS.2019.2909559

Zhao, Y. (2019). AI in Industrial Energy Management Systems. *IEEE Transactions on Industrial Informatics*.

Zhao, Y. (2019). *Edge Computing in Industrial Internet of Things: Opportunities and Challenges*. Elsevier.

Zhao, Y. (2019). IIoT and Digital Twin for Smart Manufacturing: An Overview and Perspectives. *Journal of Industrial Information Integration*, *15*, 1–11.

Zhao, Y. (2020). *The Role of Digital Twin in Manufacturing: Optimizing Production Systems and Enhancing Efficiency*. Springer.

Zheng, Y. (2019). *Urban computing*. MIT Press.

Zhong, G., Xiong, K., Zhong, Z., & Ai, B. (2021). Internet of things for high-speed railways. *Intelligent and Converged Networks*, *2*(2), 115–132. DOI: 10.23919/ICN.2021.0005

Zhong, S., Zhang, X., & Lin, X. (2018). *Edge computing: Technologies and applications*. Springer.

Zhou, L., Yu, L., Du, S., Zhu, H., & Chen, C. (2019). Achieving differentially private location privacy in edge-assistant connected vehicles. *IEEE Internet of Things Journal*, *6*(3), 4472–4481. DOI: 10.1109/JIOT.2018.2876419

Zhou, W. (2019). Artificial Intelligence for Cybersecurity in IIoT Systems: Opportunities and Challenges. *IEEE Access : Practical Innovations, Open Solutions*, *7*, 118127–118141.

Zhou, X., Ke, R., Yang, H., & Liu, C. (2021). When intelligent transportation systems sensing meets edge computing: Vision and challenges. *Applied Sciences (Basel, Switzerland)*, *11*(20), 9680. DOI: 10.3390/app11209680

Zhou, Z., Chen, X., Li, E., Zeng, L., Luo, K., & Zhang, J. (2019). Edge intelligence: Paving the last mile of artificial intelligence with edge computing. *Proceedings of the IEEE*, *107*(8), 1738–1762. DOI: 10.1109/JPROC.2019.2918951

Zhuang, Z., Wen, D., Shi, Y., Zhu, G., Wu, S., & Niyato, D. (2023). Integrated Sensing-Communication-Computation for Over-the-Air Edge AI Inference. *IEEE Transactions on Wireless Communications*.

About the Contributors

Minakshi is an accomplished academician with 18+ years of experience in computer science and engineering domains. Currently an Assistant Professor at King Khalid University, she has taught at esteemed institutions like Uttaranchal University and Tula's Institute. A prolific researcher with 80 Scopus publications, 18 patents, and 3 software copyrights, she has received accolades like Outstanding Section Volunteer Award (IEEE UP Section), Research Excellence Award, and HOD of the Year Award. Adept at curriculum development, research guidance, project management, and team leadership, Dr. Minakshi brings a holistic approach to education, fostering student success through quality instruction and innovative pedagogical methods.

Tarun Kumar received his Ph.D. degree from the National Institute of Technology Patna, Bihar, India. Dr. Kumar has more than 20 years of experience in teaching and is currently working as an Associate Professor in the School of Computer Science at the University of Petroleum and Energy Studies (UPES), Dehradun, India. His research interests include cloud computing, IoT, and DNA computing. Dr. Kumar has published several edited books, book chapters, patents and papers in conference proceedings and refereed journals. He has also participated in many international conferences as an organizer and session chair. Dr. Kumar is a senior member of IEEE, ACM, IEEE Computer Society, and a Member IEEE Computational Intelligence Society. Dr. Kumar brings a holistic approach to education, fostering student success through quality instruction and innovative pedagogical methods.

Kapil Joshi is an associate professor at Uttaranchal University, Dehradun. He earned his Ph.D. in Computer Science and Engineering from Uttaranchal University in 2022, specializing in Image processing. Dr. Kapil's research interests include Image processing, Artificial intelligence, Machine learning etc. He got "Best Researcher Award" in International Scientist Awards 2021 On Engineering, Science and Medicine 07&08-Aug-2021, Pondicherry, India and organized by VDGood, technology factory. He is having more than 100 papers published in Scopus/SCI. He has published various patents also. He has organized many conferences, seminars, workshops etc.

Akash Saxena is a distinguished Principal at the Department of Computer Science and Information Technology at Compucom Institute of Technology & Management in Jaipur, Rajasthan. With over 21 years of experience, he is an expert in Data Mining, Network Security, E-Commerce, and Cloud Computing. Dr. Saxena holds a Ph.D. in Computer Science from Maharaja Ganga Singh University, along with M.Phil and M.Tech degrees. His impressive academic contributions include over 70 papers in international journals, 35 in international conferences, and 21 in national conferences. He has authored 11 books, holds 6 patents and 3 copyrights, and has guided more than 45 research scholars. Dr. Saxena is also actively involved in professional organizations like CSI and IEEE.

DIlip Kumar Jang Bahadur Saini is having above 20 years of teaching experience. He got his PHD from Sathyabam Institute of Science and Technology, Jeppiaar Nagar, Chennai in 2024. He is working on various research projects which are funded by government agencies. He is having various publications which are indexed by Scopus/SCI. He was awarded by Best Researcher Award 2021 from Innogen Research Foundation Hyderabad on 5 Sept 2021. He was awarded by Performance Excellence Award 2021 from Global Education and Corporate Leadership (GECL-2021) Award by LWT way Tech India Pvt. Ltd, Rajasthan India at Tulas Institute of Technology, Dehradun on 21 Dec 2021.

***

Beneta Mary A. is a faculty member in the Department of Computer Science and Engineering at St. Joseph College of Engineering, Sriperumbudur. She is dedicated to imparting knowledge and fostering innovation in computer science education. Her academic interests support both teaching excellence and student development.

Vivek Agarwal is a dedicated academician with 11 years of teaching experience. He holds a B.Tech and M.Tech degree and is currently pursuing a Ph.D., showcasing his commitment to continuous learning and expertise in his field. Over the years, he has mentored numerous students, contributed to academic excellence, and demonstrated a deep passion for education and research.

Harishchander Anandaram completed a PhD in bioengineering, an M.Tech., and a B.Tech. in bioinformatics from the Sathyabama Institute of Science and Technology, Chennai, in 2020, 2011, and 2009. In his bachelor's and master's theses, he worked on analysing resistance in HIV protease inhibitors based on molecular mechanics and machine learning studies, a collaborative project with IIT Madras. In his PhD thesis, he worked on pharmacogenomics and miRNA-regulated networks in psoriasis, a collaborative project with Georgetown University, USA; JIPMER, India; CIBA, India; and ILS, India. His thesis illustrated a multi-disciplinary approach by combining computational biophysics and molecular biology machine learning. While doing a PhD, he had the opportunity to collaborate with international researchers and have publications in reputed international journals in bioinformatics and systems biology. He has received the prestigious "Young Scientist Award" from "The Melinda Gates Foundation" for his research abstract on "The Implications of miRNA Dynamics in Infectious Diseases.". To date, he has reviewed more than 200 manuscripts in systems biology.

Mangaiyarkarasi D. is an Assistant Professor in the Department of Artificial Intelligence and Data Science at Sri Sairam Engineering College, Chennai. She is passionate about teaching and research in AI, with a focus on fostering innovation and practical learning. Her academic efforts support the growth of intelligent technologies in engineering education.

Saru Dhir, presently working as Associate Professor in the Department of Information Technology, at Amity University Uttar Pradesh, Noida. She completed her Ph.D. in Computer Science & Engineering in 2017. She filled the Patents on "An environment friendly green tablet PC"(Amity CRN 773) and "An Agricultural System For Early Blight Detection Without Connectivity". She is having more than 13 year experience in teaching as well as in research. She has published more than 40 research articles in international journals, book chapters and conference. Her research areas are: Software Engineering, Agile Development, Software Testing, Cyber security and IOT. She is the member of Professional Bodies such as IAENG, CSTA. She is also serving as a Guest Editor of Special Issue on Intelligent Systems and Application, International Journal of Intelligent Information Technologies (IJIIT), IGI Global (Scopus Indexed). She is the editor of book series "Advanced Computing Techniques: Implementation, Informatics and Emerging Technologies", published by Bentham publisher.

Atharv Gupta is the student of B.Tech. CSBS at Amity University Uttar Pradesh, Noida. He is sincere to his work and academically strong. He aspires to build his future work around his areas of interest, i.e., business and technology.

He is strongly motivated and commited towards the innovation of new and efficient technologies that help mankind.

SudarvelJ. working as an Assistant Professor of Management at Karpagam Academy of Higher Education. He produced five Ph.D. Scholars and four Ph.D. Scholars are under his guidance. Further, to his credit he published more than five articles in Scopus indexed journals and published more than 50 articles in international journals. He is acting as a Subject Experts in Board of studies of various autonomous colleges.

Vinay Kumar Kasula has a master's in technology from Osmania University, followed by a second Master's from Northwest Missouri State University. A deep-rooted interest in research and advanced technologies has driven his academic journey. This passion led him to pursue and complete a Ph.D. at the University of the Cumberlands, where he graduated in 2024, focusing on areas including Blockchain, Artificial Intelligence, Deep Learning, Machine Learning, Data Analytics, and Cybersecurity. With over a decade of industry experience, currently as a Senior Systems Analyst, he has applied and expanded his expertise in these domains, continually exploring and integrating innovative solutions to meet evolving technological challenges. This blend of education, research, and practical experience fueled his commitment to advancements in these cutting-edge fields. He has many publications in the allied field including conference papers and journals publications and many in the queue.

Naresh Kumar is a Professor in the Applied Computational Science & Engineering, G L Bajaj Institute of Technology and Management Uttar Pradesh. He is having 18 years of Experience in Teaching and research. He has received his Ph.D. in Computer Engineering from University Institute of Engineering and Technology, Maharishi Dayanand University Rohtak. He completed his Master of Technology in Computer Science & Engineering from Kurukshetra University, Kurukshetra in 2004. He has presented several papers in international conferences and published work in peer-reviewed and science cited journals. Dr. Kumar has also authored a book "Objective Computer Science - Training Minds and Creating Opportunities" by Inkart Publishing. He is active reviewer of many top journals of IEEE, IET, Springer. He is also CISCO Certified Trainer for Cisco Network Security, CCNA, CyberOps. His area of research is Information Extraction, Big Data Analytics and Computer Networking.

Sanjay Kumar BTech(IT),Rajasthan Technical University kota,, MTech(CSE),Rajasthan Technical University, kota, PhD (image Processing) Galgotias University, Greater Noida (U.p) Dr. Sanjay has Worked as software engineer, Wipro Technology, Banglore currently Have more than 12 yrs of vast experience of R&D in Image Processing And 5G . Author of various national and international research papers published in on various prestigious platforms. Guided so many research projects on various Data driven Technologies like IoT, Images processing, 5G.

Anto Gracious L. A. is an accomplished academic professional in Information Technology and Computer Science, known for his dedication to education, technology, and research. He holds a B.Tech in IT from C.S.I Institute of Technology (2006), an MBA in Technology Management, and an M.Tech in IT from Francis Xavier Engineering College (2011). He began his career as a Programmer at Software Solutions Integrated Limited, later transitioning to academia in 2011 as an Assistant Professor at Marthandam College of Engineering and Technology. Over eight years, he excelled in teaching, led the Software Development Cell, and earned multiple awards for his contributions. He later served at St. Xavier's Catholic College of Engineering and currently holds a position at R.M.K. College of Engineering and Technology. A prolific researcher, Anto focuses on machine learning, wireless sensor networks, and healthcare technologies. His work is widely published, and he has received accolades such as the Best Paper Award and multiple Best Faculty Awards.

Pushpa Mamoria has served in various academic and administrative roles at renowned educational institutions for over 20 years. She is presently working as an associate professor in the Department of Computer Application, School of Engineering and Technology, at CSJM University Kanpur. Before here, she served at the Indian Institute of Information Technology, Allahabad (IIITA) from 2005 to 2007. Apart from her teaching assignments, she worked as a head of the department and member of the proctorial board and is now working as a convener of the alumni association, hostel warden, program officer NSS, and engaged in other academic & administrative assignments. Her main research interests are in digital image processing, artificial intelligence (AI), machine learning (ML), fuzzy logic, soft computing techniques, IoT, big data, data science, Indian Knowledge System, and social studies. She has published/presented several papers in reputed international and national journals, conferences, and symposiums. She completed a PhD from the Department of Computer Science, School of Information Science & Technology, Babasaheb Bhimrao Ambedkar University (a central university), Lucknow, in 2018, with an M.Tech. from the School of Computer Science and Information Technology, Devi Ahilya Vishwavidyalaya, Indore, and a B.E. in Computer Science and Engineering from Shri G. S. Institute of Technology and Science, Indore (SGSITS). She has supervised M. Tech., MCA, and B.Tech. theses and is presently supervising MCA, BCA, and PhD students under her guidance.

Nirav Narendrakumar Modh is a skilled software engineer with over 14 years of experience delivering innovative solutions across web and mobile platforms. Currently a Consultant at Infosys Limited, he specializes in full-stack development with a focus on interface design, user-centric solutions, and mobile app engineering. Nirav creates scalable, intuitive applications using cutting-edge technologies. With expertise in mobile application development, he aligns technical solutions with business objectives. Known for his leadership, Nirav holds a B.Tech in Computer Engineering from Nirma University, Ahmedabad, India (2008). He is committed to staying at the forefront of digital innovation.

GirijaP. is a faculty member in the Department of Information Technology at Panimalar Engineering College, Chennai. She is actively involved in teaching and research in the field of IT and emerging technologies. Her academic contributions reflect a commitment to student success and innovation in technical education.

AbithaR. is an Assistant Professor in the Department of Artificial Intelligence and Data Science at Vel Tech Multi Tech Dr. Rangarajan Dr. Sakunthala Engineering College, Chennai. She is committed to academic excellence and research in AI and data-driven technologies. Her work focuses on empowering students with practical and theoretical knowledge in emerging tech fields.

VelmuruganR. presently working as an Associate Professor in Commerce, Karpagam Academy of Higher Education, Coimbatore. He started his career as a Project Fellow under UGC Sponsored Major Research Project at NGM College, Pollachi. He has 18 years of teaching experience has 15 years of research experience. To his credit he produced 22 Ph.D. Scholars and 5 M.Phil. Scholars. At present 1 scholar submitter his thesis, 6 Ph.D. Scholars are under his guidance. Moreover, to his credit he published 168 articles in various International Journals, of which 58 articles are published in Scopus Indexed Journals and 15 articles in Web of Science and 76 articles in edited volumes. He also participates and presented 27 papers in various International Seminar / Conference and 54 National Seminar / Conference. He acted as an external examiner for various M.Phil. and Ph.D. Viva voce examinations. He acted as a Vice Chancellor nominee for Doctoral Committee Expert at Bharathiar University, Coimbatore and Periyar University, Salem. He acted as a Chairperson at various National Level Conferences. He also acted as an Expert for Syllabus Scrutiny Committee, Question Paper Scrutiny Committee and Expert members for Board of Studies at various reputed Colleges. Considering his meritorious contribution, he received awards like Best Paper Presenter, Best Research Supervisor and Best Faculty Awards from various research foundations and councils. He too acted as a resource person for 27 Guest Lectures, 30 Workshops and 10 faculty development programmes.

Ravikumar RN is an experienced educator with 11+ years of teaching in Computer Science across India and overseas. Currently an Assistant Professor at Marwadi University, Rajkot, he specializes in Advanced Java, Machine Learning, Data Science, and AI. He holds a Mini MBA from the Swiss eLearning Institute (2015), an M.E. in Computer Science Engineering from VMRF University (2013), and a B.E. from Anna University (2010). Completed PhD at Amity University, Jaipur, he is dedicated to research, professional development, and advancing education through technology.

Sivaramakrishnan Rajendar is an Associate Professor in the Department of Computer Science and Engineering at Vel Tech Rangarajan Dr.Sagunthala R&D Institute of Science and Technology, Chennai. He specializes in advanced computing technologies and contributes actively to research and academic development. His work reflects a strong commitment to innovation in computer science education.

Basudeo Singh Roohani is currently working in the department of Computer Sc & Engg. at IMS Engineering College Ghaziabad. He did B.Tech in Computer Sc. & Engg. from Bundelkhand Institute of Engineering & Technology(BIET), Jhansi, M.Tech in Computer Sc. from Uttar Pradesh Technical University (UPTU), Lucknow and Ph.D(p) in Computer Sc. & Engg. from Dr. A.P.J. Abdul Kalam Technical University Lucknow. He is having Research interest in the field of Design & Analysis of Algorithms, Machine Learning and Deep Learning. He has twelve years of administrative experience as head, Computer Sc. & Engg. Deptt. out of twenty five years of experience at various reputed Institutions, to monitor all operations and activities within the department. He has attended 19 FDPs, Seminars, Workshops, Conferences and Training Program. He also presented 11 research papers in National and International Conferences. He has published 07 Patents. He has published 05 Book Chapters. He has also published 09 Research Papers in reputed journals. He has also worked as Conference Paper Reviewer.

Aarthi S is a dedicated Assistant Professor in Computer Science with over six years of teaching experience. She is currently pursuing her Ph.D. at Marwadi University, Gujarat, and holds an M.Phil. and MCA from Bharathiar University, Tamil Nadu. Throughout her academic career, Aarthi has specialized in programming languages such as C++, Java, and C, and contributed to research in recommender systems and AI-related data privacy. She has published journal articles, contributed to book chapters, and actively participated in technical workshops. Known for her student mentorship and engagement in academic events, Aarthi remains committed to fostering innovation and excellence in computer science education.

Senthilkumar S. is currently working as Assistant Professor in Finance and Management, Skyline University, Nigeria. His qualifications are MBA, M.Com, M.Phil, MS, and PhD. He has rich experience in teaching and academic of 18.2 years. He had published 58 papers Publications in National and International Journals and Proceedings. He Authored 4 books in Research Methodology, Corporate Finance, Principles of Accounting and Business Policy & Strategic management. Participated and presented 62 papers in National & International Seminars and Conferences. He acted as resource person and Guest lecture around 25 Programmemes. He guided 225 projects in M.B.A., 36 M.Phil, and 9 PhD. He got Authorized Guide ship for PhD & M.Phil from Indian Universities such as Anna University, Karpagam University, Bharathiar University, Periyar Manimai University and AMIET University and Vinayaka Mission University and Bahir Dar University, Ethiopia. He performed as Foreign examiner for evaluating PhD Thesis around 18 Thesis of Indian universities such as Bharathiar University, Visvesvaraya Technological University, University of Mumbai, MS University and Bharathidasan university.

Vineeta Singh is presently working as an Assistant Professor in the Department of Computer Science & Engineering, School of Engineering and Technology, Chhatrapati Shahu ji Maharaj University Kanpur, India. She has more than 8 years of teaching experience in different Engineering and Technological Institutions. She has guided more than 120 B.Tech. level projects and more than 2 M.Tech. level Projects. She has received her Ph.D. Degree from the Harcourt Butler Technical University Kanpur India in 2022 and M.Tech from Dr. APJ Abdul Kalam Technical University Lucknow in 2015. She passed out B.Tech with honours from UPTU Lucknow India in 2009. She was B.Tech branch topper. Her area of research includes Deep learning, Image Processing, Cyber Security, Data Mining and Biometrics. She has presented and published more than 30 international conference papers and published 11 SCIE indexed journal research papers and 6 are in pipeline. Additionally, she has published 6 book chapters and 11 are in pipeline. She also worked as reviewer in different international conferences organized by IIT BHU (ANTIC-BHU) Varanasi and NIT Arunachal Pradesh. She is also working as reviewer in SCIE indexed journals such as IET Image Processing, Scientific Reports, Signal Image and Video Processing, Journal of Scientific and Industrial Research and many more. She is also associated as an editor with five ongoing projects as edited Books pertaining to renowned publishers. She is also involved with three projects (Indian patent grants). She has two Indian Granted Patents "Artificial Tree for oxygen production and atmospheric purification" and SMART BOOK FOR TRACKING STUDENTS' LEARNING

PROGRESS and third one is in process. She has three design based grants accepted and 6 in process. She has one UK design grant.

Rinki Singh is currently serving as the Head of Department and Associate Professor in the Department of Computer Science and Engineering at Satyug Darshan Institute of Engineering & Technology, Faridabad. With over 22 years of academic and research experience, she has worked with several reputed institutions across India. Dr. Singh has guided numerous undergraduate and postgraduate students in their academic and research pursuits. Her core areas of interest include Compiler Design, Machine Learning, and Deep Learning. She has published a number of research papers in reputed SCI, Scopus-indexed, and international journals. An enthusiastic lifelong learner, she has successfully completed several MOOC courses, including multiple NPTEL certifications, and has been a topper in many of these. Her passion for teaching, research, and continuous learning has significantly contributed to the academic excellence and innovation in her department.

Siva Subramanian R is a faculty member in the School of Computing at SRM Institute of Science & Technology, Trichy campus. He specializes in computer science domains including artificial intelligence, data analytics, and software development. With active involvement in research and teaching, he contributes significantly to academic and institutional growth

C.V. Suresh Babu is a pioneer in content development. A true entrepreneur, he founded Anniyappa Publications, a company that is highly active in publishing books related to Computer Science and Management. Dr. C.V. Suresh Babu has also ventured into SB Institute, a center for knowledge transfer. He holds a Ph.D. in Engineering Education from the National Institute of Technical Teachers Training & Research in Chennai, along with seven master's degrees in various disciplines such as Engineering, Computer Applications, Management, Commerce, Economics, Psychology, Law, and Education. Additionally, he has UGC-NET/SET qualifications in the fields of Computer Science, Management, Commerce, and Education. Currently, Dr. C.V. Suresh Babu is a Professor in the Department of Information Technology at the School of Computing Science, Hindustan Institute of Technology and Science (Hindustan University) in Padur, Chennai, Tamil Nadu, India.

KannadadhasanSuriyan is working as an Associate Professor and HoD in the department of Electronics and Communication Engineering at Study World College of Engineering, Coimbatore, Tamil Nadu, India. He completed his Ph.D. in the field of smart antennas at Anna University in 2022. He has thirteen years of teaching and research experience. He obtained his B.E. in ECE from Sethu Institute of Technology, Kariapatti, in 2009 and his M.E. in Communication Systems from

Velammal College of Engineering and Technology, Madurai, in 2013. He obtained his M.B.A. in Human Resources Management from Tamil Nadu Open University, Chennai. He has published around 110 papers in the reputed international journals indexed by SCI, Scopus, Web of Science, and Major Indexing, and more than 250 papers have been presented or published in national and international journals and conferences. Besides, he has also contributed a book chapter. He also serves as a board member, reviewer, speaker, session chair, and member of the advisory and technical committees of various colleges and conferences.

Index

F

G

H

I

L

M

P

Q

R

S

T

U

www.ingramcontent.com/pod-product-compliance
Lightning Source LLC
LaVergne TN
LVHW080912300926
849162LV00003B/655